Inside
Maya 5

by

Mark Adams
Erick Miller
Max Sims

With contributions by Adrian Dimond,
Will Paicius, Daniel Naranjo, and Daniel Roizman

New
Riders

Inside Maya 5

Copyright © 2004 by New Riders Publishing

International Standard Book Number: 0-7357-1253-0

Library of Congress Catalog Card Number: 20-01098735

06 05 04 03   7 6 5 4 3 2 1

Interpretation of the printing code: The rightmost double-digit number is the year of the book's printing; the rightmost single-digit number is the number of the book's printing. For example, the printing code 03-1 shows that the first printing of the book occurred in 2003.

Printed in the United States of America

Publisher
Stephanie Wall

Production Manager
Gina Kanouse

Senior Acquisitions Editor
Linda Anne Bump

Development Editor
Audrey Doyle

Senior Project Editor
Kristy Knoop

Copy Editor
Krista Hansing

Indexer
Lisa Stumpf

Manufacturing Coordinator
Dan Uhrig

Cover Designer
Aren Howell

Proofreader
Lori Lyons

Composition
Amy Parker
Gloria Schurick

Media Developer
Jay Payne

Marketing
Scott Cowlin
Tammy Detrich
Hannah Onstad Latham

Publicity Manager
Susan Nixon

Contents at a Glance

Introduction

Part I   **Maya and the Production Pipeline**

    1   Using Maya Well   3

    2   Project Overview   17

    3   Digital Studio Pipeline   33

    4   Technical Considerations   51

    5   MEL   81

Part II   **Modeling**

    6   Formats   111

    7   Methods   139

    8   Sets   175

    9   Props   217

   10   Characters   289

Part III   **Technical Direction**

   11   Layout   333

   12   Node-Based Architecture   349

   13   Making Advanced Connections   369

   14   Particles and Dynamics   419

Part IV   Animation

    15   Character Animation in Maya   479

    16   Character Setup Pipeline for Animation   575

    17   Rigging Characters for Animation   609

    18   Shading   697

    19   Lighting   733

    20   Rendering   775

Part V   Appendix

    Appendix A   Intermediate and Advanced MEL   833

Table of Contents

Part I   Maya and the Production Pipeline

I   Using Maya Well   3

What Maya Can Do 4

Applications 4

Tools 5

Characteristics 7

Maya's Development 8

Maya's Roots 8

Your Development 10

Resources 10

Approach 15

Summary 15

2   Project Overview   17

Beginnings 18

Plan A 18

Regrouping 19

Plan B 23

The Pitch 24

Fleshing It Out 24

The Killer B Plan 29

(Story)boards 29

The Book 30

The Budget 31

Summary 32

3   Digital Studio Pipeline   33

Preproduction 34

Story 34

Visual Considerations 36

Technical Considerations 37

Production Setup 39

Modeling 39

Articulation 40

Shading 42

Layout 43

Set Dressing 44

Production Flow 46

Animation 46

Lighting 47

Effects 48

Rendering 49

Summary 50

4   Technical Considerations   51

Getting Cozy 52

Commands 53

Command Defaults 53

Hotkeys 58

Shelves 64

Marking Menus 68

The User Interface 69

UI Elements 70

Menus 73

Viewing 74

See the Big Picture 75

Set Some Boundaries 75

Stay Centered 76

Managing Files 77

Projects 77

File Naming 77

Summary 79

5   MEL   81

What Is MEL? 81

What Can MEL Do and How Is It Used? 82

Maya's Embedded Language: Some

Specific Essentials 84

The MEL Command Line and Script Editor 85

Using the Script Editor 88

Intro to Programming: A Crash Course on Programming

Using MEL 91

Catching Return Values into Variables 92

Arguments, Arrays, and Control Structures 93

MEL UI Control Exposed 100

Adding a New Item to a Pre-Existing Default Maya Menu 102

Adding a New Menu to the Global Maya UI 104

Summary 106

Part II   Modeling

6   Formats   III

What's Not Available 112

    Implicit (Blobby) Surfaces 112

    Octrees 112

    Point Clouds 112

Format: The Big Choices 113

    Fidelity 113

    Efficiency 113

    Precision 114

    Continuity 114

    Flexibility 114

    Shading Needs 115

Polygons 115

    Flexible Topology 115

    Positional Continuity 117

    Arbitrary Shader Space 119

NURBS 120

    Parameterization 120

    Rectilinear Topology 124

    Trimming 125

    Smooth Surfaces 125

    Deformability 126

Subdivision Surfaces 129

    Flexible Topology Plus Hierarchy 129

    G1 Continuity 131

    Arbitrary Shader Space 133

Surfacing Decisions 134

    Characters 134

    Cars 134

    Fire Hydrant 136

    Storefronts 136

Other Modeling Possibilities 137

    Paint Effects 137

    Blobby Particles 137

    Hair and Fur 138

Summary 138

7   Methods   **139**

  Set Your Sights 140
    Get Their References 141
    Artwork 143
  Plan Your Journey 148
    Take Big Steps 148
    Use Travel Guides 149
    Take Baby Steps 151
  Handle the Details 151
    Avoid Sharp Edges 151
    Put a Lid on It 159
    Cut Corners 162
  Handle the Ups and Downs 164
    Tunneling 165
    Potholes and Speed Bumps 170
  Summary 173

8   Sets   **175**

  Roughing It In 175
    Have a Plan 176
    Have Standards 177
    Know the Code 179
    Mock It Up 180
  Building Blocks 182
    Curbs 182
    Sidewalks 190
    Streets 197
    Beach 198
  Building Buildings 201
    Planning Department 201
    Solid Foundations 202
    Details, Details 206
  Pass It On 212
  Summary 214

9   Props   **217**

  Basic Prop Guidelines 217
    Space 218
    Simplicity 220
    Structure 222

Simple Prop Models 224
  BigBone 225
  Hydrant 238
The Car: A Complex Prop Model 261
  Body Panels 263
Summary 288

10 Characters   289
Functional and Aesthetic Criteria 289
  Advantages of Subdivision Surfaces 290
Additional Criteria 291
  Level of Detail 292
  Extraordinary Points 292
  Texturing 294
Creating Spot and The Jerk 294
  Getting Started 294
  Modeling Spot 298
  Modeling The Jerk 311
Summary 330

Part III Technical Direction

11 Layout   333
What Is Layout? 333
Visual Clarity 337
  From Storyboards to Animatics 339
Summary 348

12 Node-Based Architecture   349
Transformations: Parent/Child Relationships 350
Objects, Shapes, and Components 352
Maya Node-Based Basics 355
  What Is a DAG Node? 355
  What Is a DG Node? 355
Node Types 360
Non-DAG Nodes 361
Viewing the Maya Scene Graph and
Node History 362
Connecting Attributes Between Nodes 364
Summary 367

13　Making Advanced Connections **369**

Understanding Node Connections 370

Some Practical Uses for Constraints 386

Quick Review: Overlapping Action 388

Using History to Your Advantage: Modifying Geometry
After It Is Smooth-Skinned 412

Summary 417

14　Particles and Dynamics **419**

Emission 420

Collisions 423

Gravity 426

Control Nodes 427

Rendering 433

Hardware Rendering 433

Software Rendering 444

Creating Water Trails 455

Summary 476

Part IV　Animation

15　Character Animation in Maya **479**

Maya Animation 481

First Steps: Planning *Your* Animation 487

Step One: Capturing Your Vision 487

Step Two: Researching the Motion 497

Psychological Research: Mini-Script Theory 501

Story Research 503

Motion Research 504

Reference Footage 505

Motion Capture 506

Video Research 507

The Principles of Animation 508

CAPS 509

The Pose 519

Final Plan 522

The Production Process 523

Breaking the Model 523

Working the Controls 526

Break a Leg! 538

Setting the Poses 547
    Setting Keys 551
    It's About Time… 566
    Graph Editor 569
    May the Force Be with You! 570
Last Tips for Motion 572
Summary 572

16 Character Setup Pipeline for Animation   575
Five Golden Rules of Character Setup 576
    Understand the Character's Anatomy 576
    Become Intimate with the Character's Motion Requirements .577
    Keep Character Controls Easy, Intuitive, and Collaborative 578
    Keep Your Files Clean 579
    Bulletproof Everything 583
The Character Setup Pipeline 584
    Eleven Common Character Setup Pitfalls Revealed 585
Summary 608

17 Rigging Characters for Animation   609
Setting Up a Character for Animation 610
Creating Clean Joint Hierarchies for Animation 610
Rigging a Simple Quadruped Character: The Dog 614
    Quadruped Spine and Hips Setup 615
    Quadruped IK Legs and Feet 616
    IK Spline Tail and Ears Setup 620
    Low-Res Stand-In Geometry 622
    Hooking Up Control Boxes to Your Character Rig 625
Creating Advanced Bipedal Character Controls 630
    The Advanced Biped Spine 630
Advanced Stretchy IK Legs and Classic Reverse Foot 648
Advanced IK Arms and Clavicular Triangle 657
Hooking Up the Head Skeletal Hierarchy 680
    Facial Controls and Blend Shape Deformers 682
    Creating Eye Controls 683
The Hair of the Jerk 685
    Smooth Binding Proxy Geometry 686
    Painting Smooth Skin Weights 688
    Paint Weights Using per-Vertex Selections 693
    Using Additional Influence Objects 695
Summary 696

18   Shading   697

Seeing the World in Shaders 698

Achieving a Look 699

Considerations Before Shading 710

    Surface Quality 710

Shading Process and Tools 712

    Multilister, Hypershade, and Visor 712

    Efficient Shader Setups 713

    Creating Libraries 715

    Material Assignment 716

    Evaluating Shaders 717

Creating Texture Maps 718

    Painted Texture Maps 718

    Scanned Textures 719

    Maya Paint Effects Textures 719

    Procedural Textures 720

    Shader Example 725

Projection Mapping 727

Summary 732

19   Lighting   733

The World in Lights 734

    Shadow Control 735

    Maya Lights in Production 743

Defining GI, Radiosity, FG, IBL, and HDRI 746

    Faking GI with Maya's Standard Renderer 747

    Faking Global Illumination with Dome Lights 748

    Creating and Preparing HDR Images 759

Color Scripts 766

Summary 773

20   Rendering   775

Rendering Efficiently with Maya's Standard Renderer 776

    Known Limitations 776

    Antialiasing 778

    Ray Tracing 781

    Motion Blur 783

    Depth of Field 785

    Tessellation 786

    Memory 788

    Animation Efficiencies 789

    Shaders and Texture Maps 789

Block Order Texture (BOT) Files 791
Shadows 791
Render Diagnostics 793
Command-Line Rendering 794
Previewing Renders 795
Preflight Checklist 797
Conducting Rendering Tests 798
Rendering with Mental Ray 799
Known Limitations 799
Common Settings 800
Multipass Rendering 812
Render Layers 812
Global Passes 814
Lighting Passes 814
Which Technique? 815
Render Farms 822
Render Farm Services 822
Render Farm Software 823
Picking the Platform 824
Hardware 825
Farm Layouts 828
Preparing for Final Output 829
Video 829
High Definition and Digital Video 829
Film 830
Summary 830

Part V   Appendix

Appendix A: Intermediate and Advanced MEL   833
What Is a Script Node? 834
Creating and Using a Script Node 834
Combining *scriptJobs* with Script Nodes 841
Launching an Executable and Returning Its Output 844
Error Handling 845
Distributed Jobs: Scripting and Error Logging 851
Advanced MEL 855
Intro to the API: Writing a Deformer 860
What Is *Object Oriented*? 860
Summary 874

Index   875

About the Authors

Mark Adams has been doing 3D modeling on computers for 20 years. He began CG work while working in the Detroit area as a draftsman (after leaving behind the crazy idea of being a lawyer). He had seen Robert Abel's work and leapt at the chance to get into the same field when the firm where he worked considered a CAD system purchase. Over the next decade, Mark spent four years each at Intergraph and then at Alias, primarily as an applications engineer learning, demonstrating, supporting, and tackling the problems du jour of their customers. In 1994, he received a call from Pixar that brought him to California to work on *Toy Story*. He has since been working there as a technical director on Pixar's feature films (plus some CD-ROMs and commercials), mainly as an Alias modeler. A full-time Alias user since 1988, Mark now uses Maya daily for his modeling needs. He recently finishing his work on Pixar's fifth and latest film, *Finding Nemo*. He shares a house in the North Bay area with his wife, two boys, two cats, and a few too many computers. He's a Leo and thinks that astrology is nonsense, except when it says interesting things about Leos.

Erick Miller is currently a technical director at Digital Domain, the Academy Award-winning visual effects company responsible for digital effects in recent blockbusters like *The Time Machine*, *Lord of the Rings*, *X-Men*, and *Armageddon*. Erick uses Maya and its robust 3D environment in his everyday responsibilities as a technical director, writing many proprietary Maya API Plug-ins and Mel scripts, rigging advanced character setups and deformation systems, as well as developing production pipelines for high-budget feature films and commercial projects that work between Maya and other 3D software applications. Since Erick has been at Digital Domain, he has contributed to many important projects; a plug-in pose based deformation system, and a proprietary muscle/skin-deformation plug-in system for Maya are just a couple examples. After wrapping up on a Maya-based crowd animation pipeline for Roland Emerick's high-budget apocalyptic end-of-the-world feature film entitled *The Day After Tomorrow*, Erick has been given the position of team lead on the feature, *I, Robot*—a huge CG character film based on the acclaimed science fiction novels by Isaac Asimov about robotics and humanity. To integrate Maya's powerful architecture into a production pipeline, he connects his artistic knowledge with MEL scripting, Maya's API, and other external programming languages (Perl, Tcl), and C/C++ APIs (RenderMan, OpenGL). Some of his other tasks include advanced character setup, complex skin deformations, RenderMan integration with Maya, and realistic cloth or dynamic simulations. Erick has a Bachelor of Fine Arts degree in Computer Graphics from the Academy of Art College, is Alias|Wavefront certified in Character Setup, and has been a Maya user since its inception at version 1.0.

Max Sims began his career as a car designer in Europe with Opel and then Renault. He joined Alias in 1989, servicing industrial design and animation clients. After leaving Alias, Max began his own entertainment design and design visualization firm Technolution, which boasts clients such as PDI, ILM, Pixar, frogdesign, and Apple Industrial Design Group. He went on to become a product manager for thinkreal, with an upstart Italian company called think3. In 2000, he joined LuuLuu.com to create digital fashion tools. As the director of 3D production, he used Maya as the primary tool to make models' bodies and drape clothing on them. Since 1994, Max has been teaching advanced rendering and modeling as well as Maya at the graduate level at the Academy of Art in San Francisco. He is now an adjunct professor at Cogswell Polytechnic, where he teaches concept design and Maya. He also teaches Painter and Advanced Alias Studio in the industrial design department at the Academy of Art. Max is still designing and can be reached at max@technolution.com.

About the Contributors

Adrian Dimond is an animation director and visual effects supervisor who currently resides in Los Angeles. Recent clients include *The Anna Nicole Show*, Korn, Cherish Productions' film *Cherish* with Robin Tunney, 3DO's *Mad Trix*, and Mattel's *Max Steel*.

Adrian began his computer studies at The School of the Art Institute of Chicago, where he also studied painting, sculpture, performance, digital audio, and video. "When I discovered the world of 3D, I realized that I could combine all aspects of fine and time arts in one medium," he says.

In his spare time, Adrian enjoys doing Perl scripting and rebuilding the front end of his car. Adrian is a very active member of highend3d.com, where he shares his insights and 10 years of experience of working in the CG industry.

Will Paicius thinks himself *Hokusai* of Character Animation in that he believes his best work is still ahead and he is continuously improving toward that goal. As a full-time professor of character animation and game design at Cogswell Polytechnical College in Silicon Valley, he devotes much of his time to Cogswell's Game Club (fuzzywoto.org), who won IGF Student Showcase Finalists for "Gates of Temlaha" in 2003. Will also teaches at DeAnza College and other schools in the Bay Area. He founded NeoCreations, a non-profit company providing students with professional sub-contracting work. NeoCreations students provided game modeling for *HydroThunder on PS2*.

 **Daniel Naranjo** is the Lead Organic Sculptor and 3D Modeler at Alvanon Inc., a 3D Visualization, Data Management and Rapid Prototyping company for the garment industry. Dan also attends art school and is a traditional sculptor. His training has focused on the priceless skills of balance, weight, and compositional proportion in regards to both organic and non-organic forms in traditional sculpture. Dan applies this valuable knowledge in his everyday work as a Lead Modeler, modeling in 3D, and sculpting models that are eventually sent to be milled via 3D rapid prototyping machines, transforming his sculpted 3D forms into real life-sized organic sculptures. These prototyped objects are used for product visualization and manufacturing. The results are perfectly accurate real scale organic forms that are sold for various visualization purposes.

 **Daniel Roizman** has worked in the visual effects industry for more than eight years. He began his career as a product specialist at Alias|Wavefront, where he worked with the development team responsible for creating Maya. Daniel has worked as the FX animation supervisor for several post-production facilities, including Kleiser-Walczak, Simex Digital Studios, and Spin Productions on projects that include X-Men, The One, Imax *Cyberworld* 3D, Universal Studio's *Amazing Adventures of Spider-Men*, and the Clio Award-winning commercial Trophomotion. In early 2000, Daniel created the kolektiv (`www.kolektiv.com`), a company conceived to assist visual-effects companies in achieving their production goals. Through the kolektiv, he authors and produces training DVDs for Alias|Wavefront, collaborating with industry experts such as Habib Zargarpour, and also develops plug-ins for Maya that are currently in use at studios around the world. To contact Daniel, purchase kolektiv plug-ins or training DVDs, or learn more about the kolektiv, visit `www.kolektiv.com`.

About the Technical Reviewer

This reviewer contributed their considerable hands-on expertise to the entire development process for Inside Maya 5. As the book was being written, this dedicated professional reviewed all the material for technical content, organization, and flow. Her feedback was critical to ensuring that Inside Maya 5 fits our reader's need for the highest-quality technical information.

 **Linda Rose** has worked in product development as a senior technical writer for Alias|Wavefront for 12 years. She has been working with Maya since version 1, specializing in dynamics and cloth simulation, and creating Maya online help. She is now a freelance writer and online help system developer. Linda resides in a 100-year-old farmhouse in Santa Barbara with her husband and daughter.

Dedication

—Mark Adams—

I dedicate this to my lovely wife, Stephanie, whose love and support made my contribution possible; and to my boys, Peter and Kevin, who put up with Dad hiding away in his office these many months when they wanted him to play instead.

This is also for my mom, who learned that this career was a better choice for her son than being a lawyer and who always had high expectations of me.

—Erick Miller—

To my grandma, Ida Dimeo, to whom I would like to dedicate my portion of this book, who helped raise me as a baby, and who died while I was writing this book. God rest her soul… and, to Monica, my beautifully intelligent wife and lifetime partner, for eternal love, emotional support, and stability.

—Max Sims—

This is dedicated to my very supportive wife, Chris Sapyta, and lovely child, Zelia Katherina Sims. I got my first nibble on this book on a very strange day. September 11 was my daughter's first birthday. I saw it all come down before she even woke up. What would we know about happiness without pain?

I also want to thank my parents, Joseph and Dinea Sims, for making me who I am and never dictating where my career should go.

I want to thank Edward and Marie Sapyta for creating such a lovely daughter for me to marry.

I want to thank the spouses and significant others of my co-authors, Erick and Mark, for supporting these two and permitting them to help me get the project done. Thanks, Steph and Monica!

I can't go on without mentioning my brothers: Chino, Marco, and Julio. My only regret is not having an o at the end of my name.

Lest I forget the in-laws: Diana, Carole, Karen, Jim, Paul, and Kathy. Oh, and then my nephew and niece, Liam and Moira.

Since we are on the subject, thanks to all of my friends who I couldn't hang with as much since I was doing this book: Jim Leftwich, Debbie Young, The Yankees, Jeff and Laurel Stvan, Paul and Robin Murphy, The Nassisis, The Weys, The Rydings (of Seattle and Indiana), The Baptistas, and the interchangeable Hodkinsons.

I want to sincerely thank Mark Adams, Erick Miller, Daniel Roizman, and Scott Clark for joining in on such a large project. This was greatly improved by your participation.

Acknowledgments

Mark Adams

Thanks aplenty go to the founders of Alias Research, who gave me the opportunity I sought to take the big turn away from the engineering-oriented use of CAD and toward the creative side of this business. Thanks also go to the people of the old Wavefront, who spurred on the competition that led to the feature-rich products we now have before us. Now that these old rivals have become one company, users such as myself can enjoy the fabulous range of tools and creative possibilities embodied in Maya.

The years I spent working for Alias were filled with people who deserve public appreciation for all the help they freely gave—particularly Kevin Tureski, John Gibson, and Milan Novacek. The other talented applications engineers I worked with also shared their secrets freely—thanks especially go to Stanley Liu, Phil Moy, Damir Frkovic, and Brad Redmond.

I can't even imagine where I'd be right now if not for Damir Frkovic, who called me back in 1994 and wondered if, just maybe, I'd be interested in working for Pixar. Now, Detroit was a nice enough place (and my sports allegiances are forever based there), but when I look out my window at the San Francisco skyline and see all the talented people walking by my office door, I remember that this entire phase of my life started with that phone call.

Of course, I'm deeply indebted to many of the people here at Pixar. In particular, I owe much to Eben Ostby and Eliot Smyrl for their continuing technical help over several films and several years. Thanks also are due to Deirdre Warin, Kelly Peters, and Cindy Cosenzo for their ability to manage production details with aplomb and for helping me keep my sanity when things got insanely busy.

I'm not sure I'd have ever weaned myself from Alias AutoStudio had it not been for the gracious support and copious Maya knowledge of many other Pixar people. Chief among these were Bryan Boyd, Bruce Buckley, and Martin Costello. Extra thanks go to Josh Reiss, who had the patience and knowledge to listen to all my Maya gripes and show me how to fix them and understand "the Maya way," even as I pined for the AutoStudio way.

Special thanks go to John Lassiter, who showed us all the magic that was possible with computer animation; to Ed Catmull, for helping found this wonderful company; and to Steve Jobs, who believed in the magic and made sure that the lights stayed on when Pixar was not yet a household name.

I'd also like to go way back and thank Kathleen Hanna, Patricia Ferrick, Jean Jorgenson, and Allen Gilbert for the fun and enthusiasm that made my early years at Intergraph so enjoyable.

As challenging as a career in computer graphics can be, people like these showed me that it can be even more enjoyable.

To Linda Bump, Victoria Elzey, and Audrey Doyle, thanks so much for your continuing support and patience as we've tried to shoehorn writing this book into our lives. Rookie authors must be awfully aggravating, but you've each been tremendous, hardly complaining a bit as you've bent over backward to keep this project moving.

Finally, thanks to Max Sims, for approaching me about this project and graciously tolerating all the difficulties I made for him as we collaborated on it from afar. Thanks also go to Erick Miller, Daniel Roizman, and Scott Clark for all of their contributions and hard work.

Erick Miller

To my mom (Anna) and Jim for all of the most valuable advice, wisdom, support, and lessons in life. To my father (Steve), Carol, Gramma, Grampa, and all of my family for their love, advice and support over the years. To Max Sims, Chris and Ziela Simms, Linda Bump, Audrey Doyle, and the other great editors, authors, and contributors to this book; Daniel Naranjo, Paul Thuriot, Manfred Reif and the LuuLuu/Alvanon crew, Darin Grant and all the amazingly talented people at Digital Domain, Steve Mauceri, Tim Coleman, Nathan Vogel, AAC and Mesmer. Finally, to all of the people who have ever helped me personally or professionally, and most especially, to all the readers of this book: I would like to give my deepest thanks, dedications and goodwill.

Max Sims

I want to thank all the current and past employees of Alias Research and Wavefront Technologies for creating such an unfathomably deep software package. It has been a pleasure and honor to have worked with you or used the fruits of your labor.

I especially want to thank the crew at the Alias|Wavefront San Francisco office. This includes Jim Lorenz, for selling me my trusty Indigo 2 so many years ago; Heather Hughes, for supporting the SF Bay Users Group beyond my wildest dreams; and Pete Billington, for his technical support and industry insight.

Back at Alias|Wavefront corporate: Thanks to Donna Teggart, Heather Kernahan, Darlyn Dimayuga, David Lau, Shelley Morden, Laryssa Struk, and Dwayne Poot, and Renukah Maharaj. Also, to Steve Spencely for designing the best UIs on the planet, Kevin Tureski for giving credit where credit is due, Dave Wharry for delivering the goods to the users group, Peter Mehstaeubler for that meeting in Santa Clara, Bill Buxton for that walk in Seattle, and all the past presidents of Alias|Wavefront—particularly Penny Wilson, for being such a good softball player; Doug Walker, for instilling faith and a future to Alias|Wavefront; and Dennis Payne, Brian McLure, and Kristen Pearce at Snader and Associates, for their generous support. Mark Sylvester, we miss you.

At New Riders, I want to thank Linda Bump for finding me and convincing me to do this. Thanks for working with my hectic schedule and the tough love. Stephanie Wall for staking so much for three harried writers.

I also want to thank Audrey Doyle, for such polished edits and talents as a good grammarian; Victoria Elzey, for guiding us neophytes through this; and Maria Raposo at ATI, Chris Seitz at Nvidia, Connie Siu at AMD, Adam Schnitzer at Lucas Arts, and Paul Thuriot at Tippet.

To all my students and colleagues over the years at the Academy of Art and Cogswell Polytechnic College, who have vitalized me and taught me in so many ways.

To all my former employees over the years, especially Bruce, Erick, Debbie, Matt S., Matt J., Mike K., Alex C., Paul T., and Sven J.

Thank you, Dave Cole, Dan Brick, Hideki Masuda, Kevin Cain, Ronn Brown, William Renteria, Josh Hartl, and Bill Barranco.

I need to also acknowledge every librarian and bibliophile I have ever met. With a special wink to Bruce G. Dahms at The Cogswell Library. I wouldn't know that I don't know without all of you, and I would have a much smaller residence without all these damn books. It feels good to put a book out.

Lest I forget two other great librarians, Gretchen Goode and Lillian Heatherton at the Academy of Art—thanks for the "Shots."

Tell Us What You Think

As the reader of this book, you are the most important critic and commentator. We value your opinion and want to know what we're doing right, what we could do better, what areas you'd like to see us publish in, and any other words of wisdom you're willing to pass our way.

As the Senior Acquisitions Editor for this book, I welcome your comments. You can fax, email, or write me directly to let me know what you did or didn't like about this book—as well as what we can do to make our books stronger.

Please note that I cannot help you with technical problems related to the topic of this book, and that due to the high volume of mail I receive, I might not be able to reply to every message.

When you write, please be sure to include this book's title and author as well as your name and phone or fax number. I will carefully review your comments and share them with the author and editors who worked on the book.

Fax: 317-581-4663
Email: linda.bump@newriders.com
Mail: Linda Anne Bump
         Senior Acquisitions Editor
         New Riders Publishing
         201 West 103rd Street
         Indianapolis, IN 46290 USA

Introduction

Welcome to *Inside Maya 5*. This book will guide you through using Alias|Wavefront's Maya animation, modeling, and rendering software in a production setting. We've written this in a unique way, taking you through all the discreet processes toward making your own short film. The book is for intermediate to advanced users who want to learn big-picture issues with the exact details of how it is done in Maya. A major emphasis is the how and why of creating a memorable piece while using a dominant tool. All the authors and interviewees are at the top of their craft and work with Maya professionally on a daily basis. All of us go through our specialized knowledge in dedicated chapters while trying to get a short film called *Parking Spot* produced. The entire digital studio production pipeline is shown here using Maya 5.

Who Should Read This Book

This book is intended for people who have a fundamental mastery with Maya. Think of this as a way of raising the hood of a car and getting inside the engine to get untapped horsepower. Users who want to know at a deeper level how Maya works and how to customize it will find this book enlightening. Power users will learn alternate approaches to their techniques and will explore in depth other aspects of Maya that they might not be as familiar with. Because no one is a specialist in every aspect of Maya, we have them show off only their expertise. The high-level overviews and workflow will be of interest to the power user (or the soon-to-be power use). All of us authors have a great deal of artistic knowledge to share with you as well. This is not just a "press these buttons" type of book; instead, it is intended to show the salient aspects of Maya from a production point of view by professionals *for* professionals or advanced users.

Who This Book Is Not For

People who have just started with Maya or 3D computer graphics (CG) might not be able to keep up with all the highly developed material in this book. People looking for a smorgasbord of menu picks will not find this here, either. Some areas and aspects of Maya, such as patch modeling, will not even be covered at all. We assume that you are not just dabbling into 3D. We also know that after reading this, you can't then apply everything to a large digital studio in a week. There is no substitute for mileage on complex systems, and this book is no exception. Even with all the pages written here, we couldn't tell you all the possibilities with Maya. If you want an idea of how Maya works and want to get familiar with it, we suggest getting *Maya Fundamentals,* by Jim Lammers and Lee Gooding, published by New Riders Press. (Yes, it sounds like a plug, but it's a great book and CD combo.)

Overview

This book attempts to show users of the software how a project would go from start to finish. *Inside Maya 5* is broken into three distinct parts. The first section describes Maya in its latest guise and shows how to customize it. The *Parking Spot* project is described in both visual and technical terms. With the context set, the next section delves into the guts of Maya. Here we follow the production process in creating the models, providing technical direction, and laying out the scenes. The last section gets very technical as well as artistic in unleashing the power of Maya. The node-based architecture and particle dynamics comprise some of the technical detail. Character setup is explained thoroughly, as is shading, lighting, and rendering. Here is more detail in each chapter:

- **Chapter 1, "Using Maya Well," by Mark Adams**—Major applications for Maya are enumerated, followed by a broad summary of its toolset and characteristics. A brief history of Maya and Alias|Wavefront is also included. Finally, the skills and traits needed to become a successful Maya user are described.

- **Chapter 2, "Project Overview," by Mark Adams**—The project on which our book centers, called *Parking Spot,* is described. Briefly, this is the story of a dog who finds his restful spot next to an open parking spot disturbed by an impatient man who needs a place to park his car. The objectives of the piece, both creatively and technically, are explained and our plan of attack for the book is described.

- **Chapter 3, "Digital Studio Pipeline," by Mark Adams**—Digital animation production studios have only recently become a reality. The process of creating an animation in such a studio is described, with particular emphasis on the flow of data through the production process. Our book's structure and Maya's tools are explained in the context of this digital production process.

- **Chapter 4, "Technical Considerations," by Mark Adams**—The environment in which a project is begun is an important factor in how easily and how well it is completed. To this end, we review the ways in which the Maya environment can be adapted to suit user needs. Customizing menus, defining useful hotkeys, tailoring shelves, and even modifying the interface itself are discussed. Recommendations are also made for efficiently navigating within and managing files and projects.

- **Chapter 5, "MEL," by Erick Miller**—The Maya Embedded Language is at the core of Maya. It permits interpreted scripting and acts as a simple yet powerful way to automate and interface directly with the Maya program. MEL is introduced and discussed clearly and in depth, as this chapter slowly builds up your knowledge of structured scripting and code authoring. Procedures, variables, control structures, loops and UI manipulation are all demonstrated in an easy-to-comprehend and directly applicable, yet fun manner. All code examples are fully tested, and included on the CD-ROM for immediate use by the reader.

- **Chapter 6, "Formats," by Mark Adams**—Modeling in Maya can be done in polygonal, NURBS, or subdivision surface formats. We examine the features, advantages, and disadvantages of each format and provide guidance for choosing among them or even mixing them. Distinguishing characteristics among these formats, such as continuity, shading, deformability, and topological flexibility, are carefully compared. Formats suitable for selected models in our project are also considered.

- **Chapter 7, "Methods," by Mark Adams**—Various useful modeling techniques are shown, independent of the project work. This both provides a useful set of techniques for general modeling purposes and saves time when we later describe how various models in our project are made. Techniques covered include creating rounded edges, working with artwork and image planes, making holes, and mitering corners.

- **Chapter 8, "Sets," by Mark Adams**—The process of modeling sets is first described and then examined in action as we walk through the process of modeling several set pieces. The street and buildings necessary for the *Parking Spot* project serve to illustrate typical modeling problems and how they are solved, with an eye to efficiency and fidelity to design intent.

- **Chapter 9, "Props," by Mark Adams**—A prop has different requirements than a set or a character, so we spend some time describing those requirements. Then we model a few. Starting with a simple prop, we work our way up to modeling a really complex model, the hero car (although not every gory detail is shown). Various modeling techniques are shown in context, with the rationale given for significant choices made along the way.

- **Chapter 10, "Characters," by Max Sims**—A lovable dog and odious jerk are modeled in subdivision surfaces. Techniques for eliminating modeling dead ends and efficient workflow are discussed. Maintaining the character's appeal and smooth flow of points are also addressed.

- **Chapter 11, "Layout," by Max Sims**—This chapter discusses the process of digital cinematography using Maya's robust camera tools to create an animatic. An interview with Adam Schnitzer, head of layout at Lucas Arts, further illuminates the art of layout.

- **Chapter 12, "Node-Based Architecture," by Erick Miller**—Maya's node-based architecture might sound technically complex, but it can easily be understood here. The varying aspects of how Maya's Directed Acyclic Graph (DAG) and Maya's Dependency Graph (DG) both function together to create the powerful combination of transforms, shapes and compute nodes that make up a Maya scene is covered. Attributes and connections are all explained in clear view, and will deepen your true understanding of how Maya works, as well as enhance your ability to harness the full power of nodes and connections in Maya.

- **Chapter 13, "Making Advanced Connections," by Erick Miller**—The next step up the learning ladder is to make some advanced connections. Techniques for complex connections between nodes are demonstrated in simple and easily understood step by step tutorials. The tutorials vary from short ("Creating a Hand Controller") to quite in-depth ("Using Particle Dynamics to Create an Overlapping Action Skeleton Rig"), and explain to you the connections that are occurring between all the nodes along the way. Each tutorial contains a nugget of knowledge on its own. This chapter gives you further knowledge of how Maya operates and, how you can use the knowledge of node connections in real world tutorial based examples.

- **Chapter 14, "Particles and Dynamics," by Daniel Roizman**—Dynamic simulations are one of Maya's greatest strengths, yet they remain one of its most untapped resources. This chapter explains the ins and outs of creating a water spray simulation, focusing on how to create high-level simulation controls, set up rendering parameters to achieve various looks, and properly integrate your final elements with other rendered layers.

- **Chapter 15, "Character Animation in Maya," by Will Paicius**—Maya's powerful animation tools are interwoven with the principles of animation. An interview with Scott Clark, an animation director at Pixar Animation Studios, sheds light on this misinterpreted art form. The correct sets of tools are combined to analyze and bring the illusion of life to the screen. Blocking, refining, and finishing off the animation complete the reality.

- **Chapter 16, "Character Setup Pipeline for Animation," by Erick Miller**—Setting up a character rig in Maya involves several key concepts and ideas, all of which must be considered within the context of the production pipeline. This chapter explains the concepts behind what makes a good character rig, and the methods involved with implementing these concepts within a production environment using Maya. Five golden rules of character setup are introduced, and common character setup pitfalls are discussed, each with Maya specific software solutions. This chapter is capped off with a special bonus interview with Paul Thuriot, the character setup Puppet Supervisor from Tippett Studios, one of Computer Graphic's most respected and celebrated CG Studios specializing in character and creature animation.

- **Chapter 17, "Rigging Characters for Animation," by Erick Miller**—A bipedal character and a quadrupedal character are both set up as digital puppets in order to make them the animated characters that they long to be. This is one of the core parts of Maya's forte. Character Setup techniques and custom controls show you how it is all done in a real world production environment. This chapter is packed full with in-depth tutorials for character setup, varying in complexity from mid-level to advanced. Rigging the quadruped setup of the dog and the bipedal setup of the Jerk are both explained in great detail through the use of rich multi-part tutorials. The clavicle, squashy, stretchy arms and legs, and complex spine setup of the Jerk's versatile bipedal character rig, as well as the four-legged Ik setup of the dog, his ears, and his tail, are all explained in much detail in separate contained rigging tutorials. Facial, jaw, and eye setups are all covered, as well as numerous skin-binding and weight painting techniques to achieve smooth deformations on your character. If you are interested in learning some new and sophisticated techniques in character setup to get the most out of your animated characters, then this chapter is definitely for you.

- **Chapter 18, "Shading," by Max Sims**—The process of creating hand-painted and procedural shaders is shown and compared here. Texture-mapping techniques also are demonstrated to eliminate confusion. Additionally, you will learn how to wire up your own custom shaders. Your observational and Maya skills needed in approaching any shader will greatly improve if you read this chapter.

- **Chapter 19, "Lighting," by Adrian Dimond**—When the scene is set, you can write with light using all of Maya's lighting tools. Efficient setup and workflow speed up this process. You'll learn here how to simulate a warm summer day and observing six-point lighting, to give you an added cinematic edge.

- **Chapter 20, "Rendering," by Adrian Dimond**—Pointers, tips, and tricks help speed up the rendering process for getting to see your final images. This is the icing on the cake for a complete short film project.

- **Appendix A, "Intermediate and Advanced MEL," by Erick Miller**—This appendix goes into more detail on how MEL can be used leveraged on a production level. Many details are covered, including the ideas and concepts behind the core of several scripts and algorithms at the heart of these scripts. Many concepts are covered, including the use and power of Script Nodes, Script Jobs, Error Handling mechanisms in MEL, writing data to ASCII text, and much more. The appendix finishes with an introduction to Maya's extremely powerful C++ API, with a fully implemented example plug-in deformer, the rippleDeformer. All source code for each example in this chapter has been fully tested, and is included on the companion CD-ROM for immediate use by the reader.

Conventions

This book follows a few typographical conventions:

- A new term is set in *italics* the first time it is introduced.

- Program text, functions, variables, and other "computer language" are set in a fixed-pitch font—for example:
  ```
  optionVar -intValue attachCrvKeepOriginal 0;
  ```

- Code lines that do not fit within the margins of the printed page are continued on the next line and are preceded by a code-continuation character ➥. Please note that the printed versions of the coded examples may have some lines that wrap in publishing, potentially causing a syntax error to occur if the code were to be typed by hand with actual returns in an editor. All code in this book has been thoroughly tested, and is included on the companion CD-ROM, in fully functional and usable form, which can be directly opened in any ASCII text editor for viewing without any possibility of syntax error due to the line wrapping or formatting of the text that occurred due to publishing.

Part I

Maya and the Production Pipeline

1	Using Maya Well	3
2	Project Overview	17
3	Digital Studio Pipeline	33
4	Technical Considerations	51
5	MEL	81

Chapter 1

Using Maya Well

By Mark Adams

As many Maya users already know, the Maya product was named for a concept in Hindu and Buddhist thought. Sometimes referred to as the "Mother of Creation," sometimes seen as the material universe itself, and sometimes understood as the illusion masquerading as reality, the concept of Maya is rooted in the nature of reality itself. In these Eastern schools of thought, reality is not what it seems. The material world is itself an illusion, one that hides the fundamental unity of all things. Maya is both the world and the illusion of its reality.

The product name is uncannily appropriate. The Maya application from Alias|Wavefront is an incredibly powerful tool that can create entire worlds, never revealing the reality behind the illusion. Fantastic creatures can romp through jungles of mysterious plants. Huge spaceships can engage in spectacular battles in galaxies far, far away. Entire civilizations can carry on their epic sagas in the grass of our own backyards. The illusions made possible by this particular Maya are bounded only by the limits of our imaginations and its technology.

But the reality is that these are real limits. Our imaginations are shaped in many ways by what has gone before. Conveniently, so is our understanding. Maya can't fill in the gaps in our imagination, but it can help us to close the gaps in our knowledge. As complex as our world is, Maya provides us with powerful tools to reduce those complexities to manageable levels, enabling us to create fresh worlds of our own.

Although Maya demands much from its users, those who seek to use it well are rewarded for their labors. From the moment a new user starts it up, Maya is a compelling product. The knowledge it requires can be gained one step at a time. The tools themselves embody the acquired knowledge and techniques of their designers, yet these can be amended with the new knowledge and techniques of their users. As experience is gained, Maya users become capable of producing breathtaking images worthy of art galleries and feature films.

Progressing from novice to expert is a goal of most Maya users. In this book, we'll try to help move experienced Maya users farther along that path. To do this, we'll explore Maya's features by demonstrating their use in an actual animation project. Tool details, background theory, production strategies, and practical advice are provided.

This chapter looks at the following:

- What Maya can do
- How Maya came to its current state
- How to develop your Maya skills
- How to approach Maya projects

What Maya Can Do

When enumerating the features of Maya, it's tempting to instead prepare a list of what it *can't* do. It can't make your morning coffee, walk the dog, and so on—but the list of its shortcomings as a modern computer graphics application is awfully short. Maya has tremendous breadth and depth in its feature set, owing in large part to its impressive lineage (described later in this chapter), as well as the hard work and brilliance of the people at Alias|Wavefront.

Applications

Maya is adept at a great many things. Most CG users are well aware of the many feature films that have used Maya to produce outstanding special effects and compelling animation. From *Lord of the Rings* to *Shrek, Titanic* to *Pearl Harbor, Star Wars: Episode I* to *Final Fantasy, The Mummy* to *The Matrix,* and *Ice Age* to *Monsters, Inc.,* Maya has been there, putting breathtaking scenes before our eyes and breathing life into characters. In just a few short years, Maya's strengths have made it nearly ubiquitous in feature film studios.

Television shows and commercials have also made extensive use of Maya. The average American television viewer probably gives little thought these days to watching a guinea pig and a rabbit talk about Blockbuster Video, but Maya users recognize the skill of the users and the power of the tools behind it all. Whether kids are tuning in to their favorite animated series or watching the latest music videos, the chances are good that Maya is right there, too.

And when kids switch on their video game consoles, chances are also good that the games they love were developed using Maya. Many of the top-selling games for Nintendo's GameCube, Sony's PlayStation, and Microsoft's Xbox rely on Maya's power to go from interesting concept to exciting gaming experience. Game developers such as Electronic Arts, Square, Acclaim, LucasArts, Sega, and Sony use Maya to keep children and adults parked in front of their games (and away from all those pesky chores they might otherwise be doing).

While product designers have used Alias|Wavefront Studio Tools for years to create everything from electronic devices (such as input devices for those video games) to jewelry, toys, and a myriad of household products, design leaders such as BMW Designworks use Maya every day to bring new ideas off the drawing board and into our lives.

Even scientists and engineers will often use Maya to visualize and understand complex data. Although Maya isn't used to calculate the collision of galaxies, scientists at NASA's Scientific Visualization Studio can use it to see what the simulation results look like. Or if you're going to court about an automobile accident, it's quite probable that if you see a simulation, it was done in Maya.

Tools

In just a few years, Maya has gone from new kid on the block (albeit one with thoroughbred parents) to the neighborhood Renaissance man. Maya is used for such a broad range of work because it has an equally broad range of tools. Even if you work with only a small slice of Maya's features, you can't help but notice the depth and detail inherent in its tools. You might not use some of the options in a given command, but you can rest assured that they're all there because other users do.

Models can be constructed a great many ways. Game developers will find a comprehensive suite of polygonal-modeling tools. Industrial designers will find the sophisticated NURBS surfacing tools capable of creating complex and precise designs.

Animators will enjoy the smooth surfaces and flexibility of the hierarchical subdivision surfaces. Each of these formats can also be utilized in a variety of ways, allowing the modeler to choose from a range of methods (including powerful tools such as Artisan) for a given modeling problem.

Shape data can also be imported or exported easily in a wide range of formats, including IGES, DXF, OBJ, RIB, and Alias Wire. Additional formats are often just a plug-in away. Animation data, including motion-tracking data with Maya Live, can also be read or written.

Character models can be articulated in many sophisticated ways, using deformers, skeletons, skinning, and constraints. From a broad selection of deformers, you might choose to use lattices, blend shapes, jiggle deformers, clusters, and wrap deformers on your character. You might then create your skeleton with inverse kinematics (IK), manipulate it with IK spline handles, and then use smooth skinning to control the surface shape during bends. Adding constraints (of which there are many types) can help ensure sane usage of the character during animation. Finally, character sets permit easy interaction with complex character controls without traversing hierarchies.

After the characters are rigged, Maya offers plentiful ways to quickly get the performance just right. In addition to conventional methods such as setting keyframes, Maya provides powerful tools such as Set Driven Key that get their power from the underlying Maya architecture, which lets almost anything be connected to something else. Or, if you prefer, perhaps path animation, motion capture, or even nonlinear animation will do the job. Tools such as the Graph Editor and Trax Editor help make great performances possible.

Technical directors can assemble shaders of great complexity and subtlety using tools such as Hypershade and the Hypergraph. By using graphical interfaces instead of requiring coding, tools such as these bring together complicated shading networks in an easily understood form that speeds along the process.

The range of effects available right off the shelf is extraordinary. From the incredible possibilities of Fluid Effects to the amazingly inventive Paint Effects, Maya dares you to create. Particle systems, dynamics solvers, fur, cloth—tremendously sophisticated tools are at your fingertips, tools that carry their weight every day in the entertainment industry.

Lighting and rendering tools brim with features. From the choice of lights to the choice of renderers (including third-party renderers), Maya gives you choices and more choices. By the time your final images have made it to the screen, you've used more power than was even imaginable on the desktop just a decade ago.

Of course, Maya leaves you with the tools to unlock even more doors with its API and the Maya Embedded Language (MEL) scripting language. If it's not in there yet, you can put it in yourself (and sell it to the rest of us). Maya gives you both a complete set of keys and the locksmith's toolkit for good measure.

Characteristics

Even with a broad and powerful toolset, it wasn't a sure bet that Maya would succeed. Great attention was given to features that don't show up on a list of commands, characteristics that set Maya apart from its competitors.

Foremost among Maya's characteristics is its adaptability. A wide variety of methods for interacting with Maya are provided. Some users, like me, will appreciate the marking menus and shelves, others will admire the HotBox, and still others will use the more conventional menuing system. Maya can accommodate each user's preferred method of interaction.

A closely related characteristic of Maya is its configurability. Menus can be changed, layouts can be added, and even the entire user interface can be rebuilt. Built on a user interface foundation that was intended to be reconfigurable, Maya offers persnickety users (such as us) the chance to just smooth over the rough edges with some hotkeys or to remake the entire interface in their own image.

Maya is also highly extensible. For artists and animators going about their daily work, MEL provides an easy-to-access scripting language with extensive capabilities. In fact, these scripting features are so rich that the entire Maya user interface is created with MEL. For serious software engineers, Maya also offers a richly featured API to allow them to add extensive new features and wrap them up within Maya or provide them as standalone applications.

Data in Maya is also made accessible. Although users may opt to store their data in a binary format, Maya provides an ASCII format, too, which makes all the data in the scene available for inspection or modification. Got a piece of problem geometry? Open the file in your favorite text editor and perform a little surgery. Even better, the file is itself made up of MEL commands. With your *MEL Command Reference* at hand, you can spelunk through even the most complex of scenes to learn how things are really done.

Finally, you can move that data easily between systems. Whether your need is importing an artist's EPS file or exporting an IGES file, Maya is set up to handle it. Want to render with Pixar's RenderMan? Export a RIB file. Developing for the web? Support for Shockwave 3D is in there. You can even develop your own custom data interfaces, from simple things such as using custom attributes to using the API to write an interface to your own special data structures. Data in Maya is inherently designed to be open and available.

Maya's Development

Unlike our universe of illusion, Maya didn't just spring into being from nothingness. It was carefully designed by veteran software engineers to bring together the best of several earlier 3D products into a modern graphics product that could handle the demands of the new millennium's projects.

Maya's Roots

Nominally created in 1995, Alias|Wavefront really started back in the mid-1980s when Alias and Wavefront were formed. Alias officially began in 1983, while Wavefront hung out its shingle in 1984. Both companies were founded by a small group of people with big ideas about the use of computer graphics. Early players in the computer animation business, the two companies were rivals as they staked out their market niches. Although both companies began by pursuing computer animation markets for film and video, distinct differences appeared as they grew.

Alias made a huge turn into the industrial design market after General Motors became enticed in 1985 with the potential of the Alias/1 software. Previously relegated to engineering-oriented software, the industrial design market quickly embraced the idea of designer-friendly surfacing and visualization software. Originally offering a product based on cardinal splines, Alias moved quickly to uniform B-splines and then on to nonuniform B-splines, which greatly enhanced its surfacing capabilities and its appeal to product designers. Coupled with powerful rendering capabilities, designers found that Alias software let them better control and visualize their designs, and they loved it.

Meanwhile, Wavefront became an established leader in the production of video animation. Primarily a polygon-based product, Wavefront's software became nearly ubiquitous in post-production houses. Offering extensive capabilities for programming, it also became widely used for scientific visualization. Amazing images of turbulent flow, galactic interactions, and swirling storms brought its power to light. By 1988, Wavefront software (Personal Visualizer) was standard issue on every Silicon Graphics computer.

As their markets and products evolved, Wavefront and Alias developed other niches, but they didn't last long. Driven by the need to match competitors' features, the companies kept innovating and imitating, trying to land the biggest share of the market. Sometimes they simply bought the competition, as when Wavefront purchased Abel Image Research in 1988 and Thompson Digital Images (TDI) in 1993. At other times, they played leapfrog with features such as particle systems and dynamics. The competitive forces were ultimately healthy for both companies, at least as far as the products go.

With their merger in 1995, Alias and Wavefront could combine their knowledge and experience to develop a fresh new product. With such a project (coding a fresh entertainment-oriented product) already in the works at Alias, it was almost an obvious solution to bring in the expertise of the Wavefront personnel. Presented to the world in 1998, the happy parents named their new baby Maya and changed the industry.

Maya was an immediate success. Designed for flexibility, raw power, ease of use, and extensibility, Maya made life easier for a great many animators. Industrial designers might still use the Studio and AutoStudio products for complex surfacing, but animators flocked to Maya. Things that had previously required complex coding were now accessible through graphical interfaces. Tab A could be moved from Slot A to Slots B or C painlessly. The guts of the product itself were viewable and alterable, thanks to a powerful new language, MEL. Maya took the tools and experience of the previous products and presented new and easier solutions to problems—and then tackled entirely new problems.

Maya changed the computer graphics business. Once the private reserve of only particularly well-funded enterprises, Maya brought more power and value. Now within reach of even the serious hobbyist, Maya has made its powers of illusion available to a market hungry for more and better media content. Maya is growing up very well.

Your Development

Although the story of Maya's development from the technology and personnel that helped shape the computer graphics industry might be an interesting one, it's not *your* story. Each Maya user is unique, as is each studio using Maya. Perhaps all we authors really know about *you* is that, because you purchased this book, you have a desire to learn more about Maya.

Maya attracts all kinds. Some Maya users are trained artists, with a keen eye for form, color, and composition. Others are computer scientists, experts in coaxing the illusion of reality from lines of code. Still others are gamers, drawn to the tools that make their pastime a reality and seeking to share their ideas of a highly entertaining time. Some carry forward their love of animation from childhood, while others need to visualize staggeringly complex scientific data. People flock to Maya from a tremendous range of backgrounds, looking to realize a vision they believe others will understand and appreciate.

But let's be honest—Maya is not for dullards.

Powerful systems require powerful controls, plus the wherewithal and experience to know how to use them. The space shuttle's controls are more than a joystick and a fire button, after all, because they're capable of doing numerous things—in the right hands. In untrained hands, that shuttle's unlikely to even get off the ground.

Although it does a commendable job of dividing the complexity into manageable chunks, Maya must still have a considerable number of controls and a skilled operator to guide it. This is where you come in, bringing your own particular talents, vision, and background to coax from Maya yet another illusion.

Resources

So how does one develop the necessary skills? Even educational programs that expose students directly to Maya barely scratch the surface of all that it has to offer. Fortunately, a multitude of resources are available to the Maya user who has learned the basic skills and is ready for more challenges.

Of course, the fundamental resource of the expert Maya user is experience itself. Nothing compares to having done something similar in the past. Even the most brilliant of users will turn to previous work and build upon it, rather than start with a completely blank slate. In some sense, though, this begs the question, as one can't simply wait for the quantity and quality of experience to assemble itself. It must be gained through personal effort and attention to details—but Maya users are a pretty sharp bunch.

Background

Simply put, there is no "right" background for a Maya user. Expert users come from all sorts of backgrounds: artists, animators, engineers, programmers, gamers, industrial designers, physicists, and more. Maya is a tool that can be applied to a broad variety of disciplines and mastered by skilled people in any of those fields.

Useful skills, however, are many. The ability to visualize a model or scene well is a major asset. Although you can work out solutions by sheer persistence, having a mind that is attuned to spatial relationships saves a great deal of time and hair pulling.

An alternative to working with spatial relationships in your head is to work them out on paper. Drawing skills are tremendously valuable to Maya users because they apply to a multitude of problems. Model design, topological planning, animation posing, storyboarding, and even shading all benefit from good drawing ability. As an added benefit, despite popular opinion to the contrary, skill with a pencil can be learned—it doesn't take a mysterious "talent" to be able to draw well enough to assist you in your Maya work.

Tip

Make sure you keep pads of plain paper and pencils near your computer work area. The back of a napkin might do in a pinch, but it's important to remove barriers to sketching out ideas.

Enjoying problem solving is nearly essential. Whatever the nature of the task is to which you set Maya, you will find yourself solving a series of small problems as you work at it. These aren't the sort of problems for which you file bug reports; they're the kind of planning and execution details that need to be worked out to get to your final result. Sometimes it's deciding where articulation controls should go, sometimes it's deciding how to set up your lights, and other times it's writing a MEL script to expedite something tedious. If tackling such details suits your temperament, then your relationship with Maya is likely to be a happy one.

Closely related to problem-solving skill is programming skill. Unless you've specifically been hired to write scripts and plug-ins, don't worry about it. Most handy MEL scripts are just a few lines long, and the language is right there in front of you, being continuously used by Maya itself, where you can inspect it.

A more important skill may be familiarity with the particular computing platform on which you'll be working. Whether it's Windows, UNIX, Linux, or Mac OS, you'll want to be comfortable with the operating system at least at a routine user level. Knowing no more than how to just open and quit Maya is asking for trouble.

Spending only a bit of time each week to learn a little more about the system will reward you later with time saved and more options from which to choose. Fortunately, few users stumble blindly into Maya unaware of this.

Experimentation

The first resource to draw on is one made easy by Maya itself: practice. At any given moment, you can experiment. Remember, whatever you're doing in Maya can be set aside while you try something you haven't done before.

It's remarkable how easy this can be to overlook. Perhaps it's because it's easy to get so absorbed in the larger project before us that we just forget that we can save the current scene and explore the alternatives. Now that disk space is utterly cheap, we simply need to cultivate the habit of saving our work and taking a quick detour to better understand the problems before us and their possible solutions.

Tip

Develop a well-understood system for file naming and project management—one that incorporates a place to put your test scenes, too. When the moment comes to experiment, it will then be easy to know where to put your file for now and where to find it later.

Sometimes the necessary experiment is as simple as trying each of the options in an option box of an unfamiliar command. Other situations might call for building some simplified test geometry and trying various operations on it.

You can approach most problems by testing possible solutions on simple examples. But even if the only way to try something is to use the entire original problem, remember that in Maya you're not committed to continuing down that path. You can try an idea, back up, try another, save it, back up again, try something else, and so on.

Maya provides many ways to experiment. You can use Undo to back up and try an operation (or a long sequence of operations) again and again. However, undos work only within a single Maya session; they are forgotten when you exit Maya.

Tip

Set your number of undos in the Preferences window to a reasonable number. The default queue size of 10 is much too small, while Infinite is much too large. A queue size of 100 or 200 works well for most situations.

Command history is another powerful aid to experimentation, one that is retained in the scene file itself. Although I don't make much use of command history myself—I'm a modeler, for the most part, and don't require history relationships for very long—I usually leave history turned on. If something goes wrong, I can often find the offending operation in the object's history stack and simply delete it. When I no longer need history on an object, I simply delete it, using a hotkey I've set up to make it easy.

Even though reliable work habits and time-tested strategies are excellent assets, break free of their grip occasionally. Try something in a whole new way or just change an option value, but try things. A spirit of exploration will advance your skills considerably faster than if you always do things in the same old way.

Education

Experience might be the best teacher, but there is still a huge need for educational resources. Although there are many formal ways to learn the field of computer graphics, there are many other options as well.

You hold in your hands one of those options—a book. Now that computer graphics is so widespread and Maya is so popular, many titles are available for learning. Some of these books target the novice, while others target advanced users. Many make extensive use of tutorial examples, with examples that have been checked carefully to ensure that the mechanics are sound and the results are predictable. Because there are multiple book publishers, many titles compete against each other for the same market demographics. Often users just elect to buy them all and glean from each what each author has to say.

Even though most sophisticated programs now offer online documentation, there is always the need for another perspective than that given by the software publisher. In books such as this one, you can find opinions and criticisms, not just descriptions of tools and interfaces. Furthermore, the examples supplied with the software usually avoid problematic situations, whereas an independent text (such as this one) can forge ahead and describe the compromises to be made while pursuing goals other than just explaining the software's features.

Of course, the Rosetta Stone of resources is the online material provided by Alias|Wavefront. An enormous amount of help is available, as close as the F1 key. From *Instant Maya* to the *MEL Command Reference*, detailed documentation is at your fingertips. Whether you're looking for a tutorial to give you a sense of particle dynamics or you're trying to find out whether an option exists for a MEL command, the Maya documentation can help.

Tip

Be sure to add your most commonly accessed online Maya documents to your browser's bookmarks. Don't forget to include the Alias|Wavefront home page and links to third-party sites that cover Maya, too.

Several third-party sites about animation or computer graphics also offer Maya resources. User-written tutorials are an especially popular way of explaining a given topic because the step-by-step detail they offer ensures that the intended material is covered. Take the time to seek out and organize those resources that you find valuable for the kind of work you're doing with Maya.

Many of these same third-party sites also offer message lists or discussion forums for exchanging information and opinions about Maya. Take the time to explore the forums and Maya resources on sites such as www.3DArk.com, www.cgchannel.com, www.cgtalk.com, and www.highend3d.com. Tremendous resources available, between the information already on the boards at these sites and the information available directly from folks who take the time to read questions you've asked.

A particularly popular list is the Maya List from www.highend3d.com, which reaches thousands of Maya users. You can easily sign up for the list on the web site, but you might want to immediately filter the list to a separate mailbox—it's busy!

Another useful resource can be a Maya user group. Although the web has lessened the impact of the actual user group meetings, it has also enhanced the potential for the groups to effectively share information and techniques. In addition, the personal relationships they foster can be an invaluable resource as careers and skills develop (besides which, it can just be fun to talk with someone who really understands what you're going through). Check with Alias|Wavefront to see if a Maya user group is available in your area.

Maya classes can be found in a number of places as well. From four-year institutions down to community colleges, Maya-specific classes have become available. Specialized schools even cater to the animation and graphic arts markets (such as the Ringling School of Art and Design and the Expression Center for New Media), offering Maya training in many contexts and levels. SIGGRAPH, too, has become a popular place to learn from the masters in Alias|Wavefront's Maya Master Classes. No longer must users rely on the right job, the right co-worker, or Alias|Wavefront for high-quality educational opportunities with Maya.

Finally, thanks to the Maya Personal Learning Edition, it's now even possible to learn Maya at home on your own computer. Although this edition is currently available only for the Maya Complete product level (a strange name, considering it's not actually "complete"), a new user can use a PLE version to learn most of Maya. It takes some determination to push yourself through the features, but with the aid of the tutorials and online help, it's possible to learn more than enough to go from novice to employed professional in the computer graphics business.

Approach

As important as any of the resources you've brought to bear on your personal Maya development is the attitude you bring. Whether you've had an exemplary academic background or bootstrapped your way into the business with the PLE, your success with Maya will certainly find itself linked to your approach to working with it.

Maya can be huge and intimidating, but it can also grow to become your greatest ally, given an attitude of curiosity and some measure of patience. You'll want to know everything right away, and you might find yourself discouraged or overwhelmed early on. That's perfectly normal. Maya's not easy, but it's not impossible, either.

Applications such as Maya don't come around every day. There is a truly incredible amount of power and subtlety to Maya, much of which simply takes experience to put to use. Maya is an even larger application, for instance, than Mac OS X. Untold man-years have been spent adding and refining features, both to make Maya usable by the novice and to enable expert users to harness all that power.

There is so much to Maya that you simply must acknowledge up front that you won't know it all. No matter how much time or how many projects you use it for, each day will teach you new things about it. Although it can be a blow to your ego, this is actually a good thing. You don't have to know it all—just enough to take care of the project in front of you.

Summary

Maya isn't for dummies—it's a robust, world-class 3D product that can do amazing things in the right hands. We see Maya work on the television, in the movie theater, at theme parks, and in our computer games. With knowledge of how to use it well, you can use Maya to make jaws drop and pulses race in appreciative consumers around the world.

Evolving from the mergers of a number of industry-leading software vendors, Maya has a power, range, and adaptability that resulted from this combined expertise. The integration and extension of features formerly developed to distinguish competing products has produced a package with enormous breadth and depth.

Robust modeling technologies, from polygons to NURBS surfacing to hierarchical subdivision surfaces, help your project to get off to a running start. Powerful, reconfigurable shading networks can provide just the look you're after. When your shots are assembled, Maya's character setup and animation tools continue the legacies of Alias and Wavefront as animation industry leaders. Whether you need forward or inverse kinematics, dynamics, particle systems, deformers, constraints, skin binding, clusters, or motion capture, it's in there.

Throughout the project, the flexible UI can be there when you need it and out of the way when you don't. Custom interfaces and new tools can be developed with the extensive API. Features such as Paint Effects, Maya Fur, Maya Cloth, Artisan, and Fluid Effects reduce exceptionally complex problems to a manageable size, allowing you to focus on the result instead of burying you in the process. When you're ready, Maya's lighting and rendering tools give you the flexibility you need to achieve the look you're after.

In Maya, beginners can get started easily enough, but expertise must be earned through experience. Reading a book, as useful as it can be, will expose you only to the ideas of others. When you've crossed the line from following along in others' footsteps to blazing new trails of your own, you'll be on your way. As the tools, techniques, and flavor of Maya become second nature and become just the background from which you work, you won't just be using Maya—you'll be using it well.

In the chapters that follow, we'll try to open your eyes to not just the particular details of Maya's features, but also why we use them as we do. We'll show you how we approach a real project, and we'll try to separate the wheat from the chaff. You've made your way into the thick of the Maya jungle—now we'll try to show you ways to make your journey less about raw survival and more about really going places.

Chapter 2
Project Overview

By Mark Adams

Although we'd love to claim otherwise, the *Parking Spot* project wasn't a story gathering dust on a back shelf, waiting to be brought to life by an inspired group of fans. Nor was it a famous commercial or short film seen by millions crying out for a book about it. No, *Parking Spot* was created just for you, the readers of this book about using Maya well. Think of it as a small piece of entertainment with a purpose, one created especially with you in mind.

In this chapter, we discuss the project itself, not the steps of any particular Maya process used in creating it. In the next chapter, Chapter 3 "Digital Studio Pipeline," we take a high-level look at the process itself; then we dive into the project's particulars in following chapters.

But here we pause to consider both the task we've set for ourselves and our objectives. In this chapter, we look at the following:

- How the *Parking Spot* project came about

- Our objectives for the project

- The details of the story

- Our plan for getting the project done

- What the final results should be

Beginnings

Like many things, *Parking Spot* came about from a combination of necessity, persistence, and coincidence.

The necessity was, of course, that we had signed a deal with New Riders to produce a book about Maya—specifically, a book about going from start to finish through an entire project. This was to be a book for people with Maya experience who want to see something taken from conception through to completion. Persistence and a few coincidences would carry us through some early difficulties and on to a well-defined project that served our needs.

So, what was that project to be?

Plan A

To be fair and accurate, the book deal was signed with a particular project already in mind. Max had proposed that the project would be a car commercial, which sounded good at the time. Cars are familiar, complex, and sexy, and their commercials are ubiquitous. A car commercial would be a well-defined, typical example of CG work—heck, it might even be entertaining.

After Erick and I were added to the team, we all met to discuss the task at hand. We needed to work out the details and divide up the assignments so we could turn our Maya book deal into an actual Maya book—the sort of book we'd want to buy.

Having had some experience modeling both cars and car parts, I was particularly concerned about the size of the piece we were biting off with the car commercial idea. Cars are *so* familiar that they have to be modeled extremely well, to fool even the casual viewer, regardless of the sort of experienced and critical reader we were seeking. Even a fairly realistic CG car (see Figure 2.1) won't pass for real easily.

The highly reflective paint, glass, and chrome finishes on a new car demand that these surfaces be created with great skill and attention to subtleties of form. We intuitively understand a car's body shape by looking at the reflections on its surfaces, reflections that act like flaw magnifiers—which is why you can immediately notice when your car door has been dinged in a parking lot. A whole car, presented seriously as the focal point of the project, might be a way to paint ourselves into a shiny proverbial corner.

Even if automotive designers used Maya (they don't—they generally use Alias|Wavefront's AutoStudio product instead), they would have a whole team of designers and a much more extensive budget than our little group. Surfaces are smoothed by specialized analysis programs, scrutinized in full-size clay models, and evaluated by test groups. Designs are revised over and over until literally millions of dollars have been dedicated to each new style that makes it into production and the advertising that slips it into your favorite sitcom.

Figure 2.1   A fairly realistic CG car.

Real car commercials also feature lots of driving around (in sets that the advertisers don't have to build for themselves first) and real people doing lots of realistic things. Focusing on the car itself (which a car commercial must surely do) quickly became an enormous threat to completing the project because it both demanded extensive resources and would likely expand the scope of the project in many directions.

Obtaining real car data was an even worse proposition because it would cut the heart out of the modeling section and we wouldn't know where to begin to get the appropriate permissions.

A new plan was clearly needed.

Regrouping

We like cars. In fact, we *really* like cars. Max was trained in the Transportation Design program at the Art Center College of Design, the Yale Law of design schools. Me, I'm from Detroit, so the love of cars has simply been drummed into my soul. Erick, well, he watches lots of sitcoms—for the ads. We're practically obsessed.

We wanted cars in our project, but we all agreed that realistic cars for a realistic car commercial could well be our undoing. As our meeting went on, we realized that we needed to enumerate our objectives and try to construct a project specifically to address them.

Defining Objectives

Foremost in our mind was that the project's scope must be manageable. Our team was small, and our project's time budget would be squeezed in between the demands of our day jobs and the publishing needs of New Riders. A grand but incomplete project was little better than no project at all (and a lot more work). As someone I know once said, "Real artists deliver."

Equally important, the project had to cover a wide range of Maya topics. No two users would bring the same understanding or needs with them to the bookstore, but our intended audience would definitely bring with them some experience applying Maya to their work. Because we couldn't know what the understanding, needs, or work would be for any given reader, we had to create a project that had both breadth and depth in its Maya coverage.

To complicate matters, we couldn't simply enumerate features and create simple examples to illustrate them. Maya already ships with extensive online documentation, and other Maya books are available that move systematically through features and exercises. Our goal was to show Maya being used to service the needs of a real project, letting the readers see how decisions are reached and real results are achieved.

For some added seasoning, we needed to be sure that the project put to use several of the latest and greatest Maya features. In our case, our project's delivery was going to depend on the (as yet) unknown release date and feature set of the next Maya release.

The project also had to lend itself to compartmentalization. Even though all of our team lived in the San Francisco Bay area (at the outset), it's a very large area and we weren't exactly neighbors. The work needed to be divided into suitably sized segments, with as many of these segments as possible being something a single Maya user could complete. Besides making a collaborative project like this ultimately possible, this seemed to reflect workplace realities, whereby teams of workers combine their specialized skills to produce an integrated whole.

This need for a distributed workload was also to ensure that there were as few bottlenecks in the publication process as possible. We needed to submit our written work chapter by chapter, balancing the need to do the project with the need to document it.

A related goal served by compartmentalizing the topics is that, ideally, each chapter can be read independently of the others. Of course, both the project and the book have parts that reference or depend on other parts, but the objective serves both masters well.

For ourselves, we wanted the project to be enjoyable and artistically satisfying. Like most people in this business, we've surely had our dreams of making that One Great Work that forever imprints our names on the minds of our peers. Even if this wasn't that masterpiece, we wanted to make something of which we could be proud, something that would hold up well to scrutiny in the eyes of fellow professionals and make them laugh at the same time.

Because we'd like our project to demonstrate our artistic skills nearly as much as our technical skills (which differentiates us from practically no one in computer graphics), we wanted to produce a piece that allowed us plenty of design freedom. No boring photorealism for us, thanks. We wanted some style!

Finally, we wanted a real story. Even if our piece ran only 30 seconds (our initial estimate), we wanted it to tell a tale that was worth telling, regardless of media. Despite the machinations we were willing to go through to include and illustrate Maya procedures, the story should at least appear to be a sufficient driving force that establishes the context and requirements of its components.

There's a bedtime story game I often play with my oldest son (who'll be six when this book comes out) in which he picks out a few assorted and unrelated things and I make up a story that includes all of them. Most of the time I manage to make up a reasonable story, despite my initial perplexity at creating one with, for example, a hippo, a bee, a tractor, broccoli, and a mountain. As we made our list of objectives, this project was starting to look like a real-life version of that game.

Limbo

After we'd finally hashed out all of our objections to the old project and our objectives for the new one, we started to discuss how we might satisfy those needs. As fun as brainstorming might seem before or after the fact, this is where our persistence came into play.

Working from an initial draft of our table of contents, we tried to think of objects or operations that might illustrate each topical area. We had expected to model, animate, light, and render shots with cars, people, sets, and props—but now we weren't sure just what would be the thread that tied them all together.

We liked the style and feature potential of including a car, but we agreed that we should adopt an exaggerated style, one clearly not intended to be photorealistic. That way, we could still deal with the same sorts of modeling operations, have more design freedom, and keep our workload manageable.

Now that our objectives didn't require utterly realistic designs, we decided to adopt a stylized design look throughout. Although this would ultimately be based in part on Art Deco, at this point we simply knew that our world wasn't like the everyday world.

We also agreed that we should try to keep the set(s) for our project as limited as feasible. A story that involves driving around through the countryside, for instance, would be substantially harder than one that takes place in a garage.

Probably because we were trying to include a car in our story, we found ourselves considering a scene set on a city street. Buildings could bound the set, a car would make sense on the street, our characters could be on the sidewalk or in the cars, and so on. It seemed like a city street scene had lots of potential, so we considered what Maya goals we might be able to achieve in such a scene.

Set modeling would be covered well because the buildings and streets are fairly typical set components. Props, too, would be easy to cover, given that mailboxes, signs, streetlights, fire hydrants, parking meters, and more are all around. Besides, a car is practically a complete course in prop modeling all by itself.

Also, because livable cities often have a few token trees planted along the sidewalks, we saw an opportunity to use Paint Effects for any such trees. Although subdivision surfaces could also be used to create some plants, we'd be foolish to not use the right tool for the job. Heck, it was easy enough that we might even plant some weeds to break up hard edges.

Characters were something more of a mystery, but we knew that we needed to work with a human (or at least a biped), to ensure that basic character issues would be covered. However, unless we wanted to make apes, Maya Fur wasn't going to get much use, so we considered a quadruped. Dog, cat, mouse, whatever—four-legged creatures were a worthwhile goal and would greatly enhance the range of character work.

So, with the modeling, rigging, animating, shading, and hair work, we knew that having at least one hero biped and one hero quadruped would allow us to explore a sizeable number of character issues.

Back and forth we went, trying to describe our topical needs and imagine ways to include examples. NURBS and subdivs could be covered by sets and props. We probably weren't going to use any pure polygons, but subdiv work used polygon commands anyway. Props weren't likely to need hierarchical subdivs, but characters would probably use them. And so on.

Dynamics? Wind. Particles? Exhaust, maybe water. Maya Live? Nope, not gonna go there. Some things wouldn't make the cut, but hopefully not too many.

When our meeting adjourned, we found that we had ripped the heart out of Max's proposal, but we had lots of fragments of ideas that might be used to bring to life a fresh new story. We gave ourselves the task of each coming up with a few story ideas that we'd offer up and decide between when we got together the following week.

Plan B

Nearly a week after our project-planning meeting, I came home tired after a long day of work and decided it was time for a nap. Evening naps for me are rare, but I knew that my wife would surely wake me so I wouldn't miss our favorite show. I had almost an hour available until showtime, and the kids were already in bed, so I was going to put it to some real use. I'd nap, watch *The West Wing*, and then knuckle down and come up with a suitable story idea.

The problem with my plan was that I'd thought it all the way through. Trying to go to sleep when expecting to later think about a problem is practically a written invitation to think about it now instead of later—so that's what I did.

In our meeting, Max had made passing mention of using a fire hydrant blasting out its water as a gag, and this came to mind as I lay down. Car, fire hydrant, character, quadruped—the bits whirled around in my mind and then suddenly fell into place. In the space of about five minutes, I went from having no idea of how we'd construct a story to having a virtually complete one.

Quadruped? Dog! Fire hydrant? Dogs love those!

Somehow, the mental image of a dog tied up out on the sidewalk near to (but out of reach of) a fire hydrant made all the pieces fall into place.

My nap now soundly ruined, I got up and called Max with my idea. We agreed to pass it along to the others on the project and consider it seriously as our new story. After a long and grueling balloting procedure (it was the first idea presented and seemed to do the trick), we decided to adopt it.

Necessity and persistence had brought me to that night, but it was a timely combination of circumstances that made the effort pay off in a satisfying story. If I hadn't gotten home early, if Max hadn't made the fire hydrant remark, if *The West Wing* hadn't been on that night—but many fortunate coincidences collectively put my mind on the track that took me to *Parking Spot*.

The Pitch

Here's how I presented *Parking Spot*:

We see the only parking space on a crowded street, which has a dog (Spot) next to it, tied to a tree and basking in the sun. Behind Spot is a toy store with a "Whatzits! Today Only!" sign in the window. Ahead of the parking space is a fire hydrant, with its red curb. The car pulls in, putting Spot into shadow and blowing exhaust in his face, which clearly annoys him.

As the man gets out, he checks his watch (it's late in the day), and we see a note ("Buy Billy's present!") in his hand. He sees a meter maid approaching from down the block and goes to the parking meter. As he reaches to put his coin in, Spot growls and snaps, keeping him from putting the coin in.

The man tries tossing a stick for Spot to fetch, but Spot doesn't go for it and instead points to his leash. Reaching over the trunk of the car won't work, either. The meter maid's getting closer.

Finally, the man goes to the window of a pet shop, next to the toy store. He points to a bone, but Spot shakes his head "no"—he wants the *big* one. When the man returns with the bone, Spot wants to be moved over to the sunny fire hydrant, too.

We next see Spot standing next to the hydrant as he takes a big bite out of the end of the big bone. Meanwhile, just as the man is about to drop his coin into the slot— BLAM!—he's blasted out of the frame by the hydrant's water. We go back to a shot of Spot grinning as he tightens up the hydrant's bolt with the wrench-shaped end of the bone. Behind him we see the toy store sign flip over from "Open" to "Closed."

We close with a shot of a ticket being placed on the man's wet windshield.

Fleshing It Out

Agreeing on the basic structure of the story was a huge step forward because it allowed us to define the necessary elements and begin to consider the sorts of peripheral items that support both the story and the book.

Although Spot is clearly not a dog to be trifled with, we wanted him to be the sympathetic figure in our story. The man in the car creates the story's problems and, so, ultimately pays for them. The meter maid's function is to provide added time pressure, forcing him to decide between his miserly nature and the mission he's there to accomplish.

Having these briefest of character sketches, we were able to flesh out many of the details.

Character Details

The man in the car would be a jerk. In fact, we simply refer to him as The Jerk. Maybe he's a salesman, maybe a spoiled rich kid. He surely talks endlessly on his cell phone. He's used to seeing the world from one perspective only: his own. He loves his car, which is somehow an extension of his self-absorption.

Character traits came easily, but we went back and forth to be sure we didn't make it all too black or too white, at least initially. While it might be easy to make the man a total jerk, annoying all who come near him, we want viewers to at least consider that he's trying to do the right thing. Conversely, we'd like Spot to at least be briefly considered a scary dog acting like a bully, not just a victim fighting back.

Spot is just minding his own business when The Jerk arrives to ruin his late afternoon basking. Thoroughly annoyed, Spot not only gets his revenge, but he also does it after getting The Jerk to get him a couple of things to make it up to him.

Once we had our characters described adequately, Scott Clark (a directing animator and talented artist at Pixar) set about the task of sketching some possible designs for them, as shown in Figures 2.2 and 2.3.

Figure 2.2   Early Jerk design sketches.

Figure 2.3 Early Spot design sketches.

After reviewing the designs and conferring among ourselves a bit, we finally selected a couple. Scott then retreated to his personal fortress of solitude and produced the artwork for our final character designs, shown in Figures 2.4 and 2.5.

Figure 2.4 Final Jerk artwork.

Figure 2.5 Final Spot artwork.

The meter maid requires no such complex understanding or artwork, however, and can be built ad hoc.

Scene Details

The design aspects of the objects aside, having our story defined meant that we also knew what was essential. We had to have a car, two stores, a sidewalk, a street, a fire hydrant, a bone, and a parking meter. Assuming that the details of the basic setup didn't change, we'd also need some other cars, a meter maid's vehicle, and a ticket. Depending on the camera angles we selected and any other features or design elements we wanted to incorporate, we might have several other objects (but we'd try to be careful).

After a brief discussion about the possibility of setting the whole story in the future, we decided that it served no story point and we would set it instead in a reasonably contemporary time frame. In fact, although we plan on interjecting some interesting twists in design history, the only time frame that actually matters is that last moment (before The Jerk's destination closes) while he tries to avoid a ticket.

The first scene and object designs were put together for the story pitch meeting (see Figure 2.6). They consisted of some embarrassingly bad sketches that tried to convey the project I saw playing before my mind's eye. However poorly drawn, these sketches conveyed the basic spatial relationships in the scene and contained the essential elements.

Figure 2.6 Initial story sketches.

One by one, key design elements would be carefully drawn up and provided for modeling reference. Miscellaneous objects, though, would be created with no special drawings—I would just make them up on the fly. Having had experience with most of the sorts of objects we'd use in our project, this wouldn't pose any problems.

More than any other object, the car simply had to have clear and detailed drawings. Max provided me with some excellent drawings of the hero car, such as the one shown in Figure 2.7.

Of course, as mentioned before, cars are really time-consuming and difficult to model well—and we were planning a parking problem. Clearly, we needed to have a plan to get this done.

We decided that we would find ways to transform our one hero car into a fleet of visibly distinct vehicles. With some trim and paint differences, we expect to be able to make these extra cars suitably distinct, especially because we'll see very little of most of them. As an added bonus, this process of modifying one object to create variants makes for some useful instructional material.

If all else fails, we might even import an old car model by Max and modify it to suit our parking needs.

Some additional objects might be needed for storefront displays and building embellishment, but we plan to tackle these as they arise. We'll let the story and the reels drive their creation.

Figure 2.7   Final hero car design.

The Killer B Plan

Every production needs a plan. What needs doing? When? Who will do it? How long will it take? Then what? Are we there yet?

Large studios ask questions like these all the time and employ teams of people organized to both ask and answer them. Small studios may not have the resources to manage these issues as directly, but they might rely instead on experienced, highly skilled production personnel who have the ability to manage their way through the mine fields that lie ahead. Large or small, successful animation projects must have some control over the methodologies and measurements used to ensure their success.

Because we've had the luxury of creating the story to satisfy ourselves, our experience could be markedly different from yours—but we still need a plan in place to know what we're attempting to do and whether we've succeeded.

For our project, there are two main criteria for success: the boards and the book. Rounding out this group of killer B's is the real stickler: budget.

(Story)boards

For tracking the progress from story concept until project completion, it's hard to beat storyboards. You lay down the story in pictures and then attempt to produce the animation shown in the pictures.

Our first pass at storyboards was as rough as rough gets, but I soon followed it up with some improved artwork, shown in Figure 2.8.

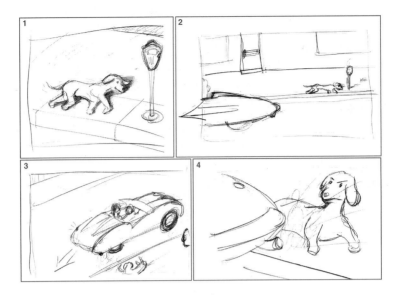

Figure 2.8 Our first real storyboards.

These storyboards would be then scanned into a Mac and made into a QuickTime movie. From this point forward, we could see how the piece played out, how long it was, what was confusing, and what made sense. We could also use these reels as historical documents, showing the evolution of both the story and the technical progress being made.

Of course, stories change. The final piece produced is almost sure to be different from the story told in early drawings. Some promising ideas get omitted for being overly long, for not moving the story forward, or because better ideas come along. Almost as soon as the story got onto boards, we found ourselves questioning various details. However, even if numerous small details change, the central core of the story remains intact.

Artistically, the storyboards are our reference point, enabling us to determine whether we've told a successful story. While numerous details of technical execution also bear on the actual completion of the project, these details are in service of the story told by the boards. No matter how technically sophisticated our use of Maya is, our project stands first on the legs of its story.

The Book

Most important of all, our project needs to serve the needs of this book. It's raison d'étre is the book. Artistic integrity and fidelity to the story are laudable goals, but just as advertisers must answer to the needs of product promotion, *Parking Spot* answers to the needs of explaining Maya.

We did, however decide that we would not artificially force any application of Maya's tools to our tasks. If we wouldn't do it that way in our normal use of the product, we wouldn't do it that way for the book, either. You won't, for instance, see any NURBS surface characters. With subdivision surfaces available to us (heck, even with just polygons), we'd never want to put up with the topological and continuity constraints that NURBS would impose on character work. It could be done, but that wouldn't help our readers understand how we'd really work, so we just won't go there.

Our guiding principle is demonstrating how we would really do a given task, explaining the considerations and decision-making process as we go. We felt that the book's value to the reader depends on that, most of all, even before the project itself.

The Budget

As we mentioned earlier, the *Parking Spot* project needed to be compartmentalized. Substantial portions of it would have to be done in isolation from the other portions, so we needed to divide up the project into appropriate segments. This was just one of the many budgeting issues we faced.

The time budgets for the project were of three kinds: publishing deadlines, screen time, and user time.

For a timely release of the book, New Riders needed material to arrive in time to be edited, reviewed, and put into book form. We needed to plan our individual assignments and compare notes with our editors to ensure that this could be done. For a group of rookie authors like us, this may have been the hardest part of the project.

Although we were making a film that had no rigid time constraints, we knew we would need to keep it short, for practical reasons. More screen time means more animation and more render time. Without being careful, we could easily create a monster. Our first guess was that the story would be between half a minute and a minute in length, but we would use the story reels to work out the precise timing. Ideally, we would choose a nice round number for the length, but we were open to giving ourselves some flexibility here.

As serious as any other budget restriction was our time. Working nights and weekends, we would be making *Parking Spot* on a shoestring. Our other work might ebb and flow, but we needed the tide of this project to move steadily forward. This requirement also strongly influenced the decidedly short nature of the film.

Other, more traditional costs of doing business applied less to us. We were making a "film," but we didn't necessarily have to get it onto film. As people with far too many computers among us, we knew we'd have the necessary hardware, and Alias|Wavefront came through with the necessary beta software. I bought a new Windows laptop just for the project (for more compatibility since I'm a Mac user at home), but I reasoned that I could sell it off when the project wrapped. Sure, I will….

Summary

Parking Spot is a short film project created to illustrate Maya techniques as well as entertain. Most of its contents are the result of deliberate efforts to create an animation project that would serve the readers, the authors, and the publishers simultaneously. The story itself, however, came about through a combination of necessity, persistence, and good luck.

Like most things in the piece, even the title suggests double meanings and hidden motives. Perhaps it's no different from any other project in that regard, but we couldn't help but get the feeling that there's a lot going on behind each and every detail of our project. Maybe it was just that we knew we'd be explaining it all in gory detail or that it might be endlessly picked apart by our peers, but we knew we needed a project that would work on multiple levels.

We hope that by explaining the genesis and objectives of *Parking Spot* we've drawn some useful parallels to your Maya work. As we go forward, we'll generally stick to the technical details, but we'll still be mindful of the other needs of the project (and now so can you).

Chapter 3

Digital Studio Pipeline

By Mark Adams

Working entirely in the digital realm has been practical for only a few years now, but it has already reached the point that small studios (and even dedicated individuals) can create compelling animation pieces to share with the world. Because of the enormous breadth and depth of Maya's features, you can accomplish virtually an entire project within its familiar confines, whether your digital studio is a team of hundreds or a team of one.

The digital studio is as much a process as it is a place, perhaps more so. Because most of the stages of the process depend on upstream results, it's an effective analogy to liken it to a pipeline. Of course, the analogy breaks down in some places upon careful inspection because many stages can be carried on concurrently, but even then a modified pipeline can be envisioned with parallel stages in appropriate places. The process has clear dependencies and a workflow that can be adequately described as a pipeline.

In this chapter, we'll describe the following:

- The stages through which our project (and its data) will pass
- The relationships of these stages to each other
- The reasons for the structure of our book
- The role of various Maya features within this pipeline

Preproduction

Before you fire up Maya and create your first object or render your first pixel, you should go through several important stages to ensure a successful result. Collectively, these make up preproduction and get your project off on the right foot. It's far better, for instance, to make a stylistic overhaul or to change major details about the story before production has begun than after the characters and sets have all been built.

So, somehow you've reached "Go" and the die is about to be cast. In this game, the best strategy will be to roll ones….

Story

Everything begins with a story. No story, no project. No project, no process. The quality of that story is fundamentally tied to the potential success of the project (at least, in a rational world), so it's important that this initial stage be well-executed. In addition, changes in the story can have enormous impact on almost all of the later stages of the process.

The genesis of the project usually provides you with the essential requirements, sometimes including the desired story line itself. However, even the most meticulously specified project will have some creative and technical latitude. The client has something in mind, which is usually grander and less specific than the final project (and its budget) can realize. And although there are often happy surprises as the work unfolds, the finite resources available make clearly defining the nucleus of the story particularly important.

Stories are rarely born fully developed. Instead, they usually evolve from an inspired concept, the rational consideration of objectives, the scrutiny of critical opinions, and the incorporation of the best of the many small "what-ifs" that occur during its development. At some point, the story is put into production ("greenlighted") and the heavy lifting begins. Although changes can and often do continue while production work is underway, unless they are purely reductive in their effect, they incur added costs. At some point, the cost of any further changes becomes prohibitive and the story must be locked.

To establish the details of the story, an initial treatment is usually followed up with storyboards. These storyboards serve several functions. First, they more clearly communicate the story than the treatment can because theyinclude information about the visual composition. Also, this shot-by-shot look at the story forces a finer-grained examination of the story's details. Using boards, story and compositional changes can be quickly made and evaluated. Finally, the storyboards can be scanned and used as the initial editorial test, and then gradually replaced by CG work as it becomes available. Storyboards are an efficient way to describe, detail, and communicate the story to both clients and production personnel.

Our story for *Parking Spot* (described in Chapter 2, "Project Overview") followed this development process. After carefully considering the needs of the piece, a concept was born that was then reviewed by the clients (ourselves and the publishers) and that gathered up details in preproduction. Our storyboards were created, scanned, evaluated, and modified (see Figure 3.1). Now, as the production work unfolds, budgets and other needs will pare back some details, while new ideas will add interest to the final product.

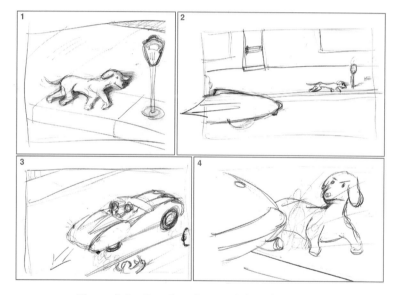

Figure 3.1   Storyboard artwork from *Parking Spot*.

Exciting visuals are unlikely to salvage an uninteresting story. A story without storyboards is likely to lack consistent or compelling compositions. Even the small gags that add texture and interest to repeat viewings will suffer if the story is treated lightly. An underdeveloped story will probably fail to realize either its visual or its narrative potential.

Treat your story as if the whole project depends on it—because it probably does.

Visual Considerations

The look of your project shouldn't be a by-product of the process, but rather an intentional choice you have made. Before beginning production in earnest, spend some time determining the visual character desired for the finished work.

Some of the visual direction for the project can come from the storyboards, but they are normally drawn quite loosely and focus much more on composition and story points than actual design details. For example, there will probably be a substantial design gap between the storyboard version of characters and their final look. For sets and props, which are often barely described during boarding, this design gap can be far more pronounced. None of this is critical of storyboarding (the idea being don't waste time drawing beautiful boards); it just points to the need for other sources of design information.

The visual design aspects of a production encompass a broad range of areas. Stylistic decisions can and should be made about character design (see Figure 3.2), set design, lighting mood, animation look, visual complexity, and level of realism. Even though these are stylistic decisions, each of these decisions carries implications for the tools to be used and technical requirements of implementing them.

Figure 3.2 Early character style possibilities.

In some cases, the visual decisions are fundamental, bringing a specifically required characteristic to the work. In other cases, they are less restrictive and open to creative interpretation by the director, art director, or animation supervisor (of course, sometimes these are all the same person). In still other cases, these decisions are a compromise between creative and budgetary forces pulling in opposite directions.

Because so many downstream processes are affected by the stylistic choices that need to be made, it's important to consider these issues once the story is understood. If budgets permit, exploration of these decisions within Maya is an excellent idea, perhaps taking the form of a test shot or sequence. Otherwise, even painting or drawing a few reference images can provide the necessary stylistic grounding for further work.

Just like the cool kids in school knew, distinctive style comes from careful preparation and attention to details.

Technical Considerations

However creative the application is, using Maya is still fundamentally a technical task. Tremendous amounts of technical skill and experience are involved in bringing most worthwhile projects to life. Fortunately, users of Maya are a clever and dedicated bunch, for whom this is as much a challenge as it is an impediment. Besides, as computers and software have advanced, we've found that we're able to embed more of our knowledge in these systems, of which Maya is an excellent example.

In a project of any complexity, some effort should be made to identify and address technical challenges that lie ahead. Some of these challenges are routine, while others are specific to the project at hand. Both deserve some careful attention to ensure that the project's goals are attainable and unimpeded by routine overhead.

The routine overhead of Maya is the easiest to address, yet is also the easiest to overlook. Throughout Maya are numerous ways to tailor its behavior to common tasks and to your working style. Maya boasts a highly configurable interface and offers extensive opportunities for extending its capabilities through scripting and programming via its API. What's more, almost the entire product is available for your direct inspection, thanks to its implementation through MEL.

Reducing this overhead can be accomplished incrementally, nipping off one rough edge after another (see Figure 3.3). Getting tired of making menu selections? Set up some hotkeys, marking menus, or shelves. Doing the same operations repeatedly? Put those operations in a MEL script. Don't like where some commands are located? Grab the menu script from the Maya product and put an edited copy in your own script directory. Each time you use Maya, you can make it better than the last time you used it—and better for each time you use it again.

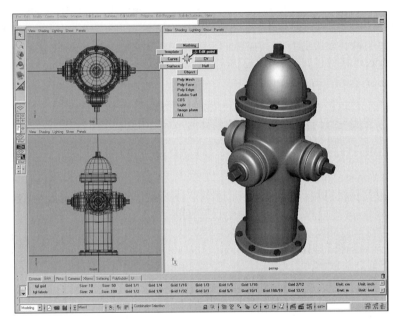

Figure 3.3   Tailored Maya interface.

This configurability can be taken many steps further via the Maya API. Although the software-development process of using the API is beyond the scope of our book, you can leverage the work of other software developers by purchasing their products or, of course, developing your own.

Other technical issues can be as simple as agreeing on standards for routine issues such as filing conventions. Whether you need to work out the logistics of storing data, customize your interface, write some new MEL scripts to handle custom attributes, or develop your own simulation system, Maya provides an extensive array of tools to tackle the job.

We'll show you the kinds of technical choices we've made in Chapter 4, "Technical Considerations."

Production Setup

Although animation production is a continuum, it can be useful to think of it as having an initial setup phase, followed by a phase in which the animation work flows through toward final output frames. In this section, we describe the stages in the digital studio pipeline that provide the necessary data for this flow.

Modeling

Modeling is the essential first step of the animation process. Without objects to animate, there are serious limits to the stories available to tell (although that hasn't stopped a few SIGGRAPH submissions).

As a production management issue, it's a good idea to inventory the models needed for a project. Budgeting and prioritizing these models enables informed decisions and allows resources to be applied wisely. Remember, almost everything takes longer than expected—particularly if you've never prepared a budget.

Although some objects in a production might not require artwork, all of the important models should have suitable design reference material available. Usually, this means creating drawings that describe the model in its key respects, often as a series of orthographic views. If the artwork comes from a separate art department, the activity of preparing this art will precede the modeling of any given object—although it can broadly parallel the activity of modeling, particularly if the model inventory is large.

With artwork in hand, the Maya artist can proceed to the creation of the model. For sets and props, these drawings can be sufficient, but characters will need additional art that shows the necessary range of motion and expression required of the model.

The modeler must choose from a variety of formats and methods for creating the model (see Figure 3.4 for an example that you'll build later), often depending upon the downstream needs of other stages such as shading or articulation. Each of Maya's available formats (polygons, NURBS, and subdivision surfaces) has its own set of characteristics and choice of construction methods.

Characters are likely to be created as subdivision surfaces (due to their inherent tangent continuity), whereas many set and prop models might be more readily made as NURBS (due perhaps to the ease of trimming or simpler shading). Some features will be added to the model to relieve the demands of shading, while others will be left for shading to provide.

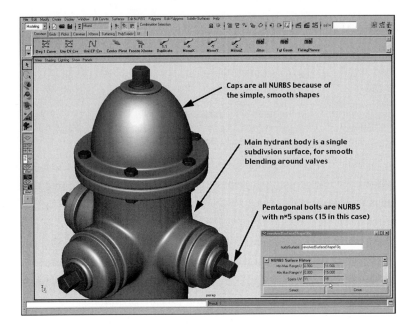

Figure 3.4 Model format and methodology choices.

Although in some sense it's the first step out of the gate for the production process, modeling affects a great many subsequent stages, so a thoughtful (but expeditious) approach to model construction is quite valuable. Having a clear sense of each model's budget is also important in keeping the project on track.

We'll lay down some modeling fundamentals in Chapter 6, "Formats," and Chapter 7, "Methods." From there, we'll plunge into the gory details in Chapter 8, "Sets," and Chapter 9, "Props." Then we'll explore a quite different kind of modeling in Chapter 10, "Characters."

Experience and a solid understanding of the trade-offs in each method and format will guide the modeler to a solution that is kindest to those who inherit his work and most effective for the production as a whole.

Articulation

Generally associated with character modeling, model articulation (also called *rigging*) applies to set and prop models as well. This process provides the necessary animation controls for each model component that must have movement not achievable through shading or simulation. Naturally, this stage must follow model construction.

Objects that employ ordinary transformations (translate, rotate, and scale) are easily handled through keyframing and often require little more than attention to the model hierarchy and relevant pivots. More complex relationships might entail deriving expressions that relate the model's components or specifying degrees of freedom and joint limits for inverse kinematics. Usually the specific values for these things can be determined after the model has been built (even *as* it's being built), so this sort of articulation follows easily after modeling.

The bulk of model articulation is indeed for characters, of course, because characters normally do the vast majority of the moving in an animation. For deformable models such as characters, Maya provides a wealth of tools for rigging. The technical director has skeletons, forward and inverse kinematics, a variety of binding methods, clusters, blend shapes, numerous deformers, and more to select from.

Character rigging is a complex activity that needs an ample budget and a ready model (see Figure 3.5). Although a substantial amount can be accomplished with a "stand-in" model, the actual model must ultimately be used to set up the character fully and pass it along to the animator(s).

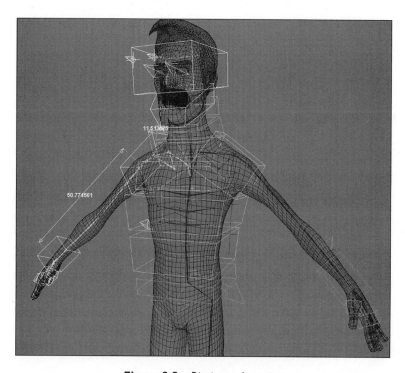

Figure 3.5   Rigging a character.

Also, because topological issues often arise with the model as it's being rigged, it's common for the model to be edited several times during the rigging process (effectively looping it back to the modeling stage). No matter—it's still moving down the pipeline.

We'll bring you along for the ride down this pipeline in Chapter 16, "Character Setup Pipeline for Animation." Keep your hands in and your heads down!

Shading

Another important stage of the pipeline downstream from modeling is shading. Depending on your studio's staffing and the particular model, shading can take place either following or parallel to articulation (in most cases, it follows).

Shading is, of course, the assignment of surface appearances to the model. It can be as simple as setting the color in one of Maya's predefined shading models and assigning it to the desired surfaces, or it can involve creating elaborate shading networks to specify a multitude of surface characteristics layered one upon another. Some studios might even choose to use other renderers (such as Pixar's PhotoRealistic RenderMan or mental images' mental ray), but the task of creating good surface shaders still takes considerable time and skill.

For simple materials, shading can be relatively straightforward—but most materials aren't simple (see Figure 3.6). If photorealism is the avowed goal of the project's finished look, the shaders will likely be complicated. The shading TD will need to plan carefully and iterate one feature at a time toward a satisfying finished look. Here again, preparing a budget and an inventory can be an invaluable aid.

Good shaders often rely heavily upon the artistic skills of a digital painter (who can be the same person as the shading TD). Real-world objects have dirt, scratches, irregularities, and surface textures that are not typically available through prepackaged shaders and texture procedures, so a skilled artist must create them. Even if a given shader isn't expected to be photorealistic, stylized shaders can carry nearly as much artistic overhead. Digital painting can be done within Maya (using the 3D Paint tool) or in other applications, such as Photoshop, Amazon 3D Paint, or Deep Paint 3D.

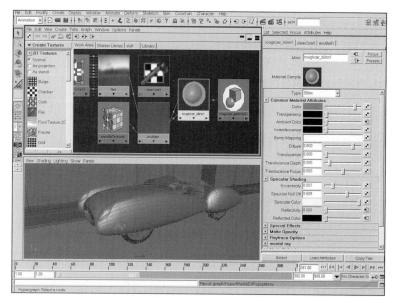

Figure 3.6   Applying a shader.

Many procedural textures available within Maya can shorten this stage of the pipeline. Building libraries of materials can also be a major aid to efficiency here. A wide variety of shaders is also available from various sources on the World Wide Web. We explore the use of shaders in Chapter 18, "Shading."

Just as good speakers are critical in the sound of a stereo system, good shaders are critical in the final look of a Maya animation.

Layout

After the critical models for a shot have been sufficiently prepared, the process of shot layout can commence. In layout, the project's storyboards begin to be realized as scenes are assembled, characters are positioned, and cameras begin to establish compositions (see Figure 3.7).

Depending on the size of your studio, layout can take place before, after, or during the shading stage of the pipeline. Layout isn't essential for shading (or vice versa), but it ought to precede set dressing and must precede the main production flow activities of animation, lighting, and rendering.

The primary activities of layout are creating and populating shots with essential elements, followed by camera composition.

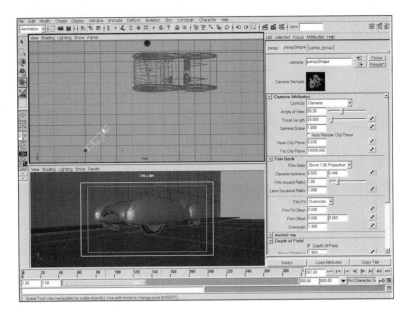

Figure 3.7 Setting up cameras and models for layout.

To facilitate the former, shots need to be explicitly tracked and the essential items within them need to be identified and available. For many projects, this also means that complex objects should be available in stand-in form. In fact, well-crafted stand-ins can often be used in lieu of finished models to permit layout work to begin substantially earlier than it otherwise might begin.

Welcome to layout—you've won a ride on the Stand-in Railroad! Do not pass *Go*. Do not collect $200. Please remain seated as you coast through Chapter 11, "Layout" (which also covers material for the next section, "Set Dressing").

When the necessary elements are all in place, camera placement commences, guided by the storyboards. Sometimes this results in more model changes (such as making a room bigger to accommodate an expansive shot), but usually this camera work produces the first images that resemble the production crew's objective.

Set Dressing

After the cameras have finally been pointed at your shots, it becomes apparent that something's missing. Actually, a *lot* of things are missing. It's the job of set dressing to turn the stark, minimalist scenes of layout and into the visually rich scenes seen in your mind's eye.

Set dressing ought to precede animation because characters shouldn't find themselves walking through the umbrella stand by the door or reaching through the lamp on the table. On the other hand, the function of set dressing is subordinate to the main elements of the scene, so if something has to give, it's the set dressing. Lose the lamp, move the umbrella stand, and do what you have to do if the action needs to happen in a certain manner.

The models used for set dressing aren't simply placed haphazardly to fill empty spaces (see Figure 3.8). They can be used to hide unsightly artifacts of other models, to balance the composition of the shot, to provide visual texture to the image, or to add sight gags for the observant viewer. Although some planning is required to have the dressing models on hand, often the actual dressing is done in an ad hoc manner, solving one perceived problem after another.

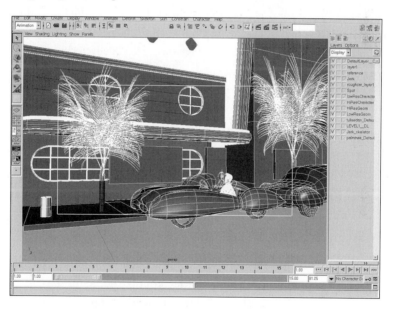

Figure 3.8   Set dressing a shot.

Even though most set dressing work is done up front, it can continue on each shot throughout its production. Despite our conviction as viewers that we understand what we're seeing, moviemakers take enormous liberties with the placement of things in shots—so, as moviemakers, we can do likewise. If the lamp gets in the way of seeing the character's face, move it. This kind of work is so common that it's often referred to as camera dressing.

Production Flow

The production setup is in place, and it's time to concentrate on the finer points of the process: getting compelling performances from your virtual actors and producing compelling imagery. You're ready to let the pipeline carry you along through the exciting work that culminates in an animation you can be proud of. You're ready to ride the flow through to the end.

Animation

Animation is often considered the real meat-and-potatoes stage of the pipeline. If your project's pipeline has properly set up this stage for you, you can concentrate on making your characters come alive on the screen (of whatever kind). Arrive here too soon, and you'll waste time scrambling for missing models, aiming cameras, and fixing broken rigging. But get here properly prepared, and it's all about the acting.

Unlike real acting, animation performances aren't delivered *in toto*, but are gradually refined. Each performance goes through stages of its own, progressing from coarse positioning to fine gestures and perhaps on to subtle expressions of emotion. The animation process needs to be structured to evaluate the performance at each of these stages, to save unnecessary rework.

First comes blocking (see Figure 3.9), in which the character is simply positioned as needed at key moments. This allows for the rendering of a simple animatic, which is especially useful for evaluating composition.

Timing is then refined and high-level posing begins. At this stage, you can begin to see an actual performance from the characters. Next, the posing is refined down through to the smallest details, culminating in a seemingly endless series of tweaks that ultimately produces the illusion of life from a collection of numerical data.

To keep the project on schedule and get it out the door, this stage *must* come to an end. At some point dictated by the budgets, good enough has to actually *be* good enough. Otherwise, a clog formed here in the pipeline can burst the whole project.

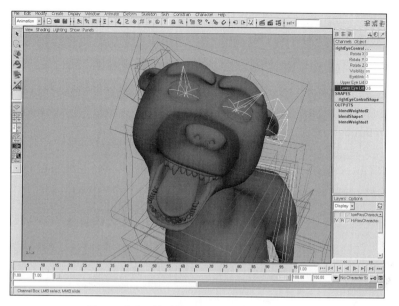

Figure 3.9 Blocking and posing a character.

Lighting

With a shot now filled with fully shaded sets, props, and characters giving the performances of their short-but-complex lives, you are finally given the opportunity to demonstrate your visual artistry. Lighting is more than simply turning on the lamps or the sun and seeing what happens. The lighting artist controls the mood of the scene, focuses interest on the relevant action, and brings out the richness and beauty of the work that has come before.

It's usually important that lighting follow animation because sophisticated lighting setups (see Figure 3.10) normally provide special lighting on each character rather than simply taking whatever happens to fall on the rest of the scene. This allows characters to be clearly delineated against the scene background and elegant effects such as rim lighting to be used to full effect. Key, fill, rim, bounce, and kicker lights are typical for characters. Controlling shadows can also take a significant amount of work, especially when they obscure characters' expressions and actions.

The lighting process requires careful attention to detail and an awareness of its impact on the rendering process. No matter how sexy a thousand points of light might seem, you pay for those lights at render time. The animation that can't be rendered might just as well not be made.

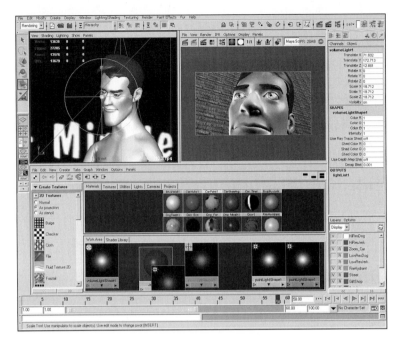

Figure 3.10 Lighting a character.

This stage can be expedited by performing a master lighting pass for each sequence, which creates a common lighting setup to ensure continuity and aid shot lighting. Each shot in that sequence can then work from the master setup to achieve the needed visual balance. We explore lighting setups and strategies in Chapter 19, "Lighting."

Exiting this stage of the pipeline can be exhilarating because the next step seems to be rendering it up and submitting it for awards.

Effects

But wait—there's more! What about the the fireworks? And the smoke? And the rain?

To be fair, effects are often achievable in parallel with the lighting effort, but not always. Even if an explosion can be created in isolation, a spray of water (such as might come out of, say, a fire hydrant) might need to have the same illumination as the rest of the scene. Effects often depend on virtually the entire shot, up to and including lighting.

Effects budgets vary dramatically, depending on the subject of the animation, much like the location of a specific effect in the pipeline. A flag blowing in the wind might need to be simulated before lighting, while a fluid dynamics simulation might need to be ready in time for animation. Similarly, fur comes up in shading and in animation. Some especially unique Maya tools such as Paint Effects can even be utilized in the modeling stage.

So, before advancing down the production pipeline from lighting to the final stage of rendering, any required effects need to be in place.

We examine some of Maya's fabulous effects capabilities in Chapter 14, "Particles and Dynamics."

Rendering

Like a ride down an amusement park water slide, rendering is your project's chance to make a big splash. All the heavy lifting by the crew is essentially done, and it's time to let the computers do what they do best: compute.

If you're really lucky, it's a simple matter of pressing the Render button and coming back later to collect your frames, but it's usually a bit more involved.

First, before you render your sequences, you'll need to feel secure that you've allowed sufficient time for all the frames to be computed. This requires running representative test frames, extrapolating the total rendering times, and comparing that result with your available computing resources. If you come up short, adjust settings (perhaps revisit the lighting stage) and try again. When all else fails, find some more computing resources or a faster renderer.

The test frames also need to be examined for unacceptable artifacts (see Figure 3.11). Even if single frames pass the test, it's important to examine entire shots for temporal artifacts. Because some artifacts can't be discovered until the final renderings have been run, it's important to allow some slack in scheduling to address last-minute surprises.

Substantial efficiencies can be gained by rendering in layers and compositing the resulting images. Even if this doesn't render any faster (it almost always does), the capability to address a problem by simply rerendering the offending element makes it a winning strategy.

Assuming that you've not found your project stuck in an intractable clog along the way, it emerges from the pipeline ready to find its way to an output device of your choosing.

You'll emerge from our pipeline after traveling down the last stage of it in Chapter 20, "Rendering."

Sure, there could still be problems, but this is Maya we're talking about here—game over! You win!

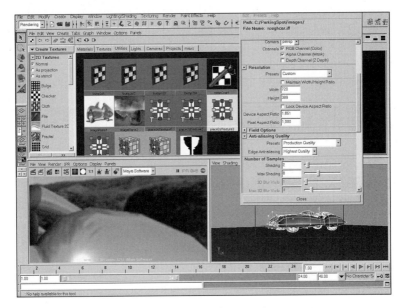

Figure 3.11 Rendering artifacts needing attention.

Summary

The digital animation studio was once only a dream, but now it's a reality. Understanding the pipelined nature of the workflow in a digital studio is key to successfully tackling the inherently complex projects taken on in animation. Budgets and planning are necessary evils, yet their potential for saving work and avoiding trouble make them well worth the effort. Going from initial story to finished work is a major undertaking, but one that Maya users worldwide gladly undertake.

Our workflow for the rest of this book closely parallels the workflow described in this chapter. As you go forward to the chapters that follow, we trust that you will find that this chapter has made the road ahead easier to navigate.

Chapter 4

Technical Considerations

By Mark Adams

One of Maya's great strengths is its adaptability. Not only does it possess many powerful tools, but the methods of interacting with those tools also can be adapted to better suit each user. In fact, virtually the entire user interface is composed of MEL files that you can examine and modify to your needs. So, before forging ahead with the *Parking Spot* project described in Chapter 4, "Digital Studio Pipeline," let's first look at some ways in which you can take advantage of this adaptability while creating this Maya project.

You're probably already aware of many of the standard means of adapting Maya to your tastes—marking menus, shelves, hotkeys, and MEL scripting. You've also likely come up with additional techniques and conventions to enhance your efficiency, organization, security, and comfort. These adaptations, techniques, and conventions all help you to streamline your work and extract the maximum from that most precious of commodities—your valuable time.

Although none is specific to any aspect of the project, each consideration inherently deals with technical aspects of using Maya. Instead of making passing mention of dozens of small (but important) items, we've chosen to acquaint you right up front with our point of departure into the project ahead.

In this chapter, you'll learn how to tailor your Maya environment to your own needs, including doing the following:

- Establishing personalized command defaults
- Making the most of your hotkeys
- Creating text-mode shelves

- Customizing Maya's UI-building MEL scripts
- Modifying and creating menus
- Navigating views efficiently
- Managing projects and files

Getting Cozy

Sometimes the hardest part of doing a project is getting started—or, more precisely, knowing where to get started. Because the clock keeps ticking along, it's important to have a reliable methodology for moving forward from concept to reality. So, before dealing with the particular methods involved in creating geometry and beyond, let's spend a short while considering getting out of the gate effectively.

In fact, we'll begin before the project itself and consider some of the meta–methods that affect the production of any project and how some of them are addressed in this project.

First, you'll want to spend some time taking advantage of Maya's many customization possibilities to set up your working environment well. Because Maya has such a broad range of user interface elements and an even broader range of commands, it can be a bit overwhelming to begin customizing—it's not likely to be something you do right away. As you learn your way around Maya, you'll find that your speed and effectiveness increase with familiarity, but there's a limit to how much performance you will gain this way. If the number and complexity of steps required to perform a task can't be reduced, your performance gains from familiarity with the tools and the process will eventually max out.

To really get things humming right along, you need to solve your own personal performance bottlenecks. Sometimes this means making the tools you use easier to access, sometimes it means reducing the number of steps a process takes, and other times it just means adopting some personal conventions.

The goal is simple: Get as cozy as possible with the interface and the tools. Although a bit of time is required to set up Maya to your liking (and considerably more time using Maya is required to really know what issues to address), your future performance gains should more than make up for the time you spend tuning it up.

In addition, as the barriers to achieving your tasks are reduced, working with Maya will become more of an extension to your thought process and less of an exercise in UI navigation and operational preparation. You'll spend more time making progress and less time pulling down menus, checking option boxes, setting selection masks, and reaching for the Undo command.

When you've spent enough time with Maya that you have learned the styles of interaction and command options you commonly use, take note of the things that are cumbersome or difficult to remember. These are the tasks that will likely benefit most from personalization.

We'll spend this chapter exploring several likely candidates for performance enhancement.

Commands

You can access commands in Maya in lots of ways: through the Hotbox, main menus, contextual menus, hotkeys, shelves, and marking menus. This provides for a lot of overlapping methods for accessing commands, some of which are better than others for specific interactions.

In this section, we look at some of these methods and how to take advantage of their strengths for your work.

Command Defaults

As you set options for various commands (for example, tools or actions) with option boxes, Maya remembers the last values you specified and stores them in your userPrefs.mel file for use the next time you select that command. This is fine if you have a command with options that rarely change or that change almost every time you use it, but many commands have factory defaults that are not quite what you normally want or which are invoked with two or more typical sets of optional values. One thing that can help is to edit the factory default option settings.

In the $MAYA_LOCATION/scripts directory are two directories that contain the MEL command scripts: startup and others. In general, the user interface is created via the startup scripts, while the specific commands and their options are handled by the others scripts.

Where's $MAYA_LOCATION?

As you know, Maya can run on several operating systems. On each of these operating systems, Maya is installed in a different location, referred to by an environment variable known as $MAYA_LOCATION. Here's where each OS installs Maya by default:

Irix	/usr/aw/maya5.0
Linux	/usr/aw/maya5.0
Windows	drive:\Program Files\AliasWavefront\Maya5.0
Mac OS X	Applications\Maya5.0

Check the Essentials section of the User Guide in the Maya documentation for more information on this and other environment variables.

Note

Although Windows systems use the backslash character (\) as a path delimiter, the other systems on which Maya runs (IRIX, Linux, and Mac OS X) use the forward slash character (/) instead. Except in the above explicit case, we adopt the forward slash as the delimiter in this book. If you're a Windows user, just use the backslash wherever you see a forward slash.

To change the behavior of any given script, copy the script from the Maya product directory to your own personal scripts directory. If the file is common to all versions of Maya that you might use, you can put it in ~/maya/scripts. Otherwise, put it in the version-specific script directory—for example, ~/maya/5.0/scripts.

Note

The tilde character (~) is a standard UNIX-style abbreviation for the home directory. So, ~/maya is where one's Maya files usually reside, but ~maya would be the home directory of a user with a login of maya. We'll take advantage of this abbreviation occasionally for clarity.

So, what kinds of things might you want to change in these scripts? Well, for starters, a command's default option values won't necessarily match your working preferences. After all, maybe you like your primitives a different standard size or your attaches blended, not connected. No sweat.

Changing an Option Default

Let's say that you want to change the default behavior of the Attach Curve command so that Keep Originals is Off. To do this, first copy the performAttachCrv.mel script from the product's scripts/others directory to your local scripts directory and find the appropriate option section in a text editor. It looks like this:

```
// keep original (for in place operations is on-1 or off-0).
        //
        if ($forceFactorySettings || !`optionVar -exists
attachCrvKeepOriginal`)
 {
                optionVar -intValue attachCrvKeepOriginal 1;
        }
```

The change is simple: Set the value to 0, like this:

```
optionVar -intValue attachCrvKeepOriginal 0;
```

When you save it and restart Maya, the Reset Options menu command now sets Keep Originals to Off, which saves you the trouble of turning it off each time.

But the really important lesson here is that Maya's "factory settings" are found in the various MEL command scripts, not hidden away in some undecipherable binary file somewhere. You are free to change them to suit your needs.

Solving Command Mysteries

In the simple case in the previous section, the name of the script was fairly obvious. Most of the modeling tools have a name like performWhatever.mel. And although in some cases a complex command might divide the work over a few scripts, you should generally be easily able to follow the optionVar settings back to the options you seek.

If it proves a bit tricky, set the ScriptEditor option Echo All Commands (in its Script menu) to see just what is being executed. You can solve many other mysteries by using the whatIs MEL command, as shown in Figure 4.1.

Sometimes the change is a little less obvious. You might need to do some spelunking through files or through the online *MEL Command Reference* to find the available choices of values. But with a little courage (or just the simple realization that you can go back to defaults by removing the edited file), you can safely change the defaults of almost any command.

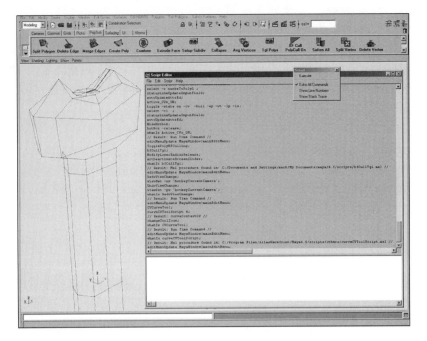

Figure 4.1   Examples of `whatIs` usage.

If `whatIs` says that what you're inquiring about is just a command, you have two ways to get further information about that MEL command.

The first is to point your browser to the *MEL Command Reference*, which should have descriptions of all the MEL commands. Each command's flags and context are described, with usage examples often provided as well. Related commands are also usually listed at the bottom of the page.

In truth, however, sometimes there are MEL commands that aren't in the *MEL Command Reference*. For that, use the `help` command in the Script Editor, which is as easy as typing in `help` followed by the name of the command, as in `help getAttr`. This produces a quick listing of the command's available flags in the Script Editor and is called, appropriately enough, quick help.

Other options are also available with the `help` command (see `help help`). You can search for relevant commands with pattern matching; for example, `help -list "*ebuild*"` identifies commands likely related to rebuilding. Also, the display of annotation strings on the help line is set with the `-rm` option and as pop-ups (on the shelf, tool box, and status line) with the `-pm` and `-pdt` options.

Keeping It Under Control

You can alter other command behaviors as well. Besides option defaults, you can change things such as slider ranges (look for the `floatSliderGrp` command), option labels, help line prompts, and even error messages.

After a while, making command script changes like these can even become habit forming—all you'll want is just one more fix to make you feel better. The more you do it, the easier it is to do it again. And again.

But be careful: Edit MEL command scripts somewhat sparingly, if only to keep your ongoing personal maintenance effort to a minimum. After all, with each new version of Maya, you'll need to go back through each of these files (assuming that they haven't changed identities!) and reincorporate your edits into any scripts that have changed between versions.

When versions change, I find that I need to actually block out hours at a time to systematically compare, edit, and test these scripts. After a few such sessions, I'm back up to speed and refamiliarized with the sorts of things I've changed and why.

In my scripts directory, I have about 30 Maya scripts that I've modified in some way to improve their options or organization. In hindsight, I wish I had changed more of them sooner—they've each made my ride on Maya a bit smoother. As my experience with Maya grows, I'm sure I'll change several more—just as soon as they find their way onto my radar.

Tip

Put distinctive comments (or actual documentation) in your edited command scripts to let you know which parts of these files were edited. When you get the next Maya release, you can then more easily migrate the changes forward. And if you share your scripts, others will better understand your changes.

Because so many of these changes are quite easy, keep in mind that much of Maya's behavior is right there in your hands, ready to be remade in your own image. Because it can be done incrementally and easily, editing command scripts is worth routinely doing. Even as you identify nagging problems, you'll know that a few simple edits can make them go away.

You'll gradually reach the right balance—when the annoyance of the remaining problems is less than the effort required to repair them. Fortunately, as your experience at this grows, this effort lessens and Maya becomes increasingly effective for you.

Hotkeys

Another exceptionally helpful way to speed up your work is to define and use personal hotkeys. Although Maya ships with many hotkeys already created for you, they're not likely to be specific to the tasks you yourself regularly perform.

The default Maya set is useful enough but is certainly not geared, for instance, toward modeling. So, by evaluating your frequent modeling needs, you can smooth the bumps in the modeling process with well-chosen hotkeys.

You might want a hotkey that executes a command with specific options, the last options used, or no options at all. Any of these can be accommodated, as can wholly new commands of your own.

For instance, if you tire of opening the Duplicate option box each time you need a simple copy (to make sure it's set to default values), make a hotkey for a vanilla duplicate command. It must be a separate command because hotkeys of menu commands will just execute those commands with whatever option settings were last used. After all, you probably won't want to worry that you might get a dozen rotated instances sometimes and one plain old copy at others, depending on the last options you've set.

In this case, it's a snap. The Duplicate menu command calls the MEL `duplicate` command, with options as indicated by their option box settings. A plain duplication operation turns out to just be a call to `duplicate` with no options.

Making It Memorable

Use the Hotkey Editor to create hotkeys that you'll remember. The hotkey that you can't remember might as well not exist.

First, review the default set provided with Maya. It's defined in the Maya product's scripts/startup/hotkeySetup.mel file, but the best way to review the defaults is to study the Quick Reference card that came with Maya.

Warning

Don't edit the hotkeySetup.mel file! Any hotkeys that you change via the Hotkey Editor will go in your userHotkeys.mel file. These will automatically override the defaults that hotkeySetup.mel creates, but allow defaults to be restored by deleting your hotkey.

Sometimes using other applications will set your expectations and associations for your hotkeys.

Because I used Alias AutoStudio for many years, I tried to make my transition to Maya relatively painless by carrying forward as many hotkeys as were useful. Wherever possible, I tried to assign the same hotkeys in both applications, taking the best from both and molding them into a powerful and efficient common shorthand.

I didn't use single-key hotkeys in AutoStudio, so since the Maya defaults make extensive use of unmodified keys, so my transition was easy. I used the modifier keys—Alt, Ctrl, and Shift—as the basis for creating hotkey categories and used similar modifiers for similar commands, all while striving to find associations that I would remember.

I thus associate, for instance, Alt+d with Duplicate and Alt+s with Save File As, for both historical and mnemonic reasons.

As another example, I've assigned camera commands to Ctrl+Shift hotkeys, which are very easy to select with most keyboards. I also strived to make those hotkeys easy to reach: Ctrl+Shift+z is zoom (one of my most commonly used hotkeys), Ctrl+Shift+d is dolly (I didn't like holding down two mouse buttons at once), Ctrl+Shift+x is track, and Ctrl+Shift+c sets my clipping planes automatically (it calls viewClipPlane -acp).

For that vanilla duplicate command, I made Alt+Shift+d the hotkey. The Shift key suggests to me an uber-application of the Alt+d duplicate that I've grown to know and love in AutoStudio. I've also used the Shift key in similar ways for other hotkeys, such as for opening command option dialog boxes.

Tip

Opening the option dialog box for a command is distinct from executing the command. You can assign hotkeys to either or both. If you often need to set a command's options, consider assigning a hotkey to the dialog box.

Each hotkeyed command fights for a place in your memory and at the keyboard. Multiple mnemonics are better than single ones. It's easier to remember my toggle Camera hotkey because my camera commands usually start with Ctrl+Shift and because I can think "Kamera" easily enough.

Whatever *your* conventions are, just having conventions makes it easier to remember your hotkeys, which increases their effectiveness.

Whatever mnemonics work for you, figure them out for those operations you do a lot. However useful you might find the Hotbox or marking menus, hotkeys are like registers in a CPU—use them for the things you access most often for best performance.

Warning

Don't make destructive hotkeys easy to select, *especially* those that write files. You can't undo an overwritten file! I have no hotkey for Save (vs. Save As) for this reason. And while I've set up a Delete All Geometry command, its hotkey uses the entire Ctrl+Alt+Shift modifier sequence, just to avoid accidents.

Mark's Hotkey Hall of Fame

Sure, we'll tell you to do things *your* way, but sometimes we really love it *our* way. So, rather than bite my lip completely, let me offer up a few personal favorites from my Hotkey Hall of Fame:

Tool	Key	Why
MergeVertices	Alt+'	Key looks like two points merging into one.
SplitPolygon	Alt+/	/ is a division sign.
DeleteEdge	Alt+-	- means deletion.
AppendToPolygon	Alt+=	Above the = sign is the + sign.
DetachCurve	Alt+5	% looks like a detach operation.
CollapseEdge	Alt+y	Y looks like the collapse operation.
InsertKnot	Alt+6	^ looks like a proofreader's insert.
DeleteHistory	Alt+H	*H* stands for "history," of course.
Revolve	Ctrl+0	The 0 depicts the circular result.
Extrude	Ctrl+6	The 6 looks like an extruded tube operation.

As you can see, many of my mnemonics are visual ones, taking their cues from the graphics on the keys. I think of graphical operations in visual terms, so this is a natural extension of my thought process.

Although less exciting (you *are* excited, right?), I have defined many other hotkeys that simply use a principal letter of the key command element, such as Alt+F for `ConvertSelectionToFaces` and Ctrl+F for picking poly faces. This consistency between hotkeys reinforces the mnemonics and keeps things orderly.

It can also be helpful to create a reference for yourself that you can review occasionally to refresh your memory. One easy way to create such a reference list is to combine your personal hotkeys (found in your prefs/userHotkeys.mel file) with the default hotkeys (found, as mentioned previously, in $MAYA_LOCATION/scripts/startup/hotkey Setup.mel), and then sort and edit the list a bit. If you do this, don't forget to remove or make obvious the defaults you've overridden. For even easier reference, you might want to group them by function so that your system becomes clear.

Tip

You know the "sacred" keys (QWERTY), right? Well, you can change those, too, if you want. I did—since R just *had* to be rotate, and W seemed like a scale factor to me. Call me stubborn. The mnemonics were just so much better for me that I had to do it (knowing full well that no one else would understand). Just in case you're similarly stubborn, don't forget to switch the modified QWERTY keys, too.

So, is anything out of bounds for hotkeys? Yes—modifier keys (Alt, Ctrl, and Shift) can't be used all by themselves as hotkeys. Otherwise, it's pretty much up to you.

Planning for the Future

You can assign hotkeys to existing commands or to new commands that you specify. If you're concerned about portability between users, machines, or new versions of Maya, you need to know that these situations are different.

If you're simply assigning hotkeys to existing Maya commands, it's easy. The Hotkey Editor records your new hotkey definitions in your maya/prefs/userHotkeys.mel file when you select Save. To then move your hotkey definitions to another machine or give them to another user, the userHotkeys.mel file is all that's required.

Tip

If you'd like a hotkey only for the duration of your Maya session, set up the hotkey in the Hotkey Editor and then choose Close—but without ever choosing Save. The hotkey definition will then be forgotten the next time you start Maya. This can be handy if you need to execute one or more MEL commands repeatedly and you'd like to make it easy to do each time.

On the other hand, if you're creating a hotkey for something new, you should try to make it as portable as possible.

The first step, of course, is to click the New button at the bottom of the Hotkey Editor dialog box (see Figure 4.2), which is accessed via Window, Settings/Preferences, Hotkeys. This activates the fields at the bottom, which enable you to create a new command for hotkey assignment.

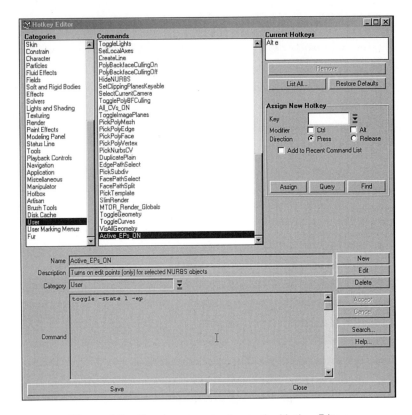

Figure 4.2 Creating a new hotkey in the Hotkey Editor.

A hotkey assignment isn't made directly to the command string that you provide, but rather to a "named command." These named commands are constructed for you automatically when you create a new hotkey, and they are stored in your maya/prefs/userNamedCommands.mel file. They appear in the User section of your hotkey categories.

If you just enter raw MEL, the named command will reference that MEL (via yet another file, userRunTimeCommands.mel). Unfortunately, if you want to provide that command to another user, you'll have to either point him to all of the right MEL files, or he'll need to enter the MEL code directly in his Hotkey Editor. Because users generally construct hotkeys to suit themselves, adopting your new and useful hotkeys will probably thus require that the person then hand-edit the desired entries into his own userNamedCommands.mel and userRunTimeCommands.mel files (rather than overwriting the existing files), which is both tedious and error-prone.

A better solution is to create each of your new commands for hotkeys in its own MEL script and then put each script in an accessible scripts directory. This allows the new hotkey to be defined simply by referring to the procedure in the script.

For example, the following simple toggle might be used to turn on or off the display of all lights in a view:

```
global proc toggleLights()
{
string $thisPanel = `getPanel -wf`;
modelEditor -e -lights (!`modelEditor -q -lights $thisPanel`) $thisPanel;
}
```

The script first identifies the view and then toggles the view state to display lights the opposite way that it had been doing. By the way, this framework can also be generally used to toggle any of the view's display categories found on its Show menu.

Another user could then use the command by simply putting it in a shared location in his $MAYA_SCRIPT_PATH and defining a hotkey that calls the `toggleLights` procedure, as shown in Figure 4.3. The procedure was written first, and then a new hotkey command that referenced the procedure was created in the Hotkey Editor. As a useful mnemonic, Ctrl+l (that's the lowercase letter *L*) was assigned as the hotkey.

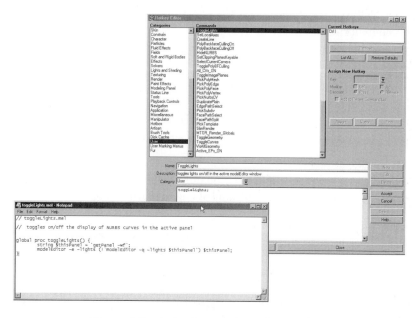

Figure 4.3 A simple procedure call as a hotkey

If you define your hotkeys this way, different users can then set whatever hotkeys they like, without needing to concern themselves with your userNamedCommands.mel file. In addition, you will be able to reference the procedure in other ways (such as through marking menus), without needing to dig through the userNamedCommands.mel file for the necessary code. .

Note

A procedure is normally remembered only within the scope in which it is defined. After its enclosing scope is completed, the procedure is forgotten and its memory is returned for reuse. However, a proc that will be used repeatedly (as with a hotkey) should be retained in memory. So, by defining a procedure as a global proc, it will be remembered for use in whatever context it's called.

In short, if your hotkey's code might be useful to others or useful in other contexts, put it in a separate MEL file as a global proc.

Of course, we three authors have been working on this project in separate locations and performing separate tasks, so there is little need to coordinate our hotkeys. On the other hand, in our professional work outside of this project, these principles have proven quite valuable.

Assign your hotkeys with some care (remember, the hotkey that you can't recall is useless), but be sure to *use* them. The total time spent navigating menus in Maya can become enormous—as can the time saved by using hotkeys.

Shelves

Of course, Maya also provides a place for putting commands that you need to access regularly—shelves. Shelves are terrific for collecting all the tools necessary for a common task. Marking menus, discussed in the next section, are also considered a kind of shelf.

I've created shelves for working on polysets, picking objects, doing NURBS surfacing, setting grids, and handling several other categories. Just the act of creating shelf categories will get your gears turning about your work process and help streamline your workflow.

An effective set of shelves offers one- or two-click access to almost all the commands you use regularly. When you're working with polygon meshes, for instance, you can leave a polygon tool shelf open that has a collection of the polygon tools that you use the most. When used in combination with a set of hotkeys, you might find that you hardly ever have to select your way through a menu. Even if you need some other non-polygonal tool (such as Create Lattice, say), you can have it waiting on another shelf just a click away.

The command navigation strategies that you use are up to you, of course, but shelves enable you to place a convenient collection of the tools you need right next to your camera window.

Command Options and Shelves

A typical way to put a tool or action onto a shelf is to drag it there from a menu while holding down the appropriate modifier keys (Ctrl+Alt+Shift for IRIX, Alt+Shift for Linux, Ctrl+Shift for Windows, and Option+RMB on a Mac). This allows any item from the menus to be placed onto a shelf. If the item is a tool, it makes that item essentially a pointer to the menu item itself.

Note

Maya distinguishes "tools" from "actions." Tools are commands that require further user input (such as selecting geometry), while actions are performed with no further input required. Instead of constantly saying "tool or action," I'll often just say "command" or "item," unless an important distinction needs to be made.

However, if you want the settings for an item on your shelf to be unique from the menu settings, you'll probably want to put the item on the shelf by dragging its icon from the tool box with the middle mouse button. It will initially inherit the currently active settings, but these settings can be changed at any time using the Tool Settings window. You can thus put two CV Curve tools right next to each other, one making cubic curves and the other making linear curves.

What about commands (like actions) that don't have tool box icons? The Tool Settings window blithely says that selected tools (such as our friend Duplicate) have no options!

Say that you want unique instances of an action, such as creating separate MirrorX, MirrorY, and MirrorZ shelf items from the Duplicate command. Open the Shelf Editor and you'll see that a Duplicate command dropped onto your shelf actually executes a procedure called `duplicatePreset` with a slew of cryptic arguments. To better understand these arguments, you can use `whatIs` to identify the source of the proc and examine it in a text editor. However, because each of these is based on your option choices, you can simply set the options and drag each variation to your shelf.

Tip

Use the MEL `whatIs` command on the command line or in the Script Editor to find the source of a given MEL command or procedure. Often it's a quick way to track down MEL procedures that you'd like to tailor to better serve your needs. Of course, not everything is a MEL procedure. When `whatIs` says you've reached a Command, you've reached a basic MEL command and a solid binary barrier to tinkering.

Don't forget, of course, to provide some identifying text for each command variant on your shelves. For most shelf items, this is a trivial matter of using the Shelf Editor to specify label text and perhaps an icon name. However, some items (typically those implemented with the MEL `superCtx` command) stubbornly resist any attempt to set their labels.

If the shelf item is written out to the shelf file as a shelfButton (most are), you can also modify the item's prompt using the `-annotation` argument. There's no interactive way to modify the prompt, but a text editor can easily modify the annotation string in the shelf file. Thus, our `MirrorX` command can have a help line message other than the default Duplicate prompt, as shown in Figure 4.4.

One other useful thing about editing the shelf file directly (in this case, the file shelf_Common.mel) is that special characters that are rejected interactively can actually be included in labels and messages. So, even though the Shelf Editor rejects attempts to label the icons –X and 1:1, this is easily done in a text editor.

```
shelf_Common.mel - Notepad
File  Edit  Format  Help
    shelfButton
        -enableCommandRepeat 1
        -enable 1
        -width 82
        -height 54
        -manage 1
        -visible 1
        -label "Duplicate"
        -imageOverlayLabel "1:1"
        -image1 "menuIconEdit.xpm"
        -style "iconAndTextVertical"
        -command "duplicate"
    ;
    shelfButton
        -enableCommandRepeat 1
        -enable 1
        -width 82
        -height 54
        -manage 1
        -visible 1
        -annotation "MirrorX: Mirror copy the selected object(s) in X"
        -label "MirrorX"
        -imageOverlayLabel "-X"
        -image1 "menuIconEdit.xpm"
        -style "iconAndTextVertical"
        -command "duplicatePreset(1,1,1,0,0,0,0,0,0,0,0,0,-1,1,1)"
    ;
    shelfButton
        -enableCommandRepeat 1
        -enable 1
        -width 82
        -height 54
        -manage 1
        -visible 1
        -annotation "MirrorY: Mirror copy the selected object(s) in Y"
        -label "MirrorY"
        -imageOverlayLabel "-Y"
        -image1 "menuIconEdit.xpm"
        -style "iconAndTextVertical"
        -command "duplicatePreset(1,1,1,0,0,0,0,0,0,0,0,0,1,-1,1)"
    ;
    shelfButton
        -enableCommandRepeat 1
        -enable 1
        -width 82
        -height 54
        -manage 1
        -visible 1
        -annotation "MirrorZ: Mirror copy the selected object(s) in Z"
        -label "MirrorZ"
        -imageOverlayLabel "-Z"
        -image1 "menuIconEdit.xpm"
        -style "iconAndTextVertical"
        -command "duplicatePreset(1,1,1,0,0,0,0,0,0,0,0,0,1,1,-1)"
    ;
```

Figure 4.4 A customized shelf set.

Note

Your shelf files are kept in your maya/5.0/prefs/shelves directory, each with a name such as shelf_SomeName.mel.

You can also assign MEL commands and scripts to shelf buttons (just drag the MEL onto the shelf from the Script Editor or the command line). Of course, as with hotkeys, it's much more portable to put the MEL into a script and then assign the script to the button.

Text-Mode Shelves

So, whatever you drag onto a shelf, you can edit any of the associated text fields and even edit the icon. But, wait, there's more! Or is it less?

Maya's shelves were initially designed with one more mode in mind: textOnly (see Figure 4.5). It turns out that, although textOnly doesn't appear on any menus, you can still easily hack the mode back in by editing just a couple of files. For your convenience, we've put the edited files (shelfEditorDialog.mel and shelfStyle.mel) on the included disk. Put them in your 5.0/scripts directory and restart Maya, and they add back in the handling of the textOnly mode.

So, if you're like me and think that there are far more commands than meaningful icons, you can use the power of English (or whatever your language might be) to easily distinguish, say, your four-span 180° Revolve around Z from your eight-span 360° Revolve around X.

Then again, if you prefer icons and don't mind using labels and icon names and perhaps drawing your own custom icons to sort out your shelf commands, there's no reason to change. To be consistent with the way most users work, I've bitten the bullet on this issue and avoided using text shelves in most illustrations—but I continue to use text shelves when no one's looking.

Figure 4.5   Text-only shelves.

Marking Menus

Although I don't normally use the Hotbox, I do use its marking menu feature. Marking menus are a very powerful concept, and Maya offers a host of ways to access them, the most obvious of which is via holding down the spacebar.

Dissin' the Hotbox

I find the Hotbox redundant (because it contains menus found elsewhere) and a bit overwhelming, so I don't use it—at least, not for getting at the main menu content. The menu commands that I use often find their way onto my shelves and into my hotkeys. Although I have little patience for traversing long menus, when I have to do it, I'd rather have fixed locations to navigate (the main menus) than a mass of commands opening wherever my cursor resides. Besides, I thought that the spacebar, also being used for marking menus and popping windows, already had enough to do.

When using the Hotbox marking menus, I use the Center Zone Only mode, which lets me set up a marking menu for each mouse button (*a la* AutoStudio). Although there are potentially 15 distinct marking menus (3 mouse buttons and 5 zones) that can be accessed via the spacebar, a zoneless configuration works well for me.

Why not use all zones? I find that I too often inadvertently select a command from, say, the North zone when I'm meaning to just make a North selection from the Center zone marking menu. I've settled for fewer marking menus so that I can eliminate command-selection errors. Besides, I don't really need the extra dozen marking menus.

Given my other use of hotkeys and shelves, the Hotbox marking menus are reserved for the really common operations, those done often enough that an associated gesture will become automatic after a short time.

To satisfy the rational side of my brain, I've given each marking menu a distinct purpose. My left marking menu is for picking, my center marking menu is for transformations, and my right marking menu is for camera manipulation.

To please the visual side of my brain and reinforce muscle memory (the key ingredient to the power of marking menus), things that "undo" on each marking menu are all to the North, common things are on the main compass points, and so on.

I've remade the marking menus to suit my working style, but doing so required determining the MEL needed to set up pick masks and selection modes and to invoke the select command. Now, thanks to well-planned picking commands on my marking menus (and a Pick shelf to handle the uncommon cases), I almost never have to visit the selection masks to get just what I want selected.

Note

Not only are there modes for Hierarchy, Objects, and Components, but there's also a Mixed mode. Here's how a marking menu command for selecting surfaces in Mixed mode (so that you can have objects from other modes simultaneously selected) might look:

```
selectMode -p; selectType -ns 1; setToolTo $gSelect
```

The end result of all this tailoring of command selection methods has been to shape Maya's tools to my thought process, choosing the methods that resonate with me. Your choices could well be different, but the capability to make these changes allows Maya users to realize tremendous performance gains. It's a tribute to Maya's design that all of this can be done to suit almost any user's preferences, without changing the underlying product in any real way.

The User Interface

For our *Parking Spot* project, we realized that not only would we be getting our project done, but we also would eventually have thousands of other Maya users looking over our figurative shoulders. To not disorient users too much, we have opted to keep to a minimum the number of obvious UI alterations. However, in the interests of educating users about the substantial flexibility of the Maya interface, in this section we'll look at a few of the useful changes that someone might make to it.

In other words, very little of the following will leak out of this section into other aspects of our book, but you might find it quite helpful to apply it to your Maya work—unless you'll have a crowd looking over your shoulder, too.

UI Elements

Maya refers to the many sections of its main window (such as the Help Line, Shelf, and Status Line) as its UI elements. You can do many things with these elements, such as show or hide them, rearrange them, or even completely redefine them.

On Again, Off Again

Any of these elements can be hidden or displayed with the UI Elements check boxes on the Display menu. Commands with hotkeys also are available for closing and opening all the UI elements (Hide UI Elements and Restore UI Elements), but use them with care.

When you hide the UI elements this way (which leaves just the workspace open), Maya takes note of what's already open, for later use when restoring them. If you use the hide only once, everything is fine and the restore command does the right thing. However, if you hide it twice in a row, Maya notes the now-closed state and uses that as the state for restoring the UI elements—which forces you to go back to the Display menu to turn back on the elements you need.

Of course, with a script that turns on just the set of UI elements that you need, you can avoid any hassle. The UI element commands shown in the following silly MEL procedure can be recombined in your own procedure to turn on or off any set of UI elements you'd like:

```
global proc UI_Off()
{
setStatusLineVisible 0;
setShelfVisible 0;
setPlaybackRangeVisible 0;
setCommandLineVisible 0;
setHelpLineVisible 0;
setToolboxVisible 0;
setAttributeEditorVisible 0;
setToolSettingsVisible 0;
setChannelsLayersVisible 0;
};
```

Placing such UI scripts on a shelf or marking menu can give you one-click access to the UI element combinations that you typically want, such as a minimal UI for modeling and a full set for complex animation work. I use a few scripts such as this for my own modeling work and put them on a shelf along with other UI-related scripts.

This Way or That Way

Not only can you turn the UI elements on or off, but you also can reorder most of them.

Why would you bother to do this?

Well, comfort, for starters. If you're making extensive use of shelves, you might find that tilting your head up an extra bit to see them, day after day, is a literal pain in the neck. A slight downward gaze is more natural and more comfortable, so adjusting the UI elements to suit your usage can be a wise move.

Another good reason to consider rearranging UI elements is to put related information areas closer together. When I mouse over a shelf command, the aforementioned annotation text is displayed on the Help Line. Unfortunately, the default position of the Shelf is at the top of the screen, while the Help Line is at the bottom. By moving the Shelf near the bottom (see Figure 4.6), these related items are brought together. Also notice that rearranging the elements doesn't alter the order of the Display, UI Elements menu—so if you use a reordered UI like this, you'll probably want to edit the buildPreferenceMenu.mel file to make the menu match the displayed order.

Yet another reason might be to put items in view based on their frequency of access. Because I hardly ever need to set selection masks or modes the old-fashioned way, and because I use hotkeys for snaps, I usually only need the Status Line to verify snap modes or to key in a name or move. Thus, I might want to move it somewhere easier to glance at.

To rearrange UI elements, the initMainWindow.mel script must be edited (remember, edit Maya product scripts in a copy that you've placed in your personal scripts directory, never in the original script file). Near the bottom of the file, the user interface elements are arranged and related to each other. The MEL code is actually fairly easy to follow, with blocks of code for each element that describe what's attached to what.

Figure 4.6 A rearranged set of UI elements.

For example, to switch the position of the Range slider and the Time slider, take these lines:

```
-attachNone     $mayaLive       "top"
-attachForm     $mayaLive       "left"    0
-attachForm     $mayaLive       "right"   0
-attachControl  $mayaLive       "bottom"  0 $timeSlider

-attachNone     $timeSlider     "top"
-attachForm     $timeSlider     "left"    0
-attachForm     $timeSlider     "right"   0
-attachControl  $timeSlider     "bottom"  0 $playbackRange

-attachNone     $playbackRange  "top"
-attachForm     $playbackRange  "left"    0
-attachForm     $playbackRange  "right"   0
-attachControl  $playbackRange  "bottom"  0 $commandLine
```

and switch them around, and reconnect the associations to produce these lines:

```
-attachNone     $mayaLive       "top"
-attachForm     $mayaLive       "left"    0
-attachForm     $mayaLive       "right"   0
-attachControl  $mayaLive       "bottom"  0 $playbackRange

-attachNone     $playbackRange  "top"
-attachForm     $playbackRange  "left"    0
-attachForm     $playbackRange  "right"   0
-attachControl  $playbackRange  "bottom"  0 $timeSlider

-attachNone     $timeSlider     "top"
-attachForm     $timeSlider     "left"    0
-attachForm     $timeSlider     "right"   0
-attachControl  $timeSlider     "bottom"  0 $commandLine
```

Save the file and restart Maya; the Time slider will now be positioned above the Range slider. Because the UI is constructed at startup, a restart is essential.

Of course, if these simple changes aren't enough to suit your tastes, you can completely overhaul the interface by setting the environment variable MAYA_OVERRIDE_UI and doing it *all* yourself. Naturally, the creation of an entire user interface is beyond the scope of this book, but it is possible.

As before, although I prefer some of the UI elements in different positions than the defaults, for reasons such as described previously, we'll generally stick to the default arrangement for the *Parking Spot* project's screen shots.

Menus

My typical workflow is a dense combination of hotkeys, marking menu selections, shelf item picks, and mouse moves. Only occasionally do I need to venture up into the menus for something unusual. When I do, however, I like to find commands easily and efficiently.

Just like the UI, menus can be modified because each menu is created with MEL, typically in a single file per menu. Any menu file can be copied to your local scripts directory and changed as desired to make it easy to navigate. Although each time you do this you add some overhead for updating future Maya releases, it can be worthwhile to make some simple changes that make frequent minor annoyances go away.

You might first want to consider changing command arrangements, moving the most often-used commands up to the top. Or, you might move commonly used commands buried in submenus to the top level, where they're easier to access. You can even add a menu from one set (such as Deform from the Animation set) to another set (such as Modeling, where the Deform menu can be very useful) (see Figure 4.7).

Even the Tool Box is created in a file (toolbox.mel) and can be rearranged, although you'll probably want to do this only if you do crazy stuff like reassign the sacred keys.

Menus aren't inviolable, so don't be afraid to do a little surgery and put your favorite tools where they're easy to reach. The MEL involved is fairly simple and usually involves only one file at a time, plucked from Maya's scripts/startup or scripts/others directories and dropped into your personal *scripts* directory for editing. As always, undoing these modifications is as easy as removing the edited file and restarting Maya.

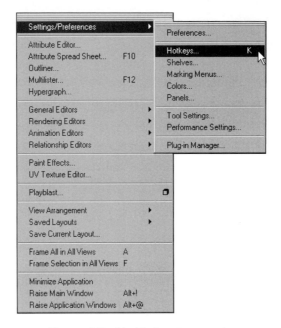

Figure 4.7 Modified menu example.

The menus shown in Figure 4.7 actually have several of these kinds of changes. First, initMainMenuBar.mel was edited to add the Deform menu from Animation mode to Modeling mode. Also in that file, the Edit NURBS menu was renamed back to Edit Surfaces (because that's what those commands really do) and the Create menu was scooted over to be next to the Edit Curves menu. Then the Window menu (WindowMenu.mel) was rearranged to put the most frequently used commands at the top. Finally, the icons in the tool box for the sacred keys were rearranged to correspond to my very personal preferences for transformation tool hotkeys.

Let your workflow and awareness of inefficiency guide you as to what you might want to change. If you access most of your commands via the Hotbox, you'll probably benefit more from menu editing than someone who relies heavily on hotkeys, shelves, and marking menus (although it didn't stop me).

It's your time, so save it and spend it as you see fit.

Viewing

You will spend countless hours working with Maya adjusting your cameras to show you what you need to see. Because viewing is such an important part of using Maya, performance gains made here will reap substantial and ongoing benefits. Let's take a brief look at how you can more effectively manipulate your views.

See the Big Picture

First, when you look at your scene, you want to see it as well as possible and not waste time trying to bring the information you need into view.

The first step in this direction is to maximize the camera's window, making the displayed view as large as is practical. I almost always (more than 99% of the time) look at single-model panel views rather than the four-view default layout. To make this easy, I've set up top-row hotkeys (F5 through F8) that bring up the particular view I'm interested in (Top, Front, Right, and Perspective, respectively). Switching among cameras takes but a single keystroke rather than popping in and out of the four-view mode and moving my mouse into the desired view.

Be aware of your camera's position, whether in orthographic or perspective views. Setting clipping planes, for instance, depends on knowing where your camera is.

Set Some Boundaries

Because clipping planes are defined in camera space, before you set them. Single views are also faster graphically. You first need to know where the camera is located. To do this, use the Select Camera command (which I've hotkeyed, of course) from the window's View menu. If it's a standard orthographic view, check the translation for the axis normal to the view (for example, the X translate for a side view). I like to keep the clipping plane math simple, so I usually set it to the default value of 100 or some other nice round number.

Setting the clipping plane values normally involves either using the Frame command or going into the Attribute Editor and explicitly setting the near and far clipping plane distances. However, by adding these clipping planes to the list of keyable attributes, the job can be easily done in the Channel Box. You can manually make them keyable by using the Channel Control window, or you can prepare a MEL script that turns on their keyable attribute for example:

```
setAttr -k on "topShape.nearClipPlane";
setAttr -k on "topShape.farClipPlane";
```

When the camera clipping planes are in the Channel Box, adjusting them is simply a matter of selecting the camera and entering the values for the near and/or far planes (see Figure 4.8).

This is especially convenient for culling geometry that you don't want to inadvertently operate on. Because the camera's at a rounded-off value, it's easy to calculate the near and far values to obtain a desired slice of a model in that camera.

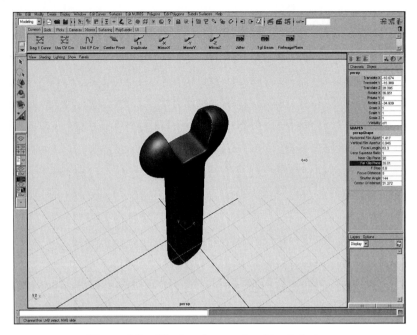

Figure 4.8   Clipping planes as keyable attributes.

Stay Centered

When the camera is pointed in the right general direction, it's important to keep it aimed where you want it and to maintain a spatial sense of the entire scene.

When modeling, my initial approach to viewing the model in a perspective camera is to do the following:

- Set my field of view to something like a "normal" camera lens (say, 45° or so)

- Adjust my distance to the model so that it just fits within the view

- Select the geometry of interest

- Perform a Look at Selection (not a Frame) operation

When that's done, I adjust my view primarily with Tumble, Track, Zoom, and Look At commands. In particular, I zoom in for a moment, do some modeling operations, and then use the Previous View hotkey to return to my "orbital" position. Only occasionally do I need to dolly in or out, which is good—the clipping plane relationships stay intact and my reference position (on the outside, looking in) has a known sense of scale and proportion.

When incremental adjustments eventually get me disoriented, I return to the previous procedure and set up again. Orthographic views are handled similarly, but without the field of view and tumbling issues.

If you're especially ambitious, you can use the camera command to define the camera's home default; then a simple selection of Default Home takes you back to a customized home position. We'll leave the details of this, though, as an exercise for the motivated reader.

Managing Files

In any project, keeping everything organized and secure is of primary importance. Haphazard organization can waste tremendous amounts of time and can put your entire project in jeopardy. On the other hand, having a well-organized system helps the process flow smoothly and minimizes unpleasant surprises.

For the *Parking Spot* project, we'll be collecting the work of three different Maya users and assembling it into a series of shots. Getting data from one set of hands into the next will need to happen dependably and consistently.

Projects

The first decision is how our animation project will be organized within Maya's project structure.

Because the animation will involve several fairly complex models, we'll want to build each model in its own project. We'll name each project after the model itself, such as ParkingMeter, FireHydrant, Spot, and so on. In each of these projects, we can work out the modeling, shading, and articulation details for the given object.

We'll then do our layout, animation, lighting, and rendering work in a master project: ParkingSpot. All our final shots will live there, as will the intermediate steps along the way and the final images we produce.

File Naming

One advantage of working this way is the capability to systematically assign filenames. Instead of resorting to arbitrary filenames that try to distinguish incremental saves from checkpoints from important versions, we'll adopt a system designed to make it easy to distinguish each type with predictable names. By utilizing a common naming scheme across our Maya projects, we can minimize the effort of staying on top of it all.

It's hard to understate the importance of saving your work as you go. Although Maya is a powerful program, we all know that, as with any complex computer program, it just *might* quit working without notice. In addition, we might find that we've gone down a dead-end path and need to back up to a previous turning point. Our system makes such potentialities easy to handle in stride.

The following file-naming system has served me well over the years and should serve this project equally well:

- Each model is created in its own project (for example, FireHydrant).
- Regular checkpoint files have an abbreviated name and a sequence number (as in FH.3).
- Incremental saves (temporary files) are named tmp1 through tmp9, and then the filenames are reused.
- Special saves are given descriptive names (as in BeforeDeforming).
- Final versions are given the project name (as in FireHydrant).
- Revisions cause the file being edited to be renamed to receive a version number (such as FireHydrant.1), and the newly edited version is given the final version name (such as FireHydrant).

We'll apply these naming conventions to each of the models and to the shots in the *Parking Spot* project. When we're done with any model (and with the whole animation), we know that we can safely delete the tmp files and can choose to cull the checkpoint files, and the finished result is clearly identified.

In the case of shots (or any models in which we create some parts separately), we'll need to distinguish temporary files from different shots, so we'll sort them out with names such as s1tmp1, s1tmp2, and s3tmp1. Also consistent with model names, shot checkpoints will be named s1.1, s1.2, and so on; the final shots will be shot1, shot2, and so on.

In addition, we'll save our files as Maya ASCII files, not as binary files. Binary files might save some disk space, but they are not editable. The enormous advantage of ASCII files is that if something goes wrong, a corrupted file can potentially be fixed in any text editor (a fact that has saved me on many occasions).

Warning

Save your files as Maya ASCII files, not Maya binary files! ASCII files can be repaired if they are somehow corrupted—binary files can't. Don't put your hard work at risk by saving in Maya binary format.

By having a plan for our projects and files, we'll be able to work confidently with the knowledge that we have a place for everything and that everything will be in its place. A sudden urge to save a file won't give rise to a filename that no one understands a month later. It will be clear what files are important, what to name the next file, and what files to consider for the CD for this book.

Summary

The Maya interface is enormously customizable, so examine your workflow and consider how you might tailor that interface to suit you. Whether you undertake a complete UI overhaul or simply set up some hotkeys that you can remember, tuning Maya to your way of working is key to using the software as effectively as possible.

Also, although we'd be flattered if you chose to do everything our way, the real point is to identify your needs and come up with ways to meet them. A minor inconvenience might add only a couple of seconds to any step of your work, but if you put up with that inconvenience day after day, you both subtract that time from your life and add frustration and wear to your life.

At least occasionally, take the time to examine your work habits for inefficiencies and recurring tasks. You might find that devoting an entire day or two with each new Maya release is most effective, or you might be content to gradually chip away at the rough edges week after week until your process has become smooth. Whatever your plan of attack is, without one you'll be missing out on much of what Maya offers its users, all while slowed down by needless friction.

Your hotkeys might never be entirely set in stone, and your UI might never be fully optimized to your working style. But steady attention to these technical considerations can reward you with steady gains in productivity and personal comfort.

Chapter 5
MEL

By Erick Miller

What Is MEL?

MEL, otherwise known as the Maya Embedded Language, exposes a direct way to execute any command within Maya. In fact, almost all of Maya's menus and windows, as well as most of its user interface, are built using MEL. By typing the corresponding MEL commands, you can also access any command that you can access from a menu. All the MEL scripts that are being executed from the menus can also be retraced from within Maya's very own internal Script Editor. In a nutshell, MEL is the direct way to send messages that tell Maya exactly what to do. MEL lets you build logic using common control structures such as loops (to repeat or iterate over a list or array), conditions (to evaluate expressions as either true or false), and functions (otherwise known as procedures in Maya terminology).

The following topics are covered in this chapter:

- What MEL is and how it can be used
- Specific MEL essentials
- Workflow: the Script Editor and external editors
- Crash course on programming your first script
- Arguments, arrays, loops, control structures, and data types
- How to modify Maya's global UI using MEL
- Some helpful further learning resources

What Can MEL Do and How Is It Used?

MEL can do almost anything that Maya can do—and actually much more, in many cases. MEL can be used to automate tasks that would have normally been tedious and repetitive for someone to do by hand. The beautiful thing about MEL is that a well-written script will almost never make mistakes (but people often do after doing the same thing—such as selecting and deleting the same five vertices of a polygon—hundreds of times). MEL can be used to design and implement everything from the very simplest of scripted character GUIs to quite sophisticated algorithms in all corners of Maya's domains—from modeling and animation; to particle dynamics, effects, and rendering; all the way to the very user interface that exposes these commands to any average user. MEL can do it all. MEL can even do file I/O, in that it can write to and read from files on a hard disk or across a network. This gives it the easy capability to create and read from ASCII log files or to create, execute, and send batch job files to a distributed network-queuing system or to a render farm. In fact, MEL can import files, export files, save files, and even execute and send command-line arguments to any external program that your heart desires.

With all these features easily accessible, MEL can be used to do just about anything that involves communicating the flow of data between Maya and the rest of your production pipeline, and automating all the unnecessary stages that may lie in between. MEL is most commonly used by the Maya TD (Technical Director) to accomplish specific tasks that are simply too repetitive or too technically complicated, or that require precise algorithmic logic to accomplish. It can then package them up into neat little scripts that can easily be sourced and executed on demand by any user on the network.

If something cannot be done directly in MEL (such as writing your own deform function for a custom deformer node), Maya has a robust application programming interface to write custom plug-ins for this very reason. And when you are finished writing and compiling your plug-in, you can use MEL to dynamically load it for your users from a single location across your network, making it very easy to update. Maya's entire Cloth module was implemented using the Maya dynamics API. The Maya Live module, as well as many third-party file format import and export parsers, were also implemented using the Maya API.

While reading this chapter and learning MEL, remember the following:

1. MEL is fun and easy.

2. The better you know Maya, the better you'll know MEL. The better you know MEL, the better you'll know Maya.

MEL was never originally designed to be a full-fledged programming language. Nor was it designed to replace any pre-existing languages that are already working quite well and that have a large user knowledge base and code base on their own. Instead, MEL was designed to be the easiest way to directly control Maya and still have the capability to add lots of logic and control into the flow of things directly within the reach of your 3D authoring environment. MEL is also platform-independent (for the most part). Although a few commands here and there are UNIX- or Windows-specific, for the most part, if Maya runs on the platform, so will the MEL.

MEL is very successful in its language design with those clear objectives in mind.

Note

If you are completely new to programming and are stepping into things for the very first time, things might get a little confusing. Don't let this discourage you! Previous programming experience is definitely not required to understand the basics of MEL scripting—or the rest of this chapter—although a little background in this area definitely couldn't hurt. If you do start to stumble a little (this happens to us all as we learn something completely different for the first time), it's a good idea to get yourself a book that provides a good introduction to C programming. A book that covers how to write and design a program from the ground up will be indispensable for all future script writing and for an overall understanding of general programming terms and methodologies.

Anyone with a background in C or C++ programming, UNIX Csh, or Perl or Python scripting can definitely benefit from this previous knowledge, but it is not required. If you don't have this experience but know someone who does, that person could probably help answer some of your basic questions about how things work. But don't worry: MEL is a much simpler language than any of these just mentioned. As a language, it was designed so that artists as well as programmers can use it effectively, with a very small learning curve from both sides. As a programmer, you are less likely to know the ins and outs of Maya itself and how to access menu commands from the UI, but you are much more likely to quickly write readable and efficient scripts with professional clarity. As an artist, you will be much more familiar with the specific commands to complete an action, but you will be less familiar with the programming side of things. So, at this point we all stand on equal ground, and the TD is right smack dab in the middle. Because of its design goals, MEL lacks many very common things that give other programming languages more low-level control and complex sophistication, such as object-oriented design and user-defined data structures. But, in turn, these sacrifices make it much easier to learn and harness as a very powerful and yet immediately usable scripting tool for all of Maya's diverse user base.

Maya's Embedded Language: Some Specific Essentials

MEL is an internal scripting language, compiled and executed by the Maya Executable as its interpreter. MEL's programming syntax style could easily and quickly be described as similar to the C programming and Perl scripting languages. The true power of MEL does not lie in a sophisticated and difficult language to learn or use. Instead, its power lies in the fact that it's a very simple and easy language that offers full control over Maya's runtime environment, including UI windows and widgets, all of the thousands of native embedded MEL commands, and the capability to create and execute your own custom scripts and functions inside the robust environment.

MEL is a top-down, function-based, procedural scripting language. Each MEL procedure should perform a single task and, in turn, return the result of that task to the next called procedure or function until the script is finished executing and all tasks are complete. Remember, MEL is a single-paradigm language. Things such as user-defined datatypes, objects, classes, methods, and templates are not conventions in MEL. Even things such as pointers or passing references to a function do not exist. Memory is managed completely by Maya; all array variables grow automatically and are deleted from memory by Maya's garbage collector as soon as the function exits scope. We'll talk more about variables, declarations, and syntax in the upcoming sections, but MEL makes it all very simple for the end user.

MEL does indeed contain all the familiar features of any useful language, including most necessary 3D, 2D, and character string datatypes; global and local variables; control structures; expressions; conditions; switches and branching, loops; variable scope; recursion; and, of course, function declarations with return types (both global and local). Hundreds of built-in MEL commands also exist for things such as string processing, math functions, file I/O, error catching, and thousands of more exposed custom Maya-specific functions and procedures in the global namespace. A few other neat things, such as triggers and events using `scriptJob` and `scriptNode`, are discussed more in depth in Appendix A, "Intermediate and Advanced MEL," the slightly more advanced MEL and Maya API section at the end of the book.

The MEL Command Line and Script Editor

Being the robust software application that it is, Maya has its own handy internal editor for writing and debugging MEL scripts, called the Script Editor. You can access the Script Editor by going to Window, General Editors, Script Editor (see Figure 5.1).

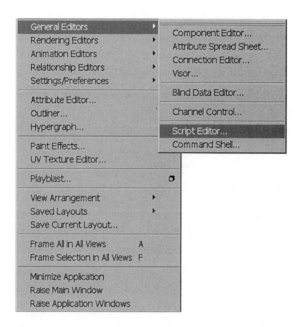

Figure 5.1   Access Maya's Script Editor by clicking Window, General Editors, and then Script Editor.

When preparing to write MEL scripts, be sure that Display, UI Elements, Command Line is checked as active and is visible in Maya's Main UI. The command line can also be helpful while writing script (see Figure 5.2). It provides a text box for entering MEL commands on the left side, as well as a read-only text box for viewing command output on the right side.

An even easier way to access the Script Editor if the command line is visible is to click the little box in the very bottom-right corner of Maya's main UI that looks like a miniature editor window. This is the most convenient way and my favorite way to launch the Script Editor. The full command line is annotated in Figure 5.3.

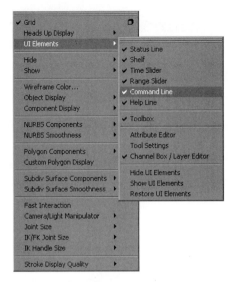

Figure 5.2 Display, UI Elements, Command Line checked as active and visible in Maya's Main UI.

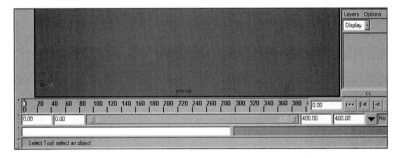

Figure 5.3 Accessing the Script Editor via the command line and Script Editor UI button.

There is one final way to launch the Script Editor, and this is the one we will use in the following exercise.

Exercise 5.1 Executing Your First MEL Command: Launching the Script Editor Using a MEL Command

1. Make sure the command line is visible, as outlined previously.

2. If you opened the Script Editor already, close it before going any further.

3. In the command line, type the following command:

   ```
   ScriptEditor;
   ```
   Don't forget that MEL, like any scripting language, is case sensitive!

What actually just happened in Maya when you typed the command to launch the Script Editor? Well, hopefully the Script Editor window opened. But for that to happen, Maya did just a few things behind the scenes to create that special little window that you see in front of you right now.

After Maya first loaded itself into memory, back when you launched maya.exe, it sourced a script that defined the command `ScriptEditor` as a default `runTimeCommand`. This defined the command to simply call another procedure, `showWindow`, and pass to it the global variable `$gCommandWindow` as an argument. This global variable contains the "real" contents (or memory location) of the Script Editor window. Maya assigned this variable upon creation of the UI element, when Maya initialized, and loaded itself (and all its other UI MEL scripts) into the computer's memory. The name of the window is stored in a global variable, to keep the variable exposed and fully accessible to other scripts, while still avoiding accidentally hard-coding a string (or word) into the MEL source code. This happens in case any naming conflicts occur upon the name assignment (even though, in this case, it would be nearly impossible).

If another child UI window element somehow was assigned the same name that the Script Editor was trying to take first, Maya still would have the correct name because it was returned to the original global variable. If the script were to use a hard-coded string, the Script Editor and possibly the whole program would probably be broken in this case. This is a good example because it is also a good way to prelude global and local variables (as well as a variable's scope, which we will talk about later). For now, understand that if you print the contents of the global variable `$gCommandWindow` by typing this into the command line:

```
print $gCommandWindow;
```

you will see this word appear in the output of the command feedback line and in the output section of the Script Editor:

```
CommandWindow
```

This is the "actual" string that the variable `$gCommandWindow` is referring to. This is because in the MEL script initialLayout.mel, one of the very first MEL scripts that Maya loads upon execution, there exists the variable declaration and assignment:

```
global string $gCommandWindow = "CommandWindow";
```

Also note that because this is a global variable, it is fully exposed to you during runtime. So, if you reassign new data to this variable, by typing and executing something like this:

```
$gCommandWindow = "foobar";
```

you will break Maya during the current open session, and the Script Editor will no longer open correctly. This is the single most important reason why global variables are bad practice unless they are used for a purpose such as the one explained in the previous example of the Script Editor.

Note

Using an external editor to write your MEL scripts is very common and often quite necessary. Many people use external editors such as Emacs, VIM, or Nedit. You are free to use whatever editor you are most comfortable with. I have seen programmers write MEL in Visual Studio, all the way down to the confused artist hacking away in Notepad. The choice is left to you. I personally use UltraEdit to write all my MEL scripts because it contains familiar things such as autoCodeComplete (Ctrl+spacebar), as well as custom syntax highlighting and a lot of really great macro, search, and replace capabilities. If you are currently not using a good text editor or want to give UltraEdit a try, I highly recommend it as a powerful Windows-based text editing application (Wordfile.txt is included on the CD for MEL syntax highlighting in UltraEdit).

Using an external editor usually promotes clearer code, fewer mistakes, and overall faster completion of your script. Why? Because there is no syntax highlighting and only one undo available inside Maya's internal Script Editor. Although Maya's Script Editor is great for testing and quickly debugging your MEL scripts, an external editor is much better for authoring them. The most effective thing to do is to write the script outside Maya and then source it using the `source` MEL command from within the Script Editor, or as a shelf button, for testing and debugging.

Using the Script Editor

After you have written a MEL script and saved it to disk, you must source it before it will work. You must do this for two reasons:

1. Maya checks your code for any syntax or logic errors that it can detect, which might then need to be fixed and debugged.

2. Maya must load the procedures that do all the work of your script into memory so that it recognizes them and so that they can then be called by name from within Maya.

By sourcing a script in the Script Editor, you are actually executing the MEL that is contained within that script. By opening a script in the Script Editor, you are merely viewing it as a text file. If any code in a script file exists outside a procedure declaration, that code immediately is evaluated and executed as soon as it is sourced. So be sure you know what you are sourcing (especially if you have randomly downloaded a script from the Internet). It is the best practice to have a quick look over the script and any comments or file header descriptions or directions ahead of time by opening the script in an editor before you source it, to make sure that it contains code that you definitely want to execute on your local computer (see Figure 5.4).

How do you source a script? Well, there are several ways. The first three you can do while Maya is running (during runtime).

The first is the most obvious way. From the File menu inside the Script Editor, choose File, Source Script. Then navigate to where you have your script saved and choose your script. Maya outputs any diagnostics into the output section of the Script Editor as soon as it is sourced. Remember, when sourcing a script, no news is good news. That means that Maya's debugger detected no syntax or logic errors.

The second way to easily source a script is to use the MEL function `source`, followed by the full path to the MEL script you are trying to source.

For example, to source the MEL script copyArray.mel (using a Windows file path) you would type this:

```
source "C:/Program Files/AliasWavefront/Maya4.5/scripts/unsupported
/copyArray.mel";
```

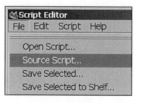

Figure 5.4   The Script Editor window, fully annotated, with history and input sections, the File menu selected, and the source script highlighted.

Note

Maya on the Mac, Windows, Linux, and Irix operating systems is almost identical in terms of MEL commands. As a trifling matter, the paths to files and few trivial system commands might vary slightly on different operating systems. As such, most examples in this book remain platform –independent—the MEL commands used are consistently platform independent based on Alias|Wavefront's support and implementation of Maya and MEL on that specific operating system.

It is quite convenient to make the command to source the script that you are writing a shelf button while you are testing and debugging. This way you can continually save backups in your editor and still save the most recent script using the path that you are sourcing in the shelf. Then you can switch back over to Maya, click the Shelf button, and immediately see any error messages that Maya might have discovered in your script so that you can interactively debug your script outside Maya.

The third way to quickly source some MEL code during runtime is the easiest and most convenient way. It's also the least permanent, which makes it great for quickly testing and debugging small procedures as you are writing them. Simply copy and paste the lines of code from your script into the bottom half (Input section) of the Script Editor. You can also use the open command from within the Script Editor to load your entire script into the Input section. Then highlight the text with the mouse cursor and simply click the Enter key on the keyboard next to the number key pad. Make sure that it is the Enter key next to the NumPad, or this will do nothing but erase your code. If you are on a laptop computer or a computer without a NumPad, use the Ctrl+Enter key combination, which has the same effect as the NumPad Enter key. As soon as you hit Enter, you should see the code that you highlighted appear in the History Output section (the top portion) of the Script Editor. This is where all commands and procedures show up after they have been executed, and it is a wonderful way to figure out what is going on as commands are being executed.

The final way to source a MEL script is to have it exist in Maya's global sourcing path on your hard drive when Maya is started. The global sourcing path goes to your user scripts directory—the ../currentUser/maya/scripts/ directory—as well as to any of the folders in the ../AliasWavefront/Maya5.0/scripts/ directory, where Maya was installed. By placing a MEL script in either of these locations, you ensure that it is sourced each time Maya is started up. The Maya source path is actually a global environment variable and can be queried or changed using the MEL commands getenv and putenv. Here is an example of querying the value of a global environment variable:

```
getenv MAYA_SCRIPT_PATH;
```

Some very helpful options also are found under the Script menu within the Script Editor—namely, Script, Echo All Commands; Script, Show Line Numbers; and Script, Show Stack Trace. These three functions can be priceless when trying to debug a script, and I always keep all three checked on.

Intro to Programming: A Crash Course on Programming Using MEL

Hopefully you now understand exactly what MEL is and what it can be used for, and you are comfortable with your scripting environment inside Maya. Now it's time to really dive into MEL and start talking about scripting. We'll start with procedure declarations, return statements, datatypes, variable declarations and assignment, control structures, and, you know, all the easy stuff!

First you'll declare a global procedure that prints `Hello World` and returns the string goodbye. Type the following into the Input section of the Script Editor, and source it by highlighting it and hitting the NumPad Enter key:

```
global proc string helloWorld ()
{
print "Hello World!!!\n";
string $bye = "Goodbye";
return $bye;
}
```

Congratulations, you have just written your very first MEL procedure, `helloWorld()`.

Now you will execute the procedure you just wrote. At the command line or in the Script Editor, type **helloWorld**();. Highlight it again and hit Enter. Now look in the Output section of the Script Editor, and notice what it says:

```
helloWorld();
Hello World!!!
// Result: Goodbye //
```

Let's break down what has happened here. The function `helloWorld` was defined as a global procedure. This means that it is visible and directly executable by name from within Maya. The word `string` between `proc` and `helloWorld` specifies the return type—in other words, what kind of variable the function will output when it is finished executing. The two parentheses after `helloWorld` are empty. This means that the procedure takes no arguments (or doesn't get anything or any variables passed into it to process). The two curly braces that surround the rest of the procedure are defining the variable's scope inside the procedure as being only local variables of that procedure. The print command outputs to standard output and prints the text to the screen. The \n is an escape sequence and is read by the print command as being a carriage return, or a new line. Next, the variable $bye is declared as a type string and is assigned the value goodbye. Finally, the function reaches its end and returns the variable $bye, which contains the word Goodbye.

Think of returning at the end of a procedure like passing the answer out of the function: If there is an answer, someone now needs to catch it or it will be lost *forever*.

Catching Return Values into Variables

Now that you have written, sourced, and executed your helloWorld procedure, try catching the return of that procedure in a variable and then printing its contents to verify that you did indeed catch the information that was returned:

```
string $catchIt = `helloWorld`;
print ("\n The result is: " + $catchIt + ".\n");
```

After executing this code, you should see this:

```
Hello World!!!
The result is: Goodbye.
```

The procedure helloWorld was called and the string goodbye was returned from helloWorld() into the variable $catchIt. In most programming languages, MEL included, the order of execution happens from right to left so that the assignment to the variable happens last. This would have to be the case. Otherwise, the computer would not know what the value of the data is for further processing. The function helloWorld() appears inside the infamous ` backticks. This is an operator for evaluation and is simply shorthand for declaring the command:

```
eval ( "helloWorld" );
```

These backticks enable you to evaluate and catch returned data from any MEL command or procedure.

Next the `print` command is called, but this time, the + string concatenation operator is used to combine the variable `$catchIt` with the regular string `\n The result is:`. This expression must occur within parentheses so that it is evaluated first, combined into a single string; then the `print` command is called, with the final resulting string as its argument.

Tip

While you are writing your scripts, be careful about syntax, case sensitivity, and, most commonly, typos. This is probably the most difficult thing about writing scripts. (Even more frustrating than solving the logic is just getting used to how picky the compiler can be and how easy it is to accidentally overlook a silly typo and immediately assume that it is a logic error in your code instead of simply looking closer to find any undetected syntax errors.) One of the most common, undocumented mistakes by beginners is accidentally using the single quote (') character, found on the same key as the quotation mark, instead of the correct backtick character, which is usually found on the upper-left corner of your keyboard on the same key as the tilde (~) character. Another very common mistake is accidentally using the = assignment operator to evaluate an expression when you mean to use the == is-equal-to operator. This is a well-documented mistake but can still cause quite subtle logic errors that might be slow to find and correct in your code. Be aware of what you type.

And always remember that MEL will tell you what your error is. Keep the options Echo All Commands, Show Line Numbers, and Show Stack Trace checked at all times (from the Script menu in the Script Editor). Maya always tries to tell you as much as it can about any errors that it can find as it is interpreting your code. These errors often tell you the exact mistake you made and on which line in the code you made it. You can then have line numbers turned on in your editor and go immediately to the exact place where Maya encountered the error so that you can fix it. Sometimes these errors will be less precise and it will take some digging to figure out where things went wrong. No matter what, don't give up or get discouraged because of errors. Errors are a normal part of writing and debugging code. Chances are, it is a simple typo or silly mistake, not a huge, discouraging failure of your logic and ability.

Arguments, Arrays, and Control Structures

Now that you can declare a function and catch its return type, let's try building something with just a small bit of logic involved. You will write a function that calls your first function `helloWorld();`, but this time the new function will take an argument of type array of strings. An array of strings is just like saying "a list of strings." You can store an entire list, with each item being a separate element, into a single variable type using an array. The new function will also include an `if/else` flow-control statement. `if` evaluates an expression down to either 0 or 1 and then makes a decision based on the result: 1 being `true` (`if`) and 0 being false (`else`). Finally, you will also include a loop, or a way to repeat and cycle through a block of commands many times, often used to sort through things that are stored in a list.

The numeric integer datatype is also introduced. In this case, you will cycle through and store, format, and print each element in the array that was passed to your function using a loop. Looping is often referred to as iterating, and often inside of your loop you use incrementing and decrementing to keep track of which number you are on. You will then pass your formatted string to the original calling function, which will then print the output of the original function. This all works in a very similar manner to the previous example, but it introduces a lot more of MEL's control structures to you.

The following script is entirely explained using comments, or anything found on the right side of the // characters. Comments are just explanations and notes for the programmer, or anyone reading the script, and are completely ignored by the compiler (Maya). Comments are introduced here as a good way to explain what you are doing in your code. The rest of the code in this book is actually overcommented for the purpose of explaining it to the reader (including the following functions). It is not necessary and is a waste of time to overcomment your own code. As a general rule, if the code itself already explains what is happening, allow it to speak for itself. The purpose of comments in production code is not to teach people to program, but to effectively communicate what is happening in the code. It is usually best to keep your comments on the outside of your functions and much more generally concept-based. This way, if the code is updated or changed, the comments do not become obsolete. It is far too common to update code and forget to update all the specific comments. If I am reading a script with too many spread everywhere inside functions, I prefer to just delete them before I begin to look at the code instead of trying to read them at all.

The following script is the first full example of everything we have talked about so far. It is included on the companion CD, and I highly suggest that you use that version instead of trying to retype it from the book (but retyping your own procedures will definitely benefit you in the very near future).

This script was written as a fun example of learning MEL. It uses most of the fundamental methods for processing data that an actual MEL script might contain.

This script searches through an array of declared names until it finds the name `Stinky Pete`. No one wants to be around Stinky Pete, so when the script finds him, the search exits. Although the script is searching through the list of names, it is also storing (or string incrementing) a goodbye message, which is printed by the first function.

This script is commented very explicitly, to walk you step by step with explanations on each command and procedure. To execute the script, just type `firstFullExampleScript()` in the script editor or command line. Have fun!

```
//firstFullExampleScript.mel
// author: Erick Miller
// Declare the global procedure
// firstFullExampleScript as the 'main'
// function, which is the procedure that
// should be called to execute the rest
// of the script. It is not necessary to
// name this function main(). In MEL (unlike
// C), you can call the first function
// anything that you want because you will
// have to call it by function name to
// execute it anyway.
// This function has been declared with no
// return types; therefore, a return
// statement at the end is not required.
//
// main procedure:
//
// firstFullExampleScript();
//

global proc firstFullExampleScript()
{

//
// Declare a string array of eight elements,
// and assign the elements to the array.
// These elements can be accessed
// individually by using their array index
// number, which is commented next to each
// element and always starts with 0.
// For example, Monica is equal to the
// variable $myArrayOfNames[3] of the eight-
// element array. Even though Monica is the
// fourth element, she is still indexed by
// the number 3.

string $myArrayOfNames[8] = {

"emptyElement", // array element $myArrayOfNames[0]

"Max",          // array element $myArrayOfNames[1]

"Mark",         // array element $myArrayOfNames[2]

"Monica",       // array element $myArrayOfNames[3]
```

```
    "Matt",          // array element $myArrayOfNames[4]

    "Stinky Pete",   // array element $myArrayOfNames[5]

    "Bill",          // array element $myArrayOfNames[6]

    "Bob"            // array element $myArrayOfNames[7]

        };

    //
    // Declare the string $getIt, and pass the
    // flow of control
    // to the global procedure
    // `firstFullExampleProcedure` passing as an
    // argument into this procedure the array
    // that was just declared.  Whatever
    // data is returned by
    // firstFullExampleProcedure will be
    // assigned as the contents of the string
    // $getIt. (enter the function
    // firstFullExampleProcedure now)...


    string $getIt = firstFullExampleProcedure( $myArrayOfNames );


    //
    // The flow of control has been passed back
    // to firstFullExampleScript();
    // Now print the contents of what the
    // firstFullExampleProcedure has returned to
    // its calling function for us.

        print $getIt;
    }

    //
    // Introducing arrays, arguments, loops,
    // conditions, comments, and much more!
    //
    // Declare the global procedure with an
    // argument of type string array and a
    // return type of a single string.
    //

    global proc string firstFullExampleProcedure( string $arrayArg[] )
    {

    //
```

```
// This calls our original function
// helloWorld(); and returns its contents
// into string $goodbyeString.

    string $goodbyeString = `helloWorld`;

//
// This declares the return string
// so that it has "scope" for the
// entire function (because its declaration
// is in the outermost block of code).

    string $longReturnString;

//
// This declares an integer for our loop...

    int $i;

//
// You are about to enter a for loop.
// A loop is simply a way to repeat or
// iterate and evaluate commands on each
// iteration.
//
// The declaration statement of the loop
// can be understood like this:
// Variable $i is equal to zero.
// While $i is less than the total number of
// elements in the list, enter and begin the
// loop.
// After each evaluation of the loop,
// evaluate $i++, which is just shorthand
// for $i is equal to $i + 1
// (called incrementing $i, increasing its
// value by one each time).
// If $i is greater or equal to total
// elements in array, then exit the loop.
// This is called a 'for' loop:
// **You can exit any loop at any time
// using a break statement, or skip to the
// very next element by using a continue
// statement:

    for( $i=0; $i < size($arrayArg); $i++ )
    {

//
// if $i is equal to zero, && (AND) the
// current array element is not equal to
// "Stinky Pete" (because we will be
```

```
// handling this special case later in
// our code - it would be a logic error to
// not test for "Stinky Pete" here). If both
// evaluate to true, then execute the code
// inside the curly braces of the if block.
// Otherwise, skip to the code in the next
// block of the else statement:


if ( ($i == 0) && ($arrayArg[$i] != "Stinky Pete") )
{


// the 'continue' statement skips to
// the next iteration of the loop
// without evaluating any of the rest
// of the code that would normally follow.
// In this case, it just skips the very
// first element if the first element is
// not equal to "Stinky Pete".

                continue;
            }
            else
            {

//
// print hello to each array element :)
//


print ( "Hello, array element #" + $i + ", " + $arrayArg[$i] + "...\n" );

//
// Check to see if the current array element
// is equal to "Stinky Pete" .  If 'true',
// then enter the block of code inside the
// curly braces of the if statement. If
// 'false', then enter the else statement
// block.




if ( $arrayArg[$i] == "Stinky Pete" )
{
print ("\n...OH NO. ITS STINKY PETE!
```

```
FOUND AT ARRAY ELEMENT #" + $i + ". RUN AWAY!!!\n");

$longReturnString = $longReturnString + $goodbyeString + " Stinky Pete!!!\n";



//
// the break statement is used to
// immediately exit a loop without any more
// iterations of the for block or
// incriminations of $i.

    break;
  }
  else
  {

//
// The return string is equal to the return
// string concatenated with the goodbye
// string (which was returned from our
// original hello world function),
// concatenated with a space and then the
// current array element accessed by its
// index $i, concatenated with period and a
// new line character (for a clear, formatted
// look to the return string output message
// later).

  $longReturnString = $longReturnString + $goodbyeString + " " +
$arrayArg[$i] +".\n";


    }
  }
}

//
// This message lets you know when the for
// block has been exited and the flow of
// control is about to be returned to the
// original calling function,
// firstFullExampleScript();
//

        print "\nTime to exit example procedure.\n\n";

//
// return the formatted message
// string to whoever called the function...
//
```

```
              return ( $longReturnString );
}

//
// Our very first Hello World Procedure   :)
//

global proc string helloWorld ()
{
      print "\nHello World!!!\n";
      string $bye = "Goodbye";
      return $bye;
}
```

See, isn't MEL fun and easy? Just wait until you start making icons and shelf buttons! Get ready for more, as we start to expose some real examples of manipulating Maya's default user interface controls.

MEL UI Control Exposed

The following script is something I wrote to demonstrate that Maya gives you full control over its own global user interface controls. Usually, the environment controls the language. Well, in the relationship between Maya and MEL, the language can also control the environment. It even enables you to do things that you might not really want to do, such as set the main Maya window's visibility to 0. If you do something like this, the Maya UI actually disappears, yet your scene is still open and unsaved, and no error has occurred (although you can almost be guaranteed that you have lost your scene in this case). In this respect, MEL can be somewhat dangerous because it harnesses full control over the Maya executable and any open Maya scene file that the user might be engaged with. The following file is explained fully in the comments that I wrote specifically for this book. This MEL file can also be found on the companion CD, to save you from having to type all this.

```
// closeAllOfMayaExceptMaya.mel
// author: Erick Miller
// This is a useful little script that will
// instantly close all open windows except
// the main Maya window.  This is an easy
// way to get rid of all the clutter whenever
// there are just too many open
// windows.
//
// main procedure:
//
```

```
// closeAllOfMayaExceptMaya();
//

global proc closeAllOfMayaExceptMaya()
{

// The Maya Main Parent UI global variable:

    global string $gMainWindow;

// build an array of all open windows:

    string $allOpenWindows[] =`lsUI -wnd`;

// loop through the array using a
// for-in repetition structure:
//

    for( $eachWindow in $allOpenWindows )
    {
        if($eachWindow == $gMainWindow)
        {

        // current window is actually
// the main Maya window:
// set visibility to false.

            window -e -vis 0 $eachWindow;

        // set visibility back to true

window -e -vis 1 $eachWindow;
        }
        else
        {

        // current window is
// ANY other window:
// set visibility to false

            window -e -vis 0 $eachWindow;                    }
    }

    // Oops. This got rid of the channel
// box (or attribute editor)
    // from the main Maya UI as well...
    // so restore its default state by
// simply toggling ChannelBox back on,
    // and making sure it's still visible:
```

```
        ToggleChannelBox;
        if (!`isChannelBoxVisible`)
        {
                setChannelBoxVisible
(!`isChannelBoxVisible`);
        }
}
```

Adding a New Item to a Pre-Existing Default Maya Menu

Did you ever wonder to yourself, "Why in the world didn't they put the Create Render Node window under the Create menu?" I have personally been wondering this for about three versions now. Well, Maya is still open to change. If you don't like Maya's default menus or want to add to them or rearrange any of them, they are all purposefully exposed directly to the user in neat global variables that enable you to add new menu items very quickly, clearly, and easily.

The following script shows how you can add the Create Render Node window MEL command in a procedure and then make it a menu item of the default Maya Create menu, just like you might have always wanted. The following script is explained fully in the comments written specifically for you, the reader. This MEL file can also be found on the companion CD, to save you from having to type from the book:

```
// addCreateRenderNodeToMenu.mel:
//
// This script shows how to add a menu item
// to the end of one of Maya's main menus.
//
// main procedure:
//
// addCreateRenderNodeToMenu();
//

/*

The following variables can be found in 'initMainMenuBar.mel':

These globals are used to name the main
menus so that users can add things to the
end of the menus without hard-coding the
name.
```

```
        global string $gMainFileMenu;
        global string $gMainEditMenu;
        global string $gMainModifyMenu;
        global string $gMainDisplayMenu;
        global string $gMainWindowMenu;
        global string $gMainOptionsMenu;
        global string $gMainCreateMenu;

*/

//
// This is a procedure declaration, used to
// launch the Create Render Node window with
// default arguments...
// This procedure is used as the command for
// the added menu item "Create Render Node"
// found in the next procedure,
// addCreateRenderNodeToMenu();
//

global proc InsideMaya_CreateRenderNodeWin()
{

// launch create render node window

    createRenderNode("-all", "", "");

}


//
// This is the function that will actually
// add the additional command to
// the end of the Main "Create" menu:
//

global proc addCreateRenderNodeToMenu()
{

// global variable for Maya's Create menu

    global string $gMainCreateMenu;

// This will build the menu, in case it hasn't been built yet:

eval("ModCreateMenu " + $gMainCreateMenu);

// set "Create" menu as current menu Parent

setParent -menu $gMainCreateMenu;
```

```
// add divider, to separate a new section

    menuItem -divider true;

//
// Add the menu item, using the
//procedure declared previously as its command
//

    menuItem -label "Create Render Node"
    -command "InsideMaya_CreateRenderNodeWin"
    -annotation "Create Render Node: Opens the Create New Render Node window.
    ➥Easy, huh?";

// Set the parent to the last one.

    setParent -menu ..;

// You can call this command in any script that is located in your
// Startup folder, and this menu item will always show up
// in the main Maya UI, as if it was already put there by
// Alias Wavefront itself.
}
```

Adding a New Menu to the Global Maya UI

Do you want to have your very own Maya menu, with all your own scripts and toolbars all under one single roof, easily accessible to all users? Well, adding a new menu as a child of the main window is a piece of cake. Read the following script. The comments contain the full explanation every step of the way. This script is also included on the companion CD, for your use and dissection:

```
// createCustomMenuItemInMaya.mel
//
// This script is an example of how easy it
// is to add your own menu items to Maya's
// main UI.  The following procedure creates
// a menu item parented to the Main Maya
// Window, called "Custom Menu".
// The first menu item uses the MEL command
// `sphere` to demonstrate using the -c
// switch in the menu command. The rest of
// the menu items are null placeholders,
// leaving the -c switch blank, simply as a
// demonstration of multiple menu items.
// Remember: Any command can be placed in
// the -c switch: a custom procedure or a
// built-in MEL command.
//
```

```
// main procedure:
//
// createCustomMenuItemInMaya();
//

global proc createCustomMenuItemInMaya()
{

// global variable for the Main Maya UI.

    global string $gMainWindow;

// global declaration for custom menu item

    global string $gMyCustomMenu = "myCustomMenuItem";

// make the Main Maya UI the current parent

    setParent $gMainWindow;
    if (`isTrue "BaseMayaExists"`)
    {

    // Create and name your custom menu:
    //

        menu -l "Custom Menu" -aob
true -to true  // make it tear-off
        -postMenuCommandOnce true
        $gMyCustomMenu;

// parent it to the previous main Maya UI.

setParent -m ..;

// make custom menu the current parent

setParent -m $gMyCustomMenu;
        menuItem -divider true;

    // Create and name custom Menu Items:
    //
    // This first menu item creates a
    // proprietary sphere :-) (Joke)
    //

        menuItem -label "Super Custom Sphere Command!"  -c "sphere"
        -annotation "Proprietary Workflow Interface module containing a
        ➤top secret Sphere command!";
```

```
// add divider, to separate menu sections
        menuItem -divider true;


//
// The rest of these menu items do nothing
// and were left blank to display the
// addition of multiple menu items separated
// by menu dividers.
// Maya gives you full control to customize
// away!
//

            menuItem -label "Custom Command 1 Goes Here!"   -c "";
            menuItem -label "Custom Command 2 Goes Here!"   -c "";
            menuItem -label "Custom Command 3 Goes Here!"   -c "";
            menuItem -label "Custom Command 4 Goes Here!"   -c "";
            menuItem -label "Custom Command 5 Goes Here!"   -c "";

            menuItem -divider true;

            menuItem -label "Custom Command 6 Goes Here!"   -c "";
            menuItem -label "Custom Command 7 Goes Here!"   -c "";

// Set the parent to the last one above.

            setParent -m ..;
    }

}
```

Summary

To conclude this chapter, it is important to note that this is really just the tip of the iceberg. There are so many other extremely useful ways to use MEL as a fully functional programming language inside Maya. The topics covered were tailored around a quick introduction to the concept of MEL and the general usage and common syntax rules that might not be clearly outlined already in the online Maya documentation. A good example of this is adding a menuItem to one of Maya's global menus. Learning to parse strings in a loop can be applied to solve many different problems, so instead an example was displayed that was both easy to understand and hopefully somewhat amusing. The importance of all these topics can be vital to learning and using MEL in the professional working environment of a digital production studio, but there is so much more of MEL to be seen. Be sure to read Appendix A if you are looking for more useful MEL tips and techniques.

Some final notes, helpful learning advice, and resources: Use the MEL commands `help` and `showHelp` by typing **help** and then the command name. By typing **help help;**, you can even get help on the `help` command! Also, if you are ever unsure of whether something is a MEL command or a procedure, or where a script is getting sourced from, use the MEL command `whatIs` to get the full path to the MEL file or find out that it is a command.

Additional resources include the "Maya On-Line Library" (under the Help, Library menu). Use the following sections: "MEL Command Reference," "MEL," "Instant Maya" (Section 10, "MEL"), and `www.highend3d.com/maya/mel`.

Part II

Modeling

6 Formats   111

7 Methods   139

8 Sets   175

9 Props   217

10 Characters   289

Chapter 6
Formats

By Mark Adams

An amazing variety of objects exists in the world around us. From the incredibly tiny parts of the dust mite to the vast galaxies of interstellar space, the objects of our world can be staggeringly different. Some things are irregular, some are symmetric, some are tremendously complex, and others are platonically simple. Manmade objects add their distinctiveness to the natural collective. But despite this enormous range of objects, computer graphics has managed to represent almost all of it using just a few mathematical formats.

Maya offers three different primary modeling formats: polygon meshes, NURBS surfaces, and subdivision surfaces. Polygon meshes have the longest heritage. NURBS came into prominence in the 1980s, and subdivision surfaces became practical in the 1990s. The demands of producing models efficiently, precisely, and flexibly drove each of these technologies, resulting in suites of tools and techniques that can handle almost any model you can throw at them.

In this chapter, we'll look at characteristics that distinguish each of these formats and consider how Maya can use these to model various objects that will be a part of production. Specifically, this chapter covers these topics:

- Modeling formats available (and not) within Maya
- Distinguishing characteristics between modeling formats (polygons, NURBS, and subdivision surfaces) available in Maya
- Continuity and how these formats achieve it
- What NURBS really means and why that's important
- How we plan to approach building various objects in the *Parking Spot* project

What's Not Available

Although Maya provides a broad range of modeling formats, not every possible format is represented. For completeness, this section covers a few modeling formats that aren't available within Maya. Each has it strengths and applications, but none of these has yet found its way into the product.

Implicit (Blobby) Surfaces

Blobby surfaces work well with organic shapes because they are designed to smoothly blend shapes into each other. Operating by a few basic rules, they typically involve placing smooth primitives (usually spheres) in proximity to each other and then specifying parameters for the blending operation. Maya allows particles to be rendered as blobbies, but it has no specific modeling operations for constructing ordinary models from them.

Several metaball plug-ins (such as MetaShapes and Flow Tracer) have been written for Maya, each with a slightly different emphasis. Depending on your needs, these might provide you with metaball modeling tools suitable for your needs. Because Maya itself still lacks specific support for implicit surfaces, however, these are implemented through existing Maya modeling (and rendering) formats.

Octrees

Imagine neatly filling an empty vessel with building blocks (a.k.a. voxels), and you've got the basic idea behind octrees. Take the concept a bit further, allowing the blocks to be of various sizes, and you've just about got the whole thing. Octrees, named for the eight spatial divisions created by three axes, are data–intensive and do not create smooth surfaces. They can be useful for applications such as topography, but you'll never miss them for the kind of work Maya does.

Point Clouds

Point clouds are another data–intensive approach to modeling, usually the result of 3D scanning systems. The typical problem with point clouds arises when converting the data to more conventional representations, such as NURBS surfaces. They find their greatest application in areas such as reverse engineering or digital-elevation models. Although some systems can do a good job of constructing a polygonal mesh (usually triangular) from the data, the necessary data-reduction and fitting algorithms make this a specialized set of tools.

For users who simply must have point clouds, Alias|Wavefront supports these in its Studio Tools product line (as do several other software vendors). Of course, the problem of fitting surfaces to the data still remains, but the resulting surfaces can then be easily imported into Maya.

Format: The Big Choices

The choice of the best method to use for building a given model is sometimes clear, but usually a range of possibilities and trade-offs must be considered. Sometimes the final solution incorporates more than one of these formats or uses one format to construct another. Many users have access to pre-existing data in some formats; others need to generate everything within Maya.

When deciding which modeling format to use in Maya—polygon meshes, NURBS surfaces, or subdivision surfaces—consider the following essential characteristics. For now, we'll just touch on them, but we'll examine them more closely when we describe each format in detail later in this chapter.

Fidelity

Foremost among modeling considerations is fidelity to the desired shape. Although it can be interesting to alter proportions or simplify detailed elements down to more basic forms, the tools must be capable of faithfully representing the object's shape as intended, regardless of complexity. Because some features might be added through shading, not all details are necessarily in the geometry of the model itself. In addition, some details might be discarded altogether as unimportant or imperceptible. However, when the necessary level of detail is established, the format used should be capable of faithfully representing the intended shape.

Each of the three major formats available in Maya is fundamentally capable of representing almost all objects, with differences that come to the fore when considering those characteristics that follow.

Efficiency

The modeling format must be both compact in size and manageable in its complexity. Although computing power has been growing at a fantastic rate, so have our expectations. Moreover, the modeler (the person, not the program) is still a limited commodity, one who must be able to effectively interact with the model when creating or modifying it. Thus, the speed with which a modeler can construct an object is usually an important factor. Faster, smaller, and simpler aren't always decisive, but efficiency is always desirable.

In our production, given the small size of our team and short production schedule, this is a vital consideration. Many of the decisions we make for modeling various objects in our production are based on the suitability and efficiency of a given modeling format for creating the object at hand.

Precision

For many CG applications, the end result is a physical object with an intended function. Automotive and aerospace designers need their parts to operate properly, so the difference between round and almost round is the difference between success and failure. Animators, on the other hand, might need to ensure that physically large shots don't introduce jittery limbs because of round-off errors. Either way, scientists and artists alike find that they need adequate precision in the scene data.

Because our production in this book involves a set of limited size and objects of ordinary scale, this is a minor issue for us. We can cut plenty of corners and take advantage of the limited resolution of images to cover up many shortcomings.

On the other hand, some objects and areas are critical, and modeling flaws should be avoided in these cases. These are primarily "hero" objects, such as the hydrant and the curbs, that will be seen very closely and that likely will have displacements in their surfaces. For these objects, it's important to achieve precision in both fit and continuity.

Continuity

CG objects must be free of unwanted gaps and sharp edges. Some objects have even more precise requirements, such as ensuring that a rounded edge has a consistent radius or that a surface highlight changes in a smooth fashion. In some modeling formats, these continuity relationships are implicit; in others, they must be carefully created. In some cases, the only way to achieve a specific relationship is with a particular modeling format.

Many of the objects in the *Parking Spot* scenes have significant continuity considerations, so this characteristic might well decide the format for several models.

Flexibility

In animation, objects very often must literally be flexible, bending or deforming in whatever way the animator desires. Modeling an object in a static position, even if it is perfectly faithful to the design intent, is no guarantee that it can be deformed properly. The format of the model is often dictated by this need for object flexibility.

Characters are the obvious models for which this is important. This is true for the *Parking Spot* production as well, although other models also will undergo some deformation.

Shading Needs

Just as animation can steer the choice of format, so can shading. NURBS surfaces inherently provide surface parameterizations (discussed in the "NURBS" section later in the chapter), but polygonal and subdivision surfaces do not. Additional shading methods exist that are independent of modeling format. Each approach has its strengths, so some models are created in a particular format because of their shading needs.

Several of the models in the *Parking Spot* production can be readily shaded by taking advantage of surface parameterization. However, the capability to map parameter values to poly vertices makes it fairly easy to work around this if another format has other advantages.

Polygons

The use of polygons for modeling objects was largely driven by early demands for simplicity and ease of computation. Detail could be specified to satisfy downstream rendering and data storage needs by limiting the number and arrangement of interconnected polygons. Although this almost always results in approximations for objects rather than models that are completely faithful to the designs, these approximations could be controlled directly by the users of CG systems.

Modern uses of polygon-based modeling still carry forward these characteristics but are freed from many of the limitations that first brought about the format. Maya offers a sophisticated set of polygon tools, enabling users to create and edit highly complex models.

Flexible Topology

Perhaps the primary characteristic of a polygon-based modeling system is flexible topology—that is, one in which the structure of shapes may vary. Aside from the fundamental requirement that the polymesh must avoid being nonmanifold, a great deal of freedom exists in such a topology.

One of the consequences of this freedom, though, is the responsibility of the user to ensure that an appropriate amount of detail exists in the mesh. For some models, this means creating multiple versions, with higher or lower amounts of mesh detail for varying situations. Game developers are particularly familiar with these trade-offs because they balance the need for speed with the desire for increased realism.

If the mesh has too little detail, nickeling artifacts or insufficient feature definition will result, as shown in Figure 6.1.

If the mesh has too much detail, it can be unwieldy to edit or to render, as in Figure 6.2.

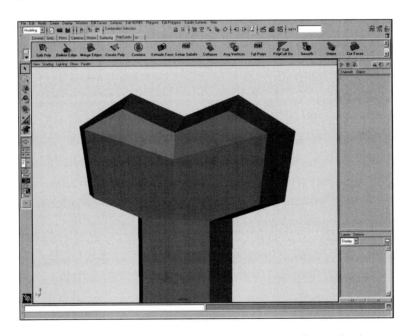

Figure 6.1   Mesh with nickeling artifacts from insufficient detail.

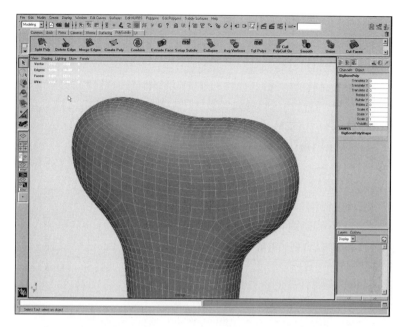

Figure 6.2   Mesh made unwieldy by too much detail.

Polymeshes consist of linked polygonal faces, which are composed of edges, which are themselves composed of vertices. This structure enables single points to be shared among multiple edges and enables single edges to be shared among multiple faces. Data is kept to a minimum, and traversal of mesh data structures can be quite efficient.

The point data itself is very precise in Maya, but polymeshes all suffer from a lack of fidelity for curved surfaces. Manufacturing applications find polymeshes unsuitably imprecise and data-intensive to be practical, at least as a modeling format (some manufacturing processes use polygonal formats). Animation applications, however, are usually forgiving enough to allow a mesh to be refined, to make nickeling relatively imperceptible.

Although polymesh topology is highly flexible, modelers must still pay attention to building manageable, well-structured meshes and avoiding flawed topologies. In the next three chapters, we examine these issues in some detail.

Positional Continuity

Polymeshes have only positional continuity, which is simple positional connectedness. But rendering techniques can make it appear as if higher orders of continuity exist. Edges can reveal nickeling even if the rendering process has interpolated vertex normals and made the interior seem smooth, as shown in Figure 6.3.

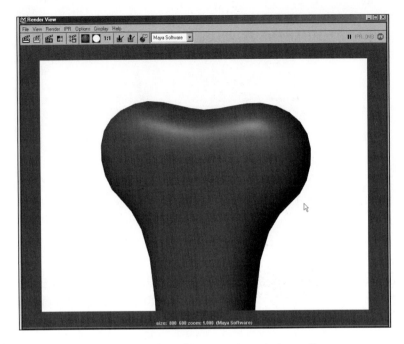

Figure 6.3 Polymesh positional continuity artifacts.

However, this simple connectedness is actually a key strength of polymesh modeling. When multiple higher-degree parametric surfaces (higher than degree 1) are deformed, their control vertices are not typically moved in ways that maintain the higher orders of continuity with each other that they might possess. However, because all that is required of polymesh continuity is that coincident CVs stay together, spatial deformations do no harm to it. Even though they are simpler, polymeshes bend easily; their more sophisticated cousins (such as NURBS) often break.

The capability of renderers to interpolate normals and achieve smooth shading (in Maya, the Smooth Shading rendering attribute enables this) is also of great utility with Boolean operations. When smooth shading is turned off, the sometimes-ragged intersection results of Boolean operators can be quite unattractive. However, smooth shading is on by default, so these areas usually blend in pleasing ways, as shown in Figure 6.4.

Of course, smooth shading is a feature that affects the rendering *within* a given mesh. Separate polymeshes which have positional continuity along their exterior edges do not benefit from the interpolation of vertex normals, so a seam will be apparent unless their neighboring faces are coplanar.

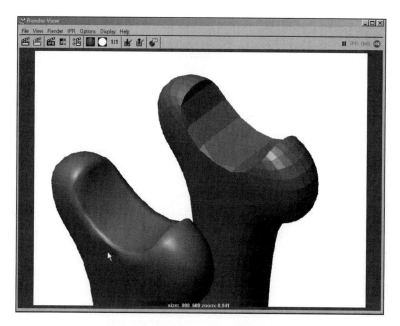

Figure 6.4   Smooth shading off and on for Boolean.

Arbitrary Shader Space

Polymeshes do not intrinsically contain parameterization values, so shading must obtain desired texture coordinates through some explicit assignment. Fortunately, Maya provides many ways to assign these coordinates to polymeshes as needed.

Texture coordinates (UVs) for polymeshes are assigned to vertices. They may be assigned at the time of the mesh or polygon creation (this is the default), or they may be assigned or edited later. In general, if the texture coordinates for a model cannot be readily assigned using the UVs associated with parametric surfaces or through procedural shaders, a polygonal mesh might be a good choice for the modeling format.

In some circumstances, it's useful to generate a polymesh by converting a NURBS surface. In these cases, the surface's UV values are converted automatically and become the UVs associated with the polymesh vertices. If complex polymeshes are being constructed piecewise in this fashion, it can be quite helpful to have each component surface pass along its parameter values.

NURBS

The development of NURBS (nonuniform rational B–splines) was an important step forward in CG modeling. Finally, a single modeling format existed that could precisely and efficiently represent a vast range of objects. In addition, these objects could be trimmed, allowing arbitrary areas to be removed from surfaces without changing the remaining areas. The end product of a long process of research, NURBS quickly became adopted as a de facto standard for CG surfacing applications.

NURBS surfaces are piecewise parametric surfaces, an almost entirely different approach to geometry representation than polygons. However, at render time, most renderers (Maya's included) convert NURBS geometry into polygons for computational convenience. To understand the choice between these formats, first let's examine NURBS more closely.

Parameterization

Parametric curves and surfaces represent geometry via basis functions and control points. The basis functions are constructed as functions of a single parameter (U), using one for each coordinate value:

$P(u) = (X(u), Y(u), Z(u));$

Each coordinate function uses the same basis, which is designed to take the respective coordinate value from each control point and produce a weighted sum. In some bases (the plural of basis), such as the Bézier basis, all the points are used. In others, such as the B–spline basis, only a specific number of them are used at a time.

In this latter case, the curve or surface is said to be constructed piecewise because distinct sections of the element (spans) use a given subset of control points. The parameter values at which one span ends and the next begins are called knot values. The geometric location where each knot occurs is referred to in Maya as an edit point, and it is the result of evaluating the appropriate control points at that parameter value using the basis functions.

Parameter values represent a space that may be traversed from beginning to end. Some bases are defined on a range from 0 to 1, but the B–spline basis simply requires that the range of knot values be nondecreasing. The specific parameter values are not particularly significant: They can easily be adjusted to a desired range by adding or multiplying a constant to all values. However, the ratios of knot values are very significant.

When all knots differ from each other by a constant value, the element is said to be uniformly parameterized because the knot interval is uniform. When any of the knot intervals fails this test, the elements parameterization is nonuniform.

Uniform B–splines thus describe elements over a uniformly spaced nondecreasing range of knot values, determining a weighted sum of the control points via the B–spline basis function. It's simpler than it sounds, honest.

The B–spline basis is actually a family of functions, not a single function, depending on the desired mathematical degree.

This basis has been carefully constructed to ensure that the weights applied to each of the relevant control points always sum to 1. This ensures that no point has excessive influence on the element and results in the highly desirable convex hull property. This property says that the element always lies within the area bounded by lines connecting the respective control points.

The effects of degree are actually quite intuitive when considering the basis functions as weighted sums of points in space. Think of each point as exerting a pull in its direction, with no point pulling any farther than all the way to its position.

In the case of two points, a straight line via simple linear interpolation is all that can be achieved. No other point is available to influence the curve in another direction. For obvious reasons, this path is a linear curve, mathematically described by an equation of degree 1.

In the case of three points, a point on the curve will surely lie within the triangle that connects the points. Different basis functions might produce different curves, but as long as these functions sum to 1, the curve will lie on the plane inside the triangle. Such curves have an extra degree of freedom and are of degree 2.

To get the curve free of the plane, four points are needed. Maya users will immediately recognize that curves of degree 3 require four points, and this is the reason. The minimum number of points required for nonplanar parametric curves is 4, and the minimum degree for such a curve is 3.

So, basis functions operating on two, three, or four points can be understood as describing linear, planar, or nonplanar cases. Actually, the cases just described represent single-span curves. For multiple spans, the B–spline basis (see Figure 6.5) specifies how to iterate along those spans, using the appropriate CVs for each span.

As the parameter is evaluated from one span to the next, the effect of one CV goes down to zero as the effect of the next CV ramps up from zero, with the curve smoothly continuing forward. A degree 1 curve continues from the position at the end of the span, a degree 2 curve continues in the same direction, and a degree 3 curve also does so with the same curvature value. This is the essence of B–spline continuity, and its basis functions were constructed to create these continuity conditions.

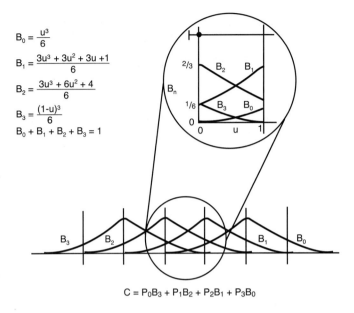

$$B_0 = \frac{u^3}{6}$$

$$B_1 = \frac{3u^3 + 3u^2 + 3u + 1}{6}$$

$$B_2 = \frac{3u^3 + 6u^2 + 4}{6}$$

$$B_3 = \frac{(1-u)^3}{6}$$

$$B_0 + B_1 + B_2 + B_3 = 1$$

$$C = P_0 B_3 + P_1 B_2 + P_2 B_1 + P_3 B_0$$

Figure 6.5   The uniform B–spline basis function.

Higher-degree NURBS can also be created and provide for higher orders of continuity, but adjusting CVs for such continuity control is best left to the computer rather
than the user.

We're almost there. What remains is a quick look at the nonuniform and rational
parts of NURBS.

As we mentioned before, knot intervals don't have to be uniform. As long as the
knot values specified are nondecreasing, they can have any value. Changing parameter
values changes the shape of the curve as the range of effect of various CVs is altered.
One particularly useful method of parameterization is to assign parameter values based
on the direct distance between successive edit points. Although it's only an approximation (the actual distance along the curves depends on the parameterization itself), it's a
useful one that we know as chord-length parameterization.

Another place where nonuniform parameterization is especially useful is at the end
spans. A straightforward application of the previous B–spline basis function to a strictly uniform knot vector actually leaves dangling ends (see Figure 6.6). But, by repeating
parameter values in the knot vector, the ends of a curve can be made to interpolate the
terminal CVs.

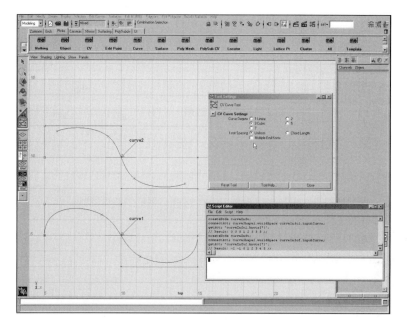

Figure 6.6   True uniform versus multiple end knot B–splines.

This is the situation normally encountered in Maya—uniform curves and surfaces are actually nonuniform at their ends. The advantage of this is that the locations and tangent directions at the ends can then be directly controlled by the user.

Finally, not all CVs must be evaluated in exactly the same manner. An additional scale factor can be specified to designate the ratio (thus the term *rational*) of a given CV to an ordinary one. Why? Because conic sections, such as truly round circles, can be accurately represented by B–splines only if they are rational.

Circles or revolved surfaces in Maya are not actually truly round. The more spans that are used, the more even the curvature will be—but it will never be precisely round unless it's rational. A circular element created with very few spans appears noticeably out–of–round, whereas a rational element always is round and is constructed with precisely the number of spans necessary (see Figure 6.7). Maya can make use of rational geometry, either imported from another program or created via MEL or the API, but the interactive package does not directly generate it.

So much for the cook's tour of NURBS. Now let's consider modeling with them.

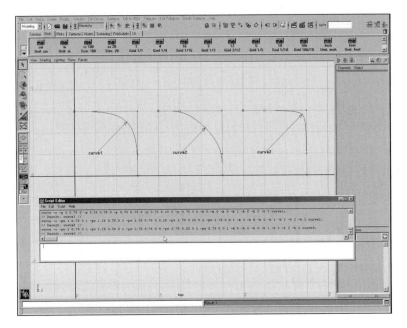

Figure 6.7 Nonrational vs. rational B–splines.

Rectilinear Topology

Much of the preceding discussion centered on curves, but the principles apply in exactly the same manner for surfaces. In fact, the primary conceptual difference between NURBS curves and NURBS surfaces is an additional parametric dimension, V. With two parametric directions, U and V, NURBS surfaces are always rectilinear in their topology, regardless of their actual shape.

This topology means that complex objects are usually modeled with a network of rectangular surfaces. Some of these surfaces might have sides of zero length (known as degenerate edges) but the topology is still rectilinear. Planning an effective arrangement of these surfaces can be a challenging undertaking, but a great deal of precision in form can be obtained.

Another consequence of this topology is that detail needed in one area of a surface must necessarily be propagated across the entire surface. Each row of CVs completely spans the surface. Highly detailed areas can sometimes be cleverly localized by extracting and modifying pieces of larger surfaces, but continuity relationships must be carefully maintained by leaving one or more rows of edge CVs alone.

Trimming

A mitigating feature of this topology is that NURBS surfaces can be readily trimmed. To trim a parametric surface, a boundary is defined in UV parameter space. Such a boundary is typically created by projecting a curve onto a surface or computing the intersection of two surfaces, but there are other methods. To be useful, this boundary must divide the surface into separate regions, but the surface shape is unchanged.

It's also very easy to undo trimming operations because the trim boundary can simply be removed, leaving the original surface.

Trimming is especially valuable when precise fillet shapes are needed. Fillets and rounds can be constructed to meet careful tolerances for continuity, without disturbing the shape of the neighboring surfaces. Of course, there's a trade-off between enough precision to avoid visible gaps between surfaces and not so much precision that the fillets are overbuilt.

The use of trimmed surface fillets can be critical for creating an area such as the wheel wells of the cars that will appear in our *Parking Spot* production, in which changing the shape of the fenders would be unacceptable.

Of course, many studios make it a practice to explicitly avoid using trimmed surfaces. In large part, this is because parametric boundaries aren't directly controllable by CVs in the same way that NURBS are. Trim curve CVs actually exist in the parameter space of the surface, so deforming the surface CVs moves the trim CVs in a different space. Such deformations almost guarantee cracking along trimmed surface edges.

Smooth Surfaces

Another definitive characteristic of NURBS is, of course, smooth surfaces. NURBS surfaces are mathematically precise entities that can be potentially manufactured or rendered to any desired precision. Any pair of UV parameter values within the surface's parameter range identifies a specific coordinate location that lies precisely on the surface.

For any point on the surface, there also exists a specific surface normal, unless it occurs at a point of tangent discontinuity. To explain this, first let's consider continuity.

The default order of continuity between spans on a NURBS element is one less than the degree of the element. This value represents the number of continuous derivatives available, which is something of a mouthful. It is expressed as C0, C1, C2, and so on, which might not help much.

An easier and equivalent way to think of continuity is as progressively matching rates of change. A NURBS surface contains position information and is, of course, positionally (C0) continuous across its knots, no matter what its degree is. The rate of change of position is slope. So, while linear (degree 1) surfaces do not guarantee slope (a.k.a., tangent or C1) continuity across knots, higher degrees do.

Likewise, the rate of change of slope is curvature. So, although quadratic (degree 2) surfaces are C1 across knots, they are not C2. For that, you need cubic (degree 3) surfaces. And so on.

The order of continuity is reduced by 1, by the way, for each repeated knot value. So, a point of tangent discontinuity is created on a cubic NURBS element when a knot appears three times in succession in the knot vector. The continuity is reduced from C2 to C1 by the first repeat, and then down to C0 by the second repeat. Repeating the knot again, in fact, would introduce a break in the element by eliminating even C0 continuity.

Deformability

A powerful thing about NURBS is that these orders of continuity not only exist across internal knots, but they also can be established across separate surfaces. Parameter values internal to a surface are inherently part of a consistent range, but across separate surfaces there is no such guarantee. For these situations, the terminology of continuity is often slightly different, expressing the geometric relationships as G0, G1, G2, and so on (see Figure 6.8).

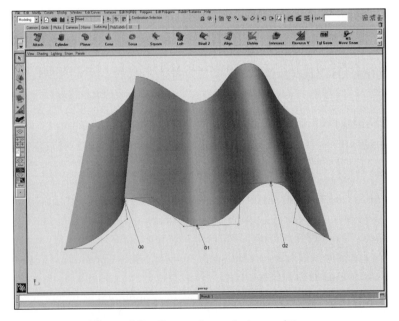

Figure 6.8   Geometric continuity conditions.

Creating the proper arrangement of points to achieve these continuity conditions can be complex as orders increase. Fortunately, Maya has the necessary aligning tools for the job. Broadly speaking, achieving geometric continuity involves arranging CVs in consistent alignments and ratios across the shared boundary.

In almost all cases, it is a trivial operation to reparameterize neighboring surfaces to establish parametric (Cn) continuity when geometric (Gn) continuity exists. Geometric continuity is usually all that is needed for modeling purposes, but shading needs might require parametric continuity.

Having the desired continuity established across surface boundaries, however, does not ensure that a NURBS object can be successfully deformed.

In fact, if knot vectors for the surfaces in question are of the multiple end knot form described earlier, creasing or cracking will likely occur under deformation (see Figure 6.9). This is because the necessary relationship between neighboring CVs is a specific geometric one, and the deformation changes this relationship.

On the other hand, if the surfaces do not possess multiple end knots, the necessary continuity relationship involves superimposing neighboring CVs atop each other. Spatial deformations will then affect these overlaid points equally, so the continuity relationships are preserved (see Figure 6.10). Note, however, that Maya does not normally create such surfaces (though it can).

Not all continuity relationships are precise—some are approximate, such as those along the boundaries of a fillet. In general, trimmed surfaces almost certainly crack under deformation, so they are a poor choice for flexible objects (unless the continuity condition is being recomputed for each frame).

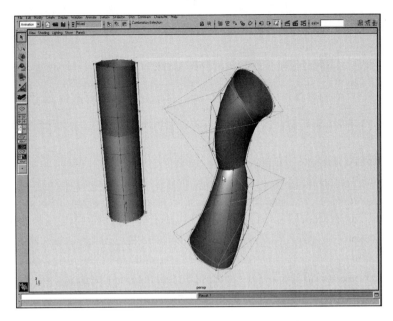

Figure 6.9 Multiple end knot surfaces under deformation.

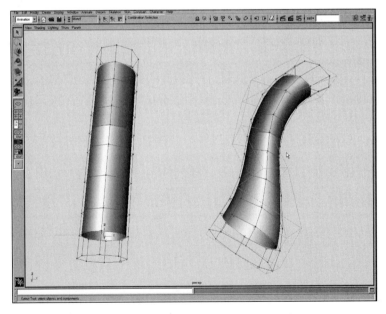

Figure 6.10 Single end knot surfaces under deformation.

NURBS modeling can at times seem like the polar opposite of polygonal modeling, but there is something of a middle ground….

Subdivision Surfaces

The smooth surfaces of NURBS are highly appealing, but so is the flexible topology of polygons. Subdivision surfaces offer both of these characteristics, providing an innovative mix of technologies.

Flexible Topology Plus Hierarchy

The basic rules for polygon mesh topology also apply to subdivision surface mesh topology. Subdivision meshes must avoid being nonmanifold, having lamina topology (faces glued on top of each other), having inconsistent normals, and so on (as described on the first page of the "Polygonal Modeling" section of the online Maya documentation). Essentially, the mesh must be consistently oriented and free of superfluous data. This is somewhat more restrictive than the requirements of polygonal meshes, but only in ways that produce a mesh with higher integrity.

Subdivision surfaces, however, add to the polygonal mesh two important characteristics: the limit surface and the use of hierarchical levels of detail.

The limit surface is the key to the power of subdivision surfaces. Faces in the mesh are progressively subdivided as many times as needed through the application of a refinement scheme. This process of mesh refinement produces ever–smaller faces that replace the previous mesh, until some predetermined limit (such as the size of the new faces) has been reached. In the case of Maya, the scheme used is known as the Catmull-Clark subdivision scheme.

Although the Catmull-Clark scheme is not simple to express, some of its results are simple to understand.

First, the scheme produces quadrilateral faces from the input mesh. In fact, after only one level of subdivision, the refined mesh is already composed entirely of quads. Furthermore, extraordinary vertices (in this case, those with more or less than four edges) are limited to just those present in the initial mesh. Thus, the structure of the resulting new mesh is highly predictable almost immediately, as shown in Figure 6.11.

Second, when applied to a rectangular array of quadrilateral faces, the resulting limit surface is identical to a uniform B–spline surface with the same input mesh (see Figure 6.12).

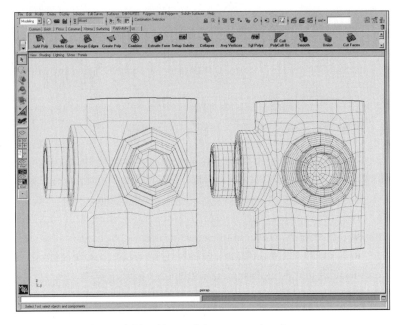

Figure 6.11   Maya subdivision mesh refinement.

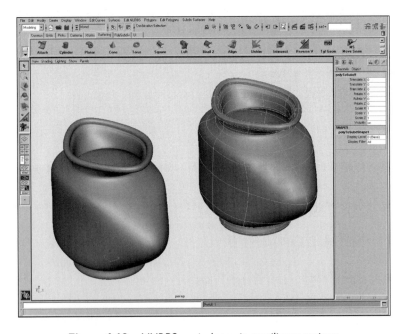

Figure 6.12   NURBS equivalence in rectilinear regions.

Knowing this can be extremely useful in designing an effective mesh. For one thing, areas within the perimeter of a rectangular array of CVs can generally be trusted to not display visual artifacts (assuming that they are reasonably positioned, of course). Also, knowing that such areas will behave just like Maya's uniform NURBS makes operations such as combining separate meshes intuitive to experienced NURBS modelers.

Maya, however, takes this scheme one step further with the addition of hierarchical levels of detail to subdivision meshes. Because a subdivision surface is by its very nature the product of progressive refinement, those refined levels can be made editable. But instead of requiring you to simply open all the resulting refined mesh data for editing, Maya enables you to specify the data that you want to edit.

The result is a powerful mechanism for adding or manipulating detail in a subdivision mesh that inherits the information from earlier levels. This permits both compact data structures and feature refinement that can inherit high–level changes. Not all subdivision meshes require the use of this hierarchy (alternate methods of adding detail are available), but it can be invaluable in many cases.

If an entirely base–level mesh is desired, the modeler must decide how to transition from coarse mesh areas into finer areas. The advantages of this approach can be better optimization of mesh size and the capability to work with all the mesh data at one time. In addition, some third–party tools exist that connect the output of a polymesh shape node to the input of a subdivision surface, resulting in a potentially improved workflow. The disadvantage is that it's substantially harder for the modeler to get a mesh without artifacts.

The choice of mesh detail representations can be based on personal preference, interoperability requirements, or the particular demands of the model. We will explore some of these choices more closely later, but the power of subdivision surfaces to handle such detail effectively is great indeed.

G1 Continuity

The topological flexibility of subdivision meshes is particularly powerful because the limit surface has tangent (G1) continuity throughout. Tangent continuity is important because it allows displacement mapping to work, by ensuring that surface normals are also continuous. This is critical because normals that are discontinuous cause cracking during displacement.

Surface normals are easily understood in the case of NURBS as the cross–product of the U and V tangent vectors. However, because no parameter space is intrinsic to polygonal meshes, it's less obvious how subdivision meshes calculate them (the edge vectors can be used). Regardless, it's enough to know that because G1 continuity exists, surface normals also exist and are continuous.

One case challenges this assumption, though—at the poles of revolved surfaces. Maya officially discourages building models with these poles because of "vanishing normals," which occur because the longitudinal vectors go to zero (even though the latitudinal vectors do not). This might pose rendering difficulties, but the limit surface still exists at the pole, and the normal there should at least be obtainable as the limit of the neighboring normals (see Figure 6.13).

As a workaround, poles can be reduced or rebuilt, but be aware that some change in surface shape will occur. Some users will be able to tolerate this limitation; others will not. It seems likely to go away eventually, just as it did for rendering NURBS.

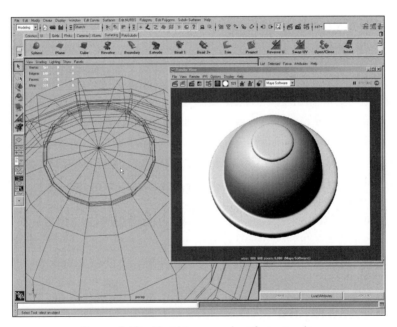

Figure 6.13   Vanishing normal artifacts at poles.

Another powerful implication of G1 continuity everywhere is that rounded edges are easy to create around an object—usually much more easily than if NURBS fillets must be constructed. If the rounded edges are the sort that can be readily described with a cubic uniform B–spline, they will probably work out well. If the edge can be constructed in a region easily covered by a rectilinear mesh, you should be able to make it smooth. Of course, if exact circular radii are needed or if the edge cuts diagonally across other mesh grids, you might need to use NURBS instead.

As desirable as G1 continuity is, it's also possible to eliminate it with creasing. Edges or vertices can be creased (see Figure 6.14), which results in tangent discontinuities. If a completely sharp edge or point isn't desired, it's also possible to "partially" crease it, which tightens it without making it entirely sharp (it does this by deferring the subdivision step for a specified number of iterations).

Finally, remember that we mentioned that rectangular mesh areas behave exactly like uniform NURBS? And that cubic NURBS have G2 (curvature) continuity? Well, subdivision surfaces in these situations also have G2 continuity. In many subdivision surface models, the majority of the limit surface, in fact, is curvature continuous. But because the main reason to use subdivision surfaces is usually the topological flexibility, you can depend on those nonrectangular regions to be only G1 continuous.

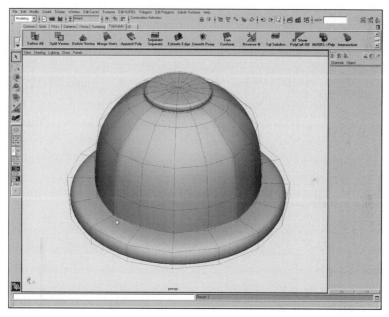

Figure 6.14   Uncreased, partially creased, and fully creased edges.

Arbitrary Shader Space

Subdivision surfaces are like polygonal meshes when it comes to providing texture coordinates, except that not as many opportunities exist to create them directly with these coordinates. Most subdivision surfaces are created from existing polymeshes or from NURBS, so they often simply inherit these coordinates.

Similar issues exist for texture coordinates subdivision meshes as for polygonal meshes, with one exception: The rules for remapping texture coordinates from a coarse mesh down to a finer mesh are more complex. From the modeler's point of view, however, they are essentially equivalent.

Also, vertices in subdivision meshes do not specify a normal because they operate more like NURBS CVs than polymesh vertices. The normals of the subdiv limit surface aren't looked up and interpolated like a poly face. Instead, they are a geometric property of the limit surface. So, although subdivision mesh vertices may hold UVs, they don't have vertex normal information in the usual polygonal mesh sense.

Surfacing Decisions

With the preceding points of comparison in mind, let's apply some decision making to some models from the *Parking Spot* production.

From the outset, we should say that few objects will be candidates for polygonal modeling, at least as a final solution. Our goal is to produce a short film relatively free of CG artifacts, of which nickeling is among the most egregious. NURBS surfaces will still have to be carefully tessellated, but they can be adjusted during the rendering phase, whereas polymeshes will be substantially harder to smooth over. Polygonal modeling will surely help along the way, but it probably won't be the final form for too much of anything.

Characters

The characters will doubtless be modeled with subdivision surfaces because polygonal models would be either too coarse or too data–heavy; NURBS models would be too cumbersome to keep from cracking. The particular details of how they will be modeled will probably vary, but clearly the end result will be subdivision meshes.

The bulk of the characters' clothing will probably also be made with subdivision surfaces, although the cloth simulations might require a polygonal mesh for the actual simulation data. The star's shoes and belt might be NURBS, but otherwise subdivs will rule.

Cars

The cars in the *Parking Spot* production have long, flowing lines, in keeping with their Art Deco designs. As with any vehicle, highlights and reflection lines are critically important indicators of surface quality. Because the audience will get a good look at the hero car (see Figure 6.15), it should stand up to reasonable scrutiny. It also will be seen from several angles, so a fairly complete vehicle will have to be built.

On the other hand, a substantial amount of caricature is involved in the designs, so there might be room to cut a few corners or alter the design slightly as needed. The focus of the production is not to make a car commercial or to cut a model from the surfaces. So, we'll look for efficiencies wherever we can get them.

Figure 6.15 Car design sketch(es).

In addition, we need more than one car. The premise of this film depends on limited parking near the destination, so we need to have models that can be readily changed into distinctly different variants (see Figure 6.16). This can probably be done mostly by changing bumpers, grilles, handles, and so on, but some body panel variations will also be needed.

Figure 6.16 Alternate vehicle sketch.

Given these requirements, most of the major body surfaces will probably be NURBS, in part because of things such as the aforementioned wheel well issue. However, much of the decorative hardware will probably be best created using subdivision surfaces, particularly because of the ease of getting rounded edges. In addition, thanks to shiny windows and a low camera angle, we can probably create very little interior geometry.

Most of the geometry will be painted metal or chrome, so surface parameterization won't be much of an issue. Tires and probably wheels will benefit from having UV spaces, so they'll be NURBS. Most of the rest of the geometry will be indifferent to shader spaces. And although we expect to squash the tires a bit, this can be done with a deformer to the NURBS tires.

Our story also calls for a parking-enforcement vehicle. Thankfully, this vehicle should be visible only from the front and can be fairly simple. Some simple signage and a flashing light will go a long way toward selling it to the viewers.

Fire Hydrant

The fire hydrant might appear at first to be a classic NURBS model. However, hydrants tend to be made for heavy–duty usage, the product of big castings with substantial radii around the edges. Depending on the final design and budget, it might be a fairly even mix of NURBS and subdivision surfaces, or it might be almost entirely made of subdivision surfaces.

Grooves in the surfaces might be modeled in or shaded in, but we can be fairly sure that the main body will begin in NURBS. We might be able to then convert it to polys, do the same for the arms, do a Boolean operation, combine them, and turn the whole thing into a subdiv. OK, maybe we'll just see when we get there.

Well, we can at least be confident that the chains on the caps will be NURBS….

Storefronts

The storefronts are largely made up of planar geometry, so we might be tempted to resort to polygons, but two considerations will deter us. First, we don't want sharp edges anywhere because they'll look conspicuously unreal. Second, we might find that having NURBS parameter spaces will make the job of shading easier because patterns such as bricks are fairly easy to map into UV spaces. So, we expect these to be predominantly NURBS.

In addition, many of the planar NURBS surfaces will be linear in one or both directions. This makes their parameterization simple (0 to 1, in most cases) and makes editing them quick and easy. We can just grab the CVs at the edges and drag them to where we want, without worrying that we've left interior CVs behind and thus distorted the parameter space.

We might also choose to make some of the objects—perhaps the doors, awnings above windows, or some walls—with subdivision surfaces. We can get rounded edges easily, as long as the shading of these objects isn't a problem when using subdivs.

Other Modeling Possibilities

Despite the tremendous range of models that can be created with polygonal, NURBS, and subdivision surface modeling, some models (or parts of models) are better handled with other methods. In fact, these methods are not modeling methods in the conventional sense of producing 3D geometry that exists in the scenes alongside the conventional models. Instead, these models are normally fully revealed only by rendering processes. Because we plan to use them for some specific items in a scene, we mention these processes (and the models for which they are planned) briefly here.

Paint Effects

The trees planted in the sidewalk could be modeled using subdivision surfaces, NURBS, or polygons, but the Paint Effects feature in Maya presents an attractive alternative. The particular details aren't critical, so we can iterate our way toward a pleasing model. The speed of making vegetation with Paint Effects will probably far outweigh the time and effort needed to arrive at the final models. Besides, Paint Effects trees look pretty good. And now Maya 5 can also output these as polygonal geometry if needed.

Blobby Particles

Near the end of the piece, the fire hydrant is opened. Needless to say, this releases a torrent of water. Clearly, this is a job not for conventional modeling, but for some particles instead. We'll give them some heft and have them interact like water droplets by using blobby particles. Most of these particles will go roaring by, but some will cling to surfaces and run down. Precisely how we do this will be worked out after we've set up our shots, but blobby particles are clearly the right tool for this job.

As mentioned earlier, blobby particles are not quite the same thing as blobby surfaces. Maya doesn't offer blobby surfaces that can be used to model directly in the scene, but it does allow particles to be rendered as blobbies. They're still implicit surfaces, but they are somewhat restricted in their range of application. Fortunately, they should be excellent for water droplets.

Hair and Fur

Both the dog and the people will have hair, and we'd like it to really look like hair. Maya Fur is just the tool for this job. Although we could probably get away with the main character being bald or having a plastic hair–shaped shell on his head, it'd be cheesy (and a poor lesson). Painting a fur coat on Spot would be even worse. So, we'll model our characters without hair and then add it with Maya Fur.

Summary

Maya provides three major formats for modeling objects: polygons, NURBS, and subdivision surfaces. Each of these formats has its strengths and weaknesses for various kinds of modeling tasks. Taken together, though, they provide a robust set of choices for the modeler. By understanding the nature of each of these formats, you can make choices that take you down the best path for your modeling needs.

For some models, the capability to deform smoothly is paramount. For others, precise control over form, highlights, and edges is most important. Still other models require the absolute maximum performance from the least possible geometry. A few more considerations, such as modeling time and effort, shading ease, and the specific toolsets for each format, will also guide your decisions.

Of course, because Maya also allows geometry to be converted from one format to another, the solution for a given model might just be to use all three. Whether each model uses purely one format, mixes them, or converts between them as the model is built, Maya provides a host of well-implemented, industry-standard format choices.

Now that you've taken the tour of the basics of these formats, let's move on to examine some common modeling methods in the next chapter.

Chapter 7
Methods

By Mark Adams

Much of the work of modeling in Maya involves the repeated application of standard techniques. Although we'll spend the next few chapters modeling the particular objects and characters for our *Parking Spot* project (described in Chapter 2, "Project Overview"), this chapter examines techniques and strategies for handling some modeling problems common to almost any project.

Early in my career, I was told by an experienced Detroit automotive designer that most of the time spent in creating a finished CG model wasn't spent shaping the big surfaces that define the form of the vehicle. Those were relatively easy. The work, he said, was mostly about putting in the rounded edges everywhere—and doing it well.

Almost two decades later, I have to say that he was right.

Applications for computer graphics since then have expanded dramatically in breadth, depth, and power. The visual richness of the medium has reached a level almost unthinkable at that time. Average citizens now take for granted images and effects that once seemed the rare and dazzling products of a few obscenely expensive advertising and design studios. Power is evident everywhere nowadays, yet one thing hasn't changed: The devil is still in the details.

No matter how powerful the software is, attention to detail makes the difference between acceptable and excellent. Making excellent models invariably involves paying attention to innumerable subtleties of form and topology. To build a complex model that looks like the image on a drawing or in your mind, you will find yourself building, rebuilding, attaching, blending, smoothing, rounding, and, most of all, *examining* your models until good enough really *is*.

Fortunately, just as a sculptor learns his tools and develops methods and strategies to shape stone to his will, you can do the same. And just as the sculptor's techniques soon become second nature to his work, so can your modeling techniques in Maya.

In this chapter, you'll learn some of the methods that I routinely use when creating my models, including these:

- Gathering reference materials

- Setting up image planes

- Using layers and grids

- Creating rounded edges

- Capping off open ends

- Making and filling in holes

My goal is not to provide a comprehensive set of techniques (which could fill a book all their own), but to give you some insights into tackling the sorts of modeling problems that lie ahead in our project (and yours). You'll see a number of different ways to approach these common problems.

But perhaps the best lesson of all is learning to see the trade-offs among the many ways in which Maya might handle a modeling problem.

Set Your Sights

Before you set off on any journey, you're well advised to have your destination clearly in mind. In our project, we've taken the time to carefully design the key elements and decide upon broader guiding principles for those things we're brave enough (or hurried enough) to do by the seat of our pants. So, no matter how caught up we get in the demands of the moment, we know where to turn to see how we're doing.

Your projects might bear little resemblance to ours, but there will surely still be models to build and budgets to respect. Although it's always tempting to just forge ahead and see where your modeling feet take you, it can be an act of hubris that you soon regret. In all but the simplest cases, it's smart to make sure you've identified just what you'll be modeling and have the appropriate reference material close at hand.

When I finally realized that my mind's eye and sense of proportion were *aided* by design references, not threatened by them, I found that my work became much easier and the burden of my ego was much less. When all is said and done, the quality of the final model and the fidelity to the design intent are what matter most. By setting your sights clearly on the end result, the whole journey becomes easier.

Get Their References

Okay, it's time to knuckle down. You've got a widget to make and maybe just an idea or a crummy little sketch to go by. Just because the art director can say, "You know, I want a basic fire hydrant" doesn't mean you know what that really means. You need some references.

You need to understand the thing you're trying to model, so try to collect whatever useful material you can in the available time.

Real Stuff

The very best source of design information is normally having the thing itself in hand. Most modeling questions that can arise from artwork will magically disappear if the thing intended can be directly examined.

If it's a car, try to get the art director to buy you one (good luck). If it's a fire hydrant, well, it'll still be useful to have one to examine (as long as you don't have to carry it in). If that doesn't work, get someone to buy you a model of it (this works especially well for cars, less so for fire hydrants). Finally, if no such model exists, perhaps a model of it can be made for your reference if it's difficult to draw clearly.

With a real example of the object for reference, even if it's only close, your modeling work will usually be substantially easier.

Sadly, for our project we found no cars or fire hydrants available that were similar enough to our design intent. In fact, as we went down our list of objects, precious little was both obtainable and needed. One friend has a Dalmatian, though, so maybe we'll see if she can act....

Photo-Real Stuff

The next best thing might be to have photo reference material. No one we know personally has a 1937 Delahaye 135 M Figoni et Falaschi (the design inspiration for our hero car) for our inspection, but photos of it will do very nicely. With an Internet connection and some skill and patience for searching, we can usually do some substantial background work for a given model—often producing a plethora of photographs to examine.

Fire hydrants are quite fake-able if you just need a background prop, but ours is a main prop in a work with a distinctive design motif. Generic just won't do, so I ran a brilliant Google search ("fire hydrant") and waded through a number (1) of results before discovering a hard-to-find site (firehydrant.org) that presented me with more than 1,000 different photos of fire hydrant designs. On a photo outing to take some images of my own, I also found plenty of variations in nearby communities (see Figure 7.1). Between these two sources, I had more than enough to go on.

Figure 7.1   Fire hydrant designs.

Of course, that was the easy part. I then dutifully looked through a few hundred of the designs and realized that Art Deco and hydrant design rarely crossed paths. Even when they did, their designs were nothing like I'd imagined. Still, I downloaded photos of various interesting designs that would serve as excellent references for proportions and details.

Some further thinking about the project led me to look for images of hydrants in action. We rarely see uncapped hydrants, so I looked all over the `firehydrant.org` site for such images but found none. Disappointed, but glad to have found such a terrific resource, I emailed the webmaster some comments on the site and happened to mention the uncapped hydrant images I'd wanted.

The next day, I got a polite reply from Jim Quist of `firehydrant.org`, who let me know that open hydrants were a safety hazard they didn't want to encourage. I explained our particular objective but understood and bid him well. To my amazement, a couple of days later I received a set of pictures from Jim that had been taken of an opened hydrant (see Figure 7.2) especially for us.

Besides illustrating the power of good karma, the fire hydrant example shows how useful photographic information can be easily obtained for model reference. I've done similar searches for parking meters and Art Deco cars with good results. Each of those will be modeled from a mix of art and reference photos, but having the reference available early in the process speeds it along.

Getting the details right is not only a good idea, but also easier than you might expect—with the right photographs. Don't forget to get images of the details—they provide the authenticity that sells the design, along with some delightful party chit-chat. For example, did you know that most valve nuts on fire hydrants have five sides to prevent tampering?

Figure 7.2   Opened fire hydrant spraying.

Artwork

Sometimes the best references are a few good drawings. If you are lucky enough to have a skilled artist who will provide you with such artwork, consider yourself truly blessed. The artist can put his or her talents to work to illustrate the important details, adding notes where necessary, and can help you take the design from concept to realization.

If you're the designer as well as the modeler, you'll have the advantage of understanding your design particularly well. Either way, you will find that good artwork makes a huge difference.

You'll want orthographic line drawings. Because the Maya window defaults are top, front, and (right) side, you'll probably want those same views drawn. Shading might actually be a drawback in these images because it can make it difficult to discern object shapes and edges.

If you're modeling manmade objects, go online and track down some manufacturers' web sites. Especially for things like fire hydrants, you might find complete mechanical drawings or 2D line art available.

We'll have drawings for at least the street scene, the car(s), and perhaps the parking meter and fire hydrant (see Figure 7.3). Although plenty of our props have some design latitude, we want to get the major design elements right, so we've got art.

Naturally, our character designs are explored on paper quite a bit, both to investigate alternatives and to assist with the modeling (see Figure 7.4). Of course, given the tight budget we're on, we might fudge a few design details—but we'll have a clear idea of what we want right from the start.

We'll work out many of the fine points during the project, but these sketches serve to guide us and remind us of our creative inspirations. Early on, it's not clear how we'll balance our efforts among clothing, facial features, hands, and hair—but we know the direction we're headed.

Figure 7.3   Typical prop artwork.

Figure 7.4   Some character designs.

Preparing Scans

The main reason for the orthographic line artwork is for use in image planes. For easy-to-use image planes, I aim for high-contrast black lines on a clean white background. Photographs are generally poorly suited for modeling image planes, by the way, because they usually suffer from poor contrast and image foreshortening (but they're often better than nothing).

If you're creating image planes strictly for modeling, you'll probably want your scans to be grayscale. I've found that 100dpi is usually about the right balance between detail and file size (that is, performance), plus it makes any required math easy.

After you've done the scanning, you'll probably want to clean up the scans so that they read better in your modeling windows. I use Adobe Photoshop to clean up most of my scans. Here's how I do it.

1. First, I open the scanned image and convert it to 8-bit grayscale, if it's not already in that format.

2. If the image is scanned at a high resolution, I use Image, Image Size to reduce the file size to a more comfortable size and to set the resolution to a convenient 100dpi.

3. Next, I open the scanned image and use Image, Adjust, Levels to set the image's white and black points (see Figure 7.5). This expands the middle range of values so that anything below the black point is pushed all the way to black and values above the white point are pushed to white. This ensures that the contrast range is high and tends to clean up erasures and smudges a bit. If the middle tones are too faint or too muddy, use the middle slider to gamma-adjust the image.

4. Then I save the file—just in case—under a new name. I don't want to over-write the raw scan, in case I make an image-editing mistake and need to start over. I wait to discard the raw scans until the image planes are set up and working well.

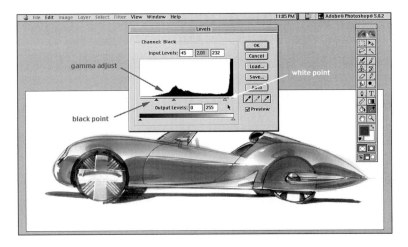

Figure 7.5   Using Photoshop's Adjust, Levels feature.

5. If I've called the original scan widgetScanRaw.tif, I'll typically call the edit-ed scan widgetScan.tif, unless it's strictly one view. In that case, I'll name it with a view direction, as in widgetScanF.tif for the front view. When mul-tiple views are on one sheet, just crop out the specific views from the edit-ed scan and save them individually.

6. I make a touch-up pass over the image, erasing stray marks and cleaning up anything that could be confusing when seen through a grid. I *don't* want to remove dimensions because they will help me set up the image plane.

7. Finally, I save the cleaned-up, high-contrast, compact grayscale file I've made as widgetF.tif. Of course, these files don't have to be .tif files, but the compact sizes and lossless encoding of this kind of image are both de-pendable and satisfying.

Setting Up Image Planes

Setting up image planes in Maya is straightforward. Just follow these steps:

1. To place your scan as an image plane, select the camera in which the image will be seen and open the Attribute Editor. Go to the camera's shape node, expand the Environment tab, and select Image Plane, Create (there's also a View, Image Plane, Import Image Command, but I go straight here). The image plane attributes are then displayed in the Attribute Editor, so specify your source image as the image name.

2. To make an image plane helpful but not intrusive, adjust the gain of the image to blend the image plane into the window background. For my light gray background (R = G = B = 0.75), I find that a Color Gain set to 0.5 and a Color Offset set to 0.25 work reliably. This dims the overall image and blends the white background into the gray, which works well for overlaying new geometry.

3. Now switch to the Channel Box. The image plane exists out there in your scene's space, and the Channel Box tells you where. You'll usually want your image planes on the other side of the grid from your camera so that they don't obscure the grid. If necessary, use the Center value that corresponds to the viewing axis of your camera to move the image plane to the other side of the zero plane.

Warning

Don't be tempted to use an image plane as a far clipping-plane tool because you'll still be able to select things behind it (even though you can't see them).

4. Uniformly scale the image plane (scaling the Width and Height attributes by the same amount) until the image is the right size. Having dimensions, especially long ones, on the artwork image is very helpful in getting these values correct. I usually display a grid against which I can adjust the scale until the image plane is the right size.

Tip

If you select multiple channel names in the Channel Box and then middle-mouse-drag in a camera window, you can change all the selected channels simultaneously. When you've set the Channel Box to Invisible Manips (Channels, Settings, Invisible Manips), this is an easy way to perform a uniform scale—such as an image plane scaling operation might require.

5. When the image plane is the correct size, it's a simple matter of adjusting the other two image plane Center values to slide it into place.

Tip

You can easily set up an image plane display toggle by searching for anything called imagePlane*. Then iterate through the list, query the value of the displayMode attribute for each item, and set it to an opposite state, as shown in the following procedure:

```
global proc tglIP() {
    string $allPlanes[] = `ls 'imagePlane*'`;
    for ($thisPlane in $allPlanes) {
        $dMode = (int) `getAttr (thisPlane+'.displayMode')`;
        int $newMode = (int) ($dMode<1) * 3;
        setAttr ($thisPlane + '.displayMode') $newMode;
    }
}
```

Assign this script to a hotkey, and voilà! For convenience, we've put this file on the CD.

6. At this point, I save the scene as <whatever>.0, which I understand to be an initial setup file. Time to get rolling!

Multiple image planes are simple to overlay—just stack them in front of each other as needed, using the Center value normal to the window. Both broad and detailed artwork can be used together this way.

Plan Your Journey

So, what's the plan?

As straightforward as that question might seem, it's one that's easy to overlook in the rush to forge ahead with the modeling. But a few minutes spent devising a strategy are surely worthwhile because they can save you from hours of frustration later.

Take Big Steps

Start by deciding whether the object will be polygonal, NURBS, a subdiv, or perhaps a hybrid of some sort. Organic characters certainly make sense as subdivision surfaces because they're irregular and will undergo plenty of deformation. Buildings might be easiest as NURBS, although subdivs might work. And so on, as we've previously discussed.

When you've got an idea of what the final geometry will be like, mentally walk through the process of getting there a couple of times. Some models can be realized in a linear process that produces final surfaces directly, but others might need to go through a few different forms to get to the end result.

An example of a directly buildable model might be one of our shop doors, while the head of the parking meter might end up as a single subdivision surface after intermediate stages as NURBS and polygonal surfaces. Your plan might also include building a nicely squared-up model and then mashing it around a bit with deformers and CV manipulation.

Be sure to consider how to make the model editable. Changes are a fact of life (perhaps the only one), so plan to make your model so that you can change it as needed.

If you have a physical model to examine, look it over and imagine the order in which you might create the component parts. You might even try drawing mesh lines or surface boundaries on the object directly (dry-erase or china markers on nonporous surfaces work especially well). Pay particular attention to how major features come together and how you'll create any rounded edges (see the section "Avoid Sharp Edges," later in this chapter).

Use Travel Guides

Even better is a 3D scan to work with because the correct proportions then are right in front of you—but few modelers have the tools for making such scans readily available. If you can't have your model digitized, make some rough approximations of the final masses. Either of these will augment the use of image planes, making useful templates over which you can construct your model.

As a rule, I immediately create a previs layer (short for "previsualization") when I've got a 3D reference scan or stand-in model as a guide, plus a construction layer where I can put all the useful construction elements after I've used them. Because layers share the same namespage as objects, you may need to make layer names distinctive (perhaps with a prefix or a suffix). Most of the time, things on these layers are kept templated, except when I need to reuse them (see Figure 7.6).

You can often create useful 3D reference geometry by intersecting surfaces or projecting curves onto surfaces and using the resulting curves as templates. These also serve especially well as snapping targets when you need to build a specifically parameterized 3D curve, although you'll need to untemplate them first.

Other layers are created for major groups of like components, such as an interior layer for a car model. Layer visibility is controlled through the use of shading overrides, which can be a problem if you're making other use of them (such as for subdivision mesh and surface separation). For this reason, I tend to hold off on layer assignments until I'm well into the model. But if you don't use any special tools that depend on the shader overrides, go right ahead with layering.

If it's a manmade object, use your grids. Snapping CVs to grids whenever possible can dramatically reduce continuity problems because alignment becomes trivial for many curves and surfaces. Because I use grids so much, I keep a special shelf for nothing but setting grid units and sizes (see Figure 7.7).

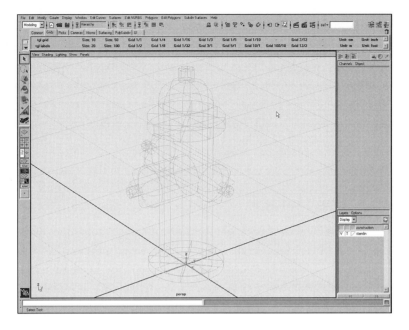

Figure 7.6   3D reference template.

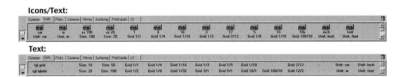

Figure 7.7   Grid shelf.

Maya stores positions and dimensions internally in centimeters but can present them to the user in several different systems of units. Feel free to change your units and grids as you work, but keep in mind that metric and English units are essentially incompatible when it comes to grids.

As a rule, I work in English units and fractional grids, particularly for architectural objects such as our buildings, because I'm most comfortable with such dimensions. You might find metric units and decimal grids more suitable for your work, but look for opportunities where grids can help you along.

Take Baby Steps

Build what you know how to build first. Our parking meter has a somewhat complex head on it—but I absolutely know how to make the post, so I'll start there. The hero car might be complicated, but putting in the wheels first will get me, dare I say it, grounded and rolling.

You might not be able to easily visualize the curvature of the car's fenders—but you can create curves atop the side view's image plane and then adjust them to also match the front view's image plane. You might not be sure about the curvature of the hood, but you know that it'll be level across the center. Like doing a crossword puzzle, filling in what you already know will help you to complete the other areas.

If you've created curves that have compatible parameterizations, the subsequent surfacing operations will proceed more smoothly. If you're going to extrude your subdiv widget from a sphere, start with a sphere with the right number of sections. Remember that interesting surfaces usually take refinement, so get the basic topology in order first and then work at fine-tuning the shape.

Handle the Details

Many details of models are typical. You don't need to reinvent them each time you encounter them (although you'll probably still have to build them). This section looks at a couple of extremely common problems: using soft edges and capping off open ends.

Topology is everything with these problems—when you understand what you're trying to make, it's often easy to find a way to make it.

Avoid Sharp Edges

Rounded edges are everywhere. Almost nothing ever appears sharp, much less *is* sharp. And because light bounces off all of those soft edges in such a familiar way, we need to put them on our objects, too.

The place to begin in understanding rounded edges is the simple NURBS curve. Its CV placement behavior exactly mimics most of the CV arrangements you'll try to create on your NURBS or subdivision surfaces.

As you know, placing a few points close together will tighten up the curve around them. The trick is in knowing "how many points" and "in what arrangement" to get the shape you're after without overbuilding your model. In addition, too many points not only makes the data set heavier, but it also makes shaping smooth features more difficult.

We'll start out by looking at NURBS and some approaches using them; then we'll examine some polymesh and subdivision surface methods.

Mastering the Point Spread

Two points, even piled directly on top of each other, won't make a cubic curve have an entirely sharp cusp. On the other hand, three points similarly piled up will make a distinct corner. Even though those two cases would seem to cover the whole range of curvature values, there's considerably more to it than that.

The problem is that we're concerned not only about the radius of the curve, but also about its *shape*. We care about its position, direction, curvature, and probably rate of change of curvature. The mathematics don't usually matter to us, but the resulting shape that those CVs produce has to pass our visual test.

Tip

A *fillet* (pronounced "fill-it") is an interior rounded corner, while a *round* is an exterior one. A *bevel* is an angled cut on a corner to reduce its angle. Some folks call them all bevels, others (like me) call them all fillets, and a few more must surely call them all rounds. Fillets and rounds are geometrically identical, but bevels are at least ostensibly different—however, polymesh bevels are what become subdivision surface fillets and rounds. The best advice is just to call 'em as you see 'em.

Most rounded corners take anywhere from two to five points to shape well. Deciding factors include the required shape of neighboring spans and the need for consistent curvature.

Using five points to go around a corner lets you keep the shapes of the neighboring spans flat, locally bind the corner's knots, and shape the interior of the corner to be fairly circular. You also can easily scale the corner radius by scaling the CVs about the middle point.

If the object is a desktop, with small, rounded edges and large, flat expanses between them, you can use just five-point corners (I throw in midside CVs unless the sides are short) and get excellent geometry. Use grid snap to keep the three CVs at either end evenly spaced and aligned with the flat sides (see Figure 7.8).

Three-point corners are more common, especially if the roundedness can taper off over a longer distance. If the shape of the corner just needs to be rounded off (not convincingly circular), this is a good way to construct it. When you have three-point corners aimed at each other (especially if a midpoint is added), the sides in between will be flat and the corners will look suitably round. The radius will gradually taper away into the flat, but you can perform a similar radius adjustment as with five-point corners; the bounds of the flats just won't be as controllable.

Most of the rounded edges in our project will be accomplished with three-point corners, especially the architectural details.

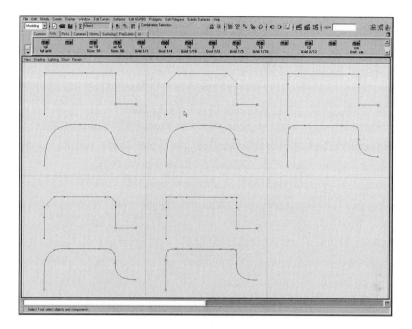

Figure 7.8   Rounded corner topologies.

Using only two-point corners won't make the sides between them flat unless other collinear CVs are added, which can be good or bad. Corner radius adjustments are limited to what two points atop each other can do, and scaling the corner radius (well, more of a hyperbola, in this case) is a little trickier. But if the model doesn't need or shouldn't have flats between rounded corners, then two-point corners can be lean and mean.

Four-point corners are like two-point corners with bonus radius adjusters. The spacing of these extra CVs can be adjusted to create a fairly consistent radius around the corner—in fact, just arranging them like a five-point L without the corner makes a well-shaped rounded corner. In addition, pairs of four-point corners *can* have flats between them.

Knowing the characteristics of these basic point arrangements will help you create the right topology the first time through.

Getting Attached

If you're modeling with NURBS, attaches are a useful way of adding a smooth, rounded edge between surfaces. Attaches, of course, manage to accomplish this by combining the two surfaces into one, so use this approach only when that won't be a problem (such as with shaders relying on existing parameterization).

Most often, when you use Attach Surfaces, you'll want to use the Blend option so that the edges of the CV meshes are averaged. You can use the Blend Bias value to favor one edge or the other, which is most often useful when the tangents on one surface are substantially larger than the tangents on the other. Most of the time, though, you'll just blend evenly, which discards the edge CVs and averages the tangent CVs.

Besides removing any discontinuity (the surface knots become a single internal knot), this has a flattening effect along the seam. So, if you detach a surface and reattach the pieces, you *don't* get the original surface back (see Figure 7.9).

However, when using Attach Surfaces to create edges, you'll usually want to insert knots to limit the shape-changing effect of the operation. The Insert Parameter value is used to specify the fraction along the first span of each surface at which to insert a knot. A value of 0.1 inserts a knot farther along a physically long span than along a short one. For an evenly spaced row of CVs on either side of the join, either start with roughly even span lengths or compensate for the scale differences with Blend Bias.

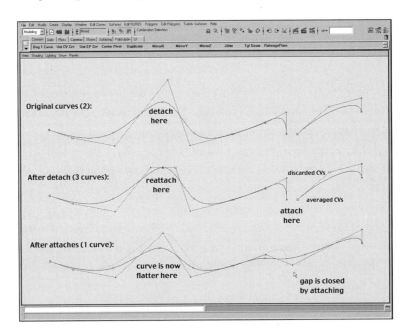

Figure 7.9   Attach behavior.

The Attach Surfaces command, of necessity, incorporates all the knot ratios of both surfaces into the resulting new surface. To keep the surface meshes from getting over-built, try to ensure that your matching surfaces are parameterized equivalently.

The easiest way to accomplish this is to model the surfaces from a set of equivalent U or V curves. By copying the initial curves and reshaping them by only adjusting their CVs, you can keep their knot ratios in sync.

The next easiest way is to use Rebuild Surfaces to make the surfaces uniform along the mating edge. You'll also need to ensure that they have the same number of CVs. I prefer to get the CV counts matched up first (by deleting or inserting rows of CVs) and then rebuild uniformly with Keep CVs selected.

In the simple parking meter example shown in Figure 7.10, I can smoothly blend the ridges by adjusting the Blend Bias to compensate for different tangent lengths. Do a rough calculation of the bias value, using a ratio of $B \div (A + B)$ for span lengths A and B, respectively; then attach them with Insert Knot turned on. You should be able to predict the results fairly readily from each set of Blend Bias and Insert Parameter values.

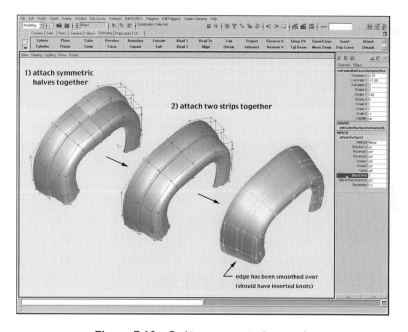

Figure 7.10   Parking meter attach example.

The upside of using Attach Surfaces to create rounded edges is that you get C2 continuity (discussed in more depth in Chapter 6, "Formats") for free and have something likely to stand up to deformation better. Plus, if you need separate surfaces, it's as easy as selecting the isoparameter curve at the desired seam and detaching.

Using Brute Force

The Surface Fillet commands are better reserved for NURBS edge situations when topologies can't readily be made compatible. Fillets generally make for heavier geometry because they're made tangent by a method akin to brute force—offset the surfaces, create curves at each knot along their intersection, loft, and refine with intermediate curves until a numerical tolerance is achieved. It's more elegant and complex than it sounds, but that's the fundamental idea.

The great strength of creating rounded edges with fillets is that you are freed of the need to precisely control your parameterizations. For the freeform varieties of the command (Freeform Fillet and Fillet Blend), having matching parameter values can produce clean results, but the fillet commands are at their best when odd intersections between surfaces must be rounded. In some cases, they're the only way to get a rounded edge without disturbing the shape of the surfaces involved.

Classic examples of fillet situations are blending in fender flares around wheel wells, cutting out designs in wheels, and intersecting one rounded rod obliquely through another. Our cars will probably have a few of these situations, with the neck of a mirror-mount one possible example of the last situation.

One of the downsides of fillets is that they tend to rely on surface trimming for their power. If history can be successfully maintained, it's possible to animate and deform filleted components, but difficulties in mapping shaders to changing UV boundaries can be a showstopper. If the history is absent, forget it—surface boundaries along fillet edges are sure to crack under deformation.

Another negative is that they create a lot of data. The fillet surfaces themselves can quickly grow heavy (especially with tight tolerances), and the trim curves add extra data to the original surfaces.

If the model is static, the situation is complex, and the surface shapes are important, then filleting is a good option. Just don't expect more from fillets than they can deliver.

Do-It-Yourself

When presented with a design that has lots of planar surfaces separated by uniformly rounded edges (a rounded box such as a die or a door, for instance), it's often easiest to simply do the filleting yourself. If the planar surfaces are aligned with worldspace planes, so much the better.

Fillets require tangent continuity, and sets its tangency the last two CVs of an element to set, so a single cubic surface span has all the CVs it takes to be tangent to elements on either side of itself (assuming that the parameterizations are compatible). So, when surfaces lend themselves to it, rolling your own fillets can be an excellent answer.

Don't start with a cube for these constructions—start with spheres, cylinders, or (if need be) circles. If roundness is more important than simple tangency, use eight-span primitives in the round direction (that is, one span per 45°), which look suitably round and provide detach locations in the principal directions. The basic approach is to dice up the larger primitives and then loft between edges to fill in the surfaces (see Figure 7.11).

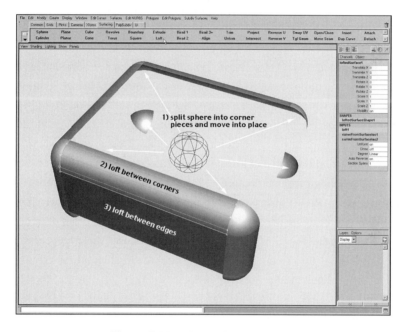

Figure 7.11   Manual filleting example.

A simple rounded cube has 8 corners, 12 edges, and 6 sides. It can be quickly constructed beginning with a sphere:

1. Dice up a sphere into eight rounded corners, and then move them into position.

2. Select the corresponding edge isoparameter curves and loft between them (degree 1 lofts make for easy repositioning and less model data) to make the 12 edges.

3. Finally, loft across the edges to make the six sides.

Naturally, if your object is symmetric, take advantage of mirroring and copying with 90° rotations to minimize the effort.

Lots of objects have this kind of configuration, with 90° rounds matching up to planar sides. Somewhat more complex profiles with planar ends (such as the curbs or parts of the fire hydrant) can often be simply handled by extruding a quarter-round profile around each end and capping off the ends (see the section "Put a Lid on It," later in this chapter).

Subdivide and Conquer

The Attach Surfaces corollary for polygonal and subdivision surfaces is the Combine operation, followed by some point snapping and vertex merging. When the object must deform and can't be shaped by a single NURBS surface, using polysets to create smooth edges is most likely the method of choice.

There are many ways to construct a rounded edge in a subdivision surface, but all hearken back to our original NURBS curve discussion about bringing numbers of CVs close together. Unless you want a sharp edge (which full creasing can give you), controlling the character of an edge is a matter of the CVs placed along it. So, the trick is to have a few methods in your repertoire that can place those CVs the way you'd like.

Recall that, in the midst of grids of quadrilaterals, subdiv meshes are equivalent to uniform B-spline surfaces. Because of this, I often create subdivs out of polymeshes converted from NURBS surfaces. I do this (rather than directly surfacing to a polymesh) so that I can see what the chunk of surface is really like and obtain the tangent rows of points that the cubic NURBS operations produce. Those tangent rows are simple to remove if they're not needed, but they are very helpful for creating rounded edges when the polymeshes are combined.

Although the Split Polygon tool can be used quite effectively to place a row or two of CVs along an edge, the facePathSplit script (available from Alias|Wavefront) is often my choice when such a row isn't already in the mesh. It walks across rows of faces, neatly splitting them in half until it meets a fork in its road. It sometimes makes mistakes, but these can be undone and the benefits far outweigh any troubles (see Figure 7.12).

Because facePathSplit works only by splitting faces into halves (a similar tool by Mikkel Jans, multiLoopSplit has a slider), sometimes you need to run it a few times in succession to get a small enough face size—but its companion scripts, facePath and edgePath, are great tools for selecting any extra faces and edges for deletion. They're also a great help in performing Extrude operations.

Maya 4.5 has also added the Edit Polygons, Cut Faces tool, which can simplify edge row creation if a planar cut across the polymesh describes the edge row adequately. It can also be used to hack off arbitrary chunks of mesh, if you feel the need.

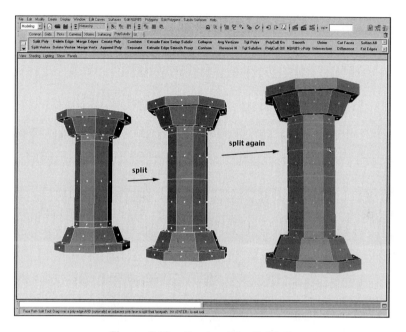

Figure 7.12   Results of facePathSplit.

Put a Lid on It

During early discussions of our story we had considered trying to lure Spot away with a stick ("Fetch, boy!"). Although we dropped the idea, the stick would have been a natural candidate for the edgePath script. You can use edgePath to quickly create a rounded edge on a tube-shape polymesh and then cap it off neatly (see Figure 7.13).

To cap a polymesh tube, follow these steps:

1. First, select the edge row of CVs with edgePath by left-clicking one of its edges; then use Edit Polygons, Extrude Edge to pull out a new row. I almost always use a standard Move transform, by the way, rather than the fancy manipulator Extrude Edge produces (because I just want to move it over a bit).

2. Next, use Extrude Edge again, but scale the row inward instead of moving it. Repeat once or twice again, scaling the central row down to 0 (or snapping all of them to one point).

Tip

Scaling CVs down to exactly 0 normally requires that you do one of two things:

- Perform an interactive scale, undo it, and then paste the undone scale string back in (with zeros you've added manually).
- Group the CVs into a cluster, scale the cluster to 0 (usually in the Channel box), and then delete history to eliminate the cluster.

Fortunately, we've added a script named zeroScaleCVs on the accompanying CD that makes scaling selected CVs down to 0 a snap.

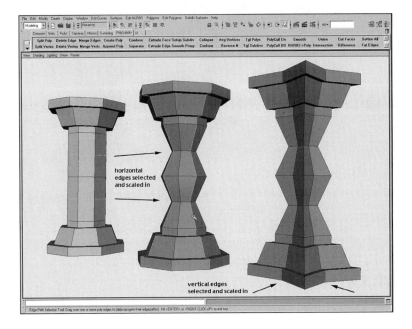

Figure 7.13   Using edgePath.

3. Then merge the vertices at the pole. If you have a lot of points converging at the center, you might want to spend a moment thinning down the mesh on the cap so that there's no pinching at the pole. Your cap is then complete.

A similar thing can be done with NURBS surfaces (see Figure 7.14), creating a neatly capped surface from an open end:

1. First, figure out how many added rows of CVs you'll need (typically three or four) and use the Insert Isoparms tool to create the required edge rows.

2. Then scale the central (pole) row down to 0. These surface CVs don't get merged or closed in any way; you just want them together in the right spot.

3. Scale down the next row around the pole to a useful tangent row size. This row *is* a tangent row and must be coplanar with and symmetric across the pole. An easy way to achieve this is by placing a circle of similar size and the same number of CVs at the pole point, and then snapping the tangent row CVs to the circle's CVs.

4. Scale and move the other CVs along the rounded edge to create the edge shape you want. I tend to use three CVs to go around an edge, but sometimes I use two CVs (or even one) to create a softer edge.

5. You might want to rebuild the surface as uniform in the direction along which you added spans (be sure to use Keep, CVs) because the initial parameter values from the Insert operation might no longer apply.

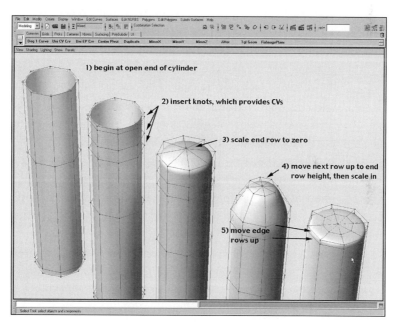

Figure 7.14 Capping a NURBS tube.

Your NURBS cap is now complete. Of course, it could have just as easily been made using two surfaces and the Attach Surfaces command, as described earlier: Duplicate the edge curve, turn on its CVs, scale it to 0, loft, fix the pole tangent row, and attach the result to the original.

Whatever way they get created, rounded edges are a product of CV placement, which almost entirely governs the shapes of those edges. Even the subdivision surface technique of creasing, refining, and uncreasing simply has the net effect of moving rows of CVs closer together.

Cut Corners

Okay, so there are lots of ways to add rounded edges to objects—but sometimes edges need a different kind of shaping: mitering. Miters are angled cuts made by woodworkers to match two pieces of wood meeting at an angle. There are miters in window frames, door moldings, cabinet doors, table edges, and more. Whether there's a rounded edge involved or not, it helps to know how to make a miter.

Here's how you might make a window frame as a single surface:

1. Begin by creating a profile curve for your frame. Create this profile about half of the window's width away from the origin.

2. Revolve that profile curve, creating a 16-span NURBS surface. You're using 16 spans here because you'll put three CVs in each corner, plus another in the middle of each side. You'll turn this surface into the frame.

3. Select the hulls going out at 45° angles. Notice how they appear foreshortened when viewed perpendicular to the axis of rotation. You'll undo this by precisely scaling the hulls back out to the corners.

4. Scale the selected CVs by 1.0 along the rotation axis and 1.4142 in the other directions (see Figure 7.15). The latter value is the amount needed to compensate for the foreshortening that occurred, which is precisely given by the cosine of the rotation angle. To undo a 45° rotation, use: $1 \div \cos(45°) = 1 \div 0.7071 = 1.4142$.

5. Use the arrow keys to pickwalk-select the four in-between hulls (the ones at 22.5° increments) on one side or the other. Once you have CVs selected and know their orientation angle, you can use simple ratios between the one-over-cosine values to compensate for further rotation.

Tip

You can use the keyboard's arrow keys to navigate up, down, left, and right through your scene, object, or mesh hierarchy.

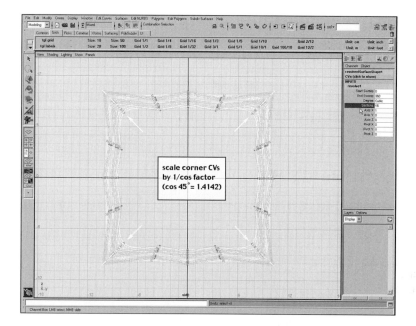

Figure 7.15 Window frame intermediate corners.

6. These are to be oriented the same as the corners, so scale them as before and then rotate each another 22.5°. These will then overlay the first set of hulls you put in the corners.

7. Select the opposing four hulls by pickwalking two steps either way; then scale them the previous amount. However, rotate them the opposite way (which piles up three hulls and makes the corners appear sharp).

8. Finally, separate the overlapping in-between hulls in the corners by some "radius" amount. You can pickwalk your way easily around the mesh to grab each overlapped row and move it. Your finished window frame should look something like Figure 7.16.

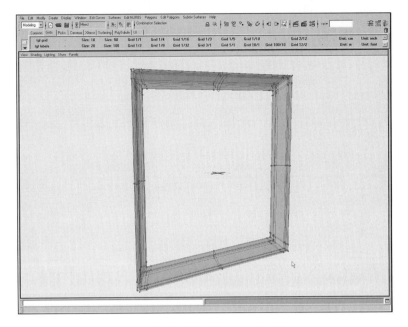

Figure 7.16   Single-surface window frame.

You can adjust the size of the window frame by simply selecting the CVs for each side and moving them. The frame will be simple, rounded, and precise.

There are several other ways to approach this problem, such as shearing the CVs or placing 16 curves and lofting a closed surface. But an understanding of this kind of applied trigonometry solution can be a powerful modeling aid in itself.

Handle the Ups and Downs

When you're driving along in your car and hit a pothole, it's usually quite unexpected. The road's designer didn't put it there to jar you into alertness. Most of the bumps and voids (tunnels excepted) along the road are the result of thousands of vehicles and the onslaught of the elements. But when you build a road in Maya, you are the road's designer, builder, traffic, and weather all rolled into one. Each hole and bump is yours to shape, to give your viewer's eyes precisely the ride you intend.

In this section, we look at techniques for creating features such as holes and bumps in both NURBS and polygonal geometry.

Tunneling

A hole that goes clear through to the other side of an object can be made in many ways, depending on the model's format, use, and precision of form required. Let's look at the benefits and drawbacks of some possible approaches to building tunnels through objects.

Going with the Flow

Often the best way of building a through hole for NURBS is to find a way to cleanly integrate it into the surfacing flow. This means that you construct your object so that features on one side of the hole have a planned correspondence with those on the other side. Typically, this means that you create your construction elements so that they are parametrically similar at corresponding locations on either side (for a discussion of parameterization, see the section titled "NURBS" in Chapter 6).

The simplest example of this is a torus. Of course, a model with a toroidal topology doesn't have to look like a doughnut—the window frame discussed in the previous section has this topology. If your model has a single hole and no emergent features that can't be embedded in the overall flow around the hole's perimeter (see Figure 7.17), you might be lucky enough to create it from a single revolved surface that you shape to suit.

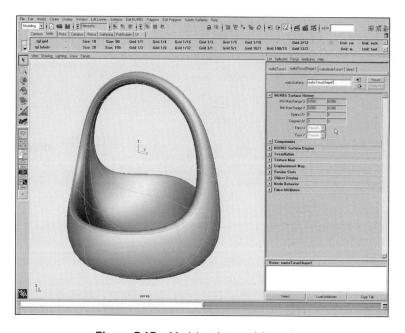

Figure 7.17   Model with toroidal topology.

The disadvantage of constructing single-surface NURBS models is that the rectangular nature of CV meshes means that each parametric direction will carry the maximum mesh detail needed by the most complicated location. Extremes of this effect can be often be seen in "sock" models of human heads (see Figure 7.18), which begin in the mouth, wrap around the face and over the head, and then go down the neck. Such models, while cleverly ensuring continuity under deformation, can be nightmares to shape due to their heavy data.

Notice that the sock model can still be seen as fairly similar to the torus, even though it's closed in only one direction. The shape of the inner hole (going down the throat) is still intimately linked with the shape of the outer hole (the outside of the neck). When such a linkage is manageable, single-surface models with holes can be an attractive option.

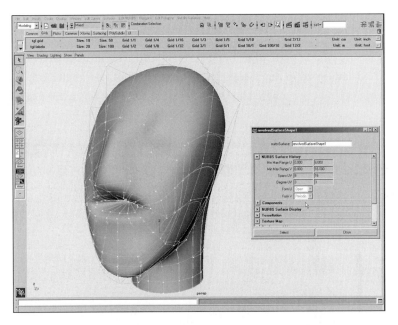

Figure 7.18 "Sock" model of a human head.

Polymesh Holes

With polygons and subdivision surfaces, of course, toroidal topologies are quite easy to construct. One need only ensure that a reasonable similarity in edge shapes exists on each side of the hole and that the edge shapes can be adjusted to create the desired hole profile.

Note

The Make Hole tool doesn't show any visual connectivity between the hole and the surrounding polygon. Especially if you are using polygon meshes to construct subdivision surfaces, this can remove some important control from your hands. This is one of the reasons I don't use it and choose to make my own holes.

In the case of an artist's palette, for example (see Figure 7.19), it would be easy to construct the thumb hole in a polymesh model:

1. Ensure that one or more faces lie in corresponding positions on the top and bottom of the polymesh.
2. Select and delete those faces.
3. Use the Append to Polygon tool to create new polygons on the side of the hole.
4. Use the Split Polygon tool to add any necessary edge detail around the hole.

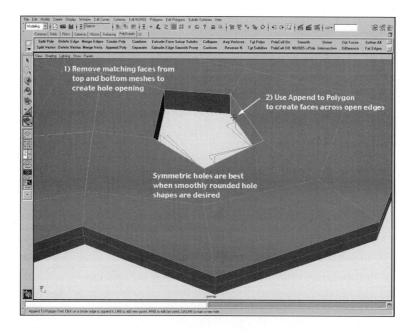

Figure 7.19 Making a polymesh hole.

You can make practically as many holes as the polygon mesh density will tolerate this way, so it needn't apply just to toroidal topologies. Just arrange to have similar edge shapes at either end of the hole if you need to maintain the hole's shape on the way through.

Subdivision surfaces behave much like uniform B-splines, so the polygon meshes that shape them will look like the corresponding NURBS meshes. If you want a circular hole, use the same number and placement of polygon vertices as you would for a NURBS circle. Thus, four-point holes through polygonal meshes will be noticeably out-of-round, whereas eight-point holes will seem quite round.

Planar Holes

NURBS models that require multiple holes must, of necessity, be constructed from multiple surfaces. This is surely the most common case for NURBS models, and it bears a strong resemblance to the previous technique of handling holes in polygonal meshes.

In the case of the artist's palette, a NURBS model would probably be easy to construct, no matter how many holes (within reason) are needed. Why? The palette's top and bottom are planar.

When creating holes between planar NURBS surfaces, the planar surfaces can be re-created in pieces after the hole has been built (see Figure 7.20):

1. Build the outer edge of the palette, perhaps by extruding a profile around a path.

2. Build the inner edge of the hole in a similar manner, ensuring that both the top and bottom of the hole surface are coplanar with the palette outer edge surface.

3. If there is a clean line of sight all around between the hole edge and the palette edge, you might be able to simply use Loft to construct the top and bottom surfaces.

Tip

If lofting between curves produces a "twisted" result, you need to either reverse the curve direction of one of the curves (not both) or use Move Seam to orient the curves so that equivalent knots are matched up. Also, curve knots are matched up by ratios, so the surface won't necessarily take the shortest apparent route.

4. If there isn't a clean line of sight (or if there are multiple holes), you need to divide up the construction curves for the top and bottom into segments that have clean sight lines and that can be lofted between. Otherwise, your surfaces will self-intersect or overlap other surfaces. Use Loft to close up the various areas until the voids are all covered.

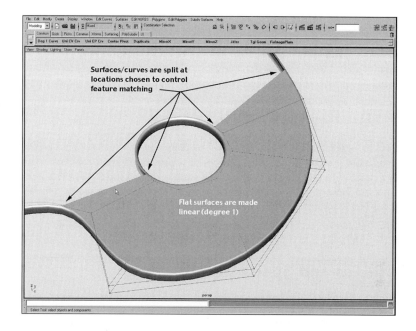

Figure 7.20   Making a planar NURBS hole.

Tip

Use degree 1 surfaces to fill in holes on non-deforming planar surfaces. They're half as much geometry as cubic surfaces and much easier to edit if you change the design later.

Planar NURBS holes can always be closed up by a suitably complex network of coplanar lofted surfaces. Because these are all coplanar, no seams are evident during rendering and the voids are tightly sealed. The only disadvantages to this approach are the inability to deform the final object without creasing and cracking, and the loss of a continuous parameter space for shading.

Nonplanar Holes

For those NURBS through holes that aren't planar, it is sometimes (but not always) possible to create a network of surfaces between the surfaces on either side of the hole that smoothly blends in. This approach can be quite similar to the planar approach, only with more of a burden for controlling surface continuity (such as surface tangency).

Much depends on the orientation of the opposing surfaces. In some cases, you might want to create the edge surfaces first and then loft over the voids (similar to the planar case, but using degree 3). In others, you might choose to start with the opposing surfaces, and then build the hole (in sections or all at once) and apply a healthy dose of commands that enforce continuity.

Tip

For best results in all cases, match up corresponding knots so that features flow as intended. Whenever possible, use uniform parameterization so that knot-to-knot matching is fully predictable. You can examine knot values by selecting edit points and looking at the Script Editor, or use Rebuild Surfaces to set the parameterization to uniform (by setting the Rebuild Type to Uniform).

Potholes and Speed Bumps

Not all holes go all the way through an object, of course. Many holes are like potholes or drilled holes, appearing almost arbitrarily in the middle of other surfaces and having distinct bottoms. Also, if you invert such features, it's easy to see that bumps and projections are essentially the same topological things.

Many of the techniques mentioned in the previous section can also be applied to such holes and bumps. In this section, though, we'll take a brief look at a couple of techniques most commonly encountered with these features: NURBS filleting and polygon Boolean operations.

Filleted Holes

The most attractive reason for turning to filleted holes is their freedom from the shape constraints of the surfaces being cut away. As long as the surfaces being filleted don't have a local radius of curvature smaller than the fillet size you're using, you can construct a good fillet. For a further discussion of the trade-offs involved in filleting, see the section "Using Brute Force," earlier in this chapter.

Note

Radius of curvature is a measure of the local curvature of a curve or surface. A true circle or sphere has a constant curvature at any location, whereas a spiral has a higher curvature (smaller radius of curvature) as you go toward its center. Radius of curvature is expressed as the size of the radius of a circle that would precisely match the curvature at a given location.

If you need a constant radius, use circular fillets. However, if you need to specify the edges along which the fillet is bounded, use freeform fillets. In the latter case, you can sometimes find ways to use the edges of surfaces directly and manually construct a surface that will hold up under deformation—or, at least, not rely on trimmed surface edges.

Warning

Avoid building surfaces directly between the trimmed edges that fillets have generated. These surfaces will be very data-heavy (because the trimmed edges are parametrically unrelated to each other) and won't fit any tighter than a standard trimmed surface.

While trimmed surfaces can require careful attention during rendering to minimize cracking along trimmed edges, their utility for creating features such as holes and bumps can be very helpful.

Whether you're constructing a footprint in the dirt or snow, a slot for a coin, raised lettering on a tire, or the edge around the tongue of a shoe, filleting can be a powerful approach to making holes and bumps.

Logical Holes

There's a polymesh corollary to NURBS filleting and operations: Boolean operations. Polygon Booleans enable you to easily add or subtract polygonal surfaces (as well as select only the common volumes).

Note

NURBS Booleans also exist, but I never use them. They produce sharp intersection edges, not the rounded edges I want. You might find them useful for quickly massing in a reference object of a design study, but you probably won't want them for making final geometry.

For scooping holes out of surfaces, the Subtract tool is the right tool. For adding a bump, the Union command does the job well.

The Boolean operations use the face normals to determine what to keep and what to throw away, so it's important that your polymeshes are properly set up. First, be sure that all your normals point in a consistent direction by using Edit Polygons, Normals, Conform. Then, if a Boolean operation produces an unexpected result (see Figure 7.21), try reversing the normal of one or both polymeshes with Edit Polygons, Normals, Reverse.

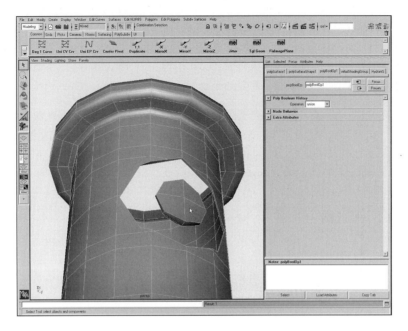

Figure 7.21 Boolean subtraction examples.

Finally, remember that Polygons, Booleans, Difference cares about the order of selections. It subtracts the second object from the first, so you might need to switch your selection order.

Tip

You can easily move any selection to the end of the selection list by choosing it in the Object menu of the Channel box.

Polygon Booleans perform a simple face-by-face intersection of one polymesh against the other and then save the desired logical result as a single mesh. Because these operations result in a polymesh with almost arbitrarily bounded faces along the intersection, you should perform a cleanup pass along the intersection boundary if you intend to use the mesh for a subdivision surface.

To make the intersection clean, I first try to adjust the edges of the separate meshes so that they cross near edges on the opposing mesh. This ensures that the odd short segments generated will be fairly close to each other. Then I eliminate extraneous edges with Edit Polygons, Collapse, doing a little moving of vertices as I go. I try to create an intersection boundary that's logically connecting vertices on one side to vertices on the other. The end result can be a very clean and attractive blended edge around the hole or projection you've made.

In the modeling that lies ahead for our project, we'll have several opportunities to use poly Booleans, and we'll explore these techniques in greater detail.

Summary

Modeling success is largely a matter of gaining experience solving topological problems and reducing inefficiencies. As your experience with Maya grows, you'll find that more of your modeling time is spent in familiar territory, which will help you make better models faster. Some problems are common, and others are unique—but a solid sense of what's possible in Maya models will soon guide you through even the most difficult modeling problems.

By recognizing the common tasks and developing standard approaches to them, you can both pay the necessary attention to detail and have more attention available for addressing the creative needs of your project.

Chapter 8
Sets

By Mark Adams

The first thing almost any project needs is a location. Characters and props must have a place in which they can interact. Cameras must be placed somewhere and be looking somewhere. Although it's possible to carry on with many early project activities in parallel, creating a set is such an essential step to so many later activities that we'll begin there—if only so that there's actually a there there.

In this chapter, we'll look at these topics:

- Getting a set off to a fast start
- Building stand-ins
- Making major set pieces
- Creating architectural elements
- Managing the structure of sets

Roughing It In

Building a complex set can seem like an almost overwhelming task. There might be dozens (perhaps even hundreds or thousands) of models to construct, each needing to properly fit into the scene and convey the necessary look. Usually each must be different from its neighbors in sometimes subtle and sometimes dramatic ways. Just getting your head around the problem can be intimidating.

Fortunately, we humans are logical thinkers. We can look at our problems from a variety of perspectives to find useful patterns, and we can plan our solutions in hierarchical ways. Building a set, whether it's a room or an entire city, can be tackled top-down. To build the set required for our *Parking Spot* project (see Chapter 2, "Project Overview"), we'll use just such an approach.

Have a Plan

At the intersection of our storyboards, the book, and the real world lies the set we need to build. Not having the luxury of copious budgets, we designed our set to be minimalist but sufficient for the necessary story and book points.

First, we examined the storyboards for necessary elements. We absolutely needed to have a street, a sidewalk, and some stores. Because the meter maid would be seen from afar, the street had to have at least enough length to it to give The Jerk time to interact with the dog. Trying to get the most from the least, we decided that two blocks would be long enough.

After mulling over our requirements for a while, I prepared a quick sketch in Photoshop that laid out the basic elements for us (see Figure 8.1) and reviewed it with Max for our required elements.

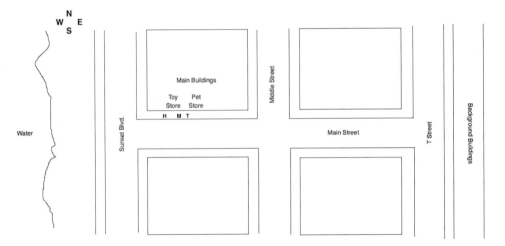

Figure 8.1 Plan view of the *Parking Spot* set.

This arrangement of elements allowed us to have light coming from the direction we needed, a manageable number of buildings and other city details, and a large expanse of sky and water (for examples of the new Fluid Effects features). Perhaps most important, it kept the horizon itself under control. Because this project's set was outdoors, this was of critical importance. We agreed that this plan view would be the plan for our set.

Have Standards

We had to agree on some other details, too, so that we would be able to successfully work together.

For starters, our set would be constructed using Z as the up-axis. If your project is exclusively a Maya project, it doesn't matter which axis you select as the up-axis (the other choice being Y-up, of course). It's important only that you all agree on what that choice will be, to avoid having to rotate the characters, props, or set pieces to bring them all into agreement. Because I've spent nearly all of the past 20 years building Z-up models, this pleased me.

The choice of up-axis can make a difference, however, if you will be exchanging data with other applications. Of course, if you've already invested substantial effort into models with the "wrong" up-axis, you can usually successfully transform from one system into another by grouping everything and rotating the whole group 90° about the X-axis.

Next, we agreed that everything would be modeled one-to-one—that is, at full size. In Maya, you can freely change from one system of units to another (for example, from inches to centimeters), so this wouldn't constrain us in any way. I could use feet when building the streets and inches when making the architectural details, changing my grids all the while to suit my needs.

Tip

If you're building models (such as sets) that have dimensions that are easily expressed, consider setting up a shelf with nothing but grid and unit settings (such as shown in Figure 7.7, in Chapter 7, "Methods"). This makes changing units and grid settings much faster and easier than doing it through the menus.

Implicit in our adoption of the overall plan was the adoption of a fixed orientation to the world. In our top view, north would be at the top and west would be to the left. In a front view, we'll be looking north.

If only one person is building the set pieces (as in our case), this decision is easily honored. However, if a crew of several people is building the set pieces and others add props and characters, it can be aggravating (not to mention expensive) to waste time orienting models before using them.

Finally, we needed to consider the origin and placement of objects in our set. Although each model is created separately in its own space, the set as a whole is the final destination and has its own space. We had to agree on just how that space would relate to our shots.

Because all the action happens in a relatively small area, the X and Y positioning was easy. We would center the XY plane about this action. Because the edge of the curb in front of the parking space conveniently divides the scene along Y, we placed the Y=0 at this edge. Laterally, we decided to make X=0 at the middle of the parking space itself. The vertical (Z) positioning was less obvious.

First, we decided that we'd rather not deal with sloping streets and sidewalks (even though real ones are sloped for drainage), so we'd make them flat. Because we weren't making entirely realistic scenes, we figured no one would notice (or they would forgive us if they did). Had they been sloped, every step and every move of the car would have been much more difficult, with no relevant story point benefiting from the effort.

Next, we found that we had several possible choices for a Z height. The characters would spend most of their time on the sidewalk, so making Z=0 at that level was reasonable. This would make vertical placement a nonissue for most of the character animation, but it would make anything in the street have a negative Z value.

On the other hand, the cars also needed to be accommodated, so making Z=0 at street level was also a sensible choice. As a result, all of the street and building geometry would have positive (or 0) Z values, which would be easy to keep straight.

Finally, the water level (at the west end of Main Street) could be set to Z=0, which would make all of the Z values positive away from the water.

Because the action takes place away from the water (and we might decide to adjust the slope of the beach at some point), we discarded the last option. For the interactive simplicity of positive Z values, we then chose to make the street level Z=0 and add the necessary offset when the action was on the sidewalk.

The decision of set orientation was ultimately not complicated for our project, but it can be for more involved projects.

Note

Set, shot, or scene?

These terms tend to be used so casually that it's often just assumed that you know the difference. In ordinary production usage, a *set* is a location. A *shot* is a single continuous camera event. A *scene* is a collection of shots that comprise a distinct set of events that advance the story (another s-word!).

Of course, Maya muddies these meanings a bit by referring to its files as scenes (which might or might not be accurate, depending on whether they contain multiple shots). Because our story really has only one scene, we'll normally be using the term *scene* in the Maya fashion (and try to be clear when we mean it the other way).

When sets are completely separate, each one can easily be dealt with in isolation. However, when sets are large and interconnected, it can be extremely important to determine an absolute reference point (and to confirm that the separate pieces match up as they should). Failing to be meticulous in this can create substantial extra work repairing mismatched features and adjusting set dressing and character positions.

One important way of ensuring that mismatches are unlikely is to agree on a system of units for your shots. Although it's perfectly alright to change your units as you model individual elements, when you start pulling things together, it's a good idea to use an agreed-upon system of units and to use your grid snaps. Although it is possible to precisely place objects otherwise, it's much simpler to just follow the standard.

In our case, the set will be modeled with inches as the standard units, reflecting our American cultural bias. This primarily affects the height of the sidewalk (and, thus, the Z value for the placement of the characters), but it also will come into play as set pieces are created, copied, and placed in relation to each other.

Know the Code

Streets, sidewalks, and buildings are such everyday things that we might just assume that we can simply model them without further ado. As it turns out, even these objects can be deceiving, in part because of their context. Just as the harvest moon or the setting sun looks larger than its midsky equivalent, the scale of these utterly familiar objects can fool the eye. In addition, numerous small details can be overlooked when trusting a quick glance or memory for design guidance.

Although I've modeled these kinds of objects many times, it was usually done to specifications provided by others, which I soon forgot when the project was done. So, to obtain some real-world data (and spare someone the effort of detailed drawings), I visited downtown Petaluma, California, one day for some city-street and building research. I took along a tape measure and a note pad, expecting that I already knew the answers. I didn't.

Despite my experience, I found that several of my design assumptions were incorrect. I'd guessed that curbs were about 8 inches high, but they were 6. Sidewalk squares seemed about 3 feet wide—they were about 4. The gutter at the edge of the curb seemed a bit more than a foot wide—it was 2 feet (sometimes 4 feet) wide. How big was the radius of the sidewalk at an intersection? By this time, I was afraid to guess.

The lesson in this is to get actual measurements, even if they will ultimately be overridden for stylistic effect. Sometimes our hunches are right on target, and sometimes they're wildly off. How tall is a door? How high is the doorknob? How big is it? What's at the base of a wall? What's at the top? How deeply set are windows and doorways? To know, you need to get out there and find out!

Of course, there are standard references for the innumerable small details of our modern world. Some can be found online (because cities need to publish their codes and standards); others are in books for the building and architectural trades. Still more information can be found in the sales literature provided by manufacturers of these items (did you know that there are "curb and gutter" machines?), so look around online if you don't feel like heading out with your tape measure.

A little error here or there probably won't make much difference. But when a whole slew of them are present, the design will surely look wrong, even if the viewer can't say exactly why. Caricature is fine, of course, but it should be based on the real thing. When a character reaches for a doorknob and it's 6 inches too high, the whole animation suffers for it. Try to be like Picasso, mastering the classic styles before inventing your own.

Mock It Up

To get things rolling, start by creating a simple mockup of your set. Build it to scale, but don't include any more detail than you need to simply orient yourself and see the scale relationships of the set.

An average city block is about 300 feet long (about 18 blocks per mile), although it's not a fixed measurement (a downtown Chicago block is 330 by 660 feet). An average street lane width is from 10 to 12 feet. Because we have no particular desire to make more buildings than necessary, we'll opt for blocks that are 300 feet long, separated by streets that are 50 feet wide. Because we're using 4-foot sidewalk squares, let's make our lives easier and say that the curb radius at the corners is equal to the sidewalk width, which we'll make three squares (12 feet) wide.

If we find anything awkward about these dimensions, we'll adjust them as needed. For now, though, we'll make some simple placeholders that can be put onto their own layer, which I'll call the reference layer.

Tip

Using layers to hold reference or construction geometry can greatly aid in reducing visual clutter, while still making useful geometry easy to access.

For our set, I started by reducing the information I had gleaned about cityscapes to the bare essentials. Beginning with a simple ground plane, I placed polygonal cubes for the sidewalks and building masses, and then I added some smaller cubes for doors and windows of primary interest (see Figure 8.2). To pretty up the corners, I used quarter-cylinders with a 12-foot radius and a top cap.

Primitive elements such as these allow for a quick examination of the scale relationships within the scene and serve as design templates for finished set models (you can load up InitialMockup.ma and have a look around). Preliminary camera exploration can be also be done, although some additional details might need to be added.

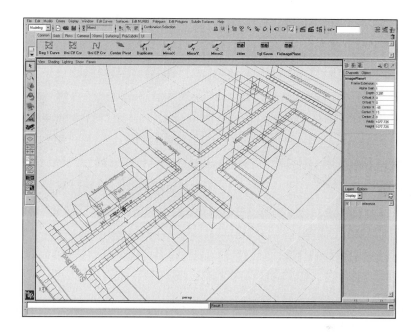

Figure 8.2 Initial mockup for the *Parking Spot* set.

To take a good look around, I first set up some cameras in positions that approximated those in the storyboards and examined the scenes they revealed. Because I wanted to return to these positions again, I used the New Bookmark command to save them. Later, when the final shots were being composed, these bookmarked views (see Figure 8.3) served as good starting points for each shot's camera.

Simple stand-ins were used for objects such as the fire hydrant, parking meters, streetlights, trees, and cars. These have the immediate effect of making the scene seem substantially more real and provide a better sense of scale.

Tip

Create your stand-in models in the same space that you will create the real model, and then transform them into place. If you'll build the parking meter at the origin, for instance, build its stand-in there, too. That way, you'll later be able to perform direct object replacement without having to compensate for the difference in modeling spaces.

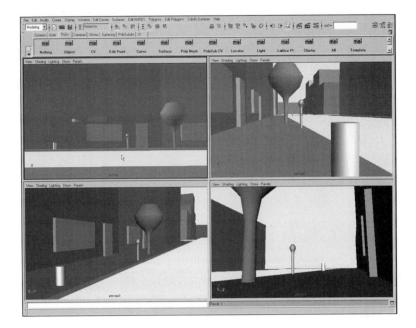

Figure 8.3 Early camera bookmarks.

Additional architectural details were also added, to see if the flavor of the style could be suggested. Many of the details were suggested by studying references to the Miami Beach Art Deco buildings. Because our storyboards had never addressed these details, it was an opportunity to work out cheap design solutions at an early stage.

The early results were encouraging. We now had a workable and visually interesting set prototype, which would serve as a template for the detailed modeling to come. Some of these simple stand-ins might also be used later if the detailed models proved too heavy to handle interactively.

Building Blocks

With two city blocks to build, let's start by building the sidewalks. Everything else is relative to them (and we know the relevant details about curbs and gutters), so in much the same way that we draw in the outlines before coloring, we'll start there.

Curbs

As I learned, curbs are typically 6 inches high and 6 inches wide, with 2-foot gutters. There are also quarter-inch radii around the expansion joints, and about a 1-inch radius at the leading edge. The joints are three quarters of an inch wide and an inch and a half deep (but often filled in with some compressible material). Because the curbs in our project will be so close to the camera (and to reduce the shading load), the expansion joints in the curbs should be modeled.

Exercise 8.1 Curbs and Gutters

Before doing any construction, I ensured that my mockup was on its own layer and that I wasn't working on that layer. I routinely use layers to sort out types of geometry, so I created a Curbs layer and made it active.

Construction a section curve for the curbs is easy using a quarter-inch grid (be sure to snap your CVs to it). Because none of the radii needs to be precisely to size or exactly circular, a uniform cubic NURBS curve (as shown in Figure 8.4) can be easily constructed in a suitable shape.

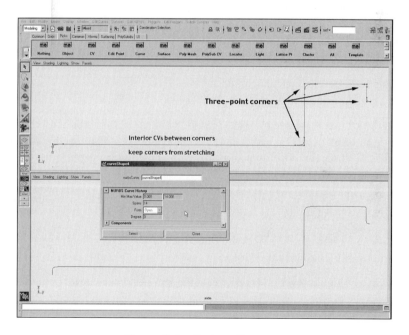

Figure 8.4 Curb profile curve.

It's easiest to create this curve already at the correct height, which is to have the gutter section at Z=0. Because there are curbs all around, it doesn't actually matter on which zero plane it's constructed (X=0 or Y=0), but the area around Spot absolutely must have these curbs. Creating the necessary curves in the side view (X=0) is the logical place to start.

Curbs aren't sectioned as often as sidewalks, so instead of making a curb section 4 feet wide, 16 feet makes a good choice. Now, the profile curve *could* be copied and the copy could be moved into position some distance off to the side. However, we need to remember the expansion joint and decide whether we want it to be a separate piece or whether it should be integrated into each curb surface.

The expansion joint can be constructed either as a separate groove (with the main curb surfaces created between each pair of grooves) or as an integral part of the main curb surface. Although it's appealing to keep the surface count down, in this case the size of the groove relative to the overall length of each curb section is very small. Putting such a small feature in a broad surface complicates the parameterization of the surface, potentially taking some simpler shading options away from the shading TD. So, in the interest of keeping things simple and leaving our shading options open, the curbs will get separate groove surfaces.

Therefore, our strategy for building the curb surfaces from this initial profile curve (which you can get in the file CurbProfile.ma) is to first get the profile curve(s) in the right spot:

1. Duplicate the curb profile curve.

   Instead of simply moving this copy 16 feet along, you need to allow for the width of the groove. A groove of 3/4 inches wide groove with a radii of 1/4 inch on either side amounts to a total width of an inch and a quarter. Half of this is 5/8 of an inch, so this is the positional adjustment to apply to the curb profile at each end, to keep the grooves centered about nice, even grids every 16 feet.

2. Move the copy an inch and a quarter. This gives two profile curves that are separated by a groove's width.

3. Now move both profiles back 5/8 of an inch. This centers the profiles on the major grid (in this case, around X=0).

   At this point, it's a good idea to create the groove profile curve. Because you might block the groove with a filler, you could just make a quarter-inch radius on either side. However, this runs the risk that a gap might occur—besides, it makes two surfaces for each groove instead of one.

4. Using grid snap again (to ensure that the new groove profile exactly matches up to the curb profile), make a curve shaped like an inverted hat (see Figure 8.5). Put it at a location where it exactly connects to a curb profile curve edit point (ideally, at a spot where the curve is locally flat, especially if that's at an end). It's not necessary to go as deep as real grooves, though, so limit the hat depth to less than 1 inch, to avoid self-intersection in the leading edge of the curb.

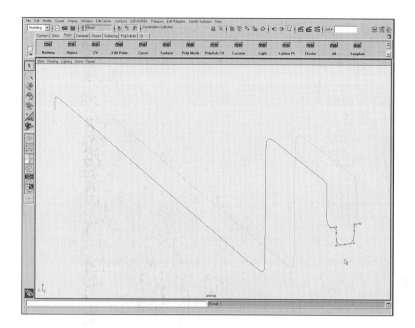

Figure 8.5   Groove and curb profile curves.

5. Create the groove surface by extruding the groove profile along the curb profile.

Close inspection of the result shows that the surface is still self-intersecting in the areas of the quarter-inch radii on the curb profile (see Figure 8.6). Because these will render badly, they need to be fixed.

The simplest fix for self-intersecting surfaces is just to move or scale the CVs involved so that their hulls no longer cross. The surface follows the shape of the hulls, so repairing the hulls repairs the surface itself.

6. Select each hull, in turn, that overlaps in the corners. It's probably easiest to rotate them out from the corner first and then scale them to compensate for the fore-shortening effect of the rotation. Lattices are another alternative for this kind of repair, offering easy shearing of surface CVs.

When the hulls have been fixed, the groove surface is ready to be propagated for building the curb surface.

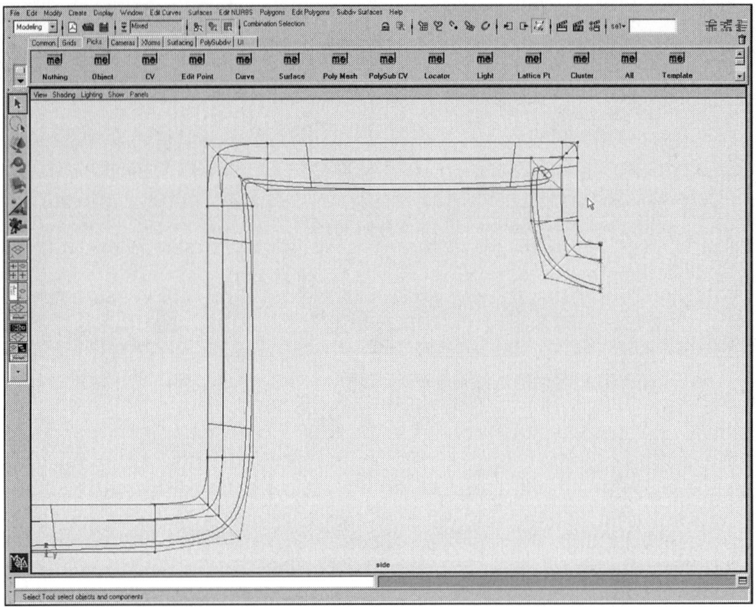

Figure 8.6 Self-intersection in the groove surface.

Tip

To see just the hulls on a NURBS surface, turn off the surface geometry display with Display, Object Display, No Geometry, or select the geometry and enter the MEL command `toggle-state off -geometry`.

Before we build lots of other geometry based on this new groove surface, we should first see if the numbers all work out. We're going to need enough curbs and sidewalk squares to cover sections of straight road, plus more to go around the corners. That means we have 276 (300 – 24) feet of straight road, which is 69 sidewalk squares long. Because this doesn't match up well with 16-foot curb sections, let's tweak the overall block length to 312 feet, which creates 72 sidewalk squares and 18 curb sections along each 288-foot straight section.

To maintain consistency with these larger dimensions, a quick modification is needed to the underlying street template.

7. Set the working units to feet and use a 4-foot grid (primarily for visual confirmation).

8. Select the sidewalk polymeshes and street-corner cylinders at the east ends of all four blocks, and move them 12 feet more to the east.

9. Select the polymesh vertices at the east ends of the Main Street sidewalks and move them 12 feet east. Using the Relative mode in the Status Line's numeric input field (Alt+` is the default Maya hotkey to direct input to this field) an easy way to move all these vertices at once.

10. Select both of the eastern blocks and move them another 12 feet to the east.

11. Move the sidewalk polymesh on the east side of T Street 24 feet to the east.

   Now the underlying template is sized correctly (at least, for ease of modeling) and we've got one good groove surface in hand. The surfaces for the remaining grooves and straight sections can be fleshed out to quickly provide all the curbs needed:

12. The curbs will be easiest to handle on their own level, so make sure you have a Curbs layer and assign the first groove to it. Also ensure that the Use Current Layer box is checked under the Layer Editor's Options menu so that each new section of curb that you make is automatically placed there.

13. Select the groove surface and name it curbGroove1. Copy it 16 feet to the east.

Tip

Set characteristics that you'll care about, such as names and sidedness, *before* creating copies so you won't have to spend extra time later setting these for each copy. To promote later sanity, append the first object featured in a series of numbered copies.

14. Create a linear lofted surface between the edges of the two groove surfaces. If you're using Loft as an action (rather than as a tool), isoparameter curves need to be selected; this is easily done via the right mouse button menu. However, it's usually easiest to use Loft as a tool instead.

   Construction history isn't needed (it might even be a nuisance), so turn it off before lofting, or remove it from the result with Edit, Delete by Type, History. Name the resulting surface curbSpan1.

   Because there will be so many of these surfaces, they should have any common characteristics set before they're repeatedly copied.

15. In this case, set the surface to single-sided display. Select both of the grooves and the new curb surface, and then open the Attribute Spreadsheet. Click the Render tab and then the Double Sided column header; then enter **0** or the word **off** in one of the highlighted fields.

16. Turn on a shaded view of the geometry and check that the surfaces are facing the right direction. If not, use Edit NURBS, Reverse Surface Direction to reverse one (not both) of the offending parameter directions, which flips the surface normal.

17. Select the curb surface and create another copy 16 feet to the east (in positive X). Then select both the copied surfaces (one groove and one curb span) and make the remaining copies needed (Duplicate with Transform is great for this) to complete the block. The reference layer geometry can be used as a guide, or the precise number of copies needed can be worked out (13 to the east, 3 to the west, if you do things the way I did). Be sure that there's a groove surface at each end of the long straight sections.

A straight, block-long section of finished curb is now in place, as shown in Figure 8.7 (and found in the file StraightCurb.ma).

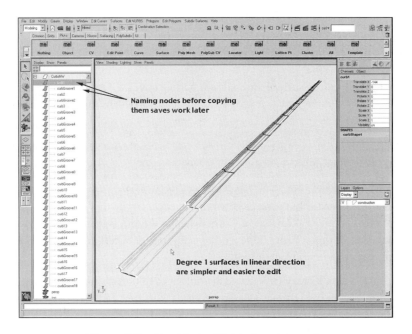

Figure 8.7 One block of finished straight curb.

The corner curb surfaces need to be constructed next:

18. Select the isoparameter curve at the far side of the most-distant terminal groove surface. Duplicate this curve using Edit Curves, Duplicate Surface Curves.

19. With the curve selected, open up the Revolve tool and set it to revolve 90° around the Z-axis, with four segments.

You can either set the curve's pivot location ahead of time or specify the desired pivot location using the Preset option in the Pivot section. The pivot location should be at the end of the curve, aligned with the edge of the groove surface (not its center), even though this nudges us off of the nominal 4-foot grid by 5/8 of an inch. You could nudge it back if it mattered, but it's currently important that the sidewalk blocks match up to the grooves properly.

Create the revolved surface and name it curbCorner1.

Tip

To set an object's pivot, invoke a transform command (Move, Rotate, or Scale) with the object selected, then set the object's pivot using the Insert key during the command. Don't transform the object, though—just set its pivot and tap the Insert key again. This doesn't work with components such as CVs, however, because the temporary component pivot location is forgotten when any components are deselected.

20. Select the last curbGroove surface, and then copy and rotate it around the corner to abut with the revolved surface. This creates a groove for a north-south curb.

21. Copy and rotate a single curbSpan surface and place it in position, next to the groove from the previous step. This begins a north-south section of curb.

22. Select both the preceding curbGroove and curbSpan surfaces, and copy and translate as many copies as needed to complete the curb sections at the intersection.

23. Duplicate and transform these intersection-related curb surfaces to complete the corner at the other end of the straight curb on Main Street. This should complete an entire section of curb for one block.

24. Group all the curb surfaces on this block and call the group curbsNW. Make mirrored copies on the south side of the street and for the two blocks to the east. Name each of these in a similar fashion (after their compass point directions).

Finally, create the far east and west curbs (down at the ends of the main street):

25. Select a north-south curbGroove surface and its neighboring curbSpan surface. Duplicate these surfaces and take them out of their curbs group with Edit, Unparent. When you do this, set the Unparent method to Parent to World, and make sure Preserve Position is checked.

26. Regroup these surfaces and name the group curbsE or curbsW, whichever applies (based on their final destination). Move this new group into position, and then select its surfaces and create as many translated copies (each 16 feet apart) as needed to complete whatever curb might be visible on Ocean Drive or T Street.

27. Make a mirrored copy of the curb group and move it into position down along the other north-south street.

Voilà! A complete set of curbs and gutters is now in place (see Figure 8.8) and is found in CurbsAndGutters.ma. These will later be grouped as needed with other set elements.

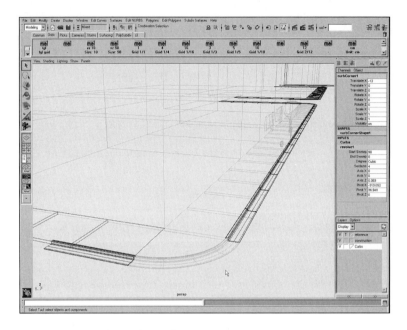

Figure 8.8 Completed curbs and gutters.

Sidewalks

Filling in the sidewalks is the next priority, which we'll tackle in Exercise 8.2.

Exercise 8.2 Creating Sidewalks

The approach in this exercise will be similar to that used for the curbs, creating the grooves and flats separately (with some additional choices to make at the street corners).

1. Once again, create a layer (Sidewalks) for the new geometry and make it active. It's easy enough to assign geometry to layers after the fact, but developing the habit of doing it early tends to save some time and housekeeping effort later.

2. Model the sidewalk grooves with the same profile curve as the curb grooves because they should have a similar profile (especially where they meet up with each other). However, this profile won't be driven along the entire edge of the sidewalk block—only the straight parts. Although there are other ways of creating these square blocks, this approach should make it easier to handle the corners.

3. Recalling that the curb groove profile is three quarters of an inch wide, with a quarter-inch radius, assume that the quarter-inch radius is typical (including the vertical edges at the block's corners). Place a pair of these profile curves along the block edge (see Figure 8.9) so that you can loft a straight groove surface between them.

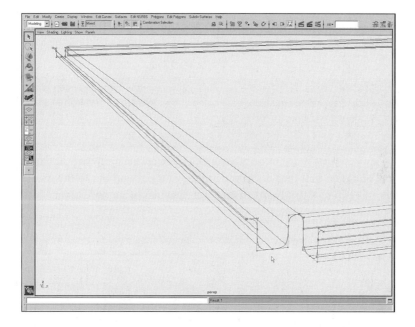

Figure 8.9   Sidewalk groove construction.

4. Copy and rotate until all the straight groove edges are put in place. All the groove edges should touch their neighbors at the corners of the block and fully bound the large, flat area in the middle. Create this flat area by simply lofting a linear surface across a pair of opposing groove edges.

5. To make the block corners, revolve the groove profile to create a quarter-inch radius surface.

Select an existing groove profile curve (or duplicate one from a groove edge surface). Set its pivot to the inner endpoint (the end touching the block) of the curve.

6. Decide whether you'd rather detach half of the curve before doing the revolve or detach half of the resulting surface afterward (I generally choose the former).

7. Revolve the profile curve 90° around its corresponding corner. A two-span surface is optimal, being both round enough and simple.

The rounded edge at the bottom of each groove corner surface leaves a diamond-shaped hole (when there are four of them meeting there) that might need filling. There are a few distinct options for doing this, if necessary (remember, these grooves are often filled by either dirt or filler strips).

One approach to closing up the holes might be to use diamond-shaped patches, but in that case the patch corners would be degenerate (when U and V are collinear, the surface normal is undefined). But because degenerate areas are likely to cause shading or rendering problems, another method should be found.

Warning

Avoid creating degenerate surfaces, where possible. Whenever the angle between U and V is undefined or when they are collinear, the surface normally is effectively undefined and shading difficulties or rendering artifacts are likely.

8. The approach we'll use is to split the two-span corners into two single-span surfaces, and then pull the CVs in the middle of the round out to the theoretical corners (see Figure 8.10). Name them along the lines of grooveCorner1 so that they're easy to select.

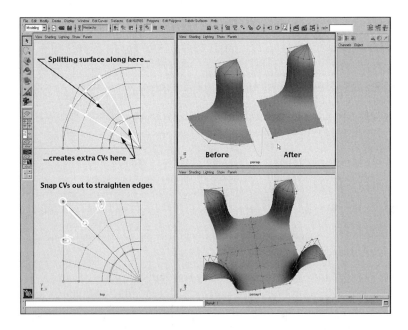

Figure 8.10   Closing corner holes by splitting and pulling CVs.

The holes could also be filled by putting in a plane at the bottom level of the groove. This is by far the simplest method. Although it theoretically should not ever intersect the corner radii surfaces (which immediately begin to rise up from the level of the hole), you'd want some confirmation from render tests, just to be sure. If you can't just use a plane, the corner-splitting approach becomes your best choice.

Fill in the grooves so you can see how the filler strip looks and make your decision about the holes.

9. Make a polygonal cube of the appropriate size (48 inches × 3/4 inch × 1 inch) to fit in the groove. Delete the bottom face from this cube. Place it into the groove so that its top is a quarter inch below the sidewalk surface.

10. Use facePathSplit to add an extra row of edges to the sides of this cube. Use it again to add three extra rows across the long dimension of the cube. Select and move the outer two new rows of poly vertices out to a quarter inch from the ends.

11. Convert this poly cube to a subdivision surface. It will have soft edges along the sides and ends. This poly-box method is a quick and easy way to create soft-edge box shapes via subdivision surfaces. Although sundiv creases could also be used, rows of CVs along edges provide finer corner radius control.

From placing a few of these filler strips, you can see that the hole in the groove isn't visible, so the method of filling them in is moot. This is great news—we'll have less geometry at the corners than expected if we use the filler strips.

The flat surface on top, the groove edges, and the corner surfaces could then be duplicated and translated 48 inches in Y into position next to the first, and then once more (Duplicate With Transform once more). Then this 12-foot row (the width of the sidewalk) could be copied and moved to make another row, and so on. However, this all makes for a *huge* number of surfaces because every block has nine surfaces—and there are a whole lot of blocks!

A superior method in a case like this is to use a single subdivision surface instead. Yep, one subdiv can be made that incorporates an entire set of sidewalk blocks. You don't even need to back up (see the file SidewalkBlock.ma for another way to generate this polymesh).

12. Select all nine of the block surfaces (the top, four sides, and four corners). Use Modify, Convert, NURBS to Polygons to generate polymeshes for them. Be sure that the tessellation method is Control Points.

13. Hide the original surfaces so that they won't be in the way for the following operations.

14. Use Polygons, Combine to combine these meshes into a single polymesh. Combine can do this all in one step, so select them all and invoke it.

15. Select the CVs of this mesh (perhaps by just using Edit Polygons, Selection, Convert Selection to Vertices) and use Edit Polygons, Merge Vertices to merge the vertices along the edges of the original polymeshes.

    If you find that the vertices won't merge, it's almost surely because the neighboring faces from different original meshes point in opposing directions. Use Edit Polygons, Normals, Conform to get all of the faces in the new mesh to agree on the normal direction; then try to merge the vertices again.

16. Now almost all that remains is some more copying, combining, and vertex merging. However, the groove corners first need to be squared up. Just pull them out in X and Y to align them with the CVs on the straight sides. This makes the entire polymesh appear square when seen from above.

17. Duplicate this mesh a couple of times, moving each one 48 inches in Y so that it abuts the previous one. Select all three polymeshes, combine them, and merge their vertices. You now have one strip across the sidewalk

18. Do the same thing in X, making as many copies as needed to complete the entire sidewalk mesh from one street corner to the next. Once they're all combined and their vertices are merged, only one step remains.

19. Finally, convert the polymesh to a subdivision surface with Modify, Convert, Polygons to Subdiv. It's ready for action now (and in the file SubdivSidewalk.ma).

A straight section of sidewalk is now ready—as a single piece of geometry. Not only will this be more efficient and less confusing, but these subdivs also offer some extra flexibility, as you'll see later.

It's a good idea to name this straight sidewalk something like sidewalkStraight1 before propagating it around to create the other straight sections. Making shorter runs of sidewalk for the north-south streets is just a simple matter of deleting unwanted poly faces.

The curved corners are a little tricky. Because it's our own design, we could choose to revolve each of the three sidewalk rows around the corner (creating concentric rings), or we could just continue with square blocks and lop off what overlaps at the curb. The deciding factor might be the aesthetics of how that overlap looks or how easy one technique is versus the other.

Keeping in mind that these corners are never seen closely, let's first look at the overlap (see Figure 8.11).

With nine blocks overlapping a circular edge, a tiny triangle is left midway along the curb edge. It's no harder to construct than any of the other areas are, but it looks a little funny. One alternative might be to join it up to one of the blocks next to it.

On the other hand, if we use concentric rings, the outer edge of the outer ring is about 18 feet long (considerably longer than the 4-foot standard block length). We could divide up the interior of the rings into sections. This would look nice, but it might be problematic to keep the grooves straight and match the curb's curvature.

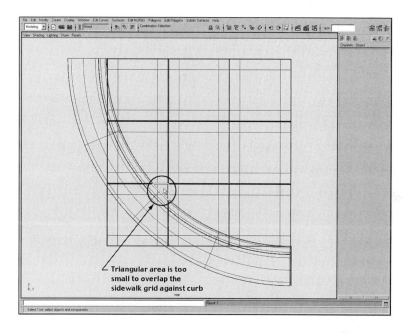

Figure 8.11 Sidewalk grid overlap pattern with round curb.

The straight-gridded approach requires that we lay down the geometry for the nine blocks and then trim away what we don't want (by projecting the edge of the curb-to-sidewalk groove onto the blocks). We should also create corners at these locations by revolving the groove profile the correct amount to blend with that curb-to-sidewalk groove.

The concentric approach is simple if we don't subdivide the flats—just revolve the grooves and patch across. However, if we want to subdivide the flats, we'll also need to construct some dividing grooves, lay them in at the correct angles and locations, trim back the flats, and construct corners.

Because both thorough approaches involve projecting trim curves and creating fussy little corners, we'll punt and take the easy way out for now: simple concentric revolved surfaces (see Figure 8.12). If we have the time later, we'll go back and make them beautiful.

One more thing needs to be added—er, removed. Some sidewalk blocks need to be removed to make room for the trees. These blocks will come from the curbside row, but the specific locations can be picked out later.

Removing these is easy because faces can be easily deleted from the subdivision surface mesh. Just select the big face at the center of the block to remove, grow the selection three times, and delete these faces. Presto! Had this been a single NURBS surface, we'd be out of luck (well, it'd certainly be more trouble).

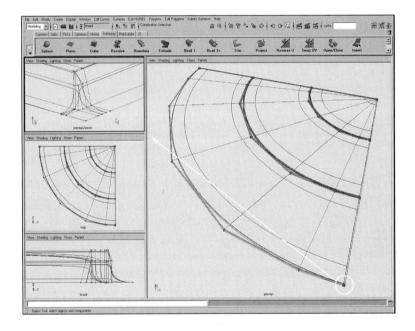

Figure 8.12   Simplest solution for sidewalk corners.

Because the mesh for the sidewalk was carefully constructed, the sides of the neighboring blocks still look appropriate. We're probably going to use grates over the openings anyway, so this might not be a problem. But even if we resort to an open dirt surface, all we'll really have to do is keep the dirt level above the groove bottom, and things will look fine.

This same face-selection technique provides one other handy advantage of using a subdiv: Any block can be selected and subtly tilted. This breaks up excessive linearity and makes the sidewalk seem more real. It also does this without opening up any cracks in the sidewalk grooves.

Streets

Finally, a truly simple element!

Having already decided what size to make the street (50 feet wide) and at what level (6 inches below the sidewalk), it's a simple matter to lay down some flat surfaces spanning between the curbs.

The curb has an outer gutter edge that's intentionally deeper than the street, to allow the street to intersect it. We need to make sure that the street actually interpenetrates this edge, so that any displacement of the curb doesn't leave a gap.

We'll place a linear NURBS plane and size it up to match up to the street width (50 feet, plus a little bit) and straight curb length (276 feet exactly). By making it this size, it opens up the possibilities of painting textures for it directly (although I don't know yet how we'll do the street's shading). To make each section easy to identify, we'll name these like our original sketch, such as MainStreetW.

The intersections are also created as planes, except that they need to be wider to accommodate the extra width of two sidewalks. So, a precisely 74-foot (one 50' street + two 12' sidewalks) plane is placed in each of the three intersections, which completes the street surfaces. Each is named to describe its location, as in MainAndOcean.

It should be noted that even though I don't know about the shaders that will be associated with the geometry I'm creating, I make a new shader for each likely material, try to ballpark its color and surface finish, and assign the shader to the geometry. This enables me to look at my geometry better than if everything was left as the default Maya gray. At this point, I've created shaders named Concrete and Street, and the scene looks like Figure 8.13 (also found in StreetsAndWalks.ma).

Now that we've got the basic infrastructure in place, we'll move ahead to the other structures that flesh out our set. Several other details can be added to our streets (drains, manhole covers, tree grates), but we'll continue on with the fundamentals before worrying about those.

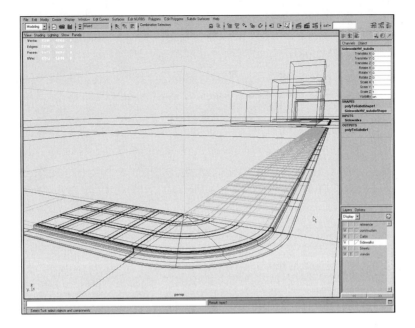

Figure 8.13 Scene with curbs, sidewalks, and streets.

Beach

But first, let's spend a little time on the beach. Not long, just enough to relax and soak up a few rays of the setting sun. Our beach detour takes only long enough to build and sculpt one easy surface.

Although natural terrain can at times be exceedingly complex (and is often best handled by specialized tools), the beach we have in mind is little more than a gently sloping surface leading from the far side of the west sidewalk of Ocean Drive down past the water's edge.

The beach surface *could* be initially created as a 50-foot-wide plane next to the sidewalk, but its shape can be helped along by lofting between a couple of typical section curves. In the long direction (along these curves), 20 spans should be enough. The surface will then need enough control points across it to add some low-frequency undulations (leaving the high-frequency details to a shader), so about 10 spans will do. Because it's a gentle, sandy beach, this should provide plenty of control.

Making these curves is quick and easy. In the Top view, use those 20 spans to create the profile where the water meets the sand. If you'd rather not count out the spans as you go, build a single-span curve, rebuild it up to 20 spans, and then push its CVs into the desired shape. Move this curve down 2 feet in Z to put it into position.

Now copy it and snap all the CVs of this curve over to line up with the beachside edge of the sidewalk. Because this curve is now flat, it needs some shaping. Because it's such a long curve, it can be hard to visualize the undulations being added. So, make this easier by rotating the curve slightly and viewing the foreshortened curve in an orthographic camera (see Figure 8.14); adjust the CVs in Z. Don't use a perspective camera for this—there will be diminished accuracy as distance from the camera's eye position increases. Also, remember to unrotate the curve when you're done.

Another way of accomplishing this is to rotate the orthographic camera itself. For a perspective camera, you'd expect to use the Tumble tool, and it's the same for an orthographic camera. Normally, Orthographic Views is set to Locked (in View, Camera Tools, Tumble Tool), but if you uncheck this option, you can tumble ortho cams, too. If you use this technique, just be very sure that you straighten the view back out and disable ortho tumbling when you don't need it.

Either of these foreshortening techniques is also useful for evaluating the shape of curves or surfaces, particularly if you're checking subtle curves for inflections.

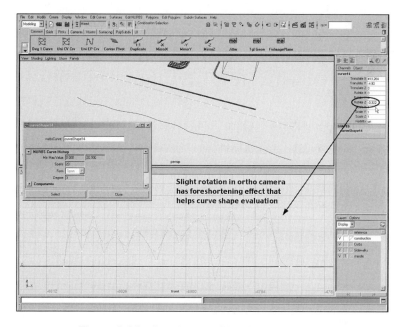

Figure 8.14   Foreshortened beach surface curve.

Construct the beach surface by using Loft to create a 10-span surface between these two curves. To change the resulting ruled surface into something more natural, pinch individual CVs together to produce soft crests, and push other CVs downward (using the Move Normal tool, perhaps) to create depressions in the sand. A suitable beach surface can be pulled into shape quickly (see Figure 8.15). My result is found in the file SculptedBeach.ma.

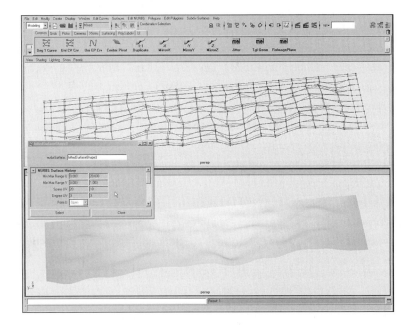

Figure 8.15 Sculpted beach surface.

Sloping down just a couple of feet to the water's edge, the beach surface should continue out far enough to ensure that the irregular surface of the water (to be provided later with Fluid Effects) won't reveal the sand's edge. Near the water's edge, we want to leave the beach surface smooth because the ocean would do the same. It's a simple matter to use Edit NURBS, Extend Surfaces, to extend the beach surface edge out into the water.

Although we could have used Maya's Artisan features to paint the surface shape—pushing, pulling, and smoothing it into shape—it seemed like too much tool for the job. In just a few relaxing minutes, the whole surface can be fine-tuned to our satisfaction with everyday tools.

Now take one more sip from your piña colada and let's get back to the city.

Building Buildings

I've always thought it odd that the finished product of the act of building is itself called a "building." Shouldn't it be called a "built" instead? But because we have this same linguistic quirk with paintings, carvings, and recordings, it doesn't seem likely to change. I'll have to content myself with building buildings, and then telling myself that they're really built. Fortunately, building them in Maya is a lot easier than building the real thing.

Planning Department

We've got simple stand-ins already that lay out the masses we'd like to achieve. This is a commercial zone in an Art Deco town, one that hasn't had the benefit of elaborate planning. Starting with a few simple drawings and some reference material about Deco style gleaned from the web, this neighborhood needs to come together quickly, but with some flair.

The buildings on Main Street are all two or three floors tall. Central to our project are the gift store and the pet store, both of which will be seen clearly from the front. All the other buildings will serve only as a backdrop against which our story is set. In their design, little needs to be done to make them look like particular kinds of stores, but there should be a common design aesthetic.

To the west, there are no buildings, just beach and open water. To the east, T Street closes off much of the view beyond, although some other evidence of a larger city lies beyond. Rather than build more city, though, we'll use a painted flat to provide any rooftops or skyscrapers we decide we need.

The critical factor in getting our two blocks of buildings to look as if they have a similar style is to use a shared palette of architectural elements. Conveniently, this is also a way to gain some efficiency in the modeling process. It's much faster to resize and reshape elements such as doors, windows, and cornices than to have to build each one fresh. In addition, the selection of Art Deco as the design inspiration is practical because it's a style based on simple forms with little extra adornment.

Common design elements for Art Deco designs (see Figure 8.16) include curved corners, long vertical and horizontal lines (from the "streamlining" influence), flat awnings, simple cornices, windows wrapping around corners, and several recurring decorative motifs. Not all of these details will make their way into our hero buildings, but most can find a place in the rest of the background buildings.

Figure 8.16 Common Art Deco design elements.

Working primarily in NURBS, we'll block in the major building forms and then progressively refine the shapes as needed. Every corner will likely have a radius, to pick up highlights and allow for any displacement that is desired. We'll also use some of the elements (such as the awnings) to cover up any shortcuts we take. Some additional items will be purely decorative, meant only to punch up the design a bit.

Solid Foundations

The place to start is the corner nearest the main action, the area with the two shops featured in our story. We'll look at how to construct the gift shop simply, but with some style.

First, a few words are needed about the construction of a typical building. As long as there are flat walls involved, the following approach is likely to succeed in building them up (no pun intended) and adding the desired details.

For walls, radiused corners (where needed) are put in place first. A quarter-cylinder with two spans is all that's needed, but Maya doesn't let you create that directly (four sections are the allowed minimum), so a circle or cylinder must be chopped up. For this, I usually just create a circle (because Maya's primitive cylinders don't offer different degrees in U and V), select edit points that delimit the section I want, and invoke the Detach Curves tool.

Created in a Top view, this resulting circle is on the XY zero plane. However, I usually want it down below the zero plane (because I don't want to see a gap beneath the building), so I lower it a couple of inches to ensure that it's closed with respect to the sidewalk edge (and not aligned with curb or sidewalk features).

The quarter-circle is duplicated and the duplicate is moved up as far as necessary to create a long building edge. The height value isn't critical at this point because it can be adjusted as needed later. Loft a linear surface between these two curves, and the edge is ready. You'll probably also find it useful to slightly exaggerate the radius so that the edges don't look too sharp.

The wall edge is duplicated and moved down to the other end of the wall. Walls are then created by lofting a linear surface between these edges. This simple kind of wall blank and its edges (see Figure 8.17) can provide the foundation for much of the exterior work ahead. We can copy these surfaces and then rescale or move edges for numerous other wall segments.

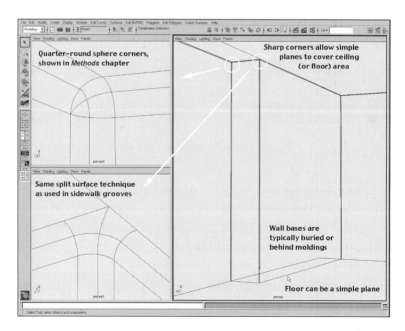

Figure 8.17   Basic wall blank with edges.

Working around ordinary windows in such walls is done by first pulling the top edge of the wall surface down to the level of the window bottom. Then duplicate the wall surface and move it up to sit atop the previous wall. Adjust the copy's top edge to the height of the window top. Finally, the process is repeated once more to make the wall above the window. This creates a three-layer wall (see Figure 8.18): one layer below the window, another at window level, and another above the window.

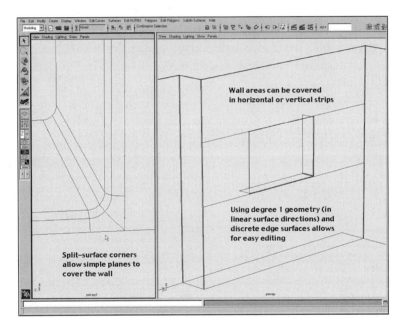

Figure 8.18 Three-layer basic wall.

Having said all that about typical wall and window setups, this model isn't typical. For starters, the windows are round, not rectangular, so the layered wall approach doesn't work (at least, not nearly as easily). The window openings in our gift shop model will be created by projecting circular curves onto the wall surfaces and trimming out the holes.

I considered several design ideas trying to incorporate the Deco style without making more work for myself than I could handle. The first design in Maya (see Figure 8.19) got things rolling in the right direction, and it evolved into the final design (see Figure 8.20 or the file GiftShop.ma) rapidly.

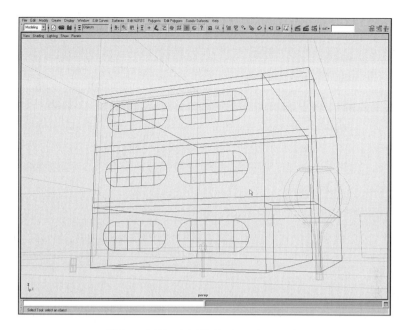

Figure 8.19   Initial gift shop design idea.

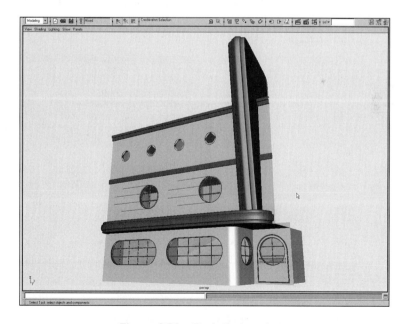

Figure 8.20   Final gift shop design.

Most of the rest of the buildings can be set up with the standard approach. Because we'd like to have a similar style throughout, we can copy many walls and corners around, moving edges and rescaling corner radii as needed. This leaves us with a series of facades, each with cutouts for the windows and doors. We can distinguish among our buildings by varying the number of floors, positions, and styles of the doors and windows, shaders, signage, and the many small distinctive details that buildings possess.

Details, Details

So far, we've just dealt with the broad strokes of setting up the building forms, with no particular concern for the fine details that will distinguish one building or business from another. Although there are more details in our final scene than will be covered here (because it would probably make for a couple hundred rather dry pages of reading), this section briefly covers some typical examples of the details we've included.

Invariably, it's the attention to details that makes a design (and a project) work well. In our *Parking Spot* project, we attempt to draw the line between creating a stylized, yet credible world and handling an entire project with very limited manpower resources. We trust that you'll find both our strategies and our results satisfying, at whatever level of detail you choose to examine it.

Doors

The shop doors figure prominently in our story, so they need to be suitably realistic, without adding more modeling work than necessary. Deco designs were very fond of glass doors with stylized handles, so that's what we'll use here—but it has the potential for adding a lot of interior work. To avoid the extra work, we'll create an alcove inside the door and use it (and the late afternoon shadows) to minimize what we can see inside.

The first step is to block in the alcove. Because we'll never see any detail inside, we don't even need to create radiused corners. The alcove is essentially just a floor and a back wall, with maybe a baseboard down at the bottom of the wall. Off to the left of the door, we might make some of the shop's interior visible, but gift stores are notoriously cluttered and we don't feel like having to model a bunch of gifts simply as filler. So, by limiting our view into the shop, we reduce our workload (and perhaps figuratively leave the door open for a simpler story point than a last-minute gift store).

With our simple alcove in place, we then create the doorframe by extruding rounded rectangular profiles. We could join them with mitered corners (as shown in Chapter 7), but the only such corners in our model are down in the lower corners, almost out of sight. As a simpler alternative, these inconspicuous corners are mitered but not attached. Although a standard door is 80 inches tall, we'll make the doorframe for the gift shop quite a bit higher, using 108 inches instead.

On either side of the doorframe, we could use a simple linear plane to close up the space. However, because the door never has to open, it's quicker to simply make the door and wall from a single surface, trimming out the window area. Radiused corners can be placed at the intersection of walls to blend one into the other.

We'll skip the details of adding a hinge, glass panel, and handle, but note that we'll continue to apply soft edges throughout wherever they'll be noticed. Our finished door (shown in Figure 8.21) is simple, but consistent with our style objectives.

An ordinary door could be copied around to do duty (sometimes double-duty) in any other buildings where doors show. Minor tweaks would be made to handles and panel shapes, but we'd leverage our investment and try not to spend time wondering if viewers will notice. Of course, because this door is distinctive, it will be only in this one shop.

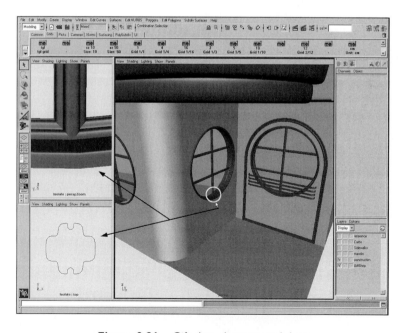

Figure 8.21 Gift shop doorway and door.

Windows

A shop is basically a sales display area, and no area is more important for display than the storefront window. Potential customers are enticed to enter the store by what they see through this window, so it must serve not only an architectural function, but also a sales function. Although we're trying to be conservative in our modeling requirements, there's no avoiding the need for the shop window to be attractive and functional.

What visually connects our window to the door area is the overhanging "awning," which is really just a flat platform jutting out from the building. This simple detail integrates the window area with the doorway.

Construction of this detail is easy. A profile curve is constructed in an orthographic window, as is a path curve. The path curve is perfectly straight along most of its length and is circularly curved at the ends (for shape control and capping off the area, I've used three separate curves). Then the profile is extruded along the path, creating the leading edge of the awning (see Figure 8.22). This "streamlined" profile reinforces the Deco style and mirrors the shape of the curved doorway entrance below.

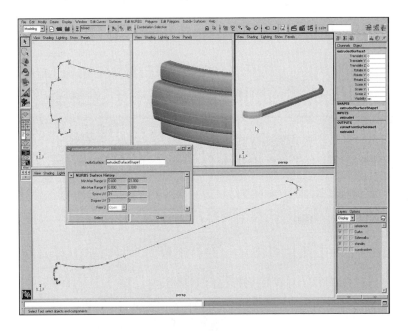

Figure 8.22 Awning construction.

The top and bottom surfaces of the awning are easily made by snipping out the straight section of the path curve and lofting between the two (now separate) curve ends. Another approach might be to simply loft between an unbroken path curve and a straight curve created between its two endpoints. For extra realism, the awning could be pulled slightly away from the wall and a small radius could be run around its wall edge to blend it into or separate it from the wall.

Deco windows are typically set back from the wall surfaces, so we'll give this look by running a deep frame (similar to the doorframe) around the opening. Then this broad opening is divided into individual panes by placing slender surfaces, first vertically with one size mullion, and then horizontally with more slender muntins. By ensuring that the muntins are a bit smaller than the mullions, we avoid any problems with coincident surfaces where they intersect.

Note

The major vertical section dividers in a window assembly are known as *mullions*, while the smaller pane dividers are called *muntins*. Mullions are big, like millions

Finally, we put in the glass as a single large plane, and we have our display window (see Figure 8.23).

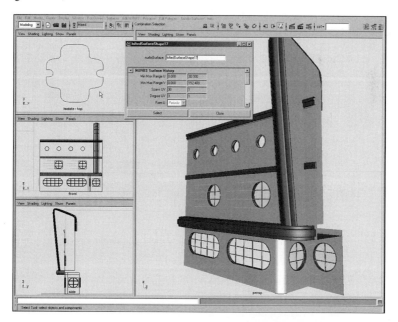

Figure 8.23   Shop front window.

But what's behind it?

To get away as cheaply as possible, we construct a display that is essentially the inside of a box (without a top or front side). The bottom of this box meets the inside bottom edge of the window frame and provides a surface for placing displayed items. The sides of the display area are the walls of the store, while the back is a simple backdrop extending up to about eye level (see Figure 8.24).

Over this we might see silhouetted figures, but we will surely see the inside walls of the store. Although we will use lighting (or the lack of it) to hide the interior, we need to put in some planes to complete the inner walls and ceiling.

The remaining windows on the various buildings are created in a similar manner, with many of the elements simply grabbed from this window and resized, removed, or duplicated. Some of these windows have round motifs and some are built around corners, but all have a common structure of frame, mullions, muntins, and panes (plus, upstairs windows might have sills or ledges). Each building, too, must have interior walls where needed to prevent its windows from showing the endless nothingness (or the next block over) behind them. With the addition of some simple curtains or blinds, the windows are completed.

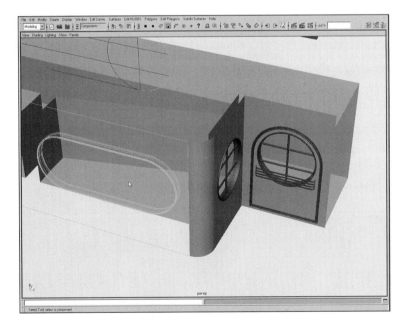

Figure 8.24 Shop display area.

Trim and Infrastructure

Many other small details ultimately sell the set as a credible city scene. Exterior building walls typically have footings at the bottom and cornices at the top. These details are usually quite simple (although in some architectural styles they can be ornate), and our Deco style lends itself to the use of simple extruded shapes for them. When they change direction, we just miter the corners, leaving rounded edges. We can make just a few basic variations and copy them around onto different buildings.

A few downspouts can be added to the sides of the buildings, if for nothing more than to add some visual texture to the scene. They're easy to make as simple extruded shapes, so they're cheap enough to barely be noticed on our budget's bottom line.

Street signs and streetlights provide an opportunity for some more creative expression, so they're designed to have a clean look consistent with an Art Deco feel. Both are essentially revolved shapes with additional adornment—the lights with their lamp housings and the signs with their sign panels.

Grooving along the shafts of each can be done in the models, sparing the shading person yet another detail. To do this, a revolved surface is first created from a profile curve, with careful attention to the number of spans used. To put eight grooves in a shaft, some multiple of eight spans must be used.

Selecting CVs along the section of the shafts we need grooved (we want them only along the long, tapering part) can be done by using clipping planes in a Top view.

Tip

To make a camera's clipping planes easily adjustable without going into the Attribute Editor, make them keyable (using the Channel Control window). This makes them show up in the Channel Box and permits easy adjustment (especially in conjunction with a hotkey for selecting the active camera).

These CVs can then be scaled as needed to make the grooves, by scaling them in or out on two of three axes.

Tip

To quickly perform scaling of CVs in only two axes, select the CVs and use the Scale command interactively. Hold down the Ctrl key and select the manipulator on the axis you *don't* want to be scaled. The other two axes will then uniformly scale together.

Street lamps can be constructed in the upright position and then can be bent over using a bend deformer (lattices can also work well). Adding the grooves to the tapering shaft and then bending it (see Figure 8.25), makes the selection of groove CVs much simpler and it's more accurate than adding grooves them to an already bent shaft.

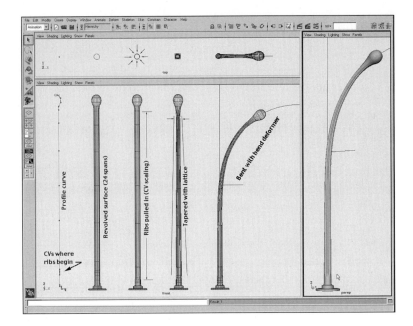

Figure 8.25   Evolution of a street-lamp shaft.

Assorted extra details are added to season the scene to taste, and then it's time to package up our creation and ship it on its way.

Pass It On

After your set model has been constructed, you should prepare it for downstream use. Even if you will be the only Maya user to lay your hands on it, taking some time to organize and double-check things now will almost certainly pay off later.

First, give the model some structure. Make it possible to turn on or off any reasonable portion of it by grouping and naming major subsections. For a model such as our city scene, start by dividing it up into blocks, streets, and sidewalks. Then divide each of these into smaller components, such as dividing blocks into buildings, buildings into facades, and facades into walls, doorways, and windows.

Naming subobjects of such highly structured models should follow some easily identified rules. Compass directions are a good idea, even if the assignment of directions is arbitrarily chosen based on where they appear to be (such as in a Top view). In *Parking Spot*, we've designated the compass directions meaningfully (having considered the sun's direction and the time of day), but even if we hadn't, we could have used street names or building identities as a naming basis.

Just try to be consistent and assume that someone might want to turn on or off some parts of the scene. You certainly don't want Maya or the renderer to spend CPU cycles needlessly considering parts of the scene that won't be seen or used in the final image.

One powerful means of partitioning set models is by file referencing. This amounts to loading up model files much like a compositor loads up images. Even if your model has been built monolithically, with every object part of a single Maya scene file, you can easily divide it up by selecting the objects you'd like to move elsewhere and using the File, Export Selection command (see Figure 8.26). If you'd like to remove the objects but automatically set up a reference to them, check the Keep Only a Reference option box.

File referencing can also help interactive performance substantially by enabling you to use a low-resolution version of a model (such as the blocking models we initially created at the start of this chapter) instead of the high-resolution version used for final renders. You can use the Reference Editor to turn on or off the versions you need, as you need them. In this way, stand-in models for sets are easily provided as a natural by-product of the modeling workflow.

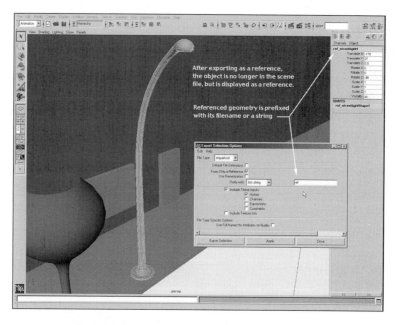

Figure 8.26   Exporting an object as a reference.

One more good reason for using file referencing is that your production might have the luxury of a whole team of people working simultaneously on a set (unlike our little project). By using file referencing, you can each access the latest versions of each other's models. You share an environment that protects you from altering each other's work, yet it provides all the detail you need, as if the other objects were a part of your own model.

Although you might be able to protect your model from others altering it inadvertently, you can't protect it from the director's hands. Expect changes.

No matter how carefully planned a story or a shot is, some elements are sure to change. Whether it's a fix to correct a minor compositional problem, a story point requiring a new gag, or a corner being cut for budgetary reasons, your set should be built in a way that allows changes to be easily made. Usually this just means ensuring that your geometry has a reasonable hierarchical structure and avoids needlessly busy data, so much of this comes for free with good work habits. But if you build a data-heavy, disorganized mess of a set model, it's a virtual lock that fate will send a slew of changes its way.

Summary

Creating effective sets is usually an optimization problem. A story needs a place to occur, but computer animation doesn't have the luxury of simply packing up the cameras and going on location. Instead, everything must be fabricated to serve the story's needs. Rather than let the problem of creating large sets get out of hand by trying to build everything to a realistic level of detail, we plan our work to add details where they matter and skip them where they don't.

Some set optimizations are achieved in advance, by keeping the story requirements under control. Others are achieved by utilizing geometry that is as lightweight, accurate, and editable as possible. Still more efficiency is gained by reusing as much existing geometry as possible, thus avoiding redundant geometry construction. A workflow that is structured in a top-down fashion can help to keep the attention to details from derailing the need to literally cover lots of ground. Finally, it's important to set up your sets for effective downstream use by making them easily navigable and efficient.

In many cases, sets can be relatively easy modeling exercises, despite their large size. The challenge of effective set modeling then becomes creating an adaptable set that gives the necessary impression of style and detail, without spending inordinate resources on their construction.

Besides setting the location, look, and era for the story, when the sets are in place, several other activities can commence. Layout, lighting, set dressing, and animation all depend on the stage truly being set. As much as any Hollywood director, the Maya director longs for three little words—words that make only sense after the set is ready:

"Lights, camera, action!"

Chapter 9
Props

By Mark Adams

Almost any animation piece created using 3D software such as Maya will require that some (often many) props be modeled. Props add the detail and clutter of real life to the potentially sterile sets of CG animation. Once the sets have been constructed and the characters have been added to the scene, then props line the shelves, decorate the shop windows, litter the streets, and are handled by the characters. Unless you're making a conversational work such as *My Dinner with André*, you'll probably need to make plenty of props.

Each prop is like a complete little project unto itself. Some easy props can be completed in minutes, while really complex props can take weeks. But despite the wide variety of budgets and levels of importance that individual props possess, there are commonalties in the process of making them.

In this chapter, we'll look at the following:

- General guidelines for modeling props
- Working with modeling artwork
- Modeling some simple props
- Doing surfacing for a complex prop

Basic Prop Guidelines

Like so many of the activities in Maya, the process of modeling props benefits from some early decision making and the use of a routine. The decisions are basic choices of things such as space, orientation, and technique. The routine brings reliability, ensuring that necessary steps are undertaken and that time isn't wasted later, because each prop model requires some spelunking to understand how it should be used.

Although the following work patterns for modeling props will become habit in time, it might help to hang a mnemonic on them. So, for your prop modeling enjoyment and edification, I hereby introduce the *Three S's of Prop Modeling*.

Space

First, a major distinction between props and set models is that set models are typically built *in place*, whereas prop models are built *to be placed* later. From this, it soon becomes apparent that an important aspect of prop models is that they must be easy to place as needed. The effort required to place, scale, and orient a prop model ideally is quite minimal because the model will already have incorporated as much of this data as possible.

To accomplish this, decisions are first typically made about the scale of objects to be used in a production. Usually, this simply means that you build things at their actual sizes. This might seem obvious, but it can be tempting to simply build without regard to the required size, just making the object fit into the default Maya windows. The thinking here is usually, "I'll just scale it as needed later." In general, *don't do it this way*—it puts off the conforming of object scales until later and can result in plenty of surprises when props don't fit the needs of the sets or the characters. It's well worth a small bit of extra time to establish the required size of a prop and build it to be that size.

With that being said, certainly sometimes 1:1 scale isn't appropriate. Planetary voyages, microscopic adventures, and even earthly terrain are often best built at an adjusted scale. On other occasions, tools upstream or downstream from Maya might dictate the application of scaling factors. What's important is that the team agree on that scale so that the models integrate smoothly into your studio's pipeline without causing extra work adjusting each model's scale.

Spatial orientation is also important. Of course, everyone on a project should be in agreement about the up-axis setting, Y-up or Z-up. Props should be built in an orientation that reflects this convention. A bottle that will be placed on a shelf should be built upright, for instance, not as if it were lying on the ground. Similarly, a framed picture is best modeled upright, as if it was ready to hang on a wall (see Figure 9.1).

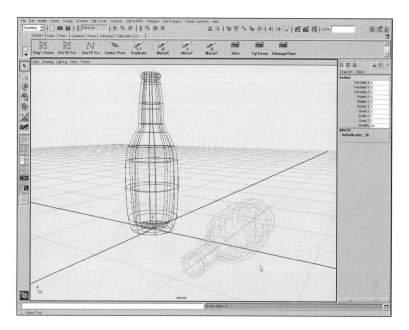

Figure 9.1 Appropriate and inappropriate prop orientations.

Occasionally, a model might be inadvertently built in the wrong view—but if multiple props from one modeler have errant orientations, it's a sure sign that the modeler didn't read the up-axis decision memo.

Props should also be oriented in a way that reflects their usage. If all of the characters are being built to face, say, in the negative Y-axis direction, then a hat for a character should be built to face that same direction. If you're building a hammer that a character will hold, build that hammer so that it's easy to grasp by a character reaching for it. On the other hand, if that hammer is meant to lay on a table, build it so that it's oriented that way from the start.

Of course, some props have multiple uses and no obvious best orientation—but most of the time you can save others downstream a bit of effort by building each prop in the most useful orientation.

Location matters, too. Even though you will usually be placing a prop (or many) in a scene, it's important that the prop be built in a useful location. In the case of the picture frame, you'd probably want to build it around the world origin, with its back up against a zero plane (where X, Y, or Z is 0). In the case of the hat, place it so that it sits on the up-axis zero plane like it was sitting on a tabletop (or a head). Let the expected usage of the prop guide you to locating the prop in space in the most useful position.

So, for most props, build them around the world origin, in the space that best suits their usage. This allows layout artists, set dressers, and animators to work most efficiently when handling them. Of course, if you're acting in all of these roles, the increased efficiency goes to you.

For props that are essentially elaborate one-off set pieces, it's reasonable to build them *in situ* so that no further transformations need be applied once the prop is added to the scene. Of course, if the precise location isn't known, fall back to the previous plan of making the prop easy to place in layout or set dressing.

Tip

One other space is important when modeling props: disk space. Resist the temptation to model all of your props in one Maya project. Build complex props (maybe all props) in their own projects, to keep directories manageable and make file-naming conventions (as discussed in Chapter 4, "Technical Considerations") easy to follow.

Simplicity

Props serve an enormous range of needs. Some are key elements in a story, requiring rich details and perhaps performing hyper-real functions. Other props are mere background dressing, noticed only in their absence or poor implementation. There might be only a few to build, or you might have to somehow cobble together hundreds. In almost all cases, however, striving for simplicity is both laudable and utterly practical.

Simplicity starts at the design phase. Large studios have artists capable of producing prop designs at a prodigious pace; small studios have at least a few heads brimming with design ideas. Besides the obvious need to keep the project under control by not designing too many props, the designs themselves ought to represent economical approaches to achieving the right look. For instance, details that will never be seen can be implied by the visible details but should never be built.

When the prop design has passed into the hands of the modeler, three additional opportunities are available for gaining economy through simplicity. By considering the potential gains of each of these, the prop modeler can magnify his or her contribution to the project.

The first depends on the skills of the modeler at recognizing problematic geometry and suggesting design alternatives. Often a difficult design to implement can be made dramatically easier by making subtle adjustments to shapes, feature locations, and topological characteristics. Usually such changes are welcomed (unless they alter an important characteristic of the model) because less work is usually preferred to more work.

The second opportunity for economy comes from the ability of the modeler to minimize the geometry of the model. An experienced prop modeler won't build a revolved surface with 32 sections when 8 will do. Excess geometry slows down every process it's associated with, from modeling through final rendering. A scrupulous habit of building models with just the necessary amount of data (and no more) should be cultivated. Of course, practicing this habit too actively sometimes conflicts with the need for raw productivity, but it's a goal to be kept in mind nonetheless.

A thorough understanding of modeling methods and their advantages and liabilities (as discussed in Chapter 7, "Methods") is a solid step in the right direction here. A particularly important technique is what I've called feature-based modeling, which stresses having specific reasons for each CV placed and being aware of the topological details of neighboring geometry. Although shapes can be carved almost by force of will (give or take an Artisan brush or some Booleans) from a primitive solid, elegant solutions come from a mix of experience, careful attention to form, and familiarity with the tool set Maya offers.

The third opportunity for economy in modeling is to not model some features at all. This doesn't mean that the features are omitted, but rather that they are passed on ahead to be added during the shading process using bump or displacement maps.

A surprising number of model details are routinely added during shading, particularly when the details are easily painted or described by a procedural shader (see Figure 9.2). Sometimes these are simple details, such as adding grooves on a bottle or knurling on a handle. And although a modeler could, for example, trim out the innumerable small holes in the post of a highway sign, it's a trivial matter to map an image of a filled circle to the transparency channel of a shader, scale it, and move on.

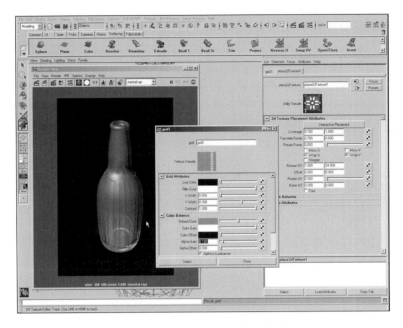

Figure 9.2 Geometric features simulated by shading.

Structure

If you want to use shading to represent a geometric feature, you have to make a special point to create a piece (or more) of geometry and put it in the object's hierarchy for the shader writer to use. This might seem like a special case, but everything in the model should have been created with an eye to making it easily shadeable. Often this is expressed through the naming and grouping of components that make up the model. This is just one way in which the structure of the model is important to the prop modeler.

Structure (or scoping, another fine S-word) refers to naming and grouping the components of a model to make it readily useable. The structure of a prop model allows it to be animated, shaded, lit, and traversed interactively. In many prop models, the structure is minimal, but hero objects rely heavily on a clearly navigable hierarchy.

Of course, animation requires that the model's hierarchy be set up with appropriate grouping and pivots. Maya's parenting and unparenting mechanisms are simple enough that creating the proper structure in a rigidly articulated model (not an oxymoron, strangely enough) is straightforward. Groups can be created or disbanded as needed, and the Outliner can be used to assign relationships interactively.

Tip

Parenting one object to another is often a simple matter of selecting the child(ren) and then the parent, and then pressing p. However, if you don't have the parent selected last, pull down the object list in the Channel Box and select the desired parent to make it the last selection.

Shading and lighting can also make use of the model hierarchy, using component names for selecting parts to assign shaders, link lights, or control visibility. Assigning concise, descriptive names to these subobjects can make clear which components are for which purpose (many models have all of this going on at once).

Even the true components, the surfaces and poly or subdiv meshes, benefit from good naming habits. Not every last surface needs to be assigned a fresh name, of course, but attention to naming for items that need to be identified for the aforementioned purposes will pay dividends later. In the end, a well-constructed model can be understood almost from the Outliner window alone.

When the hierarchy has been set up, model pivots need to also be set properly. This usually matters only for animating components, but pivots are occasionally used for other purposes, too. Pivots need to be set and checked carefully, to ensure proper results.

The typical way to set a pivot in Maya is to invoke a transformation command (like Move or Rotate), tap the Insert key, adjust the pivot location(s), tap Insert again to resume the transform command, and then exit the transform by selecting some other tool (assuming that you were intending only to adjust pivots). This leaves the pivot in the new location—but it leaves the object or component vulnerable to an inadvertent transform, so be careful.

To avoid inadvertent transforms, the Attribute Editor can also be used to set pivots. After selecting an object and opening the Attribute Editor, you can enter the desired pivot locations (there are two—a rotate pivot and a scale pivot) directly in the Pivots section of the object's transform node. You'll probably want to set it in world coordinates, but fields are also provided for entering pivots in the object's local space (notice that changing a pivot in one space also changes it in the other space, because the two spaces are just alternative coordinate systems).

Tip

A different way to set pivots is to access the object pivots directly and then use the Move tool to position them. Each object or component has a .rotatePivot and a .scalePivot attribute (there's no .movePivot attribute, by the way), which can be selected in place of the object and then moved to the desired pivot location.

The MEL command for setting the rotate pivot for an object named foo to the local space origin is as follows:

```
setAttr -e foo.rotatePivot 0 0 0;
```

To set both pivots of all selected objects to the world origin, use this command:

```
xform -ws -rp 0 0 0 -sp 0 0 0;
```

Some production processes (as well as some tools) favor freezing an object's transforms (declaring the object's data to be in the identity transform state), while others lose valuable data when this is done. For instance, a single bolt can be copied many times, but shading it might be easiest if all bolts reference an initial position at the world origin. The transformations that brought the bolts from the origin to their unique individual positions are lost when the identity transform is substituted, resulting in more work when trying to shade them. Still, identity transforms make many situations easier, so your prop models need to leave transforms in an intentional state.

Tip

It's a good idea to freeze transforms only when necessary and only to the minimal amount required (just a subobject, perhaps). Also, if important transforms are being frozen out and there isn't already a file from which you can later get the original transforms, save a clearly named file with an original version of the object(s) before freezing transforms.

Finally, as a rule, don't establish any more hierarchy for model navigation than necessary until the model is nearly complete, if only to not waste time. For most things, the geometry will need to be created before any decisions are made about what to call what. But whenever it's ultimately done, adding appropriate structure to a prop model ensures that it can measure up when it's drawn into service.

Simple Prop Models

We'll begin by making a few relatively simple prop models from the *Parking Spot* project (described in detail in Chapter 2, "Project Overview"). Then in the next section we'll tackle something considerably more complex. Going through this process a few times should make the process of prop modeling clear (we'll also cover a few modeling techniques).

BigBone

Just about the simplest of the props is the big bone that Spot gets from the pet shop. It's a caricatured bone, meant as a tasty reward for a *really* good dog to eat, like an oversize Milk-Bone biscuit.

Exercise 9.1   Building the BigBone

Artwork for such a model is probably unnecessary, so we'll wing it without any drawings.

1. First, create a Maya project called BigBone in which the model files will reside. Most of the standard subdirectories are unnecessary, so create only the Scenes, Shaders, Textures, and Images directories.

Note

Although you can just select Use Defaults in the New Project dialog window, it can be clearer for simple props to just enter names in the few fields that will be needed. In this case, only the Scenes, Shaders, Textures, and Images directories are likely to be needed.

Next, it's time to determine just how big that bone really is. After a few minutes of considering the dog's size, the size of the valve nuts on the hydrant, and what the bone might look like in the store window, a size of about 15 inches long by 3 inches wide by 1 inch thick seems about right.

2. Starting in the Front window (assuming that characters will reach out and grab a vertically oriented bone), create half of the bone profile as a uniform NURBS curve using the CV Curve tool (see Figure 9.3) and adjust its shape until satisfactory. My initial curve is found in the Maya scene BigBoneCurve.ma.

Note that the beginning of the curve is on the YZ plane and the beginning tangent is normal to this plane (that is, parallel to the X-axis). The curve will be revolved about the Z-axis, so we want to avoid a point at the ends of the surface.

3. The other end of the curve ends at the XY plane (at Z=0). To make both ends the same, mirror the curve by duplicating it and inverting the scale on the Z-axis (see Figure 9.4). Join the two ends using the Edit Curves, Attach Curves command with the Blend method selected. The result is a nicely symmetric curve with a classic "bone" shape.

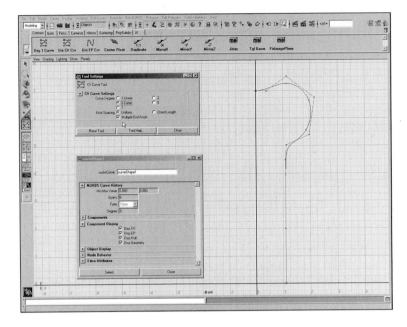

Figure 9.3 Initial BigBone curve.

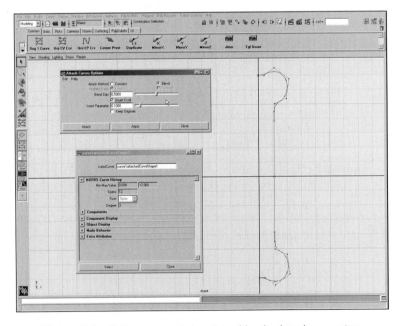

Figure 9.4 BigBone curve halves joined by the Attach operation.

4. Revolve this curve to make the initial BigBone surface.

Using the Surface, Revolve tool to create a cubic surface about the Z-axis, you can see that the resulting surface (see Figure 9.5) looks more like a dumbbell than a bone—but you can fix that.

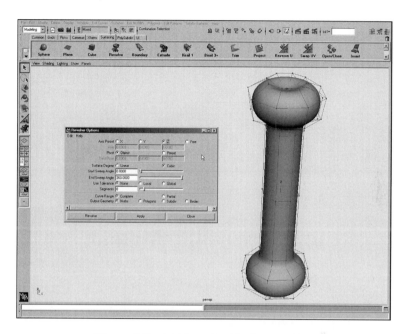

Figure 9.5 Initial revolved BigBone surface.

5. The plan here is to flatten the front and back of this surface to get a shape close to the desired one. So, scale the CVs at the "corners" of the bone (as seen from the Top view) as well as the matching CVs along the midline (see Figure 9.6). This quickly makes the BigBone into less of a dumbbell and more of a bone.

6. The resulting shape is still too thick, at least at the ends, so flatten the ends some more by selecting just the CVs that protrude too far in Y at the ends, and scaling them down in Y until they lie about where those along the shaft do.

This produces a bone surface (see Figure 9.7) which doesn't bulge out in Y anymore.

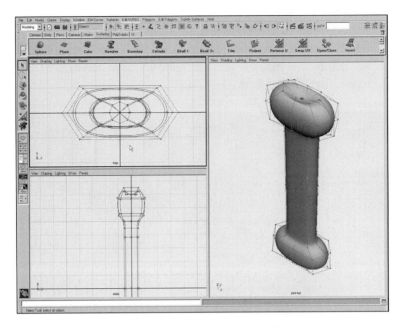

Figure 9.6 First flattening pass in the Top view.

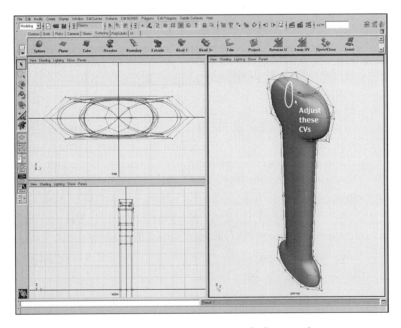

Figure 9.7 Flattened ends on the BigBone surface.

7. The flattening operations have created some distinct ridges at the front and back of the BigBone surface ends. To remove these, simply select all four of these CVs (two at each end) and scale them down in Z until they are down to about the level of the next CV row on the bone. Then, because there's now a little hiccup in the mesh caused by bringing our ridge-making CVs close to the untouched CVs near the pole, select these too-near CVs and scale them down a bit, too.

The result (see Figure 9.8) is getting pretty close to the Milk-Bone shape we initially imagined.

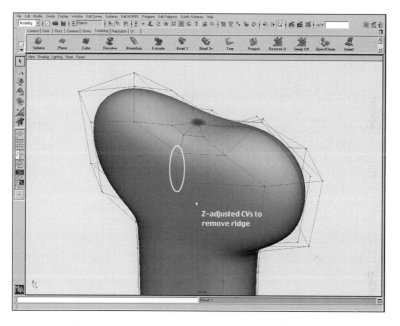

Figure 9.8   Ridges removed from BigBone surface.

The BigBone is still a little too oval on its edges, though, so the extreme X-axis CVs in the ends could be scaled in a bit. A little experimentation shows that this ruins the bone-shape profile created in the initial curve.

8. A better approach is to scale the CVs on either side of the extreme X-axis CVs in X. Because this is a surface, this also affects the profile (moving the surface out beyond the curve profile). So, when the edge shape is better, scale in a bit all of the aforementioned CVs until the shape is back at the profile curve (see Figure 9.9).

We need to make a similar profile improvement at the top and bottom of the ends. The most extreme Z-axis CVs pull up the ends of the bone, but not enough to match the initial profile anymore. The answer is once again not to pull up these extreme CVs, but to pull up their neighbors.

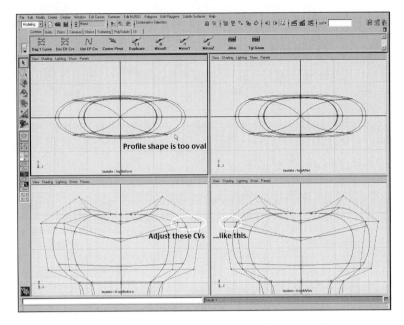

Figure 9.9   Improved end profiles at BigBone ends.

9. First, though, widen these CVs so that they line up in X with the extreme-Z CVs. This needn't be exact—merely reasonably close (see Figure 9.10).

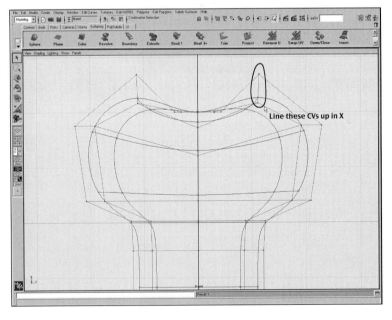

Figure 9.10   Lining up extreme-Z tip CVs on BigBone.

10. Next, do the vertical adjustments (to better match the bone profile curve) by grabbing the extreme-Z CVs and their profile-shaping neighbors and scaling them in Z. This should bring the bone surface shape back into agreement with the profile curve (see Figure 9.11).

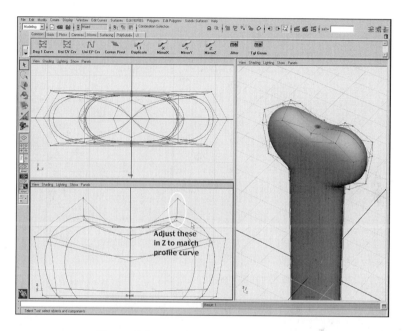

Figure 9.11   BigBone ends fully improved.

The result is now pretty darn close to the intended shape, but the dimensions are just a bit off. The bone is a little too wide in the handle, mostly, and maybe a bit short. Fortunately, these are really easy problems to fix.

II. To slim down the handle, just go to the Front view and grab the CVs along the handle area (there are five rows of CVs there). Scale them down in X until it's more manageable for poor Spot (see Figure 9.12). Of course, Spot lacks opposable thumbs, so it's all a cheat anyway, but at least it will look more plausible with a slimmer handle.

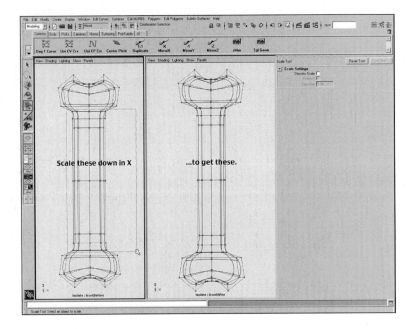

Figure 9.12   BigBone handle slimmed down.

12. Finally, to get the desired length, just select the CVs for each end and move them in Z. To make the bone the intended 16 inches long, move the end CVs about an inch farther out. Now the basic BigBone is complete (see Figure 9.13). Save this for use before Spot takes a bite out of it (or you can just load up my file BigBoneMainSurface.ma).

To take the chomp out of it, we'll do a simple NURBS trimming operation.

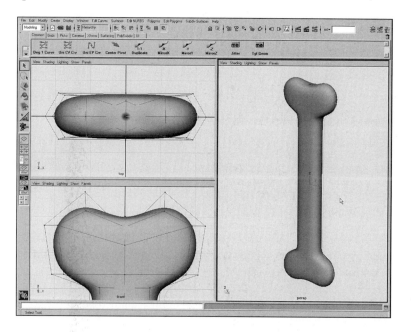

Figure 9.13 BigBone main surface completed.

13. First, create a curve that describes the shape of the bite mark required. Because this is supposed to somehow work on the valve nuts of the fire hydrant, it's a good idea for the curve to generally match the shape of the nut itself. Because these nuts are five-sided, create a linear NURBS circle with five sections in the Front view as a template. Draw the curve (see Figure 9.14) to describe the shape of Spot's bite. Because the curve is intended to look somewhat irregular yet fairly symmetrical, create it freehand and massage it a bit so that it has a credible dog-induced shape.

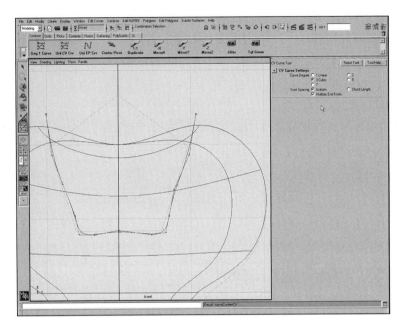

Figure 9.14 Spot's bite curve shape.

14. Duplicate the bite curve and move it to one side of the bone end, completely outside of the bone surface. Move the original to the other side, and then use Loft to construct a surface between them. If the interior shape of the bite needs adjusting, create this lofted surface as a cubic surface with two spans (see Figure 9.15). It's unlikely that you'll fuss over this shape, but it's handy to already have the CVs in place if you do.

15. With the bone surface and bite surface now passing through one another, use the Intersect Surfaces tool to generate curve-on-surface entities for both surfaces. Then trim the surfaces using the Trim tool and examine the result (see Figure 9.16).

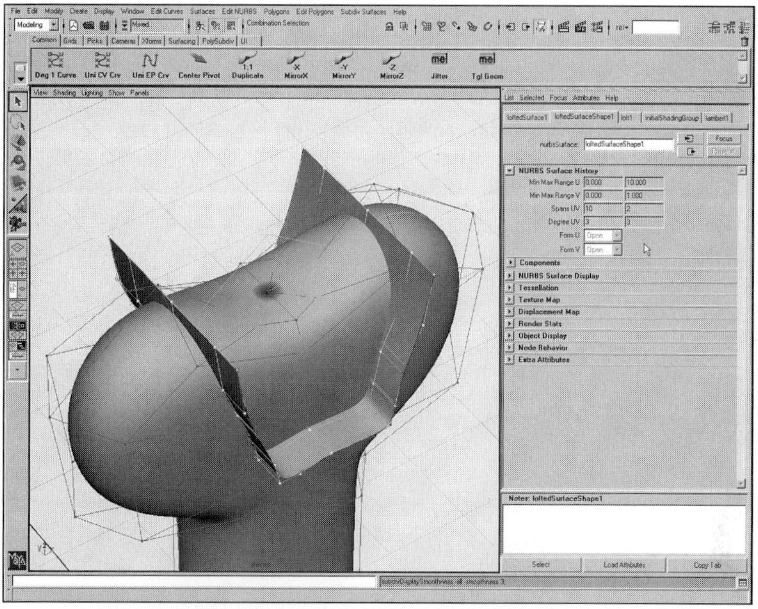

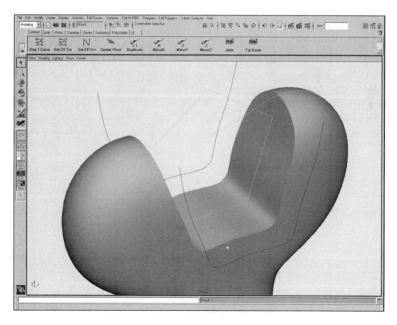

Figure 9.15 Lofted bite surface through end of BigBone.

Figure 9.16 Result of trimming out bite in BigBone.

16. The result looks awfully sharp (and the sharp edges could cause shading difficulties), so undo the intersection results and use the Circular Fillet tool instead. Use a radius of 0.05 inch and enable curve-on-surface creation to achieve a resulting fillet that looks promising. After trimming, it looks just about right (see Figure 9.17).

Note

Circular fillets are constructed by offsetting the two surfaces in their normal directions. If you don't get the fillet in the location you wanted (there are four possible locations), reverse the normal of one or both surfaces to produce a fillet in the required location.

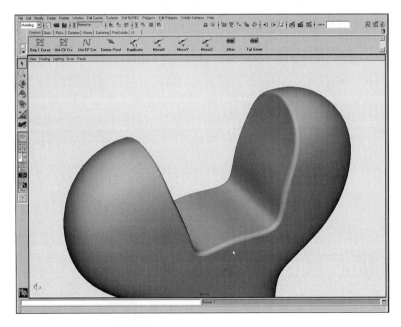

Figure 9.17 Result of filleting the bite in BigBone.

Good enough! The bone won't be seen too closely or for too long, so that'll do. The geometry is ready.

17. Now group, name, and set the resulting surfaces to a consistent normal direction (in case the shading approach cares about such things). Grouping and naming are straightforward, but to set normal directions, just select the new object (named BigBone now) and open the Attribute spreadsheet. Click the Render tab and set the Double Sided attributes to Off (entering 0 is a handy shortcut). If any surfaces are inside out (see Figure 9.18), use the Reverse Surface Direction tool to reverse either U or V (not both) for the offending surfaces. If you don't care to have single-sided surfaces, feel free to set Double Sided back to On (1).

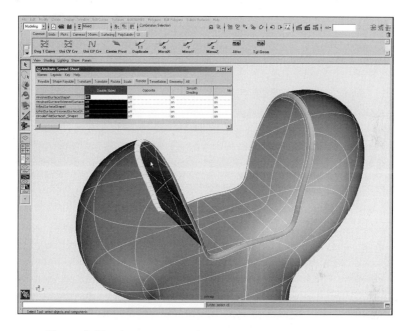

Figure 9.18   Inconsistent surface normals needing to be flipped.

18. Now it's time to assign a surface shader that's suitable. If you try to call the shader BigBone, you'll find that the name's already taken (by the object you just named). Shaders and objects share the same namespaces, so use a naming convention that easily distinguishes between them (such as adding a suffix or prefix to all shader names).

With the shader assignment in place (even if the shader details aren't ironed out yet), the model is ready to go (see Figure 9.19).

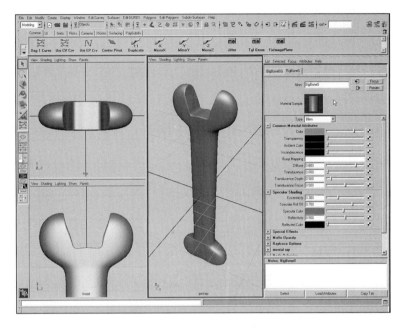

Figure 9.19   Ready-to-use BigBone model.

19. To ensure that the model used is only the object itself (and not the construction curves, which are also in the file), pick just the BigBone object and export it to its own file with the File, Export Selection command. If you'd like to compare yours with mine, check out the scene file BigBoneReady.ma. Leave previously saved files in the BigBone project, in case you need them later. The exported file will be used to incorporate the BigBone into the *Parking Spot* project for the appropriate scenes.

Although the BigBone model isn't a difficult model, it has given us an opportunity to show some prop-modeling decisions in action. Now let's move on to another prop, one that will make use of subdivision surface techniques.

Hydrant

A fire hydrant is also a relatively easy prop, but it has one feature that makes it challenging: fillets. And they're not just polite little fillets, the kind you don't really notice— they're big, fat fillets, the kind you can't help but see as integral to the design.

But that's not all: We want some grooves—big, distinctive grooves. The grooves should help turn the raw, utilitarian shape of the standard fireplug into an object with character. Somewhere among all the fillets and grooves and functionality should emerge a style. Ideally, it'll be an Art Deco style (although we might just settle for something less).

As mentioned in Chapter 2, I spent some time online and out around town studying fire hydrant designs. Although most share a common basic form, there are actually quite a few different styles (`www.firehydrant.org` has photographs of more than 1,600 varieties!). For our needs, however, we'd like it to be fairly tall and classically structured (minimalist designs need not apply). After downloading a few promising diagrams and photographic images, I picked one design (which shall remain nameless) as a starting point. This is what we'll create in the next exercise.

Exercise 9.2 Building a Fire Hydrant

The image was traced and modified in Adobe Photoshop to have the essential proportions and features (see Figure 9.20) for our model. Although it took a little bit of time to prepare, having an orthographic image as a template (for use as an image plane) was well worth the time spent. For a description of the process of setting up image planes, see the aptly named section "Setting Up Image Planes" in Chapter 7.

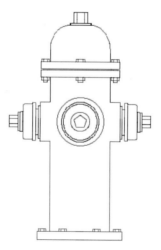

Figure 9.20 Fire hydrant design sketch.

The fire hydrant generally has a form that is composed of a central revolved surface, into which three other revolved surfaces intersect. This shape could be represented by filleted NURBS surfaces or by a single subdivision surface. Because of the potential for fairly complex displacement in the shaders (fire hydrants tend to have thick paint and substantial weathering), a subdivision surface is a more robust solution, so this model will end up in that form.

1. To begin, draw the initial profile curves as uniform CV curves, using the image planes in the Front window as a visual guide (see Figure 9.21). To make life easier, snap most of the points on these curves to a 1/8-inch grid (I moved features a bit, too, as I saw the curve taking shape). Also, remember to build the model around the up-axis (we've been using Z-up), with the center of its base at the world origin.

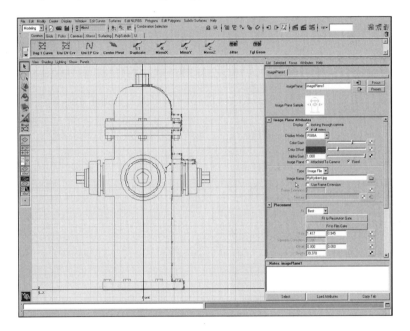

Figure 9.21   Initial fire hydrant profile curves.

The central profile is actually best made from two curves, a top cap and the main lower section (into which the side and front pipes attach). Doing it this way instead of making one continuous curve ensures a tight, flat join (which reflects the hydrant components themselves).

2. Duplicate the side pipe profile curve because it will be resized later for use as the front pipe profile. Then round off the interior end of this curve. This produces a deep bowl shape when it's revolved and ensures closure (in case you are able to see inside it when the cap is off at the end). Also, make the section protruding into the cap long and thick enough to accommodate screw threads in its shader.

Notice that corners created with three evenly spaced CVs give a consistent feel to the rounded edges. CVs between these corner details can be relatively few, mostly included to keep interior curve spans from getting too long. One exception is in the area where the side pipe profiles meet the main body curve. In these places, only two CVs are used (which will later facilitate having three-CV edges in the subdivision mesh where the pipes intersect).

Also notice that these curves should not include the pentagonal bolt head profiles at the ends because these can later be added separately much more easily.

3. Set the pivot points for all these curves at the endpoints about which they should be revolved. Now create revolved NURBS surfaces from each curve, using 16 spans for the main profile and 8 spans for the side and front pipe profiles (see Figure 9.22).

This combination provides a good matching of spans between the pipes when the subdivision surface control mesh is later assembled (if you'd like to take a shortcut, open HydrantFirstRevolves.ma and go forward from here).

Note

A little later, when you convert these NURBS surfaces to subdivs (polygons, actually), the surface CV positions will be kept fixed. This ensures that the subdiv surface regions will look like the initial NURBS surfaces. I use NURBS surfaces this way as placeholders for the final surfaces, to provide a predictably accurate mesh for each surface region and to force more conscious planning of the mesh structures.

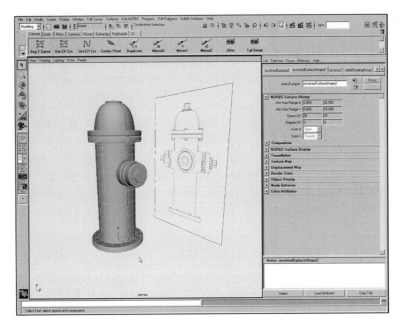

Figure 9.22 Revolved surfaces for hydrant and side pipes.

4. Because the hydrant is symmetric about X, create only one side pipe (I made the one on the right) at first. Before proceeding to make the other, however, notice that the side pipe surface doesn't intersect the central surface—its CV mesh needs to be adjusted to intersect the CV mesh of the central surface.

Achieving this intersection is easy. Simply go to the Front window, grab the CVs along the inside edge of the surface, and slide them farther inward. Both the end CVs and their associated tangent CVs need to be moved together, to keep the spacing between them the same (this spacing will affect the blending of the fillets later). Do the middle (extreme Y-value) CVs first; then do the "corners" and use the Top window to see when you've moved them far enough in X that the edge CVs are inside the central pipe mesh.

It's also important to be sure that both the front and back pairs of CVs are selected during this operation. In other words, make sure that your selections haven't been limited by too-tight clipping planes or the use of backface culling.

Tip

To be sure that an image plane doesn't obstruct your view, set its depth in your window to be fully behind the objects in the window (not at the default position on the zero plane). You might also want to set the image planes to be displayed only in their own camera windows (by setting the image plane's Display attribute to Looking Through Camera).

5. Now that you have a well-shaped side pipe surface, mirror it over to the other side (using the Duplicate command with a –1 scale in X).

   Because I do mirroring operations so frequently, I keep mirror command icons (one for each of X, Y, and Z) handy on my Common shelf. Each of these commands is actually just a simple line of MEL, such as `duplicate`.

6. For improved viewing, a shader (HydrantS) should be created and applied to all surfaces created so far. I made mine a bright yellow blinn shader and made sure that its highlight spread well enough that I could read the surface shape confidently.

   After studying the shape of the curve for the side cap, you might realize that the top cap has no hole for the pentagonal bolt to go. But because Maya's construction history has been on all along, it's a simple matter to fix (if you didn't catch it before).

7. Select the last CV on its curve and move it back from the axis enough to make room for the bolt. Then add a few points (using Edit Curves, Add Points) to create an edge profile for the hole. The surface automatically updates, and the problem is solved (see Figure 9.23).

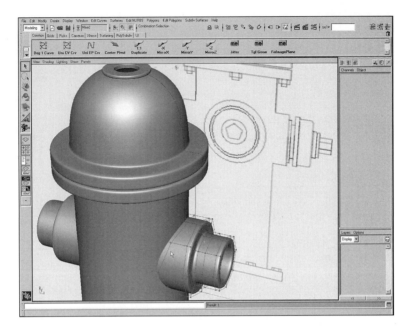

Figure 9.23 Left side pipe and top hole added.

The side cap shape is distinct enough from the top cap that a new curve should be used (instead of an adjusted copy), following the same method as before (grids and three-CV corners).

8. In the threaded interior area, move the CVs up a bit in Z to make them distinct from their neighbors on the side pipe surface. For the hole in the cap's end, make the curve periodic with the Open/Close Curve tool. Then set the curve's pivot at the location of its first CV and revolve the curve to make the side cap surface (see Figure 9.24). Finally, assign the new side cap the HydrantS shader and mirror it in X to make the other side cap.

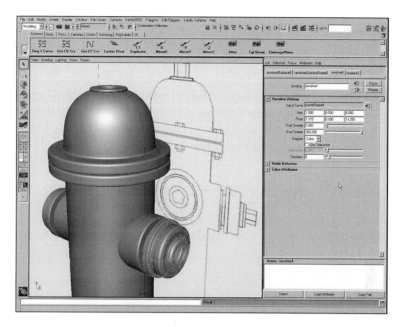

Figure 9.24 Side cap surface.

9. The front pipe and cap are basically just a larger version of the ones on the side, so make copies of each and rotate them –90° in Z. This provides the raw front geometry, but it needs to be scaled up a bit.

10. To make scaling easier, apply the Freeze Transforms command to these two surfaces.

   This redefines the current transform as the identity transform and orients the axes for these surfaces the same as the world axes.

   Although the surfaces can then be scaled up the 20% or so seen in the artwork, this puts the front and side pipes a bit too close together. It would be better to leave a little space between these pipes, so a more appropriate scaling factor needs to be determined.

11. First, pick the front pipe surface and use the Center Pivot command (you won't want the pipe moving out of place as you scale it).

12. Next, scale the pipe by eye (using the overall scale manipulator) to determine the necessary scaling factor (about 1.1 seems to work). However, this scaling affects all three axes, so undo this rough scaling. You don't want the front pipe and cap to protrude any more than the side ones—the scaling should be applied only in X and Z. Fortunately, there are better ways of setting the scale you want.

Before Maya 4.5, relative uniform scaling on two axes had to be done via a key-in or by undoing a single-axis scale value after scaling all axes. For example, you could select the front pipe, invoke the Scale command, and then enter the scaling factor (1.1 1.0 1.1) as a relative scale in the status line's numeric input field. Or, you could scale interactively, undo the scaling, and then paste the undone command from the Script Editor into the command line, edit the scaling values, and execute the command (whew!). Or, you could compute the scale factors and edit the scale values in the Channel Box. Each of these approaches is somewhat awkward.

Nowadays, however, you can perform two-axis uniform scaling by simply holding down the Ctrl key as you drag the middle mouse button. To indicate the correct pair of axes, start your drag on the axis icon (the little cube) of the axis you're *not* scaling. Using the normal axis this way is especially helpful if the final value needn't be nicely rounded off. Use this feature to scale the front pipe surface up about 10% in X and Z.

Now that this pipe surface has been scaled up, it might need a bit of CV tweaking to match its inner edge with the central pipe (like you did with the side pipes).

13. Go to the Top window and see whether the front pipe mesh needs adjustment to bring its CVs within the central pipe mesh. If it does, move the edge and tangent CVs inward toward the central pipe, as before.

    Scaling the front cap will be a little trickier because you want to leave the hole area untouched.

14. In the Top or Side windows, select the CVs behind the boss on the front.

    The numeric input field doesn't work when scaling (or rotating) CVs, nor does the Channel Box, but the two-axis scaling operation does. However, because you scaled the front pipe by an exact amount, getting precisely the same scale factor applied to the front cap requires the command-line technique.

15. Scale the selected CVs (everything not affecting the hole shape) an arbitrary amount interactively using the scale manipulator. Now undo that operation.

    On the Command Feedback line appears a message that shows the undone scaling command (open the Script Editor if it's scrolled out of this field). This command shows not only the scale factor that was used, but also the pivot location used—the real objective behind the undone Scale command. CV pivots are generated on the fly, but you can let Maya do the figuring for you and just grab the result you need this way.

16. Now copy the scaling command from the Command Feedback line (or Script Editor) over to the command line, and edit it to have the precise scaling values used on the front pipe. Be sure to leave the pivot information intact.

For instance, the following MEL command:

```
scale -r -p 0cm -15.71625cm 36.195cm 0.6789 0.6789 0.6789
```

will become this:

```
scale -r -p 0cm -15.71625cm 36.195cm 1.1 1.0 1.1
```

17. Ensure that your selection is still intact (you've still got those CVs selected, right?), and execute the edited command by pressing Enter. The front cap should now precisely match the size of the front pipe again.

Of course, you could probably have just fudged it, but it's useful to be able to exactly match values and locations when you need to, even when they're only transient.

For a little more visual interest, the shape of the cap can be rounded a bit. The resulting front cap and pipe are shown in Figure 9.25.

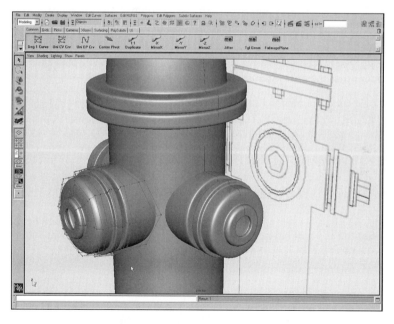

Figure 9.25   Front pipe and cap added to hydrant.

Now it's time to integrate the various pipes into a single subdivision surface model. This entails converting each of the separate NURBS surfaces into polygon meshes, and then combining these meshes into a single polymesh. The resulting polymesh will then be converted into a subdivision surface.

Although it's a bit unconventional, I prefer working this way for most complex subdivision surface modeling. This enables me to leverage the advantages of NURBS, polygons, and subdivision surfaces at useful stages in the modeling process.

I use NURBS curves to carefully shape contours and to build smooth NURBS surfaces. The construction tools for NURBS are comprehensive, and the display and selection options are robust (taking advantage of the inherent parameterization). Cubic NURBS surfaces are invariably used because subdivision surfaces are akin to degree 3 NURBS surfaces, not some other degree.

These surfaces are destined, then, to be converted into polygon meshes (although I keep the NURBS around, just in case). During this stage of the modeling process, I assemble the polygon meshes into a single larger mesh. Polygonal operations such as Booleans and combining meshes go smoothly, allowing me to focus on the topology of the mesh being constructed.

Ultimately (in fact, typically several times), this larger mesh becomes the subdivision surface control point mesh. Almost as soon as I've joined two polymeshes together properly, I convert the new mesh to a subdiv and examine the resulting smooth surface. Because most of the shape typically comes from the NURBS mesh interiors, I can focus on the joins to ensure the blend quality I'm looking for, confident that the rest of the surface will look as expected.

18. Converting the NURBS surfaces is easily done using the Convert NURBS to Polygons command. Select each of the four pipe surfaces (don't forget the big one in the middle), specify the tessellation method as Control Points, and click Apply.

It's a good idea to then either template the NURBS surfaces or put them on a hidden layer. I normally keep the original surfaces around (templated on the *construction* layer) as a shape reference, but I drop the construction history for the polygon mesh.

19. After the surfaces have been converted (see Figure 9.26), the four intersecting polymeshes need to be brought together into one mesh (you can use my file HydrantPolymeshes.ma for this, if you like).

Because their points don't all match up initially, you must choose between two ways of making them match. The first method is to manually edit the polymeshes and snap together nearby points. The second method is to use Maya's Boolean operators to intersect and trim the meshes so that they match. The latter is generally simpler, so you can try it first.

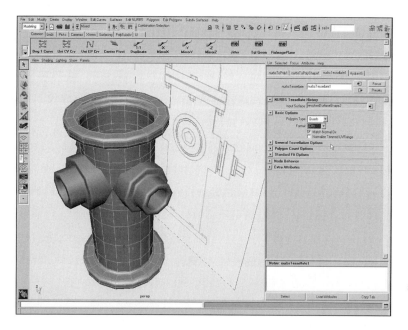

Figure 9.26   Polygonal meshes extracted from NURBS surfaces.

If you select the center and right pipe polymeshes and then use the Boolean, Union command, it might not give the expected result (see Figure 9.27). In my case, most of the right pipe simply disappeared!

Here, the face normals of the two meshes don't agree. The Boolean operators assume that the polymeshes are outward-facing about their enclosed volumes (although they need not actually be enclosed). But if the actual normals don't adhere to this assumption, you're in for some surprises.

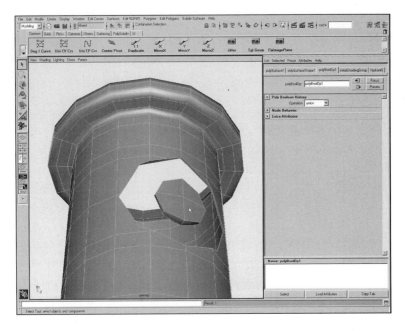

Figure 9.27 Unintended results of polymesh Union command.

20. To view the normals, you have a few easy choices. You can use my preferred method, which is to turn on backface culling (with Display, Custom Polygon Display or a hotkey equivalent) and just look at the mesh (in either shaded or wire-frame mode). Another simple check is to use the Attribute Spreadsheet to turn off the Double Sided attribute (found under the Render tab) and then turn on shading. Finally, if you'd rather see normal vectors drawn, select the polymesh and turn them on with the Display, Polygon Components, Normals command.

Tip

Although using a single-sided shaded display to check normals works reliably for polymeshes, it doesn't always work for NURBS surfaces. The surface normal for a NURBS surface is computed as the cross-product of the U and V vectors, so inverting the mesh inverts the normal. Maya compensates for this in the display, but the NURBS Boolean commands still see the geometric normal. When the product of the three axis scales is negative, the displayed normal isn't the same as the geometric normal.

21. If you find any pipe meshes inside out like this (they are typically brought to your attention by unexpected Boolean results), use the Edit Polygons, Normals, Reverse command to bring the offending mesh into agreement with the others. When the normals are properly set, the expected result will be obtained when the union operation is performed (see Figure 9.28).

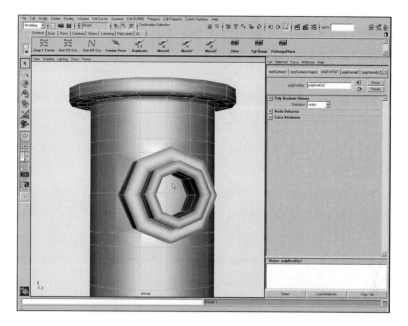

Figure 9.28   Better result from polymesh union.

Well, almost. The deep interior of the right pipe is being lopped off by the Union command. Although you could split off that section, perform the operation, and rejoin the pieces, there is an easier method.

22. Simply remove the center pipe's faces in that location. Pick the middle CV in that area of the center pipe, convert your selection to faces, and then delete the faces.

23. To ensure that the meshes still fully intersect, vertically scale down the outside corners of the removed faces to bring them within the bounds of the side pipe mesh.

Now the Union command does the expected thing (see Figure 9.29), joining the two meshes without lopping off the inside end of the pipe.

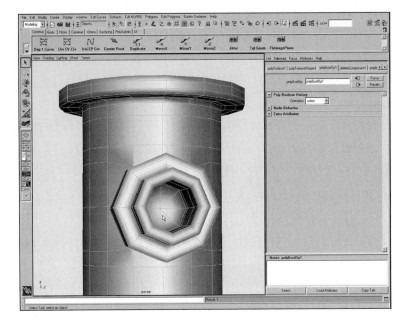

Figure 9.29 Desired result from polymesh union of pipes.

The same procedure could be performed on the opposite side, but it's easier to take advantage of symmetry.

24. Cut off the left half of the mesh by picking the faces on that side and deleting them. As it turns out, you can now toss the left pipe mesh, too, because the right side incorporates it already. The remaining right side mesh is almost ready to be mirrored (see Figure 9.30).

But before mirroring this mesh and combining the two parts, this side needs some cleanup along the edge created by the union.

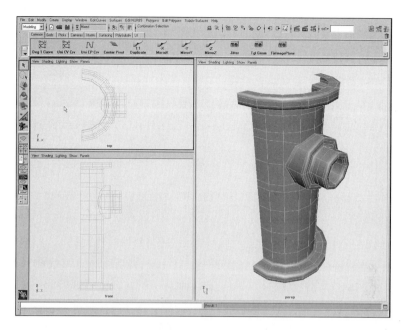

Figure 9.30 Left side of combined mesh removed.

25. Using the Edit Polygons, Split Polygon tool, make new edges that connect the side pipe mesh corners with original CVs in the center pipe mesh.

You can remove any unwanted edges with Edit Polygons, Delete Edge. Remember, don't get in the habit of simply backspacing away unwanted edges; this leaves vertices behind that subdivs won't like along edges.

You might also find it useful to remove some edges by collapsing them with Edit Polygons, Collapse. This removes an edge and merges its former endpoints at the midpoint.

The goal is a well-behaved mesh with edges that flow smoothly around and across features. Making a mesh composed predominantly of quads is especially helpful in avoiding surface irregularities. By working with these three commands (Split Polygon, Delete Edge, and Collapse), Boolean edge results can be cleaned up to gracefully blend features from each original mesh.

26. Finally, after the Boolean edges are tidied up, make one more pass with Split Polygons and create a clean set of edges encircling the side pipe (see Figure 9.31). This helps keep the resulting fillet around the pipe nice and even.

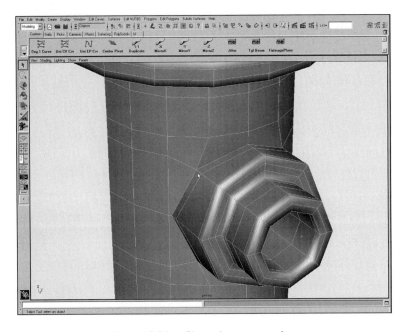

Figure 9.31 Cleaned-up union edge.

27. To get a quick preview of how the subdivision surface (and the fillet, in particular) will look, use the Modify, Convert Polygons to Subdiv command to generate a subdivision surface (keep the original mesh, by the way). If the subdiv isn't produced, check the Script Editor for more information—it usually tells you just what's wrong.

    When you have the subdiv surface, examine the results in shaded mode at a fine smoothness setting. When it looks good, throw it away—you'll make another one from the full mesh shortly.

28. Mirror this good-looking mesh in X and join the two meshes using the Combine command. This makes a single polymesh that contains all the points of both, but they're not fully together yet.

29. Merge vertices along the join line by selecting them and using the Merge Vertices command. If you haven't accidentally moved any edge CVs, the left and right halves will have precisely matching CVs along the YZ plane.

30. To check whether the merge was successful, select the mesh and then use the Custom Polygon Display tool to show heavy border edges (check Highlight, Border Edges and set Border Width to 2 or more).

You shouldn't see any bold edges along the seam. If you see just a few, you probably have a few CVs that weren't close enough to each other for the Vertex Merge operation. Snap these together and merge again; this should eliminate the bold edges.

On the other hand, if none of the vertices merged, then one side of the mesh needs its normals flipped to match the other side.

31. Use the Edit Polygons, Normals, Conform command to reconcile the difference. Just select the whole mesh, execute the Conform command, and click an orange area. Now you'll be able to get those vertices merged, which is essential for getting the needed subdiv.

32. Convert this polygon mesh to a subdiv, and give it a good hard look at a fine smoothness setting. It should now look like Figure 9.32.

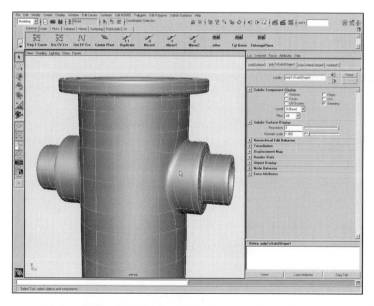

Figure 9.32   Subdivision surface from merged polymeshes.

Although there might be some minor artifacts around the resulting fillets between the arms and center pipe, they should be minimal and perfectly acceptable for a fire hydrant casting.

33. Undo the subdiv conversion (or throw it away, if you kept the original polygon mesh) and repeat the same basic procedure for integrating the front pipe into the mesh (although I'll skip the gory details).

Note

I keep disposing of these subdivision surfaces, by the way, because the act of merging polygon meshes (or running them through Boolean operations) breaks the subdivs anyway, leaving a merged polymesh and a subdiv without a polygon proxy. Although there are ways to get the polygon mesh back, it's easier to treat the shaded subdiv as an evaluative device until the overall mesh is cobbled together.

Even though pulling features out of a subdiv in polygon proxy mode is relatively easy, getting those features to really match your artwork and dimensional requirements can be difficult. But adding known features into a base mesh this way enables you to combine NURBS accuracy with polymesh flexibility.

34. When you've got the front pipe blended in, convert the mesh one final time to a subdiv. This one you'll keep. The final main body of your hydrant should look like the one in Figure 9.33.

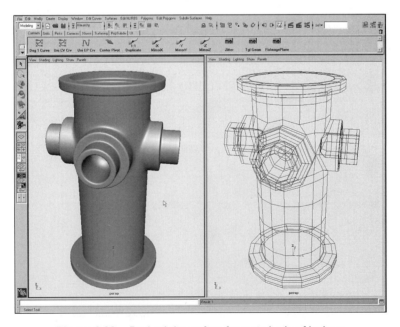

Figure 9.33 Final subdiv surface for main body of hydrant.

The pentagonal bolts are next.

Because there are five sides and you are generally using three CVs to go around corners, there will be at least 15 CVs going around the bolt surfaces. The plan is to take a revolved surface and make corners by grouping CVs close together. However, because the bolts also need round bottoms, there will need to be an area at the base where this grouping doesn't occur.

35. Start with a simple NURBS profile curve built beside the Z-axis that fits within the hole at the top of the hydrant. Create a revolved surface there from this curve with 15 spans. Then select every third hull going around this new surface (minus the base CVs that need to stay put), and rotate them about Z to bring them close to a neighboring hull.

Because of the number of spans (and the resulting CV spacing), the rotate pivot needs to be adjusted to be above the origin before you do the rotation (see Figure 9.34). Maya's automatic CV pivot generation simply uses the center of the CVs' bounding box, which doesn't work the way you might expect when the point distribution isn't symmetric about the world axis directions. Anyway, by tapping the Insert key, you can set the pivot back on the Z-axis where it belongs before doing the rotation.

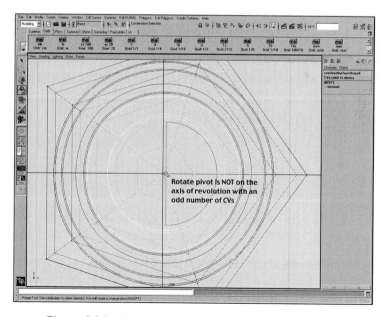

Figure 9.34 Rotate pivot skew with odd number of spans.

Because you'll perform this rotation more than once (one more set of CVs will go the opposite way), you might want to use the command-line technique mentioned previously to perform equal CV rotations in both directions.

36. To get fairly crisp corners, first rotate the selected CVs about the Z-axis toward their neighbors on one side. Through a little trial and error, I found that 21° worked well.

37. Then, by pickwalking back one row, select the other set of CVs and rotate them the opposite amount (−21°, say) about Z. This is the place where you could paste the previous rotate command onto the command line and edit the rotation amount.

The result is the desired clustered corners, as shown in Figure 9.35. With perhaps just a bit of adjustment to the hole size on the top cap, the bolt will fit perfectly.

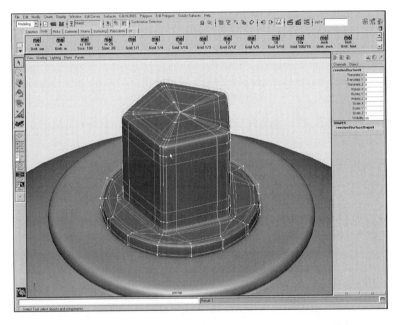

Figure 9.35   Pentagonal bolt corners created by rotating CVs.

38. Create a simple shader and assign it to the pentagonal bolt. Because the base of the bolt can also be cleverly made with the necessary rounded undercut, this bolt will be copied and used on the side and front caps, too.

For now, make one copy. Only a minor scaling operation should be necessary to widen the base to match the cap design as it was drawn. Select the CVs around the base and scale them to fit, using the two-axis CV scaling technique used earlier.

After you've copied the resulting bolt onto the other caps, the hydrant should really be taking shape (see Figure 9.36).

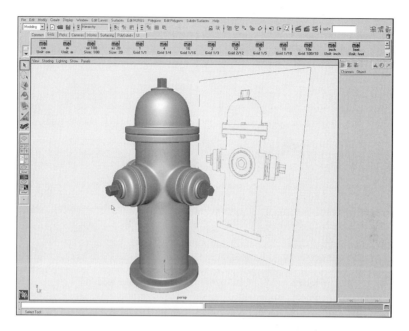

Figure 9.36   Hydrant with all pentagonal bolts added.

39. Construct hexagonal bolts in a similar fashion, only with 6 corners involved (so there are 18 spans instead of 15).

Then place these false bolts (there are no threaded bodies, just the bolt heads) in appropriate locations around the base of the hydrant and on the flange joining the top cap and the main hydrant body. On the underside of the flange, add the missing bolt ends, simply penetrating the hex bolts with simple revolved bolt profiles.

Of course, these bolts could have also been created quite easily with subdivs (and perhaps some creasing), but we chose the scenic route for these. These hex heads should also be randomly rotated in Z, so as not to appear too regular in orientation (see Figure 9.37). The hydrant geometry is now essentially done (HydrantFinal.ma is provided for your reference).

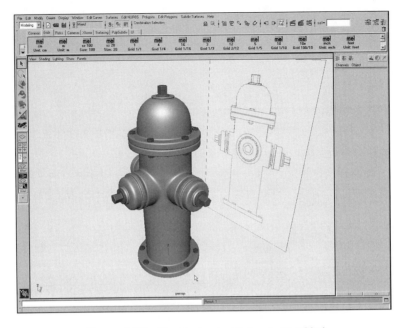

Figure 9.37   Final hydrant with hex bolts added.

If you later need to displace the top of the hex bolts (or the pentagonal bolts, for that matter), they can be converted to subdivs and their pole CVs can be merged. However, if this is done, care must be taken to keep the valence (the number of edges at a CV) at the pole from getting large (four is ideal). If there are too many edges meeting at a point, there will be a distinct pucker at that point.

40. Finally, the model needs some grouping and naming. The cap on the right will be removed when Spot turns on the water, so group the bolt and cap surface together and name it RightCap. A few additional groups and names can be added for clarity when shading or in case subobjects need adjustment.

The fire hydrant still has room for some additional details, such as grooves or chains on the caps, but it's basically ready for use. Some of these details might be added in shading; others might be left off for want of the necessary time or budget. It's time to move onward and upward—or at least over to the parking spot.

The Car: A Complex Prop Model

Although he's a bit of a jerk, our main character drives a cool car. It's not the sort of car you see on the street every day—it's one of a kind. Of course, in our fictional world there are other unique vehicles, but this car needs to express something about its owner as well as its world. And it does.

Max's early concept sketch (see Figure 9.38) shows a sporty, almost jaunty vehicle, the likes of which would make an egocentric movie star proud. The implied level of self-absorption it exhibits adds depth to the shallowness of our antihero. A major goal of modeling this car will be to maintain that characterization in the finished model.

Figure 9.38   Early concept sketch of The Jerk's car.

Later sketches provide the necessary views for a model packet (see Figures 9.39 and 9.40).

Figure 9.39   Top-view sketch of the car.

Figure 9.40   Side-view sketch of the car.

As you follow the next few exercises, these side and top views will be used as image planes, allowing us to obtain much of the character by simply matching the design sketches. In addition, Max has provided a reference view that we will also use, showing more of the car's form from an elevated angle (see Figure 9.41).

Figure 9.41   Reference sketch of the car.

Because a car is a complicated model, we won't cover every detail of the modeling process required (that could be an entire book of its own). Instead, we'll focus on the major forms and the overall approach required to successfully integrate these major forms with the minor details.

Body Panels

Let's start by creating the main body panels. It's not going to be possible to work from the inside out (although real automotive design goes through a "package design" phase that does essentially this). To put in the seats, steering wheel, and so on, we need a literal frame of reference. And before we can go anywhere with the exterior surfacing, we'll need our artwork in place.

First, the design sketches need to be matched up to the modeling windows as image planes. It's unlikely that all the features will match up in each view, but it's important to have the image planes placed to scale and aligned as closely as possible with each other.

Two competing means of aligning the sketches normally exist. Either the wheelbase or the overall length of the vehicle can be used to establish the scale. Because you can't actually see the wheels in the top view, aligning the overall body size is the obvious choice.

So how long is this car? Wheelbases for sporty cars are typically in the 100- to 110-inch range, so let's try 108 inches as the reference measurement. When the side view of the vehicle is placed as a Front view image plane (this conforms to standard view conventions in the automotive industry), the overall vehicle length is about 142 inches. This looks good, so we'll use that measurement (actually, the frontmost and rearmost positions of the vehicle) to position the Top window image plane.

Although the sketches are fine quality, the scans of both images needed to be rotated slightly to align the images with the axes. And although the color in the images is pleasing to look at, it's best removed for purposes of drawing geometry over it. Also, to ensure that the image planes don't obstruct grids or geometry, they are pushed back enough to be entirely behind everything of interest.

All of these image plane procedures and more are described in detail in Chapter 7, in case you want to set up your own image planes for this exercise. My final image plane setup (also found in the scene file CarImagePlaneSetup.ma) is shown in Figure 9.42.

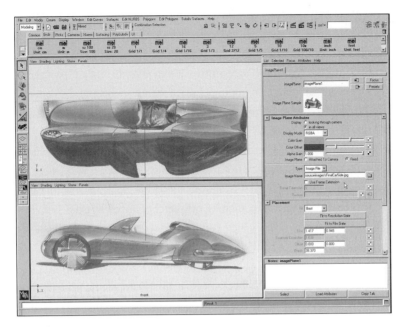

Figure 9.42 Final image plane setup for the car.

Exercise 9.3 Creating the Car Body Panels

Although I might normally create an auto body entirely in NURBS, this design seems more suited to a subdivision surface. Overall, the design is broadly given by two graceful "speed curves," like two flattened teardrops melding into each other. Perhaps literally building such a shape (assuming that you don't get lost in the details), will successfully capture the graceful, aggressive form Max has designed.

As with the hydrant, NURBS surfaces will be used initially, and then subdivision surfaces will be created from them. In part, using a single subdiv is a convenience that allows tangent continuity to be obtained all across a busy surface. This will be particularly helpful when pulling the cowl shapes up from the rear deck surface. It might be a bit challenging when working around the wheel wells, but the continuity solution is worth it on such a highly reflective surface as an auto body. Besides, we won't really have to even open the doors, so a big continuous surface is even functional.

This car is unlike any other car I've modeled, so it seems that the best place to start is someplace where it's clear what the surface shape is. The rear deck is such a place. First roughs must be built of the trunk and hood; then the fender flares can be pulled in and the details can be cut out as needed.

I. Create your first curve, which will describe the center line of the trunk (see Figure 9.43). Work in the Front view and use the image plane to guide you.

Space the control points for this curve relatively evenly, with an eye toward maintaining a graceful, positive curvature (avoiding flat spots or unwanted inflections). Don't forget that the CVs don't go right on the image plane curve, but are placed "outside" the radius of the curve (the CVs "pull" on the curve from out there). A good initial curve shape can save much work later.

Because cubic NURBS curves are locally more curved near CVs, having too few CVs would tend to make areas between them flatter than desired. Of course, too many CVs would be a nuisance. Spacing them roughly one every 8 inches seems like a good compromise.

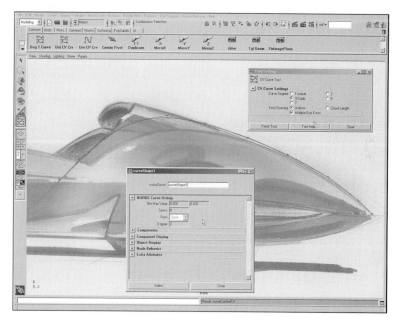

Figure 9.43 First curve, describing trunk center.

2. Copy this curve and move it out to the crest of the rear fender flare. Make a lofted surface with four spans between these two otherwise identical curves. This surface won't be used directly, but it will be used to obtain additional curves by extraction.

3. Scale down the outer curve a bit, using its rearmost endpoint as the scaling pivot. The lofted surface will change because of its construction history to reflect this curve modification.

4. Next, copy the outer curve and rotate it down 90° about X, using the same rear-most CV as its pivot.

5. Flatten this curve somewhat to correspond to the profile of the rear fender as seen in the Top window. Because you don't really want this curve to abut the previous curve (the outer curve of the loft), move it down about an inch and move the previous curve inward an inch or two.

6. Duplicate this third curve and rotate it another 90°. Reshape it to match the lower fender profile and move it inward, below the outer loft curve (but not exactly, to keep the two curves visibly distinct for picking).

    This now gives a top, middle, and bottom curve for describing the fender (see Figure 9.44). These curves are also found in the scene file CarRearDeckCurves.ma.

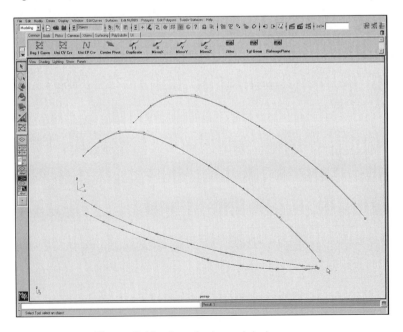

Figure 9.44   Rear fender and deck curves.

You've nearly got the set of curves needed for constructing the rear deck.

7. Duplicate the interior isoparameter curves from the lofted surface by selecting them and using the Duplicate Surface Curves tool. Template the lofted surface because you might find that you need it again to regenerate a curve. Delete the history on these new curves, however, so that they can be freely reshaped.

These curves will be used to construct a new lofted surface. Each curve will describe the character of the surface in its local area. For obvious reasons, such curves are known as *character lines* (although the term is usually reserved for important feature-defining curves).

However, one more curve is needed between the top and middle fender curves because there's a big gap that a lofted surface won't bridge well.

8. To obtain this, make yet another loft between the top, middle, and bottom curves. It's important that this be a cubic surface because you need a rounded surface from which to grab the necessary curve.

9. To generate in-between isoparameter curves, set Section Spans to 2 before executing the Loft tool. After duplicating the desired isoparameter curve (the upper one, between the top and middle curves), you should have the curves and surfaces shown in Figure 9.45.

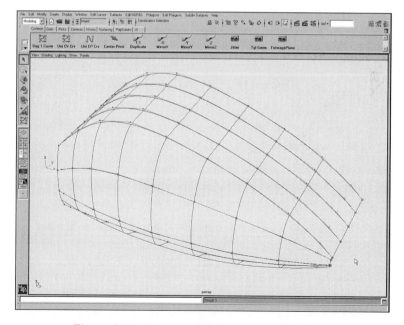

Figure 9.45   Rear construction curves and surfaces.

At this point, it's tempting to think that you could simply attach the two existing surfaces—but the attach wouldn't likely behave well near the back corner, so let's stick to the original plan.

10. Create a fresh lofted surface from the planned curves. It should look much as intended (see Figure 9.46).

Figure 9.46   Rear end lofted surface.

Even the depression inside the fender crest is much like the design intent. It's definitely off to a good start!

Although you could work at refining the rear shape some more, either by adjusting the construction curves or by manipulating CVs in the surface, it's more important to block in the front end first, so let's move up there.

The front is distinct from the rear in one important respect: It has a couple of big holes. No, not the grille—the wheel wells. Seeing these makes the initial assumption of using subdivision surfaces for the whole body a bit suspect again—at least, for this area of the body.

Automobiles are like big mirrors that amplify surface imperfections as reflected light plays off them. An arbitrary hole (relatively speaking) cut out from a reflective subdivision surface is just begging to show lumpy, bumpy artifacts. Our budget (not to mention my patience) might not accommodate massaging a subdivision surface enough to keep these artifacts under control. But we'll cross that bridge when we come to it.

So, it's possible that the front wheel well might have to be made from one or more trimmed NURBS surfaces. Fortunately, the wheel well is quite close to the front corner. This might actually be an advantage if it comes to using NURBS, enabling you to hide surface imperfections by trimming them away.

11. Once again, draw an initial uniform CV curve in the Front view. However, you can't really see past the fender to the center line of the vehicle. So, copy the curve you've drawn as it appears in the image plane, and then move it out to the crest of the fender, where it really applies.

12. Adjust both curves a bit to fit as they should. Scale down the center-line curve in X, using the windshield end as the pivot. Lengthen the fender curve a bit, using a similar pivot location, until its end is at the door seam (see Figure 9.47). These two curves will be used as the rails in a birail surface.

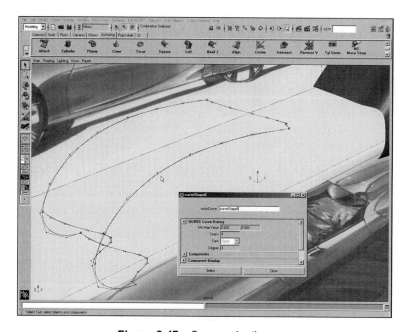

Figure 9.47 Front end rail curves.

13. Add your interior section curves next, starting with the front profile of the nose as seen in the Top view.

It's important that this curve connect to parametrically identical locations on the two rail curves, so set the rails to have only their edit points displayed (using Display, NURBS Components, Custom Settings) and snap the endpoints of the profile curve to corresponding edit points.

Note that the grille detail should be ignored for now, as if the hood and nose were all one big surface.

Now it's time to create additional profiles.

14. Copy the nose profile and move it into position up at the windshield end of the rails. Reshape it by moving CVs (not edit points) to follow the shape of the windshield. Fudge a bit as needed to allow for the mismatch of the Top and Front image plane artwork. Turn it near the end to follow the door cut line.

It's important that the CVs making up the indent in the nose profile correspond to those of the indent where the windshield meets the door cut. This ensures that the indent naturally flows up the hood edge to the door cut line.

15. Create another profile by copying the nose profile, and move it all the way around to the underside ends of the rails. Down there, the indent should basically disappear, so ease the CVs into a smoother shape.

16. Finally, an interior hood section is needed. Copy the windshield profile curve and place it between matching rail curve edit points. Reshape it as needed by moving CVs, with an eye toward carrying features through from the neighboring curves.

After a bit of CV adjustment to all the curve shapes, these birail curves (also found in the scene file CarFrontCurvesReady.ma) should be ready to use (see Figure 9.48).

17. Use the Surfaces, Birail 3+ tool, selecting the profile curves and rails as prompted.

This produces a surface, but that surface needs a little work (see Figure 9.49). The few options available in this birail tool won't change the surface in any appreciable way. However, its basic structure is pretty close to what's desired, so let's wrestle it into shape.

Figure 9.48   Front end birail curves ready for surfacing.

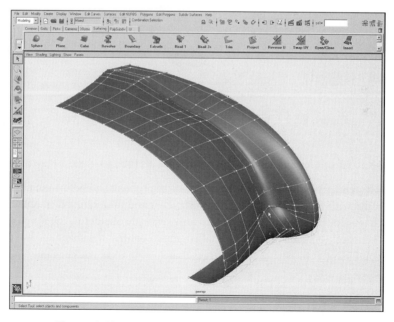

Figure 9.49   Front end surface created by Birail 3+ tool.

18. Most egregious are the multiple knots at the profiles. Use the Edit NURBS, Rebuild Surface command to remove them (choose the aptly named No Multiple Knots option for Rebuild Type).

Now the surface structure looks workable and the desired shape can be obtained by moving around CVs. After a bit of work, a pleasing front end surface can be obtained (see Figure 9.50). For simplicity, let's call this surface the hood.

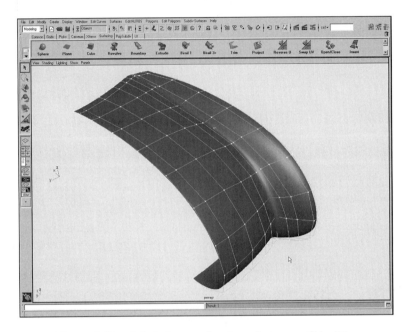

Figure 9.50   Rebuilt front end surface after some CV editing.

Next, a front fender needs to be created, so it's time to make a few more curves.

The fender poses an interesting topological problem. It needs to maintain continuity with the hood surface just constructed and maintain a desirable highlight shape along the side—yet there are only really three sides to the shape (ignoring the wheel well cutout). It'll be challenging to control the shape of the surfaces, so you'll have to construct some curves that specify what you're after.

Let's start with a body side profile. Because you're eventually going to join the front fender with the surface at the back, you'll grab the body side edge curve from the back fender.

19. To do this, first select the isoparameter curve at the frontmost edge of the rear surface and duplicate it. Then pick the edit point on this curve three spans up from
the bottom (that's all the curve you need) and detach the curve there. Now move
that curve up to the rear corner of the hood surface (you'll need to set its pivot at
the detach location and snap it into place with vertex snap).

This curve needs some additional shaping.

20. First, snap all of its CVs to the same X coordinate as the point where you just
placed the curve. Next, the tangent CV at the top needs to be at the same height as
the endpoint. This makes the curve meet the hood surface level with the crest of
the fender flare. Then make the curve longer so that its lower end is down at the
level of the door bottom. Finally, puff it out a bit in the middle so that its fattest
part matches what you see in the Top view.

21. Now duplicate this curve and move the copy forward (back in X) three spans
along the hood edge. This curve needs to be a little taller than the previous one
(the flare is at a peak in this area), so scale the upper CVs up to reach to the flare.
Leave the bottom three CVs where they are, to ensure that the highlight stays level
across that part of the surface.

At this point, you should have constructed curves that look like those in Figure
9.51.

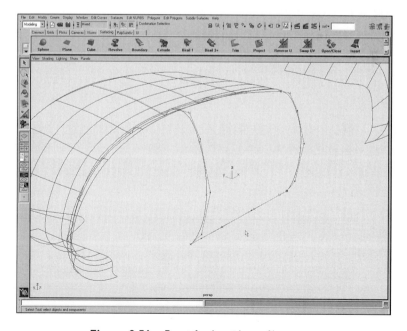

Figure 9.51   Front fender side profile curves.

The plan here is to make a four-sided front fender surface, so you still need the bottom curve. Again, by grabbing a surface edge, you can quickly have a curve with the right topology.

It's a good idea to use Display, Hide, Hide Unselected Objects to make sure that only the intended objects are available for the selecting, detaching, and surface construction operations ahead.

Although the hood edge already exists as a curve, it's a good idea to build from the surface edge rather than the original curve.

22. Pick the isoparameter curve along the hood edge and duplicate it. Then pick the edit point three spans in from the back end of this curve and use Detach Curves to snip off the part needed. (Because the previous curve was moved forward three spans along this curve, the useful chunk is the rearmost three spans.)

Warning

Don't assume that surface edges and construction curves are identical, even if you meant them to be. Often there are subtle differences in shape or parameterization. Be sure you construct from the right source geometry.

23. Connect this curve between the bottom two profile curves, and level it out.

Now that all four sides of this fender area are in place, you can use the Surfaces, Square tool to construct the surface.

24. Open the Square command's options. Setting Continuity to Tangent is the obvious choice in this tool; set this option and invoke the tool. Pick each edge curve in order as you go around the opening (the hood edge is one of these) and build the surface.

Note

When creating multiple surfaces with the Square tool, it's a good idea to pick curves in a consistent order (such as bottom, left, top, and right). This ensures that surface UV orientation and normals are consistent, which makes pickwalking and some surface-editing operations much easier.

You'll see that there's an extra span being added along the rear edge. This is because the rear profile isn't actually tangent with the hood surface, and Maya adds the span in an effort to achieve tangent continuity (within the tolerance you specify). You can either try to align it (tweaking the surface or the curve) or change the Continuity option to Implied Tangent, which says to simply interpolate tangent values along the edge.

25. Implied Tangent is fine in this circumstance (because you can reshape the rear surface edge later if you have to), so use the Channel Box to switch the continuity type. Select the new square surface and click the input node (probably called squareSrf1). Notice how, by using the Channel Box, you can adjust the continuity type for each edge independently. Change the hood edge Continuity Type to Implied Tangent. The surface updates, now without the extra span.

That takes you only partway across the fender. The front portion still needs to be built.

26. The lower part of the front segment can be bounded by making a couple of curves. A quick way of constructing these curves is to make a uniform edit point curve between the curve ends, and then rebuild it up to two spans and align the ends (using the Align Curves tool) to achieve tangent continuity.

27. Copy the bottom curve and move it up a couple of spans on the front surface (the nose section of the hood); fashion a suitable top curve from it.

28. When you've created these curves, build another square surface. Setting the Continuity Type to Tangent should work along both neighboring surfaces, resulting it what you see in Figure 9.52.

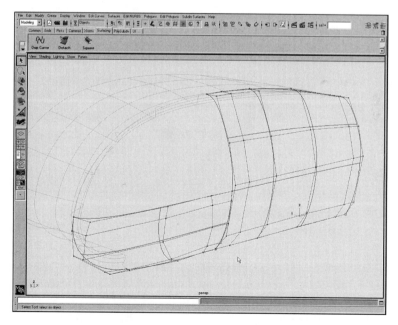

Figure 9.52   Square surfaces in front fender area.

Remember that much of what you see here will be trimmed away when you create the wheel well. So, now you need to finish up the remaining triangular region.

29. Rather than try to make it all a single surface, add one more curve paralleling the hood edge, leaving a small triangular region right in the middle of the wheel well area. Using the now-familiar process of duplicating an edge and snipping off the section you want, construct this curve to bound the edge of the area rolling around the flare.

   However, as I looked at this region in the Front view (see Figure 9.53), it became apparent that if only the top span in the big side panel were a little lower, I could entirely hide the triangular patch down in the middle of the wheel well. So, that's exactly what I did. If your geometry is similar, you can fix it, too.

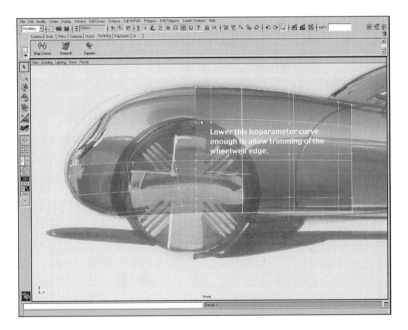

Figure 9.53 Front window view of wheel well area.

30. Turn on the CVs for the side panel and lower the CVs a bit.

   But suddenly the lower front surface disappears! What's happened? Well, the isoparameter curve that was being used to match the upper-edge curve of the disappearing surface no longer matches the curve. Of course, if history wasn't on, that surface wouldn't have gone away—but it's actually useful (albeit a little unnerving) to have such an obvious sign that something has gone awry.

Nonetheless, it's time to go back and refit the side profile curve to the newly reshaped surface. Because this area will be trimmed away, it's simple to just roughly snap and line up the necessary CVs and carry on. When the curve is touching the isoparameter curve again, the square surface that disappeared (the lower front panel) will reappear.

31. Shape the curve that you grabbed from the top fender edge into place. Make it flow from the middle isoparameter curve on the lower front surface to the upper isoparameter curve on the side panel surface. This should all now stay within the wheel well, as seen in the Front view image plane.

32. To make your work even easier, notice that the back portion of the lower front panel also lies within the wheel well area. Use Edit NURBS, Detach Surfaces to get rid of the entire chunk (it was doomed anyway). This makes it even easier to get a clean, simple shoulder surface; you can now easily adjust how the newest curve meets the edge of this newly smaller surface.

The Surfaces, Square tool is also a good choice for building this fender shoulder, especially because it offers easy edge continuity adjustment (via the Channel Box), even after the surface has been created. Use Square to create a tangent surface that now completes the area around the wheel well.

After constructing this shoulder surface, the fender looks something like Figure 9.54 (mine is in the file CarFrontShoulderSurf.ma).

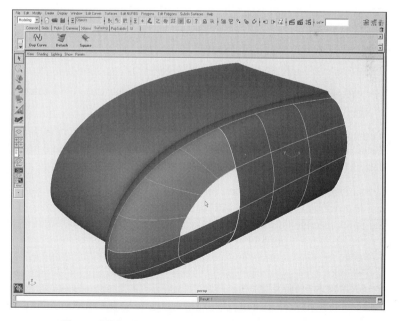

Figure 9.54   Front fender with surface patches in place.

Although you could obsess a bit about achieving tangency all over, you don't actually require it here—yet. The plan is now to merge these separate surface patches into a few larger ones. To do this, you really want well-behaved surface meshes with equivalent neighboring topologies.

Another hitherto unspoken goal has been to build surfaces so that their edges correspond to the body panels themselves. This makes it a much easier task to add fillets around the body panel edges.

It must be said that this is certainly *not* the way production surfaces are made for real automobiles—but it's a great convenience for building a car prop such as this. Chunks of surface can be shaped locally and then joined together, allowing the process of attaching to handle the continuity problems for you.

First, separate the hood section from the fender crest.

33. Select the isoparameter curve running along the groove between the two, and use the Detach Surfaces tool (you don't need to use Keep Originals).

Although the goal is fewer surfaces, you've actually got one more for a moment. There's now an inside shoulder surface running the length of the fender flare.

34. Use Detach Surfaces once more to separate the top part of the side panel (which mates to the shoulder surface) from the bottom.

On the opposite side of this new surface is a set of three surfaces that you'll pull together using the Edit NURBS, Attach Surfaces tool.

35. After setting Attach Method to Blend, use Attach Surfaces to attach these surfaces pairwise. Now the discontinuities between them are gone. There are now long shoulder surfaces on either side of the fender flare.

36. The two shoulder surfaces can then be attached—but this attach operation doesn't go quite so well.

As immediately evidenced by the mass of extra flow lines, there is clearly a parametric mismatch (see Figure 9.55). This calls for a pass with the Edit NURBS, Rebuild Surface tool to make them conform well.

37. Rebuild the surfaces in the long direction, keeping the CVs where they are and parameterizing from 0 to the number of spans. You might need to do this only to the outer shoulder surface, but try the Attach Surfaces command to see. If necessary, do the inner shoulder surface (and the hood, while you're at it).

After rebuilding the surface(s), the Attach operation produces a much better result. The entire shoulder is now a single smooth surface.

This leaves the lower fender side panel, which is no longer continuous with the shoulder. It's not obvious, but it will surely show up if you see the side of the car with reflections, so it should be fixed.

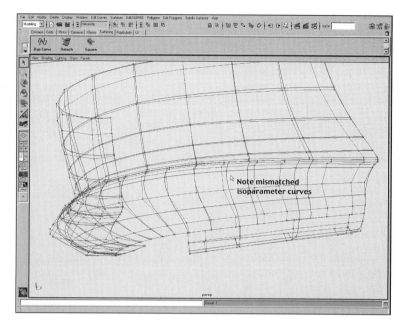

Figure 9.55 A parametric mismatch during surface attachment.

But how? The side panel is only partially in contact with the shoulder, so the Align Surfaces tool won't do the trick. One answer is to split the shoulder again, dividing it at the location where the side panel ends. Then the Align tool should be able to work on it.

In theory, that'll work. However, for reasons unknown, it didn't work for me. No amount of option tinkering seemed to generate a satisfying result. So now what? (By the way, this isn't really an indictment of the Align Surfaces tool, but an opportunity to see an alternative alignment approach. It could well be that I did something wrong.)

When faced with a continuity problem like this, it's usually possible to manually construct a solution. The underlying principle here is to get CVs aligned with each other across the seam (for a deeper discussion of continuity see Chapter 6, "Formats").

38. By constructing straight lines between the tangent and border CVs of one of the surfaces, it's possible to use them to provide perfect tangent continuity snapping targets. These curves are easily created as linear CV curves or edit point curves. Set the pivots for each of the curves at the tangent CV end, and then scale the curves by a consistent amount (I simply double their size).

39. Now just snap each of the tangent CVs on the other surface to the ends of the scaled curves. Voilá! Perfect tangency (see Figure 9.56).

The front end is now a smooth set of four surfaces. It's time to bring the front and back together.

Joining the front and back is really just a continuation of the methods used up to this point. Character lines are laid down to match existing curves and surfaces, as well as to match the artwork. Surfaces are then built using these curves. If your surfaces have been faithful to the art up to now, it should go smoothly. Of course, the art can't really show everything, so roll up your sleeves.

Just like in life, the easiest place to start is at the bottom.

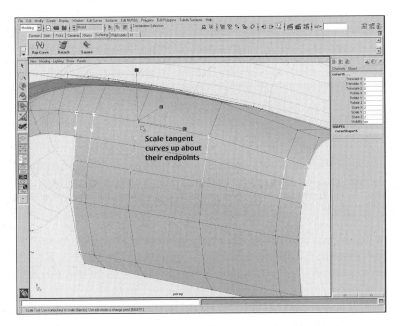

Figure 9.56 Manual tangent continuity setting between surfaces.

40. Create a single-span edit point curve between the bottom edges of the front and back surfaces. Immediately rebuild this curve to have a useful number of spans (4 is good for this) with the Rebuild Curves tool (keeping CVs).

As soon as this curve was in place, though, it was apparent that my back surface had too deep of an undercut. So, before doing any work on the door curve, I spent a moment bringing out the lower edge of the rear deck surface. After a bit of fussing with some of the shortcomings of this surface, it was ready to have the curve fitted up to it again.

41. When your curve is in place, copy it and move it up a couple of spans to match the edge between the side panel and the front shoulder surface. At the other end, match it up to the rear surface two spans up from the bottom. Take a moment to do some checking against the art in both the Front and Top windows. The curves shown in Figure 9.57 are ready to use (you can get them from CarLowerBodySideCurves.ma).

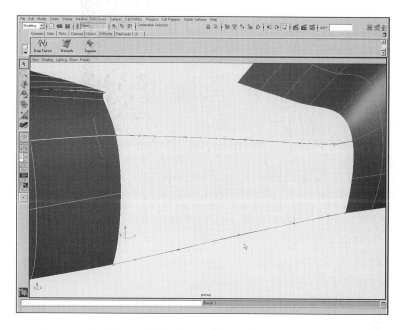

Figure 9.57   Lower body side curves.

42. Turn to your reliable Surfaces, Square tool and build this surface.

43. Use a similar procedure to construct the top section of the body side. Create a suitable top curve and build a Square surface to complete the body side.

When both surfaces are in place, it starts to really look like the car in the artwork (see Figure 9.58).

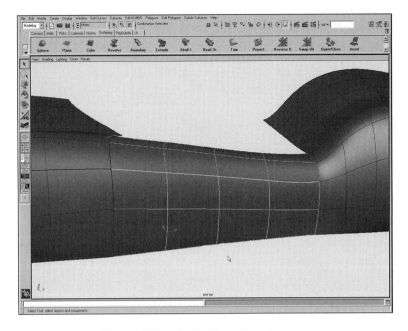

Figure 9.58 Body side surfaces in place.

44. To take a look at the whole thing, mirror the surfaces in Y by grouping them all and mirroring the group.

For an extra dose of reality, the wheel wells can be trimmed out. A circular curve can be constructed in the Front window and projected onto the front fender surfaces with the Project Curve on Surface tool. Then the Trim tool can be used to trim the surfaces back.

Except for some nagging concerns about surface continuity, it should be looking pretty good (see Figure 9.59). If yours isn't (or even if it is), feel free to load up CarFullBodyPreview.ma and look it over.

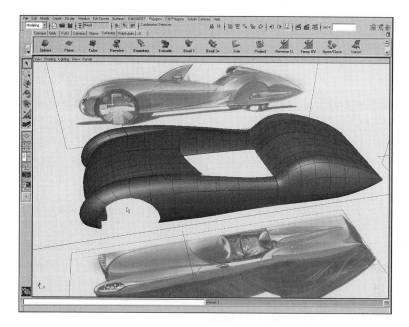

Figure 9.59   Full body panel preview, complete with trims.

Now what?

All along, we've known that subdivision surfaces offer unmatched surfacing flexibility and continuity. Yet we've been leery of some of the topological issues with incorporating precise details and achieving design fidelity. So, we've been building surfaces that individually were faithful to the design and addressed continuity issues as they arose.

But just what's involved in taking that big step to an all-subdiv car model? Let's see.

Each of the surfaces we built was designed to maintain topological similarity to its neighbors, to achieve surface continuity. This is also an excellent approach to building a complex subdivision surface. Although many approach subdivision surface modeling by starting with primitives such as cubes and spheres, and then extrude or pull faces and edges to shape the topology and features, converting NURBS surfaces into subdivs is a powerful methodology that enables you to carefully control the individual surface forms.

45. The first step is to turn the CV meshes of the surfaces into polygonal meshes with the Modify, Convert, NURBS to Polygons command. We'll avoid going directly to subdivs because there are several polymeshes to attach together first.

In this case, simply select all of the surfaces and execute the command. This operation is nondestructive and produces the polygonal meshes shown in Figure 9.60.

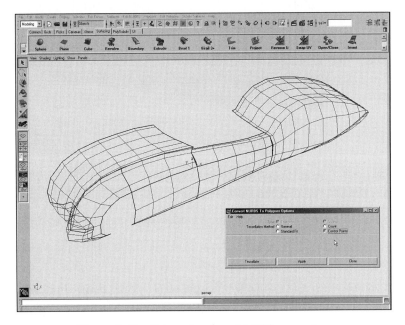

Figure 9.60 Polymeshes from NURBS conversion.

With the NURBS curves and surfaces turned off, it might become apparent that not everything was as aligned as was hoped. In addition, those surfaces that were detached will have an extra row of tangent CVs on either side of the split. Before attempting to sew up these polymeshes, you need to get their topologies to match up better.

The tool Edit Polygons, Selection, Select Contiguous Edges makes it easy to grab the extra tangent rows (so does the script edgePath that you saw in the previous chapter).

46. Simply select an edge and then let the tool select all those edges that are connected to it (within angular constraints that you can specify). Doing this a few times quickly removes the extraneous edges (at least, with regard to subdivs) by using the Delete Edge tool.

Note

The edge CVs along a detach boundary are actually closer to the surface than the original CVs were before the detach operation. When reattaching meshes, be aware that these CVs need to be adjusted outward to avoid flattening the merged surface in that area. It can be useful to keep a copy of the undetached surface for providing snapping targets for this adjustment.

When the meshes have been culled in this manner, it's time to make them match up.

47. Walk along each edge and snap the CVs together. If desired, extra edges can also be easily inserted as you examine the mesh using the Split Polygon tool.

When you're done, the spruced-up meshes should look like those in Figure 9.61 (from my scene file CarCleanedUpPolymeshes.ma).

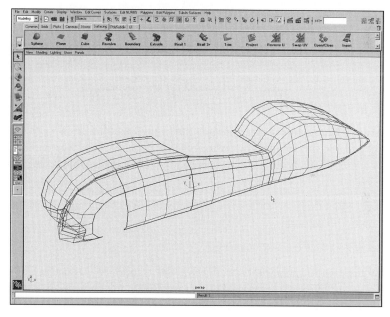

Figure 9.61   Cleaned-up polymeshes before combining.

48. Pick pairs of neighboring polymeshes and use the Polygons, Combine command to join them. Continue (as in the previous fire hydrant example) to check polymesh normals and merge vertices until they all belong to a single polymesh.

The resulting single mesh (see Figure 9.62) has all of the clear flow of the original surfaces. Plus, it can offer the added guarantee of tangent continuity inherent in subdivision surfaces.

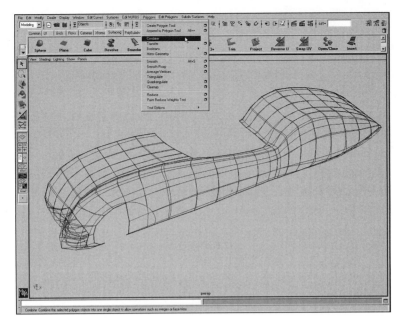

Figure 9.62 Combined car polymesh.

49. Mirror this mesh in X and combine the two halves. Now it's time to generate a subdivision surface to show the overall vehicle body shape. Use Modify, Convert, Polygons to Subdiv to generate a car body surface made from a single subdiv (see Figure 9.63).

Notice that there are no seams up the middle or any telling artifacts from discontinuities. It's smooth.

So, what about those wheel wells?

50. By constructing a simple capped polygonal cylinder and using the Polygons, Boolean, Difference command to remove it from the body mesh, it should become clear that the anticipated artifacts around the wheel well aren't so bad after all (see Figure 9.64). You can examine the results I had by calling up my scene file CarWheelwellSubdivTest.ma.

Of course, to perform the difference, a complete intersection edge must exist, so it's necessary to extend the bottom edges around the wheel well area a bit and close them up with Append Polygon. Some time will also be needed to clean up the edges around the rim of the wheel well—but it's well worth it.

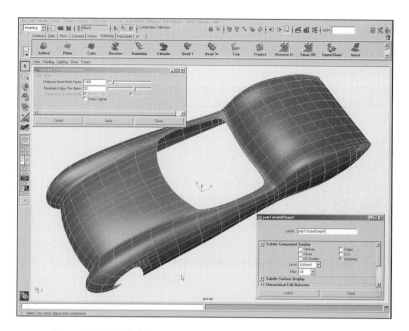

Figure 9.63   Subdivision surface from combined polymeshes.

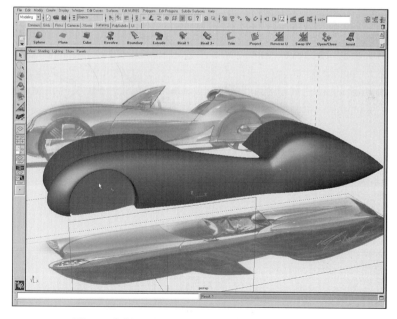

Figure 9.64   Wheel well subdivision surface test.

There will be no fearing reflections off this car.

Even though there's plenty of work left, it has become clear that the car's body can really be a subdiv. The humps behind the head rests can be easily pulled up from the mesh, perhaps using Maya's hierarchical features or perhaps just adding the detail to the base mesh. Ditto for the grille and the "swoosh" over the rear wheels.

With the car's body in place, whether it's made from NURBS or subdivision surfaces, additional details can be added as the design demands and the budget permit. Real automotive design processes go on for months or years, with every small detail scrutinized for style and functionality. In our production, we'll add the essentials and strive for a distinctive style, but we'll cut whatever corners we can.

Although it's a main prop, the car is much like the bone or the fire hydrant. It needs to serve a function, express a design sensibility, and add to the story. But most of all, like any other prop, it has to be made first—and Maya, like its namesake, offers a multitude of ways to bring it into existence.

Summary

The techniques of modeling in Maya could fill a book of their own. However, the process of modeling props has some commonalities. Props are built to be placed, handled, or moved around. They need structure and simplicity, and they need to be built to scale. Sometimes they have artwork, sometimes not, but the process of modeling them requires constant balancing of beauty, time, technical requirements, and effort.

In many respects, modeling techniques are expressions of personal preferences and acquired habits. But Maya offers a huge range of tools, wide enough to suit almost any methodology and tackle any prop-modeling problem. Of course, how you get it done is up to you—which is how it should be, after all.

Chapter10

Characters

By Max Sims

Our animation project (an overview of which is provided in Chapter 4, "Technical Considerations") stars two characters—Spot, a dog, and The Jerk, a man—both of which need to meet certain functional and aesthetic criteria. This chapter discusses these criteria and provides insight into how we met them for our project using the modeling and design features in Maya. Specifically, we cover the following:

- Modeling well-parameterized characters that can be sent down the production pipeline
- Using subdivision surface modeling techniques for organic characters
- Creating and testing appealing characters that are worth animating

Functional and Aesthetic Criteria

Whenever you set out to create a character, you need to take into consideration several functional and aesthetic criteria. In terms of function for this project, the models must fit the criteria given by the character setup department. This means that the topology of the surfaces must bind well to the inverse kinematics skeletons. Point placement at the joints should allow for bending and wrinkling. Overall surface smoothness is important for texture mapping and, consequently, rendering. The flow of points is equally important because their consequences are felt all the way down the production pipeline. The technical director (TD) for this project sends the models to character setup, and later they go to the animator for animation. At that point, the models need to have all their points in the right place so that problems don't arise. The models must flow smoothly in more ways than one. Any compromise done at modeling could result in extra time and effort spent by the motion TD and animators.

Regarding aesthetics, the models should be attractive and appealing. There are far too many bad character designs out there in 3D land; they're downright ugly. Knowing our limitations, we got our professional colleagues involved. I knew that I was not the best character designer, but I also knew what I wanted. So, to get the most aesthetically appealing look for the characters in this project, I commissioned Scott Clark, an animation director from Pixar, to design the two characters. We went through three successive design refinements before settling on versions of Spot and The Jerk, keeping in mind that the characters will be in an Art Deco universe and that they are actors that will tell a story. Scott drew the bodies and detailed head drawings that I could trace over in Maya. I also had Erick Miller, our TD, sit in at later design meetings to ensure a smooth transition for setup.

For the Spot character, we had three main concerns: modeling, design, and animation. In terms of modeling, we needed to make sure that we were using the best modeling method for characters. This meant subdivision surfaces. On the design side, we needed to ensure that Spot would fit into our designed world while exhibiting universal appeal. We had to make sure that Spot could withstand scrutiny from both the motion TD and the animator. This meant that he needed to have the right points in the right place to make their lives easier. The joint placement and point placement needed to match to get Spot to articulate nicely.

The Jerk also had to fulfill the criteria of looking like the jerk that Mark and I had envisioned. The design had to be definitive and had to credibly exist in our imagined world. Functionally, the character needed to be somewhat cartoonish, so all of the controls needed for a real person were not there. Another factor was clothing. All the people we knew who were great at Maya Cloth were busy in their day jobs; they might not be available to do cloth and write a chapter on it. We decided to give The Jerk the T-shirt and jeans look that could be done either as a texture map or as a full-on cloth simulation.

Advantages of Subdivision Surfaces

With all of this in mind, we decided to create both Spot and The Jerk using Maya's relatively new subdivision surfaces (subdivs) rather than build him from a traditional NURBS patch model. Subdivs have many advantages over NURBS. For instance, many studios still rely on a technique called *patch modeling*, in which small strips of NURBS surfaces are socked together with an internal tool that keeps all the adjacent edges tangent to each other during animation. This is possible, but a high level of finesse is required to do this with Maya's Global Stitch tool. With subdivs, you never need to worry about continuity issues such as multiple edge tangencies and global stitching. You can model as a complete volume, adding and subtracting with ease. Furthermore, you can leverage all of Maya's polygon tools to help work around tricky elements. Plus, subdivs are supported in Pixar's RenderMan, which will come in handy when we try alternative renderers later in the project. With this format, we come closest to the ultimate goal of a single-skinned character with multiple openings. Only real skin is better.

Subdivs aren't perfect, however. The main disadvantage of subdivs is rooted in the fact that they have not been available very long in commercial software, and they have been available in Maya only since Version 2.5. Even then, Maya users couldn't render their subdiv models without first converting them back to polygons.

Furthermore, each successive version of Maya since 2.5 has demonstrated increased functionality in the subdiv arena, to the point that today users can take full advantage of features such as 3D painting, match topology, and better blend shapes. However, these features are nonetheless relatively new, and often workflows and processes such as subdiv modeling are not as refined. A modeler can run into a blind corner, with no resort but to start over. The beauty of NURBS is that they have been around for decades, and software engineers farther down the production pipeline know exactly where the U and V are on a surface for items such as particle sampling or texture space. Despite these caveats, you should learn subdivision surfaces and embrace the future.

Although many high-end studios still do not support subdiv geometry, subdiv support is an emerging trend. And the good news for Maya users is that, with Maya 5, you can also convert Paint Effects or Fluid Effects into Polygon. Truly unparalled! You might find it easier to create your shapes in subdivs and then convert to NURBS if that is the only format that your company supports. You might be more comfortable with NURBS as a modeling medium as well, and you then can convert to subdivs. This production is trying to emulate reality, not show all of Maya's details. Therefore, all the characters will be done using subdivs, not the patch method.

Additional Criteria

As noted earlier, the functional requirements for our models of Spot and The Jerk are that they smoothly transition downstream to animation and rendering. We can ensure this in several ways, as the following sections illustrate.

Level of Detail

The two character models must be bound to a skeletal structure, to accommodate enough detail at the joints. To do this, we need to make sure at subdiv levels 0 or 1 that there are enough vertices to bind to the skeleton when it is rigged. During the modeling process, great care must be taken to make sure that the model's surface flow lines are even and ordered. The best way to do this is to build the models first as polygonal boxes and then convert them into subdivs later. You also should test the conversion at various steps to make sure that the model is not going down the wrong path. To ensure that Erick Miller had a good enough model to rig for animation I consulted with him early on for what he needed. His biggest requirement was for most of the detail to be at subdiv Level 0. The original polygon model's vertices correspond exactly to the Level 0 points.

As discussed in Chapter 6, "Formats," Maya has a unique hierarchical subdivision surface-modeling system. This means that you can model in extreme detail at multiple nested resolutions. In production, going further than Level 3 detail is more than sufficient. If you went to Level 12, it would be at 1/4096th of level 0. This kind of functionality is great and demos well, but it is impractical until the hardware can keep up.

Extraordinary Points

The other modeling consideration in the subdiv world is extraordinary points. These are areas in which many surfaces flow into one. Figure 10.1 shows a good example: Notice how the fingers go into the palm to create a spider-web pinch point. This effect happens in a lot of cases and just needs to be acknowledged. The trick is to make sure that the progression is gradual. In Figure 10.2, take into consideration that the fingers will flow into the palm and simply create a palm that has four polygons running down the entire hand.

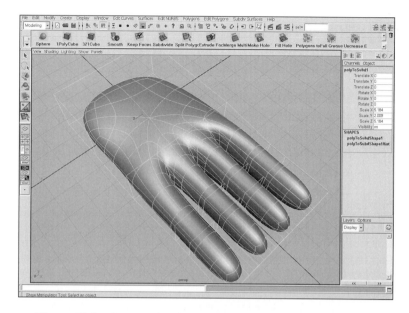

Figure 10.1   An example of extraordinary points pinching too much.

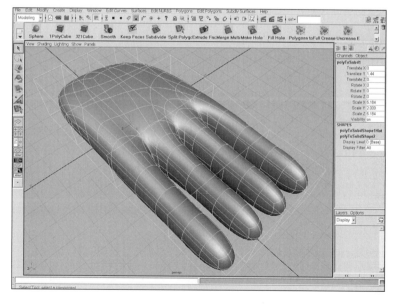

Figure 10.2   A much more optimized hand in terms of surface flow.

Texturing

Texturing is another consideration when creating models. Your modeling affects texturing in the shading process. The UV texturing capability in Maya's subdivs is similar to polygonal texturing. Both have the capability to get an image and lay the polygons over it to assign placement. This is relatively time-consuming compared to NURBS texturing. Maya has an excellent 3D texture-painting tool that requires new UVs to work properly. The other possibility is to do projection maps based on orthographic views, negating a lot of problems. This is discussed in more detail in Chapter 20, "Rendering."

Tip

You can skin a cat (or, in our case, a dog and a human) in many ways. For instance, you can pre-set all of Maya's modeling tools to output subdivs in the Window, Settings/Preferences, Preferences|Modeling option box. Any modeling tool, such as Loft, then creates a subdiv surface rather than a NURBS surface. NURBS and polygons can be converted to Subdivs after the fact. You might feel more comfortable with these formats and know that things can go round-trip.

You can also just start with a subdiv primitive and add volume to the shape. My personal preference is to start with a four-sided polygonal mesh and flesh out the basic form by extruding faces. This ensures you good subdivs to begin with, so that you don't run into problems when you convert a detailed poly or NURBS model. You are simply adding to a complete volume and avoiding attaching disparate surfaces. If you do this, make sure that you keep most of your detail at the polygonal proxy form, to match your subdiv base mesh of 0. That allows good binding points to your skeleton later.

Creating Spot and The Jerk

Now it is time to manifest our designs into a real model. The next section covers the process of creating Spot and The Jerk. You will do things such as create a custom modeling shelf to speed up your production, and then move on to sculpting the shapes of the characters using subdivision surfaces. You will hopefully gain insight into the relatively easy process of fleshing out form to the more nuanced art of sculpture.

Getting Started

Before we set out to build our models, we're going to take advantage of the high level of customization in Maya and create our own modeling menu shelf. It's beneficial to create your own modeling menu shelf for projects in which you'll be using a small number of controls often. By customizing your menu shelf, you can access those controls that you use most often, without digging into menu after menu.

Exercise 10.1   Creating a Custom Modeling Menu Shelf

In this exercise, you create a very simple polygon and subdivision surfaces modeling tool shelf.

1. To start, make sure that the shelf UI element is showing (see Figure 10.3). If you don't see the shelf, go to Display, UI Elements, Shelf to display it.

Figure 10.3   The shelf UI element in Maya.

2. Left Mouse Button (MB) over the Shelf menu items and select New Shelf. Name the shelf PolyModl.

   You have just created a new shelf and named it PolyModl. At this point, your shelf is empty. Not only do you automate your most used menu picks, but they have all your favorite option settings.

3. First we will add the menu tab for the custom shelf. Maya has somehow managed to use different key combinations to do this for each operating system: Ctrl+Alt+Shift for UNIX, Alt+Shift for Linux, Ctrl+Shift for Windows, and Option+RMB on a Mac. Press and hold the add-to-shelf keys for your OS while you select Create, Polygon Primitives, Cube.

   An icon appears on your shelf. Your new shelf should look like Figure 10.4.

   That was easy! Now we're going to customize the shelf even further.

4. To preset a different option box setting, open the option box for Create, Polygon Primitive, Cube. Change Subdivisions Along Width to 3 and Subdivisions Along Height to 2. Click Apply at the bottom if you want to make a cube with these settings (to confirm that it's what you want), or select Save Settings from the Edit menu on the Polygon Cube Options window (if you're sure). One of these must be done to establish the new settings.

5. Repeat Step 3 by pressing the add-to-shelf keys for your OS and clicking Create, Polygon Primitives, Cube one more time. Notice that the menu pick is now set to the new options set in the option box.

   Because you don't want to have the same name and icon for the two different types of cubes, you need to edit their nomenclature with the Shelf Editor.

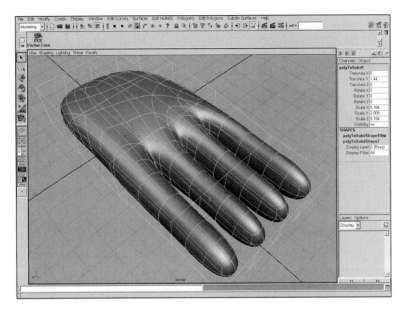

Figure 10.4 Your first menu shelf item.

6. LMB over the Shelf menu items and select Shelf Editor. The Shelf Contents tab should show the word Cube on two lines.

7. Highlight the first instance of the word Cube and, in the Labels and ToolTips area, rename it 1 Poly Cube. This is the string that appears when your shelf is displayed in one of the combination icon/text modes. To add text that overlays the icon image, enter it into the Icon Name field.

8. Rename the second instance as 321 Pcube. I like to have very short names so that I can see the label name when I mouse over it. By default your second cube icon will have the same label that you gave the first one, however, it will probably be best to make your labels unique.

The changes that you make to your shelves in the Shelf Editor take effect immediately, so you can just click Close when you're done. However, if you want to have these shelf changes in future Maya sessions, click Save All Shelves instead.

If you need to get rid of an icon, just Middle Mouse Button (MMB) and click-drag the icon to the small trash can icon in the upper-right corner (see Figure 10.5.).

Figure 10.5   You can place icons that you no longer want in the trash can.

You will now get the tools that you will use most often to the PolyModl shelf without needing to modify options in the option box.

9. Select Polygons, Smooth and then Polygons, Tool Options, Keep Faces Together.

You've just made a custom shelf for fast subdivision surface modeling workflow. You can reuse this anytime you want to model in this method.

10. While again pressing your OS's key combination, click the following from the Edit Polygons menu to add them to your shelf:

> Subdivide
>
> Split Polygon Tool
>
> Extrude Face
>
> Merge Multiple Edges
>
> Make Hole Tool
>
> Fill Hole

11. From the Subdiv Surfaces menu, add these tools to the PolyModl shelf:

> Full Crease Edge/Vertex
>
> Partial Crease Edge/Vertex
>
> Uncrease Edge/Vertex

12. Finally, add Modify, Convert, Subdiv to Polygons to your shelf. You can continue using the Shelf Editor to modify the order, labels, and icons as you see fit.

You now have a menu system that permits quick surface modifications. The context-sensitive RMB marking menus take care of the rest of your needs as you model along. The next two exercises use this shelf that you just created to do the organic modeling of Spot and The Jerk.

Modeling Spot

Spot, the dog, is a simple, semi-caricatured quadruped. Because I tend to think of objects that I will model in subdivs as if I were carving in marble, I rely on the original polygonal model of Spot to be the basic stones that I will detail and refine into the final form. I think of the overall form as one complete volume first, see if it looks right, and start over if it doesn't. I add details only after I am pleased with the basic form. After all, if I don't have the basic proportions right, why should I consider the subtle nuances?

Tip

For this animation project, I grew a model to a certain point and then scrapped it to see if I could rebuild it with yet one more order of efficiency and elegance. You should do something similar in your projects. Allot the time to experiment with your models rather than just using the very first thing you have built. I am not saying that you should build your models in full detail multiple times. Instead, you should do as most sculptors do and make maquettes before you make the final sculpture. You won't get things right the first time, so consider this a 3D sketching exercise.

You often don't see what the sketches led to the final piece. I would like to show some of my thinking that led to the final model. The basic procedure is to build from a primitive polygonal shape and then test it as a subdiv model. Look at Figures 10.6 through 10.8 to see some of the ways I thought of building the basic dog shape.

When I was creating the dog model, my basic procedure was to build from a primitive polygonal shape and then test it as a subdiv model. Figures 10.6 through 10.8 show some examples of ways in which I thought of building the basic dog shape.

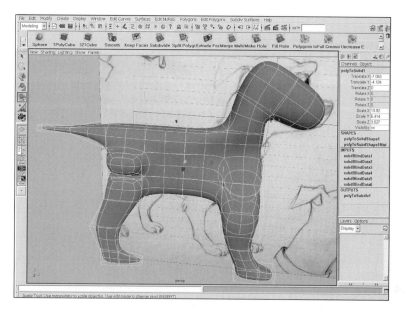

Figure 10.6   A polygonal cube, with more material extruded using the Extrude face command.

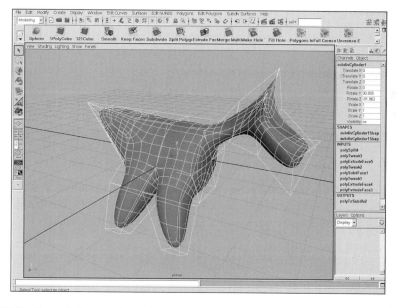

Figure 10.7   A rough form made with a cylinder—good for the body but not to shape the head.

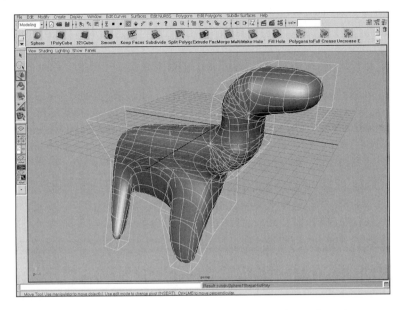

Figure 10.8   A modified box that uses wedge faces to transition the neck to the snout.

In the next exercise, you make a simple maquette to test the surface flow of the Spot character.

Exercise 10.2   Subdivision Surface Sketching

In this exercise, you use the menu shelf items that you created in the last exercise.

1. Create a primitive poly cube with your 1 Poly Cube shelf command and select the front face using the context-sensitive marking menu. Use the menu shelf items that you created in Exercise 10.1. Select Face and then Edit Polygons, Extrude Face.

   As a result of these actions, you will get a Translate Scale Rotate (TSR) manipulator that you will use to translate the new face out and away from the original cube. This is a fundamental way of adding more volume to your model.

2. Select the top face and press the g key to repeat the Extrude Face process. Pull up a neck.

3. Extrude again (by pressing the g key) and move the selected face up in the Y axis. Immediately select the rotate manipulator and start to turn on the Red X Rotate axis about 45°.

Tip

You can also get quick, dependable angles by clicking the Modify, Transformation Tools, Rotate Tool option box and then turning on Discrete Rotate and setting Step Size to 15.

4. Repeat the extrusion and rotation to start the head form.

5. Extrude again, and this time scale by 75%. Then extrude a snout straight out.

6. Select the two side faces on the left and right sides. Extrude them again, moving them first out and then down. Select the rotate manipulator.

    When you rotate, notice that the other side spins in the opposite direction. This is where you will forget about bilateral symmetry and start to just work on the side closest to you. If you had two faces extruded together, you would need to make sure that Polygons, Tool Options, Keep Faces Together is checked off. This is something you will turn on and off with great frequency, depending on what you need.

7. Select the faces that will form the legs and extrude. Pull out the legs even though they are at a 45° angle. Use the Translate tool (or the w key) instead of the TSR manipulator to move the legs into place. This moves the faces together in the same direction rather than in opposite directions.

8. Select the faces on the two legs and extrude them straight down. Do that again, but do a shorter extrusion for the paws (about one quarter of the length).

9. Select the front lowermost faces on the leg to form the paw, and extrude them slightly.

10. To form a tail, select the back of the entire dog and extrude the face, pull it out, and scale it to make the transition to a tail.

11. Extrude again and pull a long, straight tail.

    Now you have the polygonal massing of a dog maquette. You can further manipulate that simple polygonal model after it is a subdiv surface. All the Edit Polygon tools will still be available to use in conjunction with the subdiv surfaces. This is where the power is to be found in easily massing up a form as a single continuous skin. Next you will test out the subdiv surface and begin to model symmetrically.

12. RMB with your cursor over the model, and press Select to select the entire model.

13. Convert the polygons to subdivs by clicking Modify, Convert, Polygons to Subdivs. The model should look almost like a seal with legs and a tail.

    We will now remove one half of the side to make a symmetrical model.

14. RMB over the model to see a marking menu with the items Coarser, Finer, and Refine. Select the five o'clock position on this marking menu, and you will see Polygon. This lets you switch to your original polygon model.

Tip

This is called the polygonal proxy because it is used as the proxy to approximate the subdiv shape. For faster interactivity, do as many of your manipulations as possible in Standard mode. Think of the base-level mesh's faces, vertices, and edges as corresponding to those of the driving polygon. When creating detail, though, in Standard mode do not revert back to add detail in Polygonal mode. An area that has had subdiv refinement will cause errors if poly faces are split after the fact. Make sure all your splits and polygon subdivides are done before refining to higher levels.

15. Turn the model to the side with the leg nubs. Right Mouse Button (RMB) marking menu over the model, select all the faces facing the negative Z-axis, and delete them (see Figure 10.9). This throws away the other half of the model so that you don't have to sculpt twice as much detail.

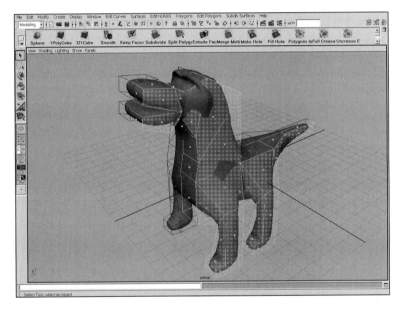

Figure 10.9   The faces to delete.

16. Switch back to Standard mode with the RMB marking menu. Select all the vertices on the open edge.

17. Switch to the Front view and move the vertices locked on the Z-axis only, by pressing the x key. The points snap to the 0 XY plane.

18. Duplicate the model by going into the Edit, Duplicate option box and checking the Instance box. Set the scale Z to −1. Now you have a perfect replica that you can model symmetrically without having to select both sides.

I like doing this when I have a lot of geometry that will be exactly like the original. It is very file space–efficient because it simply redisplays the original geometry. It doesn't speed up the renders as fast as one would think, though, because the pixels for the object need to be calculated.

19. You can now select an edge and Subdiv Surfaces, Full Crease Edge/Vertex. Move it around, and see that the other side reflects the same change.

You can see quite quickly that the massing model achieves the desired doglike form. When you analyze it, you can see that it needs to be beefed up in certain areas. The side is only two faces, and we need to add a belly. Perhaps four divisions are needed along the side. More detail is required around the mouth. A separate gum and teeth model can go inside the muzzle. This model is one of many variations I have tried to get to the optimal balance of a light polygonal proxy with enough detail to hand over to a character setup person.

You can see the finished model for Exercise 10.2 by setting your project to Spot and then opening Dog_sketch.mb in the Scenes folder. The next exercise is similar to Exercise 10.2, but you will delve much deeper into subdivs.

Exercise 10.3   Modeling Spot, the Dog

Using the previous sketch model, we could add more polygons, split off parts, and reattach them. This would be more complicated than starting on a fresh path, however. In this exercise, you model the finished dog so that it is suitable for handing over to a character TD. This exercise takes you through the process of importing artwork, developing the form, and reining all of the detail.

1. Set the project to Spot and create a new scene.

2. Make the Front view active and then select View, Image Plane, Import Image. Retrieve Side_Spot.iff from the CD Spot/source images folder. Set the Center Z to –.1.

3. In the Attribute Editor, make sure that the image plane is set to display in all views. Also, if Color Gain is set to .4 and Color Offset is set to .3, this will gray down your image so that you can see active and inactive geometry easily.

4. Create a 321 Pcube from the Poly Modl shelf created in Exercise 10.1. Make it active, and in the Channel Box set Subdivisions Width to 4. Based on Exercise 10.2, the sketch model showed that we need more area for the dog's belly. So, scale the cube to fit over the main body of the dog in the Top and Front views.

5. In the Front view, select the vertices of the new cube and move them to the positions shown in Figure 10.10. You are moving them to conform to the rough silhouette of the dog in the image plane.

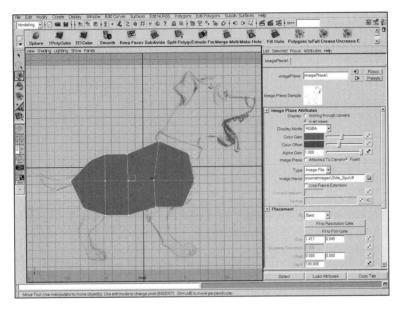

Figure 10.10   The image plane settings and the first poly cube.

6. Select the center bottom and top vertices, and scale them up in the Z-axis only.

7. Select the upper-right vertices and move them down. This sets the face to be perpendicular to extrude a neck.

8. RMB over the model and select the face that corresponds to the base of the neck. Extrude the face. Repeat the extrusion three more times, to make enough geometry for the jaws and eyes.

9. Now you'll make a transition surface for the jaw opening. Select the faces for the jaw area and make sure that the Polygons, Tool options are set to Keep Faces Together. Extrude it a short bit.

10. Turn off Keep Faces Together in Polygons, Tool Options, and extrude the same jaw faces again.

11. Scale in the faces slightly, to make sure that they are not joined together and to taper the muzzle. Move the vertices to conform to the Side and Top view images.

12. Go to the Side view and import the heads_frontdetail .jpg image from the accompanying CD. Highlight the Channel Box Inputs for Width and Height. Scale the image plane to 15.2, to get the head to align to the brow and to the neck base/collar. You might need to fine-tune it. The Center should be set to X –15.

13. Now use the head detail image to get the jaw line and silhouette to match. Do this by moving the closest vertices to align to the image plane.

14. Test the subdiv surface with Modify, Convert, Polygons to Subdiv menu. Orbit around to make sure everything is together; set the display to Shaded mode using the 5 key, and set it to a high-resolution display using the 3 key. Press the z key (or Undo) to revert back to your polygonal original.

At this point, your model should look like that in Figure 10.11.

Figure 10.11   The subdiv model exhibiting good surface flow and a light build.

In Figure 10.11, you can see that the model is close to what we want, but you will need to get more of the desired point positions with your subdiv vertices. That's what you'll do next.

15. Start by extruding the tail face. Scale and rotate the new face to be square in the Front view.

16. Go to the Edit Polygons, Extrude Face option box and, in Other Values, set Divisions to 2. Immediately translate the face out to the end of the tail. Taper the extrusion on the end, and fatten it in the middle by scaling it down and up.

17. Shift+click the right front shoulder face of the dog and the polygon edge. Open the Edit Polygon, Wedge Face option box; set Wedge Angle to 90 and Wedge Divisions to 2. Don't worry about the other side.

18. Move the new vertices to conform to the upper shoulder. Make sure that the face angle for the leg that you will extrude is set to flow naturally to the elbow.

19. Extrude the face for the leg, still making sure that Divisions is set to 2 in the Other Values menu. Keep rotating slightly to eliminate the kinks in the joints.

20. Repeat Steps 17 through 19 for the hind legs.

21. Select the roof of the mouth and set the option box for Extrude Face to an Offset of .5 and Divisions of 1. Move the face up to form the upper palate.

22. Select the lower jaw face. This time set the Offset to .1 and then move the jaw face down.

23. Select the first four faces of the jaw and scale them slightly to form the mouth.

24. Now you'll move on to the ear. Use the Edit Polygons, Split Polygon tool to split the polygons on the back of the head to form an extrusion for the ear. Continue this down the head and to the nose base.

25. Extrude the face into four divisions, making a small length for where the ear will flop.

    At this point, you're ready to work on the eye area.

26. Extrude an eyebrow and offset-extrude the eye socket.

27. Convert the polygons to subdivs. Turn the model to the side without the legs. RMB marking menu over the model and select all of the faces facing the left side. Delete them (see Figure 10.12).

28. Switch back to Standard mode with the RMB marking menu. Select all the vertices on the open edge.

29. Switch to Front view and move the vertices locked on the Z-axis only, with the x key depressed. The points will snap to the 0 XY plane.

30. Duplicate the model by going into the Edit, Duplicate option box. Set Scale Z to –1 and Instance. This permits you to see the model symmetrically, so that you do not have to model both sides.

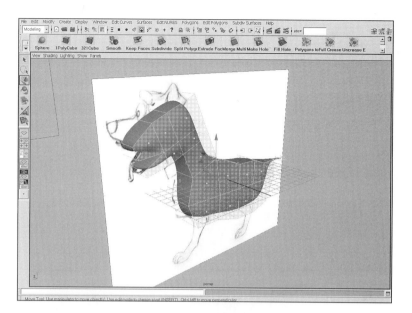

Figure 10.12   Delete these faces.

At this point, you should be ready to try your hand at sculpting out the shapes you've just built. You can sculpt in two distinct ways: You can move subdiv points in NURBS or use polygon tools.

Also at this point, you can successively refine the specific area where the model needs detail. For the Spot model, it will be better to move polygon points in order to hand off to the animation rigger. Also, the model is probably a bit too mechanical in shape, so we will need to randomize the proxy shape a bit so that it feels right.

The model so far has been based on orthographic views that do not convey what the three-dimensional reality of the character will be. It is time to think of the head as a sphere and to give the eyes their initial neutral expression. It is helpful now to assign a Blinn shader to the model and to set up two opposing directional lights, with one being colored. This will distinguish what features are being sculpted, and the shader will give us a nice highlight to work with. A hero character can take two full-time weeks to get the shape right. Then it might need some massaging when it comes back from the rigging department for functional reasons.

In the next exercise, you start to give the model some "life."

Exercise 10.4 Subdiv Surface Editing

In this exercise, you add more detail and maintain a good flow of faces. Think of this as a well-gridded model in which the spacing is generally uniform and is going in the general direction of the surfaces. We will avoid grids on the surface that are willy nilly because this will make sculpting much more difficult; in this exercise, you will know where every point is and why it is there.

1. Starting with the mouth, split the top, side, and bottom faces of the upper jaw to form the nose, as in Figure 10.13.

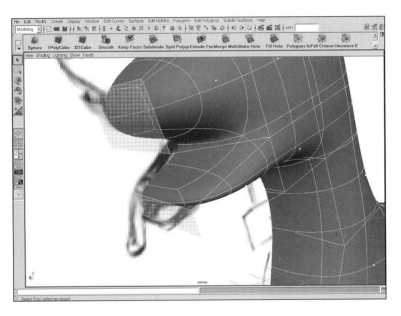

Figure 10.13 Split these faces to form the jaw.

2. Continue splitting along the upper jaw to nearly the tip of the ear.

3. Select the edges of the mouth and elbows, and partially crease them.

4. Select the subdiv vertex at the ankles and partially crease them as well.

5. Select the nose base and fully crease it. Your model should look like Figure 10.14.

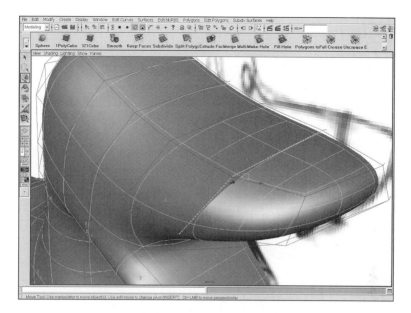

Figure 10.14   The nose base that will be creased.

6. Go back to Polygon mode. Select the front face of the paws, and split it into three vertical faces. Extrude out the claws and scale them slightly.

7. Revert to Standard mode. Select the three subdiv claw faces and refine them with the RMB. Pick the center Level 1 vertex and pull it out.

8. Hit Refine again on that Level 1 point. Now select the center Level 2 vertex, pull it out, and then move it down. Partially crease the tips (see Figure 10.15).

9. Move the Level 2 points around to get the toenail shape the way you like it, moving each point separately to get random organic results.

10. Delete the instance model. Duplicate it again as a regular noninstanced model.

11. Make sure that all the polygon points and Level 0 vertices are exactly on the center line, and switch both sides to Polygon mode. The new side might have its normals facing in. Check by going to Display, Polygon Components, Long Normals. Duplicate –1 in the Z direction. You will notice that the Normals on the copy are now facing in; this is undesirable. Delete the copy. Now you can use a more specific tool.

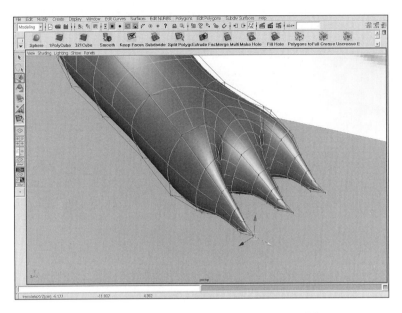

Figure 10.15 Two of the nails have been creased; one Level 1 point remains.

12. Turn off the normal display and pick the Subdiv model. Set Subdiv Surfaces, Mirror to mirror things in Z. The copy that it produces will be set up properly to then attach.

13. Open the Subdiv Surfaces, Attach option box. Set the Threshold to 0.2. This lets the two sides become one surface.

Note

The mirror threshold should be set to something larger than 0, to accommodate any imprecision of your point placement. Always look at the option box of any unfamiliar tool to see what the options are. Often in Maya, that will be the difference in whether a tool works for you.

Now we have the basis of our dog character and have done some tweaking using primarily the polygon model. More detail is better achieved by judiciously splitting polygons. Minimal work has been done in the subdiv refining, and we go to only Level 3 on the toenails. We tweaked the model with the current points to get the dog looking appealing in all possible views (see Figure 10.16).

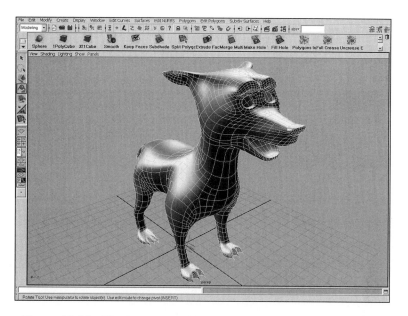

Figure 10.16   The final dog model ready to be sent to character rigging.

Erick Miller, the character TD, wanted a model that would be easy to bind up in the polygon proxy, to ensure a trouble-free setup. This means that the 0 vertex points and polygon vertices are in the same place. There must be enough detail for the skeleton to bind up to the points. Luckily, the dog was designed with a very cartoonish slant, to make all our jobs easier. If we had done a more realistic dog, it would look the same in terms of surface flow, but a lot more detail and modeling tedium would have been involved. Time and aesthetic decisions here did not permit perfect realism.

In the next exercise, you model The Jerk character and use the same techniques used for Spot. In this exercise, however, we'll place more emphasis on the big picture.

Modeling The Jerk

The Jerk was designed to be an obnoxious antagonist who displays a healthy dose of narcissism and resembles my archenemy. I had Scott Clark design the character based on the actor who most resembles the embodiment of a jerk. Through a wide set of iterations of what a jerk could be, we started to hone in on the actor. Figure 10.17 shows the first pass. Figure 10.18 shows a target set to be refined. Too many characters in 3D animated pieces are designed to one sketch and then appear unappealing to audiences.

The Jerk was carefully designed and then resolved into what the drawings in Figure
10.19 came to be.

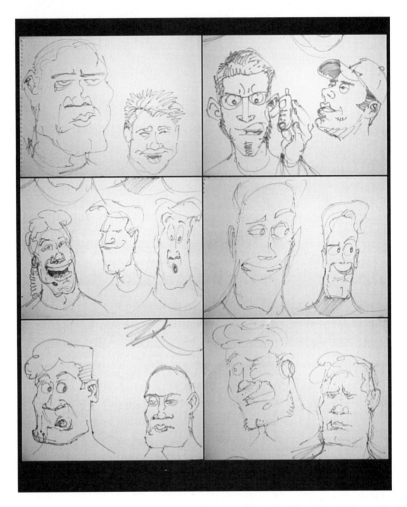

Figure 10.17 A wide set of jerks explored in art direction (sketches by Scott Clark).

Figure 10.18   Further refining, done to hone in on The Jerk (sketches by Scott Clark).

Figure 10.19 The final character sketch for our infamous Jerk (sketch done by Scott Clark).

The head also was designed to be at a specific level of detail. Scott presented us with a range of choices from complex to simple. We opted for simple as the most appealing and worked toward that as an ideal. Figures 10.20 through 10.23 show the range of complexity and body types.

Figure 10.20   The complex head design (sketches by Scott Clark).

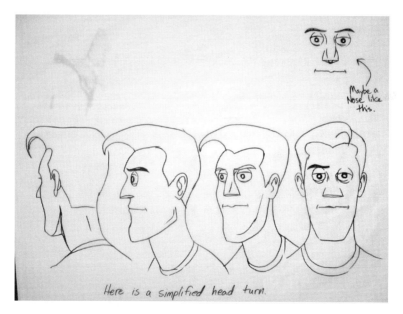

Figure 10.21   The simple head design that was chosen (sketches by Scott Clark).

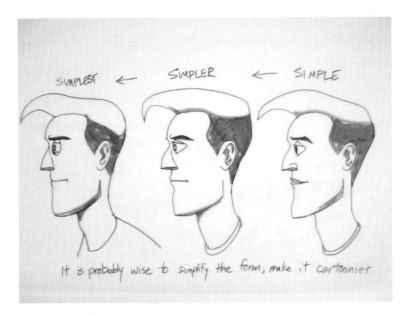

Figure 10.22 A head design that is even simpler (sketches by Scott Clark).

Figure 10.23 The three options on the body type that were offered; the middle one was the easiest to execute (sketches by Scott Clark).

Creating a good character design is as important as making a good model. If the design is not there, the effort expended will not be worthwhile. Realize that the best work is not always done solely by you; collaboration is the key. This is why Scott designed this and Daniel Naranjo finished off the model for the project. Next you will model The Jerk based on the elements shown here.

Exercise 10.5   Building The Jerk

The Jerk is a cartoonish and simplified human form. The model will be constructed in the same manner as the one for dog: using a polygonal box method. The legs and arms will be very simplified because we will be draping cloth over the character. We will also create some simple musculature seen through the clothing. The face will be neutral because the facial expressions will be sculpted later. The objective here is to add volume, starting with a cube. The resulting polygons will turn to a smooth subdivided surface. The Jerk will be built with only one side, and then mirrored and attached later. The advantages of modeling this way are that the character can be one volume, with detail inserted where needed. Most of the detail will be at the 0 base level mesh, which is, of course, the same as the polygon vertices.

1. Set the project to The Jerk from the CD.

2. Import the image sourceimages/Jerk_head.JPG as an image plane into both the Front and the Side windows.

3. Scale the images uniformly until they are the right size; then adjust their Center attributes until they're in just the right spot. Figure 10.24 shows the scene with both image planes displayed.

   An alternate method will be used to make the body image.

4. Create a polygonal plane with proportions of 512 by 612 (the image size). Make a shader with the Jerk_body.tif image mapped to the incandescence value, and apply it to the plane. Orient and scale this plane in the Front window to align it with The Jerk side image planes. Make the head drawings overlay the head in the body drawing.

5. Create a poly cube primitive and set Subdivisions to Width 4, Height 3, Depth 1.

6. Scale the cube nonproportionally to fit the Front view torso (see Figure 10.25).

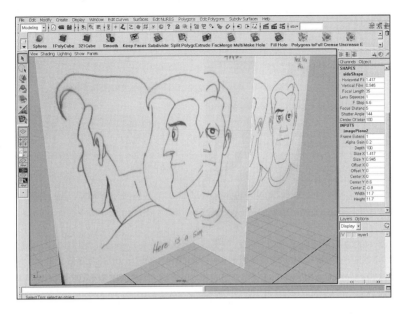

Figure 10.24 The two images aligned in space so that the Front view is set back slightly from the side.

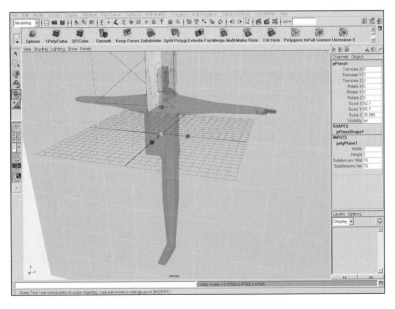

Figure 10.25 Start massing the model with a simple cube. The Jerk looks like the blockhead that he is!

7. Select the two rightmost bottom poly faces and make sure that they are set in the Tool options to be together. Extrude to half the knee, again to the center knee, and once more below the knee. We are giving The Jerk kneecaps that we can break later (just kidding—they're actually to bend with the skeleton). Rotate the leg slightly to separate.

8. Keep extruding to the ankle and extrude a short face below the ankle for the foot. Extrude the front face out for the foot while scaling slightly. Extrude the toes and move the vertices down to make a flat foot.

9. Move the top side face to extend out an arm just as was done with the leg, with extrusions on the elbow and the wrist. See Figure 10.26 for an idea of what it should look like.

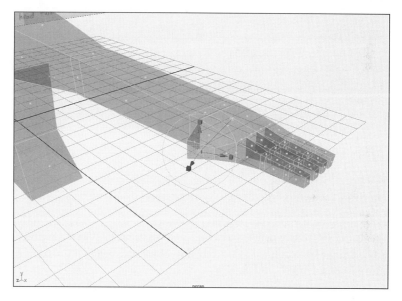

Figure 10.26 The hand and fingers to be extruded, pulled with enough detail for the knuckles and thumb.

10. After the wrist, extrude a palm. This is an area of higher detail that must transition into the arm. It will be broken up so that the area flows from one division to two, and then to four for the fingers.

11. Select the four sides around the palm, but not the front face. Use the edit Polygons, Subdivide on the side faces to make four little polygons out of one.

12. Using the Split Polygon tool, break the front surface into four vertical strips.

13. Extrude the four faces seven times, to make joints for the knuckles. If you work that G key hard, your model should look like Figure 10.27.

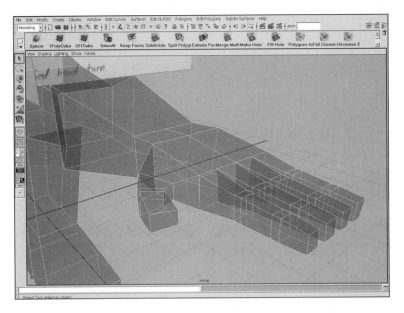

Figure 10.27 A fairly detailed hand, with two extruded faces per joint.

Now that the hands are finished, you can move on to the head.

14. Make sure that Keep Faces Together is turned on in the Polygons, Tool Options menu. Select the two center faces on top to make a short neck. Repeat to make an angled face that is aligned to the jaw line. Select the edge on the collarbone, and move it up slightly.

15. Select the front window-facing image planes. Use the Attribute Editor to turn off their display by setting Display Mode (found under Image Plane Attributes) to None.

16. Go to the Side and Front views to start shaping the head. Extrude a jaw by scaling it out from the neck. Use the Side view primarily to get the basic head shape into six extrusions. More detail will be put in later at the center strip for the mouth and the nose. Another band will be used for the eyes and ears. Use the two views to roughly match the profiles in Figure 10.28.

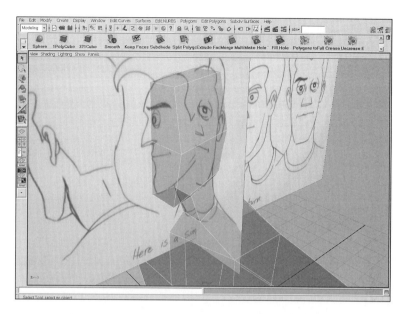

Figure 10.28   A simple massing representing the head.

17. Perform the Polygon to Subdiv conversion in the Modify, Convert menu. Switch to Polygon mode from Standard mode with the RMB marking menu over the model.

18. Hide all the image planes in Perspective view.

19. Select all the faces on the character's right side, as was seen in Figure 10.29, and delete them.

20. Select the body and switch to Standard mode. Open the Display, Subdiv Surface Components menu and turn on Edges and Vertices. Now the edges and vertices will always be up and viewable, without having to RMB select them.

21. To ensure good center-line tangency, keep the two rows of 0 points snapped parallel to each other. Snap the edge row of points it horizontally in X to the 0 ZY plane. This will facilitate the mirroring and attaching of the other half of figure later.

At this point, you're ready to model the nose.

22. Switch to Polygon mode and extrude a face for the nose. Delete the side face at the center line. Move the vertices in place to the Side and Front views.

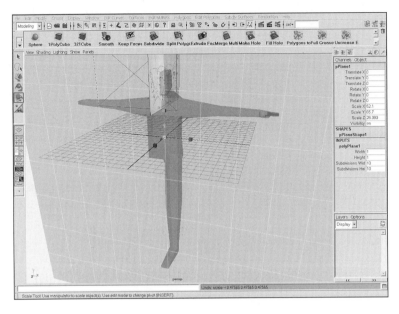

Figure 10.29 Make sure you have a straight line along the
new opening between the shoulder and the leg.

23. Switch to Standard mode. Select the bottom edges of the nose and fully crease
them. Select the edges at the intersection of the face and the boxed edge, and
partially crease them (see Figure 10.30).

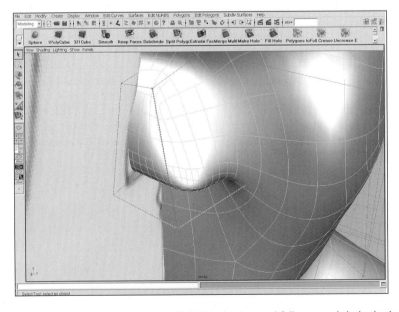

Figure 10.30 The partially creased highlighted edges and fully creased dashed edges.

Now, on to the ear.

24. Revert to Polygon mode and, starting at the top of the head and moving down to the collar bone, split the polygon in half. You should by this time feel a snapping point at the exact center when you do this. Select the face closest to the ear in Side view. Extrude with an offset of .2. Select the face and scale it in.

25. Reset the option box for Extrude Face. Extrude the basic ear from the stem. Scale and move it into place. Repeat the Offset Extrude and then a Reset Extrude that will be moved in to the inside ear (see Figure 10.31).

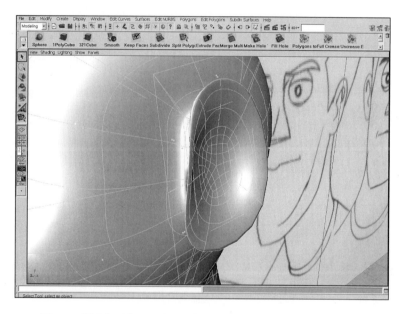

Figure 10.31 The ear being fleshed out from polygon extrudes, with the subdiv surfaces leading the way.

Now you're ready to create the mouth. Think of the mouth as being more extruded faces, but this time going into the head.

26. Select the two faces on the mouth area. Keep the faces together. Extrude them five times for a lip and mouth bag. Start to sculpt the slight M shape that upper lips have (see Figure 10.32).

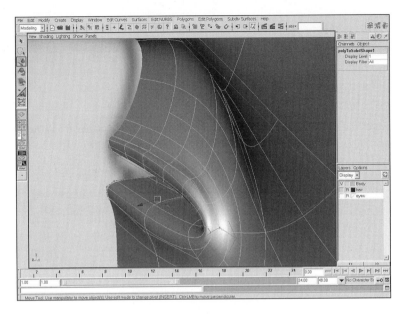

Figure 10.32 The highlighted lip edges, which will be shaped with the push, and points that will form the lip and mouth.

It will help to see The Jerk's eyes when doing the final sculpt. This will make your judgment of basic appeal more realistic. You can import the Jerk_eyes.mb file and position it or create your own.

27. If you want to create your own eyes, get a primitive NURBS sphere with the axis on the X. Adjust the sliders for Start Sweep Angle and End Sweep Angle to have the eyelid partially open on the bottom and top. Rotate the sweep angle 180° in the Y so that the eyelids are facing out.

28. Get another sphere that is slightly smaller, and detach the cornea area. Center the pivot and then reverse it. Reattach it using Edit, NURBS, Attach Surfaces with Knot Insertion on (see Figure 10.33).

29. It also helps to have a shader for the eyes, so get Eye Shader.mb from the CD. Assign the shader to the eye. Make another sphere between the size of the eyelid and the eyeball. Assign a transparent Phong shader to it and begin sculpting. Look at Figure 10.34 to see how it should be wired up.

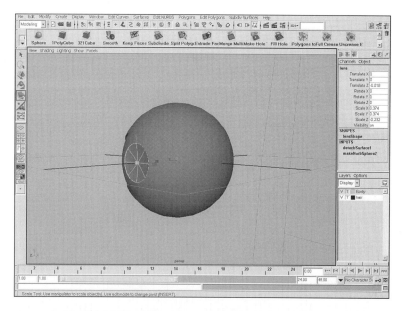

Figure 10.33   The cornea after the detachment—ouch!

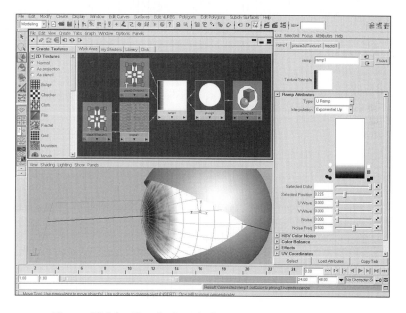

Figure 10.34   The shader, which uses a Ramp mapped to the incandescence with a fractal for the blues of The Jerk's eye.

30. At this point, you should be ready to sculpt the exact shapes for The Jerk. Make sure that you sculpt with all the Level 0 points and crease where sharper areas are needed. The lips and ears will get creases in key areas, much like the nose did in the previous exercise. Look at Figure 10.35 to see what the final shapes should look like.

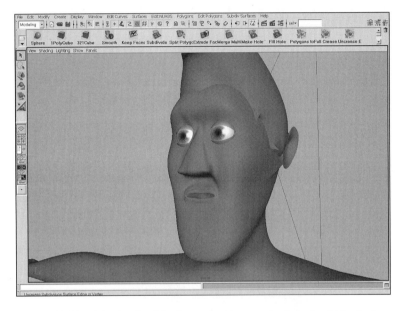

Figure 10.35   The head will look cartoonlike, yet the face should look alive. The dashed lines show where creases have been made.

Note

A character model might take weeks to get to the approval level from the art department. It might come back to you from the character riggers for purely functional revisions. When I created the first pass of the model, it was to get something to Erick Miller for testing set up and, of course, to explain it now. It would have gone significantly faster if I hadn't needed to write about it as I did it. We had the very talented sculptor Daniel Naranjo finish off the model. The artistry and sculptural ability still are the most desired, not the buttons you push. Make sure that you allot enough time to really sculpt, analyze, and critique when you model your next character.

Some final tweaking of the fingers is all that's needed.

31. Model in the volumes and tucks in the fingers with a small crease, and tug up those edges (see Figure 10.36). Look at your own fingers, and see the fleshy volumes and the tucks and folds that appear when you bend your finger.

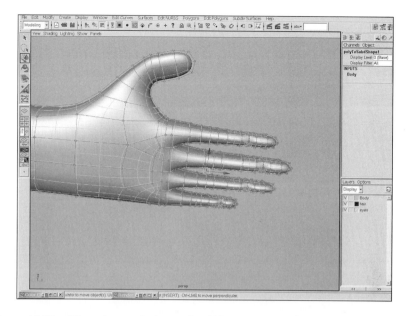

Figure 10.36   The point at which you should begin pulling and creasing the finger tucks.

32. Select the nail edges and fully crease them, as shown in Figure 10.37.

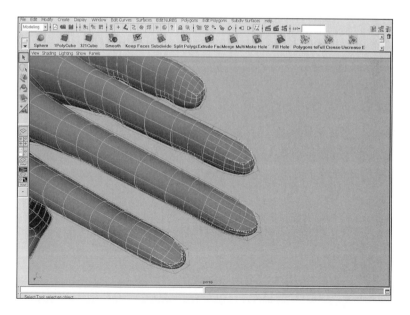

Figure 10.37   Creased nail edges.

Your final hand model should look like Figure 10.38.

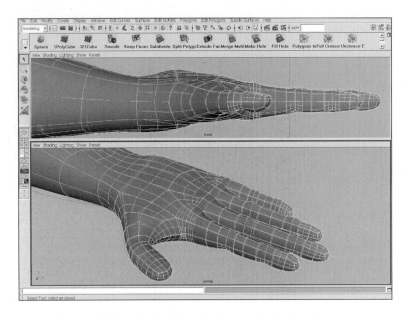

Figure 10.38   The final hand, with enough detail to keep the
cartoonish flavor without looking mechanical.

Now you're ready to create the moussed hair for The Jerk.

33. Create a subdiv primitive cone. Pull the top points off to side, as in the image
planes.

34. Pull down the Level 0 points that will comprise the hairline. Do this in a Shaded
mode to see that surfaces intersect according to the artwork.

35. Create the sharp points by fully creasing the vertices at Level 2 (see Figure 10.39).

When the hair is done, The Jerk needs to be mirrored just like Spot before him.

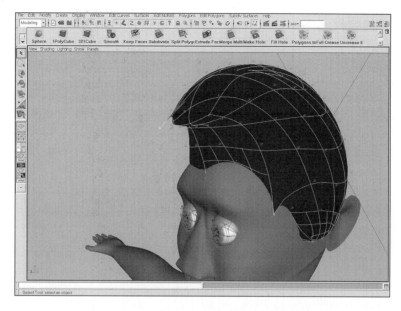

Figure 10.39   The Jerk's coif and his Level 2 mousse job.

36. Select the surface and Subdiv Surfaces, Mirror in the X plane. Pick the Subdiv Surfaces, Attach with Threshold of 0.05, and he should come together and look like Figure 10.40.

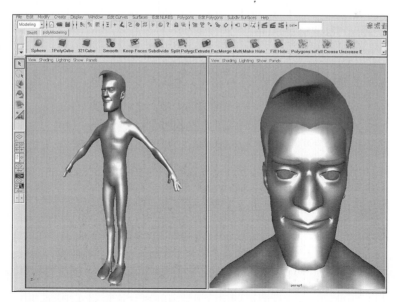

Figure 10.40   The Jerk, ready to do what he does best: aggravate Spot, the dog.

Summary

Distinct advantages exist when modeling in subdivs: the model is a complete volume and has one continuous skin. These advantages are outweighed by NURBS patch modeling when it comes to characters. Luckily, the subdivision surfaces can be easily converted to NURBS or polygons. Keep in mind surface flow at all times. Before you start on a fairly laborious model, consult the character-rigging people to find out their technical criteria. Take the time to draw a variety of character proposals before you even switch on Maya.

Think of modeling in subdivs as creating a volume and then adding to it with the extrude face functionality. Be judicious with the surface flow, and add detail with the Split Polygon tool. Try to do 3D sketches of the model before you commit to the final version, as in the first exercise. Sculpt away with the subdiv vertex, and then add detail with hierarchical refining for areas such as the toenails in the final dog. It is important to keep a relatively simple shape in regard to the poly proxy/level 0 so that edges can be creased, as with the nose detail on The Jerk.

Part III

Technical Direction

11 Layout   333

12 Node-Based Architecture   349

13 Making Advanced Connections   369

14 Particles and Dynamics   419

Chapter 11

Layout

By Max Sims

This chapter describes what layout is in 3D animation. It also demonstrates why Maya is an excellent choice for doing layout of any kind, and it will details the general sequencing of the short film done for this book. In addition, we'll describe the storyboard, animatics, and final editing stages. We describe concepts of blocking and staging the actors with the camera in general terms and then in terms of using Maya. Specifically, you will learn about these topics:

- Layout concepts
- How to make clear images to explain a story
- Cinematographer-like control of Maya cameras
- Quick visual editing techniques with Maya and other tools, including nonlinear editing systems such as Adobe Premiere

What Is Layout?

Layout is a term used in traditional animation to describe the visual composition of elements on the screen. Both the cinematography and the staging of the characters and background elements fall under the heading of layout. In 3D filmmaking, the camera, characters, and props are infinitely moveable. This freedom to adjust everything in the shot at any time adds a dramatic new dimension to layout for animated films.

In a large digital studio, the layout department first translates the drawn story-boards into rough assemblages of 3D models. Determining the placement of the characters through the frame and, consequently, their composition onscreen is the role of the layout department. This department also is responsible for specifying all of the camera moves, which must receive directorial approval. The resulting spatial and temporal continuity from shot to shot is one of the most important aspects in imparting a clear story to the audience.

The layout department uses low-resolution characters, props, and sets to quickly visualize a shot. They iterate quickly from shot to shot. Mere hours might be spent mocking up a shot before it is presentable. Often these shots metamorphose repeatedly before they are ready to move on to the animation department for character animation. Because final animation can be very time-consuming and expensive, the rough shots allow them to rapidly experiment in the early stages. The editors and the director can (and will) freely adjust the shots during this early stage of production to improve storytelling.

Layout encompasses the creation of animatics as well as cinematography. Shots are called animatics when they are in a rough form, devoid of any detailed animation. The animatics are helpful representations of editorial content, showing the essence of the framing and movement within each shot. Characters typically float from one mark to the next, performing only the most essential of poses.

Considerable overlap also occurs with conventional cinematography in 3D layout. A traditional director of photography helps photograph the director's vision on film. He finds the appropriate lenses for a given shot and is in charge of lighting. In 3D production, however, layout is responsible for the camerawork, not the lighting (the lighting phase comes later, between texturing and final rendering). After the lens choice and camerawork are completed here, they normally do not change farther downstream. The animators thus have to worry about the arduous process of performance for only the given composition.

Layout gives storyboards life and dimension. This department helps translate the 2D storyboards into tangible 3D moves. This is at once a quick visualization process that allows a lot of experimentation and that yet specifies the final composition with a very critical eye.

The Role of the Layout Artist: An Interview with Adam Schnitzer

Adam Schnitzer is an excellent layout artist who is currently in charge of layout at LucasArts, a games company. Here are his views on the art form:

What is your background?

I have an MFA in fine art/painting from Stanford University. I spent 12 years as a landscape painter, selling work in galleries in Los Angeles, New York, and San Francisco. I started out in games as a background painter at Rocket Science Games in 1993. Then I spent three years at LucasArts doing background painting and eventually transitioned into creating 3D environments for games such as Grim Fandango. I went to Pixar in 1997 and spent three years there doing 3D layout on *A Bug's Life, Toy Story 2,* and *Monsters, Inc.* Then I came back to LucasArts in 2001.

What is your current role at LucasArts?

I have been working on integrating layout into the game-production process. Cut scenes (the game industry term for the noninteractive cinematics of a computer game) have been with games for a long time. But they are often created late in the game-development process and the process of doing them has often been somewhat chaotic. One of the reasons I was hired back at LucasArts was so that I could bring some of the animation production systems from Pixar, particularly the layout process, and help to establish them at LucasArts.

How do you define layout?

Layout involves two crucial decisions in the creation of a shot in animation: where to put the camera and how the characters move in front of the camera. Another word for *layout* might be *staging.* The layout artist is responsible for blocking out where and when the characters move through a shot, and for camera placement and movement. When a layout artist is finished working on a particular shot, the shot length is set, the action is timed to the dialogue (if there is any), and the basic poses and "marks" that each character has to hit in the shot are nailed down. Also, the camera position, focal length, and movement (if any) are polished. When the shot is handed off to the animator, the director has approved all of these things, so the animator must work within the parameters established through the layout process.

How do you go about setting a shot or a sequence?

Before a shot can be worked on in layout, some other things must already be done. The voice files need to be recorded and edited. The storyboards must be finished. The models must be built. The virtual "set" must be assembled. With all these elements in place, the layout artist can load the set and characters into the computer and place the characters in the set. Different layout artists work

continues

continued

differently, but in general, you start by taking a crack at blocking out the character movement first, conforming as closely as possible to the storyboards and also conforming to the pacing of the voice files. Then the camera is positioned and movement is developed, along with the correct FOV (field of view) for the shot. But shots are not developed in isolation. The layout artist is responsible for making sure that shots cut together properly, so he works on whole sequences of shots. A first pass is done through the whole scene, and the shots are viewed together. Adjustments to timing, camera movement, and blocking are then made to each shot to achieve the best cinematic flow for that sequence.

What is the biggest change from the 2D storyboard to 3D?

The biggest change is usually in the scale of things. Characters that are actually very different in height (such as Buzz and Woody from *Toy Story*) are drawn in the boards as if they were the same height. Shot compositions often change. Shots that are conceived as two separate shots in the boards are often married by a camera move. Other shots are eliminated altogether.

What do you look at for hiring layout artists?

Mostly, we need to see a good cinematic sense. Layout artists come from all different disciplines. Some of the ones at Pixar were former stop-motion camera operators. Others were former live-action cameramen. Others, like myself, came from a painting background. Some came from a programming career. But in addition to a familiarity with 3D software, a demonstrated knowledge of cinema is essential. What makes a good cut? How do you express the meaning of a moment with the camera? What goes into lens choice? What makes a good composition? An applicant's portfolio should show evidence that he or she has some answers to these questions.

Do you use Maya for layout?

I do now that I am working at LucasArts. (Pixar uses proprietary software.) LucasArts has pretty much become a Maya-only studio, as far as 3D software is concerned. I am now in the process of getting it to do all the things that I am used to being able to do from working at Pixar.

What is your advice to those who want to improve their layout skills?

Watch a lot of movies. But don't watch just as a spectator. Really analyze what the cinematographer and editor were doing with each sequence. This can be tricky because the goal of the filmmaker is to make all the camera work and cutting invisible so that the audience can become immersed in the action. A student of layout should get a film on DVD and use the pause button a lot. Think about where the director chose to put the camera. Consider the pace of the cutting. Why does the camera move in a particular way? Analyze all aspects of the staging of each shot, and try to understand why each decision was made. With the best directors, nothing happens by chance.

Visual Clarity

Visual clarity is extremely important to the layout process (see the accompanying sidebar). Clear and consistent composition is one of the fundamental principles to achieving visual clarity.

Consider how actors are positioned onscreen. A standard cinematic device, called the 180° rule, is almost always employed (see Figure 11.1). To understand this, draw a line between two characters that appear together in a scene. The camera will be kept on one side of that line (as seen from above) and will not be permitted to wander over to the other side. This guarantee that from shot to shot, the characters are always on the same side of the screen, facing in consistent directions. We are so used to this device that any deviation from it is immediately confusing (and is thus avoided).

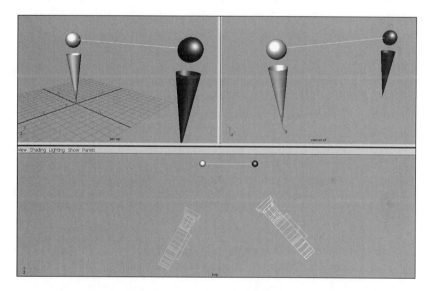

Figure 11.1   This is a graphic representation of the 180° rule. Notice that the view from both cameras keeps the characters in the same screen position.

Note

Many CG artists adore movies yet are unaware of film conventions that have been around for 100 years. See Appendix A, "Intermediate and Advanced MEL," for recommendations on books on staging and setting up shots.

Consider the animation project that we're completing in this book (for an overview, see Chapter 4, "Technical Considerations"). When an over-the-shoulder shot is done of The Jerk, he will be on the left, with Spot in the far-right background. When we cut to a reaction shot of Spot, he remains on the right, with The Jerk receding into the background.

Another term for this is the stage line. You can violate the line, but only as long as it is explained. In the case of this film, The Jerk comes out of the car and the car blocks our view from the street. The stage line is shifted when The Jerk gets out of the car and is on the sidewalk. The three-dimensional flexibility of Maya helps a great deal when figuring out where to place the camera in such situations.

All of the 2D and 3D animated movies created today are thoroughly scripted, storyboarded, and prototyped before the really expensive production starts. Animators do not have the same luxury as their live-action colleagues of shooting and reshooting. The production pipeline for a 3D film must accommodate this preplanning and provide the capability to get a rough preview before countless hours are spent animating and rendering. It is far less expensive to see that a shot or action doesn't serve the storytelling in the layout phase (even more so in the storyboarding phase) than it is to make that determination deep in the animation phase. This same approach was used for our production, small as it is.

The mechanics of scene assembly also need to be addressed. During the layout phase, this scene was done with one complete model and low-resolution mockups. At a large production facility, a more comprehensive pipeline would involve models in progress. The set pieces might be completed and some details might be omitted. When a new item is approved, it might be added. Maya has a file-reference system that can be used to refer to both the low- and high-resolution models. The layout can be completed with the low-res models first, and then the high-res models can be inserted when the detail is needed or when the scene moves upstream in the production pipeline. The Maya scene brings in the link to set pieces, props, and the entire mise en scéne (all of the elements in a finished scene). If the referred link is updated, then the next time the layout scene is brought up, the changes are there. Another method is to simply put the high- and low-resolution models in separate layers. You can then move quickly in low-res, displaying the high-res to make further refinements. On the whole, though, keep it simple so you can navigate and experiment quickly.

From Storyboards to Animatics

The process of transferring the script to the screen is greatly aided by using Maya, even if the end result is not computer graphics. Mark Adams drew up storyboards on 3 × 5 index cards very early on in the process of doing our short film. After all, this was from a proposal by him; it helped sell his idea to the rest of the crew that it met the criteria for doing this book and was within the scope of our budgetary constraints. His storyboards set the paradigm of what would drive the staging in the film. We used the index cards because they can be rearranged as a form of nonlinear editing (see Figure 11.2).

We quickly made some of the rough characters and props in Maya to see if they all hung together. Simple things such as widening the sidewalk assisted in the storytelling and gave the camera more space to move. The characters, props, and sets were slowly being finalized and then built for real with all of this previous knowledge.

It also helped to do a "location scout." This is done in live-action films when an advance crew visits possible locations for shooting. If a movie requires a desolate arid landscape, the location scouts try to find an appropriate setting that meets the needs of the production. They return with video footage and hundreds of photographs. We did the digital equivalent on our one and only street set to see where the camera could be best located. This was very helpful for constructing interesting shots and planning the forthcoming animation.

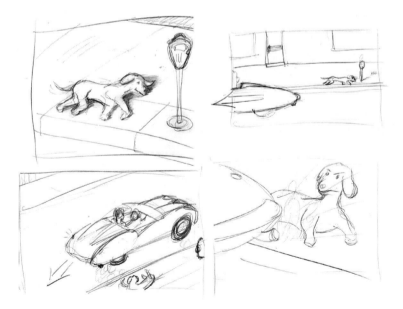

Figure 11.2   Using index cards to lay out this sequence is much faster than modeling and rendering the sequence in Maya. (Drawings by Mark Adams.)

We needed to iron out the story a bit before real production commenced. What did we think was funny? Where would The Jerk and Spot act? Staging and blocking the actors were crucial to getting the humor and tension needed for even a short piece as this one. I decided to add tension to the scenes by using a telephoto lens whenever The Jerk and Spot confronted each other. Some wide master shots would help in setting the scene to get us into this little world.

After some experimentation on the shots in 3D, I had a much better idea of what was needed in 2D. We drew up storyboards that were scanned and then put into Adobe Premiere editing software (see Figure 11.3). The shot duration was scrubbed in the timeline with a still, and a simple pan-and-scan technique was used to indicate camera movement. This would be useful to show other team members what the general pace of the film would be. The beauty of using an editing package is that you can easily print to tape. Maya can render out to the .AVI format on the PC and Quicktime on Macintosh directly by setting it in the Render Globals. That allowed us to view the shots on TV, to get a better feel of what the final would look like.

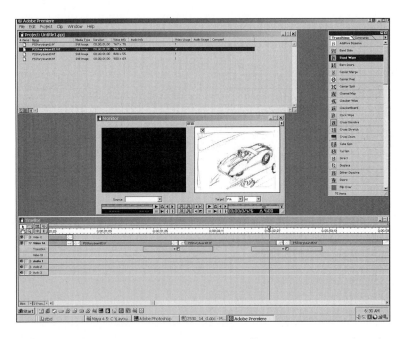

Figure 11.3 A great way to prototype your films is to use a storyboard inside Adobe Premiere.

The next step involved rendering out the animatics that had the 3D camera moves and rough movement of the actors. At first we did it with only one camera. Then in the layout phase, I used the same technique as in the forthcoming exercises, but with individual cameras. The files were rendered in hardware and then put into Premiere. A scene in which The Jerk comes down the street could be animated once with three cameras around it to show different views. This would give us more coverage during the edit stage, without having to reshoot (see Figure 11.4.).

Two important aspects to keep in mind during the layout process in Maya are the types of cameras you'll be using and how to control them. The exercises that follow cover these aspects in detail.

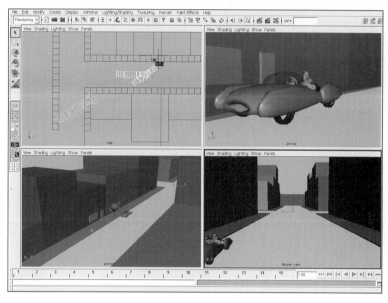

Figure 11.4   One animation of the car coming down the street can be filmed by multiple cameras.

Exercise 11.1   Camera Tutorial

Consider the camera as another actor in your piece. It guides your viewers in terms of the storytelling. The first matter to consider is camera choice. Maya has an extremely versatile set of cameras. The first order of business is to open the Attribute Editor for the camera and explore the range of filmback and lens choices. By default, Maya has a pretty average camera that is best suited for modeling, not for attaining cinematic realism. Let's explore in Maya how the different lenses and filmbacks relate.

1. To begin, copy the Layout project on the CD that accompanies this book to your hard drive. Set your project to Layout, and open the file Layout_Cameras.mb. in the scenes folder. This contains the low-resolution files of the street scene, a simple approximation of the street furniture, Spot, and The Jerk and his car. Make sure that your preferences are set to Z-up.

2. In your Perspective window, select View, Select Camera and then View, Camera Attribute Editor. In the Attribute Editor, set the controls to Camera and Aim.

    Reselect the Camera. You should see a white dot and circle in your frame (see Figure 11.5).

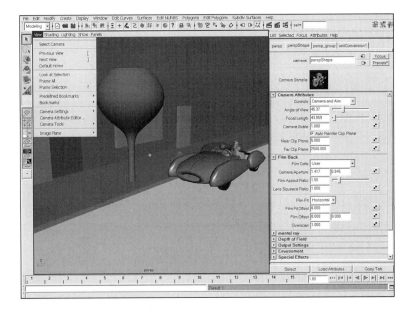

Figure 11.5 This is what your window will look like with Camera selected and the Attribute Editor up.

3. Highlight the focal length number. Hold down the Control button and then LMB-drag your mouse. This gives more precise control to any slider. In this case, go from 10 to 200.

    Notice that the subject gets closer. But also notice the grid angles on the floor plane (see Figure 11.6). A tight telephoto lens brings the subject closer to you and, in cinematic terms, might construe tension or spying on something. As the tension rises between our characters, we will start to increase the focal length. Conversely, a wide-angle lens will be good for an establishing shot or a POV.

4. Try tumbling around in various focal lengths, each time making The Jerk the center of interest by selecting him and then hitting the f hotkey.

5. In the Camera Attribute Editor, go down to the Film Back section and open the choices in the Film Gate. You will see a big variety of formats, including Vista Vision, 16mm, 35mm, and even my own format, Imax (just kidding).

These were intentionally designed to help visual effects artists exactly match the camera that was used for background plate photography. Luckily, we can use these film gates to get the camera to behave like a real one. This will help the audience clue in on what is generally accepted today as reality: cinematic illusion.

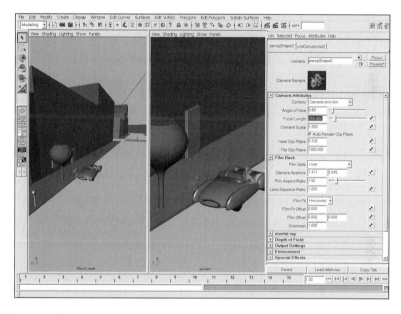

Figure 11.6   The camera on the left has a wide-angle 24mm lens; the one on the right uses a tight telephoto effect with a 350mm lens.

6. Set Film Gate to 35mm 1.85 Projection (see Figure 11.7) and set the focal length to 35.

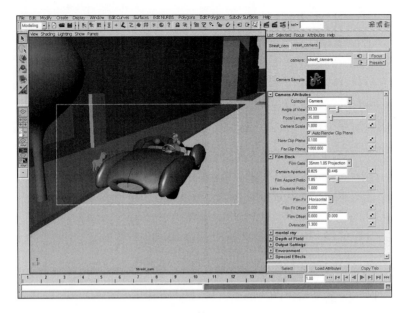

Figure 11.7 Our antagonist is framed up for his first shot.

This gives us the kind of camera we will use throughout the production. The aspect ratio of 1:1.85 means that the height is 1 unit and the width is 1.85 times the length. This is the traditional 35mm film proportion that you see in the movie theater.

7. Now you need to conform the resolution to the camera. Go to your Perspective window and select View, Camera Settings, Resolution Gate. Open Render Globals. In the Resolution tab, try the various presets and notice the Device Aspect Ratio number change. Observe the white center target and frame when Camera is selected.

   We need 1.85 and we are going out to video, so we chose a letterbox format. This will be rendered later and composited in Adobe After Effects for letterboxing.

8. Check View, Camera Settings, Film Gate to see where the image will be delineated.

   The width for video is 720, so divide that by 1.85; this results in 389.189.

9. On the Resolution tab, uncheck Maintain Width/Height Ratio as well as Lock Device Aspect Ratio. Insert 720 for the width and then 389 for the height (see Figure 11.8).

   The Device Aspect Ratio will be 1.851, which is as close as it will get. Now we have a nice feature film-style camera.

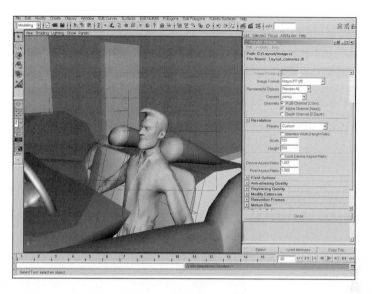

Figure 11.8   The resolution and aspect ratio are now synchronized to a cinematic framing.

10. As a final step, check off View, Camera Settings, Safe Title and Safe Action.

This is where the action can occur, without the main elements getting cropped off when viewed on a TV.

This was a simple exercise in thinking about how to frame up your images inside Maya. Hopefully you will experiment with a variety of lenses, focal lengths, and aspect ratios to help drive your story. Now that you know more about what you can do with the camera, let's start telling a story with the camera.

Exercise 11.2   Animating a Quick Shot Sequence

This is an exercise in doing rapid visualization for layout purposes. We are trying to simply get the timing of our actors and their correct placement onscreen. We will leverage Maya to assemble fast cuts for editorial content and camera placement. Most people rush into animation and give the camera moves short shrift. Another excess occurs when people discover that they can animate cameras in 3D and then tend to over-do it. The results are the clichéd flyover camera without any logical motivation. In this exercise, perform a logical series of cuts and a motivated camera move. These are the first shots in the short film *Parking Spot*.

1. Open the file Parking_Spot Opening.mb on the CD that accompanies this book.

2. You'll see that the camera is pointing down the street. Click View, Select Camera and open the Channel Box. Make sure your Range Slider and Time Slider are on in your UI Elements menu. Select Frame 1 in the time slider and press s to set a key. Set the range slider to 300 (see Figure 11.9).

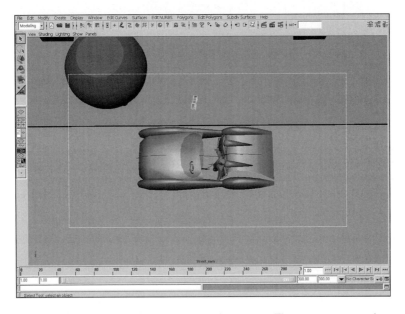

Figure 11.9   Here is a bird's-eye view of the scene. This is a rare time when a symmetrical composition is used.

3. MMB-Drag to Frame 60 in the slider. The camera does a roll to reveal the dog from up high. Track the camera down and zoom in slightly. The dog should appear in the frame at the top slightly. Set a keyframe at 60.

   You've just created a pan tilt shot that gives you some context for where you are.

4. Zoom in from above toward the dog while maintaining it in the right bottom third of the screen. Track down to eye level, set a keyframe at 90, and MMB-Drag to Frame 120.

5. Now come in closer, like a dolly shot, and frame Spot's head, as in Figure 11.10. Set a keyframe at 140.

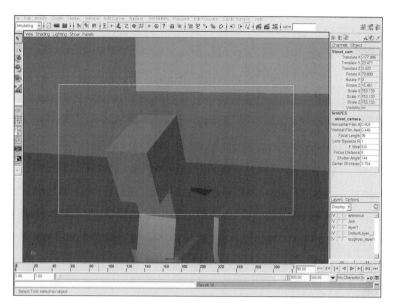

Figure 11.10 A close-up shot of Spot's indignant pose (imagine it with me—
this is the early stuff).

6. LMB-scrub to Frame 1. Then MMB-scrub to Frame 180. Set a keyframe. This is a
quick way of reproducing a shot.

7. Activate the perspective and Graph Editor with the tool setting on the left (see
Figure 11.11). Use the f hotkey to see all of the animation curves. Now play the
animation.

You will notice that the sequence has a somewhat fluid movement. This might be
as far as many novice animators go. Next you'll control the camera's movement.

8. Select keyframes 60 through 180. Set the tangent type to Linear. Play the animation.

The camera is robotic in movement, possibly reminding you of early Siggraph
reels for which the software engineer wrote a cool new algorithm but didn't know
the previous material here. Try out the same frames with the tangent type set to
Stepped. Now the camera stays put and cuts from shot to shot, with the exception
of the first pan tilt. Experiment with mixing the tangent types on the frames to try
what-ifs on each shot's transition.

Next you'll add basic character and prop animation. The goal here is far from per-
fection: It's merely to get the timing and position of the elements onscreen. The
purpose is to convey story points to see if they will actually work out. At this early
point in the film, the dog is resting on the only sunlit portion of the sidewalk. The
Jerk is pulling up in the car; Spot notices him in the corner of his eye.

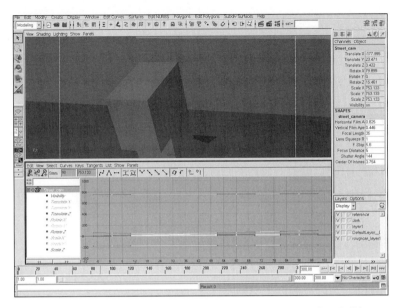

Figure 11.11   The key to getting good movement is in the Graph Editor.

9.   RMB-scrub to 150. Set the picks to Hierarchical, pick the car, and set a keyframe. Move the keyframe in the X to 0. MMB-scrub to 180 and set a keyframe.

10.   Pick the dog and set a keyframe.

11.   Rotate the dog in Y −180. MMB-scrub to 195 and set a keyframe. This is Spot's quick reaction.

This is how fast and crude the layout portion can be. If you find yourself spending more than two hours on a shot, you might be overdoing it. Of course, this is not always the case. For a feature-length film, the animatics for every shot can be done over and over again. A film can have up to 2,000 separate shots. Try to go through the shots quickly and not be a perfectionist. Character animation is *not* the point of this phase: This is strictly to get the camera move to set the parameters for the real animation.

Summary

We explored in this chapter how a team goes about the process of giving the story more concrete form in layout. You learned to control the camera and use Maya's animation for quick iteration of entire scenes. Prototyping and iterating let you explore many possibilities efficiently. Think of doing the cinematic equivalent in Maya at every stage in production.

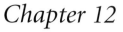

Chapter 12
Node-Based Architecture

By Erick Miller

A few basics about nodes in Maya are essential knowledge. Without a crystal-clear understanding of these pieces and how they all work together, you will never truly know what is going on inside the software. It is easy to quickly brush over a concept and dive straight into a tutorial for direct results. But chances are, you will be missing the most important part of the learning process: being able to apply what you learned as an abstract concept to solve any particular problem that is set in front of you.

This chapter provides a basic explanation of how to use Maya's architecture, which is truly an elegant and extensible 3D software system. Maya has often been described as a big "tool box" full of useful (and sometimes undocumented) tools. Maya represents its tools in the form of nodes. The goal of this chapter is to introduce you to generic techniques that will allow you to use all of Maya's node-based tools, not just the ones you are taught to use.

This chapter prepares you with a solid foundation for the rest of the node-rigging tutorials that you will be completing in this book by discussing transformations, node connections, and other issues that Maya users need to consider. These include issues related to attributes and nodes types, specifically the following:

- Transformations in Maya, including parents, children, transforms, shapes, objects, and components
- The difference between DAG and DG nodes, and the many ways to access them in Maya
- DG cycles, node types, and read-only non-DAG nodes
- Connections among multiple nodes, including history, and attribute connections

Transformations: Parent/Child Relationships

Everyone should know by now that when you move a parent, the child moves with it. This is because the child actually exists within the coordinate space of the parent. The parent/child relationship is a relatively simple concept. However, not only is it an extremely important thing to know, but it also is a vital concept to understand and use to its full capability.

Anyone who works in the game industry will tell you that the "coordinate space" in which a node is animated is often very important when it comes time to export the data to the game engine. In the film industry, when exporting data among multiple packages, the same thing holds true. If the coordinate space doesn't match, it will literally shift, move, and possibly scale everything around that is different so that nothing lines up.

The same concept holds true in many other areas of computer graphics. Indeed, group nodes and null nodes are much more than just a nifty way of hierarchically organizing your data in Maya's Hypergraph or Outliner. When a node is created at the world level in Maya, it exists relative to the coordinate space of the world (otherwise known as the world transform identity matrix), and the location of the object's pivot controls the point from which each transformation is calculated. If you freeze the transforms of a node that is a child of the world (through Modify, Freeze Transformations), you are redefining the zero of the object's transform matrix and pushing the world translations from 0,0,0 world space into the shape node of the object. In other words, the local point coordinate locations of the components of the node, like vertices of a polygon or the CVs of a NURBS surface, will now be in world space. If a node has a "parent" or is grouped, this means that the node no longer is a child of the world and is now a child of the parent's transform matrix.

It's simple: Think of getting in a car. You are a child of the world while you are walking on the ground. The moment you step into the car and sit down, you are within the coordinate space of the vehicle. When it begins to move, you move with it. Even though you are just sitting still, you are still moving; therefore, you are within the confines of a new coordinate space.

You can create parent/child relationships between only "object"-level nodes with the following techniques:

- To create a parent for multiple children, select all the nodes you want to be the children, select the parent last, and hit the lowercase p key on your keyboard. You can also access the menu item Edit, Parent. Shift+P is the default hotkey to un-parent a node, or remove a node from a hierarchy of transforms and make it a child of the world level.

- To create a group node (a null parent node), select any node or nodes, and hit the key combination Ctrl+g (lowercase g).

Tip

One of the most evident ways to view your nodes and the hierarchies of group nodes is to use the Hypergraph window (select Window, Hypergraph). When viewing a list of children under a single parent, it is often desirable to simply reorder the children so that one comes before another in the list. I've actually known people to unparent and reparent nodes just to get them in the correct order; but this is not necessary. Simply hold down the Ctrl key on your keyboard; click and hold the middle mouse button and drag the node that you want to reorder right on top of the node that you want it before. The MEL command to perform this action is called `reorder`.

You can create new parent/child relationships between objects and shape nodes with the following technique by first creating a NURBS sphere and a polygon cube from the Create menu. Select a shape node (a geometry node *without* translate, rotate, and scale attributes—in this case, nurbsSphereShape1) and a transform (parent) node (any node *with* translate, rotate, and scale attributes—in this case, pCube1), and execute the following MEL command in the command line:

```
parent -shape -relative;
```

What just occurred might seem strange: You have just parented a NURBS shape node under a polygon's transform node. You might ask, "Now what type of node is it and what have I actually just done?" It might seem confusing or complicated, but the answer is as simple as the action. You simply parented two shapes under a single transform. Maya's GUI doesn't directly expose this ability because it could be misinterpreted by average users. But through the simple MEL command, you have caused it to occur. Knowing that this is possible can be incredibly useful if you are trying to reparent a geometry shape under a new transform for many different reasons, whether for modeling purposes, for character rigging, or simply for taking a shape out of its current parent and giving it a fresh new transform.

Tip

One last thing: Sometimes Maya actually creates an additional transform parent node for you, without you actually wanting it to. The additional transform node that is inserted into your hierarchy is simply Maya's way of automatically calculating the difference between one object's coordinate space and a new parent's coordinate space, and then putting a node in between to compensate for the differences between the two.

How do you get rid of this annoying transform node? The process can sometimes get tedious, but it is actually quite easy. You need to realize that you can reliably remove this extra transform node only if its object transforms are reset to defaults (all translates and rotates are zeroed out and scales are set to 1) from the original coordinate space in which its identity exists. Of course, if you remember which hierarchy the node was a child of previously, you can simply unparent the transform's child node back into the coordinate space where it was before the improper parenting took place. In other words, you can just put the node below the extra transform back into the original hierarchy where it came from, and everything will work just fine. Otherwise, if you simply set the attributes back to 0 on the transform, you will "see" the calculation that Maya was trying to protect you against. Your object will move, rotate, or scale the opposite amount through space, based on the difference between the coordinate spaces of the two nodes above and below. You can now unparent the child node; the transform is no longer automatically created, but now your child node has transformed in an inappropriate way.

This, of course, is entirely undesirable, and that is why Maya was keeping it from happening by putting the extra transform node there in the first place. Don't fret. It's relatively easy to get rid of this node. Simply calculate the difference for each attribute as if you were to zero out the transform above—by adding each one of the extra transform's attributes (translate, rotate, and scale) onto its child. Then just negate that undesired transform by setting its transforms and rotates back to 0 and its scales back to 1. You can now safely unparent the node from the pesky transform and back to its original parent. This process can become tricky when your nodes are rotated on a different axis;
depending on the complexity of your hierarchy, this might require a coordinate space transformation calculation, which is quite a bit trickier. The best advice is that if it isn't absolutely necessary to remove these transforms, just leave them there. Otherwise, simply remember that you need to get the child reset into its correct original transform space before Maya will allow you to be rid of the nodes.

Objects, Shapes, and Components

The object and component levels in Maya should be fairly well understood. Objects exist in Maya as nodes. These nodes can transform through space as entire objects (as previously stated), like a car can drive down the road. The objects in Maya must also be built from something, just like a car's body is built from steel, aluminum, and rubber. The separate pieces of a node that comprise its actual existence are known as *components*. The components of a node exist within the object's shape node, while the transforms (translate, rotate, scale) of a node exist within the object's transform node. Therefore, it only makes sense that deformers—and most other creation history (see the section later in this chapter entitled "Viewing the Maya Scene Graph and Node

History" for a more detailed explanation of history) and DG nodes—are connected to the shape rather than the transform node. Where else would the deformers go to access the components of the object? In fact, the shape node defines the behavior of the node; you could think of the transform as simply an outer shell for translation, but not creation. This definitive nature also accounts for why it is possible to have multiple shape nodes as children of a single parent transform (from the last example of the previous section).

The shape node is an inherent child of the transform node. This structure is entirely reliable and holds true for almost any visibly selectable node that exists in Maya. There are several easy ways to visually see the object, shape, and component relationships represented through the UI:

1. You can see the inherent transform (parent)/shape (child) relationship in the Hypergraph if you go to Window, Hypergraph and then choose Options, Display, Shape Nodes. Figure 12.1 should help you understand how the transform moves the shape (and, therefore, the object's components) through space.

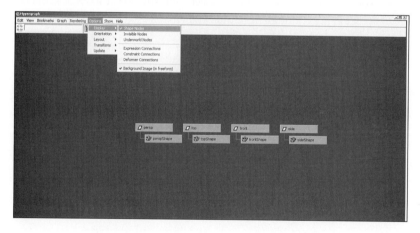

Figure 12.1   Click Options, Display, Shape Nodes in the Hypergraph to display the shape and object relationship while still in Hierarchy mode.

2. You can access the components of a node by hitting F8 on your keyboard or by clicking the Component Mode button in the top bar of the Status Line of the Maya UI (see Figure 12.2). You can also right-click over any geometry (such as NURBS, polygons, subdivision surfaces, or lattices) and choose a component-marking menu item from the displayed options.

Figure 12.2 Access and select a node's components to edit some of the node's properties, such as its shape.

3. You can also view components while in Object mode through the many Display, Component options (such as Display, NURBS Components and Display, Polygon Components) under the Display menu (see Figure 12.3). Note that if you keep them turned on, it can get confusing for other people opening the file because the components clutter the view. It is usually best not to keep component display on in this mode.

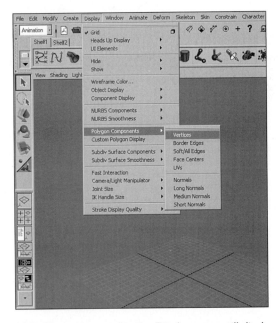

Figure 12.3 The options under the Display menu will display a node's components even while you are in Object mode.

Maya Node-Based Basics

Connections between nodes, the attributes of a node, and the hierarchical relationships of parents and children are all related topics that can work together to help you solve almost any creative visual dilemma or create any user-controlled behavior inside your Maya scene. A lot of the time, the node connections are limited more by the user's intuition than by what is possible in the software. The tricky part, of course, is knowing how all the nodes work and what ends the particular functions of the attributes on the nodes serve. Knowing how a node's inputs and outputs can work together, and how you can harness the power of connecting necessary attributes to create a network or hierarchy is one of the most important things you need to know to begin understanding Maya's powerful node-based architecture.

Defining connections between nodes in Maya is truly a creative process. You can force almost any attribute to have a dependency connection to directly control any other attribute, as long as the two attributes are of a compatible type. You can also force any transform node's transformations to control the transformation of another node using connections, parenting, or constraints. If connections are not possible, you can always just insert one of the many conversion nodes, use a conversion function in an expression, or write your own conversion in MEL or in the API to process the attribute's data into a more compatible form.

What Is a DAG Node?

The acronym DAG stands for directed acyclic graph. A DAG node is simply a way of representing complex relationships in hierarchical data—hierarchies of parents and children. Anytime you view your objects in the scene Hierarchy mode of the Hypergraph or Outliner, you are viewing Maya's representation of a DAG. Basically any node that you can select in object mode from inside one of your 3D view screens (such as your perspective camera), move around using the Move tool, and parent under other nodes is considered a DAG node in Maya.

What Is a DG Node?

The acronym DG stands for dependency graph. A DG node is used to get data through input attributes and then process and output that data through its output attributes. DG nodes come in many types, but all share one similarity: They input and output data. A great example of a DG node is a Multiply Divide node; it takes numerical data as an input and then simply multiplies it and outputs the multiplied data. Anytime you view your objects in the input and output connections (sometimes called upstream/downstream) mode of the Hypergraph, you are viewing Maya's representation its dependency graph.

The Input Output Dependency Graph

Let's speak hypothetically for a moment and start with an easy, real-life conceptual representations of what a dependency graph really is. Think of a DG as a river or a stream. What is at the beginning of a stream? For this example, let's say the source of the stream is an artesian well (a natural occurrence of water springing from the ground). The artesian well is, therefore, the first node in our graph, and it produces the water and data that flow down our stream. The compounds (or elements) contained inside the stream's water represent our data. Let's then say that in the water, the data that we are interested in is a contaminant—calcium carbonate—that needs to be processed and removed before the water can be consumed by humans. So now we have an artesian well node, which outputs calcium carbonate data into our stream.

Downstream of our artesian well, we have a water treatment node. The water treatment node's job is to process only the calcium carbonate data and remove it from the stream. The nature of the water treatment node is to split the compound data (calcium carbonate) into two separate pieces of data: calcium data and carbonate data. So, after the stream passes through the water treatment node, it contains these two modified elements derived from calcium carbonate. This results in two new streams, each following separate paths, which we will hypothetically call the river and the creek. Both the river and the creek have downstream nodes to process the output data from the water treatment node. The calcium data is contained within the water of the creek, and the carbonate data is contained within the water of the river (both the creek and the river are still really just flowing streams of data). The destination of the calcium water in the creek is simply a holding tank node, which captures the amount of calcium that is extracted and outputs nothing.

Downstream of the water treatment node, following the river's carbonate water path, is a water distribution node that branches out of the stream into an array of thousands of separate pipes (also just streams of data). The final destination of each pipe is an individual shower and faucet node. When you turn the knob, water comes out—you can shower with it or drink it. This entire process is a simplified version of what happens during the process of water softening and could easily be represented using a DG network. The process of turning the water faucet on could even be correlated to the process of rendering, or drawing data to the screen.

Figure 12.4 shows what our hypothetical DG network would look like in Maya. In the Hypergraph, select the node you want to view upstream and downstream of, and use the menu command Graph, Input and Output Connections to display the data. An actual Maya file with the following node network (purely as a hypothetical example) is included on the CD, in the file WATER_TREATMENT.mb.

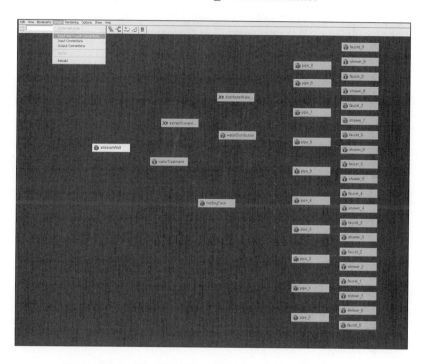

Figure 12.4   The input and output connections of our node network, as re-created in Maya, for a visual representation.

Creating a DG Node

A DAG node is simply a transform node (such as a group node), and a DG node is an upstream or downstream dependency element of the input output data graph. Almost all nodes in a Maya scene are either DAG or DG nodes— this includes shaders, materials, lights, cameras, deformers, animation curves, constraints, geometry, particles, expressions, and nulls. Furthermore, any DAG that has a transformation space and any DG that has compatible input attributes can be directly connected.

Easily understandable examples of DG nodes that can be connected to DAG nodes are several of the utility nodes found inside the Hypershade, on the Utilities tab of the Create Render Node window (see Figure 12.5).

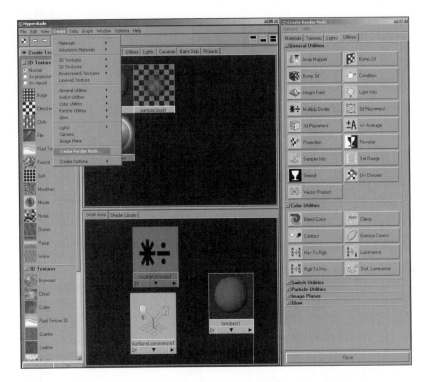

Figure 12.5 In the Create Render Node window, you can create many nodes that can be used to help render your scene, as well as add, subtract, multiply, divide, and create conditions on transform attributes of any DAG node.

One particularly helpful node is the Multiply/Divide utility node. To create a Multiply/Divide utility node, follow these steps:

1. Select Window, Rendering Editors, Hypershade. The Hypershade window opens.

2. Now choose Create, General Utilities, Multiply Divide.

3. Press Ctrl+A to open the Attribute Editor of the Multiply/Divide node.

4. Notice the two attributes, input1 and input2. The input attributes take numbers (either those typed in by hand or those from connecting another node's numerical attributes into the inputs). The value is then calculated by the node and stored in the output attribute.

   The output attribute is hidden because it is a "read-only" attribute and is meant only to output its data into other attributes. You will see how easy it is to connect output data of a node to input data of another node at the end of this chapter.

Cycles in the Dependency Graph

The dependency graph in Maya is a node network with one-way connections (edges) from node to node, which should contain no dependency loops from any downstream node in the graph back to any node existing upstream. In other words, DG connection edges are all one-way streets, traveling in the same direction from the output of one node to the input of the next.

Tip

Maya allows cycles to exist in the dependency graph but does not guarantee proper evaluation or stability of the network and the flow of data. Again, this is sort of like driving the wrong way on a one-way street. You can do it, and you might get away with it if there is no traffic. But you are still breaking the law, and you are also endangering the integrity of your passengers (your data) as well as other drivers and pedestrians. So always beware of the error message "Cycle On *node* may not evaluate as expected. Use 'cycleCheck −e off' to disable this warning." Try to find out what attributes the data is actually cycling back into. If there is a cycle in your graph, Maya often has extreme difficulty attempting to perform undo on attributes whose values are a result of cycled data. A common example of creating a cycle occurs when attempting to point- or orient-constrain a parent to one of its children. Figure 12.6 shows another simple but common example of a cycled dependency graph.

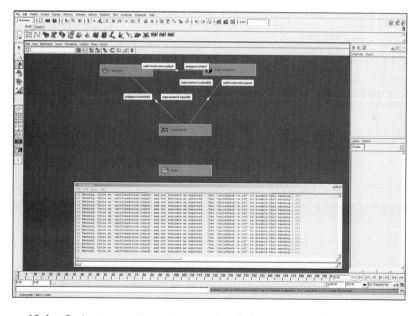

Figure 12.6   Cycles in your dependency graph will almost always produce undesirable and unrepeatable results that often cannot be reversed with the undo command.

Node Types

Every node that exists has a type. All node types are registered with Maya if the capability to create the node exists. The node type is stored in the shape node of the object, not the transform node. The transform node is always just universally of the type transform. A node cannot have "no" type. The closest thing to having no node type is being of type unknown (which, by the way, still seems to be a type). The easiest way to interactively see the node types in your Maya scene is to type the following into the Script Editor:

```
nodeType `ls -sl`;
```

Next, click and hold the middle mouse button, and drag the text into your shelf so that you have it as a button that you can click anytime.

Then select a single shape node (any one you are interested in) and execute the MEL command by pushing the Shelf button. The node type prints in the Script Editor window.

If you are interested in seeing a long list of all known node types in Maya, select Window, Hypergraph and then choose Show, Auxiliary Nodes (the last option in the menu). The window that pops up contains a list of all node types inside Maya. You can also read through a list of all currently registered node types in Maya by executing the following MEL command at the command line:

```
print `ls -nodeTypes`;
```

This list of nodes is literally the entire Maya tool shelf of registered node types (including any plug-in nodes). In most cases, Maya's UI gives access to the creation and automated connections of these nodes, although many exceptions exist. Some nodes in Maya are actually hidden from the user altogether, usually because they have not been fully implemented into the GUI of the software; however, this doesn't mean that they can't still be used. You can create any one of these nodes by hand simply by using the `createNode` command:

```
createNode wtAddMatrix;
// Result: wtAddMatrix1 //
```

Note

If the node that you created by hand is undocumented, you must look at its attributes and try to figure out what it's supposed to do all by yourself.

Non-DAG Nodes

Non-DAG nodes are simply just DG (dependency graph) nodes. This means that they are some sort of compute node that exists without a transform. Many non-DAG nodes in a new Maya scene are nodes that must exist for the scene to function properly. For the most part, default scene non-DAG nodes are not meant to be edited or modified by selecting and editing in the modeling windows. DG nodes are usually included as a part of a user-created dependency graph. Default non-DAG nodes are also almost always read-only and are not meant to be deleted. Again, Maya sometimes allows you to modify the attributes of its default non-DAG nodes, but the stability of your Maya scene will often be at risk. Some attributes of default scene DG nodes are exposed to the user through built-in UI elements, such as the default Hardware Render Globals. If Maya has not exposed the attributes of a default non-DAG node through a UI element, it is probably not necessary to attempt to modify these nodes by other means (unless you really know what you are changing).

Here are just a few examples of read-only, default non-DAG scene nodes that Maya absolutely needs to guarantee stability within your scene:

- layerManager
- globalCacheControl
- defaultHardwareRenderGlobals
- ikSystem
- characterPartition
- renderPartition
- defaultRenderLayer
- globalRender
- renderLayerManager
- strokeGlobals

To view many of the non-DAG nodes, select Window, Outliner and then choose Display, (uncheck) DAG Objects Only. The nodes that show up are non-DAG nodes.

Viewing the Maya Scene Graph and Node History

If components of an object's shape node are directly influenced by connections between nodes downstream and by the destination attributes of the shape in a dependency graph connection inside Maya, that node is said to have *history*. A node's history can generically be thought of as any data that exists downstream of it in the dependency graph that influences its creation. Specifically, history is anything that influences the creation of an object's shape node (such as "make" nodes, deformer nodes, and so on). The process of deleting history does not guarantee that it gets rid of all dependency graph connections to the node. In fact, there are often extra set nodes or intermediate nodes that do absolutely nothing and are left connected in your graph even after you delete history. This could be good or bad, depending on the circumstances. Therefore, it is always wise to be consciously aware of how, when, and why a node could be building up invisible dependency nodes and history—either during its creation or while it is in production. History is usually unnecessary data that inexperienced modelers and riggers leave floating around due to general neglect, and it often adds many unneeded megabytes to the total file size and makes the file less stable to edit and interact with.

On the other hand, history can be an excellent tool because any attribute that influences the node's creation can be modified after it has been created, including being keyframed and connected to any other attribute. In fact, one of the coolest things about Maya is its powerful construction history—but only if you are aware of how and why you are using it or keeping it around.

History and attribute connection are actually exposed by Maya almost every chance it gets. The following are just some of the places that will immediately tell you what the situation is with a node's input and output history and its direct upstream/downstream connections:

- Channel Box, Input/Output notation under shape node name
- Attribute Editor, arrow buttons and upper tabs
- Right click (in view port), Inputs, All Inputs
- Right click (in view port), Outputs, All Outputs
- Hypergraph, Graph, Input and Output Connections
- Hypershade, Graph, Input and Output Connections

Of these, the two best ways to view a node's dependency graph are through the Hypergraph and Hypershade windows, in Input and Output Connections view. These two windows are so much related to each other that it is amazing that Alias|Wavefront doesn't collapse them down to a single window. Both windows are simply visual interfaces for viewing the data stream of your entire scene graph, or of parts of it. The only difference between them is that the Hypershade does not show any objects other than material/texture/lighting/shading–related nodes by default. This window is used primarily for creating shading networks and connecting nodes that will help with rendering, lighting, or texturing your scene.

The Hypergraph, on the other hand, shows all object-level nodes by default, except for material/shading nodes. This window is used for organizing and grouping your scene when in hierarchy mode and for connecting (or viewing connections of) node attributes when in Input Output Connections view. Both the Hypergraph and the Hypershade are absolutely invaluable editors, and you should become very intimate with them if you want to truly harness the power of node networks in Maya. Both editors will also show any node you want, as long as the nodes are selected and you view input and output connections with the nodes still selected.

Note

To me, the real difference between these two editors, besides functionality, is that the Hypershade dynamically renders little swatch icons of your shaders, which update as you change values. This provides you with a nice feedback preview of how things will look before you render. The Hypershade also lacks a "Scene Hierarchy" View mode, which the Hypergraph has, enabling you to view the hierarchical transformation order of your grouped nodes; it also does not dynamically render the little icon previews. Nodes in the Hypergraph are all represented with standard vector icons, so the Hypergraph always loads large data graphs a lot faster than the Hypershade. The Hypergraph is my personal favorite, and I use this window most frequently for navigating a scene's nodes. It possesses the perfect combination of the functionality of both the Hypershade and the Outliner, in one single quick and understandable window. I vote for the Hypergraph as Maya's most useful window!

To view a node's attributes, all you have to do is select and look. The attributes of a node are everywhere. The two most popular places are the Channel Box and the Attribute Editor. A few more advanced places to see an object's attributes are the Attribute spreadsheet (for changing the same attributes on multiple objects at once), the Connection Editor (for directly connecting one attribute to another), and the Channel Control window (for changing the keyability and locked state of attributes).

You can also print a list of a selected node's attributes by typing the following into the Script Editor:

```
print `listAttr`;
```

Next, click and hold the middle mouse button, and drag the text into your shelf. Then select a single node and click your new Shelf button. A list of all attributes on the selected node prints in the output section of the Script Editor.

Connecting Attributes Between Nodes

The task of directly connecting objects that contain attributes and process data can easily be thought of as a form of visual programming. Creating a dependency graph to achieve a certain goal or to solve a particular problem, all from scratch, can be very fun and an interesting learning experience. Now that we have thoroughly discussed many aspects of DAG nodes, DG nodes, and history, let's make a simple connection between a couple of nodes to establish this idea.

Exercise 12.1   Connecting Two DAG Nodes

Let's start with a utility node called a Sampler Info node and the default shader. A Sampler Info node is a really useful node for Maya's rendering engine that outputs helpful surface-shading data on a per-shading sample basis (during a render). Alias|Wavefront's definition this node is that it:

> Provides you with information about each point on a surface as it is being "sampled," or calculated, for rendering purposes. Sampler Info can give you information about a point's position in space, its orientation and tangency, and its location relative to the camera.

We will use the Hypershade and the Connection Editor to make a simple connection between these two DG nodes.

1. Create a sphere by clicking Create, Nurbs Primitives, Sphere.
2. Create a Sampler Info utility node from the Hypershade by clicking Create, General Utilities, Sampler Info (see Figure 12.7).

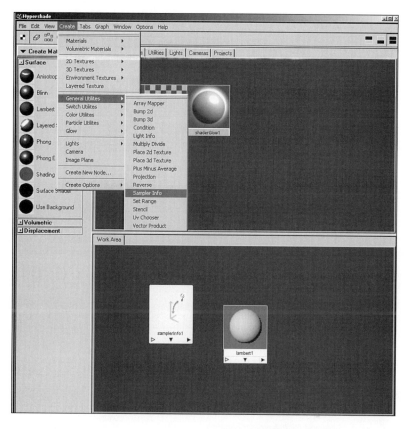

Figure 12.7   The Hypershade contains access to many important nodes.

3. Now, with your Sampler Info node currently selected, hold down the Shift key and add-select (Shift+click) the Lambert default shading group.

4. Still from inside the Hypershade, click the Input and Output Connections button (the little button with two arrows), as shown on the upper-left side of Figure 12.8.

5. Next, with the Shift button held down, use your middle mouse button to Shift-drag the Sampler Info node directly onto the Lambert default shading group. This action opens the Connection Editor window and automatically loads the nodes that you are trying to connect. You can also access the Connection Editor by going to Window, General Editors, Connection Editor.

Now that the Connection Editor is open, it is time to connect two attributes. As a simple introduction to a very useful node, you will connect the Sampler Info Facing Ratio attribute on the left side, to control the Color G attribute of the shader on the right side.

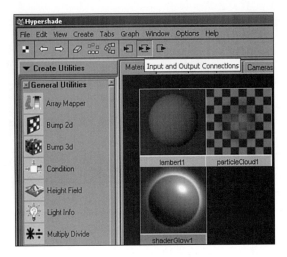

Figure 12.8 The Input and Output Connections button.

6. Click the Facing Ratio attribute so that it is currently highlighted. Next, expand the Color attribute on the right side of the Connection Editor window by clicking the little plus icon next to its name (see Figure 12.9). Now make a direct connection by simply clicking the Color G attribute.

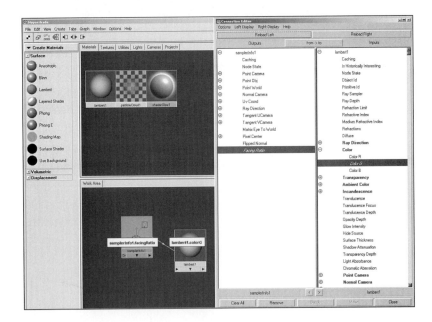

Figure 12.9 The Color attribute of the Connection Editor window expanded.

You should now see your shader change color. It should be green near the interior and should have a radiated violet around the edges. This color change is the result of the "facing ratio" data controlling the Green channel of color. The facing ratio attribute outputs a value between 0 and 1, based on the angle between two vectors, the surface normal on the geometry at the point being shading, and the direction in which the currently rendering camera is pointing.

Now do a render and see the results. Try experimenting a little with connecting the Facing Ratio attribute to other attributes on the shader. A completed example node network is included on the CD in the file FACING_RATIO_SHADER.mb.

Summary

The material in this chapter is meant to serve as an introduction to Maya's Node based Architecture and should create a strong foundation to begin understanding that Maya simply works as a toolbox of transform and compute nodes with data being passed between those nodes through connections between attributes. Really understanding what node connections are and how they can be used is vital to completing Chapter 13, "Making Advanced Connections." In addition, really understanding transforms and shapes will prove to be priceless when doing the character setup and rigging exercises later in the book. Having a foundation of nodes and knowing how to connect their attributes is a basic building block for creating shaders, creating character rigs, writing MEL scripts and expressions, and so much more.

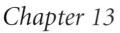

Chapter 13
Making Advanced Connections

By Erick Miller

Maya gives you a powerful capability to create multiple types of user-defined attributes. These user-defined attributes can control or be controlled just like any other normal node's attributes can. For example, you can use an attribute to control the on or off state of several weighted point constraints, creating a blended control that allows a character to smoothly pick up and put down an object. Giving full control over your setup using a few basic keyable attributes makes your file easy to use, modify, and update later, when changes need to be made.

This chapter covers how to create customized control by creating nodes, adding attributes, and connecting attributes to gain control over your attributes by using connections. The chapter includes several exercises that range in difficulty level from easy to medium to semiadvanced, and that cover a broad range of useful and practical techniques for creating relationships between nodes and attributes. Specifically, you'll learn how to do the following:

- Create a standard hand and finger controller using a set-driven key, a constraint, and the Connection Editor
- Use weighted constraints to pick up a randomly moving object
- Use particle dynamics, weighted constraints, and inverse kinematics to create an overlapping action skeleton rig
- Modify geometry after it is smooth-skinned, and transfer UVs onto a skinned character without leaving any construction history behind

Understanding Node Connections

The two easiest and most common ways to understand node connections—by applying them in a practical way to solve a common problem—involve using straight connections in the Connection Editor and creating animation curve-driven connections using the Set-Driven Key window.

Set-driven keys is a truly wonderful feature of Maya. A set-driven key enables you to create your own relationship between two attributes without writing any expressions or hooking up any complex node networks; the Set-Driven Key window pretty much does all this for you. The basic idea to keep in mind before you begin the exercises in this chapter is that by creating node connections, your end goal is simply to cause one attribute to modify the value of another attribute (using some sort of defined relationship). A set-driven key lets you do just that. As an example, when this attribute is set to, say, 5, you can tell it that you want this other attribute to be set to –15, but as the first attribute changes back to 0, you want the second attribute to also smoothly go back to 0. This is a simple example, but hopefully it begins to open up the idea of controlling attributes and using set-driven key relationships to do so.

Exercise 13.1   Creating the Standard Set-Driven Key Hand Control

In this exercise, you open a file of a hand skeleton that is ready to be rigged with custom controls for the fingers and the wrist. Then you create a locator as a node that you can add your new controller attributes to. Finally, you add multiple attributes that will control many different aspects of the hand, concentrating on keeping a balance between simplicity and total control for the animator who wants to bend the fingers.

1. Open the file Chapter13Hand_begin.mb from the accompanying CD.

   In this file, you will find a generic hand and arm skeleton for this tutorial. Any nodes that are referred to by name that were not created through the instructions of this tutorial will exist in this file as a starting point.

2. Create a locator and rename it left_handControl.

3. Next, point-snap the left_handControl locator to the left_wrist node by holding down the v key on you keyboard and using the Move tool with the middle mouse button to drag the locator directly onto the wrist in the 3D view.

4. Perform the menu command Modify, Freeze Transformations. Now scale your left_handControl to 3 so that it is larger and easier to select (see Figure 13.1).

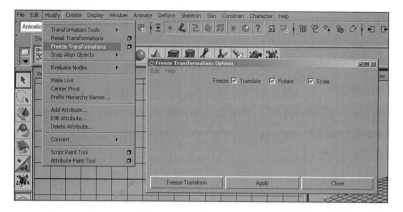

Figure 13.1   Freeze Transformations zeroes out the transform attributes of the controller.

5. Point-constrain the left_wrist to the left_handControl joint by selecting the left_handControl first and then the left_wrist, and then clicking Constrain, Point. Point-constrain the left_handControl to the left_armEnd joint by selecting the left_handControl and then the left_armEnd, and clicking Constrain, Point again. This keeps the wrist attached to the locator control at all times.

Note

Using point constraints is appropriate for this exercise because you are dealing with forward kinematics only on the arm joints. You could have made the locator a parent of the wrist, but that would not allow you as much freedom later when you want to also control the rotation. If inverse kinetics (IK) were applied to the attaching arm, it would also make sense to point-constrain the IK handle to the left_handControl so that the hand control also controlled the positioning of the IK. For those of you who are not sure about forward kinematics versus inverse kinematics, here is a brief synopsis:

Forward kinematics (FK) is the hierarchical transformation of joints purely through the means of parent and child relationships. When you rotate a parent, all of its children rotate with it, around the parent's point of pivot.

IK uses a "solver," or a mathematical solution, to compute the rotation of a joint hierarchy, based on the positions that are input into the solver to solve for the rotation of the parent joints to correctly place the location of the child. IK is great for sticking parts of hierarchies that are naturally children (such as hands or feet) onto surfaces (such as a desk or the ground).

Next, you want to cause the rotation of the left_handControl to control the rotation of the left_wrist joint as well as the rotateY of the left_forearm joint. This will consolidate all of the wrist's rotations into the rotation of a single control. You can easily do this in the Connection Editor.

6. Go to Window, General Editors, Connection Editor (see Figure 13.2). Select the left_handControl locator, and click the Reload Left button in the Connection Editor. Now select the left_wrist joint and click the Reload Right button.

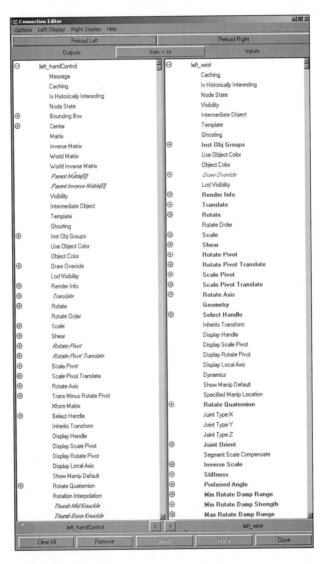

Figure 13.2   The Connection Editor simply connects one attribute to another so that the "from" attribute is controlling the "to" attribute.

You are now ready to make a connection from the left to the right. The left-side (from) attribute will control the right-side (to) attribute.

7. Scroll down until you see Rotate, and highlight it by clicking it on the left side. Then, while it is highlighted on the left, highlight the Rotate attribute on the right by clicking it.

You should now see that the rotate attributes on the wrist joint are being controlled by the rotate attributes of the locator (see Figure 13.3).

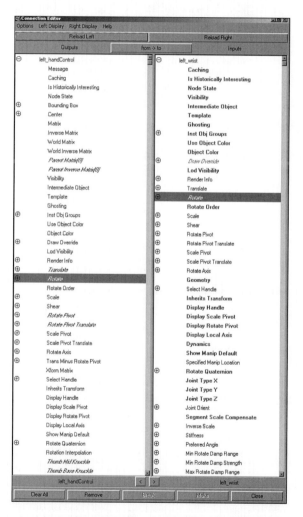

Figure 13.3   Notice that the rotate channels are highlighted. This signifies that the connection has been made.

8. Select the left_forearm joint, and click the Reload Right button in the Connection Editor. Click to expand the rotate attribute, and highlight the rotateY attribute.

9. Keeping the left_handControl loaded on the left side, scroll down on the left side of the Connection Editor until you find the rotate attribute, and expand it so that you see the three X, Y, and Z rotate attributes. Click the rotateY attribute so that it is also highlighted (see Figure 13.4).

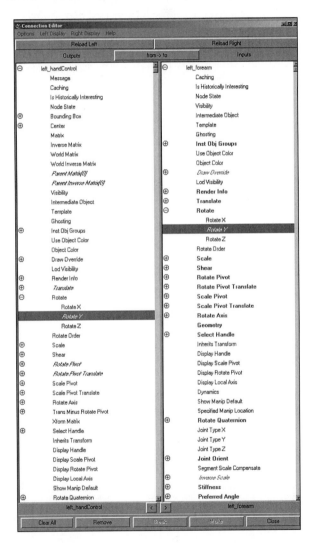

Figure 13.4   Connecting attributes in the Connection Editor is as easy as a click.

10. You have now connected the rotateY of the controller to the rotateY of the fore-arm. When you rotate the locator, the appropriate joints will rotate with it properly.

Note

Step 10 worked correctly and seemed so simple because the local rotation axis of the wrist joint matched the world orientation of the hand control locator. (To view or edit a joint's local rotation axis, select the joint, go into Component mode, right-click the Question Mark Pick Mask, and select Local Rotation Axes.) The local rotation axes (LRAs) of your joints are editable XYZ axis handles that can change the orientation that your joints rotate from. They are very important because they determine which axis your joints will rotate upon, as well as how your joints will rotate in relationship to each other. We talk more about LRAs in Chapter 16, "Character Setup Pipeline for Animation." For now, you should at least understand what they are and why they are important.

Now you'll lock and get rid of any extra attributes you don't need, and then add some extra attributes that you will rig up to control the fingers.

11. First, to lock the attributes that you don't want anyone to touch—in this case, just the scale attributes of the left_hand control node—select the scale attributes in the Channel Box, right-click the attribute names, and choose Lock Selected.

12. To hide all the rest of the unnecessary attributes, go to Window, General Editors, Channel Control. On the left side of the Keyable tab, highlight all the attributes that you don't need to set keys on—in this case, all translate, scale, and visibility attributes—and then click the Move button. Your attributes disappear from the Channel Box and no longer clutter the view (see Figure 13.5).

13. Now, with the left_handControl locator still selected, add attributes for the fingers by going to Modify, Add Attribute.

This brings up the Add Attribute window that lets you add any attribute that you want to any node in Maya.

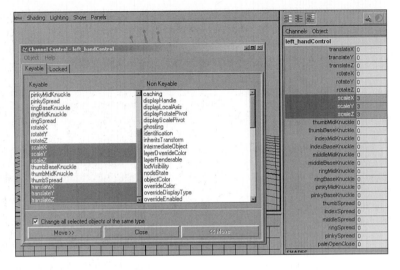

Figure 13.5   The Channel Control window enables you to hide attributes so that they cannot have keyframes set on them and are also not viewable in the Channel Box.

14. The Add Attribute window has a few settings. Under Attribute Name, add the following attributes for the fingers:

> thumbMidKnuckle
>
> thumbBaseKnuckle
>
> indexMidKnuckle
>
> indexBaseKnuckle
>
> middleMidKnuckle
>
> middleBaseKnuckle
>
> ringMidKnuckle
>
> ringBaseKnuckle
>
> pinkyMidKnuckle
>
> pinkyBaseKnuckle

Each attribute controls bending knuckle rotation of separate fingers, for ultimate poseable finger control.

Leave the remaining settings at their defaults, which are as follows:

> Make Attribute Keyable: Check Box: On
>
> Data Type: Float
>
> Attribute Type: Scalar
>
> Minimum: –20
>
> Maximum: 90
>
> Default: 0

15. To make the fingers spread open, add these attributes:

> thumbSpread
>
> indexSpread
>
> middleSpread
>
> ringSpread
>
> pinkySpread
>
> palmOpenClose

Use the same settings given previously, except for the minimum and maximum values:

> Minimum: −30
>
> Maximum: 30

Tip

To help automate this process, you can use a few simple MEL scripting techniques (if you are comfortable with trying some scripting) to add all of the similar attributes at once. First, declare a procedure, with all the necessary arguments. Then inside the procedure, write a loop to create and make keyable all the attribute names passed in as an array:

```
global proc addSameMultipleAttrs( string $attrs[], string ⮕$nodeName,
int $min, int $max){
   for ($each in $attrs)
   {
         addAttr -ln $each -at double -min $min -max
         ⮕$max -dv 0 $nodeName;
         setAttr -e -keyable true ($nodeName+"."+$each);
   }
}
```

Now declare your array of knuckle-bending attribute names, and then just pass them into the procedure that you defined earlier:

```
string $attrKnuckleNameArray[] = { "thumbMidKnuckle",
"thumbBaseKnuckle","indexMidKnuckle", "indexBaseKnuckle",
"middleMidKnuckle", "middleBaseKnuckle", "ringMidKnuckle",
"ringBaseKnuckle","pinkyMidKnuckle", "pinkyBaseKnuckle" };

addSameMultipleAttrs $attrKnuckleNameArray left_handControl -20 90;
```

Do the same for the finger-spread attributes because they have different min/max values:

```
string $attrSpreadNameArray[] = { "thumbSpread", "indexSpread",
"middleSpread", "ringSpread", "pinkySpread", "palmOpenClose" };
addSameMultipleAttrs $attrSpreadNameArray left_handControl -30 30;
```

You should now have a multitude of attributes on your left_handControl locator node that, so far, do nothing. The wrist is point-constrained to the locator, which, in turn, is point-constrained to the arm_end (which forces the wrist to stay connected to the arm). The locator's rotates are directly controlling the wrist joint's rotates. Here is where things really get interesting. Let's hook up the finger controls.

16. Click Animate, Set-Driven Key, Set Options box. This loads the Set-Driven Key window (see Figure 13.6).

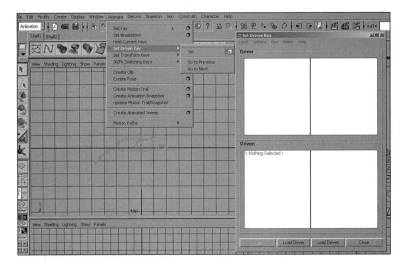

Figure 13.6 The Set-Driven Key window.

Note

Using set-driven keys is probably the most popular technique for controlling an attribute's behavior because they are so simple and easy to understand, yet they offer a wide range of remappable, editable, user-defined control. When you make a set-driven key connection, you are simply setting a key that will be animated into position based on the attribute you use as the driver. A set-driven key simply creates a function curve relationship between the driver and the driven. Set-driven keys actually use keyframe nodes, which are accessible for editing in the Graph Editor. The only difference between a regular keyframe and a set-driven key is that a regular keyframe uses time as its driver, and a set-driven key uses another node's attribute as its driver. The driver's attribute actually replaces "time" as the input to the animation curve's input attribute and allows fully customized animation curve-based remapped interpolation node attributes.

You will use the left_handControl.thumbMidKnuckle as the first attribute to begin driving the rotation attributes of your joints.

17. Select the left_handControl and, with the Set-Driven Key window open, click the Load Driver button. Next, highlight the thumbMidKnuckle attribute on the right side of the driver section of the Set-Driven Key window.

18. Select the thumb joints that you want the thumbMidKnuckle attribute to drive. I selected left_thumb3, left_thumb2, and left_thumb1. Click the Load Driven button, and highlight all three on the left side as well as all three rotate attributes on the right side of the Set-Driven Key window (see Figure 13.7).

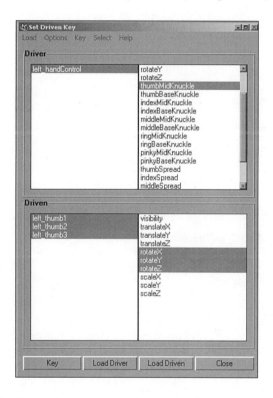

Figure 13.7   The Set-Driven Key window, ready to define the attribute connection relationships.

19. Click the Key button from within the Set-Driven Key window.

This initial keyframe keys the rotates at 0 whenever the thumbMidKnuckle attribute is at 0.

20. Next, change the thumbMidKnuckle attribute to its maximum value of 90. Rotate the thumb joints into their appropriate position for the upper knuckle to be bent down all the way, as shown in Figure 13.8.

Press the Key button in the Set-Driven Key window. This sets a keyframe that rotates the thumb joints to be set fully bent down (by approximately 90°) at the midKnuckle, which will be activated by an animation curve when the thumbMidKnuckle attribute is set to 90. All you are really doing here is defining a relationship between the rotation of the thumb joints and the thumbMidKnuckle attribute.

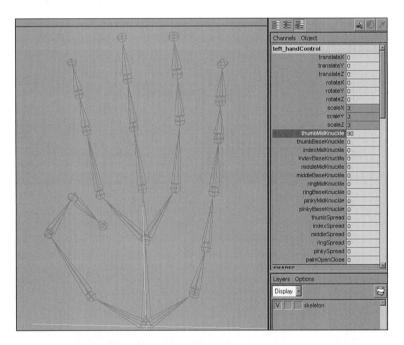

Figure 13.8 The thumb joints have now had a set-driven key applied so that they are controlled by the highlighted attribute.

21. Now set the thumbMidKnuckle attribute to its lowest value, –20. The thumb joints should move based on this attribute control until the thumbMidKnuckle attribute hits 0. Then the joints will stop. This is because there are no keys for the –20 position. Bend the thumb joints backward until they have reached their extreme back position for the upper knuckles. Hit the Key button in the Set-Driven Key window.

22. Test the control by selecting the left_handControl and highlighting the attribute so that it is selected in the Channel Box. Then, with the middle mouse button held down, drag in the 3D view window.

This activates the "virtual slider" for the attribute. The virtual slider is a commonly used control that enables you to scroll through attribute values without actually typing in numbers in the Channel Box or changing sliders in the Attribute Editor.

23. Repeat steps 16–22, mimicking the entire set-driven key process for each attribute and the corresponding set of joints that the attributes should be the driver of. Remember, you must first load the attribute as the driver, then load the joints as the driven, then key them at zero, and finally key them at their extreme low pose and extreme high pose.

You should now have a finished hand control, with attributes that control the bending of all the fingers and the rotation of the wrist. Each attribute controls the rotation of different sets of joints. A finished file, Chapter13Hand_finished.mb, is supplied on the CD that accompanies this book. You can open and examine this file to get a clear idea of what the finished setup should accomplish.

Exercise 13.2   Using Weighted Constraints to Grab a Randomly Moving Object

This next exercise shows a simple example of how you can use weighted constraints to smoothly blend between two moving objects. In this example, you will make an animated hand grab and hold on to an object. You can apply the concept of using weighted constraints to any problem that requires blending an object's transform attributes from one place to another.

1. First, open the file Chapter13Constraints_begin.mb from the accompanying CD.

You should see an animated arm (with the completed hand controller from the previous exercise). There is also an animated box that moves vertically in front of the arm and contains a quick expression to cause it to animate randomly in its translateY direction (see Figure 13.9). The arm is animated to grab toward the top of the box, where the constrained object will sit. The static (nonanimated) cylinder is the object that the hand will grab.

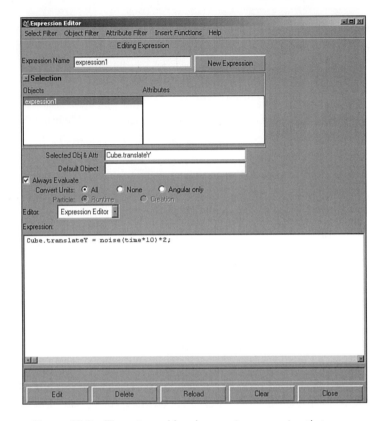

Figure 13.9 The animated box has a noise expression that causes its translateY channel to jitter randomly up and down.

2. Scrub through the animation. Notice that the cylinder object that you want to grab is not moving with the jittering box, as it should. You will fix this first.

3. Create a locator. Name it constrainToBox, and make it a child of the box by selecting the locator, Shift-selecting the box, and hitting the p key on the keyboard.

4. Next, create a point constraint to the box's child locator by selecting the constrainToBox locator, Shift-selecting the cylinder, and performing the menu command Constrain, Point.

   Now your cylinder should move anywhere the locator moves. You can easily move the cylinder exactly to the position on top of the box that you want by simply moving the locator into place.

5. Next, create a child locator of the hand the same way you did for the box. Name it constrainToHand, and make it a child of the hand by selecting the locator, Shift-selecting the left_palm joint, and hitting the p key on the keyboard.

6. Create a point constraint to the hand's child locator by selecting the constrainToHand locator, Shift-selecting the cylinder, and performing the menu command Constrain, Point. Play back the animation.

You will now see that the cylinder is exactly halfway between the hand and the box (see Figure 13.10). This is where the weights of the constraints come into play.

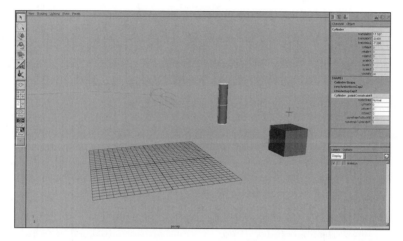

Figure 13.10   Notice that the cylinder is stuck halfway between the hand and the box because of the separate influence of two point constraints.

7. Select the cylinder and look at the SHAPES listing in the Channel Box. In the list there should be an item called Cylinder_pointConstraint1. Click this Channel Box listing; the list expands another attribute list. In the new list are two attributes that are of interest here: constrainToBoxW0 and constrainToHandW1 (see Figure 13.11).

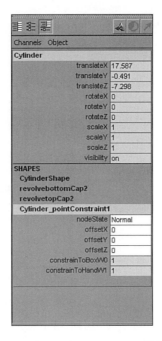

Figure 13.11   Note the constraint weight attributes: constrainToBoxW0 and constrainToHandW1.

These two attributes cause the constraints to be either on or off. But they are not simply Boolean attributes. These attributes are floats that can be blended smoothly from 0 to 1; therefore, they can smoothly move from being constrained to the box to being constrained to the hand. When both attributes share the same weight setting, they are equally weighted. Therefore, the result of the constraint is equally halfway between both constraint goals.

8. Open the Hypergraph and Outliner windows, and find the cylinder node.

You should notice that a constraint node, Cylinder_pointConstraint1, is now a child of the cylinder (see Figure 13.12). This is the node that is now controlling the translation channels of the cylinder geometry.

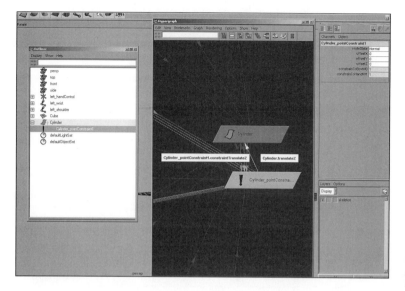

Figure 13.12   Notice the point constraint node that is a child of the cylinder; it actually uses a constraint calculation to control the cylinder's translations.

9. Select the cylinder's Cylinder_pointConstraint1 child node.

You should see the same attributes that were in the Channel Box earlier. These are the attributes that you will keyframe to get a smooth blend when the hand picks up the cylinder as it is cruising by.

10. With the Cylinder_pointConstraint1 node still selected, set your current time to about frame 61 in the timeline. Set the attribute Constrain to Box W0 to 1. Set the attribute Constrain to Hand W1 to 0. Now set a keyframe on both attributes by hitting the s key on your keyboard.

11. Next set your current time to about 63 in the timeline. Set the same attributes as in step 10, but swap their constraint weights—set the attribute Constrain to Box W0 to 0, and set the attribute Constrain to Hand W1 to 1. Set another keyframe on both attributes by hitting the s key on your keyboard, and play back the animation.

You should see a nice blending animation as the hand grabs the moving object when it glides by (see Figure 13.13).

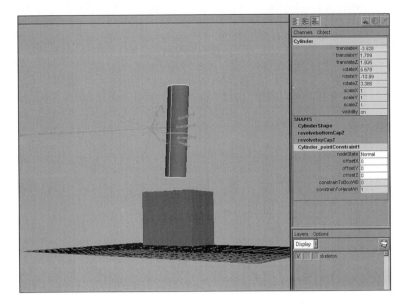

Figure 13.13 Set-driven keys control the weights of the weighted constraints.

You might need to adjust slightly and keyframe the positions of your child locators, constrainToBox and constrainToHand, so that the position of the cylinder goes exactly where you want it when the hand picks up the object. You also might want to add a few keyframes to the arm and hand animation, as well as the cylinder node's rotations, so that everything rotates and lines up into place when the hand grabs it.

You can find a completed example file, Chapter13Constraints_fin.mb, on the accompanying CD.

Some Practical Uses for Constraints

Constraints are extremely useful tools. The idea of using weighted constraints to blend multiple transform attributes can be a general solution for many other problems, not just for picking up or grabbing objects.

In fact, constraints can be used to control any transform attribute of an object in many powerful and creative ways. Here is a rundown of some of the most common types of constraints:

- **Point constraint**—Directly controls translate X, Y, and Z, as covered in the previous exercise.

- **Aim constraint**—Causes any object to point at or aim in the direction of the target object. This constraint can be very useful for creating a character's eye controls so that the character is always "looking at" the position of a locator. This constraint can also prove very useful for forcing lights or cameras to always point at a certain object.

- **Orient constraint**—This constraint is very similar to the point constraint. The big difference is that this constraint controls the rotation of an object. A great use for the orient constraint is to blend the weighted constraints of a single joint chain into two duplicated joint chains, to have multiple controls attached to a single character rig. Exercise 13.3 emphasizes this technique as a major building block to the tutorial.

Note

One of the best things about point, orient, and scale constraints, as opposed to direct connections, is that they cause the constrained object to transform as if it is within the same hierarchy as the object it is constrained to. This is great when you are doing character setup because often you need to have objects that move with other objects but that are not in the same hierarchy. This, in combination with the fact that they all have weighted attributes so that you can blend multiple constraint objects, can make constraints some of the most powerful, unique, and valuable transformation nodes in Maya.

- **Scale constraint**—The scale constraint is similar to point and orient constraints, except that this constraint controls the scale attributes of an object.

- **Parent constraint**—Ths is a new constraint type found in Version 5. It is very useful for making one group in a completely different hierarchy move as though it was a child of a new hierarchy. The default of this constraint is to maintain the offset between the constraining object and the constrained objects, so that the initial constraint operation does not actually transform the objects being constrained. Blending between multiple parent contraints could yield extremely useful behavior for various character setup techniques.

- **Geometry constraint**—This constrains a transform node directly onto the surface of any geometry node. The constrained object moves perfectly down the surface of the target object. This constraint is great for things such as tears running down the cheek of a character, or for an insect that has to land on and then crawl along the surface of a piece of geometry.

- **Normal constraint**—This constraint causes your constrained object's rotation to point in the direction of the target geometry's normals. You can view normals by selecting the object and using the menu command Display, NURBS Components, Normals (for NURBS), or Display, Polygon Components,

Normals (for polygons). Normal constraints work quite well in conjunction with geometry constraints because your constrained object will move along the surface, as well as correctly point upward as it moves over ridges or bumps in the surface.

- **Tangent constraint**—Usable only with NURBS curves as the target objects, this constraint constrains any object to the tangent of the NURBS curve at the closest point to which the object is nearest the curve. This constraint can be very useful if you want the direction of a NURBS curve to control the direction of your object, while still leaving the translation attributes available to be keyframed or controlled by another constraint.

- **Pole vector constraint**—Pole vector constraints are usable only with a Rotate Plane (RP) IK handle as the constrained object. This constraint causes the IK handle's pole vector to always aim toward the target object. The benefit of this is that the pole vector of an IK handle controls the direction in which the center joint in the chain is pointing. For example, in an arm, the pole vector would control the direction in which the elbow is pointing when the arm bends. In a leg, the pole vector would control the direction of the knee. If you use a pole vector constraint on an IK handle, it gives you an additional level of control over your character's motion—control that you would otherwise have only by using the IK handle's twist attribute, which is not as intuitive.

Quick Review: Overlapping Action

The concept of overlapping action is one of the basic principals of animation. Overlap is the idea that the main body of an animated object is leading, and another secondary part of the animated object is lagging behind a little, like an antenna on an alien character's head. Anything that is generally floppy or bendy in nature, such as a dog's ears or tail, will naturally have overlapping action when the dog's body or head moves. If the dog jumps in the air, the tail and ears will flop around much more in reaction to the force of the motion than if the dog was simply quietly walking by.

Overlapping action is something that will really sell an animation. When the timing and main action of a motion are solid, it is then usually just tedium to add all the necessary subtleties of overlap that will really polish off and finish the animation. Therefore, I have often heard animators express the request that things with floppy, droopy, or generally dynamically bouncy properties be somehow automatically and dynamically set up to have this reaction occur naturally, as they would in real life.

The following tutorial explains a technique that solves this problem. It also allows total control for the animator to still pose the skeleton as it flops around, as well as remove the "floppiness" completely, just in case the automatic overlap is not wanted in some situation.

Exercise 13.3   Using Particle Dynamics, Weighted Constraints, and Inverse Kinematics to Create an Overlapping Action Skeleton Rig

Because this technique involves many steps and can become somewhat involved, I will first provide a brief description of our general goal for this tutorial. Then I'll give a broad overview of the actual steps within Maya. You will then be able to launch into the moderately elaborate series of steps, prepared with a full overview and understanding of all the steps that you will be performing.

To create a skeleton rig that will animate with automatic overlapping action, you will be using a small part of Maya's robust Dynamics Engine, with particle goals on a soft body curve's particles. To apply this motion to a controllable and animatable skeleton, you will use Maya's Spline IK Solver, in combination with Maya's cluster deformers and weighted constraints on duplicate skeleton rigs, to pose the rig and still seamlessly blend dynamic and nondynamic skeletons during animation.

First, you'll use spline IK with a soft body curve to drive one of the skeletal duplicates (this will be the floppy skeleton) and regular spline IK on the second duplicate (this will be the regular skeleton). You will then use weighted point and orient constraints to blend the two skeletons. You will point-constrain the original's root node to both duplicates' root nodes.

Next, you will orient-constrain each original joint to the two corresponding duplicate joints, one by one. This will create a weighted constraint network that will enable you to blend the regular spline IK and the floppy spline IK. You will create a locator with a few custom attributes and use a set-driven key to control the blending of the constraint weights between the floppy and regular skeletons, as well as an attribute to control the soft body particle's Goal Smoothness attribute, to add more or less floppiness.

Then you will create clusters on the soft body goal spline IK curve and the regular spline IK curve. You will point-constrain each goal curve's cluster to the corresponding cluster on the regular spline IK curve. This will enable you to deform both curves by moving a single cluster so that whether you are using the floppy skeleton or the regular skeleton, it will move into the same "goal" pose.

You will create a locator for each of the regular spline IK's clusters and then parent each cluster to the corresponding locator so that the locators are easy-to-grab controls that can be used to position the skeleton or animate the skeleton into a pose. Next you will organize your node hierarchy and clean up or lock object attributes that are not supposed to be edited. Finally, you will make a few other connections so that the rig can simply be scaled and positioned into any new scene, and reused for multiple characters for any floppy or bouncy body part that you will ever need to set up. For your convenience, a fully completed file, Chapter13_OverlapAct_fin.mb, is also included on the CD.

1. Open the scene Chapter13_OverlapAct_begin.mb on the accompanying CD.

   This scene contains an empty skeleton hierarchy that you will be using to set up your "floppy" rig. All that is in this scene is a single FK joint hierarchy. First, you will duplicate this joint chain twice and then use prefixHierarchy to rename each hierarchy so that you can keep track of which skeletons you are using. Notice that when you open the file, there is an extra joint that is not parented to anything and that just seems to be floating in space. You will use this joint later, but you can ignore it in the next few steps for duplication and initial setup.

2. Make sure that your duplicate options are reset to defaults. Select the parent joint, joint8, and duplicate it twice by hitting Ctrl+d on your keyboard so that there are now three identical joint hierarchies.

3. Select joint8 and go to Modify, Prefix Hierarchy Names. Type **baseBindSkeleton_** into the dialog box and hit OK. Select the parent of the second duplicate, which should be named joint11. Go to Modify, Prefix Hierarchy Names and type **regularSplineIKdriven_** into the dialog box, and hit OK. Finally, go to the last duplicate, joint12. Use Modify, Prefix Hierarchy Names to rename the hierarchy prefix to **softBodyDynamicDriven_**, and hit OK (see Figure 13.14).

4. Select the parent node of the softBodyDynamicDriven hierarchy, Shift-select the parent node of the regularSplineIKdriven hierarchy, and Shift-select the parent node of the original baseBindSkeleton hierarchy. Perform the menu command Constrain, Point and then Constrain, Orient.

   This begins your weighted constraint network by point- and orient-constraining the original root to the two other skeletons' roots. Note that only the root needs to be point-constrained because the root is the only node in the joint chain that will drive translation.

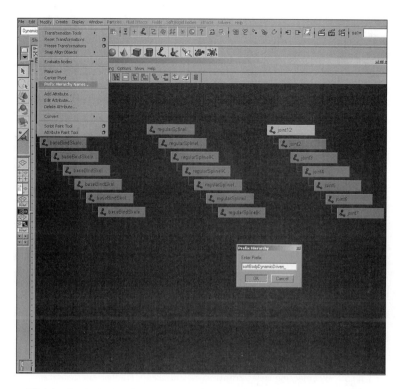

Figure 13.14   Prefix hierarchy can be used to quickly rename and identify your nodes.

5. Select the next joint down in the softBodyDynamicDriven hierarchy, softBodyDynamicDriven_joint2. Shift-select the next joint down in the regularSplineIKdriven hierarchy, regularSplineIKdriven_joint2. Then Shift-select the next joint down in the baseBindSkeleton hierarchy, baseBindSkeleton_joint2. Perform the menu command Constrain, Orient (see Figure 13.15).

6. Now select the next set of three corresponding joints, always one down in the hierarchy: softBodyDynamicDriven_joint3, regularSplineIKdriven_joint3, and baseBindSkeleton_joint3. Perform the menu command Constrain, Orient.

7. Select each of the three corresponding joints, always one down in each hierarchy, and perform Constrain, Orient. Be sure to always select the baseBindSkeleton last because this is the joint that you want to constrain. Do this for each set of three corresponding joints until you finish with the last three joints, softBodyDynamicDriven_joint7, regularSplineIKdriven_joint7, and baseBindSkeleton_joint7.

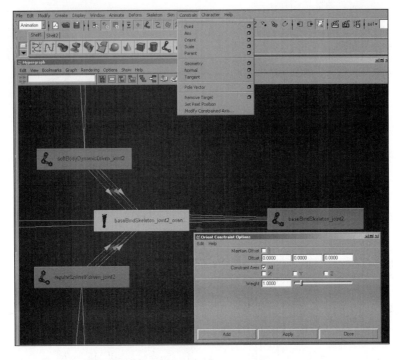

Figure 13.15 By selecting three transforms and creating an orient constraint, you are averaging the constraint between the first two nodes onto the third selected node.

Tip

You can use the g key on your keyboard to quickly repeat the last used menu command (in this case, for your orient constraint).

When finished, you will have created weighted orient constraint connections from the softBodyDynamicDriven and regularSplineIKdriven hierarchies that will drive the blending of the rotations onto the baseBindSkeleton hierarchy.

Next you will create a locator that will serve as the main controller for your rig and that will contain the attributes that the animator will use to blend between the dynamic and nondynamic hierarchies.

8. Create a locator. For lack of a better name, name it FloppyChainController.

9. Next, you'll create the attributes that will control the blending of the constraint weights. Perform the menu command Modify, Add Attribute. Use the following settings, and click OK (see Figure 13.16):

> Attribute Name: dynamicFlopOnOff
>
> Make Attribute Keyable (on)
>
> DataType: Float
>
> Minimum: 0
>
> Maximum: 1
>
> Default: 1

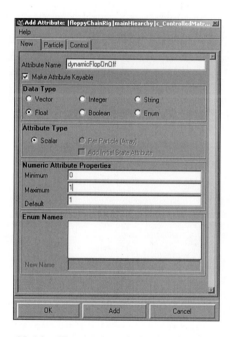

Figure 13.16   This attribute will be used to control the constraint weights using a set-driven key relationship.

Now you will use the dynamicFlopOnOff attribute to drive the weights of the constraints that you just created.

10. Load the options for the set-driven key by going to Animate, Set-Driven Key, Set Options box. Select the FloppyChainContoller locator, click the Load Driver button, and highlight the dynamicFlopOnOff attribute as the driver attribute in the upper-right section of the Set-Driven Key window.

11. Open the Hypergraph window and fully expand the baseBindSkeleton hierarchy. The constraint nodes that you previously created should now all be visible as children in the baseBindSkeleton hierarchy. Select all seven constraints. Six are orient constraints, and one is a point constraint. With all seven constraints selected, hit the Load Driven button in the Set-Driven Key window (see Figure 13.17).

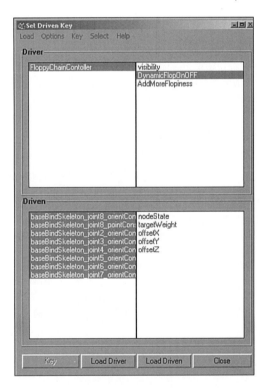

Figure 13.17 The Set-Driven Key window, which you will be using to create an animation curve-driven relationship between the dynamicFlopOnOff attribute of the locator node and the constraint's weight attributes.

Next, you need to establish the set-driven key relationship between the dynamicFlopOnOff attribute and all the constraint weight attributes of the seven constraints that you are about to "drive." You do this by first setting the key that will control the off state for the attribute. The off state will activate the regularSplineIKdriven_joint#W1 attributes to be 1, and the softBodyDynamicDriven_joint#W0 to be 0. This enables you to blend between the two skeletal hierarchies using a smooth interpolation between 0 and 1. When the off state is established, you can key the on state. Because the constraint weight attributes all have different names, you must key each constraint one at a time from the Driven section of the Set-Driven Key window. This is a bit tedious but should really help reinforce your understanding of set-driven keys. These steps could be quickly automated with a script, but for the sake of learning, you will manually key them one at a time here.

12. Select the FloppyChainController locator node, and make sure the dynamicFlopOnOff attribute is set to 0. Also make sure that the FloppyChainController is loaded in the Driver section of the window and that the dynamicFlopOnOff is the currently highlighted attribute on the right side of the Driver section.

13. In the Driven section of the Set-Driven Key window, make sure that all seven constraints are loaded, as shown in Figure 13-17. Highlight the first constraint on the left side of the Driven section. Then highlight both the softBodyDynamicDriven and regularSplineIKDriven constraint weight attributes on the right side.

Highlighting the attributes on the right is a very important step because this tells Maya which attributes to drive with the curve you will be creating. The constraint weight attributes are the ones that end with W0 and W1, respectively, for each constraint node.

14. Make sure the dynamicFlopOnOff attribute is still set to 0. Then set the softBodyDynamicDriven weight attribute to 0 and set the regularSplineIKDriven attribute to 1. Hit Key in the Set-Driven Key window.

You have just built your first relationship with the attributes. In other words, the rule that you just established creates an animation curve (which currently has only one keyframe) so that when the dynamicFlopOnOf is equal to 0, softBodyDynamicDriven weights animate to 0 and regularSplineIKDriven weights animate to 1.

15. Highlight the next constraint on the left side of the Driven section of the Set-Driven Key window, as well as the same two corresponding constraint weight attributes (softBodyDynamicDriven and regularSplineIKdriven) on the left side. Set the softBodyDynamicDriven weight attribute to 0 and the regularSplineIKdriven attribute to 1, and hit Key in the Set-Driven Key window.

16. Repeat this pattern for each of the remaining five constraint weight attributes in the Driven section of the Set-Driven Key window. Be sure that both of the constraint weight values are always highlighted and that you have set the softBodyDynamicDriven weight to 0 and the regularSplineIKdriven weight to 1. Hit the Key button (see Figure 13.18).

You know that you are finished setting the off state of your dynamicFlopOnOff attribute when all seven of your constraint weight values have been keyed from the Set-Driven Key window, with the dynamicFlopOnOff attribute set at 0, the softBodyDynamicDriven weight at 0 (on each constraint) and the regularSplineIKdriven weight at 1 (on each constraint), and all of your constraint weights show up in light orange in the Channel Box. The light orange color signifies that an attribute is being controlled by another node—in this case, a set-driven keyframe.

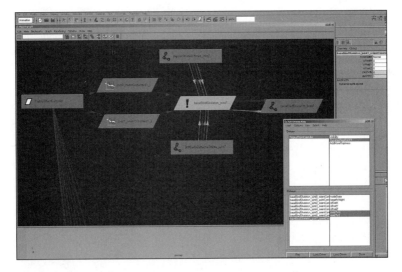

Figure 13.18 Notice the animation curve nodes that have been inserted in the node connections. This animation curve takes the dynamicFlopOnOff as an input, and outputs directly into the constraint weights that you just keyed.

Next, you want to set the on state for your dynamicFlopOnOff attribute. Keep the Set-Driven Key window open because you will do this exactly the same way you set the off state. But first you must change the attribute value of dynamicFlopOnOff from 0 to 1.

17. Select the FloppyChainContoller locator, and set the attribute dynamicFlopOnOff to 1. This turns it to its on state.

18. With the seven constraints loaded in the Driven section of the Set-Driven Key window, the FloppyChainContoller still loaded in the Driver section, and the dynamicFlopOnOff attribute still highlighted, highlight the driven constraint node on the bottom left. Also highlight both the weight attributes on the bottom right, change the softBodyDynamicDriven weight to 1 and the regularSplineIKdriven weight to 0, and hit the Key button in the Set-Driven Key window. You should start with the very first constraint at the top of the driven list and end with the very last, exactly as done in step 16, but with the new weight attribute settings (see Figure 13.19).

Now you have established a direct relationship between the weight attributes of all your constraints and the dynamicFlopOnOff attribute of your locator. Whenever the dynamicFlopOnOff is changed, the weight attributes will blend between their values according to the attribute settings that you keyed them to correspond to using set-driven keys. Easy!

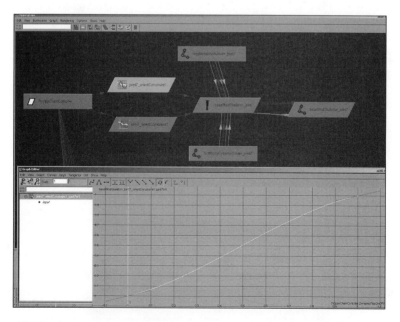

Figure 13.19   This curve animates from 0 to 1 based on the dynamicFlopOnOff attribute, which now fully controls the settings of your constraint weight attributes.

Next, you will quickly clean out the attributes from the Channel Box and create another custom attribute.

19. First, open Window, General Editors, Channel Control. In the Keyable tab, highlight all the attributes on the left side except for dynamicFlopOnOff, and hit the Move button. This hides your attributes (see Figure 13.20).

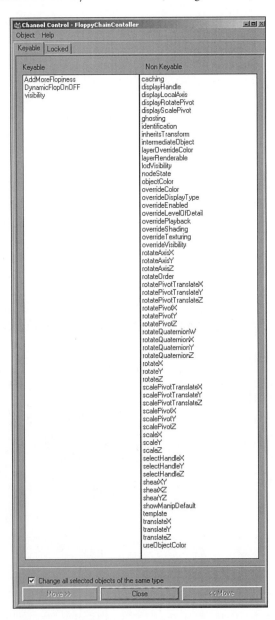

Figure 13.20   Clean up some of the unwanted channels by using Channel Control so that they are no longer keyable and do not show up in the Channel Box.

20. Next go to Modify, Add Attribute. Use the following settings:

Attribute Name: addMoreFloppiness

Make Attribute Keyable (on)

DataType: Float

Minimum: 0

Maximum: 1

Your result should look somewhat like Figure 13.21.

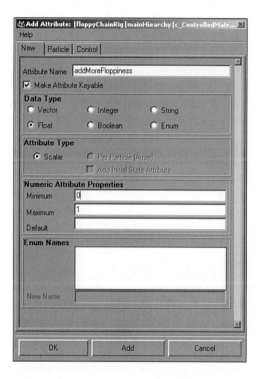

Figure 13.21   This attribute will later control particle dynamic attributes of a soft body particle shape.

Now you're ready to set up the skeleton with spline IK and add a soft body curve, with the original curve as a goal to the soft body's particles. Before you do, though, it helps to understand what soft body particles and particle goals are.

Soft body particles and particle goals are a really cool toolset from Maya's Dynamics Engine. A soft body is simply geometry whose vertices positions are actually controlled by the position of particles. As the particles move through a dynamic simulation, so do the vertices of your geometry. When you create a soft body, Maya automatically creates the particle object with one particle per vertex and connects everything for you nicely. You can then add a goal object, which tells the particles to always attempt to move their position toward the position of the goal. The goal weight simply tells the particle how hard to try to actually hit the goal's position in space. When the goal weight is 1, the particles move exactly toward the goal during simulation. If the goal weight is 0, the particles don't even try to move toward the goals. Of course, then, if a goal weight is .5, the particles try 50% to hit the corresponding goal position. This is very powerful because you can then add different weights per particle. Because the particles drive the vertices, you can create a really cool dynamic automatic floppiness based on different goal weights along the NURBS curve of a spline IK handle. Herein lies the foundation of this tutorial, and it is also what you will do next.

21. Open your Hypergraph or Outliner window, and select and hide the nodes joint10, baseBindSkeleton_joint8, and regularSplineIKdriven_joint11 by Shift-selecting the nodes in the Hypergraph, and hitting Ctrl+h on your keyboard. Make sure that the Visibility attribute on joint10 is both unlocked and set to Keyable by using the Channel Control window (found under the menu path Window, General Editors, Channel Control) before attempting to hide it.

    You're hiding the nodes that you don't need to see so that you don't accidentally select something that is not necessary. You will make these nodes visible again later. The only hierarchy that should currently be visible is the softBodyDynamicDriven joint hierarchy.

22. Next, go to Skeleton, IK Spline Handle Options box and use all the default settings, except uncheck the Auto Simplify Curve option (see Figure 13.22).

23. With the Auto Simplify Curve tool active, drag a selection around the root joint, softBodyDynamicDriven_joint12, and then drag a selection around the very top joint at the end of chain, softBodyDynamicDriven_joint7.

    You should now see that Maya has created an IK spline for you, and a NURBS curve is now controlling the rotational orientations of your joints.

24. Next, select the curve that was created, as well as the IK handle, and hit Ctrl+g on your keyboard to group the nodes. Rename the IK spline handle as goalCurveSpline_IkHandle, and rename the group as ik_curves_clusters_drivenSetup.

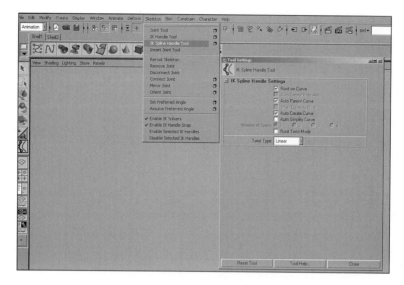

Figure 13.22   The IK Spline Handle tool.

25. Now you're going to create the soft body connections. First, with the curve selected, go to the Soft/Rigid Bodies, Create Soft Body options box. Change the pull-down menu to Duplicate, Make Original Soft. Make sure that the Make Non-Soft a Goal check box is activated and that the goal weight is set to .65. Hit the Create button (see Figure 13.23).

Figure 13.23   Creating your soft body particle system is as simple as clicking the Create button.

26. Rename the curve with the child particle object to c_Controlled_softBodyCurve. Rename the copied curve that is now under your ik_curves_clusters_drivenSetup group to goalCurve. Select the particle object and rename it SoftBodyCurveParticles.

27. Make the c_Controlled_softBodyCurve a child of the ik_curves_clusters_drivenSetup group by selecting the curve, Shift-selecting the group, and hitting the p key on your keyboard.

28. Next, select the SoftBodyCurveParticleShape node (be sure it is the shape, not the transform), load up the Set-Driven Key window, and load the currently selected SoftBodyCurveParticleShape as the driven node, with the GoalSmoothness as the driven attribute. Load the FloppyChainContoller with the addMoreFloppiness attribute as the driver.

29. Set the addMoreFloppiness attribute to 0. Set the Goal Smoothness to .75, and hit the Key button in the Set-Driven Key window (see Figure 13.24).

    Notice that the particle system shape is connected to your NURBS curve, which is driving the IK solver of your skeletal hierarchy. The animation curve is the set-driven key, which sets one of the particle attributes that makes the animation of the particles overlap more during the dynamic simulation.

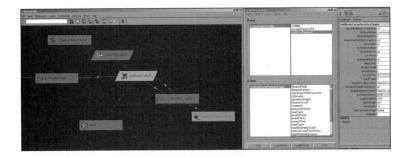

Figure 13.24 The animation curve is the set-driven key.

30. Set the addMoreFlopiness attribute to 1, and set the GoalSmoothness attribute to 2. Hit the Key button again in the Set-Driven Key window.

    At this point, it appears as though nothing has changed. But when you are finished setting up the rest of this rig, you will see how changing the attributes of your addMoreFloppiness attribute affects the dynamic simulation.

31. Next, select the SoftBodyCurveParticles particle object, go into Component mode, and turn off all components. Then turn on only the pickmask "particles" (see Figure 13-25). This step is to prepare your selection mode for selecting only single particle components.

Figure 13.25   The particle object is selected, and Component mode is activated with the Particle option as the only component for selection (notice the state of the pickmask buttons along the status line).

32. Drag a selection around your entire curve and scene, being sure to select all your particle component nodes. Open Window, General Editors, Component Editor. Open the Particle tab inside the Component Editor, scroll to the very end, and progressively set your goalPP attributes from larger to smaller, using the following values:

p[0]	goalPP: 1
p[1]	goalPP: 1
p[2]	goalPP: 1
p[3]	goalPP: .8
p[4]	goalPP: .7
p[5]	goalPP: .55
p[6]	goalPP: .5
p[7]	goalPP: .5
p[8]	goalPP: .5

These settings will actually make your curve flop around more at the tip than at the base (see Figure 13.26).

Creating particle goals in Maya is a cool way to make a particle dynamically follow or move toward the goal object, similar to the particle being attached to the goal with a piece of elastic—the particle overshoots the goal, then moves back toward it, and settles. The goals and their weights create the dynamic overlapping action.

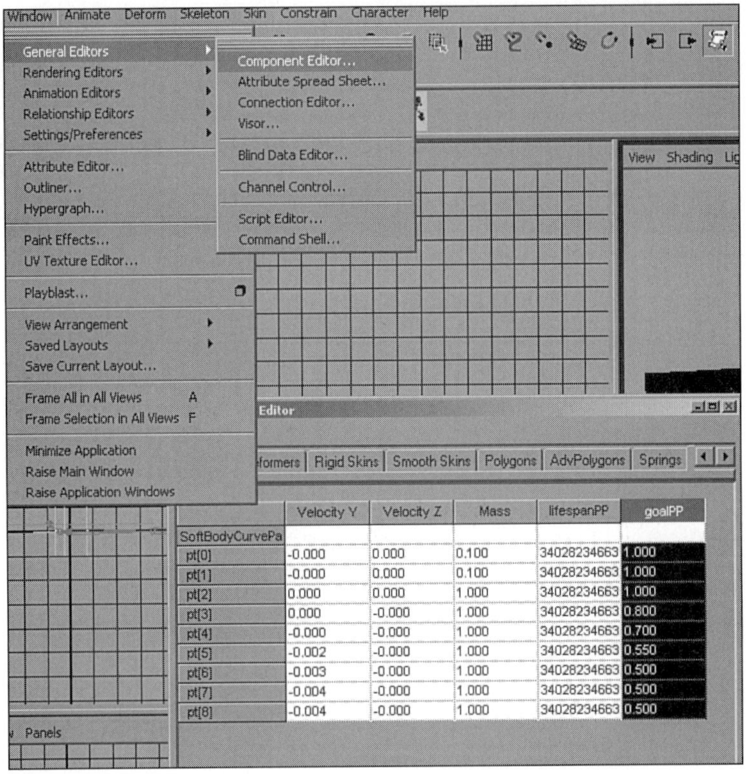

Figure 13.26 These weights affect the per-particle goals of your soft body particle system.

33. Next, hide the c_Controlled_softBodyCurve. Select the goalCurve node and go into Component mode, this time with only the CV pickmask active. Select the first two CVs on the curve and perform the menu command Deform, Create Cluster. Select the last two CVs on the curve and perform the menu command Deform, Create Cluster again. Select each remaining CV one at a time, each time performing the menu command Deform, Create Cluster.

You should now have a bunch of clusters that, if moved together, will move the entire goalCurve node (see Figure 13.27).

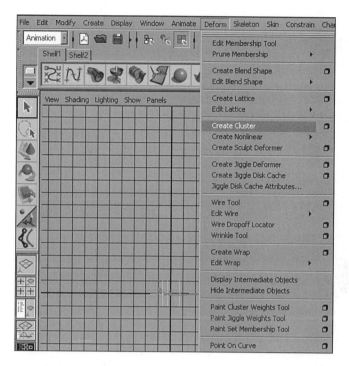

Figure 13.27   Create cluster deformers in order to deform the
CVs of the spline IK curve's soft body goal curve.

34. Shift-select all the clusters and parent them to the ik_curves_clusters_drivenSetup
node. The expected message "Warning: clusters were grouped to preserve position"
appears. Rename these new groups so that they all have the prefix
goalCurve_ConstrainedCluster for each cluster group node.

35. Next, create seven locators. Name them controller1, controller2, controller3, con-
troller4, controller5, controller6, and controller7. Point-snap each controller node
directly on top of each cluster (in order from first to last) by activating the Move tool
and holding down the v key on the keyboard while dragging the Move tool from the
round center handle toward the cluster (see Figure 13.28).

36. Select joint10 and rename it to also have the prefix baseBindSkeleton. Make the
baseBindSkeleton_joint8 hierarchy a child. Now select all the controller locators
(1–7), Shift-select the new baseBindSkeleton parent node (joint10), and group
them by hitting Ctrl+g.

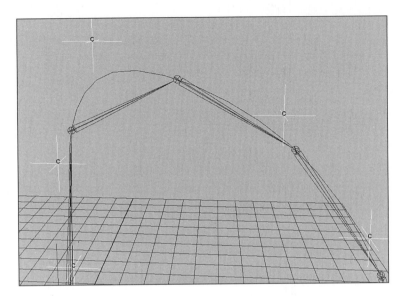

Figure 13.28   Parent your clusters to locators.

37. Rename the group mainAttachNode. Select the SoftBodyDynamicDriven_joint1 parent node and add a group above it by hitting Ctrl+g. Rename this node constraintTargetSkeletons, and make it a child of mainAttachNode with the p key.

This cleans up your grouped hierarchies and also creates a group node that makes the entire rig scaleable to different scene sizes.

38. Next, without selecting anything, and hit Ctrl+g three times. This creates three null nodes, each a child of the previous. Rename the top node floppyChainRig, the next mainHierarchy, and the last TRANS_ROTATE_SCALE_MATRIX. Select TRANS_ROTATE_SCALE_MATRIX and hit Ctrl+d to duplicate it. Make sure your duplicate options are set to the defaults. Rename the duplicate c_ControlledMatrixStack.

39. Select ik_curves_clusters_drivenSetup, Shift-select floppyChainRig, and parent by hitting the p key. Then select mainAttachNode, Shift-select c_ControlledMatrixStack, and again parent by hitting the p key.

The last couple steps simply continue with the grouping of the nodes.

Note

These specific grouping steps and the specific grouping hierarchy order serve two important goals. First, they organize the node tree. Second, and much more important, they enable you to translate and scale the entire rig so that you can import it into any file and continuously reuse it for different projects as needed. You also need a particular hierarchy that allows the clusters to control the curves, and you need the goal curve to remain in the correct space coordinates. Pay close attention to the grouping order, and make sure you are doing it exactly as specified in these steps. You can always double-check against the finished file that is supplied on the accompanying CD.

Now it's time to finish the grouping and connect a regular spline IK rig to the scenario.

40. Start by selecting controller1, the one nearest to the root node, Shift-selecting the FloppyChainController, and parenting using the p key. Point-snap the FloppyChainController locator to the root joint, softBodyDynamicDriven_joint12 (see Figure 13.29).

You are almost finished. All you need to do is create the regular spline IK and constrain the soft body clusters to clusters that you will create on the exact same CVs of the regular spline IK curve.

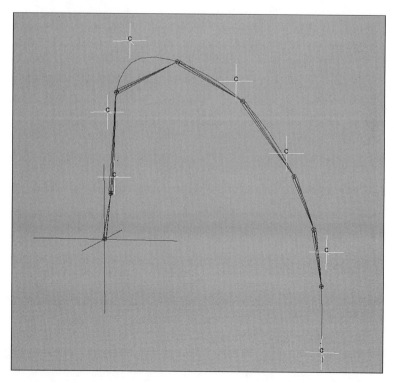

Figure 13.29   The floppy chain controller is snapped and parented to the root of the hierarchy.

41. Temporally hide the floppyChainRig parent node. Unhide the regularSplineIKdriven_joint11 parent node by selecting it in the Hypergraph and going to Display, Show, Show Selection.

42. Next, go to the Skeleton, IK Spline Handle Options box, and use all the same default settings as in step 22. Be sure to still uncheck the Auto Simplify Curve option (see Figure 13.30).

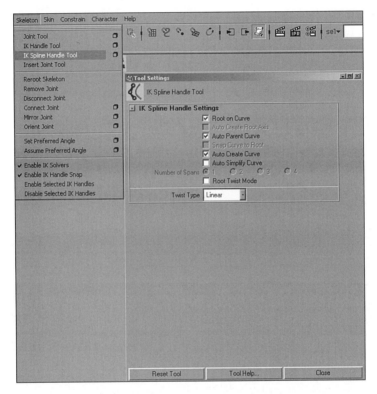

Figure 13.30 Use the same IK spline options as you did when you created the first IK spline handle.

43. With the IK Spline tool active, drag a selection from the very first joint, regularSplineIKdriven_joint11, and then drag a selection around the very top joint at the end of the chain, regularSplineIKdriven_joint7.

You should see that Maya has created a second IK Spline Solver and Handle for you, and a NURBS curve now controls the rotational orientations of your regularSplineIKdriven joint hierarchy.

44. Select the curve that was just created, and rename it regularSplineIkcurve. With this new curve selected, go into Component mode, this time with only the CV pickmask active. Select the first two CVs on the curve and perform the menu command Deform, Create Cluster. Select the last two CVs on the curve and perform the menu command Deform, Create Cluster again. Now select each remaining CV one at a time, each time performing the menu command Deform, Create Cluster.

You should now have a bunch of clusters that, if moved together, will move the entire regularSplineIkcurve exactly the same way that the clusters of the goalCurve move its CVs (see Figure 13.31).

Figure 13.31   Create a cluster for the same CVs on this curve as you did on the first curve (which is now a soft body).

45. Next, select each cluster, one at a time, and parent each one to the nearest controller locator node, starting with controller1 and ending with controller7. Remember, the message "Warning: clusters were grouped to preserve position" is to be expected; it is actually a good thing that Maya groups your clusters so that their local transformation space can be modified without directly changing their transform values, instead changing those of a parent (see Figure 13.32).

Figure 13.32   This warning message is expected.

46. Now select the new IK handle and rename it regularSpline_IkHandle. Shift-select the regularSplineIkcurve and parent them both to the ik_curves_clusters_drivenSetup group hierarchy.

47. Select the regularSplineIKdriven_joint11 parent node and make it a child of the constraintTargetSkeletons group. Hide both the softBodyDynamicDriven_joint and regularSplineIKdriven_joint parent nodes.

48. Select the floppyChainRig and perform the menu command Display, Show, Show Selected. Expand the entire ik_curves_clusters_drivenSetup hierarchy in the Hypergraph by right-clicking over the node and choosing Expand All from the pop-up menu.

You should now see three curves (one with a particle child object), two IK handles, and seven grouped clusters. You will be concerned with the clusters. These clusters control the soft body goal curve. You want these clusters to move with your controller locators as well, but you do not want to make them children of the controller locators because that would put them in the wrong transformation space. So, you will point-constrain them instead.

49. Select each controller locator node one at a time, Shift-select the corresponding closest cluster node, and then click Constrain, Point. Do this for each cluster that is a child under the ik_curves_clusters_drivenSetup hierarchy (see Figure 13.33).

50. Next, go to the menu item Edit, Select All by Type, Clusters. Hit Ctrl+h to hide the currently selected items. Also hide the ik_curves_clusters_drivenSetup node.

51. Select the baseBindSkeleton_joint10 and baseBindSkeleton_joint8 parent nodes, and show Selected. Open the Connection Editor (Window, General Editors, Connection Editor). Select the TRANS_ROTATE_SCALE_MATRIX node and load the left side (from). Select the c_Controlled_softBodyCurve node and load the right side (to). Highlight on both sides the full translate, rotate, and scale attributes.

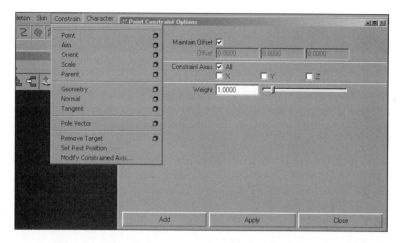

Figure 13.33   Point-constrain the goal curve's clusters to the clusters of the nondynamic spline IK curve. This puts the dynamic skeleton in the same location as the nondynamic skeleton.

This causes the TRANS_ROTATE_SCALE_MATRIX node to directly control the position of the c_Controlled_softBodyCurve node. This is very important because controlling the translations in any other way will result in errors.

52. With the Connection Editor open and the TRANS_ROTATE_SCALE_MATRIX node loaded on the left (from) section, select the c_ControlledMatrixStack node and load it into the right (to) field. Make the same connections as before: translate, rotate, and scale.

53. Next, lock all transform attributes on all nodes in the entire hierarchy, *except* for the controller# locators, the mainAttachNode, and the TRANS_ROTATE_SCALE_MATRIX. Do this by selecting all nodes except those listed, highlighting the attributes in the Channel Box, right-clicking, and choosing LockSelected from the pop-up menu.

You are now finished with the Automatic Overlapping Action rig! You now have a generically rigged chain of joints that will automatically bounce around dynamically with the control to change the dynamics, as well as to switch off the dynamic skeleton entirely.

Using the rig is super-easy. Open the file Chapter13_OverlapAct_fin.mb from the accompanying CD. This is a fully rigged and reusable setup that has been completed using the steps in the tutorial. You can use it by translating, rotating, or scaling it into place with the TRANS_ROTATE_SCALE_MATRIX node.

When you get it into place, you can animate with keys or simply point- and orient-constrain the mainAttachNode wherever you want (for example, to the rear end of a dog where his tail attaches to his body). This rig will work in any file where you use it. To test it, set all attributes on the FloppyChainContoller to 1, and animate the mainAttachNode traveling through space as if it were on a character's head while he is walking. When you play back the animation, you should see the rig bounce around dynamically. It can result in a quite appealing effect. Remember, you can turn this off completely by changing the dynamicFlopOnOff attribute to 0. You always have control over the target pose of the skeleton, whether the floppiness is on or off, by moving and keying the controller locator nodes. However, the location won't update if its floppiness is set to 1 until the animation is played back, due to the dynamics solver. Therefore, it might be a good idea to select the particles, change their start frame to something before the actual animation starts, play through the animation from there, and then use the menu command Solvers, Initial State, Set for Selected to update the particle's initial state to match the first pose that is in your character animation.

Using History to Your Advantage: Modifying Geometry After It Is Smooth-Skinned

The following tutorial focuses on a real-world production challenge that can occur while using the Maya software. The premise for this situation can and often does occur due to the nonlinear nature of production.

Exercise 13.4   Transferring UVs onto a Bound, Smooth-Skinned Character

Here is the basic premise for this exercise:

The character model has traveled through the modeling phase of the production and has passed into the character-rigging phase. But then a huge problem arises in the geometry of the character.

At the last minute, you realize that somewhere along the line, a miscommunication was made and the wrong geometry was used to bind the character and paint the smooth-skin weights. In fact, the geometry that was used doesn't have UVs for texturing.

For this scenario example, you go through a full workflow, to make geometry modifications (transferring UVs) to a bound smooth-skinned character, without adding any extra undesirable node history to the geometry.

The bound character model does not have UVs, so you will use a tricky technique of transferring UVs to the intermediate shape node of the bound geometry to achieve the desired result.

1. Open the file nonLinearWorkflow_start.mb, found on the accompanying CD.

   Notice that the character's geometry is already bound to the joints with a smooth bind. If you open the UV Texture view, however, you will see that there are no UVs on the geometry (see Figure 13.34).

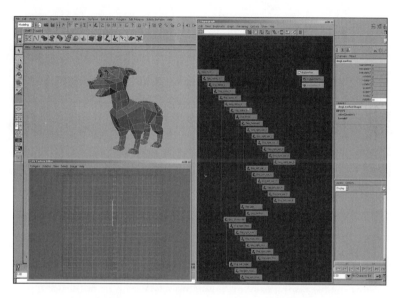

Figure 13.34   This model is smooth-skinned and weighted, but it is the wrong model! Here you go through the steps involved to transfer UVs to the geometry without adding any unwanted history nodes to the geometry.

2. Make sure that your Hypergraph menu's view options have shape nodes, underworld nodes, and hidden nodes turned on (see Figure 13.35).

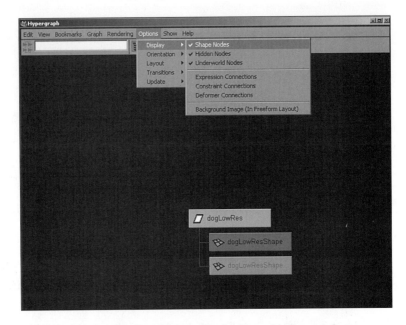

Figure 13.35   Be sure that you have Options, Display, Shape Nodes, and Options, Display, Hidden Nodes checked to On in your Hypergraph window.

First, you'll import the geometry that has the UVs on it that you want to transfer. It is important to note that the geometry with the UVs on it is an exact duplicate of the current mesh, but it has had an automatic mapping procedure applied to it.

3. Import the file nonLinearWorkflow_importUVs.mb from the accompanying CD for this chapter.

4. Next, select the imported model. Notice that it has UVs.

The next step is to transfer the UVs from the imported character onto the bound character, without leaving any trace of node history behind (see Figure 13.36).

Normally, if you transferred the UVs onto the geometry of the skinned dog, Maya would insert a node called polyTransferUv after the skin cluster's deformations. The trick to transferring the UVs without leaving any history behind lies deep within the secrets of the Hypergraph and the way Maya connects your nodes to create its dependency connections.

Notice the hidden node in Figure 13.36, just below the dogLowResShape, called dogLowResShapeOrig. This is the node that you will be examining for the moment.

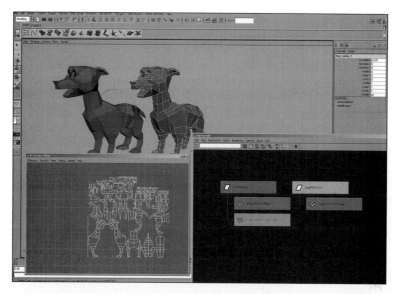

Figure 13.36   Notice that the imported model has UVs. These are the UVs that you will transfer onto the bound mesh, without leaving any unwanted node history behind.

At the base of the node connections that form the node network to deform your geometry lies a polygon-shape intermediate node. This is the node that starts the entire flow of data that creates your character's geometry and sends the skin cluster the vertices from which to deform. This is also the node on which you will perform your history operations. Then you will delete history on this node.

5. Select the dogLowResShapeOrig node, open the Attribute Editor by hitting Ctrl+a, and, in the Hypergraph window, perform the menu command Graph, Input and Output Connections (see Figure 13.37).

6. In the Attribute Editor for the dogLowResShapeOrig node, expand the Object Display portion and uncheck the Intermediate Object check box.

7. Next, select the imported mesh that has the UVs and Shift-select (to add to the current selection) the dogLowResShapeOrig node. Now perform Polygons, Transfer, Options, and make sure only the UVs option is checked. When this is completed, select only the dogLowResShapeOrig node, and perform the menu command Edit, Delete by Type, History (see Figure 13.38).

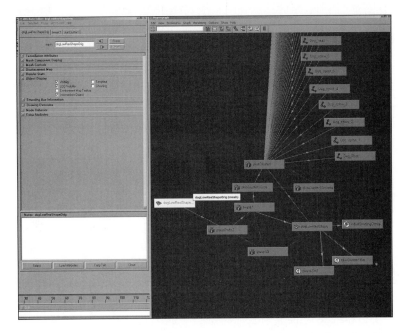

Figure 13.37 The dogLowResShapeOrig node is a polygon mesh node with its intermediate object attribute flagged on. This node actually begins the data flow that creates your character's deformations.

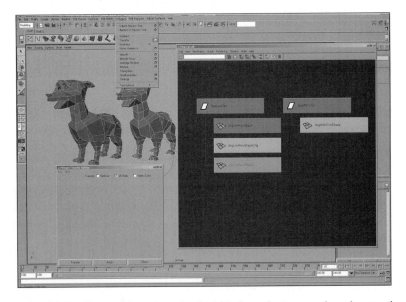

Figure 13.38 The trick is to transfer the UVs from the imported mesh onto the dogLowResShapeOrig and then just delete the history from the dogLowResShapeOrig.

8. Finally, set the Intermediate Object check box back on for the dogLowResShapeOrig node.

You have now transferred the polygon UVs, without adding any polygon UV transfer history nodes to your geometry.

You can now delete the imported model from which the UVs were transferred. A completed file, nonLinearWorkflow_finished.mb, is found on the CD.

This technique can be used under many different circumstances, with many different geometry modifications, as long as the vertex order of the mesh does not change and any modifications to the intermediate shape node can be baked into the file by deleting history while still maintaining all the smooth-skinned weights that were applied to your rigged character. Another example of this involves triangulating your character's bound mesh, which would work the same way as transferring the UVs did.

If your character's point order does need to change, Maya has also implemented an Import and Export Skin Weight Maps capability, which allows the transferring of weights between characters of different resolutions, but with the same UV space. The workflow involved for this would be to export the skin weight maps, make the modifications to the geometry's point order, delete history, rebind the modified mesh to the exact same joints that it was previously bound to, and reimport the weight maps that were previously saved.

Summary

If you are given a specific problem, a powerful exposed architecture enables you to creatively take full control over nodes and connections to build or construct any sort of predefined behavior. By linking nodes that previously had no distinct relationship, you can almost always solve even the most difficult problem. This is the strongest thing about the way Maya works: It exposes as much as possible to the user without dumbing things down with too many useless features that do some sort of special hidden magic. It exposes to you the raw data inputs and outputs, and it enables you to connect directly to the attributes that hook into the computation for any node directly. Yet, somehow, it still makes it possible to build complex relationships between attributes in a completely intuitive and creative way. This is the major advantage of Maya: It is both simple and complex at the same time. Don't you just love it?

Chapter 14

Particles and Dynamics

By Daniel Roizman

Dynamic effects such as smoke, dust, fire, and rain are often used multiple times in a production. Their simulation in Maya is often made up of several fields, particle expressions, and custom attributes working together and playing off each other. It is important to "wrap" up these attributes into one set of controls so that other people in the production can easily implement them into their scenes, or simply to have them in a library so that you can easily add them to your next scene.

This chapter teaches you how to create a spray of water that collides with geometry and slides down it in a controlled manner. Specifically, you'll learn the following:

- How to control and direct the emission of water from a high-pressure source—in this case, a fire hydrant—with a simple set of controls

- How to prepare particles for hardware rendering and generate elements for compositing

- How to create particle creation and runtime expressions, and use several important mathematical functions

- How to control the movement of particles on a surface using goals and expressions

In this chapter, you will learn a lot of the nuances of Maya's dynamics system, as well as both aesthetic and technical approaches to solving problems using dynamics. By following the step–by-step instructions and learning the meaning behind each step, you will hopefully walk away from this chapter with a better understanding of how to solve problems with Maya as well as how to make a great water effect.

For the *Parking Spot* project, I was asked to create a fire hydrant spraying a car. Having worked with particles for the past eight years on a variety of projects, I have often found myself staring at objects in the real world and trying to break them down into particle terms. Whether it be exhaust fumes from a diesel engine, the spark of a lighter igniting a flame, or the water coming off a sprinkler head, I am constantly analyzing their motion, density, size, color, and so on. In Maya, you have the luxury of being able to apply some real-world physics to particle systems, but also blend in your own creativity. In most cases, effects call for a blend of the two. When working with live-action elements, CG effects are usually used instead of practical effects because either the effect would be harmful to those around it, as with a fireball, or the behavior of the effect needs to be stylized in such a way that practical effects cannot do.

In the case of the *Parking Spot* project, creating the fire hydrant spray requires both a sense of realism, in that we all know how water spray should look and behave, and a cartoonish type of stylized spray and motion. This affords a lot of flexibility in the design of the effect; when developing the effect, it is important to build in enough flexibility to provide control over both the realism and the stylization.

Emission

In the file 14baseScene.ma, there is a stripped-down version of the set from the *Parking Spot* project. In the animation, water from a hydrant bursts out and sprays the car. This section focuses on how the water is emitted from the hydrant.

The first step in creating the spray is to emit particles into the scene. To simulate the emission, you can use a directional emitter with a spread of .5 and rename it waterEmitter. The emitter should be placed inside the fire hydrant (see Figure 14.1).

Generally, you can adjust the directional emitter through a manipulator by hitting the T key and clicking the manipulator handle until the direction manipulator appears. Now you can control the direction of emission by dragging the direction manipulator around your screen in 3D space. The resulting direction vector is shown in the Channel Box of the emitter under Direction X, Y, and Z (see Figure 14.2).

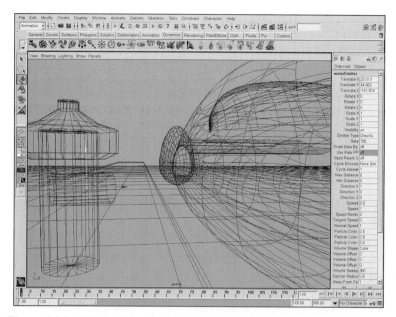

Figure 14.1   The emitter positioned near the back of the fire hydrant spout, with the speed of the emitter set to 50 and the spread set to .5.

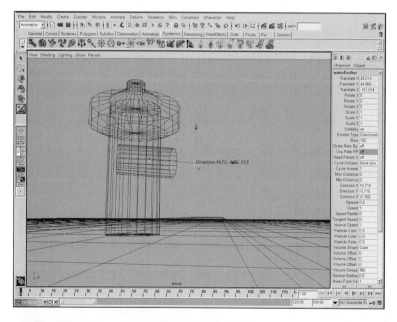

Figure 14.2   The values of the Direction X, Direction Y, and Direction Z attributes in the Channel Box changed via the direction manipulator.

Although this technique works, I find it better to simply pick a direction in one axis—for example, Direction X—and give it a value of 1; then rotate the emitter using the rotation manipulator to aim the emitter. This way, you can either create an Aim Constraint between the emitter and a target so that it always points at the target, or you can easily animate the direction of emission by rotating the emitter. This is far easier than figuring out what value to place in Direction X, Y, and Z to point in a given direction.

I usually set the render type of my particles to Multistreak when I am working on their motion. Multistreak particles have a streaked tail that bases its length and direction on the velocity of the particle. This gives you a good visual indication of where the particles are going and how quickly; it can be difficult to judge the motion of the particles when you have thousands of points moving in different directions (see Figure 14.3).

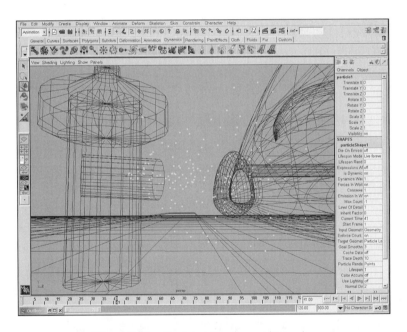

Figure 14.3 Particles drawn as multistreaks.

I use multistreaks instead of streaks because, with multistreaks, I can fake having more particles in my simulation: The multistreaks are made up of multiple streaks per point (see Figure 14.4).

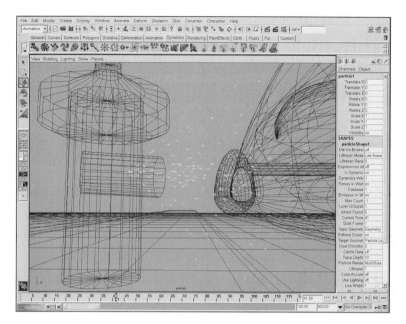

Figure 14.4   Particles drawn as multistreaks. Notice how even on a still frame, the velocity and direction of particles are visible.

When I am happy with the motion of my simulation, I can set the particle render type back to whatever I need it to be.

Collisions

As you saw in Figure 14.4, the particles now emit from the center of the fire hydrant and move through the surfaces, instead of flowing through the pipe.

Before you can collide the particles with the pipe, you first need to make sure that the normals of the collision surface are facing the correct way. In this scene, the pipe has its normals pointing outward (see Figure 14.5).

If you were to reverse the normals on the geometry (by clicking Edit Polygons, Normals, Reverse), collisions would work correctly. But texturing and lighting would be affected, and any UV mappings would be reversed as well. Instead, duplicate the pipe and rename it to a name that indicates that it is being used for dynamics (adding a "dyn_" does the trick). Set the render attributes of it to have Primary Visibility off, turn off Casts Shadows as well as Visible in Reflections and Visible in Refractions, and then reverse the normals (see Figure 14.6).

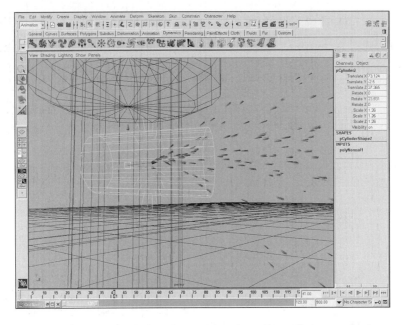

Figure 14.5 Normals indicating that the surface is facing outward.

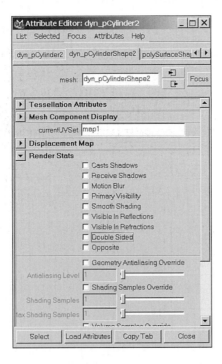

Figure 14.6 Adjusting the render attributes for a surface in the Render Stats section of the Attribute Editor for a shape node.

Setting all of these render attributes will ensure that even if you forget to hide the geometry or it gets accidentally shown down the production pipeline, it will not affect your renders.

Now you can collide the particles with the geometry by selecting the particle first and then the collision shape, and then going to the options of Particles, MakeCollide. Set Friction to .1 and Resilience to .2, and hit Create. Even though water is very slippery, it still has friction and should slow down when it collides with an object. As a result, the spray should come out of the pipe at varying speeds. When water collides with an object, it breaks up into smaller particles and merges with other particles. It does not simply bounce off the surface; it splatters. This is why you should use a relatively low resilience. Again, the bouncing of the water off the pipe will result in the water looking more realistic because it will come out of the pipe in random directions (see Figure 14.7).

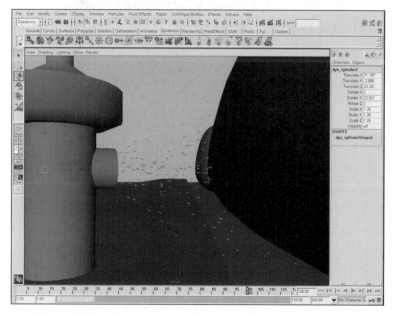

Figure 14.7   Particles colliding with pipe and coming out of the opening instead of passing through the geometry.

You can even take it a step further and add a little bit of a lip to the inside of the pipe, to cause the particles to bounce off the end of the pipe in a more erratic way. Any subtle detail that you add to your collisions will give the simulation more realism. If the particles bounce off the lip that you added and back into the pipe, rather than arcing outward, you can either change the shape of the lip to bounce the particles in the desired direction or set the resilience of the collision object to a negative value.

By using a negative value for resilience, the particles bounce through the collision object instead of off it. This type of effect can be very useful because it enables you to quickly change the direction that your particles are traveling in without using a field.

The Conserve Attribute

To simulate the loss of motion, particles have a Conserve attribute that controls how much of the particle's velocity is maintained from the previous frame. You should always set the Conserve attribute with a value less than the default setting of 1 because all objects, even in the void of space, experience some form of resistance and lose some of their momentum.

Conserve has a direct effect on your ability to control the motion of your simulation. If an object conserves 100% of its momentum every frame, it is very difficult to change its direction. For example, if a particle is emitted in the x-axis at a speed of 1 unit/second and you want to add gravity to it so that it begins to arc and eventually fall straight down, you could never achieve this effect because the particle is carrying 100% of its speed in the x-axis every frame. You would simply get a long arcing motion. I recommend initially setting the Conserve attribute of your particles to .985 and then determining from there how much higher or lower to go.

For the spray, a value of .975 works very well, allowing the water to shoot out and lose its speed at a believable rate.

Gravity

Gravity is very important in the way we perceive the realism of a simulation. If your gravity is not set correctly, dynamics will not look correct in your scene. If you have ever seen footage of astronauts on the moon, several cues tell you that they are not on Earth. The obvious ones are that the sky is black and you can see stars and the planet Earth behind them. But the way in which they rise and fall as they walk, the way dust gets kicked up and slowly settles—essentially, the rate at which objects fall—gives the viewer a "feeling" of what looks right and indicates that they are on the moon and not a movie set.

Gravity in Maya is calculated in meters per second, regardless of what units you are using—inches, feet, or meters. Therefore, the default setting of gravity in Maya of 9.8 means 9.8 meters per second squared.

You need to determine the scale of your scene and set gravity accordingly. Because you rarely build your character in centimeters—such that a 6-foot-tall person is 182.88cm, meaning that the top of the head is located at Translate Y = 182.88—you need to figure out what scale you are using and set your gravity based on that factor. If one unit in Maya is really 1cm in your scene scale, then your gravity setting would simply be 100×9.8 because 100cm is 1m.

In this scene, I will assume that the fire hydrant is 1m tall. Using the Distance tool, you can see that the fire hydrant is 57.67 units tall (see Figure 14.8).

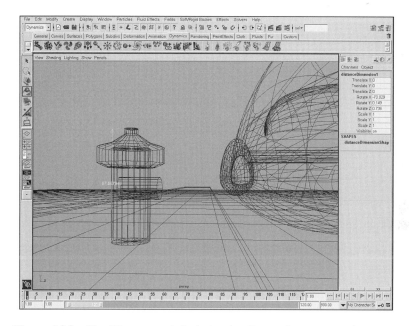

Figure 14.8   The Distance tool displaying the distance between two locators.

Therefore, the magnitude of the Gravity field should be set to 57.67 × 9.8, which is 565 rounded off. This number may seem extremely large, but here's how my comrade Adrian Graham likes to explain it: "Drop a cube that is 1 unit in size using a magnitude of 9.8. Now imagine that the cube is 1/100th of its size. If you leave the gravity at 9.8, it appears to be falling too slowly. Therefore, you need to increase gravity proportionally, which means multiplying it by a factor of 100. Think of it this way: The bigger the object is, the slower it appears to fall. Therefore, the lower the magnitude is.

I'll set the magnitude of the Gravity field to 565 for realistic results.

Control Nodes

This is a good point at which to start creating the control node for the particles. The speed at which water comes out of a pipe is determined by the pressure of the water. The volume of water moving through a space determines the pressure. Therefore, the relationship between the size of the pipe and the amount of water moving through it determine the speed at which the water is moving. If you were to calculate this through true physics, you would need to know the radius of the pipe and the volume of water.

This, in turn, would drive the speed of emission. But these factors don't need to be shown to the user because most people wouldn't know that you are moving 1,000 cubic meters of water through a pipe that is 20cm in diameter. The speed of the emitter, therefore, should be X and the rate should be Y. The user simply wants to adjust a single attribute to control how much water comes out of the pipe. However, underneath all of this you do want to relate the speed of emission with the rate of particles being emitted. That way you could easily control whether water is gushing out of the pipe or simply trickling out with a single attribute.

The following exercise takes you through the steps used to create the relationship between speed and rate.

Exercise 14.1   Water Flow Control Setup

We will begin with an empty group node.

1. Create an empty group node and name it waterSetup.

2. Using the Channel Control window, lock the Translate, Rotate, and Scale attributes.

   All of the objects that make up the water effect will be grouped underneath this empty group node. You don't want the user accidentally moving the control node because this will move all of your setup.

3. Group the emitter and particles under the waterSetup node.

4. Using the Add Attribute window, select Modify, Add Attribute, and add three float attributes: one called Pressure, one called Rate, and one called Speed.

5. Create an expression that controls the rate and speed of the emitter using these attributes as multipliers. Select waterEmitter and then select Window, Animation Editors, Expression Editor. Add the following:

```
waterEmitter.rate = waterSetup.pressure * waterSetup.rate;
waterEmitter.speed = waterSetup.pressure *waterSetup.speed;
```

The Pressure attribute will be used to control the flow of water. A value of 0 will mean that there is no water flowing through the pipe. A value of 1 will mean that the water is moving at its maximum speed through the pipe.

6. Set the Pressure to .5.

7. Play back the animation and adjust the speed so that the particles are moving at a speed halfway between a trickle and a gusher.

At this point, you'll notice that regardless of how high you set the Speed attribute, the particles always seem to fall too quickly and never really appear to burst out of the pipe (see Figure 14.9).

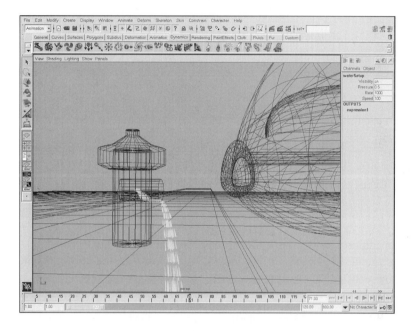

Figure 14.9   Water trickling out of the pipe, even with a speed value of 100.

The reason for this is that the force that is pushing the particles out of the pipe is occurring only on emission, so the particles get only an initial push in the z-axis. However, gravity pulls the particles down with a tremendous amount of force, and the friction of the pipe is causing the particles to slow down too quickly. In the real world, the volume of water in the pipe would cause the pressure to rise and continue to push the water outward. Because you are not using true fluid dynamics calculations, you must simulate this pressure using the tools at your disposal. A Uniform field can be used to continue to push the particles out of the pipe.

8. Select the particles and create a Uniform field. Set the direction of the Uniform field to 1 in the z-axis, set the volume type to Cylinder, and then translate, rotate, and scale the field to match the size of the pipe (see Figure 14.10).

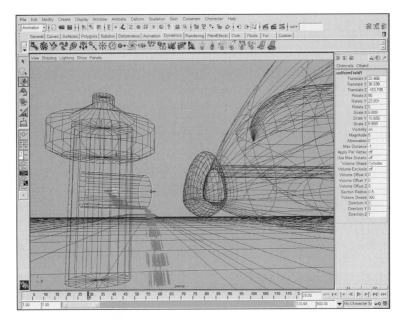

Figure 14.10 Simulating the force that is pushing the water out of the pipe by setting the Uniform field volume type to Cylinder and matching the size of the pipe.

9. In addition to setting the direction of the field to 1 in the z-axis, set the direction of the field to 1 in the y-axis. This will better simulate the upward spray of water as the particles leave the pipe.

   Remember, although Maya's particle system might use certain aspects of physics, such as gravity, friction, and mass, thousands of other factors affect the motion of objects in the real world. In the simulations that you create, you will most certainly need to fake these factors using the tools at your disposal.

10. Open the expression that you created for the waterEmitter's rate and speed, and add the following line:

```
uniformField1.magnitude = waterSetup.pressure * waterSetup.speed * 24;
```

   You multiply the value by 24 because magnitude is the amount of force exerted per second, not per frame. That is why, if you change your frame rate from film, 24, to NTSC, 30, objects continue to move at the same rate per second, not per frame. But emitters, on the other hand, provide a burst of speed on their first frame, and that speed is not based on the frame units. Therefore, if the speed is 50, the particle is born with an initial velocity of 50 and the Uniform field will need to have its magnitude set to 50 × 24, or 1,200, to maintain the current velocity.

11. Set the Speed attribute of the waterSetup node to 100.

12. Next, set the rate so that it looks like you have enough particles to warrant the speed of emission. By this, I mean that the volume of particles needs to represent the speed of emission. Again, this can be calculated using physics; for our needs, though, you can just eyeball it and determine when it "feels" right.

13. Set the Rate attribute of the waterSetup node to 1,000.

14. When you have these settings working, you can lock or key the speed and rate attributes at this value and simply dial in and out the pressure to control the flow of particles. Although this is a very simple setup, you can see that you have a good level of control over your simulation.

Because the particles are moving so quickly, they appear to be emitting in chunks or steps (see Figure 14.11).

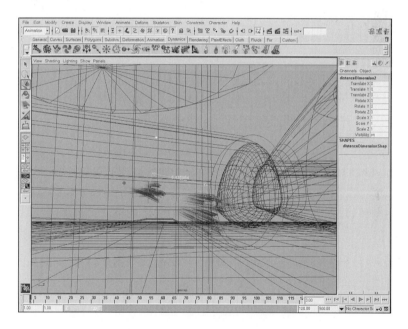

Figure 14.11   Particles emitted with a high velocity and moved a large distance over a single frame, resulting in large gaps.

Note

This is a common problem when working with particles moving at a high rate of speed. The reason for the chunkiness is that the particles are emitted with a very high velocity. As a result, they move a large distance over a single frame, resulting in a large gap between the next set of particles being emitted.

Several techniques exist for closing the gap and removing the chunkiness. One of the commonly used techniques that I do *not* recommend using is to increase the Oversampling attribute of the Dynamics Controller node. By increasing Oversampling, Maya calculates the dynamics of the scene multiple times per frame. This causes the emitter to emit multiple times per frame instead of just once, which creates smaller gaps. However, this technique affects every aspect of dynamics. So, for example, if the Conserve attribute of the particle object is set to .9, the particle would lose 10% of its velocity with each sample, instead of losing 10% per frame. Fields also are calculated multiple times per frame, so all Magnitude and Conserve settings, and any other influence on your particle system will need to be adjusted accordingly. If you know in advance that you might need to use Oversampling, I highly recommend setting it *before* you begin building your simulation so that all your attribute values are set based on the current Oversampling value.

15. Because the chunkiness problem is related to emission, the better place to correct it is at its source, the emitter. As you saw in Figure 14.11, the distance between the gaps is roughly 5.5 units. Using the Max/Min Distance attributes of the emitter, you can simply set the Max Distance to 5.5. On playback, you will see that the gaps are now gone (see Figure 14.12).

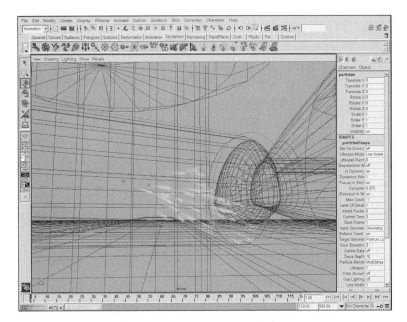

Figure 14.12   One continuous stream, created when using a Max Distance setting of 5.5 to bridge the gap between the last frame of particles and the current frame of particles.

Note

If you want, you can create a much more complex expression to control pressure, speed, and rate so that the relationship is not linear. For example, you could factor in the diameter of the pipe that the water is flowing through and base the pressure, speed, and rate on the diameter of the pipe and the volume of water flowing through it.

Rendering

Now that you have the motion of your particles looking correct, it is time to render them. Particle rendering in Maya is somewhat of a minefield where you are guaranteed to suffer some casualties. The most lacking feature in particle rendering is its incapability to match the motion blur of software-rendered geometry. Other deficiencies are its lack of proper alpha channels, differing tessellation from the software renderer, and hardware-rendered particles' incapability to be lit or shadowed.

Two methods of rendering particles exist: hardware rendering and software rendering. Each method has its own set of advantages and disadvantages. For many of the effects that you create, you can generate elements using both of these methods and combine them in the compositing stage to create a final effect.

Hardware Rendering

Hardware rendering uses your graphics card to draw into an OpenGL window, the Hardware Render Buffer, and take snapshots of the window every frame. It is called a render buffer and not a render window because Maya can render multiple passes of a frame, storing each pass in a buffer and then combining them all together to create a final image. Using this technique, you can create a stepped motion blur of an image by stepping between one frame and the next, capturing an image for each increment and then combining all the images to form one frame (see Figures 14.13, 14.14, and 14.15).

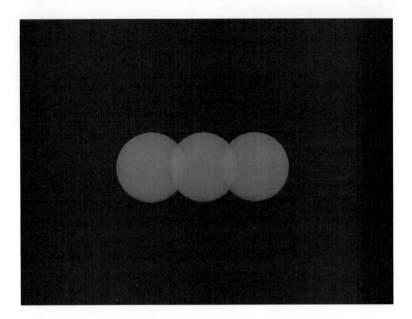

Figure 14.13 Hardware-rendered sphere with three render passes.

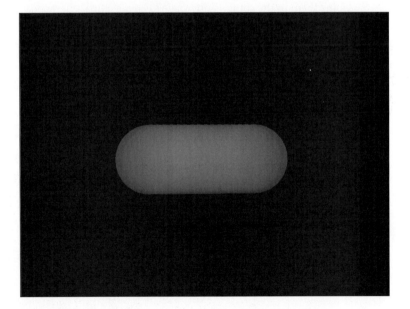

Figure 14.14 Hardware-rendered sphere with 16 render passes.

Figure 14.15   Software-rendered sphere with 3D motion blur.

Depending on how many steps or passes you select, the resulting image may pass as looking blurred. However, there is no blurring of pixels: It's just one image layered on top of another with varying amounts of transparency. For certain particle-rendering types, such as sprites, this technique actually produces very nice-looking blurred images, but that depends on how much your sprites overlap and what their opacity is. The key is to make sure you have enough overlapping particles in your scene so that you do not notice where the stepping is occurring (see Figures 14.16 and 14.17).

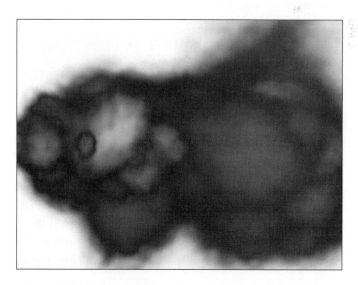

Figure 14.16   Hardware-rendered sprites with no motion blur.

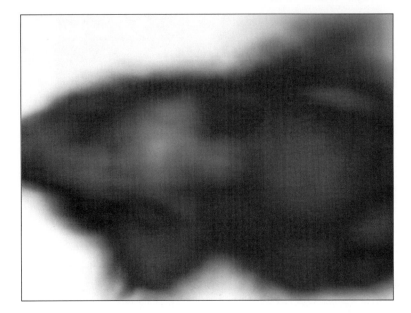

Figure 14.17   Hardware-rendered sprites with 16 render passes.

Because rendering is occurring in the graphics card, it can range from fast to blazingly fast, depending on your graphics card. For the most part, however, frames can take anywhere from 1/10 of a second to render to a minute per frame, depending on the resolution, number of passes, and amount of data in your scene.

However, as mentioned before, the speed of hardware rendering does not come without its share of corner cutting and lacking functionality.

In Version 4.5 of Maya, some particle render types do support hardware shadows—namely, points, multipoints, and spheres.

Hardware Particle-Render Types

Maya can use several different shapes to draw particles in hardware. The benefit of the buffered rendering is that, for particle-render types such as multistreaks and multipoints, instead of drawing one point or streak to represent the position of a particle, multiple points or streaks are drawn at a user-specified radius (multiRadius) around the particle's position. During each pass of rendering, Maya jitters or randomly repositions each of the points/streaks around the particle, which results in a much softer look in the final frame. By adjusting the multiRadius, pointSize/lineWidth and number of passes, you can give your particles a soft, gaseous outline or a slightly blurred, dense volume (see Figures 14.18 and 14.19).

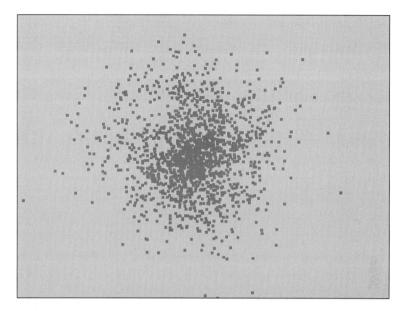

Figure 14.18   Hardware-rendered multipoints with zero render passes.

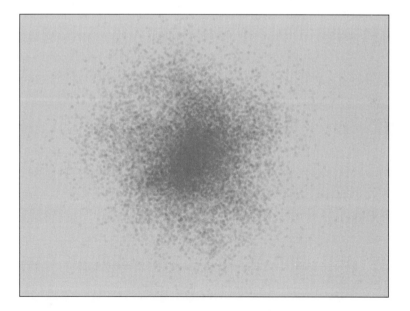

Figure 14.19   Hardware-rendered multipoints with 16 render passes.

Compositing Hardware-Rendered Particles

Compositing particles is tricky, especially when working with hardware-rendered particles. When compositing geometry, it is fairly intuitive because the alpha channel of the geometry is usually solid and geometry is either in front of or behind an object. Particles, however, represent volumes that are usually both in front of and behind other objects in a scene. Take, for example, an effect such as rain. You would usually set up one large emitter to encompass your entire scene where rain is falling and then render out the rain using the Hardware Render Buffer. But when it comes time to composite, you want to put objects that have been software-rendered in front of and behind the rain. If you had a Z-Depth channel for your particles and your geometry layers, in the comp, you could easily do a Z-Depth layering and everything would line up.

Unless your render type is set to a geometry-based type, such as spheres, or you are instancing geometry to your particles, the Hardware Render Buffer cannot create a Z-Depth channel for your particles. Multistreaks (which you would most likely use for rain), as well as streaks, points, and multipoints, do not create an impression in the Z-channel of your image. There is some reasoning behind this: How do you create a Z-Depth channel for a volume, where the color of the final pixel drawn onscreen is often determined by all the pixels behind it? To help in compositing hardware-rendered particles, you can turn on the Geometry Mask option in the Hardware Render Attributes window. Geometry mask is similar to the Use Background shader in software rendering; it creates a holdout in the scene without rendering geometry (see Figures 14.20 and 14.21).

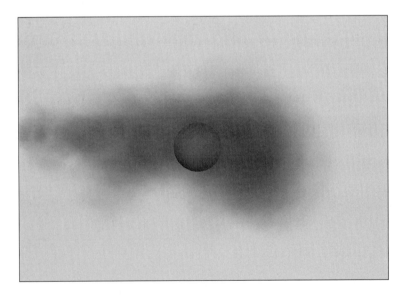

Figure 14.20   Hardware-rendered sprites with red sphere.

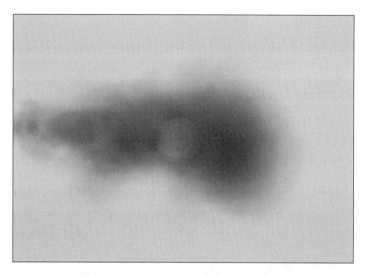

Figure 14.21   Hardware-rendered sprites with geometry mask for sphere.

In theory, the cutout of the geometry in the particle render should line up with the soft-ware-rendered image. Unfortunately, this does not really hold true, for a couple of reasons.

During software render, NURBS surfaces and even Sub-D surfaces are tessellated into triangles based on your tessellation settings. What you are seeing in the Hardware Render Buffer is not the same tessellation as in the software renderer, so the cutout will not be an exact match, especially in areas of high curvature. To correct this problem, you can turn on Display Render Tessellation for each surface that is cutting out the par-ticles. If you are using Sub-D surfaces, you cannot get the hardware-displayed tessella-tion to match your software-rendered tessellation.

If you are using motion blur in your scene, be it 2D or 3D, your geometry mask will not line up with the software-rendered image. Using hardware motion blur often exac-erbates the problem because the blur of the Hardware Render Buffer not only does not result in stamped-looking images, but also does not even use the same approach to motion blur as the software renderer (as you saw in Figures 14.13, 14.14, and 14.15).

It is often better to not use motion blur on your particles if they need to line up with the cutout of a software-rendered element. Unfortunately, this drastically affects the look of your particles because motion blur is a key aspect of the look of a rendered image, especially when dealing with objects such as particles that are very small and that tend to move quite quickly, resulting in blurred streaks.

Assuming that you have a good approach to getting correct geometry masks and that you are solving the motion blur issues, the next area you need to tackle is the alpha channel.

Alpha Channels

Depending on your graphics card, you might or might not have Hardware Alpha available to you. Although it sounds like an option that you can't do without, it actually is more of a hindrance than help. In some situations, the alpha channel generated by the hardware in your graphics card is okay, such as when working with solid geometry or particles with an opacity of 1 (see Figure 14.22). However, the results generated for transparent objects are often inaccurate and tend to cause problems in the compositing stage as compositors work to fix an alpha channel that is completely wrong (see Figure 14.23).

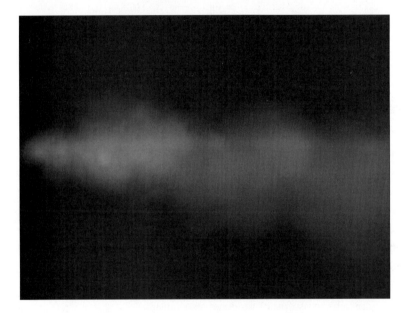

Figure 14.22 Hardware-rendered smoke on a black background.

Many people use the luminance of their rendered image as their alpha channel because they are often rendering grayscale images of smoke or dust. However, this is the wrong solution. By using the luminance of the image as your alpha channel, you flatten the look of your particles (see Figure 14.24). By "flatten," I mean that you remove all shading information from them: The darker areas will have a lower alpha value and will, therefore, show up less in the final image. The dark areas of your particles are just as important as the light areas, and the alpha channel should represent how much the layer behind the particles shows through (see Figure 14.25).

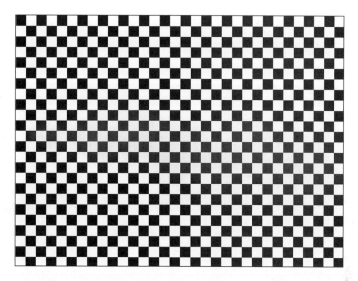

Figure 14.23   Hardware-rendered smoke with Hardware Alpha, composited on top of a black-and-white checker pattern.

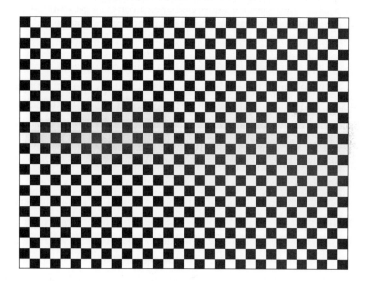

Figure 14.24   Hardware-rendered smoke with the alpha set to Luminance, composited on top of a black-and-white checker pattern.

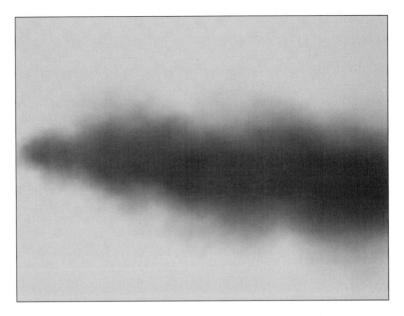

Figure 14.25 Darker blue smoke not layered correctly, even after adjusting the levels in the alpha channel using compositing software.

Even with Hardware Alpha available, Maya does not appear to properly calculate the alpha channel of an image—at least, not if you are using an opacity value of less than 1 (as you saw in Figure 14.23). When particles are drawn, they are drawn from back to front, layering on top of each other. If you were to layer a blue pixel on top of a green pixel on top of a red pixel, all with an opacity value of 1, the final pixel drawn would be blue because the blue pixel would not show through to the green or red pixels behind it. The resulting image would have a blue pixel with an alpha value of 1.

However, if the opacity of each of the pixels was .5, you would end up with blue pixel mixing with green and red pixels because all of their colors would be mixed based on their opacity. The resulting pixel would be 50% blue, 25% green, and 12.5% red. The first pixel with an opacity of .5 would have 50% of its color represented in the final value. The second pixel, green, would also have 50% of its value showing through—but rather than being 50% of the final pixel color, it is 50% of what is left showing through the first pixel, or 50% of 50%, which is 25%. The last pixel, red, is then showing 50% of 50% of 50%, which is 12.5%.

As for the alpha channel, this is where Maya seems to give strange results. Theoretically, if all pixels have an opacity of .5, the alpha would never be 100% white. Think of it as having a piece of cake that you are sharing with someone: You take the first half of the cake, and the other person takes half of the remaining half. You continue to each take half of what is remaining until, eventually, the piece is so small that you can't cut it in half and you eventually just eat that last bite. If each pixel is showing half of itself through to the next, the opacity should keep getting larger. You are showing a little bit less behind each pixel until eventually you hit a threshold, and the alpha should get pretty darn close to 1; there are so many particles that you can no longer see all the way through them.

Unfortunately, this does not happen and Maya somehow figures an alpha value that just doesn't work. I have been unsuccessful in figuring out how Maya calculates the alpha value, but it does not accumulate it using the same technique by which the color value is calculated. A simple example is to take two particles and give one an opacity of .5 and the other an opacity of 1. Line them up in the viewport so that you are looking through the particle with an opacity of .5 and into the particle with an opacity of 1. Render the image and look up the pixel values in an image editor such as PhotoShop. You would assume that because the pixel behind has an opacity of 1, the alpha should be solid because nothing should be showing through that particle. However, the alpha channel ends up being .75.

To summarize, even though the resulting color information of your image is correct, the alpha channel is not; you need to figure out another technique of deriving the alpha value.

The method that I like to use for generating an alpha channel is to use a green-screen technique. When rendering effects that do not require a distinct palette of colors, such as smoke or water spray, I tend to use the RGB values of my particles as storage for data instead of color. For a smoke effect, for example, the important information that you need is the shading information of the smoke—namely, its intensity. The color of the smoke can be corrected in the compositing stage. By either placing the shading information in a single channel, such as the red channel, or separating it into areas of shadow and highlight, with shadows going into the red channel and highlight going into the blue channel, you leave the green channel free for any information you want. By leaving the green channel empty, you can set the background color of your image to green and then set the Hardware Render Buffer's alpha source as the green channel (see Figure 14.26).

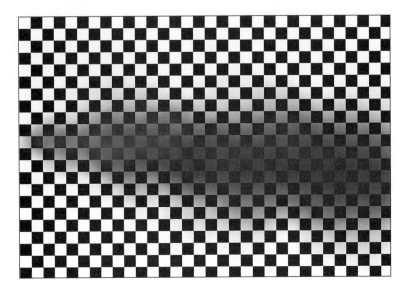

Figure 14.26   Smoke properly composited on top of a black-and-white checker pattern, using the green channel as the alpha for the image.

If you cannot use green or another color as your background color because it interferes with the color of your particles too much, you can simply render out two passes for your particles, one with your color information and another with an RGB value of 1 over a black background. The resulting image can then be used as a mask for the color pass.

Software Rendering

Software rendering solves some of the issues faced in hardware rendering, such as creating proper alpha channels and having the tessellated geometry line up correctly. Using software rendering, you also get shadows being cast by other objects in your scene affecting your particles, as well as self-shadowing (particles shadowing themselves).

However, even software-rendered particles cannot be motion blurred. The reason for this is that when Maya calculates motion blur, it looks at where the triangle that is currently being sampled is now and where it was at each sample in time that you set your motion blur settings to. Then it calculates which direction to blur the particle.

In the case of 3D motion blur, the color of the pixel at each of those times is calculated as well, so the results are very good. With 2D motion blur, however, Maya simply calculates a motion vector and blurs the final pixel based on it. When it comes to particles, in the case of blobby particles that are a type of metaball geometry, the surface is an iso-surface; as such, it gets recalculated when the blobs move. Therefore, the triangle that is currently being sampled might not exist at the given sample in time or might be located in a completely different position, so no blur is calculated. In the case of cloud particles, you are dealing with a 3D volume. The current pixel that is being sampled also is made up of the hundreds of pixels behind it, each moving at a different rate and in a different direction. Therefore, Maya cannot calculate where the blur should happen. This is the same reason why Spotlight fog cannot be motion blurred.

Workarounds exist for faking motion blur, even in software. To create motion blur, Maya needs to be capable of looking at where a triangle is at each sample taken so that it can calculate a blur vector. In the case of 2D motion blur, Maya does this calculation and then simply blurs the final pixel in that direction. Because cloud and blobby particles are both spherical in shape, if you were to instance geometry and spheres, the renderer would then be able to blur those spheres. But you don't want to simply blur spheres; you want to blur blobs or volumetric clouds here. This is where you can exploit a limitation of the software renderer to your advantage. When doing 2D motion blur on an object, Maya does not evaluate the shader on the object to figure out whether it is transparent. It simply looks at the triangles of the tessellated object and calculates its motion vector; then it blurs the final pixel color. This is why you do not get proper results when performing a 2D motion blur on a transparent object. So if you were to assign a surface shader with 100% transparency and Matte Opacity set to 0 to the instanced geometry, the final pixel color would be that of the blobby geometry underneath. That color would then get blurred correctly based on the geometry that is sitting on top of it. (See Figures 14.27, 14.28, and 14.29.)

Figure 14.27 Software-rendered blobby particles with 2D motion blur—no blurring occurs.

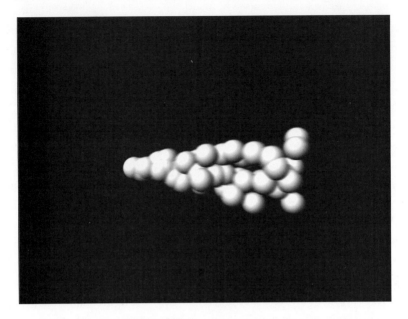

Figure 14.28 Software-rendered blobby particles with instanced NURBS spheres on top and 2D motion blur.

Figure 14.29 Software-rendered blobby particles with transparent NURBS spheres instanced and 2D motion blur—blobby particles now blur.

The key to this technique is in making sure that the geometry that is being instanced is slightly larger than the blob or cloud particle. If you are using radiusPP to control the size of the blob or cloud particle, simply use radiusPP to control the scale of the instance in the Instancer Options section of the Attribute Editor for the particle.

In many cases, this technique works. However, if you have a lot of particles, you will need to instance a lot of geometry, which can make your scene quite heavy and, in some cases, too heavy to render.

When a small, fast-moving object is motion blurred, it usually ends up looking like a streak. In the case of cloud particles, a volumetric rendering type of particle, this look can be achieved instead using the tube particle render type. Tubes are similar to the hardware render type, a streak, in that the length of the tube is determined by the velocity of the particle. The faster the particle is moving, the longer the tube is. You also have control over the radius of the tube at its tip (radius1) and base (radius0), so you can create a tapered-looking tube. This results in a fairly good simulation of motion blur.

For blobby particles, the workaround is not as easy. You want to follow a similar approach as you would with tube particles, creating a tapered tail trailing behind the blobby particle.

emit Function

The `emit` function in MEL enables you to emit new particles into a particle object using a command. When used inside a particle runtime or creation expression, the `emit` function gives you a tremendous amount of control over your particle simulation, enabling you to place particles in specific locations with specific attributes. Depending on how the command is implemented in your expression, it can be extremely computationally expensive.

You usually want to generate the MEL command through a procedure such as a `for` loop:

```
for ($i = 0;$i < 1000;++$i){
    vector $randPos = sphrand (1);
    emit -object particle1 -position ($randPos.x) ($randPos.y) ($randPos.z);
}
```

Although this function works correctly, it calls the `emit` function 1,000 times. Imagine if you had 1,000 particles using this function: It would call the `emit` command 1,000 × 1,000 times, or 1 million calls.

A more efficient way of writing this command is to generate one long command and execute it once:

```
string $cmd = "emit -object particle1 ";
for ($i = 0;$i < 1000;++$i){
    vector $randPos = sphrand (1);
    $cmd += (" -position " + ($randPos.x) + " " + ($randPos.y) + " " +
    ($randPos.z));
}
eval $cmd;
```

Using this technique, the number of function calls is limited to one per evaluation of the expression.

To create the streaked tail of the blobby particles, you need to get some information about the current particle, its position, and velocity. Then, based on some variables, you need to emit the tail.

First, you need to create a new particle object called blobbyTrailParticles that the waterEmitter will emit particles into. If you were to emit the particles into the same object, they, in turn, would emit particles, creating a huge number of particles very quickly. In the script editor, type the following:

```
particle -n "blobbyTrailParticles";
```

You will need to change the render type of the new blobbyTrailParticles to Blobby, click the Add Attributes for Current Render Type button to add the Radius attribute, and then set the radius to 0.1.

Set the render type of the (waterEmitter) particle object to Point or some other non–software render type. The reason for this is that blobby particles from different particle objects do not blob together, so the lead particle and the trail particles will not join into one object and will give undesirable results.

You will also need to set the life-span mode of blobbyTrailParticles to Constant and set the life span to .03, which is the equivalent of living for one frame.

In the runtime expression for blobbyTrailParticles, type the following:

```
vector $direction = unit (velocity);
```

unit

The unit function returns a normalized vector and is very important to understand when working with particle expressions. If a particle is traveling in the x-axis at a rate of 10 units per second, its velocity would be <<10,0,0>>. But if you just wanted to know what direction the particle was traveling in and didn't care about the speed, you would use the unit function, which would return a value of <<1,0,0>>. So, the unit function returns a direction without the speed.

mag

The mag function, on the other hand, returns the speed at which a particle is moving. Because a particle can be moving in all three axes at the same time, you need an easy way of determining how fast it is moving. Another use for the mag function is to determine distance or length. If particle A is located at <<10,5,0>> in space and you wanted to know how far away it was from locator2, which is located at <<-20,42,3>>, you would simply write this:

```
float $distance = mag (<<-20,42,3>> - <<10,5,0>>);
```

The mag function always returns a positive number because the distance between particle A and locator2 is the same, whether you subtract particleA from locator2 or locator2 from particle A.

For the purpose of this expression, the magnitude of the velocity is being used to find the speed at which the particle is moving. Therefore, you write this:

```
float $speed = mag (velocity);
```

Now that you have the direction and speed at which the particle is moving, you need to determine how long you want the tail to be and how many particles you want to emit into the tail. You need to add two new attributes to the particle object as regular float vectors, tailLength and density. For now, set tailLength to 1 and density to 0.1.

Next, you add the emit command to the runtime expression:

```
string $emitCmd = "emit -object blobbyTrailParticles ";
```

Then begin the for loop:

```
for ($i = 0;$i < $speed * density;++$i){
```

The number of particles emitted is based on how fast the particle is moving and how dense you want the trail to be. As the particle slows down, it emits less particles into its tail so that when the particle stops moving (speed = 0), no tail is emitted. This simple relationship between speed and density ensures that, regardless of how fast the particle is moving, the tail always retains its density and does not appear to be stamped.

linstep

The `linstep` function is another key function to know when working with particle expression. Like the `unit` function, the `linstep` function normalizes a numeric range. Given a certain range, the `linstep` function returns the percentage of the way through that range that a number is. So, for example, you know that 7.5 is halfway between 5 and 10; using `linstep`, you could find that out by writing this in the script editor:

```
float $percentage = linstep(5,10,7.5);
// Result: 0.5 //
```

For the tail of the particle, you want each particle that is emitted to be slightly farther away than the last one. So you need to know how many particles will be emitted and where you are in that range:

```
x float $weight = linstep (0,$speed * density,$i);
```

Now that you have a weighting for the particle, you can move it in the direction of the velocity by the value that you set for the length of the tail, using the weighting to determine how much this particular particle should move:

```
     vector $newPosition = position -
<<tailLength * $weight * $direction.x,
tailLength * $weight * $direction.y,
tailLength * $weight * $direction.z>>;
```

You now start to build up the emit command, adding the new position:

```
$emitCmd += (" -position " +
$newPosition.x + " " +
$newPosition.y + " " +
$newPosition.z);
```

Finally, you can end the `for` loop and execute the `emit` command using the `eval` function:

```
}
if ($speed * density > 0)eval $emitCmd;
```

As you can see in Figures 14.30 and 14.31, the trail particles lag behind the emitter particles. This is because, by default, Maya evaluates expressions before it applies dynamics. So, when the expression for emission is calculated, the position of the particle has not been affected by the Uniform field and other forces of the particles; it is basically using its position from the previous frame. By setting Expressions After Dynamics to

True, the dynamics of the fields are applied to particles before the expression runs, so the position that is being used in the expression is up-to-date.

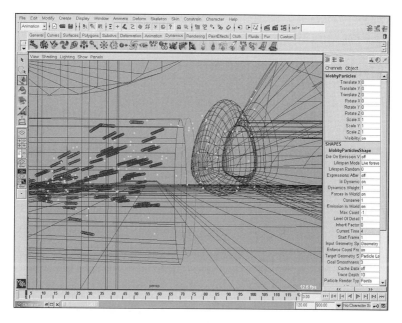

Figure 14.30 Blobby trail particles trailing behind the emitter particles.

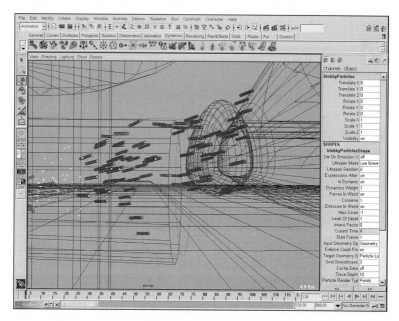

Figure 14.31 Trails now lining up with the emitter particles after setting Expressions After Dynamics.

The trail particles are currently just a tube of blobby particles, without any tapering. To create a tapered tail, you need to add opacityPP and radiusPP, as per-particle float array attributes, and also add opacity and radius as scalar float attributes to the blobbyTailParticle object:

```
$emitCmd += (" -attribute radiusPP -floatValue " +
(blobbyTailParticlesShape.radius * (1 - $weight)));

    $emitCmd += (" -attribute opacityPP -floatValue " +
(blobbyTailParticlesShape.opacity * (1 - $weight)));
```

For radiusPP, you want the particles to be large at the front of the trail and to taper off at the end. Therefore, you need to invert the weighting of the particle so that the first particle, with a weight of 0, will actually have a value of 1 (1 − 0). And as the particles taper off, you also want them to become more transparent. Therefore, you also should assign a per-particle opacity to them, with the opacity tapering off as well.

In Figure 14.32, you can now see the difference between the tapered and nontapered tail. If you want to have more control over the shape of the tapered tail, you can connect a ramp to the tail particle's radiusPP and drive the input of the ramp with an arbitrary attribute tail that, in turn, is set by the emit function. By default, ramps that are connected to a per-particle attribute are driven by the normalized age of the particle.

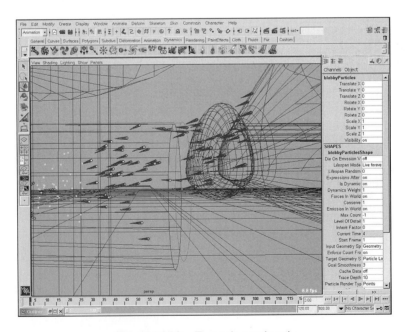

Figure 14.32   Tapered particle tail.

ParticleSamplerInfo

Because blobby particles use regular Maya shaders, you need a way of connecting the per-particle opacity values to the transparency of a shader. The particleSamplerInfo node enables you to drive attributes of a shader on a per-particle basis. When the particle is sampled during the rendering process, the particleSamplerInfo node passes information about the particle to the rendering node.

To create a particleSamplerInfo node, go to the Utilities tab of the Create Render Node window. Under the Particle Utilities section, select Particle Sampler Info. By default, if you drag and drop this node onto a material, it connects the outColor to the Color attribute of the material. Also by default, if you drag the particleSamplerInfo node onto the transparency attribute of a material, it connects the outTransparency value to it. Because opacity and transparency are opposite of each other—that is, an opacity value of 1 means that you cannot see through it, whereas a transparency of 1 means that you can completely see through it—Maya automatically converts opacityPP to what the renderer thinks of transparency (1 – opacityPP).

Figure 14.33 shows a particle tail that has been software-rendered without the particleSamplerInfo node controlling transparency. Figure 14.34 shows a particle tail that has been software-rendered with the particleSamplerInfo node controlling transparency.

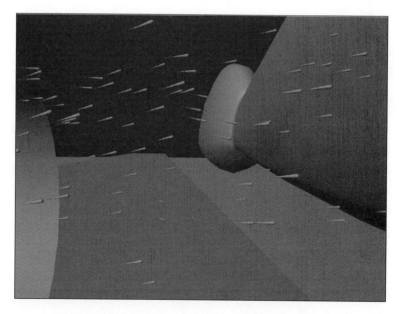

Figure 14.33 Particle tail software-rendered without particle
sampler info node controlling transparency.

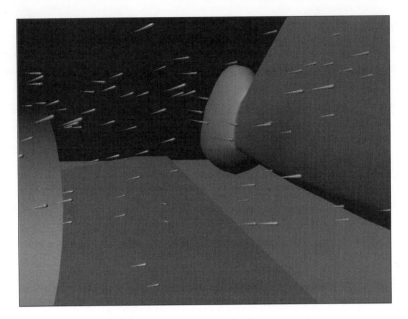

Figure 14.34   Particle tail software-rendered with particle
sampler info node controlling transparency.

The blobby particle now appears to have a streaked trail following behind it.

Caching

Now that the settings for the particles have all been configured, it is time to render the particles.

Before you render your particle simulation, you should always cache the particles disk first. Particle simulations are made up of emitters, fields, and expressions. Each of these types of input has a certain level of randomness, whether it be the randomness of an emitter or the randomness of the lifespanRandom attribute of the particle shape. Although there are ways of ensuring that each of these inputs uses the same random seed each time the simulation is played back, it is often more difficult to guarantee the randomness than it is to simply cache all the values to disk. Most important, based on my experiences with Maya, it is rare to have an entire simulation render correctly on the first try. If you need to rerender certain frames without a particle cache, there is no guarantee that the particles will be in the correct position.

Note

> Although particle disk caching can require a large amount of storage space on disk, it requires only one frame's worth of data to be stored in memory at a time. For example, if you have a 300-frame animation containing 30,000 particles, it might require 1GB of storage space on disk. However, each frame of the animation would require only 3MB of memory to be used. If you used memory caching, you would need 1GB of memory to store the values for the particles.

Multiple Passes

When rendering particles, as mentioned earlier, it is always best to generate multiple passes of the effect that can be composited later. For an effect such as water spray, you have streaks of water particles that are moving in a very directional manner at high speed. In some areas many water droplets merge to form large blobs of water. Mist and spray get caught up in the stream and add volume, but they also escape the stream and float away. Each of these elements has its own render properties: opacity, color, and specularity. Each of these elements can be rendered separately, some using the Hardware Render Buffer and others in the software and then brought together in the final composite to create the finished look.

Creating Water Trails

To learn how to create water trails, open the file 14waterDropsStart.ma, which you'll find on the CD that accompanies this book (see Figure 14.35). Play back the scene.

The particles that were set up in the previous chapter are just one element of the final effect. In this section, you'll learn how to make the spray appear to interact with the car by having it collide with and roll down the windshield. You'll be using the collision of the particles to trigger their goaling to the surface. Instead of having the particles initially emit from inside the fire hydrant pipe, the emitter has been positioned at the end of the pipe so that the only object that the particles will collide with is the windshield. A radial field also has been added to the particles to make them appear to burst outward.

You'll want to make this stream of particles collide with the windshield and roll down it, leaving a trail of water behind it. Several techniques can be used to get this type of effect, each with its own advantages and disadvantages.

Figure 14.35   Fire hydrant spraying water onto a car, as shown in
the file 14waterDropsStart.ma.

You could simply make the particles collide with the geometry, set the resilience to 0 (so that the particles don't bounce off the surface), and then have the particles fall with gravity. This technique would work if you were not dealing with a liquid. When liquids move along a surface, they tend to stick to the surface and not simply fall with gravity. A simple example of this is the way that water hangs from the ceiling in the bathroom after you have a hot shower. Even though the water is being affected by gravity, it tries to stick to the surface that it is on. Even if the ceiling had a slope to it, the water would fall with gravity down the slope and would congregate at the lowest point—but still, it would not fall. So, the simple behavior of collisions does not suffice for liquids.

Another shortcoming of this technique is that the friction setting for collision objects is set uniformly for the entire object. When water moves along a surface, its motion is dictated not only by gravity and the slope of the surface, but also by the texture, specs of dust, greasy spots, and so on. When the droplet of water comes in contact with any of these things, it has a tendency to slow down, change direction, pause for a moment, and so on. These variations in the drop's motion in some ways define what type of liquid the drop is made of. A heavy liquid such as mud would not be as affected by these factors and would tend to move in a very linear fashion, whereas water might zig and zag quite a lot.

Exercise 14.2   Sliding Water Down a Surface

In this exercise, you learn how to slide particles down a surface using a combination of collisions, goals, and expressions. Due to some limitations of goals in Maya and the fact that the water needs to collide with multiple surfaces, this exercise is fairly technical.

Because you are using goals, you need to determine when to turn on the goals for the particles and when the goals should be ignored. As the particles are flying through the air, you want the goals to be off; when they hit the surface, you want the goals to turn on. When the particles reach the bottom edge of the surface, you want the goals to turn off so that the particles can fall with gravity again.

The first step is to find the "hit" point. You do this using collisions.

1. Select the particles and then the windshield. Under the Particles menu, select Make Collide.

   On playback, the particles now bounce off the windshield.

   The next step is to make the particles stick to the surface at the point at which they hit the surface.

2. Select the particles and then the windshield. Under the Particles menu, select the Goal Options box.

   This brings up the options for the goal command (see Figure 14.36).

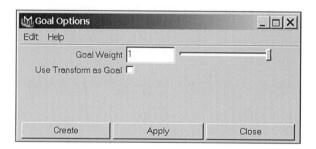

Figure 14.36   Setting an initial goal weight for the particles in the Goal Options window.

3. Set the Goal Weight to 1 and select the Create button.

   On playback, the particles move to the CVs of the surface (see Figure 14.37).

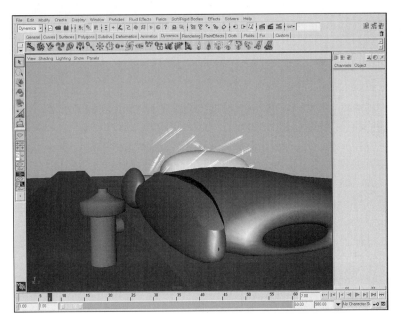

Figure 14.37 Particles moving to the CVs of the windshield surface as they are emitted from the fire hydrant.

This is because, by default, the goal for the particles is set to 1, and the particles are trying to stick to each of the CVs of the surface.

Next, you'll make the particles goal to the surface only when a collision occurs.

4. Open the Attribute Editor for the particles. Under the Add Dynamics Attribute tab, select General.

5. In the window that appears, navigate to the Particle tab and select collisionU, collisionV, goalU, goalV, and traceDepthPP (see Figure 14.38).

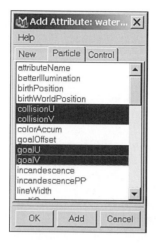

Figure 14.38 The Particle tab of the Add Attribute window, where you can add predefined attributes to your particles that Maya can make use of internally to pass or receive information.

6. Select OK to add the attributes to the particles.

Because you will be using the UV parameterization of the surface in your expressions, it is always best to rebuild the surface with a 0 – 1 UV parameterization using the Edit NURBS, Rebuild Surfaces menu item.

7. Open the creation expression for the particle object by right-clicking goalPP in the particles attributes. Add the following lines:

```
//  initialize the goalPP with a value of 0
//
goalPP = 0;

//  initialize the goalU and goalV with a nonzero value
//  a zero value dramatically decreases Maya's performance
//
goalU = 0.1;
goalV = 0.1;

//  initialize traceDepthPP with a value of 1
//
traceDepthPP = 1;
```

Essentially, you are setting some initial values for the attributes that you added.

Note

When you add a goal object to your particles, Maya creates a goalPP attribute automatically. Internally, Maya initializes the value of any particle that is born with a goalPP value of 1, not 0. For other attributes that are internal to Maya, there is no way for you to know what the default value will be, so it is always a good idea to set initial values for any attribute that you add to your particles. This is true even if the value you are initializing it with is 0.

In the creation expression, goalPP is now being initialized with a value of 0 so that the particles do not try to match the goal position.

When you create a goal object for your particles to follow, Maya initially sets the target position for your particles to be either the vertices or the CVs of the surface, in the case of polygonal or NURBS geometry. However, when using NURBS geometry, you have the ability to set the goal position based on the UV parameterization of the surface. This means that you can have a particle stick to a specific UV coordinate of that NURBS surface.

Note

Because of a bug/performance issue in Maya, when your particles have a goalU or goalV value equal to or less than 0 or equal to or greater than 1, playback performance decreases drastically. We therefore initialize goalU and goalV with a nonzero value—.1, in this case.

The last attribute that is defined is traceDepthPP. The dynamics solver in Maya can calculate multiple collisions per frame. For example, if your particle dropped into a very small tube, it might collide with the walls of the tube more than once per frame, bouncing from one side to the other repeatedly.

In the Attribute Editor for the particle object, under the Collisions tab, is an attribute called traceDepth. The default value for traceDepth is 10, which means that, on each frame, Maya will calculate up to 10 collisions.

8. Because the water drops stick to the surface that they collide with rather than bouncing off it, initialize the traceDepthPP with a value of 1.

Note

We do not initialize collisionU and collisionV because these attributes are read-only and are set internally by Maya. When colliding particles with a NURBS surface, Maya has the capability to return the UV coordinate of where the collision occurred on the surface. You will use this value to assign the goalU and goalV values so that the particles stick to the point on the surface that they collided with.

9. Open the runtime expression for the particle object and add the following lines:

```
//  check for a collision
//
if (collisionU != -1){
    goalPP = 1;
    goalU = collisionU;
    goalV = collisionV;
}
```

10. Play back the animation, and you'll see that the particles seem to disappear when they hit the windshield. This is because the particle render type is set to Multistreaks, which base their tail length on the velocity of the particle. Because the particle is stuck to the surface, it is not moving and has no velocity. Change the render type of the particles to Points, and you will see that the particles are stuck to the surface of the windshield (see Figure 14.39).

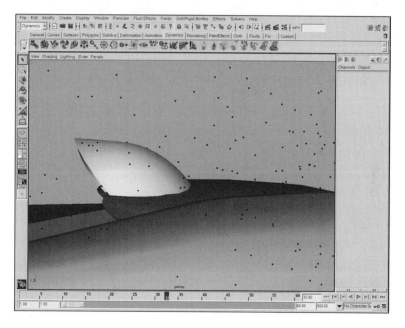

Figure 14.39 Particles sticking to the windshield at the point at which they collided.

When a particle is not colliding with an object, its collisionU and collisionV attributes both return a value of -1. When they collide with a NURBS object, the value returned is the UV parameter on the surface where the collision occurred. Figures 14.40, 14.41, and 14.42 show the collisionU values of a particle that collides with the windshield.

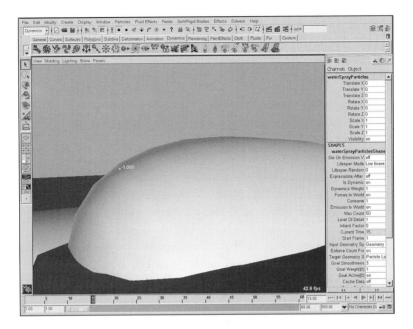

Figure 14.40 Frame 15, showing that the particle has not yet collided with the surface; the value of collisionU is −1.

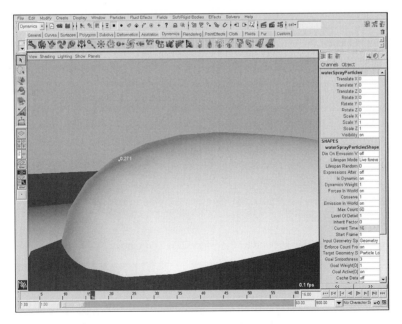

Figure 14.41 Frame 16, showing that the particle has collided with the surface; the value of collisionU is .271.

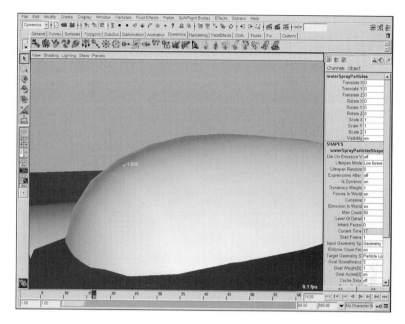

Figure 14.42   Frame 17, showing that the particle is now
goaled to the surface; the value of collisionU is −1.

When a particle is goaled to the same surface that it is colliding with, results can sometimes be unpredictable. In theory, the goalUV puts the particle directly on the surface, which should always result in a collision. Yet Maya returns a value of ·1 for collisionU once the particle is goaled to the surface, indicating that no collisions are occurring. This is due to a discrepancy between the collision surface and the goal surface. This discrepancy is more clearly illustrated when the particle is sliding down the surface.

The particle is stuck to the surface using goalU and goalV. UV parameterization is basically a separate coordinate system from XYZ space. Using UV coordinates, you can move along an object in surface space, not world space. Because water drops move along a surface, you'll want to adjust the coordinates that the particle is goaled to, goalU and goalV, to make the particle move along the surface.

To do this, you need to determine which way the surface is oriented.

Select the windshield and turn on its Surface Origins, Display, Nurbs Components, Surface Origins (see Figure 14.43).

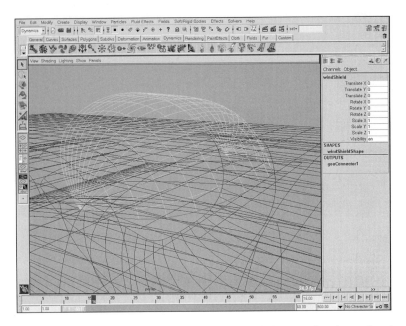

Figure 14.43   The surface origins of the windshield, showing that the surface is parameterized with the U value running horizontally and the V value running vertically.

This brings up a set of curves that indicate where the parameterization of the surface begins. From this you can see that the U parameter of the surface, as indicated by the red line and the red U, moves along the horizontal axis of the surface. To slide the particle down the surface, you would need to move it in the V direction.

In the runtime expression for the particle object, add the following line:

```
//  shift the goalV parameter by adding .01 to it
//
goalV -= .01;
```

When you play back the animation, you will now see that the particle gets emitted, hits the surface and sticks to it, and then slides down the surface.

If you step through the animation with the render type of the particles set to Numeric, you will see that the collisionU value of –1 sometimes changes, indicating that a collision has occurred.

Tessellation

When Maya calculates collision with a NURBS surface, it first has to convert the surface to polygons. This conversion is done through the geoConnector node. When the surface gets tessellated into polygons, it does so using a very simple count-based algorithm. The tessellationFactor of the geoConnector node indicates the number of triangles that Maya will tessellate the nurbsSurface into. The default setting of 200 is barely adequate to represent the shape of a simple sphere, let alone that of a more sculpted form such as the curvature of the windshield.

Although the collision tessellation might not be true to the shape of the NURBS surface, the goalU and goalV positions are, in fact, 100% accurate and do not use the tessellated geometry as their goal. That is why Maya sometimes indicates a collision as the particle is moving along the NURBS surface and is not necessarily making contact with the tessellated collision surface. Try setting the tesselationFactor of the geoConnector node to 10,000. On playback, you will notice many more collisions.

We initialized the traceDepthPP attribute with a value of 1 during the creation of the particle. After the particle has collided with the surface, no more collision needs to be calculated, so you can simply set the traceDepthPP to 0 after the first collision has occurred. A value of 0 indicates that no collisions should be calculated for that particle. You will notice a marginal increase in performance because Maya still seems to want to look for collisions, but it will not calculate any collision values. This also ensures that the first part of the expression gets calculated only once.

In the runtime expression, add the following line inside the first `if` statement:

```
   //  check for a collision
//
if (collisionU != -1){
    goalPP = 1;
    goalU = collisionU;
    goalV = collisionV;
    traceDepthPP = 0;

}
```

noise Function

Now that the particle is colliding with the surface and sliding down it, you'll want to add some randomness to its motion. The first step is to add a zigzagging motion. Several techniques can be used to add this motion, the simplest of which is to use the noise function.

The `noise` function returns a value between –1 and 1 using a Perlin noise field generator. The Maya documentation does a good job of explaining how the `noise` function works, but in layman's terms, I like to think of the `noise` function as a noisy curve that runs from 0 to infinity. The value that you provide to the function dictates where you are sampling the curve. Unlike the `rand` function, the `noise` function produces the same result each time you sample at the same point. This means that every time you execute this command, you always get the same result:

```
noise (10);
// Result: -0.465903 //
```

And because the noise behaves as a curve, if you sample it at values of 10.01, 10.02, and 10.03, you will get a smooth interpolation of values as follows:

Sample	Return
noise (10.01)	-0.474992
noise (10.02)	-0.483307
noise (10.03)	-0.490858

On the other hand, if you sampled it at 10, 11, and 12, you would get much more random return of values:

Sample	Return
noise (10)	-0.465903
noise (11)	0.376804
noise (12)	-0.420169

To zigzag the particle along the surface, you'll want to adjust its position in goalU, which runs horizontally along the windshield.

First, change the attributeName of the value that is currently being displayed for the particle from collisionU to goalV.

In the runtime expression for the particle, add the following line:

```
goalU += noise(frame) * .01;
```

On playback, you will see that the particle now zigs and zags back and forth as it slides down the surface. The motion is too chaotic because the parameter that you are sampling the curve at is changing too quickly. The `frame` value comes from the current frame that Maya is on, which is incrementing by a value of 1. To smooth out the randomness, sample the noise function in smaller increments. Simply divide the frame by a factor of 10 or 100, or any value you choose that gives the desired results:

```
goalU += noise(frame/10) * .01;
```

The greater the number is that you are dividing the frame by, the less chaotic the zigzagging motion will be.

The value returned by the `noise` function is then multiplied by .01. This multiplier acts as the amplitude of the noise. By multiplying the results by .01, you essentially change the range of numbers returned by the noise function to between –.01 and .01. Because you are incrementing the goalV attribute each frame with the results of the `noise` function, it is important to remember that a change in value of .01 in either direction is essentially a shift of 1% along the surface—the UV parameterization of the surface ranges from 0 – 1.

You can add a similar noise function to the goalV attribute of the particles, but you do not want the goalV value to ever increase. This would make the particle move back up the surface, which a water drop would never do:

```
goalV -= abs (noise(frame / 10 ) * .01);
```

On playback, the particle appears to slow down and accelerate at different points in time.

When you play back the animation, you'll notice that all of the particles are zigzagging at the same time and by the same amount. This is because the `noise` function always returns the same values for the same queried parameter. Because all of the particles are using `frame` as the parameter for the `noise` function, they are all getting the same value returned. To correct this, you want to have each particle sample a different point along the `noise` function curve. To determine this unique point at which to sample the `noise` function, simply use the ID of the particle. To ensure maximum randomness, multiply the ID by a factor of 1,005 or some other number that feels lucky to you.

Additionally, if you want to vary the randomness even more, multiply goalU and goalV by different amounts, thereby having each attribute follow a different random number stream:

```
goalV -= abs (noise(frame / 10 + particleId * 2005) * .01);
goalU += noise(frame / 10  + particleId * 1005) * .01;
```

Now when the animation plays back, the water drops will appear to move in a more random manner, sometimes slowing down in their decent speed and sometimes in their side-to-side speed.

As mentioned at the beginning of this chapter, when Maya encounters a goalU or goalV value that is less than or equal to 0, or greater than or equal to 1, playback performance suffers. Because goalU and goalV are both being incremented randomly, you need to limit their value ranges to values between 0 and 1, not including 0 and 1.

Add the following lines to the end of the runtime expression:

```
if (goalU >= 1 || goalU <= 0)goalU = clamp (.001,.999,goalU);
if (goalV >= 1 || goalV <= 0)goalV = clamp (.001,.999,goalV);
```

You should notice a significant increase in playback performance as particles bunch up along the boundaries of the surface.

When a drop of water reaches the bottom of a surface, it has a tendency to stick to it rather than fall with gravity. It sticks and fills with water from the water that has trailed behind, or until it merges with other water droplets and becomes too heavy to cling to the surface and eventually falls off.

The easy way of having the water droplet fall off the surface would be to set its goalPP to 0 when it reaches a value of .999 in goalU. Remember that you are clamping the goalU and goalV values to between 0 and .999 to increase playback performance.

This simple if statement will cause the water drop to fall off the edge as soon as it reaches it:

```
if (goalU == .999)goalPP = 0;
```

On playback, you'll notice that this doesn't make the water feel like a heavy drop.

Rather than just setting the goalPP to 0, you can simulate the drop filling with water by decreasing the goalPP by a random number every frame that it is at the bottom of the ledge. This ensures that each drop falls differently:

```
if (goalU == .999)goalPP -= rand (.01,.1);
```

On playback, the particles now appear to hang and slowly break away from the surface. Depending on the values you use in the rand function, you can delay or speed up the falling of the drops.

This effect of water falling off the edge isn't really useful for the windshield of the car, but for other areas, where the water does need to roll off, it can be.

Water Trails

When a drop of water falls on a surface, it leaves a trail behind it. Depending on the type of surface that the water falls on, the trail of water will either stick to it and be absorbed by it or will seem to follow behind the drop.

In the *Parking Spot* project, water is spraying on a windshield, which is quite a smooth surface. On a surface such as this, water tends to bead up rather than leave a trail. To create a more interesting effect, we had the drop leave a trail behind. The steps to do this are outlined in the next exercise.

Exercise 14.3   Emitting a Water Trail

In this exercise, you will use per-particle emission rather than the `emit` command to emit a trail of particles.

1. Select the waterSprayParticles object.
2. In the Particles menu, select Emit from Object.
3. Set Emitter Type to Directional.
4. Set Direction X Y Z to Zero.

    This creates an emitter and attaches it to every particle in the dropParticle object.

    On playback, the resulting effect looks more like fireworks or asteroids than water drops (see Figure 14.44).

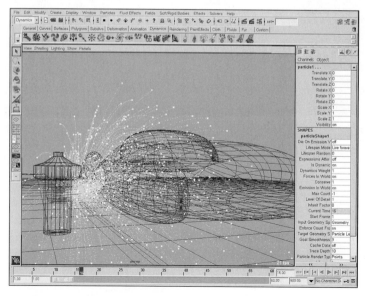

Figure 14.44   waterSprayParticles emitting a trail of particles.

You want the trail of particles to be emitted only as the particles slide down the surface. In Version 3.0 of Maya, Alias|Wavefront added a feature called Per-Point Emission Rates that enables you to control the rate of emission on a per-particle basis.

5. Select the newly created emitter, emitter1. You can find the emitter parented underneath the waterSprayParticles node.

6. Rename the emitter trailEmitter.

7. In the Particles menu, select Per-Point Emission Rates.

In the Attribute Editor for waterSprayParticles, you will see that a new attribute has been automatically added, named trailEmitterRatePP.

If you open the Hypergraph for the emitter, you will see that there is now a connection between waterSprayParticlesShape.trailEmitterRatePP and trailEmitter.ratePP (see Figure 14.45).

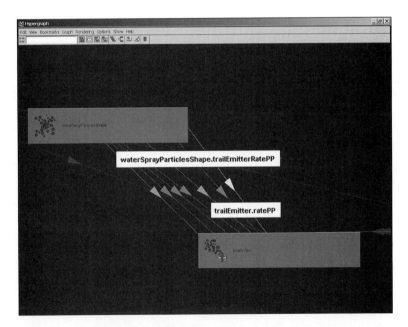

Figure 14.45   The trailEmitterPP attribute automatically added to waterSprayParticles and is connected to the emitter when Per-Point Emission Rates is selected.

In the runtime expression, you can turn on emission when the drop particle makes a collision and then turn it off when it falls off the edge. First, you need to initialize trailEmitterRatePP in the creation expression.

8. Open the creation expression for the waterSprayParticles object and add this:

```
trailEmitterRatePP = 0;
```

9. Open the runtime expression for the waterSprayParticles and add this to the first if statement:

```
//  check for a collision
//
if (collisionU != -1){
    goalPP = 1;
    goalU = collisionU;
    goalV = collisionV;
    traceDepthPP = 0;
    trailEmitterRatePP = 100;
}
```

10. Add this to the last if statement:

```
if (goalU == .999){
goalPP -= rand (.01,.1);
trailEmitterRatePP = 0;
}
```

11. Set the speed of the trailEmitter to 0.

Depending on how quickly the drops are moving along the surface, the trailEmitterRatePP might need to be increased if you notice too many gaps in the trailing particles.

12. On playback, you can now see the trails being left behind the drop particles. Two aesthetic issues are immediately noticeable (see Figure 14.46).

13. The long, smooth, arcing trails can simply be adjusted by varying some of the values in the noise functions. Instead of editing the expression each time you want to adjust the motion of the drops as they fall, you can create add some controls to the waterSetup control node that you created to control the fire hydrant.

14. Rename particle1 to trailParticles.

15. Turn off Inherits Transforms for the trailParticles in the Attribute Editor, and parent it under the waterSetup node.

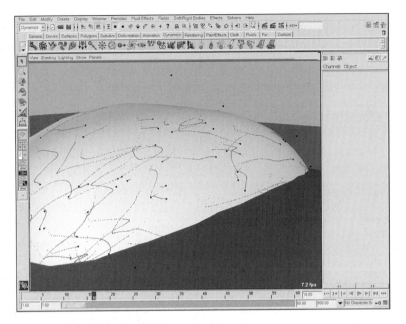

Figure 14.46 The trailing particles, which resemble figure-skating etches in ice rather than trails of water on a windshield.

16. Add the following attributes to the waterSetup node as Float, Scalar attributes: hFrequency, hAmplitude, vFrequency, vAmplitude.

In the runtime expression for the waterSprayParticles, you need to change some of the hard-coded numbers to instead be driven by these attributes.

17. Open the runtime expression for the dropParticles and change the following:

Replace this:

```
goalV -= abs (noise(frame / 50 + particleId * 2005) * .03);
```

With this:

```
goalV -= abs (noise(frame * waterSetup.vFrequency +
particleId * 2005) * waterSetup.vAmplitude);
```

Replace this:

```
goalU += noise(frame / 10  + particleId * 1005) * .01;
```

With this:

```
goalU += noise(frame * waterSetup.hFrequency  +
particleId * 1005) * waterSetup.hAmplitude ;
```

You can now control the motion of your drops through the Channel Box by selecting the waterDropSetup node (see Figures 14.47, 14.48, and 14.49).

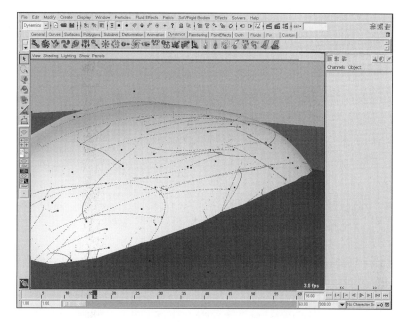

Figure 14.47 hFrequency = .03, hAmplitude = .01, vFrequency = .01, vAmplitude = .01. With a low horizontal frequency, the water changes direction horizontally less frequently, creating long arcs.

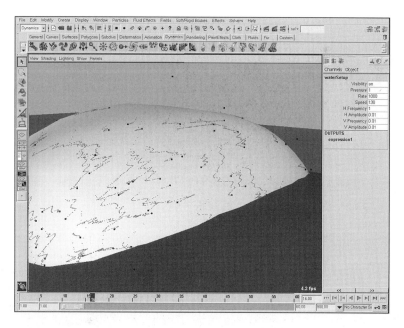

Figure 14.48 hFrequency = 1.0, hAmplitude = .01, vFrequency = .01, vAmplitude = .01. With a high horizontal frequency, the water changes direction horizontally frequently, creating squiggly arcs.

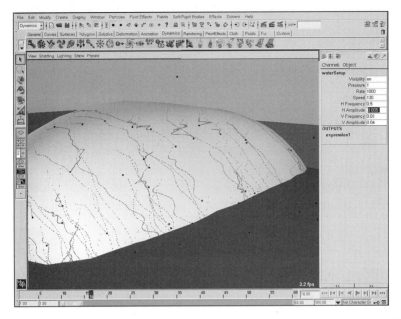

Figure 14.49 hFrequency = .5, hAmplitude = .005, vFrequency = .01, vAmplitude = .04. With a medium horizontal frequency and very small horizontal amplitude and medium vertical amplitude, the water changes direction horizontally frequently but does not move a large amount in any direction. This maintains a random-looking, yet fairly straight vertical trail down the windshield.

As you can see, many different looks can be achieved by simply adjusting these four variables. In addition, you can add controls for the emitter rate so that you can easily adjust the density of the trails if they become too sparse.

18. To make the trails appear to follow the drop, set the life-span mode of the trailParticles to lifespanRandom, and set the lifespanRandom attribute to .5 and the life span to 1.

In this file, the only object that the water will slide down is the goal object, which, in this case, is the windshield. If you want to apply this same effect to any surface that the water collides with, you must create a particle object for each surface on which a collision occurs. This is because, although Maya enables you to have multiple goal objects for a particle object, there is only one goalPP attribute. This means that you cannot have a particle goal for multiple surfaces and control which one it sticks to on a per-particle basis. To work around this limitation, you need to have a particle object for each surface, goaled to that surface. You would then add a collision event to the waterSpray particles that would execute an event procedure similar to the following procedure:

```
global proc waterCollision(string $particle, int $id, string $surface){
//   notice that there is a " " blank space before the name that I am
//   matching
//   this is because Maya returns a blank space before the name of the
//   surface
     if ($surface == " windShield"){
          //   here, we get the collisionU and collisionV values for the
          //   particle
          //   note that the variables I declare are arrays since the
          //   particle
          //   command could be returning values for multiple particles
          float $u[] = `particle -attribute collisionU -id $id $particle -q`;
          float $v[] = `particle -attribute collisionV -id $id $particle -q`;
          //   since we will be using the emit function to add particles to
//   an existing particle node, we must emit with a position
          float $pos[] = `particle -attribute position -id $id $particle -q`;
          //   this if statement gets run if the name of the collision
          //   surface is windshield
//   we therefore want to emit into the windshieldParticles object which is
          //   goaled to the windshield geometry
//   the goalU and goalV attributes of the emitted particles get initialized
//   with
//   the collisionU and collisionV values of the particle that just collided
          emit -object windShieldParticles -pos $pos[0] $pos[1] $pos[2]
               -attribute goalU -fv $u[0] -attribute goalV -fv $v[0];

     }
}
```

Rendering

Rendering the water drops and trails should be done using software rendering with a blobby particle render type and raytracing enabled. The blobby particle attributes radius and threshold work in conjunction with the number of particles in the drips and how much each particle overlaps with its neighbor. There are no magic numbers that give smooth, seamless results; however, it is a good idea to always ensure that you have particles overlapping with each other with a high threshold. A good rule of thumb is that the smoother you want the surface to look, the larger the radius and higher the threshold should be. When working with a threshold that is larger than 1, you will need at least two particles to overlap to get any resulting surface.

Compositing

When water moves along a surface, it tends to leave a trail behind it. That trail can be either water spots on a shower door or a simple discoloring of a surface that indicates that the surface is wet. It can be quite difficult to generate these types of elements in the software renderer procedurally and have them line up with the water drops that are dynamically moving along the surface.

By rendering out additional elements from your simulation, some with trails of particles that live forever, some with different particle render types, and so on, you allow for a lot of flexibility in the compositing stage. A compositor can use those passes to either darken, add a subtle bump effect, or displace and distort the software-rendered elements.

Summary

As with any other technique, this one has its advantages and disadvantages. To achieve greater realism, you need to add more realism to the expressions and setup. A large drop of water should move faster than a smaller drop, should zigzag much less, should leave a larger trail, and so on. If you assign a random value for the drop particles in their creation expression, you can then use the mass of the particle to determine the radiusPP of the blob particles, as well as modify the goalU and goalV values to either increase or decrease them with each frame. The more variables relate to each other, the greater the chance will be that your simulation will look natural and organic.

Many layers are needed to simulate the high-pressure spray of a fire hydrant. In this chapter, you learned how to create a thick volume of water using hardware rendering, as well as how to have that water interact with geometry in your scene using software-rendered blobby particles and expressions. You also gained greater insight into the speed and power of the Hardware Render Buffer and how to overcome some of its limitations.

To learn more about Maya's particles and dynamics through my training videos and plug-ins, visit the kolektiv web site, `www.kolektiv.com`.

Part IV

Animation

15 Character Animation in Maya   479

16 Character Setup Pipeline for Animation   575

17 Rigging Characters for Animation   609

18 Shading   697

19 Lighting   733

20 Rendering   775

Chapter 15
Character Animation in Maya

By Will Paicius

> *The art of character animation is to try to catch lightning in a bottle...one volt at a time.*—Brad Bird

If animation is the art and technique of making things move, character animation is that subset of animation in which these moving objects appear to the audience to be alive. This "live" character is the basis for the word *animation*: in Latin, *anima* means *soul*. Hence, anything with a soul is alive. So, character animation is about giving the illusion of life to character objects.

As a process, character animation is, therefore, the study of movements and techniques that convey to the audience the sense that our character object has emotion and thought (see Figures 15.1, 15.2, and 15.3). By learning these movements and how the audience responds to them, we as animators can predictably create movements to convey to the audience the desired character thought and emotion through the behavior of our characters.

Figure 15.1

Figure 15.2

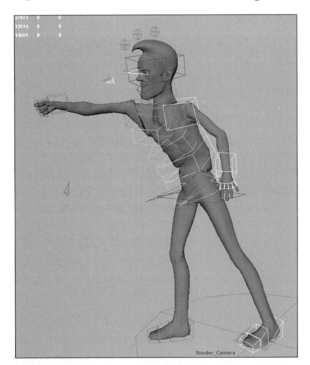

Figure 15.3 The character animation process proceeds from the expectation drawing (Figure 15.1), to the action research (Figure 15.2), and to the animated implementation of the selected motion (Figure 15.3).

If we are successful, the character will seem convincing and will have a personality to which the audience can relate. If the audience loves or hates the character, the animator was successful. If the audience does not care or is confused, the effort was not successful.

Ultimately, the audience is the measure of the success of any animation we undertake, including the *Parking Spot* animation we're creating throughout this book.

In this chapter's study of character animation, we examine the following:

- How to define your character
- How to define your character expectations
- Reference, acting, and planning
- Blocking and animating
- Principles of animation
- Tips on applying these principles to Maya
- Performance evaluation

Maya Animation

Computer animation has taken the entertainment world by storm. The popularity of computer-animated films such as *Ice Age* and *Stuart Little* is based on both today's computer graphics developments and animation's past. Learning the lessons of the past and incorporating them into the fast-changing world of computer graphics is the challenge for today's animators.

Character animation was perfected before computers were available, using other media. For example, *3D animation* originally referred to puppet animation and stop-motion photography. These animated objects had three dimensions, after all. Consider, for example, Ladislas Starewich.

Starewich (1882–1959) invented the 3D stop-motion puppet-animation film in 1910. Starewich's early films using animated bug parts pioneered the idea of puppet animation (his first film done in 1910 was *Lucanus cervus*). Sadly, audiences' appetites for puppet animation have been fickle over the years, and puppet animation's popularity waxes and wanes from time to time.

Traditional, or PGI (Pencil Generated Imagery), animation was perfected by Disney in the 1920s and 1930s. The learning from this period was codified for the apprentice animators in Frank Thomas and Ollie Johnson's book *Disney Animation, The*

Illusion of Life (Abbeville Press, 1987). One entire chapter of *The Illusion of Life* is dedicated to defining their classic "Principles of Animation" to help aspiring animators.

Today, computer animation pioneers at Pixar Animation Studios—and almost every studio—incorporate the learning of this animation tradition, and often many traditional animators, into the new art form. These same principles that were developed before computer animation still apply, but newer principles are unique to computer graphics animation. Animators need to learn both sets of principles to be successful with computer graphics programs such as Maya.

Maya was created with an object-oriented programming approach that permits keys to be set for any attribute. Objects can be thought of as nodes, where attributes—color, size, position, and the like—are collected. You might know that any attribute whose values can be changed can be keyframed. So, if you can make anything change in time with Maya, you have done animation.

But here we examine this deeper level called character animation. *Character animation* is an attempt to make something move with compelling and believable motion so that your audience thinks the object is alive. Character animation is anthropomorphism in action. In this chapter, we use *animation* to mean character animation, and we explore some of the ways professionals get results with Maya.

In Maya, this animation tradition is carried on through the development of tools and techniques that help animators do their pioneering work. Because Maya is an open system, tools and programs can be developed *within* Maya using MEL, the Maya Embedded Language. CG companies, such as Pixar, can utilize the tools provided by Maya and, when necessary, create their own custom tools using MEL.

Maya provides all animators and technical directors with this ability to customize the animation tools. You do this by learning MEL, and it is not that difficult to learn. Animators who can use MEL are highly valued. Maya doesn't use MEL; Maya *is* MEL. And although other high-end CG programs provide such a capability, none is as popular today as Maya.

The tools in Maya, whether stock or custom, help the CG animator to continue the long tradition of animation. And although CG animation is most popular today, it is likely to join traditional and puppet animation in a rich future that appreciates all forms of animation media.

See if you can find these threads in our interview with Scott Clark. Scott is an animator by day, and he teaches animation at night at San Francisco's Academy of Art College.

Scott Clark Interview

What is your background?

I studied drawing, painting, design, and animation at the Rhode Island School of Design and graduated with a BFA in Illustration in 1996. During my last two years in school, I participated in two internships: one at Chuck Jones Film Productions and the other at Pixar Animation Studios.

I was lucky enough to meet Chuck Jones and speak with him about animation. My time at Pixar came as *Toy Story* hit the theaters and Pixar's name had yet to be established. My original goal had been to become a drawn animator at a studio such as Disney. My initial experience at Pixar showed me that I liked—and was actually good at—computer animation.

What is your current role at Pixar?

Currently, I am a directing animator on John Lasseter's next project, *Cars*. Pixar will be releasing two other films, *Finding Nemo* and *The Incredibles*, so I'm doing a lot of testing and preproduction for *Cars* right now.

I started at Pixar in 1996 by doing work on the *Toy Story* CD-ROM. I cut my teeth by doing a lot of the animation for Heimlich and the circus characters in *A Bug's Life*. I also animated a lot of the main characters on the Academy Award–winning *Geri's Game* and *Toy Story 2*. My first directing gigs came from two *Toy Story* McDonald's commercials and a short piece for the 2000 Academy Awards Presentation. My role on *Monsters Inc.* was as a directing animator.

How do you define animation?

Animation literally means to "bring something to life." Whether it is a cartoony Tex Avery character falling apart into pieces or a realistic dinosaur chomping on some unfortunate soul in a modern monster movie, animation allows us to believe in something that really isn't alive. The best animation will always show us a bit of ourselves in the characters.

In other words, we enjoy watching animated characters because we recognize all our own human traits, flaws and all, in the characters. Anyone can pull up a computer program and move stuff around these days, but it takes a talented animator to make you believe that an inanimate object has thoughts, feelings, emotions, a future, a past, and a life outside of the screen.

How do you go about animating?

This is a broad question, but it's common. Animation is like any other craft that must be studied and built upon through years of experience, much the same way an actor or painter grows throughout his or her career. Learning how to animate isn't simply reading about the principles of animation in a book or learning a program on a computer.

continues

continued

Animation involves performance, timing, acting, physics, and story. When it is done correctly, the audience should forget they are looking at drawings, models, or renderings and should believe in the character and story being told. The audience should identify with that character and be involved in the story. If an animator does his or her job correctly, the craft is invisible. No longer is the audience aware of the illusion of life on the screen or that the animator had a part in creating it. The audience simply believes in the character!

My animation process has been built from the knowledge and wisdom of animators both young and old, from computer to drawn. My inspirations come from classic animators such as Chuck Jones, Frank Thomas, Ollie Johnson, and Ken Harris, or from modern animators such as Glen Keane and Richard Williams. I'm constantly inspired by the work I see done by other animators around me or by great acting performances I see in live-action movies. I think it's imperative that an animator have the observational skills of a scientist and an artist.

Rather than sitting at a desk and putting down the first, most likely clichéd choice, I do research by going out into the world to find the specific and unique choices. I still plan my shots the way traditional animators do: through thumbnail sketches to find the most entertaining poses that tell the story clearly. I act out my shots in front of a mirror to observe the motion I want to put in a character and to feel how emotion affects the physicality of a character. I use video reference to find the subtle quirks in actions. I usually begin with simple pose-to-pose blocking, filling in the action with more straight-ahead animation as needed. I layer and rework the timing first before polishing off the shot with overlapping action and smooth arcs.

What do you teach your students at the Academy of Art?

I start the class from the basics by animating three bouncing balls: a basketball, a bowling ball, and a beach ball. I encourage the students to actually play with them in real life, to get the proper sense of physics and weight to each ball. About half the assignments are physics-related (animate a character jumping over a ball, animate a realistic walk cycle). The rest of the assignments are acting related—an attempt to get an entertaining, believable character on the screen, whether it be comic or tragic. I keep the assignments simple and give restrictions on the frame range. Anyone who can animate a character that appears to have thoughts and emotions can do the simpler stuff—like a flying logo or a spaceship. It doesn't work the other way around.

What are the common problems and benefits of computer animation?

Computer animation is an amazing medium. A lot of people, including executives at major Hollywood studios, mistakenly think it is better than previous media such as stop-motion or hand-drawn animation because it is newer. What they don't realize is that the story is the most important, not the animation that tells it. You can have an amazing actor cast in your film, but if you give him wooden dialogue and horrible direction within an inadequate story, the audience really won't care about the character. The animation is the heart of the film and the acting that drives the main story. The story is the skeleton.

Computer animation is great at subtlety. You can get really small movements, such as the small darting of the eye, that are simply impossible to do with traditional methods. When polished, computer animation can give a smooth, realistic look. It combines the flexibility of layering and timing that you get from drawn animation with the dimensionality of stop motion. It is easier to stay on model, and you're not limited to linear time or gravity bringing down an armature on your set (see Figure 15.4).

Figure 15.4   This is our example of a character model sheet. Note how Spot behaves and how he remains Spot in various poses.

Note

Traditional animators had quite a challenge when drawing their characters in different poses. The characters would squash and stretch in response to the circumstances and forces they experienced. However, they were not supposed to change in volume. That meant the drawings had to look like the model sheet drawings, even though the character was put into extreme situations. Keeping the drawn character's appearance in line with the model sheet was called "staying on model."

continues

continued

However, computer animation has the same limitations as any other traditional method; the ability of the animator still shows through. All the same rules of filmmaking still apply, and although we call it 3D animation, we're really composing an image for a two-dimensional screen. The computer fills motion between poses evenly, so it is easy to get either floaty, smooth, and weightless motion or unnatural pops and jitters. I've seen animation in major Hollywood movies that looks like the characters are being affected by the gravity of a different planet than Earth! It is also really difficult to convincingly show contact between characters and objects. Things such as clothing and hair still have to be simulated and can't be controlled easily by the animator. There is a graphic quality of exaggeration and design that will always be possible only with drawn animation.

What do you look for when hiring animators?

At Pixar, we're looking for animators who are good actors and storytellers, ones whose choices are unique and original. Usually they've had professional experience and obviously aren't afraid of the computer. We've hired animators experienced with traditional hand-drawn, stop-motion, computer, and puppetry techniques.

What is your advice to improve animation skills?

If you like to draw, set yourself up with a computer with a pencil test program. Or get into a computer program and start playing around with it. But start simple. Don't try to make epic films. Do short scenes that challenge your current abilities. Start by animating a bouncing ball. Animate a box jumping over a ball. Keep it simple and short. And watch anything that has a great quality of timing about it, whether it is a Chuck Jones cartoon or a Buster Keaton film. Observe what makes it funny. Try to get that same timing into your own work. During my art-school days, I remember learning a lot about painting from copying master paintings. Always work from the general to the specific. Work loosely and quickly with your blocking, and tie it down as you go. Like anything else, getting better at animation will take a lot of practice.

Thanks to Scott Clark for his frank insight into the real world of character animation! Did you notice in the interview those threads we mentioned earlier? In this chapter, we weave those threads into a character performance. But before we do that, we must begin with a plan.

Ollie Johnston says that an animator should allocate about half of his animation time to planning. An animator friend reports that her informal surveys of animators at a major studio where she works revealed that only about half of the animators actually planned their animations. Their response puzzled her. She inquired why these animators did not regularly plan their work; most said they did not really know. Some animators added that things seemed to have gone better when they did. They just forgot to plan.

So, lest we forget, let's look at this process of planning an animation.

First Steps: Planning Your Animation

The process of planning your animation can be summarized in four steps. First, you define your expectations and record them. Next, you research the motion you will animate. Third, you add context to the motion. Finally, you create a composite performance, bringing the best of your ideas into a single performance. With this guide, we can proceed.

Character animation is hard. At least, it is not as easy as is widely believed. It requires patience, attention to detail, and vast amounts of energy. You must also know your tools very well so that you can spend your energy telling your story well.

Animating characters is a lot like creating blind contour drawings in drawing class. First, you have to slow your mental processes way down to get attuned to the details. Then you have to focus on the task, to the exclusion of all other tasks.

Life-Long Learning Heroes

You will never stop learning about all the things that go into good character animation. The roots of skills in character animation delve deep into psychology, anatomy, kinesthetics, acting, performance, human perception, and computer science, among many other fields. Because of the scope and breadth of this work, it is difficult to provide a comprehensive methodology for character animation.

So, I present a methodology here that best reflects the teaching of many people in the character animation field. Significant among these people are Wayne Gilbert and Dave Sidley, from Industrial Light & Magic (ILM). As a long-term student of their tutelage, I have included much of their influence in the methodology I am presenting. Additional great teachers include Rex Grignon, Paul Davies, Ron Thornton, Steve Bailey, Kyle Clark, Jimmy Hayward, Oren Jacobs, Dave Sidley, and Wayne Gilbert among so many others. I dedicate this methodology to these and all my great teachers.

Step One: Capturing *Your* Vision

The first step in doing any animation is to know the predisposed attitudes and visions of the animation sequence or motion. You must do this before the research process ever begins, to preserve the energy derived from "your vision." Performing this much preparation work is important because character animation represents one of the few truly creative steps in production.

You see, most of the important creative decisions for any animation project are made in the preproduction phase of the project. In preproduction, the colors, staging, characters, location and settings, dialogue, lighting, and cinematography are designed. In fact, the only things you see on the screen that are not decided by the art department in preproduction are the character's behavior and his facial expressions.

Character animation defines the character's performance on a second-by-second basis in production. To keep that creativity alive, especially after adjustments from the director, lead animator, and the like, you must record your initial vision. Capturing your vision first keeps you, the animator, excited about the animation and holds the key for your personal satisfaction.

In the animation-planning step, you want to define two important things: energy sources and preconceived misconceptions. *Energy sources* are those parts of the internal movie of your imagination from which you get power and awe. These visions are the ones that will empower you and drive you to finish this *Parking Spot*, or any other, animation.

Professional animators are often surprised by how different their expectations are when compared to reality. We watch things move daily, but we don't really see what is happening until we focus our attention on the study of these motions. So, a good reason to define your expectations is to help root out misconceptions about how things move.

By misconceptions, we mean to describe the mind's impression of how movement takes place. Our impressions might not be accurate when compared to reality. However, they are valuable because these are areas where our understanding of real world movement need a tune up.

People say "blind as a bat," yet bats have perfectly good eyesight and are not blind at all. At night, when vision is less useful, bats navigate by echolocation, a sonic location skill that they use for night hunting and navigation. Yet, we can use this information for both planning a bat animation and incorporating expectations into our plan.

Consider making an animation of a horse running. How do the legs move for a horse? What is the firing order of the legs? Does a horse move front left, front right, rear left, and rear right? Or is it front left, rear right, and so on? Stop and think about your expectations about how horses run. Surely, you have seen horses run.

It might be difficult to define this horse motion, but you won't really know until you try to write it down. Stop for minute now and commit to how a horse walks. Don't read on until you have written your impression.

Did you get the horse movement? The correct answer is that horses have a transverse gait. They move front left, front right, rear left, and then rear right.

Consider the section in Chapter 2, "Project Overview," in which we discuss how the *Parking Spot* project was being created. You might remember Mark Adams's vivid vision of the water splashing from the fire hydrant and onto The Jerk. Just from reading that section, you get an indication of the energy Mark had for this shot: his vision. A vision like this creates the energy in a scene and keeps the animator's interest and commitment.

The other major reason for defining what you think you know is that your vision of the motion will be at least preliminarily based on your imagination of what the scene will look like and how the characters will behave. You will quickly lose this preliminary vision when you begin researching and investigating the motion. You must try to capture as best you can your vision that gives your animation life.

This idea of capturing your preconceived ideas has existed for artists for many years. Natalie Cooper, scriptwriting consultant and teacher for ILM, Pixar, and others, provides us with insight about Picasso's inspiration. Picasso recognized that his paintings were attempts to capture the visions in his mind's eye. His vision was both the source and the goal of his paintings.

To help clarify this capturing of ideas, Picasso said that when he painted, he got a vision, an idea. This was the one true essential vision of what he wanted to paint or draw. This idea was the impetus for him to try to create that vision in physical media. The process drove him to work at this vision until he could get no closer. His final painting was his best attempt to satisfy that first vision.

Animators, too, have visions of how their characters will move and what they will be doing. However, before research destroys that kernel of an idea, the animator must capture it, to keep the work that follows alive and purposeful. This is why there is such a sense of relief at the end of a sequence. The work is as close to the idea as time and sense permit.

For the animator, it is useful to resolve in shorthand the motion and excitement of the scene as the animator sees it. This can be done using simple drawings using pencil and paper. For these character motions, most professional animators use simplified versions of their characters to show the position and movement in a simplified form. It is like a blueprint for the motion.

Many animators use stick figures to define the poses of the characters in the flow of the performance. Often these poses are linked to a line of dialogue or an imagined line of dialogue that best fits the character and the circumstances.

Begin with a drawn previsualization. I recommend starting with stick figures such as those shown in Figures 15.5 and 15.6. Because we are working with The Jerk character, the stick figure has similar proportions to help with his movement. The character stick figure can be manipulated into poses and give an idea of what the movement might look like.

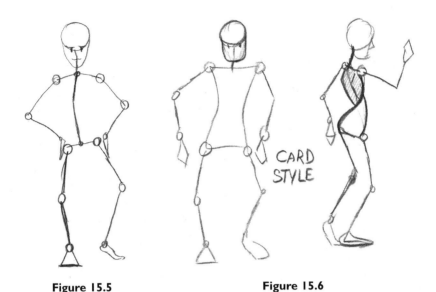

Figure 15.5   **Figure 15.6**

Figure 15.5 shows a simple character structure that an animator can use easily to describe the poses the character will take—simple, yet effective. Figure 15.6 shows a card-style character that is like the card soldiers in *Alice in Wonderland*. Some animators like this style because it shows the torsion of the torso more clearly.

Note

One of the best references for simple drawing techniques that support the planning of animation projects is Wayne Gilbert's *Simplified Drawing for Planning Animation*, available through www.anamie.com.

When you begin to draw your character thumbnails, you might want to use a mannequin to help with the perspective and pose (see Figure 15.7). Mannequins are often good for simple poses and for getting a clear picture of where the weight of a pose should be. However, I often find that wooden mannequins have very limited motion, and this makes posing extreme poses more difficult. There are mannequins for people, horses, and more; some can get very expensive. However, I recommend exploring this avenue to see if you can get results.

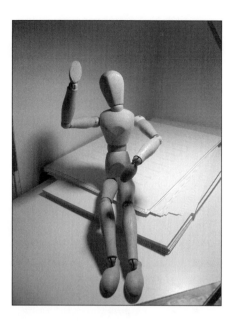

Figure 15.7   This is a small standard female mannequin
who is posing on my drawing table. The movement is not very flexible,
but within limits, it can give a good approximation of a pose.

Increasingly, today's modern animators find it useful to use programs such as Poser to get the character poses that they want. If you haven't tried to use programs such as Poser, you might discover a font of creativity, if only for a while. And there are ways to export the Poser-posed character into Maya, to use as reference for your character.

Note

Reiss offers a Maya plug-in program for bringing your Poser character into Maya. For more information, visit www.reiss-studio.com.

I still prefer the traditional drawing method because it is portable enough to do while waiting in a grocery line or while commuting.

Another advantage to using the pencil-and-paper method is that you can define the text or subtext that forms the character's thoughts, intentions, and motivation on a pose-by-pose basis. Text is often considered to be what a character actually says or does, such as shaking hands and saying "Hello." Subtext is what is really going on in the character's mind, such as shaking the hand of an evil villain and trying not to let it show that he knows who he is (see Figure 15.8).

TEXT:
Howdy!

SUB-TEXT:
HOPE THEY
DON'T NOTICE
I'M
NAKED !!!

Figure 15.8   This pose shows the written
text and the subtext. The text is a wave for hello.
The subtext is embarrassment from being naked!
Both play a role in the pose and the story.

In acting, "the method" describes a way of dealing with text and subtext. The actor vocalizes the subtext and then the text. So, in the example of shaking hands, the actor says, "You dirty bastard" and then "hello." This new expression of "hello" is more complex and interesting than the first one because it contains both text and subtext. This more complex form of communication is necessary for a good story and audience appreciation. In the take, the actor thinks the subtext and says the text.

Note

For a great book on how actors do their magic, check out *Strasberg's Method: As Taught by Lorrie Hull: A Practical Guide for Actors, Directors, and Teachers* (Ox Bow Press, 1985), by S. Loraine Hull. The book is out of print, but copies are available through used-book channels.

When you define both text and subtext, be sure to show which is which. I often use parentheses or a different colored pencil to provide this distinction. If you are working with actors who have already been audio taped, you will have to work with the director and videotaped looping session to get the text and subtext queues.

Getting on with our scene, we have to look at the text of the script to get our own visual perception of the scene and action. For our scene, we've select the part of the story in which The Jerk approaches the dog, Spot.

As The Jerk gets out of the car, he checks his watch (it's late in the day) and looks at a note that reads "Buy Billy's present." He turns to see an approaching meter maid who is just down the block. The Jerk goes to the meter, but as he reaches to put in the coin, Spot snarls and snaps, thwarting his first effort.

So, we begin the process of establishing our first impressions for this sequence of shots. In animation, the scripts are often longer than they are in film. In film, we know that a page of a script is about a minute on the screen. However, in animation this might not hold up.

Therefore, the first thing to do is to watch this scene play out in your head. Let your imagination give the scene life and feel what is the most important part of the shot. Your mileage might vary, but my strongest image is that moment when The Jerk goes to put in the coin and is confronted by Spot.

If you are game, this is the right time to stop reading and begin sketching your stick figures for the shot we defined here. I would appreciate seeing your work, if you want to send it to me (`Will@deanima.com`). Stop and do the poses now!

Back? Okay, here is my vision: I imagine The Jerk leaning forward with an outstretched arm and then, after Spot's growling and snapping, pulling back in fear. To me, this seems to be the strongest part of the sequence because it best represents the conflict between our protagonist (Spot) and our antagonist (The Jerk).

Figure 15.9 shows a version of our story from one of my animation students at Cogswell Polytechnic College, named James Bettencourt. His drawing shows the poses that he imagines for this action. Note that he has written in the thoughts of our character in each pose. This idea of a mini-script is examined later.

Figure 15.9   This image shows the poses imagined or expected by animator James Bettencourt. He uses a simple stick figure, but the poses are clear.

Let's assume that I am the animator for The Jerk. My first step is to create a line of action for The Jerk's poses. A *line of action* is a traditional animation approach that creates lines that represent the pose. My imagination says that there are at least three poses. The Jerk goes toward the meter with a coin. He must have gotten the coin from his pocket, so that might be a pose. He cringes from Spot's snarling and nipping (see Figure 15.10).

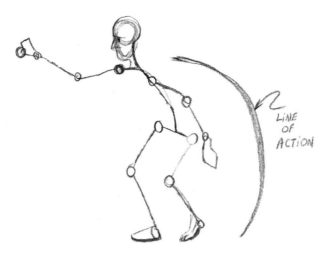

Figure 15.10   This image shows a line of action at the right
and the pose that follows that line of action at the left.

The strongest line-of-action changes occur when a line of action is reversed. In the image, The Jerk's approach toward the meter is a forward-sweeping line, shaped like a loose, backward C-shape pose leaning to the left. This shape is reversed when he pulls back from being startled by Spot: a forward C-shape pose (see Figure 15.11). The contrast between these poses provides an interesting change in pose from the side. Yet, you still have to deal with the coin pose.

Figure 15.11   This image shows the startled pose that
immediately follows the pose in Figure 15.10.
Note the reversal of the pose shapes from
concave in Figure 15.10 to convex in this figure.

Some directors would prefer to have a neutral pose to catch the audience when the aforementioned reversal takes place. However, others would contend that the audience will be better set up by the forward C-shape for this pose as well because it, too, contrasts better with what follows. My imagination has The Jerk in a contorted pose in which he is still looking back toward the meter maid and digging in his pocket for an appropriate coin. This weird pose can help set up the audience with some anticipation that something is about to happen.

What does it mean to hold a weird pose? Well, it is an attempt to create an interesting and, hopefully, funny image that Frank and Ollie call the tableau gag in their book *Too Funny for Words: Disney's Greatest Sight Gags* (Abbeville Promotional, 1990).

The tableau gag happens when your animation brings the character into a funny still pose. One of the best examples is just after the pie is thrown into the protagonist's face and we watch the eyes open behind the whipped cream. The camera holds on this tableau while we laugh at the misfortune of the protagonist.

Examples of the *line of action* and the poses are shown in Figures 15.10 and 15.11. I imagine that these are being shot in nearly a full shot from the side, to give the poses the best staging. These are by no means the only way to shoot this scene, but it is the vision that I see and that fuels my working with it. My vision will be modified by my research, but I know and have put down my vision for review.

Figures 15.12 through 15.16 show my thumbnails in order.

Figures 15.12 through 15.16 These are the key poses I imagined for The Jerk in this scene of *Parking Spot.* Notice that I am reversing the inflection in each pose.

If you are a working animator, you will keep this kind of work in a notebook or on sheets of paper that you hide from anybody else. You can get some insight from Disney animator and author Shamus (Jimmy) Culhane. Culhane wrote two books on animation: *Talking Animals and Other People* (DaCapo Press, 1998) and *Animation from Script to Screen* (St. Martin's Press, 1990).

Culhane says that you should not tell your visions to others, for two reasons. His first is: When you explain your vision to others, your story has been told and there is no reason to animate it. The motivation wanes.

His second reason is that the other animator might steal your idea. Because this is your resource, you should treat it with care. You will need this later for motivation and insight.

Now if you have completed these exercises, we have defined what we expect in the scene. We can now begin to research the scene and determine whether we were accurate and precise. I have just done a part of the scene in which The Jerk does a few moves.

However, you can easily see the process and extend it to the entire sequence or other sequences using the same technique. For example, often we expect animals to behave in a particular way, only to discover that our expectations are not accurate. But this will be revealed in the research part of our character animation journey.

You might not have gotten the same results as I did, and that's to be expected. You will—and should—see differences between animators. Some animators believe that you can animate only yourself. So, if your results differed from mine, you now have two exercises to complete this learning process. Let's go.

Step Two: Researching the Motion

Before you can create a character's performance, you have to know how the character will behave: the character's nature. One's behavior is often the result of both physical and mental history.

Whenever actors are interviewed on the Bravo Channel's television series *In the Actor's Studio*, they are quick to point out the time they spend researching a role. Dennis Quaid spoke of spending three months with the New Orleans homicide division before he was comfortable with his role in *The Big Easy*. Quaid explained that he became familiar with the difficulty homicide police face as they deal with the most extreme situations daily. These policemen and women become affected by the violence and can survive only by becoming hardened to the world's cruelty.

This kind of research that the animator does for each character is called *acting research*. Animators are called "actors with pencils" just for this reason. Animators use pencils (or, in our case, the 100-pound pencil known as a computer) to create performances that reflect the character's thoughts and motivations. We want to research the character to define who he is and how he moves.

But before we do this research, it is important to understand the goal of the research process. We want to create a composite performance based on our observations, experiments, and sense of motion. We will select from these inputs a composite performance that best entertains and moves the story forward.

Unlike the role of actors, who must create a performance on demand, we have the luxury of planning and editing before we even begin to animate. Unlike editors, who must get the best shots from among those taken, we can plan our actions in advance to create the scene we want to convey to the audience. Animation has elements in common with the actor and the editor, but our lot is very different.

So, we want to gather information and performances from people we can see and meet to fill up our reservoir of performances from which our final performance palette can be drawn. We can begin by simply watching people who are like our character. Or, we can begin with questions about who the character is.

To begin our research, we might start with some superficial analysis of the scene. The shot we plan to animate has a simple text. The actions are as follows: first, find the coin; second, try to put the coin in the meter; and third, pull back in fear. This is our superficial or text-level analysis: This is what our character does. It does not tell us much about *how* this action is performed—in other words, the subtext.

Let's add some subtext to the scene that gives color and character to the action. Look at what makes The Jerk work. Find what is important to The Jerk. Find out why that is important to him. This will help us understand his motivation and inner conflicts, which will form the texture of our subtext.

Who Is The Jerk, and Why Do We Care?

Before you can create a character's performance, you have to know how the character will behave: the character's nature. As noted earlier, one's behavior is often the result of both physical and mental history.

One of the most important parts of research is to define who your character is. It is not enough to approach this task without preparation because it is from this basic understanding that the animation will proceed. Every character, whether human or not, interacts with its world in a unique way.

A character might limp due to a childhood injury, a bane of his frailty. The limp might be faked to invite the sympathy of strangers. Each character brings to a story the baggage of where it has been and what it is doing. We who would walk in his path must know the character's history and habits.

The most effective way of discerning who your character is, is to begin to define a *backstory*. The backstory has information about the character that supports the role played in the animation. So, let's look at the character of our Jerk, as explained by Max Sims:

- **What is the Jerk's biggest fear?**—He fears that others will discover he is a phony. He really is a phony. He claims to be a great salesman, but, in fact, The Jerk landed a recent big sale merely because he was in the right place at the right time.

  This big sale did not result from anything he did or did not do; he was just lucky. He claims it is skill. Many people are fooled into thinking The Jerk is a cool guy. But The Jerk is benefiting from the work of others and won't admit it.

- **What is The Jerk's orientation to the rest of the world?**—The Jerk believes that the world centers on him. Anything that anyone does is to please or soothe him. If a person is not pleasing him, The Jerk will try to cajole them into compliance. If that fails, The Jerk will go out of his way to make sure that that person will not get in his way.

  He has no pets. They would complicate his life. It is all about him!

- **Could The Jerk actually fight with someone?**—The Jerk could definitely fight with someone. He might not win, but he'd put up a good fight. He probably would come out even.

- **Why is The Jerk a salesman?**—He enjoys the lifestyle. You really don't have to do anything, as he is proving. He loves to flaunt the trappings of success: He drives the coolest car and owns the coolest things—and why not? He believes he deserves them!

- **Is The Jerk athletic?**—His father was a football coach. His mom was a housewife. He played football for his dad but stopped at the high school level. He was so-so at football and got his place on the team because of his relationships. The Jerk played quarterback, but he was pretty much unremarkable in his years playing. This lack of skill prevented him from pursuing a career in sports.

- **Does he have a girlfriend?**—He has several girlfriends, each of whom does not know about the others. He does not want them to know about each other. Most of these women are gold diggers. They wanted somebody handsome to be around who would spend money on them. They, in turn, are attractive and help him show off. Relationships are superficial. The Jerk is a philanderer.

- **What is his favorite hobby?**—The Jerk likes to cruise around in his car or make the scene—anywhere that he can be seen, and be seen to be cool. That's his hobby. He does not play sports, but he loves to watch and bet on football games. He likes to show off his media center and drink beer with the guys. He drinks only to be social.

  He plays golf, but he cheats. His scores are not that bad, but he cheats nonetheless. When he plays with customers, he keeps it honest, allowing them the chance to beat him. He might lose if he is playing against a promising client.

  He has never been injured, and he is a great dodgeball player. He is a Teflon kind of guy: Nothing sticks to him.

- **What college did he attend?**—He attended Loyola University on the north side of Chicago. He was a Catholic but is no longer practicing. In former days, he was an altar boy. But, as with many today, he has lost the spirit.

Well, there is some insight into who our Jerk is as a person. Although this might seem pointless, it gives us tools with which to build a characterization of The Jerk. We can look with some new insight into his behaviors and how he manages to move.

We might be able to put ourselves into his character as an improvisation and try to behave like The Jerk would in our own daily activities. This can be illuminating to try to think like The Jerk and behave in your own environment. Improvisation is an important keystone in the animator's world for just this reason. It is very useful to use improvisational exercises to find the character.

As you can see, becoming the character you are animating is the key to getting a believable performance out of your character. Often beginning students move the character around the stage without understanding what the character is thinking. They are surprised that the audience sees that the character is not thinking anything. In this case, the character is just moving like a digital puppet, with no intentions. Audiences tune out characters that are just going through the motions to move.

So, acting is an important skill and should be developed. Improvisation is one of the most important elements of performance skills as applied to animation. Improvisation gives the animator a way to explore what the character is thinking and doing. Pantomime is a valuable skill for animators because it forces the animator to show thoughts visually, but pantomime is inherently "pretending" to move and act. We are searching for the truth of our Jerk character.

Note

Ace Miles is an animator, mime, juggler, ventriloquist, fire eater, sword swallower, and more. He has been a mentor and inspiration to me. Ace has taught at local colleges and showed the relationship between his skills, especially animation and acting. Look for his award-winning animation work from FatBox and his live-action performances all around the San Francisco Bay area.

Now, along with acting, we can do some research about the psychology of our character.

Psychological Research: Mini-Script Theory

Animation teachers point out that there is a difference between acting and action. *Action* is movement based on external forces. The wind blows our character and the empty cup in the gutter with the same force. There is only reaction to the wind, no motivation.

Acting, however, means engaging the character's will: an internal motivation. The story is based on the protagonist's desire being thwarted. Without internal motivation, there is no story. Character animation, then, must consider internal motivation.

Just as a script provides a dialogue for the character's performance and suggests his or her motivation in a play or movie, the *mini-script* is a mental dialogue defining the character's second-by-second thoughts during a given performance. *Mini-script theory* can be defined as the process of delineating the second-by-second thought process that a character experiences while performing a particular behavior or set of behaviors.

The idea of mini-script theory is based on the work of Taibi Kahler, who noted that people's life scripts are recapitulated in their moment-by-moment behaviors. Kahler's work informs character animators who use this moment-by-moment thought process to create the motivation for the performances of their digital actors. Creating and refining this thought process informs the pose and the performance of the character.

Recently, the mini-script has resurfaced in lie detection studies as *microexpressions*. A microexpression is momentary slip, or "leak," of true reaction, lasting only a fraction of a second, before the control of facial expression can be regained. This is a good tool for animators to use for facial expression work, allowing a means to convey plot and subplot on the same face.

Note

Microexpression is part of a continuing investigation on behavioral lie detection. You can learn more from the review article by Michael Decaire at: `http://www.suite101.com/article.cfm/forensic_psychology/54808`.

The utility of this process of assigning some thought patterns to specific behavior patterns is that the poses tend to have better behavior continuity and the character has a defined business at each pose. All too often, characters are moved without thought or mental dialogue, and the performance seems flat and thoughtless. Character animators consider the inner dialogue that the character experiences as he or she performs behaviors on a second-by-second, pose-by-pose basis.

For a character to show what he or she is thinking, the animator has to know and define that inner dialogue to guide and define what the character is thinking. Thus, the behavior can better tell what the character is thinking. By defining this thought process the animator is better able to give continuity of thought, intent, and feeling to a performance.

Consider, for example, our protagonist checking the mailbox. In itself, this might not be a very entertaining performance. If we add motivation, the performance changes and our interest piques. The protagonist leaps and pirouettes toward the mailbox, anticipating that epistle from the love object. Or, the protagonist moves with dread toward the mailbox to collect another batch of ultimatums and threats from the unrelenting bill collectors. The performance will vary according to the internal dialogue of the character—his or her mini-script.

However, mini-script theory has roots that go back to the tradition of the masters. For example, in *The Animation Process, Notes on a Lecture by Ollie Johnston*, Ham Luske presents these statements by the noted lecturer:

- **Don't illustrate words or mechanical movements.** Illustrate ideas or thoughts, with the attitudes and actions.

- **What is the character thinking?** The thought and circumstances behind the action make the action interesting: For example, a man walks up to a mailbox and drops his letter and walks away, or a man desperately in love with a girl far away carefully mails a letter, in which he has poured out his heart (what I would call subtext).

- **Don't move anything without purpose.** The facial expression should not be contradicted by the body. The entire pose should express the thought.

The idea of mini-scripting was well entrenched in Disney from the beginning, although it was not called by this name then.

The Jerk is in this world for himself. He has found a niche in which he can be regarded as successful even though he does nothing to deserve it. The Jerk believes that it is better to look good than to actually be good. He has to be perfect.

People who have to be perfect are usually disappointed because the world is not perfect and things can happen. They set themselves up for failure by assuming that surely some things can be trusted. Maybe this is a reoccurring theme to his life: over-plan, run into difficulties, struggle and fail, and then put a spin on the story to look good.

You can imagine that anybody who tries to be perfect will run into difficulties. This personality has to ignore failures and live in a fantasy, or to put effort only into sure things that will be likely successes. Risk-averse behavior, coupled with low tolerance for failure, means that spin will be put on everything to make it all seem triumphant.

If you know someone like The Jerk, you might hang around this person and note the behaviors. You can even ask backstory questions and inquire about specific attitudes and the like. This kind of research can give your character the memories that bring it life.

Story Research

Most well-written stories have what's called a *story arc*. The arc describes the changing values in a story over time. Values such as love or happiness can have positive or negative states. We can be in love at the start of a scene and then hopelessly forlorn and rejected at the end. The scene can start with our hero in a state of sadness, and at the end of that scene the hero can find bliss. Hopefully, each scene we work on will show a turn in value. So, the audience will watch such scenes with interest to find out what will happen next.

Because things generally crescendo toward a peak in the story, the timing and level of action will necessarily change during the course of the story. That is, if there is a fight at the beginning of the story, it should be less violent or challenging than the fight in the middle of the story. If not, the middle will seem tame to the audience.

So, too, the action in our story should be tempered in timing and exaggeration to meet the expected level of this part of the story. Thus, we must examine the story to see whether this scene is played to the hilt or if it has to be the quiet before the storm.

If your animation is intended to fit in a larger context, it should reflect that context in mood, tone, timing, and spacing. You must examine and research the story to ensure that your part will integrate with the larger whole.

Motion Research

Consider our first stop in researching the motion to be the use of live-action reference or motion research.

Motion research is one of the most rewarding areas for an animator to pursue. In this area of research, you and your team or friends act out your character's performance. This means that each actor uses improvisation to perform the action as they all interpret the script and context.

For many years, it was taught that long, full-length mirrors were useful for performance environments. It was thought that the actor could watch and perform at the same time and take down notes on the performance. It never worked well.

After years of trying, most have come to the conclusion that when you try to be both actor and audience for a performance, both sides suffer. It is clear that a better way is to perform these motions using a video camera or the equivalent. This method provides a faithful recording of the performance and a freer performance without worries of recording.

When captured in the camera, the video can be studied for weight distribution, timing, and the like. This frees the actor to act and become the character.

Note

For an example of this acting out of the character's behavior, see the file JamesActing.avi, on the CD that accompanies this book. James Bettencourt again acts out this scene for reference.

Tip

It should be noted that videotaping in front of a full-length mirror can also record another view angle at the same time. Good planning of your camera angle will permit this.

This additional improvisation can help reveal more of the character's motivation and subtext. Using a variety of actors, composed of any willing friends, coworkers, relatives, or the like, provides a variety of interpretations of the motion. This is a good thing.

The more different approaches you can cajole from your actors, the richer the palette is that your action can be modeled after. Here, variety is to be sought. Find the nuances among the performances, and use them to inform your final composite performance.

Reference Footage

Early in 1876, California's Gov. Leyland Stanford made a bet. As a horse lover, he thought that when horses ran, sometimes all four of the horses' hooves were off the ground. The betting parties put up a reward of some $20,000 to anybody who could prove the result one way or another.

Edwierd Muybridge was an experimental photographer who was enchanted with photographing motion. His early studies suggested that he might be able to resolve Stanford's bet. And $20,000 was a lot of money in those days!

Muybridge did finally resolve the bet after three years of work. He did it by using multiple cameras tied to fine thread that fired the cameras as the horses ran through them, one by one. Muybridge invested this reward for solving Stanford's bet into many motion studies that are published in his books on human and animal motion. You can find these books in libraries or even buy copies on the Internet.

Muybridge proved with his technique that horses do leave the ground with all four legs during the run cycle. Today we use this as the definition of a run: when, during the motion, all legs are off the ground for a part of the motion. Stanford won his bet and later donated his horse farm. The farm became the university named for him: Stanford University. It seems strange, but for the last 100 years, nobody has supplanted Muybridge's research on motion. And today, as in the years before, the images Muybridge took have been used as motion reference for animators.

Many web sites have turned the image sequences of the Muybrige publications into short movies or animated GIFs. You can find these through your favorite search engine. They can be more useful than the book because they are already scanned into the computer and are ready to use.

Note

More modern sources for motion exist, although few seem to hold up against Muybridge's work. One to look at is the *Human Figure in Motion,* by Holiday Interactive. This is a CD-ROM that has a variety of motions captured in front and side views, and it serves as a good reference for animation. You can find it at www.finley-holiday.com.

The advantage to using reference footage is that it is ready to use, with no performance necessary. The disadvantage is that you can almost never find an action that matches what you want to do. Many of Muybridge's motions are old and outdated. The actions are for things that are rarely done a mere 100 years later. However, this can provide ideas for motion.

Motion Capture

Occasionally, reference motions are available from motion-capture systems on the web. Motion capture is very controversial, as was its former counterpart, rotoscoping. The issue revolves around whether motion capture is sufficient to supplant hand animation of a character, and whether it is desired or artistic.

Pixar allegedly called motion capture the devil's rotoscope. Yet, motion-capture footage increasingly is finding its way into animation (consider the performance of Andy Serkis, the English character actor who supplied the voice of Gollam/Smeagol in *Lord of the Rings: The Two Towers*, done using motion capture and Maya). Here is a brief look at motion capture from my perspective.

Motion capture is a tool, among many, that can be used to get the animation job completed. Misuse and poor application of the technique should not be used to condemn the process, although many such misapplications exist.

The Fleischer brothers invented rotoscoping in 1926. The patent was for a method that would allow Max Fleischer to photograph Dave Fleischer, who was wearing his Koko the Klown suit, and project the movie, frame by frame, onto a tracing screen. The result was realistic motion, but it did not work.

Critics and audiences alike found the rotoscoped motion to be flat and lifeless. Characters who were animated the traditional way had much more appeal. Photorealistic motion was not what the audience expected from animation. Audiences wanted more than just a copy of reality. They weren't sure what was missing; they just wanted more.

As you might expect, Disney examined rotoscoping and used it for parts of *Snow White*. However, Disney later denied using it and rejected the technique because the animation looked too stiff and flat. Disney's examination convinced them that they wanted—even expected—to see more exaggeration in the movement.

These experiments with rotoscoping led Disney animators to their famous "believable, not realistic" philosophy of animated motion. This same philosophy re-emerged when the idea of motion capture became popular just a few years ago.

The problem with motion capture is the same as that of rotoscoping. However, newer solutions to the problem are arising. First, you can instruct a talented actor to overact or exaggerate the motion in a particular way so that it shows up in the mocap performance.

Today well-trained animators and directors for motion capture can get believable performances from the relevant performers. Good planning and technical direction can provide the necessary motion reference.

Furthermore, newer tools in analytical and editing software have enhanced the possibility of controlling the performance with greater accuracy. However, even if you believe that mocap is evil, it can serve as reference motion to help inform your animation of what realistic motion would look like.

In less than five years, according to many researchers, software will be available commercially that will be capable of converting any video source to three-dimensional data sets. This means that you could capture a clip from *Top Hat* and have your character dance like Fred Astaire.

Video Research

One area that provides resource information for movement is the DVD and videotape collection that many people have already gathered. Finding a spot in a film with the appropriate motion can be difficult, but if your memory is good, you can use this kind of reference.

If your collection is small, you can use a Blockbuster or other video rental source to find the movie in question. Often the recycling of motion from one film to another can be advantageous, if the first movie was successful.

Tip

Some web sites allow you to search movie databases for pertinent scenes. One such site, `http://us.imdb.com`, is often recommended.

As you can see, there are many potential sources of motion reference. The best is that which the animator and his team perform. This provides the most complete experience for the animator and generates data directly relevant to the motion in question.

After the composite performance is created from the reference footage, it can be recorded as a series of poses that work as shorthand for the motions selected. Some animators prefer to act out the final composite performance and videotape it to ensure that the timing and feeling are right. When the composite performance is set, you can then compare it against the principles of animation, covered next, for development of a final composite.

The Principles of Animation

It seems that there are no rules in animation. Any rule you can name can have both an animation that is both successful and one that breaks the rules you cite. So, it seems that we will have no clear guidance in how to construct an animation.

However, the animation researchers at Disney in the 1920s and 1930s put together a series of principles, not rules, to help guide the animator in planning and making the animation. These principles are based on research and testing done during those days. They remain intact even now by all considered masters in animation. Let's take a look at these principles to help understand how they can inform our animation.

You can find any number of animation principles from many sources, but the one main source for the principles of animation comes from the book *Disney Animation: The Illusion of Life* (Abbeville Press, 1987), by Frank Thomas and Ollie Johnston. In this book, Thomas and Johnston present their classical "12 Principles of Animation." They are as follows:

- Appeal
- Solid drawing
- Anticipation
- Secondary action
- Arc
- Follow-through and overlap
- Exaggeration
- Staging
- Timing
- Straight-ahead versus pose-to-pose animation
- Slow in/slow out
- Squash and stretch

These principles are so important that most advanced animation classes usually start from these. For example, Richard Williams uses these principles for his live seminar. Williams is the animator of Roger Rabbit from the Warner Bros. film *Who Framed Roger Rabbit?* and is the author of the *Animator's Survival Kit* (Faber & Faber, 2002). Williams considers these principles fundamental, so mastering them is a good first step.

Most students find it difficult to remember these principles. George A. Miller, a psychologist who published his landmark paper, "Magic Number Seven, Plus or Minus Two: Some Limits on Our Capacity for Processing Information" (*The Psychological Review*, 1955, Volume 63, pages 81–97), showed that people can remember 7 things, but not 12. See, it's not your fault—you were just drawn that way!

So, to help my students remember these principles, I break them down into functional blocks that make them easier to remember and apply. We use these principles when examining animation, which we call *dailies*, and they help to analyze the animation movement. Therefore, I present the grouping I use to help you remember and apply the principles of animation.

CAPS

One of the first things I present is the framework for this memory aid: CAPS. CAPS is a program built by ILM for Disney to automate the color on their animated films by computer. Then it stood for Computer Assisted Production System. Here, we use CAPS to remember the groups of principles.

C Is for Character

The first set of principles from Thomas and Johnston apply to character design. The two principles here are *appeal* and *solid drawing*. Appeal reminds us that our character must have some attractive design. This holds true even (and especially) for villains. This does not mean that everything has to look like a fuzzy bunny to be acceptable.

Appeal is more of a character's state of being and presence to the audience. It suggests the nature of the character's personality. Consider The Jerk. He is good-looking and thin. He is attractive on the outside, but not so on the inside. His good looks are a great counterpoint to his black heart. He is the paragon of the worst marketing person.

The second principle is called solid drawing, which came about in the 1920s to correct a problem with drawn animation of the day. People drew the characters as if they were flat. The rubber hose movement, despite its charm, was considered poor animation. Disney animators knew they could give the illusion of depth to the characters and proved this over the years. You can see how Mickey Mouse has changed as this principle developed.

You can see that as we move to computer animation, this principle still applies (or should apply) to Flash and other 2D media for animation in the computer. However, in the 3D world of Maya, this principle is a given. We make our objects and world in a virtual 3D space so that characters have depth and volume *automagically*.

Because 3D computer animation has this solid drawing principle built in, the principle can be disregarded. As long as you are building 3D models, you comply with the solid drawing principle. But beware of substitutes.

Many sources, both on the web and in books, try to replace this solid drawing principle with some other homemade principle. I have seen everything from "Know your medium" to "Personality" and more. Although these principles might have their place, they are not what Thomas and Johnston set forth. Stick with the genuine principles at the start.

Thus, we have examined two of the classical principles of animation related to characters. Ten to go.

A Is for A.S.A.F.E.

The second set of principles governs movement. Whenever an action takes place, we apply these principles to make our movement *action-safe*, or A.S.A.F.E. These principles are applied whenever we animate and whenever we critique an animation. They are a great way to examine classical animation as well.

Anticipation

Our first action-safe principle is anticipation, the first A in A.S.A.F.E. Anticipation is an action or a series of actions that sets up a bigger or more important action. You can think of anticipation as a wake-up call to the audience to get their attention. When we have their attention, we can deliver the action we need for them to see. Anticipation sets up the audience for the next action.

Because we are set with limbs that rotate, we often rotate back in preparation for moving forward. Anticipation often involves movement in the direction opposite to the main action.

Another example is the wind-up before the punch. The arm and shoulder move backward before the punch is delivered forward. The anticipation sets up the audience for the delivery of the action: a KO punch.

It is common to underestimate the utility of anticipation. Professionals know that anticipation provides extra footage, if you are getting paid by the foot. It is easy to add some anticipation to an action, to stretch it out or make it sweeter.

Secondary Action

The second letter in our A.S.A.F.E. scheme is S, which stands for secondary action. To understand what secondary action is, we have to first look at primary action.

The action necessary in the delivery of the next beat of the story is called the *primary action*. Primary action is the reason the scene is in the movie. The director has chosen an action to convey this beat, so we are animating that action.

However, we might also want to add some quality of character or color, some subtle tone or texture to this primary action. We can do this through a concurrent action that supports and adds meaning or character to the action. This subordinate action is called *secondary action*.

Secondary action can be due to the primary action, such as when the ponytail of a girl walking by bobs in rhythm. However, secondary action can reveal the subtext of the character—for example, when the character shakes hands with one hand and holds a tight fist with the other. We can use these secondary actions to add subtle nuance to action and meaning.

Secondary action must remain subordinate, or it becomes the primary action. If it becomes the primary action, it changes the beat of the story and the story itself. Make sure that the story remains the primary focus by keeping secondary action secondary.

When you think about secondary action, think of what else needs to be said in that beat of the story. Think of a way to put this into a physical action that is supportive of the primary action. This can be done for subtext or for nuance creation.

For example, consider our Jerk. He looks toward the meter maid and stares. Okay, but what is he thinking? Maybe his mini-script says, "Oh no, she's coming. No. Don't come. No. No." He can stare at the meter maid, which is our story beat, but he can shake his head and move his lips to "No. No." silently. This adds flavor to his stare and reveals more about what the character is thinking. We still know he is looking at the meter maid, but we added the sense of what he is thinking.

Arc

Arc is the motion of a ball joint. The limbs of mammals and many other creatures are based on ball joint construction. Hence, when we move our arms or legs, we move in arcs, rotating the limbs at the ball joint. The arc makes a natural and expected movement.

However, this is not just circumstantial. Disney animators in the 1920s and 1930s studied what audiences wanted to see. They discovered that people were attracted to the curved shape of an arc much more than the straight line. So, when we design paths of motion, we make sure that they take the form of an arc from the point of view of the camera.

Consider a pitcher. It would be possible to deliver a ball by throwing straight from the shoulder. However, it is much more interesting to show an arc of action for the pitcher. This simple change makes for a dramatic effect on the audience.

Disney conducted an analysis to which many authors ascribe the title of the most influential and powerful document ever generated by animators at Disney. This memo simply tries to get the animator to think of movement as an entity, not just the way to get from pose A to pose B. They said to think of motion as a unit and to put into that motion the arc, timing, and feeling of the beat. The idea of a motion path that has an arc from the POV of the camera is part of this concept, which we deal with later in the final stage of our animation exercise.

Follow-Through

Unless you are applying dynamics or some kind of animation procedural to the objects you are animating, your character will have no momentum. Because weight is only simulated in computer graphics, you must add it deliberately. This is not true in the real world.

In the real world, when a pitcher releases a ball, for example, his arm does not stop. The force and momentum of the pitcher's arm result in the continuation of the throwing motion in the arc of the pitcher's arm. This kind of motion that continues at the end of the main motion is called *follow-through*.

Actions don't just stop. The force and motion of the real world are almost expected by audiences today from 3D work, as it was in traditional animation. Often the follow-through completes the action and can include a twist for an action.

For example, a ballerina arches in anticipation and then executes a jump that is her main action. The follow-through could be that she slips and falls on her butt. The setup and action are in the ballet tradition, but the follow-through is far from typical for a ballet. This juxtaposed twist on her expected action gives a punch line to the follow-through.

Exaggeration

Robert McKee is an author and teacher of story telling in the movie tradition. His book, *Story: Substance, Structure, Style, and The Principles of Screenwriting* (Harper-Collins, 1997), has been a landmark for film screenwriters and has informed all the major animation studios. McKee, a Fullbright Scholar, is an award-winning film and television writer who has also served as project and talent development consultant to major studios.

McKee reminds us that if people wanted to see everyday behaviors, they would not go to theaters, but they would sit outside or at work and watch people behave normally. He suggests that what we really want is to see people pushed to the edge of their capabilities and limits. It is here that we really see what the characters are made of.

For animators, this means that we push the poses to the limits of the character's ability and rigging. The actions must be pushed further and be more demonstrative than ordinary actions. In short, make poses and actions bigger, bolder, and more "extreme."

A better understanding of this results later from our examination of the animated poses from planning and the dailies from our final animation.

P Is for Physicsssss

You probably noticed that I did not spell *physics* correctly. This is to help you remember the next group of animation principles. These principles are the only way animators have to communicate weight and the material nature of the objects you create in 3D.

Slow In, Slow Out

The first of these principles is called slow in, slow out. This is a single principle, and it means that you animate with momentum in mind. In the classroom, I have students play with a bowling ball and a super ball. The bowling ball has a dense mass; and when students push it, it takes quite an effort to get it moving.

When they try to stop the bowling ball, they are even more surprised at the force that is contained in a dense object that is on the move. So, for an object that is heavy, such as our bowling ball, movement is slow into an action and slow out of an action. The degree of slow in, slow out depends on the weight of the object.

This is key in communicating weight to your audience. A weight lifter picks up a heavy weight. If he lifts it easily, the audience does not think he is strong, but rather, that the object is light. If the audience sees that the object moves very slowly at first and then more quickly, the impression of weight can be achieved.

Slow in, slow out is now a default in most animation programs. Whenever a couple of keys are set, the program automatically puts in slow in and slow out, whether we want it or not. I have often called this the tyranny of slow in, slow out because in about half of the cases, I don't want this on my motion. Maya, like many other programs, does have this *automagically* enabled. So that tells us a lot about our object's weight. What about the nature of the material in the object?

Squash and Stretch

Squash and stretch is a principle of balance. When an external force acts upon an object, a level of deformation characterizes the changes it goes through. These distortions are relative to the forces applied, but they must be applied uniformly, or the audience will become bored and lose the magic of the moment that keeps them engaged.

Consider the bouncing ball exercise from 2D animation. The ball squashes on the ground when it hits because it has momentum or force pushing it down. The ball deforms according to the nature of its materials—the elasticity and such. Metal balls seem to deform less and have a more elastic bounce, while rubber balls have a lossy deformation that absorbs more of the energy as the ball's shape changes.

Like Scott Clark, other Pixar animators who also teach animation taught me about Lasseter's principle of animation called *faithfulness to materials*. In the world of 3D animation, the traditional squash and stretch doesn't match the audience's expectations for near-realism. For that reason, Pixar animates rigid bodies as such, while finding other ways to accomplish squash and stretch.

If you look at *Luxo, Jr.*, for example, there is squash and stretch, but it is accomplished through rotation at the joints. The lamps are made of steel, and the limbs don't bend. Only the hinges bend, but this is enough to accomplish squash and stretch.

Lasseter is cited as having said that problems combining the squash and stretch principle and the faithfulness to materials principle are based on character design. For example, consider a canister-model vacuum cleaner. We want the vacuum cleaner to act like a dog. The solid metal body will have to bend like the back of a carnivore to simulate the dog's movement. However, this violates Lasseter's principle of faithfulness to materials.

One fix to this problem is to redesign the character to include a bellows at the midsection of the canister vacuum cleaner. This bellows, made of rubber or some other more flexible material, allows the behavior we want with the structure we need.

S Is for STS

The last group of principles that completes Disney's classic 12 has to do with the idea of staging and presentation. These three principles are grouped together by the fact that they integrate the method of animation with the presentation of the motion.

The first principle in this group is called straight-ahead versus pose-to-pose animation. It is reported that most of the animation done in the industry is essentially pose-to-pose. For this reason, the *Parking Spot* animation is also pose-to-pose. However, this does not mean that straight-ahead animation has no relevance.

Straight-Ahead Versus Pose-to-Pose

Straight-ahead animation has a longer history, going back to 1910, when Starewich animated his bugs on film. Starewich's films used dead bug parts assembled with pins for hinges. The film was advanced one frame, and the character was posed again for movement from the previous frame.

However, because the time elapsed between poses was about 1/24th of a second, each new pose was only slightly different. The key idea was that the film was advanced one frame at a time, the character was posed, the frame was exposed, and the process moved forward one frame, straight ahead.

Straight-ahead animation is used today for stop- and go-motion puppetry. This long history of straight-ahead animation informs both real-world 3D animation and computer graphics 3D animation. The style of straight-ahead animation gives a unique look with smoother-looking motion.

If you want to learn this technique, you can use computer graphics to animate a character straight ahead, one frame at a time. Remember to put motion onto every part of the character in each frame. This keeps the fluidity of motion associated with straight-ahead animation. It is an exercise that every student of animation should undertake.

The difficulty in using straight-ahead animation in production is that when the animator begins, there is no way to know how long the animation will take. That is, neither the duration of the final shot nor the time to produce it is known. That makes it very difficult to determine how long a shot or a sequence will take in the movie. Things done straight-ahead have a unique style, but if there is a problem with the shot or sequence, the animator has to start over from the beginning.

Unlike the production-unfriendly straight-ahead method, the pose-to-pose approach works like the computer 3D software. From preproduction work, we know where our character has to be and when. We can pose the character and keyframe that frame in time. The sequence is exactly as long as we wanted it, by definition.

For the animator, the work is to get the movement between the key poses to look as good as possible, and the animation is complete. Furthermore, this production scheme allows for another of Lasseter's principles, called the layering principle, to take place.

Layering allows parts of the animation to be done at different times and by different people. For example, a junior animator can do the blocking, putting a character or stand-in model in the key locations and facing the right direction.

With this layer done, the scene can go simultaneously to lighting for preliminary lighting setup, to facial animation for the lip synch and facial expression, and again to the body pose animator. Layering allows for a division of labor in the animation industry.

So, is pose-to-pose better than straight-ahead animation? Well, the jury is still out in this regard. Many animators love the look of straight-ahead animation; it has a kind of life and movement that have mesmerized audiences for a century. Yet, pose-to-pose animation is very common in the industry.

One reason for the popularity of pose-to-pose animation is that computer software has been made to automatically provide the in-betweening for the animation. Even though this in-betweening is mechanical and needs human intervention, it is easier to edit than to make all the keyframes.

Furthermore, there is a strong influence today on poses. To a degree, this is due to both minimalism in animation production and the influence of Anime (Japanese traditional animation) and Manga (Japanese graphic novels). With production budgets smaller each year for television series, the simplification of animated films reduces the number of poses and in-betweens.

The popularity of Anime and Manga among artists and studios is a fact of globalization. However, the history of Anime, with its roots in Manga, is essentially an illustrated version of the Manga. Characters move between poses quickly, and what happens between poses is less important than the pose itself.

By contrast, Western animation has always been focused on what happens between the keyframes. The way characters move is the focus of Disney animation. So the stage is set to resolve these two styles into our new media. The relevance of pose-to-pose animation in this environment is clear.

The Hybrid

Many authors have suggested that a hybrid between these two styles exists and that such a hybrid gives the best animation. Sadly, there is really no such thing. You can set keyframes and move straight ahead to get to that pose, but most likely it will not be in the allotted time. So, you will have to scale or manipulate the animation in one way or another. This is messy business.

In fact, most animators use pose-to-pose animation to generate the number of shots needed in a modern production. The ease of computer-assisted animation is too strong of an inducement. Although there is evidence that animation experience in each method informs the resulting animation style, the hybrid is an unlikely result of two different methods.

Kinematics

It should be noted that either straight-ahead or pose-to-pose animation can be used for inverse or forward kinematics. There is no necessary relationship between the straight-ahead or pose-to-pose animation and inverse or forward kinematics. Again, the animator's preference and the desired outcome of the animation control the final choice in production.

Staging

Staging has to do with showing the animation so that the audience can read it clearly and easily. You can test whether the pose reads well by using Maya's IPR Render feature and clicking the Display Alpha Channel button. This displays a silhouette of the pose.

The silhouette should read clearly to the audience (see Figures 15.17 and 15.18), or the pose must be rethought (see Figures 15.19 and 15.20).

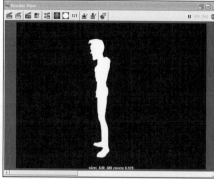

Figure 15.17 and 15.18   The silhouette for The Jerk is not very interesting in this staging of his pose. Neither the RGB image at the left nor the alpha channel silhouette reveals anything about The Jerk.

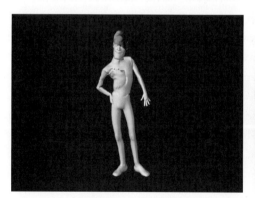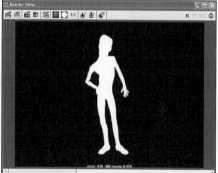

Figure 15.19 and Figure 15.20   These images show a much better staging of The Jerk's pose. Note the negative space created between arms and torso. This helps to make a pose more interesting and revealing.

Staging has as much to do with composition as animation. The roots of this concept date back to early theater. The people in the cheap seats should be able to understand and tell what's going on without having to hear well. That is, the story is in the actions and animation, not in the dialogue.

It is said that theater is based on dialogue, while film, including animated film, is based on visuals. If you watch television animation, the show is basically illustrated dialogue. You can test for yourself if you turn off the sound and watch the visuals. If you can tell what is going on, at least some of the story is in the visuals.

Notable among those shows that fail is *Beast Wars*. If you turn off the sound, you will still see impressive visuals and great CG character design. However, you will have no clue about the story and issues pertinent to that story without the audio channel. This is CG illustration, not animation.

Staging, then, implies that you have animated the story and will present the story in a convincing and worthy camera. Good staging tells a story. Great staging informs, involves, and influences the audience.

Timing

Two kinds of timing are present in any animation: small and big. By *big timing,* we mean the pacing of the film as it moves from the inciting incident through crisis of conflict and out to the denouement. Big timing describes the pace of the story of the animation.

Small timing refers to the timing of an action, shot, or gag. If you consider a simple action as a bend of the character, you can see the effect of timing. If the character bends slowly, he might be bowing in reverence or the like. However, if the bend speeds up, the action seems more military and subservient. If we increase the speed still, it seems that the character is ducking a thrown object or attack.

In these cases, the action is the same, but the timing is different. The change in timing changes our perception of the action. This is but one of the effects of the power of timing.

Timing is one of the most difficult things to learn, but it can be learned. Timing is explored in our implementation process during planning and animation. It is all-pervasive and all-encompassing.

So there is our last installment on the road of learning the 12 principles of animation. To get our four categories, we can use the CAPS *aide du memorie.* This functional breakdown of the principles of animation should make application, as well as memorization, easier and more effective. We will apply these principles where appropriate to our animation.

We can use these principles, and especially our action-safe (or A.S.A.F.E.) principles, to examine and develop our composite performance. We can use the A.S.A.F.E. principles to critique our animation and find places to strengthen our story and action.

The next step is to explore the action and behavior of the character, to understand what it can do and to determine whether it can perform our motion. This process, called breaking the model, is discussed next.

The Pose

Theater is about the narration and dialogue, while movies are about visual storytelling. The audience's view cannot be controlled in the theater the way we can control it in the movies. Consider how strange it would be to go to a play in which the audience had to physically move in toward the stage to simulate a close-up. Even if they took turns, the audience's experience would be boring.

However, one very important lesson learned from the theater carries over to film: the pose. The theater audiences toward the back of the theater (a.k.a. the cheap seats) have to be able to tell what is happening onstage without being able to hear everything. This is accomplished visually by the actor's poses.

In Kabuki, a traditional Japanese theater, the actors have the advantage that certain poses are known to trained audiences to mean certain things. When the actors strike a pose, the audience has a clear understanding of what that pose connotes. This close tie between the actor's body language and the audience's interpretation is quite a contrast with Western theater.

Note

Good reference and resource for Kabuki arts can be had from Mary Mariko Ohno, who teaches Kabuki in the Tacoma, Washington, area. Her web site is `http://webforce.nwrain.net/ kabuki/Academy.html`.

In Western theater, we don't have clear guidelines for the meaning of a pose. One can kneel in reverence, prayer, or despair; to plead; and so on. Therefore, actors and animators have to be clever when selecting the pose. The pose should be as clear as possible and as close to the connotation that you can muster.

For example, Figure 15.21 shows a number of poses from a pose library, with some connotations. Each animator should work to build a reference set of poses to help clearly communicate a character's feelings to the audience. You can improve your library of poses through testing. However, in my own testing, giving students just the poses and asking for the meaning or emotion of the pose, it is clear that Western theater supports no standards.

Figure 15.21   The Pose library shown here shows a starting point for you to build a library of poses. It is useful to create poses for different emotions for reference when you have less time to get an appropriate pose. The rows across show angry/mad poses, then sad poses, and, finally, glad poses.

Remember that these poses are not defined by set meanings; they depend on many factors, including connotation and audience. Therefore, we have to find a way to define the net effect of the pose on the audience.

One of the most effective ways to do this is to use the dailies procedure for evaluation of the scene. After the final poses are set, get a group of like-minded animators together to watch the sequence and the poses. This will provide some feedback on what is working and what is not.

It is better to work with trained and experienced animators in this endeavor. My mom always thinks that whatever I have done is great. This helps my ego, but not my art. Your work will be only as good as the level of your dailies participants.

I have seen a lot of work go up on web sites that are supposed to be oriented toward character animation. My experience with this goes something like this: A new animator puts up a horrible piece that looks not at all like human motion. Three of the five (likely inexperienced) animators say the piece is awesome. One says the character is too tall, and the other says the character's shoes should be brown. Although this is a bit of an exaggeration, it is essentially typical of what you get from nonprofessional or uncommitted critique.

This criticism is not to slam the web sites or the desire to get good critique for development of skills; rather, it's a concern based on respect for these very values. To those who would be better animators, I recommend that you find a local class or animator and get feedback. Professionalism here is in your best interest.

Now, to go back to Japanese tradition for a moment, you can look to Anime and Manga for good pose reference. Typically, the Japanese are very economical by using one pose for an extended time and then moving on to another. They focus on getting into the pose and holding it.

Western (that is, Disney tradition) animation has always been about what happens between the poses. The motion and its beauty are the focus of our tradition. Western audiences want to see how characters move between poses, unlike the Japanese art.

However, we can benefit from both traditions by incorporating the Japanese and American poses to build up the strength of our poses. Then, we can revert to our Western tradition to build up beautiful motion between the poses. In this way, we can learn from the newer films in both Japan and the West that seem to me to be converging on this combination.

It is often useful to remind animators that this is a visual medium. We call "digital illustration" the use of animation to supplement a theatrical story done for TV or movies. The information for these theatrical works is in the audio channel, not in the visuals as movies.

What Western animators are working for is the kind of physical acting that tells the story in the video channel. This is much harder than you might think. Complex ideas and emotion can be challenging. Again, this is why the West relies on dailies with experienced animators to help convey the story visually.

This dependence on visuals is often the motivation for animators to take classes in areas such as Kabuki, pantomime, and improvisation acting. If you have not had a lot of experience in these areas, they can be good places to start developing this sense of body acting.

So, the pose is an important step toward communicating to our audience. The skill in acting in animation is similar to that of silent-film acting, and these can serve the animator as additional sources of timing, pose, and gag-acting resources.

The poses that we plan to use in this exercise can now be reviewed in light of the meaning and connotations our test audiences experience, and we can apply the principles of body acting into our animation. These rich sources can help us to achieve animation rather than digital illustration.

Final Plan

Armed with this information and any other relevant research, we can construct the final plan. We want to start with a floor plan for blocking that includes a camera position, if we know one. Then we need our pose plan with script and mini-script. Finally, we need any notes that are pertinent to our project, such as lead animator inputs and director inputs.

The floor plan is a simple scale diagram of the stage that you will be using for the scene. You need it to be to scale because the locations of the characters' poses need to fit in the space allowed. Take the time to ensure that this is the case for your animation. Figure 15.22 shows a scale drawing that you can load into Maya for reference.

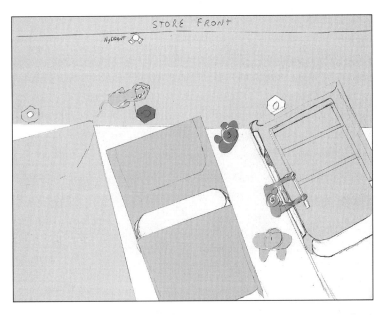

Figure 15.22   This image shows the aerial view of the location used in this shot. The scene shows a parking meter behind each car. At the center car there is a dog, Spot, who is tied to the parking meter for now. The Jerk approaches from stage right.

Next, complete your pose sheet, which should include as complete a set of text and subtext as possible. The poses should show the action without benefit of reading the captions. The pose should tell the story without words.

When the final plan is together, this is a good time to visit the director, the lead animator, or whoever will be controlling the animation. Getting early feedback is important. We like to say that making early mistakes means inexpensive or less painful corrections. Get used to getting feedback from informed sources.

The Production Process

At last you can open Maya 5. To get familiar with the character rigging and controls on The Jerk, the first step is to break the model. But when you're familiar with the model, you can begin to set The Jerk into his poses. Next you will examine pushing the poses to their most extreme. Finally, you will examine the motion paths to enhance the motion between the poses.

Two more poses should be added to every animation plan that you produce. These are key poses before and after the times you will be animating. These poses should follow the flow of your animation and should fit into an expanded scene, if required. However, expanding the scene is not the reason.

Whenever a character starts from a dead stop, the animation at that juncture looks strange. Often we get to see the start of animation as if we just activated the character from a dead start. To avoid this, always animate a bit before and after the actual animation sequence by a pose. This ensures that your character is alive at the start of a shot and continues to live at the end of the shot.

Now you will get your chance to begin to apply all of this planning. If you have been following along, you should have a pretty good idea of what you want The Jerk to do. If not, you can rewind to the start of the chapter and start again. When you are ready, we will be here.

If you are ready, roll up your virtual sleeves and get ready to animate. As you read through the next few sections, you will get a feel for The Jerk's rigging and what you will be able to do with him.

Breaking the Model

To begin working with our character, The Jerk, launch Maya 5. The BreakingJerk.mb scene, on the companion disk, was specifically prepared for use with Maya 5. This file will not work in Maya Personal Learning Edition, however.

If you have not done so before, you might want to create a project for your work, to keep things organized as you explore these activities. You can work from the CD, but I recommend that you copy these files to a project folder. This way, you can save projects in process and do not have to navigate to another project while you are working. If you need it, this might be a good time to review the concept of projects in Maya; this can be reviewed in the *Instant Maya Manual* that comes with Maya 5.

Launch Maya 5 and load the file BreakingJerk.mb. Select File, Open Scene. From the dialog box, navigate to the CD or, if you have moved the folder onto your computer, to the location of the file BreakingJerk.mb. The scene should show The Jerk in a starting position (see Figure 15.23).

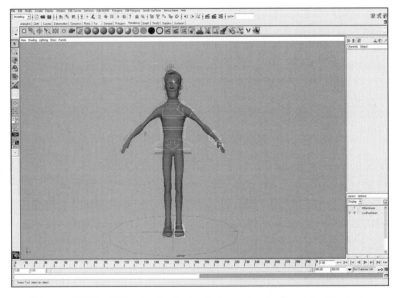

Figure 15.23 This view is the beginning point for breaking The Jerk.

The first thing you'll notice about The Jerk, besides his obvious appeal, is that he's been attacked by a spline-graffiti artist. There seem to be a number of lines, boxes, and circles made up of curves. As strange as it might seem, you will animate these lines and boxes and figures made up of curves, and not the character itself. Typically, in a professional studio, your character will be rigged with controllers such as these.

To understand these controllers a little better, let's take a look at them one by one. Let's exercise The Jerk to find out what kind of limitations might be in his movement. Frankly, my first approach to this is to start moving the character's controllers one by one and then in conjunction with each other to find out where the character model starts to break.

This process of *breaking the character* is an effort to find out how much exaggeration can be put on the character as it's currently configured. Often it's useful to use your pose sheets as the basis for both pushing the poses and testing the character. By pushing the poses, I mean to strike the same poses but to really accentuate the exaggeration of the pose, nearly to the point of being ridiculous. If your character can hang together with extreme poses, he will perform well in the actual animation.

Don't be afraid to really push the character. Your job at this point is to determine the limits of the useful envelope of the character controls while maintaining the character's appearance. This should involve both playing and evaluating the space in which your digital actor can perform.

To view the results of your breaking-the-character activities, it's important to view The Jerk with higher-resolution geometry. You'll notice two layers showing in the Channel Box. We often use lower resolution as a stand-in for setting up the scene, and then review the scene again after substituting in the high-res geometry. This way, we get the fastest possible user interface when setting poses and managing motion paths by using the lowest geometry. Then we can play back the results of the animation in the high-resolution version of the model.

If you are not sure how to use layers and what the different layer switches mean, this might be a good time to review layers in the "Using Maya: Essentials" tutorials. The column on the left of the layers control turns the visibility off and on. You can control the visibility of the models by clicking in the boxes next to the layers.

After completing this exercise, you should feel confident knowing what the character can and cannot do as far as movement goes. In an industrial setting, it's common to find that you'll need to modify the character's rigging to get the kind of motion you want. I am sure, however, that you'll find The Jerk rigging sufficient for all the motion needed to make this a successful animation learning session. Steve Bailey taught me that the true skill in animation is not having a perfectly rigged character, but finding a way to make the character perform as it is and still make it look believable and convincing.

It is important to understand the technical director (TD) and his issues when you work in a professional situation. Knowing what you want the character to do should now be much easier because you did the preproduction exercises, and you can share ideas of poses and motion with your TD. This relationship can make or break an animator, so do everything you can to be gracious and grateful to your TD.

It is good to learn what TDs learn. Be sure to read Chapter 17, "Rigging Characters for Animation," even if you do not intend to undertake such a role.

In professional environments, it's important to understand what the TD has to go through to create a rigged character for animation. It's better still if the animator understands both what a TD goes through rigging a character and the difficulties and challenges in creating great character rigs. This kind of understanding will make it much easier for you to communicate with the TD exactly what is needed for the shot. And such knowledge can help the TD to understand and create the rig that meets the animator's needs in the shot ahead with a minimal amount of effort.

Working the Controls

Below The Jerk model is a mesh that looks like a hover platform. This object is called the Jerk_MAIN_TRANSFORM. This moves The Jerk and all his controllers and things at once (see Figure 15.24). At some studios, this is called a *Jerk Null* (really!) because you can jerk the character out of the scene. At other studios, this is called a *character root*, but the function is the same: It lets you remove or place The Jerk to or from the scene.

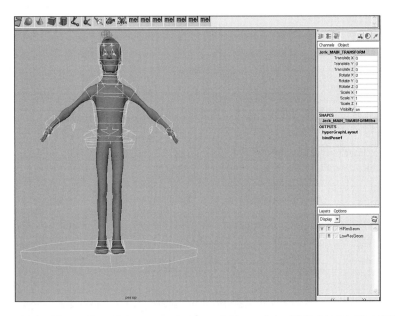

Figure 15.24   Notice that all the controllers are children of the JERK_MAIN_TRANSFORM. This sets a reference point for The Jerk's motion in the scene. It can also be used to remove The Jerk from a scene.

Select the Jerk_MAIN_TRANSFORM and press the W key. This enables you to move, rotate, or scale the whole character. Explore moving this controller and finding out what it does.

After the Jerk_MAIN_TRANSFORM is placed in a scene, it is not a good idea to animate it. The motion of The Jerk within the scene should be done below the Jerk_MAIN_TRANSFORM in the character hierarchy. Remember, you should avoid moving anything but the controllers.

Jerk_CharacterMainRoot

Select the Jerk_CharacterMainRoot and explore what it does. You are looking for the range of movement that looks acceptable to the deformation that the character experiences. You want to define a range of movement that works.

The first set of controls we will examine is the waist and hip controls. The waist controls, called Jerk_CharacterMainRoot in our model (see Figure 15.25), are the first level of animation in freestanding characters. The hip controls are called Jerk_CharacterMainRoot in our model (see Figure 15.26). I like to think of these controls as the fifth Shakra for my character, the center of his or her power and movement.

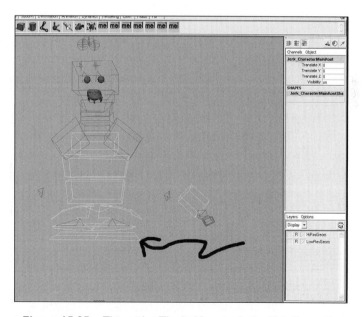

Figure 15.25   This grid at The Jerk's waist is the MainController.
It can be only translated, not rotated or scaled.

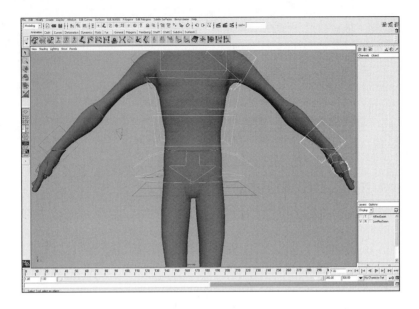

Figure 15.26 This is the grid with The Jerk's body visible. The grid is located at the fifth Shakra and is the center of gravity for our character.

Moving this control involves using translation. This is clearer when the MainController is selected. The Channel Box shows us that we can use translate channels, but rotate and others are missing. If you select the MainController and apply the Rotation tool (keyboard shortcut e), you notice that the rotation spheres icon is grayed out, and moving them does not rotate the main controller—or The Jerk.

To break this part of the model, move the main controller all over the place and note the effect it has on The Jerk. You might notice that pulling him upward (in the Y direction) results in him growing very long legs. This is telling you that his body, arms, and legs move with the main controller. However, the feet are independent.

It is clear that this main controller can be used to move his body around, even off the ground. The only limitation is that of having to move his feet to follow and continue the illusion. The main controller is also useful for moving his hips from side to side and position to position.

Notice that if you want to return to the original position or pose for this controller, simply select it, highlight the parameter values in the Channel Box, and use the keypad to set them to 0. Good rigs will have a setting at 0 for these controllers, to get them back to starting position.

Jerk_HipsAndPartialRootControl

Right above the Main Controller is another rounded grid called the Jerk_HipsAndPartialRootControl (or JHAPRC); see Figure 15.27. Selecting this controller reveals in the Channel Box that rotation is now available. We can both move and rotate this controller. Well, go ahead and play....

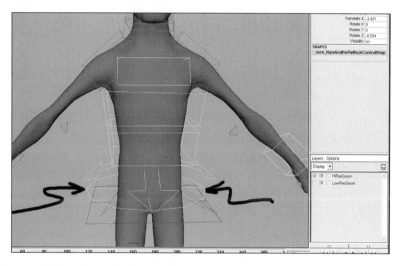

Figure 15.27   The Jerk_HipsAndPartialRootControl is shown here. It is just above the grid that is the Main Controller. This provides local hip rotation to the character.

Notice that moving this JHAPRC controller is very similar to moving the main controller. That is, if you move The Jerk down, below the main controller, he bends his knees and stoops. If you pull up this controller, the legs begin to stretch again, reminding us that his feet controllers are independent.

Notice also that rotating the JHAPRC results in The Jerk rotating at the hips. He cannot bow at the hips, but he does an Elvis impression: His hips slide back and forth in an almost obscene way (see Figure 15.28). Only our Jerk could be this wicked! So, this kind of movement will be used to fine-tune the rotation at the hip.

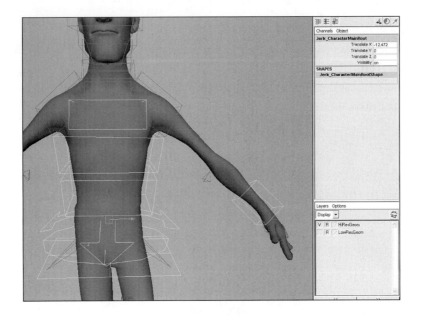

Figure 15.28   Note that the Jerk_HipsAndPartialRootControl translation
does not bend at the torso, but moves the entire torso as a unit.

Note

Deformations resulting from a rotation of more than −55° and 45° start to break the model
for JHAPRC rotation in X. Rotation in Z beyond 25° or −25° breaks the model. Furthermore,
without moving other things, such as The Jerk's stomach and feet, the Y-axis rotation is limited
to about 75°.

Jerk_ElvisControlBox

Yep, riggers like to have fun with controller names, too. From the name of this
controller, we get an idea about what it will do. Select the Jerk_ElvisControlBox controller that looks like four arrows joined at the center (see Figure 15.29). You saw some
of this kind of action earlier, but here you get a little more.

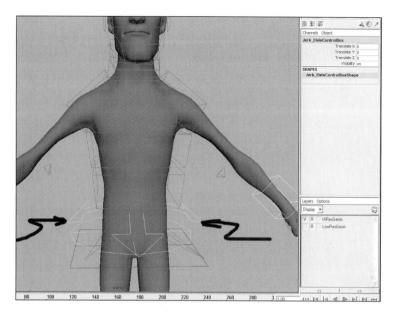

Figure 15.29   The arrow gadget is the Jerk_ElvisControlBox controller.

The Jerk_ElvisControlBox controller will only translate, and you might find it much like what happened with the earlier controllers. Although the Jerk_ElvisControlBox does behave like the previously tested controllers, there are some differences. Notice that moving the Jerk_ElvisControlBox controller has a flexible connection with the torso that was not there with the JHAPRC controller (see Figure 15.30). Thus, each controller gives a subtly different kind of movement.

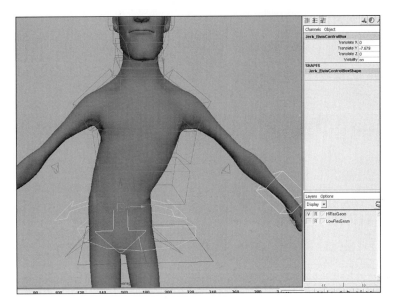

Figure 15.30 Note that the Jerk_ElvisControlBox translation shows the torso bending when affected by the lateral translation.

Translations are limited, much like we discussed earlier with JHAPRC. However, any movement up or down creates a breaking of the model at the chest (going up) and at the legs (going down). The up-and-down stretch was more flexible when we used the JHAPRC controller. However, this should be used with strong limitations.

Motion created by moving the Jerk_ElvisControlBox controller up and down or even to the sides must be very limited. Most people cannot move this way in the real world, and the motion does not look believable, much less plausible. So use this motion with care, in context with your character.

Jerk_SpineTopControlBox, Jerk_SpineMiddleControlBox, and Jerk_SpineBottomControlBox

These three boxes are treated together because they usually move together in the character. However, when we look at *lead and follow,* later in the chapter, we revisit these as a group.

The model breaks quickly when you move these three controllers to the side or back. This is the kind of movement that you get at the chiropractor or maybe in a bad football accident. Depending on the needs of your scene, this is a low-probability move.

The power comes in when we select all three of these controllers and use rotation. This rotation gives The Jerk the ability to make a good bow and bend to the front and sides. Remember to select all three, one at a time, holding down the Shift key. You might want to create a MEL script selection button for these, which you can do from the Script Editor. Highlight the script lines and, holding the middle mouse button, drag them to the shelf; you will have created a selection button, to save time (see Figure 15.31).

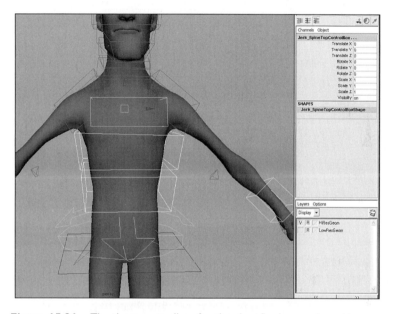

Figure 15.31   The three controllers for the chest/back are selected because they are usually moved together.

Rotation for all three seems to be limited to about 20° and −20°. Beyond this, we see the model breaking. You can see in the image how the character is breaking at the chest with 25° rotations. Remember that each box we selected is rotating some 25°, which is quite a bit more than our bodies can.

Rotation to the sides allows The Jerk to move again about 20 degrees without discomfort. Beyond this, the model breaks in the shoulder areas. The neck will have to be adjusted to compensate for the chest rotations.

Notice that scale has been left in the Channel Box and that these can be used for scaling the chest. This provides a method to create periodic breathing effects using these controls in scale.

Jerk_mainNeckControlBox and Jerk_NeckMiddleControlBox

Select the two lower neck controllers, which are marked in green. These two controllers work in tandem, and with the third above, to provide movement of the neck (see Figure 15.32).

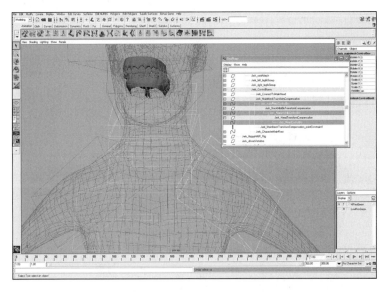

Figure 15.32   This shows the three green controllers for the neck region.

When you Shift+select these two controllers and rotate them, the neck allows the head to rotate with very good volume control on the neck. The rotation limits of –34° and 26° allow the head a full range of rotation in the Y-axis. This means that he nods "yes" using this Y-axis rotation.

The side-to-side rotation on the X-axis, as in shaking his head to say "no," shows limitations at about 8.5° and –8.5° rotation. At this point, the neck becomes creased and seems broken. (There is help in rotating further from the next controller, as you'll see later.)

Explore the limits of the rotation of these controllers. You are getting the hang of how this character can move and how he can support your animation plan.

Rotating on the Z-axis is almost unlimited in keeping the model together. It might not look right, but the model will hold together.

The rotation on the Y-axis is enhanced when the Jerk_HeadControlBox is added to the selection (see the next section). Also, when the limits of the selection are reached, you can select and rotate the Jerk_HeadControlBox a bit more and keep the model from breaking severely.

Jerk_HeadControlBox

This control moves the head as a unit. Notice that the head has several controls as we move farther up the spine, but this is the one to use to move the head around all at once.

The Jerk_HeadControlBox has controls in the Channel Box for rotation, scale, and translation. However, only the rotation has real meaning for this character. If you are planning a very cartoon style of animation in which the neck stretches as the head moves, the translation controls might make sense, but I suggest that you don't try it.

Select the Jerk_HeadControlBox. Make sure that you have not selected the topmost box on his head, which also has the same name. You can rotate the head from this location because that is how the axis bone in human necks rotates the head. Try it: Your goal is to get familiar with the movement and effects of using this controller for the head position (see Figure 15.33).

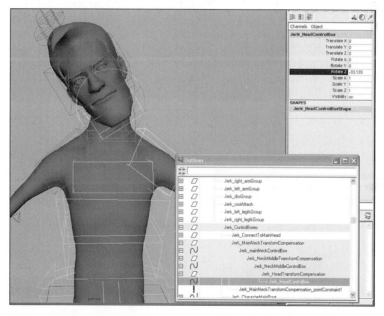

Figure 15.33 This shows the rotation of the Jerk_HeadControlBox some 33° on the Z-axis. The head looks somewhat disconnected from the neck when not used in consort with the other neck controllers.

Rotation on the Y-axis moves the head forward and backward. The head moves well until the head penetrates the body, but it looks very weird as it approaches the insertion. This gives a very useful range of rotation for our character.

Rotation on the X-axis has no creases in the neck up to 65° and –65°. If you push beyond that, you can compensate some of this with the aforementioned controllers. However, most heads don't move much beyond this angle. The movement looks good in this range using only the Jerk_HeadControlBox rotation.

Rotation on the Z-axis is smooth until the head intersects the body. The movement is very unnatural, but it does work well.

Jerk_headControlBox and Jerk_jawControlBox

These two controllers are located on the head. They have the same name as the top neck controller and should not be confused with the head controllers. You can see these two controllers selected in Figure 15.34.

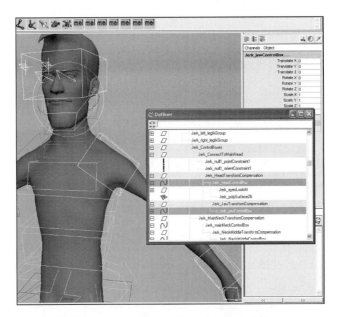

Figure 15.34 The head controllers are shown here; when not selected, they are blue. Note that the top controller has the same name as that on the top of the neck.

These two controllers have little use for us, but you should explore them nonetheless. Get familiar with what range of motion can support your animation.

Neither of these controllers is fully implemented yet, as is often the case for the hand-in-glove nature of the animator's relationship with the TD. A very limited range of motion works for these to give a sense of emotion, but most heads, if built correctly, don't move relative to other parts of the head.

That being said, notice that motion is available for these controllers—for instance, the lower controller adjusts the chin and can even elongate it when rotated. These controllers can help give a sense of facial animation. (Facial animation is beyond the scope of this chapter.)

Jerk_frontHairControl, Jerk_midBackHairControl, and Jerk_midFrontHairControl

You might want to select one or all of these spheres and explore what happens when they are manipulated. You might find a condition that helps your plan. However, it might be best to leave these alone until you are confident in applying dynamics simulation. You are looking for things that will help you realize your plan and find what might go wrong later. Explore.

The spheres at the top of the head are controlled through the Jerk_headControlBox, which has a couple of attributes to add hair dynamics to The Jerk. If you want to explore this facet of the character, you can turn on the dynamics by typing a 1 value into the Channel Box for hair dynamics on T. Also, you can adjust the dynamics with the other attribute, called Hair Floppyness. This adjusts the degree that the hair will move. (See Figure 15.35.)

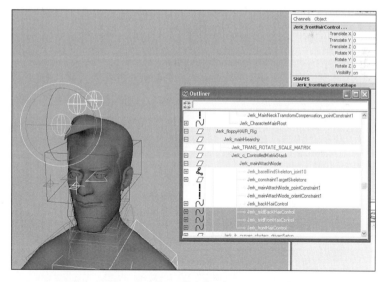

Figure 15.35 These spheres control the deformation of the character's hair and allow for dynamics to provide some secondary action to the hair geometry.

To test these dynamics, use the Jerk_HeadControlBox to set head rotations left and right over several keys. When you play back the animation, the hair will move with dynamics simulation. This advanced feature is, again, beyond the scope of this chapter, but you can explore this limited implementation for more.

This concludes the stack of controllers on the spine and the head. Notice that these controls work well together to create the illusion of character motion in the body. There is no need to put additional keyframes on the bones or geometry of the character.

Break a Leg!

Now you will test the appendages, starting with the feet. Because the appendages are the same on both sides, you will examine the left-side appendages only.

Jerk_left_reverseHeel

Select the Jerk_left_reverseHeel controller, and explore its effect (see Figure 15.36). You will notice that the leg follows the foot and tries to bend appropriately to the foot's position. The controller also allows you to rotate the foot from this controller. Make sure you have only this controller, not the two at the end of the foot.

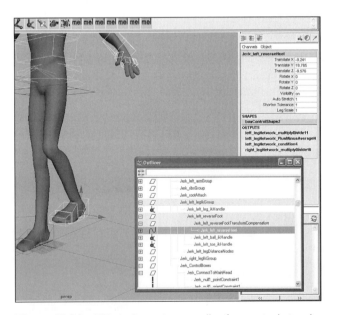

Figure 15.36   This is the main controller for manipulating the leg and the foot. The Jerk_left_reverseHeel provides almost all the control you will need for moving The Jerk's leg and foot.

Translation of the Jerk_left_reverseHeel activates the inverse kinematics for the left leg and causes the leg to bend, depending on the location of the heel. The heel has room for flexibility and runs into problems only when it is brought close to the body. Legs don't bend this way, except in rare football accidents, so this is a limitation of the model rigging.

The Jerk_left_reverseHeel also has rotation capacity. Rotating on the X-axis moves the foot along its long axis. This can be done to nearly 90° and −90° with workable mesh deformation, even though our real-world counterparts cannot move in this way.

On the Z-axis, the foot lifts up and down, as in a tapping motion. The useful range is about −30° to 20°. This is enough to show a realistic range. The foot breaks at the ankle where rotation beyond this range creates deformation of the ankle bone area.

You will notice some additional attributes in the Channel Box. These controls, such as autostretch, were specifically built into the rigging to maintain continuity in the mesh when the leg is stretched. This attribute is there to help create freedom in moving the character. However, these controls are not explored while we are breaking the character.

If you want to explore these controls, move slowly. Change one parameter at a time to make the effect of each clear. If you change too many things at once, it might confound the effect of one attribute. Happy exploring!

Jerk_left_reverse_ball

The next controller down the foot from the heel is the Jerk_left_reverse_ball. This controller has only rotation enabled in the Channel Box. You can use this rotation to move the heel up and the knee forward. (See Figure 15.37.)

Rotation on the Z-axis moves the heel up to look good until it rotates more than 57°. Beyond that rotation angle, the ball-to-toe geometry creases heavily. Rotation of −10° is the limit in the other direction; rotation beyond this gives the impression that the foot is not continuous. Rotation on the Y-axis seems just plain wrong.

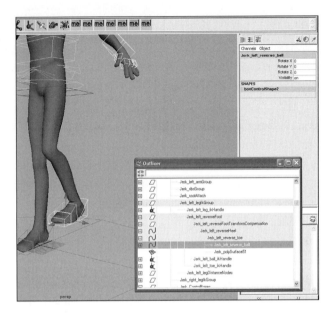

Figure 15.37   The Jerk_left_reverse_ball is selected and shows
the grayed-out move manipulator. This shows that the
Jerk_left_reverse_ball cannot be moved; it can only be rotated.
You will notice that only rotation is available in the Channel Box.

Now, what is meant by "wrong" is that this controller rotates the whole foot, just as the heel did. However, whenever there is the possibility of redundancy in controls, it is often good to use only one of the controllers by convention, to enhance the process of debugging a pose and finding problems in a short time. For our animation, we will limit the rotation of the foot to the Jerk_left_reverseHeel.

Jerk_left_reverse_toe

This is the third controller on the foot and the farthest from the heel. It has the capability to rotate the foot from the toe fulcrum. This is useful between −20° and 37° on the Y-axis. On the Z-axis, rotation from the toe of 37° to −37° works reasonably well (see Figure 15.38); beyond this, the ankle collapses again. By convention, we will not use the X rotation because it is redundant with the Jerk_left_reverseHeel.

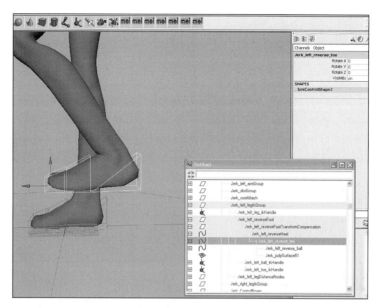

Figure 15.38   The Jerk_left_reverse_toe controller is shown with the move manipulator grayed out. This indicates that you cannot move the Jerk_left_reverse_toe controller independently. Only rotation is provided.

Jerk_left_legPoleVector

This describes the key controllers on the leg. One more that should be noted: A pole vector, or up vector, as it is called in other software, controls where the knee points. This helps the IK solver put the leg into the desired plane.

The Jerk_left_legPoleVector controller looks like a spike coming from the hipbone and protruding forward from The Jerk's hips (see Figure 15.39). Selecting this controller reveals a Channel Box with only rotation and visibility available. Rotation in the Y-axis makes the most sense: It points the knee in the same direction as the bone. This provides a simple way to control the direction of the bend of the leg. Using the Z- or X-axis control does little to affect the direction the IK solver points.

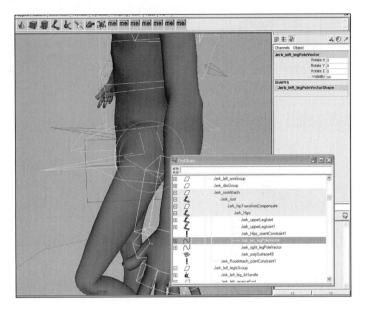

Figure 15.39 The Jerk_left_legPoleVector is shown in the figure.
This controller looks like a bone sticking out of the thigh of our character.
The only manipulation that you are allowed to effect is rotation.
This points the knee in the same direction as the bone.

Use the Jerk_left_legPoleVector to help orient your leg direction.

The arm, hand, and shoulder controls are examined next. We will break the arms and see the effects we get from the hand and shoulder.

Jerk_left_armIk

The box on The Jerk's wrist is the Jerk_left_armIk controller. This one is set up with an elaborate IK solver and shoulder deformer. You can see this when you select the Jerk_left_armIk and translate it from front to back on the Z-axis. Watch the shoulder roll with some convincing behavior.

The human shoulder is a wishbone support of the arm's ball joint, but it can also slip forward or backward a bit. This complex motion presents difficulty for the TD to automate because the motion is complex. Here, we have a good version to help ease the animation burden.

To break this Jerk_left_armIk controller, you can move the arm in the same way that real-world motion takes place. Looking from above the shoulder, you can see the shoulder movement as you move the Jerk_left_armIk controller on the Z-axis. The shoulder appears to work well.

However, if you push this rotation, there is a point at which it stops. For example, look at the situation when the hand is moved on the Z-axis to the place where the arm starts to stretch, and then add movement toward the body on the X-axis. The shoulder and arm twist and collapse (see Figure 15.40).

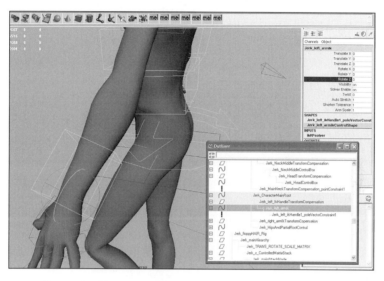

Figure 15.40   The Jerk_left_armIk affects the location of the wrist and rotation of the hand.

One important thing to notice is that whenever the hand is raised above the shoulder, a series of ridges appears on the chest below the armpit. This can be used in shots in which staging hides that side of the character. However, this area is not attractive when viewed straight on.

Because our scene will not involve The Jerk's arms above his head, the rigging will work as long as we stay within those limits. If we had to use his arms above his head, we would have had to get the rigging modified.

The Jerk_left_armIk controller also rotates the hand at the wrist. The character's hand can be rotated into any position by using the rotation controls. The rotation will be relative to the arm position, so there are no clear rules about rotation angles. However, I have rotated the hand beyond the normal range of human hands without a pinch or deformation, so this should work well for our purposes.

Solver options again are present in the Channel Box, with names such as Auto Stretch and Shorten Tolerance. These should be left in their default settings. Twist creates unseemly results and should not be used. The pole vector is better at determining the angle of the shoulder to the elbow.

Each finger and the thumb have pretty much the same control sets on their controllers, so we will examine the Jerk_left_pinkyFinger_4 controller. Note that these same controls exist for each of the fingers and the thumb.

Jerk_left_pinkyFinger_4

The Channel Box for each finger control contains rotation controls that work a bit differently from the ordinary key framing of a set position (see Figure 15.41). But first, let's not use the translation of the box. This creates a very cartoon-style motion in which the finger stretches to any length. This kind of movement works only in the most extreme Tex Avery–style animation; that is not our intent in this project.

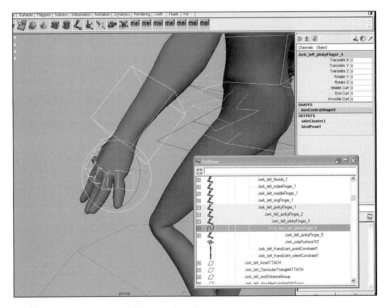

Figure 15.41 Rotation of the fingers is done by selecting the controller Jerk_left_pinkyFinger_4 and using the Channel Box attributes. Select the desired attribute and adjust with a middle mouse button drag.

Rotations are enabled for the Jerk_left_pinkyFinger_4 controller as well. We won't be using these controls either because they rotate the finger in an unnatural direction. Only in *The Exorcist* is this kind of movement acceptable.

You will want to control three more attributes in the Channel Box: Knuckle, Middle, and End Curls. These represent and control the joints in the finger. To set keys for these attributes, select the name of the attribute in the Channel Box.

Then, with the name highlighted, move the cursor into the viewport and Middle Mouse Button (MMB) drag in the window. This rotates the finger in the appropriate axis and enables you to pose the finger. To save a key for this posed finger, Right Mouse Button (RMB) click in the Channel Box and go to Key Selected.

Note that you can always go back to the base pose by Left Mouse Button (LMB) selecting these attributes and typing 0 for all values.

Jerk_left_armPoleVector

Lurking in the background is a pole vector object named Jerk_left_armPoleVector (see Figure 15.42). This object controls the place toward which the elbow will point. This allows independent control over the elbow position. The Jerk_left_armPoleVector is colored a very light yellow, and it blends on my computer with the background. If you did not notice it, you can follow the point of the elbow to it, or use the outliner or type in the name at the top of the interface where the text string selection gadget is. This works a little differently from the leg pole control, but it does the same job.

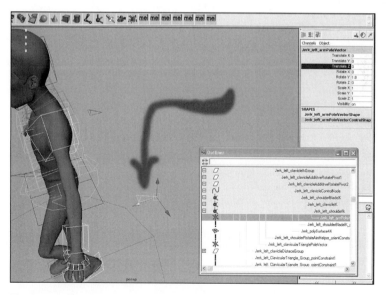

Figure 15.42   The separate "floating bone" is the Jerk_left_armPoleVector, which shows the direction that the elbow points to. If there is no slack in the arm, it might not seem to point much.

The Jerk_left_armPoleVector controller can be placed anywhere on the screen. However, this can have disturbing effects on the look of The Jerk's arms. It is possible to rotate the elbow inside out, which makes The Jerk look strange. Therefore, use discretion in setting the Jerk_left_armPoleVector controller.

Jerk_left_clavicleControlNode

The last stop on our tour of controllers takes us to the Jerk_left_clavicleControlNode controller. This one has translation, rotation, and twist attributes, but it is strongly recommended that you don't use these. They will almost certainly make the resulting Jerk look distorted. (See Figure 15.43.)

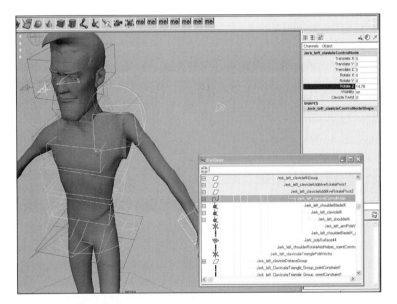

Figure 15.43   Rotation on the Z-axis shows the effect of manipulation of the Jerk_left_clavicleControlNode. The shoulder is important to convincing motion and must be well understood. Explore the limits of movement and the effect of the shoulder rotation in conjunction with the hand position.

Now that you have taken a tour of the controls, you should be both more familiar with how to animate The Jerk and what the limitations of his movement will be.

Setting the Poses

In this section, you apply your knowledge of how The Jerk moves to set him in poses that match the planning poses.

Exercise 15.1   Setting the Poses to Match the Planning Poses

Begin setting the poses by adjusting the controllers explored earlier.

1. Load the scene JerkRiggedBase.mb from the CD-ROM.

   If you have a traveling shot, the first step is to begin with the blocking. That is, your character should be placed at the position indicated by your scale drawing at the time your character is supposed to be there. The character need not be posed yet, but the timing of the gross movement between marks is set.

   It is often useful to have the character facing the right direction at each mark. This process is a little different from the one used next, but it's very similar to the one used later, when we address the motion.

   For stationary shots, such as this one, in which minimal traveling will take place, the character can be animated nearly in place. Imagine that we placed The Jerk in the scene where he will be close to the center of his action. We can move him later into the final scene by merging this animation with the final scene. We will use some stand-ins from the main scene to get a reference for our actions.

   We will use a simple box to stand in for the cars on The Jerk's left and right. We can assume that our production assistants or low-level animators responsible for blocking put these stand-ins in the right place so that we can proceed, but in the real world, mistakes happen. It is a good idea to make sure that the stand-ins are current with the scene before starting the animation process.

2. Move in the Perspective window to get a good three-quarter view of The Jerk from the front right (The Jerk's left) and get a full shot. A *full shot* is one in which you can see the whole body of the character or subject. This shot should match your planned camera angle and focus.

   One of Lasseter's principles of computer animation is *animate to the camera*. Although this has several corollaries, the first and most important is that you should have clear in your mind where the camera needs to be in this shot. In the real world, someone in the art department, or perhaps the cinematographer, will do this. In your own production, you will do this.

   Maya lets you create a camera for just such a purpose. You create a camera from which the scene will be rendered. You need to worry only about what the camera sees, nothing else. If the camera does not see the action you are creating, the action is lost. For the animator, the only thing of concern is what this camera sees.

Note

You should use only one camera to define the direction of the pose and the action. This is the camera that will be critical to the staging of poses and business. *Business* is a term that dates back to vaudeville and refers to the actions that an actor takes when performing some larger action. For instance, Humphrey Bogart did a facial tick to show that he was annoyed. You can use the perspective camera to move about the scene and adjust things, but the camera to which you will animate must stay locked down in its position.

3. Create a Render Camera by opening the Outliner, copying the perspective camera (using the Crtl+d keys), and renaming it. You can rename the new duplicate camera by selecting it in the Outliner and renaming it Render Camera.

4. Now that you have your Render Camera in place, you can select the transformations (translate and rotate, at least) on the left of the Channel Box. Then right-click to reveal the expanded menu. You will notice an entry below called Lock Selected. This prevents you from inadvertently moving the Render Camera and losing its position.

5. Check your camera view. To view the scene from the Render Camera, simply select the Panels menu on the viewport: Panels, Perspective, Render Camera, or Panels, Perspective, Perspective to return to perspective mode. Thus, you can move the character with the perspective view and return to the unadulterated Render Camera when you want.

   Whatever adjustments you make to the character's poses, always check the result in the Render Camera. The heads-up display shows which camera you are looking through by listing the name at the bottom of the viewport. Make sure your poses and actions will look good in the Render Camera and that you will be *animating to the camera.*

6. Set the Render Globals to point to the new Render Camera by choosing Window, Rendering Editors, Render Globals. In the dialog box, make sure Image File Output is expanded. Toward the bottom is a field called Camera. You can select the Render Camera that you just created from the pull-down menu.

Exercise 15.2 Keying the Poses

Working pose to pose, begin in Frame 1 of the animation. You can set the frame by either moving the slider in the timeline or typing the desired frame to the left of the timeline in the current frame indicator. For this stage, it is often easier to adjust the character with the full-screen perspective view.

1. Load the scene JerkRiggedBase.mb. Even if you have had this scene open for the previous exercise, open it anew. This minimizes unexpected strangeness.

The character should be available for IK animation. Remember to select only the controllers, nothing else. It is often useful to select Show, None and then Show, NURBS Curves. This hides everything else but the controllers that are NURBS curves. Because they are NURBS curves, they do not render; they have no width for the camera to see.

2. In the Perspective window, select Show, None and then Show, NURBS Curves. Make sure you can see all the controllers. Hold down the Shift button and drag-select a marquis over all the controllers.

3. Now open the Script Editor. This can be done by selecting the icon at the lower-right side of the Channel Box (see Figure 15.44).

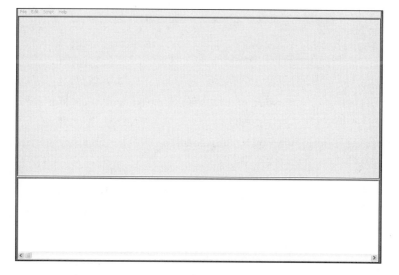

Figure 15.44 The Script Editor is the small icon shown at the lower-right side of the interface. The open window is the Script Editor interface dialog box.

4. Select the Edit, Clear All menu item. This clears all the entries in the interface dialog box (see Figure 15.45).

Figure 15.45 This shows the Script Editor recording the clear all call. The Script Editor shows the `Select -r ;` MEL command.

5. Now LMB-click in the viewport to deselect the control boxes. You will note in the Script window that the deselect function (`select -cl`) call appears in the window.

6. Select the control boxes by holding down the Shift key and drag-selecting all the control boxes. (See Figure 15.46.)

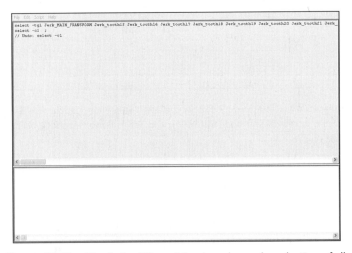

Figure 15.46 The Script Editor dialog box shows the selection of all the controllers in a one-line MEL script. This sets up the next step: creating a repeatable selection MEL script.

7. Now highlight these two MEL commands and MMB-drag them to the Shelf (see Figure 15.47). Maya recognizes that you are trying to create a MEL command and creates an icon to call the MEL script that you just created. This button will be useful for your keyframing activities. You just created a MEL script; nice going!

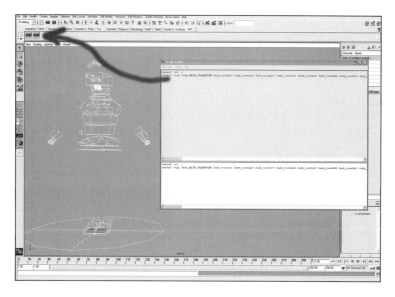

Figure 15.47   The highlighted region in the Script Editor is the MEL script you are writing. This script dialog box was cleared to clarify this step. However, there is no real need to clear the Script Editor if you are sure what you are copying into the Shelf.

8. You can test the new button by selecting and deselecting the control boxes using your new MEL script. When you are comfortable with the way it works, you can continue. At that time, close the Script Editor.

9. Select Show, All, and you can begin the posing process. First, however, you should review the ways to set keyframes and how they are affected by your method.

Setting Keys

Your computer never has enough power to afford a professional animator to be sloppy. So, there is value in examining alternatives in setting keyframes. A keyframe can be created in many ways, but there are differences in the results. This can affect the interface response time, where most animators live.

Maya has a plethora of methods for creating keyframes. For example, you can simply select the object to keyframe and press the s key. This sets keyframes on every attribute in the Channel Box: translation, rotation, scale, and visibility. As you can see, if you want to control only rotation and translation, you get much more than that. That means that Maya has more to do each time you move something in the interface.

Other means of setting keyframes in Maya yield similar results. For example, by turning on the Autokey function by clicking the icon at the lower-right side on the timeline bar, keyframes for all attributes in the Channel Box are again set.

Remember that Autokey sets keys for whatever you move in the current frame. If you forget to advance the frame, it is very easy to overwrite a pose without your conscious consent. For this reason, I call this Autokey technique "auto scene destroy" because it makes it so easy to mess up your scenes.

You can also LMB-select the attributes in the Channel Box and, with these attributes selected, RMB-open the menu that enables you to set keyframes for the selected attributes. This is a bit mouse intensive, but it puts keys only in the attributes you want. The only problem is that you are adding a lot of mouse action, and carpal tunnel syndrome is a real threat.

So, for these reasons, the Shift key is preferred. For translation keys only, hold down the Shift key down and press the s key. This sets keys for selected objects in Translation. Remember that the w key is the keyboard shortcut for translation. The Shift+e key combination does the same keyframing for rotation, and Shift+r sets keys for scale.

So, for reasons of efficiency, the Shift-key method can help reduce the bloat in the Maya interface and help set keys only where they are needed. This technique is also much friendlier to healthy carpal tunnels. Your mileage may vary.

In the exercise that follows, you begin posing The Jerk character. Remember to make sure that the poses are exaggerated but still look realistic. If you want to go for a more cartoonlike look, or Tex Avery style, you can push the poses even further. The idea of pushing poses is important to releasing the animator's energy.

Exercise 15.3   Posing The Jerk

To begin, load the JerkRiggedBase.mb scene. If you have it open, reload it to ensure that your starting point is as needed here. Start the pose by setting the center of gravity (that fifth Shakra thing I mentioned earlier). The pose methodology begins from the "inside out," By that, I mean that the force should follow from the source to the center of gravity. Then work from the inside out for each of the controllers. This exercise shows the process for one pose as a sample.

1. Select the Jerk_CharacterMainRoot and press the w key to enable the translation manipulators. Adjust the position of the center of gravity for this first pose. To review which pose you are doing, the planned pose is shown in Figure 15.48.

Figure 15.48 Use the plan drawing to help pose The Jerk for his first pose.

The rotation of the hips and the angle are shown in the plan drawing. This makes it easier to pose the character. So, we adjust The Jerk's pose to match.

2. First the hips are moved over the foot that is supporting his weight. From the plan drawing, that is his right foot. I selected the Jerk_CharacterMainRoot controller and moved The Jerk's weight onto the right foot. I like to view the quad view plane mode so that I can see all directions at once (see Figure 15.49).

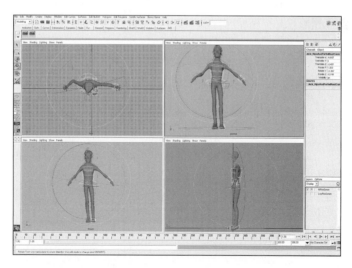

Figure 15.49 This view shows the four views of the hips as they are positioned. The weight of The Jerk is now on that right foot. His nose is over the right-foot shoelaces.

3. Next, to get the rotation on the hips, rotate the Jerk_HipsAndPartialRootControl. This gives you the angle on the hips that was established in the plan drawing (see Figure 15.50).

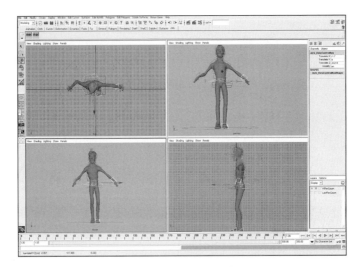

Figure 15.50 This shows the Jerk_HipsAndPartialRootControl adjusting the angle of the hips.

Next work outward from the hips and adjust the chest area.

4. Select the chest as the three boxes controlling the chest area. Then provide a rotation in Z to get the chest rotated into the angle set up in our plan diagram. Move this to taste. My version is shown in Figure 15.51.

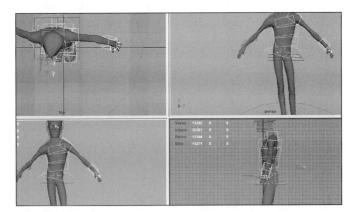

Figure 15.51 This figure shows the rotation of the chest to get that angle defined in the plan diagram. This causes the right hip to be up and the left hip to drop. This is complimented in shoulder angle. The angle of the shoulder usually does complement the angle of the hips.

5. Next you adjust the legs and knee rotations. The character in the drawing has the right leg pointing straight ahead, but the left knee is rotated toward the screen right. To effect this change, you must select the Jerk_left_legPoleVector to rotate the knee and angle of the leg. Rotate the Jerk_left_legPoleVector on the Y-axis to rotate the leg and open the stance (see Figure 15.52).

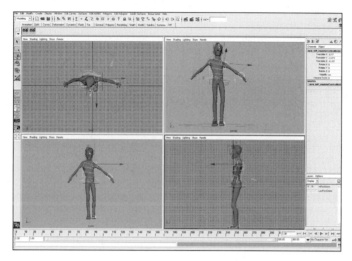

Figure 15.52   The Jerk_left_legPoleVector controller is selected and the rotation is used to open the stance. Here, I am using the selected Channel Box Attribute for rotation in Y. Then, with this attribute selected, the MMB is dragged in the viewport to adjust the rotation.

The next step for this pose is to adjust the left foot.

6. To do this, select the Jerk_left_reverseHeel controller and adjust the rotation in Y. Also, translate the foot over in X and Z to loosen up the pose (see Figure 15.53).

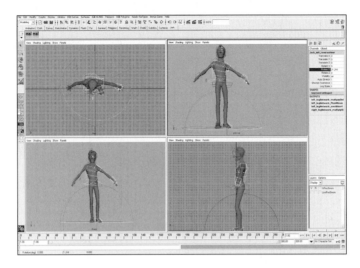

Figure 15.53   This is the opened pose after adjusting the Jerk_left_reverseHeel for both rotation and position. The legs look a bit straight and stretched out at this point, so some adjustment in the Jerk_CharacterMainRoot is in order.

To correct for the stretching of the legs, an adjustment in the Jerk_CharacterMainRoot is now necessary.

7. Simply select the Jerk_CharacterMainRoot and move it down and back a bit until the legs look more natural (see Figure 15.54).

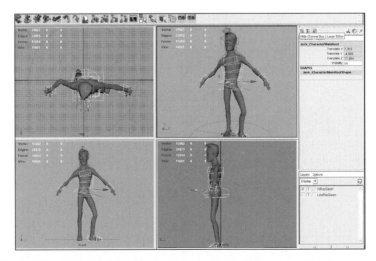

Figure 15.54   This figure is after an adjustment to the Jerk_CharacterMainRoot controller. The adjustment moved the Jerk_CharacterMainRoot controller down and forward a bit to get the legs set with just a bit of bend. Legs without bend don't seem natural or believable.

Next, adjust the rotation of the hips to make them more natural with the hips and leg situations.

8. Rotate the hip at the Jerk_HipsAndPartialRootControl. Rotation here gives the pose a better angle (see Figure 15.55).

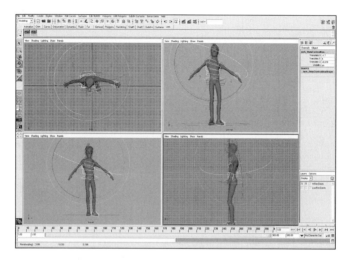

Figure 15.55   Here is a slight adjustment to the hip rotation accomplished by rotating the Jerk_HipsAndPartialRootControl. Note that the rotation opens the stance toward the camera.

9. Select the chest stack of three controllers and rotate the chest toward the camera.

Notice that in the reference diagram, the shoulders are also tilted opposite to the hips. You can accomplish that with these controllers. My finished version is shown in Figure 15.56.

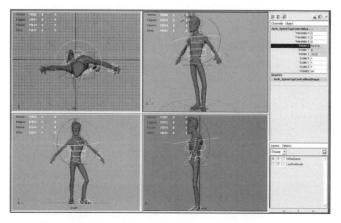

Figure 15.56   The chest stack of three box controllers is used to adjust the chest and torso. The stance is open to the camera and has a loose feel.

Because the shoulders will follow the arm positioning, you should next work with the arm controllers.

10. First, use the Jerk_left_armIk to position the arm like the planning diagram. Then position the other arm using the same technique (see Figure 15.57).

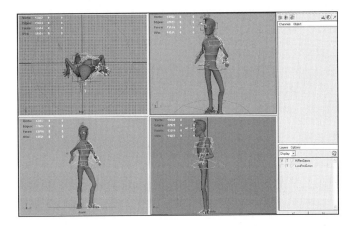

Figure 15.57 The Jerk_left_armIk and the opposite member were used to set the arm positions. Notice that the arms bend when slack is provided to the elbow. You can correct the hand and elbow orientations in the next adjustment.

11. The hands did not follow the direction of the wrist and look limp. You can correct this by selecting the Jerk_left_armIk again and switching to the rotation mode. For this controller, rotation controls the direction of the hand. Use this control to adjust the hands into position (see Figure 15.58).

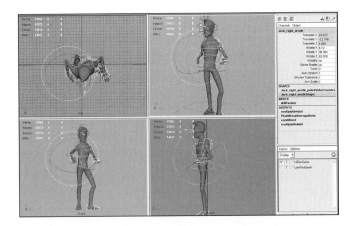

Figure 15.58 The hand rotation is corrected for current arm position using the Jerk_left_armIk and Jerk_right_armIk controllers with rotation.

12. To get the elbows in position, use the Jerk_right_armPoleVector control. The position of the Jerk_right_armPoleVector controls where the elbow will point. This means that you have control over which direction the arm bends (see Figure 15.59).

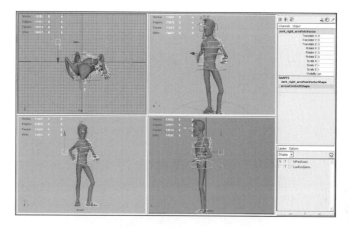

Figure 15.59   The Jerk_right_armPoleVector is used to correct the arm bend direction.

The result of this correction is shown in Figure 15.60.

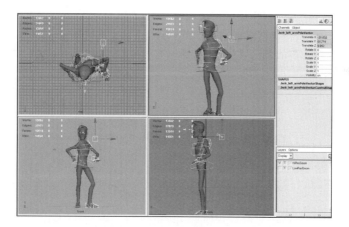

Figure 15.60   The arm bend is corrected in the arms for this image. Compare this to the planning diagram.

The pose is shaping up, but the shoulders need adjustment.

13. Select the shoulder controller, Jerk_left_clavicleControlNode. Use rotation to adjust the position of the shoulders in the view. Ignore the effect on the arms and hands; they require at least one more adjustment. Get a feeling in the shoulders of the weight and force in the pose. My adjustment for the shoulders is shown in Figure 15.61.

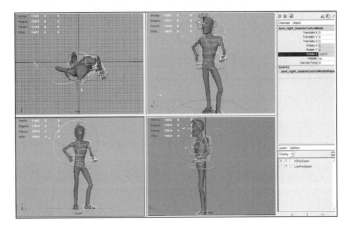

Figure 15.61   The shoulder adjustment has helped the pose of the body.

Although the shoulder adjustment has upset the hands and arms, you can adjust them again to get a proper pose. My version is shown in Figure 15.62.

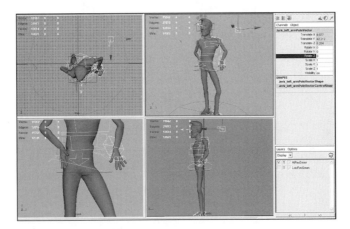

Figure 15.62   The hands and arms are on pose now for this exercise. To get to this pose, the Jerk_left_armPoleVector had to be adjusted to get a pose that matched the one in the planning diagram.

14. For the final adjustment to the pose, you can adjust the head position. Use the three controller boxes at the neck in green. They allow a rotation of the head to match the planning diagram. Rotate the head using these controllers to match (see Figure 15.63).

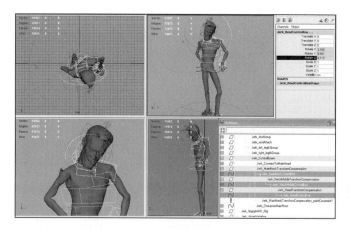

Figure 15.63   The adjusted head completes the adjustments to your first character pose.

The completed version of the pose exercise can be found in the file JerkPose1Finished on the CD-ROM.

This exercise showed how to set a pose to match the planning diagram. This might be new for some, but others will find that it makes the practice of setting poses possible and less intimidating. How did you do?

If you found this easy, great—you still have a few more poses to set. In case you found it hard, repeating the experience for more poses should help with your confidence as you build up this sequence.

Exercise 15.4   Adding Time to Poses

In this exercise, you copy the previous key settings from the first frame to the second before you start to set the second pose. This is done to ensure that all adjusted keys have known keyframes in each frame. Later, when you move these keys in time, it will become problematic if you leave keys undefined for any keyframe.

1. When The Jerk is in the pose you want, make sure that the key poses are set for all the parameters you want.

For this frame only, I usually Shift+select all the controllers, or use the handy MEL button we created on the shelf, and set keys in translation and rotation (see Figure 15.64). I do this because if any controller is moved later and has no keyframe set in the first frame, the later pose will back-fill and change your first pose.

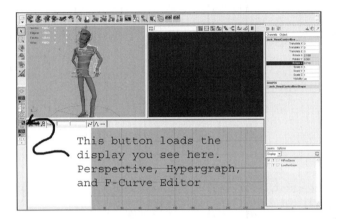

Figure 15.64   This figure shows the button used to set the three-viewport view in Maya's Toolbox.

2. To check your animation keys in Frame 1, use the three-view preset on the left side of the Maya display. It has the Perspective and Hypergraph views on top and the Graph Editor below as a double-wide viewport. Then, at the left on the bottom, there are arrow keys that control the viewports. Select the bottom double-wide button and select Dope Sheet from the expanded menu. (See Figure 16.65.)

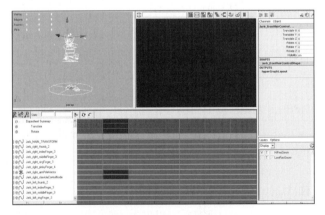

Figure 15.65   This figure shows the Dope Sheet replacing the Graph Editor, or F-Curve Editor. This is the configuration that you should have to proceed.

Note

The Dope Sheet is often professional animators' method of choice for changing the timing of groups of objects or an entire scene. The advantage is that the display treats all the actions as one line element, and control is crisp and clear. The rows are keys for one attribute across time, while the columns are keys in the same frame. This is a spreadsheet-like layout to help clarify the scene in terms of keys, like the old exposure sheet (X-Sheet) from traditional animation.

There is a caveat in using the Dope Sheet: Selecting the Dope Sheet Summary does not guarantee that all nested nodes in the character rigging will be affected. This means that if you are not careful, you can have floating nodes without keys set. This becomes a problem if later you set a key in a previously unkeyed attribute.

Setting a key later means that all previous frames will take that value. This can screw up all previous keys. So, a word to the wise: Set keys for all parameters (see Figure 15.66).

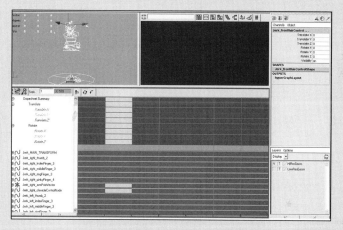

Figure 15.66   The selected keys (lighter) in the Dope Sheet Summary are not selecting any of the nested nodes or nodes that have not yet gotten keys. For safety sake, you should create keys for all of these animated attributes.

3. To set your keys, make sure that the controllers are selected, and then execute a Shift+w and a Shift+e.

   This latter action triggers an error message about setting rotation on rotation-protected attributes. Ignore it. You just set the keys that are necessary for your next step (see Figure 15.67).

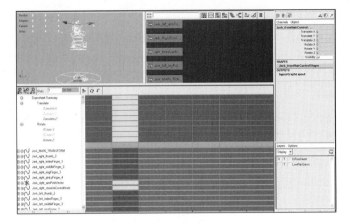

Figure 15.67 This figure shows the newly created keys for the previously unkeyed set. This means that all the controllable attributes are now set to predictable values. The lighter gray color shows that these attributes are keyed in zero state.

4. The keys need be selected to copy the full compliment. You can do this by selecting the Dope Sheet Summary and scrolling down to ensure that all the keys are now selected (see Figure 15.68).

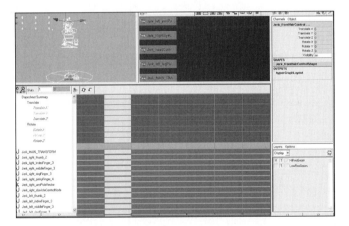

Figure 15.68 All the keys are now selected.

5. With the cursor in the Dope Sheet graph area, RMB-click and hold. This brings up a context-sensitive menu. Select Edit, Copy. This copies all the keys that you set in Frame 1. There will be no change in the display of the Dope Sheet.

6. Now move the frame to Frame 2. You can do this by RMB-clicking the timeline and dragging the current frame marker to the second frame. If it is hard to see, as it was for me, set the frame range marker to 10 frames so that the entire range is only 10 frames long. This makes navigating frames easier.

7. With the frame indicator in the Frame 2 position, right-click again in the Dope Sheet graph area and choose Edit, Paste.

This copies the frames from the invisible Clipboard to Frame 2. Now both frames are identical with keyframes for all the controllers (see Figure 15.69). Nice work! You are now ready to move The Jerk into the second pose in Frame 2. Make sure you get the sense of the planning diagrams in all five poses.

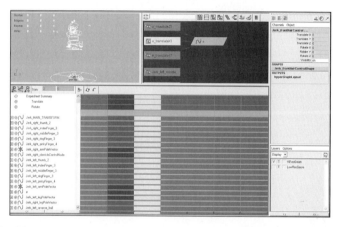

Figure 15.69   The successfully copied Frame 2 keys are now exactly like those in Frame 1. From this known state, you can begin to set the next pose in Frame 2.

At this point, you should ensure that The Jerk is keyed to preserve his pose. You can check by scrubbing back to Frame 1 using the timeline, and then scrub back to Frame 2. If you missed a key, adjust the pose now and make sure it is keyed.

When you have achieved the second pose, use this procedure to copy the finished second pose into the third frame, and begin working on that pose. As you can see, the idea is to use the previous pose as the starting point for the next pose. This helps ensure that no floating attributes will wreak havoc later in the process. Peace of mind is worth the extra effort.

Continue until all the poses are lined up from the first pose in Frame 1 through to the fifth pose in Frame 5.

You will find my five poses scene on the CD-ROM in the file Jerk5Poses.mb. You can use that as reference.

Now you can add a jump-start pose and a close-out pose. These poses are used to make sure that your character comes into the scene alive and leaves the scene alive. You might have heard the saying that one should cut on action. In animation, you will have to assume the cut in and out, and animate beyond this both before and after.

You can find my scene, 7PosesJerk.mb, on the CD-ROM for reference.

A good rule of thumb for setting these poses is to remember Tom Marsh's recommendation: The nose of your biped character should be above the shoelaces of the supporting foot. Tom Marsh is a genius in figure drawing who teaches at the Academy of Art College. His advice is pertinent and timely. So, when The Jerk shifts to his right leg, his head should follow, by means of rotating the torso controllers.

Set keys on the controllers to get the pose you need. Remember to push the poses and make them read. Use the alpha trick from earlier to help make sure the pose is clearly readable. When you have completed the pose, make sure your keys are recorded. Then it's off to the next pose.

Here is a summary that might help clarify the steps:

1. Set the pose.
2. Copy the pose using the Dope Sheet.
3. Adjust the pose-setting keys on the controllers.
4. Move through all the poses, frame by frame, for each pose in order.

It's About Time...

Now you can adjust the timing of the poses using the Dope Sheet. To do this, you will use the timing for these actions based on your reference footage and final plan. We used the reference footage from our planning process section to put together a sense of timing for the shot.

To summarize, we want the action to be slow into the coin placement and fast out of the barking dog. The search for a coin in an imaginary pocket is slow, like a tableau gag. The Jerk searching for a coin, and then finding it, picks up the pace. With ease, The Jerk reaches out toward the parking meter, but Spot jumps up and scares him back. The fastest move should be the jump back.

It is not a bad time to revisit the concept that we should have additional poses: one before the action planned and one after. So, maybe he has just been looking for the meter maid before the coin gag, and afterward, when he starts to regain his composure from Spot's startling entrance, he tries to look cool again.

The arc of the action and the timing provide some guidance to the animator. You must be sure that the action in this scene is in accord with the overall action of the whole story. That means that if the action here is really fast and furious but the scenes before and after are slow, this one might stand out.

Worse yet, if this scene is more animated than the big finale, the audience will experience letdown at the climax of the story. (This is a bad thing!) If that takes place, the story does not arc, but it peaks in this scene and crawls to the end. You must realize that you are animating in a larger work, and the actions in this area must fit the overall timing.

When setting the timing for poses, you might find it easier to set two pose keys for each pose: one when the pose is struck and one for when the pose ends. In this way, you can add a pose in between as a breakdown to set a drift. Here's what I mean.

If your character stops moving on the screen, it will appear to be dead. This is an unfortunate side effect of what we are alluding to: Living things can't stay still. In traditional animation, this is called a *moving hold*. The idea is that you add a pose, very similar to the pose you struck, but subtly different. The audience sees the character as still alive.

In Maya, you can set two kinds of keyframes. The normal keyframe sets a value in time for the attribute(s) selected. The breakdown works in the same way, except that it remains relative to the neighboring two keys when they are scaled, or manipulated. The breakdown can be useful when setting up a drift pose in Maya.

The drift pose is like that moving hold frame in traditional animation, and it adds subtle movement to the character holding the pose. If you are careful about where in the moving hold you put it, you can keep the character alive even after you edit the surrounding keyframes.

This gives us keyframe, breakdown, keyframe. This structure acts as a unit. When scaled, the breakdown keeps its relative position as the group is scaled. You can scale such a group in the Dope Sheet by LMB-drag-selecting the range with both end keyframes and the breakdown in the middle. Then use the normal scale tool (the r keyboard shortcut) and MMB-drag to scale.

If you don't want to deal with breakdown frame controls, you don't need them. You can get a similar effect by controlling the curves in the Curve Editor (you will see more about how this works in just a bit). But first, as we reach the end of the pose and timing setup, you should be aware of an alternate way to accomplish these steps a different way.

Some animators say they like to set the poses at the time they are supposed to take place. Here, we set the poses first and then moved them into place. Other animators like to copy the previous pose right to the place in time where the plan says it should go and set the pose. In either case, you wind up here, where we are. However, you should feel free to use the approach that works best for you.

Note that Maya has the capability of running the animation process in different frame rates. As you probably know, most film is done at 24 frames per second, while television is about 30 frames per second (29.97, to be exact). So, the number of frames between the poses can vary.

Some animators prefer to use 30 frames per second, following the belief that there are more frames and, therefore, more control. Others like the traditional animation approach that you can get with 24 frames per second. For you, it really is just a preference because Maya can convert back and forth.

To control the number of frames per second, go to the Animation Preferences icon at the bottom right of the screen; this is located to the right of the key button on the timeline bar. This icon opens the dialog box that controls animation settings. In this box, you will find a setting for time, as shown in Figure 15.70.

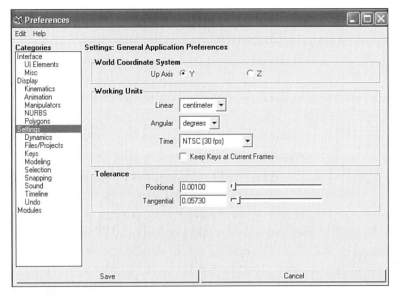

Figure 15.70   This is the dialog box from the Preferences, Settings menu. Notice that the center area has a setting for frames per second, here set to 30 frames per second.

Graph Editor

After the pose and timing are set, you can begin to evaluate the motion. Unlike traditional arts, which have had thousands of years to develop an aesthetic, little work has been done on what makes motion beautiful. So, we are at the frontier in this regard and must take all the guidance we can find. Fortunately, Disney's animators have provided some help.

The idea of beautiful or artistic motion is informed from Disney's principles. Particularly useful are the A.S.A.F.E. principles. We want to apply them to our animation to keep the motion effective and believable.

With these in mind, you can begin to approach the Graph Editor as the chief tool for making adjustments for our character's motion. The Graph Editor is a bit counterintuitive, so we will try to make the Graph Editor a bit easier to understand.

Most of us are familiar with the idea of a graph, a Cartesian coordinate system that shows a line, or the like, that plots the relationship of one parameter to another. For example, the stock market routinely plots things such as the price of a stock over time.

If you are like me, you unfortunately invest when the stock price is high and watch the stock price fall over time. After losing much of its value, the stock is sold, after which it is free to climb in value again. This is how I remain a teacher and an author instead of retiring.

However, the relationship between the parameters can be mapped: In June, the stock was at $150 when I bought. In August, the stock dropped to $100. In October, the stock rallied to $110. Then, in December, the stock dropped to $25, where your author sold again to ensure his dependence. The graph shows the stock price over time.

The Graph Editor in Maya does the same. The horizontal line is usually the timeline, just like stock or business graphs. The timeline might be in terms of frames instead of months or days, but this is still a measure of time. The time coordinate on the horizontal seems almost a convention.

The vertical parameters scale depends on which parameter you select in Maya. You will notice that there are some differences between scale values in the Graph Editor. The Graph Editor shows values that are context-sensitive for the parameter you choose.

This means if you are working on a translation, the values are set in Maya units. For rotation parameters, the scale is set for degrees, as you might expect. Scale parameters are set for multiplier values. Transformation values seem predictable.

However, if you are working with a graph of a custom attribute, you might see a scale that shows from 0 to 1. This is a percentage scale, which can be used for a variety of attributes that interpolate between two values.

For example, if you create two shapes and want to animate the shape between these two, the scale between 0 and 1 will represent the shapes in between. It is important to note that these shapes are interpolated on a linear scale. That means that each point location of the first shape linearly moves toward the point location of the second.

Most of the automatic in-betweening that Maya does follows the linear interpolation. Linear interpolation is not as interesting as the curved or arc paths discussed earlier, so we have to find a way to view our motion and give it some curved and interesting motion. This can be done using ghosting.

May the Force Be with You!

One of the most important steps for beginning animators is making the transition from pose orientation to motion orientation. As we said before, the Western tradition of animation includes a focus on how things move between poses. To show the motion clearly, you must understand the force behind the action.

In the late 1920s, Don Graham was holding training sessions at Disney's studio to help define what this new animated style was to become. Unfortunately, there were no records of these sessions, except for the animator's notes and a few memoranda that were circulated within the studio. Don Graham's *Animation of Forces vs. Animation of Forms* (1937) relates to this change in focus, from pose to action. This memo was restricted to Disney employees, for obvious security reasons. A copy of this paper can be found at `http://carlos.Mclinn.net/DonGraham.html`.

However, the memo surfaced again when it became the subject of an interview with John Lasseter in the late 1980s. While at SIGGRAPH, Lasseter stated that this memo from Don Graham is the single most important piece of information for animators. The secret lay in the approach to motion: seeing the *force* behind the motion. If you can see the motion as an applied force, the motion has its own kind of beauty. You take a giant step toward becoming a real animator.

Force can be generated from outside the character. The character can be affected by a strong wind, a bat to the back of the head, or any other external source. This kind of force, however, does not give the character "character." In this case, the character is acted upon: simple action.

A living force is generated from within our character in the form of thinking or emotion. This internal activity is communicated through the character's behavior as *acting*. So, the illusion of character is based on the expression of this internal force. The result is character animation.

Whether acted upon (action) or performing (acting) from within, the character's path of action springs from the force generated. Animators must understand the force applied to make a strong statement visually. You can see how this approach will eliminate many of the beginning character animation mistakes.

For example, if a character holds a stance in which his weight is centered between his feet, he cannot lift one leg without first taking care of force. (Try this one now. Don't shift your weight, keep it centered, and try to lift that foot.) In this case, the character must shift his weight to the support leg before he can move the free leg. Force is leading you to better animation.

To incorporate force into our animation, you have to analyze the way force is transmitted through the joints of the character. If the Jerk puts his hand to his chest, this might be seen as a form for the arm to assume. However, if we see this as a force working through the key points, we define the forces at the wrist, the elbow, and such. This gives more of a force than form result.

Now, using motion paths (Animate, Create Motion Trail), you can see how the motion is flowing. To this visualization of the motion, you can add your sense of motion. To adjust the motion between the poses, it is often useful to use the preset in the toolbar for the combination of viewports that shows the Graph Editor, the Perspective view, and the Hypergraph. You can do this by clicking the lower icon that shows this arrangement.

Change the Perspective view to the Render Camera by selecting in the viewport Panels, Perspective, Render Camera. This allows you to animate to the camera. Turn on ghosting as before. You can now adjust and fine-tune the animation from the Graph Editor.

Remember that this is not the only way to adjust your animation. If you have preferences that make you more efficient and effective, use those. However, this is presented to show how to create the motion based on the methods common to the professionals.

The task now is to review each movement in terms of the action-safe, or A.S.A.F.E., principles that we discussed earlier. Make sure that the character's movement shows good anticipation, secondary action, and follow-through. Thinking through the motion in this way focuses on complete action.

For exaggeration, our character rig imposes some limits, but use all the bandwidth that provides. The motion should be set in arcs. The motion paths will again be limited by the model rigging.

Last Tips for Motion

One of the best lessons for analyzing animation is the rule of force. Whenever your character is standing, one or both legs should support the weight. Make sure that the weight is removed from a leg before you move it. Go over the animation and review the placement of the hips, which is the center of gravity, and make sure that the hips are over the supporting leg.

Many animators feel that this is not right, but you can actually find glitches in the motion of the character by examining the animation Graph Editor. Motion should be crisp and should show snap. However, whenever there are short, sharp curves, they usually connect to short, jerky movements. Smooth curves make for smooth motion. Discontinuities are often problematic. The Graph Editor can make debugging such a glitch much more visual.

The rigging on The Jerk is great for full-body motion, and, for medium- to wide-angle shots, he works great. However, another of Lasseter's principles could be used in the next step of this animation: facial animation and lip synch. Although these are out of the scope of this chapter, they can be done after or even at the same time as the body work. This is made possible by the fact that animation can be done in layers.

The advantage of layering is that many animators can work on one assignment. This allows for specialized labor and more efficient production. The disadvantage is that it often requires a level of coordination and communication between the animators that is not generally supported by specialization.

Summary

The process used by many real-world animators consists of equal parts of planning and execution. The planning is done to ensure the accuracy and power of the performance. The execution is an attempt to realize the planning in animation.

In the process, we have touched the surfaces of many important aspects of an animator's skills and how they apply to the daily tasks of animation. In the process, I hope you found answers to some questions, but mostly, I hope you discovered that it is now no longer hard to get started animating.

The only way to learn to animate is to animate. You cannot "study" animation and become a great animator. You must exercise your skill to grow.

You must show your animation for dailies. Animation is basically communication. You cannot communicate to yourself; you must have another person, an audience. Get feedback from trained animators. If you are not in a group of these, find one, start up a group, take a class, go to a conference, or do whatever it takes. As Steve Bailey used to say, "Just get it done!"

The best outcome for me is that you will begin to apply this overview to animating your own stories. Remember, the only way to learn to animate is to animate. Get feedback from good teachers or from industry representatives. Don't use forums online; they are often misleading and inaccurate.

Have fun creating life. Only animators and gods do this work.

Chapter 16

Character Setup Pipeline for Animation

By Erick Miller

Character setup: Rigging. Boning. Chaining. Binding. Skinning. Enveloping. Puppeteering. Articulating. These are just some of the computer graphics industry's terms used to describe the processes that a character setup artist or technical director (TD) is involved in from day to day. Character setup is, most simply, the creation of an inner skeletal structure with easily accessible character deformation controls that enable animators to quickly and intuitively breathe life into the body of a character through animation.

In this chapter, we discuss all the phases of character setup:

- The five golden rules of character setup

- The character setup pipeline

- Eleven common character setup pitfalls

- Special bonus: Interview with puppet supervisor Paul Thuriot of Tippett Studios

Five Golden Rules of Character Setup

You should consider and understand many things when setting up a character. The five golden rules of character setup are a result of conglomerating all these things into a generalized summary of guidelines:

1. Understand the character's anatomy.
2. Become intimate with the character's motion requirements.
3. Keep character controls easy, intuitive, and collaborative.
4. Keep your files clean.
5. Bulletproof everything.

We discuss each rule in the sections that follow.

Understand the Character's Anatomy

Know your character's internal structure, including its entire anatomy, musculature, skeletal and bone structure, and anthropomorphic portions.

This is probably one of the biggest, most important requirements that you will ever have when setting up a character for animation. It doesn't matter whether your character is realistic, caricature, robotic, or fantasy; if it moves, it has a hierarchical structure that defines its capabilities for motion, as well as specific pivots for bending joints and skinned deformations. Grasping this anatomic layout of your character is absolutely vital when you design the initial skeleton and set up the controls and attribute sliders of your characters.

Study human and animal anatomy, and find as many ways to apply it to the creation of your character's skeleton. Depending on what kind of character or creature you are setting up, you must think of and understand different types of anatomical structures. If you are setting up a realistic dog, by all means, study canine anatomy. Consult an expert; if you can, sit down and have an in-depth discussion with a veterinarian about exactly how its skeletal structure affects how it moves in real life. If it is a cartoon-style dog, study cartoon animation carefully. A cartoon character has its own unique anatomy that is based on real life, but it is incredibly more flexible and capable of hitting just about any pose imaginable. Understand that a cartoon character will be able to squash and stretch, and generally get pulled and pushed all around in any fashion that the animator might feel is appropriate to exaggerate its personality for that shot. In our dog example, we have a careful mixture of both cartoon and realism, so you can see certain techniques from both sides.

Remember, anatomy comes first. The character's joint limitations, where the portions of the body stem from that movement and drive the character's locomotion, and generally how the character can move and deform are all dictated by its anatomy. When you fully understand this, you immediately can begin testing how the skeletal structure will be represented in 3D in the computer. You will almost always need to add or change the real representation of the skeletal structure to compensate for the limitations of 3D. This is where your creativity and understanding of the character, as well as the features of Maya, will really begin to take form.

Become Intimate with the Character's Motion Requirements

Know your character's motion requirements, special movement capabilities, or any specific motion that will be necessary for your character to achieve.

Depending on the type of character and the type of shots or interaction that your character needs to have with other things in your scene, the animation requirements of your character might change. It is of utmost importance that you, as a rigger, be completely aware of this and know fully what your character will need to do. You will need an entirely different character rig if your character crawls up a wall during an earthquake than if your character is a four-legged creature that gets swept off its feet by a gushing stream of water and then slides on its back into a river. What if your character needs to sprout wings and fly away? What if your character needs to pick up and shoot a bow and arrow? Of course, the animators will have a fun and challenging job either way. It is your job to make the character controls fit the type of motion required for the character's shots as much as possible.

The controls and skeleton hierarchies that you create will be completely at the will of the motion requirements, so study the character concept, learn how it fits into the script and storyboards, and ask questions about the nature of your character's motion abilities ahead of time. Also keep in mind that it never hurts to make your character capable of acting out motions that go a little beyond what its initial requirements define, as long as it's in the same ballpark. You never know when the director might get a new idea and want to add something, or the animator might need a control that wasn't quite thought of during the initial animation testing phase. It is always great to just tell an animator, "Oh, you need that control? Just turn on the special attribute on the wrist node, and it will do exactly what you need!" The only way you will ever be able to think this far ahead is if you actually understand better than anyone else how the character's mechanics will need to move and work with each shot.

Keep Character Controls Easy, Intuitive, and Collaborative

Always make your characters 100% intuitive to use, easy to control, and simple to quickly pose for instant feedback to the animator.

Never allow the manipulation of a character control to change the pose of other portions of the body, except for the portion of the character that intuitively makes sense. This includes *never* using things such as expressions or weighted constraints to do things such as keeping the hips halfway between both feet. Never make it difficult to accurately create pose-to-pose animation on the character. This is a key concept.

Always group your attributes together under nodes that make sense. For example, use a single controller for the face that contains all the facial expressions as well as the eyes' "look-at" capability. Have another for each arm that contains the fingers, and another for each leg. Always hang attributes on to controls that make sense for the animator. Simpler controls, with the most options that are easy and intuitive to use, always make for better animation because the animator can work faster and more confidently, without having to "fight" with the file.

Always listen to the animator. Building a character rig is a huge collaboration because you are creating a file that other people (people who might not "think" like you do) will be using for an extended period of time to deliver a vital portion of work: the character animation. If the setup must be changed because the character isn't capable of easily performing a certain motion required for the animation, it is your job to fix this for the animator. Sometimes this means just showing someone how to access a feature or attribute that already exists; other times it means changing entire portions of your skeleton rig or hierarchy. Don't hesitate to change your rig; it will only slow down the animation process if you don't, and the animators will probably blame you for it later. The challenge of building complex setups that meet the requirements of the animators is actually one of the most interesting things about rigging a production-worthy character. It is also one of the best ways to fully understand what it takes to build really great character rigs.

Tip

To help with communication issues even further, Maya 5 has two really great new features:

- A new feature called Notes enables you to type short messages and attach them to any node in a file. The Notes feature exists in the Attribute Editor of every node so that the note can be easily accessed, read, and updated for different versions of a file. This makes it very easy to explain what a certain node does or to explain that other nodes should not be changed, touched, or animated by any means.

- The new menu command Create, Annotation enables you to create hardware-drawn text labels that stay attached with an arrow pointing to any selected object. These act very much like a locator would in a scene, except that they display any text that you type in the text field of the node. These annotations are amazingly useful at explaining and labeling character rigs—and, of course, they will not software-render, just like locators.

Keep Your Files Clean

Always pass off "clean" files, catch other people's mistakes, and be a general filter for cleaning up bad data. You are the hub for the technical setup of this file—this is your job, and you should take it very seriously. Never be sloppy. A "good" Maya character TD doesn't leave any unnecessary node history or ungrouped, duplicate, or unintuitively named nodes in his scene.

For example, if you receive a model from the modeling department and deformation history is still attached to the file, by all means, get rid of it. If the character is named polyMesh12, by all, means give it a suitable name. If your file has a bunch of garbage nodes that are ungrouped or are just floating around, by all means, either group them or delete them. And, biggest of all, never create unnecessary or unexpected node history on a character after it has been bound and has entered the character animation pipeline.

Clean up any files that pass through your hands. One of the most important and vital things to do at this stage is to guarantee a file that is clean and will not "break" later. This means double-checking the model for any problems that might have been overlooked, using that keen and precise technical eye that only a character TD has.

A few standard things should definitely be quickly checked to confidently move a character's geometry into the skinning process:

1. Double-check the geometry. Run the menu command Polygons, Cleanup, Options Box, and check the Nonmanifold Edges check box and hit the Apply button. Double-check for nonduplicate vertices by selecting all the verts in component mode and hitting the Delete key. Double-check all the normals, and

make sure they are all pointing in the correct direction (outward). Make sure the vertex normals are unlocked by using the menu command Edit Polygons, Normals, Set Vertex Normal, Options Box; check the Unlock Normals check box and hit the Apply button.

2. Double-check the UVs, and make sure they are there and are laid out perfectly, ready for the final texture maps.

3. Double-check the parameterization, resolution, surface direction, or anything else that might affect how the character will move through the rest of the production process.

4. Do not move forward with geometry that is not perfect in every way. This means that the model should be ready to texture and should be bound to a skeleton for deformations so that it can now take this split road down the production pipeline into texturing and character setup.

Although there are semiadvanced techniques for updating geometry after a mesh has been bound (such as swapping out the intermediate object's geometry shape node at the beginning of the deformation chain), these kinds of techniques should be a last resort, used only when absolutely necessary. This is because they will work only if the vertex count of your model doesn't change. If you can catch a geometry mistake now, it can potentially save you time and effort during the tight deadlines to come.

Here are a few good steps to clean a scene of excess trash before rigging and skinning:

1. Always group and name Directed Acyllic Graph (DAG) transforms of your geometry if this wasn't already done for you. Make sure that all the geometry's transforms are frozen (Modify, Freeze Transformations) and, optionally, that the pivots are centered (Modify, Center Pivot).

2. Select every single geometry node, make sure the names are all appropriate, and especially make sure that the shape node and the transform node names both match (as in, NodeName and NodeNameShape).

3. By this point, I like to take a few steps that will make sure I've deleted any node that doesn't belong in my scene:

   a. First, I go to Edit, Delete All by Type and tear off the menu. (If you grab the little double bar at the top of all of Maya's menus, you can tear off the menu itself and then use it as a command palette for quick-clicking without having to navigate through the menu again.) I then rapidly click down every single command, starting with History and ending with Strokes.

   b. Next, I execute a command to delete all deformers. (Although they should all be gone by now, it never hurts to be absolutely sure.)

```
delete `ls -type weightGeometryFilter`; //delete all
➥deformers.
```

c. Next, look upstream, and make sure no additional hidden shape or intermediate nodes are hanging off the transform. You can guarantee their deletion by executing this MEL command:

```
delete `ls -io`;  // -io means intermediate nodes
```

This gives you some errors, telling you that some read-only nodes couldn't be deleted, but that's okay. If there were deleteable intermediate geometry nodes in your scene, you just wiped them out once and for all.

4. Next, use Edit, Select All by Type, Geometry, and then Graph, Input and Output Connections in the Hypershade. Break all connections to all nodes upstream by selecting all the arrowed lines connecting them at once and then hitting the Delete key. This includes breaking connections to any shading groups, display layers, or whatever else might have been sloppily left connected to your geometry. Look upstream at every single node's dependency connections, to guarantee that no random sets or extra shape nodes are hanging around from the deformers used during the modeling process.

5. Next, run the menu command File, Optimize Scene Size, with all options checked.

6. Finally, select only the geometry transform nodes and export selection into a Maya ASCII, with all the Include These Inputs check box options turned off (see Figure 16.1). This exported file is then opened in a text editor, such as UltraEdit or Notepad or Windows, BBedit on Mac, or Pico or Vim on UNIX. Delete any unnecessary `requires` lines at the header of the file, and then resave the Maya file in ASCII text mode with the same .ma file extension. This can then be imported or opened as the final cleaned geometry file that will be used to rig the character. Unless you are using some sort of proprietary or third-party plug-in that is necessary for the model to load, the only `requires` line that should be in the file is the one that says this:

```
requires maya "5"
```

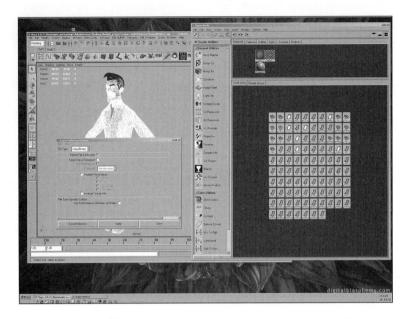

Figure 16.1   The polygon geometry nodes, completely cleaned from
all input connections, as displayed in the Hypershade window.

Sometimes I even export all the polygon geometry as separate .obj files, with no export options checked, and then bring these objects back into Maya, one at a time, to guarantee that all the geometry is in a clean and default state that Maya will deal with properly for the rest of production.

All of these additional steps might seem somewhat tedious or even paranoid just to prepare a file. Undoubtedly, this will require backward and forward communication with the modelers and texturers. As experience will teach you, however, the cleaner your file is to start, the smoother things will run in the production. That single bit of assurance can prove to be truly priceless farther down the line.

Bulletproof Everything

Always bulletproof your rigs, and everything will run as planned because there is a smaller chance that characters will break. By "bulletproofing," I am talking about removing or hiding all attributes and nodes that an animator does not need and that could potentially break the character rig if they were modified in the wrong way. Hiding all nodes, locking all attributes, and making attributes nonkeyable is definitely a step in the right direction, but this will still not stop an animator from immediately opening up the channel control and unlocking them, sometimes just to see what it does. Curiosity killed the cat, and it can just as easily kill your character rigs and cause annoying animation transfer compatibility issues in your production pipeline. Plus, because you created the file, you almost certainly will be the one troubleshooting and fixing any problems that occur later.

There are several ways around this. Undertaking good preparation and planning is one of them. Practicing good communication is another. Most likely, if you tell an animator specifically not to touch something, that person (hopefully) will not touch it. Schedule a production meeting with the animators who will be using your file, and gather feedback about how things are working for them. During this meeting, communicate to the entire group exactly what they are and aren't supposed to do to the character rig when it is passed out for the testing phase and the full-blown production phase. It is also vital to make sure that you have an appropriate system in place for versioning your files so that an older version never accidentally makes its way into the production. A simple way to do this is to hook up a hidden node with a hidden attribute that contains a version number that you can update and check using MEL as you release new versions of your file.

Set up your files with a clear understanding of how they will fit into the production pipeline later. Have a full understanding of how your file will progress through the pipeline, how the model will have textures applied to it, and then how the animation and the rigged-up character with textures will become a part of the same file. Always realize that if something can break, it will. If your scene has many nodes that are all selectable and capable of modifying the character in an unwanted way, be sure to lock them down, template them out, and generally bulletproof them as a final step before handing off the file to be animated.

The Character Setup Pipeline

The "life" of a character begins the second you start laying out its joints and determining how the controls will cause the character to move and interact with its environment. Many steps are involved with character setup, and most steps can be accomplished during the initial model creation or after the model is finished. The bulk of your work should really be spread out in an intelligent and planned scheme so that it works as much as possible in concurrence with the animation, texture painting, shading, lighting, and rendering budgeted time schedule. You should be able to publish updates of the rigged character into the pipeline as they are completed and needed by each department. This is how things need to work to function properly on a schedule in a real production environment with real deadlines, whether it be in the film or the game industry. Specific stages must occur to integrate the character rig seamlessly into the rest of the production to achieve full time/output efficiency.

The typical character setup pipeline can be broken up into the following generalized stages. Each stage is designed to be a separate element that could be preceded with an additional prerequisite stage or replaced entirely with a similar combination of stages. Depending on a specific production's needs—a commercial versus a feature film versus a game production versus a viz/sim project—each will have specific caveats that further define the details of the stages involved with the pipeline, depending on how many departments are involved, what the timeframe is, and how the data I/O pipeline needs to function (for example, file formats the 3D data needs to be converted from or into for the final digital output formats). Figure 16.2 shows a prototype of a character setup pipeline.

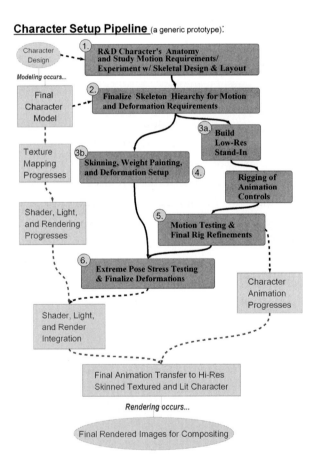

Figure 16.2 Basic workflow for the input and output of data in the general stages of the character setup pipeline for a typical character-based production.

Eleven Common Character Setup Pitfalls Revealed

This section describes specific areas of character setup that can become pitfalls or cause later problems in the character's file if they are not handled or set up properly either before or during the character rigging process. These areas include the following:

- The joint axis: orientation and scale
- The processes of moving and editing joints after creation
- The processes of changing and editing geometry after binding
- When to use IK and when to use FK
- How to design easy-to-use skeletal controls
- Pose compensation
- Rotation order and gimbal locking
- Geometry/node history
- Multiple deformers and deformation order
- Geometry normals and texture coordinates
- Skeletal compatibility for animation transfer, skin weights transfer, or general pipeline integration

Some of these issues are rudimentary, but it is amazing how often a file can become heavy and difficult to work with because one of these issues was overlooked or handled inappropriately. The following sections carefully explain how you should handle or combat these pitfalls to make life easier for you and the rest of the character's pipeline.

The Joint: A Fundamental Axis of Orientation and Scale

Joints and bones in Maya are particularly unique because they allow so many different levels and forms of transformation to occur on them. All affect the skin cluster that they are bound and weighted onto.

A joint not only can be rotated from its rotate pivot, but it also can be translated, scaled, constrained, regrouped, and parented to any other node. This directly affects its pivots and relative transforms. This behavior provides much interactive freedom when setting up and laying out a skeleton, enabling you to do just about anything you want. Unfortunately, it also opens up many places to make a mistake or to create a skeleton with some portions of its axis pointing in an incorrect or unintuitive direction and orientation.

How a joint rotates is controlled by its local rotation axis. You can interactively edit the local rotation axis by selecting the joint, going into Component mode, and clicking the question mark. Unfortunately, this does not reorient the transform (scale) axis of the joint.

If you plan to scale one of your joints, you should be sure that the scale axis lines up with the local rotation axis and points exactly toward the next joint in the hierarchy. Note that scaling a joint in Maya is very similar to changing its "bone length" in other software applications. Maya scales joints by scaling the current joint and then sending that scale into a .inverseScale attribute of the child joint. This behavior causes the current joint to scale and the children joints to remain in the same scale. This is usually desired behavior, but it can be deactivated in the Attribute Editor of the joint by deselecting the Segement Scale Compensate check box.

Tip

How do you fix the .inverseScale connections if they break? Sometimes the parent's scale attribute becomes disconnected from the child's .inverseScale attribute. This could be because of some "by-hand" reparenting or reordering of your skeletal hierarchy, or it can happen if you export your joints by themselves with the History check box deselected in the Export options. I have seen misguided people go through and reconnect each joint by hand. Well, there is a much easier and quicker way to fix this: Simply select the root of your "broken" hierarchy and duplicate it by hitting Ctrl+d on your keyboard. Maya does all the fixes and reconnects each joint for you. Because it knows that these attributes should be connected, it is smart enough to check for this and reconnect them for you.

A great new feature in Maya 5, previously available only by using the `joint` MEL command, enables you to orient the rotation and scale axis of your joints through the user interface of Maya. This new option is found under the menu Joint, Orient Joint. It is about time this option is available, considering that in the last four versions of Maya this command existed only in MEL.

Even though this UI version is available, the `joint` command is still a very useful MEL command by itself and can easily help battle the problem of correctly orienting your joint axis. As mentioned previously, the `joint` command is an essential bit of knowledge for anyone creating joints in Maya. Read all about it in the MEL documentation for the full list of specific flags and options. Here are a few `joint` commands that are frequently used for orienting joints; they can be typed into the command line while joints are selected:

- `joint -e -oj xyz;`—Reorients the rotation axis of the selected joint in the xyz directional axis

- `joint -e -zso;`—Zeros out the orientation of the scale axis to line up with the rotation axis

- `joint -e -ch -oj xyz -zso;`—Reorients the rotation axis and zeros out the orientation of the scale axis at the same time for the entire hierarchy of joints

Moving Joints After Creation or Smooth Binding

This is a very basic thing, yet can pose several annoying problems for a skeleton as it is being designed or built. Moving a joint is quite easy. Just select the Move tool, and move it, right? The problem is that the entire joint hierarchy moves along with the joint. This is fine if you want this behavior, but usually you want to move just the placement of a joint, without moving its children. There is a simple way around this.

Instead of using the Move tool, use the Joint Creation tool to select the created joint, and then move the joint around the screen using the middle mouse button. This enables you to interactively move any joint after it has been created, without actually moving the joint's children.

Even better, by pressing the Insert key, you can select a joint and interactively move the joints using the Move tool without moving the children. After you select a joint, switch to the Move tool, and push the Insert key, you are moving in pivot mode, effectively moving the pivot of the joint instead of the joint itself. But because a joint's location is actually defined by the location of its pivots (relative to its parent), the joint's translates will move as well—but without moving any of the children.

The `joint` command is another handy MEL command that contains a flag, `-co`, to enable you to numerically move a joint without moving its children. If you need to modify a joint position in a script, this is the command and flag to use. Using this MEL command, you can create any MEL script with the following code snippet as a quick hack to move a joint using any method (such as a constraint or any other unknown MEL function), and then easily move the children back where they belong:

```
// move the joint somewhere first, then:
string $joints[] = `ls -sl -type joint`;
float $mvPos[3] = `getAttr .translate $joints[0]`;
undo; // this will undo your previous move…
joint -e -r -co -position
$mvPos[0] $mvPos[1] $mvPos[2] $joints[0];
```

Next, we'll talk about a really useful script that uses a simple technique to move a joint after it has been smooth skinned. It creates new transform nodes and hooks them into your skin cluster. These nodes also end up being the new nodes that you use to paint weights with (but because weights are stored in the skin cluster, you don't lose any of your already painstakingly painted weights). This trick is so easy but so little known that it definitely deserves an explanation.

First, a skin cluster works because of an input attribute called .matrix[]. This is an array attribute that has a new element for every joint or influence object that the skin cluster uses to deform your geometry. Each matrix element is simply connected to the .worldMatrix[0] attribute of your bound joints, as shown in Figure 16.3.

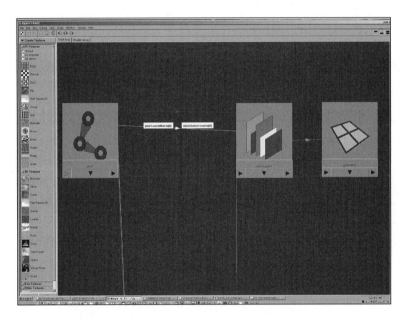

Figure 16.3 Each matrix element is connected to the .worldMatrix[0] attribute of your bound joints.

When the joint moves, the transformation matrix of the joint gets sent into the skin cluster's deform function. The skin cluster then multiplies each vertex by the cumulative weighted transformation of each influence, and voilà! The skin cluster just outputs new point positions for your vertices, and you get a nice, smooth deformation based on how smooth the weights are painted.

It is quite simple to just create a new transform node with zero transforms that is a child of the original bound joint, and then quickly hook up the new node's .worldMatrix[0] attribute, replacing the connection that was previously being occupied by the joint. Figure 16.4 shows an example of this.

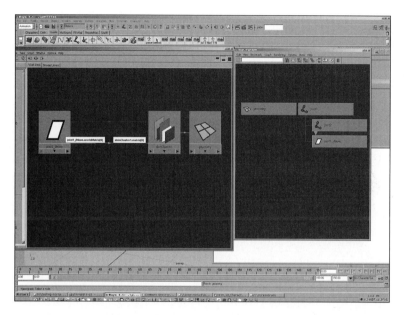

Figure 16.4   A new transform node with zero transforms that is a child of the original bound joint; the .worldMatrix[0] attribute has been rerouted into the skinCluster node.

After this parenting and new connection has been made, the joint's transformation matrix no longer directly controls the skin cluster's calculations; instead, a child of the joint does. This means that you are now free to move the joint using the Insert key, which activates the pivot mode of the Move tool. You also can reorient your joints all you want, using the Skeleton, Orient Joint commands to create entirely different origins and orientations for your bound joints, without harming your already bound geometry.

Warning

Remember that moving a joint will cause local rotation axis problems. The joint's axis no longer will point toward its child, which is unintuitive and generally unwanted behavior. Be sure that you always reorient and align the local rotational axis of your joints after you have moved them.

Changing and Editing Geometry After Smooth Binding

In an ideal production environment, your character's model usually will be fully approved and will never change after it has been handed to you for character rigging. Unfortunately, reality sometimes brings surprises. It might be necessary to have a somewhat nonlinear workflow when the geometry of your character model needs to change after the skinning and perhaps all the weighting and even the animation has been finished. This might seem like a daunting or impossible task, but you can use a couple of advanced techniques together to swap out pretty much any semisimilar geometry and keep your joint's weighting.

When your production pipeline or schedule demands it, you can change the model or even swap in new updated models after your character has been bound with two very straightforward solutions:

- You can plug the updated model's .outMesh attribute in the Connection Editor (if it's polygons) directly into the .inMesh attribute of the intermediate object mesh shape. This is the base input data for the deforming geometry's dependency graph (DG) input/output data stream (for NURBS, it's the .worldSpace[0] output attribute, which goes into the .create attribute of the deformed mesh's intermediate object). This gem of a technique enables you to swap in and out entirely different models, but with one limitation: The vertex count or order can't change, although the shape and UVs can. Vertex order is a general limitation for all of Maya's vertex-indexing data structures in general. This technique works really well if you have a character model and the modeling department is able to sign off on the resolution of the character. However, the rest of the model still needs subtle detail tweaks, slight proportional changes, and entirely new UVs. As long as the vertex order and count don't change, the skinCluster will update correctly using the swapping technique.

- If the resolution of your mesh (the vertex count or order) needs to change but the UVs will stay the same, you can use Maya's built-in menu command Skin, Edit Smooth Skin, Export Skin Weight Maps, Options Box. Maya then writes out a bunch of texture images that it can load back in from a text file that contains all the necessary links to reapply the weight data. The cool thing about this is that it does not rely on the resolution of the mesh whatsoever. Thus, your vertex count and order could change, as long as the UVs are generally in the same place for the weight maps to be imported and assigned properly. Another cool thing about this built-in technique is that, although you are importing the weight maps as bitmap image textures, it doesn't ever actually store the images as textures in your scene file. Instead, it stores the weight data on the skinCluster node, as if you had just painted it on.

- If the resolution of your mesh, the shape of your model, and the entire layout of your UVs all must change, you can use a combination of the above two methods. You can first swap out the newly laid out UVs, next save out the weights for the geometry, and then rebind the new model and load in the .weightMap file. It has also been suggested that a low-res wrap deformer can be used as a mechanism for swapping in high-resolution models in such a way that the low-res model is bound to the skeleton and acts as a wrap deformer to the high-resolution geometry. Wrap deformers are great, but they don't give you control when it comes to detailed finessing of character deformations. Therefore, this is the least desirable solution.

When to Use IK and When to Use FK

IK should be used only when a character needs to place and hold its limbs on an object. This can include pushing off the ground or a wall with his hands, or grabbing and swinging from an overhead bar. It is almost an absolute convention that any character's legs will have IK attached to them because, when a character walks, the feet need to be attached to the ground. In plenty of cases, an FK skeleton must be used as well, so let's take a look at some of those.

FK can be used if a skeleton is swinging around naturally, with freely swinging hands or feet. FK works particularly well if the end of its joint hierarchy doesn't need to plant itself on another object. Perfect examples of using FK to animate a hierarchy are with the swinging arms of a running character and with the spine/back joints of most characters.

Many animators prefer FK over IK, even if it means setting more keys, just so that they don't ever get that "pulled" look on the hands or the feet. Experience shows that most animators prefer the "natural arcs" that occur from FK over the linear pulling motion that occurs in IK. Therefore, it is very important to not only know whether the shot requires IK or FK, but to also take the animator's preferences into consideration.

Note

Maya allows a good deal of freedom when using its IK solvers. Many useful capabilities, such as rotate plane solvers and pole vector constraints, enable you to control the base rotation vector of the joint chain. Some very useful FK-to-IK keyframing capabilities can even use quaternion keyframes for interpolation, enabling you to set clean keys between an IK handle and an FK skeleton.

Designing Skeletal Controls

Skeletal controls should generally be designed to encompass all the capabilities of the character. At the beginning of the process, you should be able to map out and determine exactly what your character needs to do and what controls are needed to achieve these requirements. Never rig a final model before you have an absolutely clear resolution behind what its controls will be and how its hierarchy will need to be controlled. You will understand what the controls need to do based on the first two rules of character setup: anatomy and motion requirements. Often you will want to design a skeleton with weighted constraints to control the orientation or position of its hierarchical children. Other controls might include set-driven keyed rotation controls, yet more controls could be direct connections in the Connection Editor. Whatever your skeletal controls are, it is important to design them so that they are simple to access, easy to use, and grouped in some sort of sequential order that makes sense.

Using visual icons works really well for character controls. Some people like to use NURBS curves in the shape of text, boxes, or circles for the visual skeleton controls of a character. Others like to use polygons that have their shader connection broken (so that they show up in wireframe only and also don't render, just like NURBS curves). Either way, this very clear and helpful to the animator because the controls are visually identifiable and easier to select with the mouse than, say, a hidden locator or selection handle.

It's also helpful to use colors that represent your character controls. It is not necessary to use a new layer for each control that you want to have a different color. Instead, just open the Attribute Editor for the node, click and expand the Display section, and then click and expand the Drawing Overrides section. Click the Enable Overrides check box so that you can modify the wireframe color of any node separately from the layer editor. This enables you to easily put all the pertinent character controls into a single layer that can be turned on or off quickly and easily, yet it still allows for color coding with a bit more control over the colors.

Pose Compensation

One of the major problems that an animator can encounter while animating a character's skeleton is the issue of pose compensation. This means that when the animator changes one portion of a character's pose, it affects other major portions of the character's pose in unappealing ways. This can make the animator re-evaluate and repose the other portions of the character's pose that were inadvertently affected by the change to a seemingly unrelated orientation of a different portion of the skeleton. This is an inherent problem in character setup for animation because it is a perfectly normal reaction for an FK hierarchical skeleton, as well as a partially natural behavior for most characters. The trick is to figure out what needs to move along with the skeleton and what doesn't.

The animator can usually fix compensation relatively quickly if the rigger has set up the skeleton rig appropriately to account for such dilemmas. One of the best ways to account for pose compensation is to classify major portions of the character into separate hierarchies, such as the feet, legs, spine, head, arms, and hands. Each hierarchy can be classified according to whether it would naturally rotate on its own. Two great examples are the head and the hands. If your head is pointed toward something because you are looking at an object, hunching your back a little bit should theoretically affect the position of your head but not the orientation, which you had already posed so that it was looking at a certain object. The same situation goes for the hands. If you have an IK setup on your arms and you need to place your hands so that they are resting on an object, repositioning the character's spine or shoulder should not affect the angle and position of the character's hands. Otherwise, it would cause the character animator to repose the hands to compensate for the changed pose of the shoulders or neck. These previous examples are exactly the kinds of things that you want to avoid in your setup—and the animators will love you for it.

When the separate poseable portions of your character have been isolated, you can duplicate them from your skeleton hierarchy onto the world level. They can then be constrained to the portion of the skeleton that they would normally be children of.

Pose compensation usually becomes a real problem with orientation more than translation because, in most characters, you would expect the children joints to translate along with the parents. If this assumption is true, all that needs to occur is a point constraint onto the appropriate connecting joints. This leaves all the rotation controls free for FK posing by the animator and allows the other portions of the hierarchy to be posed using either FK or IK; their rotations will not affect the rotations of the joints lower in the skeleton.

Rotation Order and Gimbal Locking

Gimbal lock is an interesting phenomenon of the Euler rotation solver, in which one axis can easily become directly overlapped with the other axis, causing the joint to be incapable of rotations in the direction of the overlapping axis. Gimbal locking is really a direct result of your node's rotation order, which can be found in the Attribute Editor for every transform node found in Maya. The funny thing about xyz rotation order is that you can actually end up in gimbal lock by a single rotation of 90° in the Y axis if your node is oriented in world space. That means that if your character's root is oriented in world space (which is usually the case), a single turn to the left or right will put his root in gimbal lock. Let's try out an example:

1. Create a locator (Create, Locator).

2. Double-click the Rotate tool and set the Rotate mode to gimbal so that Maya displays the actual rotate axis in the viewport.

3. Now, with the Rotate tool active, type the value of **90** in the rotateY channel in the Channel box. Now, whether you rotate on the Z axis or the X axis, you are rotating in the same direction. This phenomenon is known as gimbal lock.

One way to make gimbal locking less likely on your character's root is to change your rotate order to either yxz or zxy. This allows your character to turn left and right as well as side to side. gimbal locking will still occur if he is turned halfway upside down, but because this is much less likely to occur than turning sideways, it is a step in the right direction.

Since version 4.0, Maya has quaternion interpolation, which solves the problem of gimbal flipping. The unfortunate truth, though, is that many animators prefer to battle gimbal locking using the Euler interpolation solver (which is the default) than use quaternion keyframes. This is because quaternion keyframes do not allow you to offset individual rotate channel keys, nor do they allow different tangency on individual keyframes. You can change the type of keyframes that are used from Euler to quaternion by going to Window, Settings Preferences, Preferences and choosing Keys on the left side; then change the New Curve Default option to Synchronized Quaternion Curves.

Gimbal lock can also be solved on a production level by using doubled joints (or just group nodes instead of joints, if you prefer). In this solution, a transform node is exactly duplicated, unparented, and then placed into the hierarchy with exactly the same orientation and axis as the original joint below it. Depending on the nature of your character control hierarchy, the child joint can then be hidden and eventually made visible for additional rotational control if gimbal lock ever becomes a problem. Using double joints is actually quite a useful technique for adding any rotational or scale override capability to your skeleton. All this means is that, instead of having one joint in certain places in your skeleton, you have two: one exactly right on top of the other, with simple parent/child relationships. You bind only the child joint, and the additional parent is there to offer extra rotational hierarchical control.

Joints like this, or nodes that are simply additional parents, are particularly useful in FK skeletons that need extra control over rotations. A good example is having double knuckle joints to be able to control the fingers with multiple set-driven keys, as well as having controls for the animator to manually rotate the knuckles to hit the exact pose they want. Another example is having an additional transform node above the wrist joint that is used to rotate the wrist; when gimbal lock occurs, the actual wrist is made visible to rotate the wrist on the necessary axis. Because double joints can get a bit confusing, it is really important to keep them named and grouped with organized, meaningful controls.

Geometry/Node History

Node history is one of the single most useful features of Maya, but it can also be one of the biggest detriments to keeping a file clean and organized, with the least amount of data needed to use the file. Node history is exactly what the name implies: all the operations that you have performed in the file. If history is being stored on the node from the modeling phase, you most definitely want to delete the history before you bind the character to the skeleton.

History can be good—if you understand what the history is doing on your node and need to keep it for a good reason. An example of keeping history on a node before character setup is using the makeNurbsSphere.startSweep history attribute node to create blinking eyes of a cartoon-style character. History nodes are fully capable of being animated, so they can be very useful.

History can also be very useless and even harmful to your file if you have too much of it before you bind your character. Plenty of reasons exist why history could be harmful, but to really understand why, you must understand what these nodes actually are.

History nodes are computation nodes, or nodes that perform a calculation on data and output new data. In other words, any history node has a specific algorithm that it performs and data that it must process. Sometimes the computations can become very intensive because of the large amounts of complex data usually attached to or associated with 3D information. Any time you can get rid of history, do so. If you need to keep history around, do it with the full understanding of the repercussions (if any) of that particular history connection.

Step through the following exercise to get a better feel for how to clean up node history.

Exercise 16.1   Cleaning Up Node History

1. Create a polygon sphere.

2. Select some vertices and create a cluster.

3. Select more vertices and create a lattice. It doesn't matter what the resolution is.

4. Now perform a polygon function on it, such as Polygons, Smooth.

5. Next, with the poly sphere selected, open the Hypergraph window and view the upstream graph (Window, Hypergraph). Inside the Hypergraph window, perform the menu command Graph, Input and Output Connections.

6. You should now see lots of nodes. Hit the a key to frame all. These are all your history nodes doing the calculations that are creating your geometry.

   Just for a moment, realize that if this were a final character model and you were to bind skin, you would have all this excess history doing so many calculations, all for nothing.

7. Go to Edit, Delete by Type, History.

   All the nodes should disappear except for the shape and transform nodes of your geometry.

Before you begin deforming a character (this includes modeling its blend shapes), it is generally appealing to delete all history, random set nodes, and remnant duplicate hidden intermediate shape nodes.

Another major detail regarding active history arises after binding a character. You should especially be careful about history after the character has been bound and weighted if you need to apply blend shapes to it later. Sometimes certain history can change the geometry inputs for your skin clusters and really mess up your ability to add or manipulate deformers or deformation order. This is why modeling is considered an entirely separate stage from character setup (as far as Alias|Wavefront is concerned):

The model should not be modeled on after it has been bound to a skeleton because of the order in which the upstream dependency graph that creates your output polygon mesh is being evaluated. Of course, there are ways around this. However, you should avoid geometry editing that is not related to strictly character deformations after a character has been bound unless you are fully conscious of how this history can be manipulated or removed, and how this process will affect the performance of your file for the rest of your production.

Multiple Deformers and Deformation Order

Additional deformers can be layered and added to a skeleton rig (which is also a deformer after it is bound) at any time to add additional deformation effects, such as relative clusters and lattices of vertices bound or parented to joints. Jiggle deformers are a relatively new type of deformer that are great for layering over animation to achieve jiggling skin effects. These effects were possible before only by using a combination of a cluster and particle goal weights. Blend shapes are probably the most common deformer that would be added after a skeleton has been bound to geometry.

Deformation history is the order in which the computation of the deformer takes place. In other words, do you want the deformation to be calculated on the vertex location where they are after the joints deform them, making the joints deform the original polygons? Or do you want the deformers to change the shape of the geometry and then allow the joints to deform it? Most likely, you want the new deformer to take place before the skin cluster node.

Editing the deformation is a simple task. Right-click over the geometry. A menu should open. Pick the Inputs, All Inputs menu item. If you have deformer history, when the menu opens, there will be a list of items representing all the computation nodes upstream of your geometry node. Deformers have the capability of actually reordering themselves without changing anything else except for their own order because all deformers were derived from the same type.

To reorder deformations, using the middle mouse button, simply click the input deformer in the list that you are interested in moving. With the middle mouse button held down, drag the deformer from the top of the list onto one of the deformers toward the bottom of the list. The deformer first in the list deforms the vertices location and then pass that data down the stream to the next deformer to modify. It should make complete sense why, then, it is necessary to have blend shape morph targets appear in the list before the joint cluster. This is necessary so that the model's vertex location moves relative to its original geometry's vertices, not relative to the joint cluster geometry's vertices. In most cases, you want the joints to affect the model last. This means that you need to either reorder your deformers after creation or use advanced deformer options such as Front of Chain for blend shapes when creating the deformers in the Options box. I prefer reordering them using the inputs so that I have complete control over the order of deformation history evaluation.

A deformer called a tweak node always exists whenever you create any other deformer on your geometry. The tweak node exists to store the component editing that is done on the shape node after a deformer has been applied. This node is necessary because the original deformer uses a copy of the shape node that originally existed when the geometry was initially deformed. Even though the tweak node exists, you still get the warning "Tweaks can be undesirable on shapes with history."

Also, if you ever need a tweak node, but for some reason Maya didn't put one there for you, you can create one by selecting the geometry you want the tweak node attached to and executing this command:

```
deformer -type tweak;
```

To exemplify the workings of a tweak node, try this:

1. Create a sphere and delete history on it.

2. Select some of its vertices and create a lattice.

3. Now select some of the same verts in the lattice set and move them across the screen. You should get the error "Tweaks can be undesirable on shapes with history."

4. Right-click and go to the Inputs, All Inputs list. Under the Node State column, select the tweak node's drop-down menu (and pay attention to what happens to your geometry) and select Has No Effect. You should see the geometry snap right back into the place where it was when you initially created the lattice.

This can be a life saver if a character animator accidentally selects and moves vertices on a high-res character (anything can happen, I guarantee!). All you have to do is select the geometry in question, go to Inputs, and swap the tweak node to Has No Effect.

Transforms, Normals, Parameterization, and UV Texture Coordinates

This is a pretty straightforward one: It is the job of the modeler and/or texturer to deliver clean files with properly built geometric elements and UV texture coordinates. Nonetheless, it is still part of the job to check that everything is correct before rigging occurs. This is important to be aware of before binding a character to joints, especially if you are creating the entire character yourself (which rarely happens in a big production studio but happens all the time when creating short student films or small productions). You must be sure that your geometry is correctly built for texturing and ready to be lit and rendered before you bind your character to a skeleton for animation purposes. If there is a mistake in the geometry or texture coordinates, you must catch it now, not when it comes time to render and everything looks wrong.

Of course, there are ways to fix these kinds of problems, but doing things correctly the first time is always the best way to go. Thus, we do not cover fixing mistakes here. The fixes will just end up adding unwanted node history anyway, which we just talked about in the previous explanation.

Let's talk about transforms first. Freeze transformations usually should happen after the characters are guaranteed to be the correct global scale and have been measured and compared against layout environments and the other characters. It makes sense to work at real-world scale, especially if you will have any cloth or dynamic simulations in your character pipeline. Some productions work at 10 times smaller than real-world scale, and some even work at 100 times smaller than real-world scale. The important part to remember is that after your character has been modeled to the correct scale, you should zero all the transforms that create the groups for the geometry. Freezing the transformations does just that: It simply zeros out the translations and "bakes" them into the shape node—the vertices. Freezing transformations (as well as deleting history) makes the geometry generally cleaner and is one good sign that it's nearing the final state for rigging.

If you freeze transformations and the model was built using two mirrored halves, the side that was scaled in negative one will have its normals flipped. Normals that are not pointing outward cause problems with both textures (bump-mapping uses the normals for its calculations), and any dynamic simulation or particle collisions that need to happen on the character require outward-facing normals (such as cloth simulation). One way to easily flip the normals of a NURBS surface is to change or swap its surface direction. You can flip and conform the normals of polygonal geometry by using the normals commands under the Edit Polygons menu: first Edit Polygons, Normals, Conform and then Edit Polygons, Normals, Reverse Options, choosing Reverse and Propagate from the Options box.

Vertex normals can also be a nasty little creature on polygon models. Sometimes, if you are transferring polygon geometry from other software applications (perhaps Houdini or Mirai), you get vertex normals that are locked in a single direction. You can fix this by using Edit Polygons, Normals, Set Vertex Normals and using the Unlock Normals check box. You can also try exporting as a .obj from File, Export options, with all options set to Off, and then reimporting your geometry into a new scene.

Parameterization of your character is very important. This means both the resolution in combination with the spacing of the surface components (either edges for polygons or isoparms for NURBS), and how they flow across the surface of the model. Usually parameterization is not a problem, and most modelers create really even parameterization as second nature. This means clear and equally spaced surface components that follow the shape of the forms that they create and that line up with each other with exact tangency, when necessary. I am mentioning this because not only is it important for textures, but it is important to have full control over the realistic deformations of a character. If the surface is not capable of bending in a certain way because there is not enough resolution or because the model was not modeled correctly, it is your job to catch this as a character rigger and mention it to the modeler. Chances are, the modeler will be happy to add that extra row of isoparms or edges into the model so that when it deforms, it will look its best. After all, this is the only thing that really matters. A couple great examples of places in a model that might need extra resolution are the rows of edges that form the model's knuckles or forehead wrinkles, or generally anywhere in the model where a wrinkle might need to occur when the character deforms.

Finally, we come to texture coordinates, or UVs. These are what define the placement of the texture maps or determine how the textures placed on the object will be laid out. With NURBS, UVs are inherent in the surface and the modeler or texturer will spend a good deal of time guaranteeing that all the NURBS surfaces' U and V directions are aiming the same way, line up with each other, and have 0 to 1 uniform surface types. If this is the case and your pipeline is properly set up for this, all you should have to do is quickly double-check the patches. If you are dealing with polygons, a texture mapper had to create the UV coordinates on the model. This isn't as big of a deal because you can actually transfer UVs at any time in a polygon or subdivision surface pipeline. Although it leaves a little bit of history on the geometry, it should be okay as long as you don't have proprietary plug-in exporters that don't read the history nodes correctly. Otherwise, a poly transfer node won't hurt your file. This is a good example of knowing when history is okay and when it is just plain sloppy.

Character Compatibility for Data Transfer

Keeping characters and their skeletons compatible is tricky business, especially if you want to keep them fully compatible through the entire pipeline and run into no bugs along the way. Of course, this issue begins to get very pipeline-specific. By this, I mean that the skin weights or animation transfer from Maya might never need to come back in, if you are going out to a game editor or game engine. Otherwise, if you are exporting it out to render in another software renderer, such as RenderMan, you will have entirely different issues, and many custom exporter tools in place (such as Mtor or Maya Man) likely already will handle this efficiently. But, for our example, let's assume that we are rendering only inside of Maya's supported renderers. So, we need to guarantee that we can keep our character's skeleton compatible throughout the entire animation production and that the animators are not accidentally doing anything wrong as they animate with the files.

This assumes that we are importing and exporting Maya's default .anim animation file format, which is sometimes incredibly picky about things that must match exactly for them to import correctly into the new scene file.

One way works relatively well for setting up a pipeline to guarantee that the skeleton hierarchy's joint names stay the same: Use file referencing for the low-res character file and a selection MEL script that really is just a macro, written specifically to select the correct joints for exporting animation. Because referencing requires a prefix string in front of every node name, this is a perfect opportunity to label your files with the version as the prefix. You can then reference the high-res file with the exact same version prefix that the animators are using for each new version.

Then, whenever an animator wants to see what the shot looks like in the high-res file, they can easily export the animation using a few very simple scripts. Then they can import it into a high-res file, the whole time never able to break or change the "real" data because the files are being referenced; the only data that the animators are saving are the animation curves that they are exporting from their file, as well as their progress shot of the referenced low-res character with animation. When new versions of the file are released, you can simply have a script that transfers only the keys directly from the character controls so that the character updates are nearly seamless for the animator (except for the fixes you make, of course). You can reference in environments, lights, cameras, and new shot layouts this way as well.

Note

Be careful with referencing. One thing that everyone involved with production data flow should know is when to use Maya's referencing and when to not use it. Ideally, you would use referencing seamlessly, in a fully nonlinear and nondestructive manner during the entire production process. The modeler would be finishing the model, and the rigger would already be working on the weighting; meanwhile, the texture artist would be concurrently creating UVs and textures, and the file would be lit and laid out all at the same time, before the model was even finished.

Unfortunately, referencing data does not work anywhere close to this way. The basic rule is that if you know that you are modifying a node and that it will need to be updated—and you know that the person referencing the file also is doing work on that node—referencing will not work (except for animation, as long as you prepare for it in advance). The scheme for transferring data in general is highly specific to your pipeline's needs. The previous outlined explanation was merely a primer to really get you thinking about what types of issues exist, all the way up to rendered frames. You also must think about how you set up the character at the beginning can come back to haunt you if you are not fully aware of your pipeline.

Special Bonus: Interview with Paul Thuriot, Puppet Supervisor, Tippett Studios

Tippett Studios, in Berkeley, California, is one of the world's most highly respected CG animation and effects houses. It was founded more than 16 years ago by Phil Tippett, one of ILM's former creature shop supervisors and one of CG's earliest, most celebrated pioneers. Since then, this studio has literally seen it all, boasting work from all the way back to *Jurassic Park* and *Starship Troopers*, to the Oscar-nominated *Hollow Man* and, most recently, their work on *Blade 2* and the Clio Award–winning "Carl and Ray" BlockBuster Entertainment commercials.

Tippett Studios owes the stunning beauty and realism of its renowned CG creature and effects work to its incredible team of artists, puppeteers, TDs, and supervisors, who together form an integrated production team, and a CG pipeline capable of translating and evolving the practical methodologies of a traditional model shop's successes of sculpture and stop-motion into the CG world of pure 3D computer-generated imagery.

Paul Thuriot is the very talented puppet (character setup) supervisor who has been with Tippett Studios for several years now and has worked on many high-budget feature films and commercials. Paul has wrapped as the supervisor for the puppet teams on New Line

Cinema's *Blade 2*, the second round of award-winning "Carl and Ray" Blockbuster commercials, and most recently *Men in Black 2*. He is currently working on Tippett's next big creature project, *Hellboy*, a feature-length film based on the popular action/horror comic book of the same title. All of the character and creature integration produced by Tippett is guaranteed to be truly amazing work, and it is always created using the Maya software as the primary 3D modeling, setup, and animation package. In the following interview, we talk with Paul and discuss how some of Maya's robust features can and should be leveraged in a production pipeline such as the one at Tippett studios.

What do you enjoy most about doing character setup at such a renowned creature shop like Tippett?

First and foremost would have to be learning. Being surrounded by so many different, talented artists in my time here at Tippett, I've grown so much artistically and technically in my field of expertise. No matter who you are, there's *always* something to learn from anyone.

Another thing is having a sense of being part of the team. Because Tippett is still relatively small, you feel as if you are part of each and every team, even if you aren't on the particular project. You really feel that you matter—and *do* actually matter—to the studio and those around you. Seeing that finished project after months of continuous (and sometimes stressful) work can be one of the best feelings of accomplishment.

Now as far and setup goes, I really enjoy the mixture of technical challenge and creativity. Sometimes it can be completely "cut and dry," but other times a level of abstract thinking can play a big role in the realm of setup. A lot of the responsibility of setup lies in problem solving, whether it's having to figure out how a creature should move or finding the perfect level of controls an animator needs to achieve a goal without over- or underwhelming him or her. That's on top of making sure that the whole process will even work on the computer!

And then there's R&D (research and development). That's my favorite thing to do for a show. In my world, R&D is so great because I can really explore new things, write MEL scripts and plug-ins, and problem-solve technical challenges that we will need to use for the next production or the studio as a whole.

That brings the experience full circle and back to learning.

How does the character-rigging pipeline generally work within the production pipeline as a whole at Tippett?

Well, the way we do it at Tippett at the moment, like many other larger studios, is split up the production among several different departments. Each department does just one specific thing, but each department has to communicate together to get this one big package done for the final production. Of course, this isn't saying that an individual person might not have to wear multiple hats!

continues

continued

So, starting out with a design of a creature, the model department comes first in the pipe. They make the model either by freeform modeling or scanning and surfacing techniques. When this stage is approved, they hand it off, to both the paint and puppet departments. Paint does the textures in parallel with what we do (in puppet), meaning that they can actually work concurrently with us.

So, once the puppet department gets the model, we start building all the actual controls for the character. We do a lot of sitting down with the animators and figuring out exactly what they want the character to do—the worst-case scenario type of thing—to really develop an understanding between us and the animators to determine just what the rig will allow the character to do. After we have a good idea, we start laying out all the joints, setting up and testing the deformations, and sending it back and forth between the animators and us for final testing.

After this stage is done, the final file gets passed off to the animation department, and they do all of their magic to animate the character and give it life. At the same time, the FX department does its thing to add yet another digital layer to the scene. This is where anything from fire and water to blowing wind or cloth can be added.

When they are all done, they publish that scene and it gets handed off to the lighting and rendering TDs, who light and shade it with the painted textures on shaders and kick off renders with RenderMan. When the renders are done, it gets handed off to the compositors, and they create the final image you see on the screen. The end goal is always to make a final image that looks the best possible, and the compositors are the last line of defense for this 2D integration with the background plate, which then gets printed to film.

But here's a realistic truth: At any one time, that "straight line" down the pipeline might get curved and go elsewhere or might just come straight back from where it came! We all make sure that we stray off the path as few times as possible, and if it happens, everyone tries to help out and get everything back on track.

But let's not forget other departments, such as match-move, roto, film I/O, editorial, plus everything that has to do with production in general.

How much character rigging would you say is done on a shot-by-shot basis, as opposed to having a single character rig that just does it all?

We really try our hardest to understand the needs of the character and to come up with an overall "Uber-Puppet" that will do just about anything for all the shots in the film. But unfortunately, that's not always realistic thinking. We know that there will sometimes be shot-specific puppets, for something that the creature has to do that your "standard," every-other-shot puppet just can't. Then if it's a major shot, we might make a specific puppet for that; if it's something small, we (or sometimes the animator) set a small control in the scene to use.

So how do you guys handle the whole issue of animation transfer from the changed animated characters to the hires renderable character? Do you bake the animation straight onto the joints and transfer it that way, or do you transfer it based on the controls or hierarchy connections? Is there a general standard to making this stage go smoothly?

That topic is actually in the process of changing right now.

Until now, animators would transfer animation from puppet to puppet via animation export and import. That's it—take the old puppet that they've been working on for a while, export the animation, and import it onto a new puppet. It works maybe 80–90% of the time, but if the hierarchy changes, new things need to be added. The process of transferring animation can take a while and can be quite painful.

But now we've developed a new tool set/workflow called Creature Creation Tools (CCTs, for short). I won't get into too much detail here, but you can think of CCTs as a scripting language (basically library extension in MEL)—sometimes really simple and sometimes extremely complex tools. The new tool set enables animators to choose their own specific set of controls for a character. They might want FK/IK switching on the left arm, FK on the right arm, FK/IK/Inv on the left foot, IK only on the right, and so on. Just choose the options from a simple character builder GUI (named Automatic Puppet Utility, or APU, by a couple of the animators). The combinations are completely up to them and whatever they feel comfortable with, as well as the needs of the shot. This is all built on a low-res, real-time, scrubbable model.

One of the multiple new tools is the capability to hook up this animator built rig to a base puppet and drive it. The base puppet is the high-res rig that has all the bells and whistles, and this is the version that ultimately gets rendered. This way, if there's an update, all animation has to do is "drive" the new rig instead.

Do you guys have strict standards for your setups that everyone sort of adheres to, or are all of the rigs pretty much built differently depending on the person who built each one?

We definitely have standards for everything. For all setups, we all try to follow the same general rules all the time.

At the same time, we've automated some major steps in the setup process, and while doing this, most of these "standards" are automagically applied. That makes that aspect much easier and gives us more time to focus on other tasks.

So, would you say that the use of MEL is pretty vital in the pipeline?

Most definitely! We've become so reliant on our MEL tools that some steps in our process would not be able to completed without them! And this isn't just the puppet department—it's the entire studio.

continues

continued

When the character is fully rigged and weighted, and the animation is applied to the final high-res geometry, how does the rendering occur?

After lighting, the TD fires off a command to our farm to render. We don't use Maya's renderer—we use RenderMan—so we have our own maya2rib pipeline tool. Maya2rib reads in the Maya scene file and a command file supplied by the painters. This command file basically says to RenderMan, "Geometry A will have texture file B with these properties applied."

You know, we have some wonderful programmers who write all this really awesome stuff, and lots of it runs hidden in the background. Not too many people see any of it happen, but, of course, it is vital to the production pipeline.

How does the final approval process work at such a diverse studio as Tippett, in which each person has his or her own responsibility and problems could pop up where? Maybe an animator or lighter is using the wrong file or has made a mistake that needs to be resolved quickly because it could jeopardize the final production.

Every morning, we have dailies, when we are all viewing, on the big screen, the shots and the progress of our collective works for the show. This is where most issues are first encountered and dealt with. Sometimes it could be as simple as maybe a TD not using the latest animation, or a comper using the wrong element in the wrong position. Or, it could be some huge issue, like something is really wrong and no one has a clue what it is! That's when everyone jumps and helps come to the solution.

Based on your experience as a character rigger, what would you say are some of the most important things to consider before and while rigging a character? For example, this might be the Five Golden Rules that I have in the first section of this chapter.

Remember what the final result your trying to achieve is. Don't overcomplicate things in a rig. Overcomplicating a puppet (especially one you aren't animating) just makes the whole thing a lot more difficult than it's really worth. Granted, yes, it might give you the ability to get some of that great deformation that happens in reality, but it might mean that the animator has to spend an extra few hours (or days) to finish the look. And that is never a good thing when the clock is ticking.

I find that doing everything on paper—laying out ideas before I touch the computer— works out really well because it makes me quickly think over the entire character, and it brings up ideas and issues that might occur while in the building process. This gives me the chance to fix things before the animator has to deal with them. A little preproduction work before starting helps make a clearer goal and makes the entire job much easier from start to finish.

I believe that Jim Blinn stated this quite eloquently, that computer graphics is "The Ancient Art of Chea-Ting." Although he was talking about rendering, it really applies to character setup as well.

Exactly!

What have you found is the most powerful thing about using Maya in a professional character-rigging production pipeline?

It's scripting cability. Definitely, scripting and API capabilities are Maya's biggest strengths.

Either writing tools that help make a lengthy and painful process as easy as hitting a button, or creating some completely new algorithm for some completely new node is exactly what I mean.

Basically, you can make Maya do *exactly* what you need it to do easily enough.

MEL is extremely powerful, and just about everything you'd need outside of Maya's standard, default tool set can be created from this.

Here's the general rule: If you need to do something more than once, write a script for it.

What would you predict or suggest as the next big fandangled enhancement or major software feature that could really make Maya a more powerful 3D software application for character rigging?

For rigging, I hope the next big feature is a muscle- and skin-deformation system.

Most studios are creating (or have created) their own versions of this, but I feel that it will really be a huge improvement to the rigging and deformation process if Maya or some other 3D software package releases it.

That about wraps things up. Is there anything else that you would like to say about getting into character setup or using Maya as a final thought for our readers?

Really the most important thing if you are interested in character setup is to understand anatomy, how things move, and why things move the way they do. Then you simply need to know the package (Maya or the like) and what it can do, and what it needs to do, and what you need to do to get it to do what you want it to do!

Study life, the way things move, and how things function in real life. Then know your software and how to use it. You have to know the rules in real life before you can break the rules on the computer.

There is always some production challenge for which there is an elegant solution that sparks new ideas, and that's what I like the most about using Maya.

Summary

The character setup pipeline is a process and a workflow for integrating your character into your studio's pipeline so that it can eventually be animated, textured, lit, and rendered. It is not only the process of character setup and rigging, but in fact it is the entire structure which exists around rigging as well as the actual steps involved with doing it. Of course, many little details involved with rigging a character demand special techniques and processes; these are discussed in Chapter 17, "Rigging Characters for Animation." The most important thing to remember is the entire process of rigging a character must take place within a nonlinear workflow so that other portions of the digital studio pipeline can continue to function as necessary.

Chapter 17

Rigging Characters for Animation

By Erick Miller

When setting up a character for animation, you need to complete several tasks. This chapter discusses those tasks in relation to the *Parking Spot* project outlined in Chapter 3, "Digital Studio Pipeline," and explains why they're important.

Specifically, this chapter explains setting up a character for animation through revealing the step-by-step workflow involved with rigging the following setups in Maya:

- Quadruped spine and hips setup
- Quadruped IK legs and feet
- IK spline tail and ears setup
- Low-res stand-in geometry
- Control boxes hooked up to your character rig
- The advanced biped spine
- Stretchy IK legs and classic reverse foot
- Advanced IK arms and clavicular triangle
- An advanced additive hand and fingers
- Facial controls and blend shape deformers
- Eye controls
- Smooth binding proxy geometry
- Painting of smooth skin weights
- Painting of weights using per vertex selections
- Additional influence objects

Setting Up a Character for Animation

The very first step in creating a character setup rig is to research and gather the animation requirements of your character, including the types of motion the character has to achieve and the types of controls the character must have to fulfill these requirements.

Next, you should analyze the storyboards for the project and get a feel for what the specific shots might need. Also look into what kind of extra controls or capabilities might need to be added for each character or on a shot-by-shot basis.

Note

One important thing to keep in mind while reading this chapter is that the characters in the project are not necessarily supposed to be photorealistic. Instead, they're 3D puppets that an animator will be controlling in both realistic and unrealistic—and perhaps even cartooney—ways to act and tell the story.

Creating Clean Joint Hierarchies for Animation

Now comes the time to actually decide how the joints will be laid out for the characters according to their skeletal structures. This is the experimental time during which you can try out different things for overall joint placement without affecting anything. Joints in Maya are very versatile (see Figure 17.1); they enable you to create and arrange them in whatever form you please.

The next step is to draw the joints in 3D space. The best workflow for drawing your character's joints is to put the 3D view ports into 4-up mode by going to the Panels menu of the 3D view port window and clicking through to the menu item Panels, Layouts, Four Panes. Next, using the Joint tools found under the menu path Skeleton, Joint Tool, begin drawing your joints in one of the orthographic windows (either front or side, but not the Perspective view—it's much more difficult to control where the tool places the joints along a third axis in that view, so it's more difficult to place them accurately by simply clicking in the view window). As you click the first joint, look in the other orthographic windows to see where it appears in relation to your character. Now use the middle mouse button to drag the joint into place in the other orthographic windows.

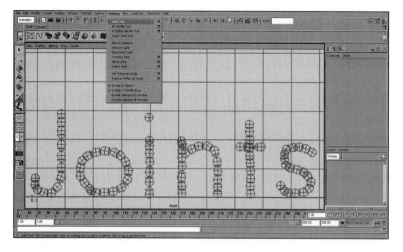

Figure 17.1 Joints are flexible.

After you have built your skeleton, you will need to orient the joints. Do this by selecting all your joints and using the Skeleton, Orient Joint menu command (see Figure 17.2).

Figure 17.2 Choosing the Orient Joint command.

If you need to move or reposition any of your joints at any point before binding, use the Insert key with the Move tool activated. This enables you to move the joints without moving the children. Be sure to never rotate or scale your joints into place, and always translate them.

After you translate your joints, you need to be sure to rerun the Skeleton, Orient Joint command, or select the root joint of your skeletal hierarchy and execute the following command:

```
joint -e -ch -oj xyz;
```

When your joint positioning is final, select all the joints, go into Component mode by hitting F8, and activate the Local Rotation Axis option. Make sure that you rotate your rotation axis (using the Rotate tool) so that the same axis (probably the X axis) is always pointing down the joint and that the other two axes are pointing in the proper direction for intuitive rotations to take place when it is time to animate the character. Never rotate a local rotation axis on the axis that would cause it to no longer point "down" the bone of the joint. Figure 17.3 shows the local rotation axis while it is being edited.

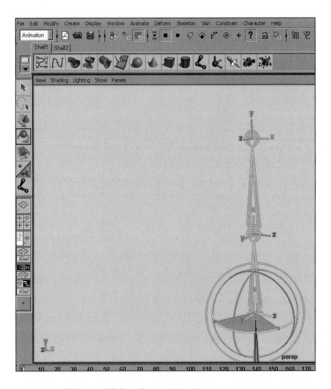

Figure 17.3   Setting local axis rotations.

Finally, after you have moved all your joints into place, oriented them correctly, and modified all their local rotation axes so that the rotations are perfect, you have only one more command to run. Select the top root of the skeleton hierarchies that you have just laid out and oriented, and perform the following command:

```
joint -e -ch -zso;
```

This zeroes out the scale orients and aligns the rest of the transform matrices associated with the joint to match the current orientation that you adjusted it to when you modified the local rotation axis. This is quite an important step, especially if you plan to translate or scale your joints. It is highly recommended that you perform this step when you are finished orienting all of your joints.

Figures 17.4 and 17.5 show the final laid-out skeletal structure of both characters in the *Parking Spot* project.

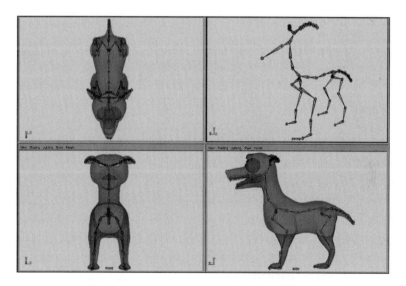

Figure 17.4   The laid-out skeletal structure for Spot.

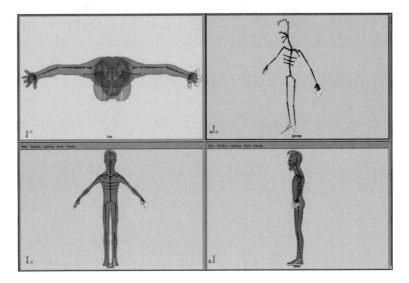

Figure 17.5   The laid-out skeletal structure for The Jerk.

Rigging a Simple Quadruped Character: The Dog

This section covers some simple techniques that you can use to quickly rig a quadruped character for animation, without having to add complex time-consuming or difficult-to-understand controls. Several advanced character setup tutorials later in this chapter go into much more detail on advanced character rigging. The techniques in this section can be used to quickly and easily get a quadruped character set up and ready for character animation.

For many characters, a simple setup is all you will need. As a general rule, it is best to keep your rigs as light and simple as possible so that they are easy to use and maintain throughout the duration of the animated piece. For hero characters whose animation might be the centerpiece of much of the shot or sequence, complex character controls could be necessary. It is the responsibility of the character setup TD to assess with the animators and supervisors of the scene what level of complexity the character's rig should have based on the complexity of the character's motion requirements.

Quadruped Spine and Hips Setup

Here we have built a simple FK spine that can be animated in a very straightforward and traditional fashion by rotating the joints.

As you can see in Figure 17.6, the spine is composed of only six joints, which are pretty much ready to have animation controls hooked up for them.

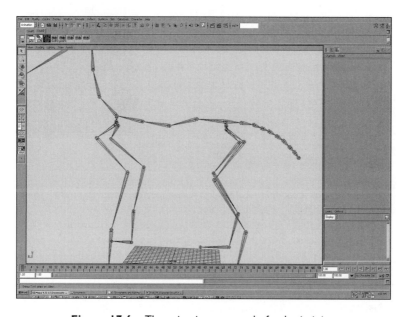

Figure 17.6   The spine is composed of only six joints.

The important part to notice in this portion of the setup is not really the spine itself, but the way the joints that create the spine are parents of the legs. The portion of the character's joints that starts the legs has an extra joint between the parent leg joint and the spine joint it is connected to. In the back of the character, this joint controls extra rotations of the hips. In the front, it controls extra rotations of the chest. Figure 17.7 shows how your spine hierarchy should connect to your legs using the extra hip joint between the hierarchies.

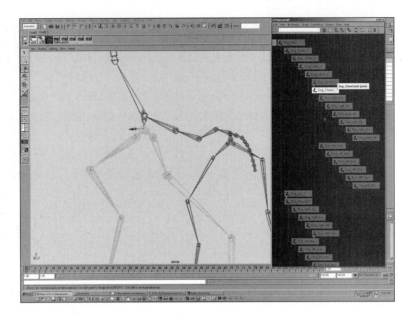

Figure 17.7 The spine hierarchy should connect to the
legs using the extra hip joint between the hierarchies.

These joints are parented in this way so that the additional rotation control can hook
IK onto all the legs and still rotate the character's hips independently. This concept of
having additional parents in a hierarchy will undoubtedly come up many more times
when it comes to rigging a character, so be sure to take note.

Quadruped IK Legs and Feet

The legs of the character are composed of four joints, stemming from the hips and the
chest. The foot is a single joint that allows for rotation from the ankle (see Figure 17.8).
A relatively simple foot control was chosen because our dog character will not need to
have individual control over each toe and claw separately.

To make the IK controls for the legs, we created two IK handles for a single leg and
hooked up a locator as a constraint to control the rotation of the ankle as well as the
position of the IK handle for the foot. Follow along with this step-by-step exercise to
see how we set up the first leg (the back right leg). You can quickly and easily set up the
character's other three legs using the same technique outlined here.

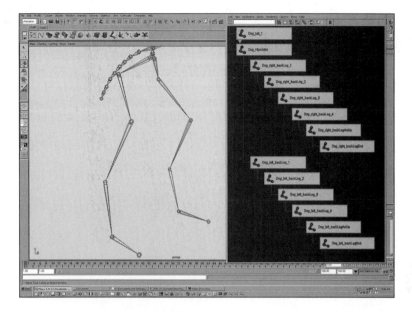

Figure 17.8 The legs of the character are composed of four joints, while the foot is a single joint that allows for rotation from the ankle.

Exercise 17.1 Creating Spot's Hind Right Leg

Begin by creating an IK handle between two joints.

1. Open the file Dog_SkeletalHierarchy.mb from the CD that accompanies this book. Use the IK Handle tool to create an IK handle from the Dog_right_backLeg_1 joint to the Dog_right_backLeg_3 joint. Name the new IK handle thighIkHandle, and freeze its transforms by choosing the menu command Modify, Freeze Transformations while it is selected.

2. Create another IK handle from the Dog_right_backLeg_3 joint to the Dog_right_backLegAnkle joint. Name this IK handle legIkHandle.

3. Create a locator by choosing the menu command Create, Locator. Point-snap it to the legIKHandle by selecting the Move tool, pressing the v key, and, while holding down the middle mouse button, dragging the locator to legIKHandle. Rename it footIkControl.

4. Create a null transform by clicking Ctrl+g with nothing selected. Next, point-snap the null to the legIkHandle using the v key, as before.

Now you will give this null transform the same orientation and transform axis as the Dog_right_backLegAnkle joint.

5. Select the null transform first, and then add to the selection Dog_right_backLegAnkle by holding the Shift key and clicking it (it needs to be last in the selection). Hit the p key to perform the parent operation. Next, perform the menu command Modify, Freeze Transformations. This zeroes out the transforms of the null and puts them into the space of the ankle joint (see Figure 17.9).

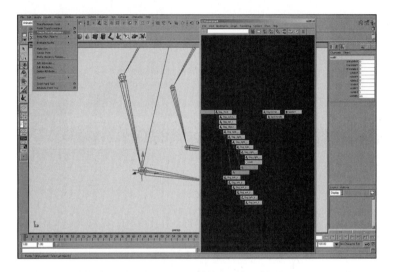

Figure 17.9 Clicking Modify, Freeze Transformations zeroes out the transforms of the null and puts them into the space of the ankle joint.

6. Now unparent this null joint back to the world level by selecting it and clicking the menu command Edit, Unparent.

7. Select and parent the footIkControl locator to the null transform node. Freeze the footIkControl node's transformations. It now has the same orientation as the ankle joint.

8. Next, select footIkControl and use the Shift key to add legIkHandle to the end of the selection list. Click Constrain, Point, select footIkControl and Dog_right_backLegAnkle, in that order, and click Constrain, Orient.

   You have just point-constrained the IK handle to this locator. You've also orient-constrained the foot so that rotating it rotates the foot and translating it moves the IK for the leg.

You are just about finished with the setup for the leg. One last step is to add a pole vector constraint.

 9. Create a locator, and name it leg_poleVector. Now move it behind the back of the character's leg, on the side opposite the side of the leg that bends inward.

10. Next, select the leg_poleVector locator and legIkHandle, in that order, and click Constrain, Pole Vector.

11. Now just group the leg_poleVector locator all by itself (to add an additional transform above), and then point-constrain the group node to the Dog_HipsJoint node. Select this new group along with the remaining IK handles in the Hypergraph, as well as the null transform that is a parent of your foot control; group them together using Ctrl+g. Name the new group IkLegControls (see Figure 17.10).

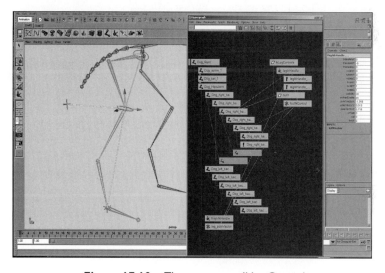

Figure 17.10   The new group, IkLegControls.

12. Repeat the previous steps for each of the other legs. This step-by-step process should go quite quickly when you get the hang of it.

13. When you are finished with all four legs, add prefix hierarchy names for each leg by selecting each node together for a single leg, clicking Modify, Prefix Hierarchy Names, and adding the prefix for that particular leg (for example, frontRightLeg_ and backRightLeg_).

14. Next, select all four of your legs' IkLegControls groups, group them together using Ctrl+g, and rename that group Leg_Controls.

15. Finally, group together the Leg_Controls and Dog_Root joint under a new group, and call it DogMainTransform (see Figure 17.11).

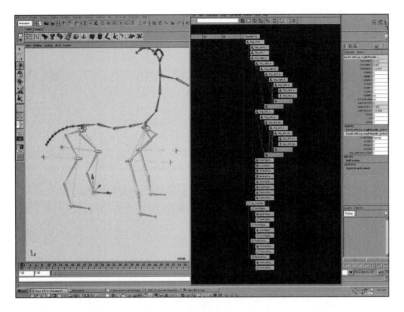

Figure 17.11 The finished legs set up for the dog.

The finished file with all the legs rigged is named Dog_LegsSetup_Finished.mb on the CD.

IK Spline Tail and Ears Setup

The technique used for the IK spline tail and ears setup is a very common combination of IK splines, with some added FK-style control. The technique you will use in the next exercise is basically to create a spline IK for the entire hierarchy of joints and then draw a low-res joint hierarchy right on top of where the IK spline curve was created (usually two to three joints is enough). Next, you'll simply smooth-bind the low-res joints to the IK spline curve. This is a nice way to get some FK feeling control and still have the ability to translate the joints for IK spline-style results.

Exercise 17.2   Character Setup for Spot's Tail and Ears

This exercise again is performed only on the tail. The exact same technique should then be used on the ears as well.

1. Start with the completed file from the last exercise, Dog_LegsSetup_Finished.mb, which you can find on the accompanying CD.

2. Go to the IK Spline tool by clicking the menu item Skeleton, IK Spline Handle Tool, Options Box. Hit the Reset Tool button at the bottom, and then be sure to uncheck the Auto Simplify Curve and Auto Parent Curve options.

3. Draw an IK Spline curve from the root of the hierarchy, all the way to the last joint in the hierarchy. In this case, it is a nine-joint tail; you create the spline handle starting from the Dog_tail_1 joint and ending at the Dog_tail_9 joint.

4. Next, using the Joint tool and holding down the c key to enter Curve Snap mode, draw a low-res four-joint hierarchy directly on top of the spline curve that was just autocreated by the IK spline tool.

5. Translate the new hierarchy upward just enough that it is not right on top of the other joint hierarchy, and rename each joint in the hierarchy TailControlJoint (see Figure 17.12).

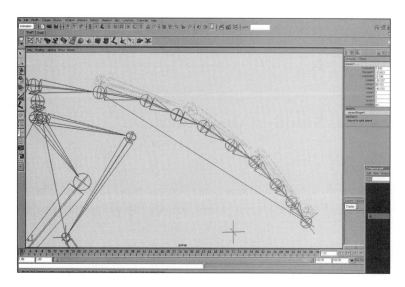

Figure 17.12   Creating a low-res control hierarchy.

6. Next, select the highest parent of the TailControlJoint hierarchy and Shift+select the NURBS curve that was created automatically by the IK spline tool. You might have to use the Hypergraph to select this curve because the joints are in the way.

7. With the current selection, click Skin, Bind Skin, Smooth Bind using the default options.

8. Select the root of the new low-res control hierarchy and parent it to the node that you want to rotate the real tail hierarchy that has the IK spline solver attached to it. In this case, I parented the new TailControlJoint hierarchy to the Dog_HipsJoint node so that when you rotate the hips, the tail wags along with them.

9. Perform these steps for both the ears. The steps are exactly the same.

10. When you are finished, group any ungrouped spline IK handles as well as spline IK curves under a new group node. Then put this group node somewhere in the character's hierarchy that will not have animation applied to it. In this case, I added a new group node to DogMainTransform and called it Dog_character. This group parents anything related to the character that should not be animated as a child of it.

11. Be sure to lock the translates, rotates, and scales of the Dog_character group node. Parent all the leftover IK controls and NURBS curves under the Dog_character group node.

   You can find the completed setup in the file Dog_TailAndEarSetup_Finished.mb on the accompanying CD.

Low-Res Stand-In Geometry

As the following exercise shows, creating stand-in geometry is a very simple process. This geometry is simply a low-resolution version of the actual character geometry, which is then cut up into a separate piece per joint using a combination of the Cut Poly Faces tool and the Poly Separate command. The cut polygon pieces are then simply made a child of the joint that they correspond to. Now, the low-res geometry moves with the joint hierarchy but is not bound or deforming, so it is extremely fast and interactive for the animator to use.

Exercise 17.3 Creating Low-Res Stand-In Geometry

For this exercise, you begin with the finished file from the previous exercise, Dog_TailAndEarSetup_Finished.mb, which you can find on the accompanying CD.

1. Import into the Dog_TailAndEarSetup_Finished.mb file the low-res dog file, called Dog_lowResPolyStandIn.mb, which you'll find on the accompanying CD (see Figure 17.13).

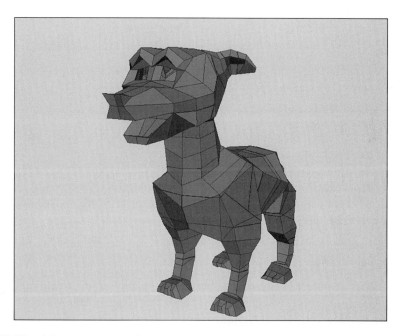

Figure 17.13 A low-res version of the character model is used for the low-res stand-in geometry.

2. Take a look at the joint hierarchy of the dog, and start to figure out where you want to cut your low-res poly object into separate pieces. A general rule is that you will need to cut your character in any place that it will need to bend, or any child that will need to rotate independently from its parent to achieve the articulation of the character's pose.

3. Select the low-res polygon character. Activate the Cut Poly Faces tool by clicking Edit Polygons, Cut Faces Tool (it might say just Cut Faces, depending on your tool settings) Option Box (see Figure 17.14).

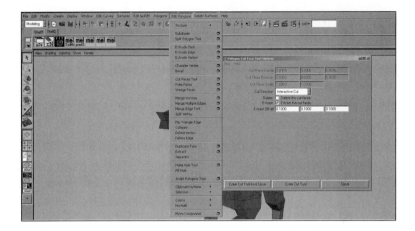

Figure 17.14   Select the low-res polygon character, and activate the Cut Poly Faces tool.

4. Now, with the options from the previous figure, drag your mouse across the geometry and watch as the Cut Faces tool creates a straight line across your geometry. This is where the polygons will be cut when you release the tool. Cut the polygons. Experiment with where you are cutting the geometry and how well it lines up with the location of the joint.

5. Next, after you have cut the polygon, perform the menu commands Edit Polygons, Separate and then Edit, Delete by Type, History.

6. Cut the geometry into a separate piece for each joint, trying not to cut across other parts of the geometry that shouldn't be split yet. Then, each time you cut, separate the polygons and delete the history. Eventually, you will be finished cutting up the entire geometry.

7. Next, one by one, select each polygon piece that you cut, and Shift+select the closest joint that you cut that piece for. Hit the p key on your keyboard to parent the geometry to the joint. Do this for each separate piece that you cut for the character.

You can find the finished file with the low-resolution stand-in character properly cut and parented in the file Dog_LowResStandIn_Finished.mb on the accompanying CD.

Hooking Up Control Boxes to Your Character Rig

Control boxes are the visual handles that the character animator uses to animate the character. The control boxes are an extra layer of setup hooked up to your skeleton's joints, IK, and hierarchical controls to give the animator a simple and intuitive way to see and select all the controls for your character that are meant to be animated. All the translation and rotation of your character should happen on character control boxes, not on random locators or selection handles that are difficult to see or select.

Control boxes can be made of NURBS curves or of polygon objects that have been disconnected from a shader. NURBS curves are the most common choice because you can isolate them for selection while animating using the NURBS Curve option in the Object Mode Pick Mask menu. You can also quickly view them on or off with the Show NURBS Curve option of the Show menu of your current 3D view port window (or from the HotBox).

Open the file CharacterControlBox.mb on the accompanying CD to see exactly what a control box is. As you can see, it is just a NURBS curve that has been shaped so that it creates a cubelike box shape—hence the name control box (see Figure 17.15). Control boxes can, of course, be any shape and size (because they are just NURBS curves), and the CVs of the curve itself can always be hand-tweaked to produce the correct shape.

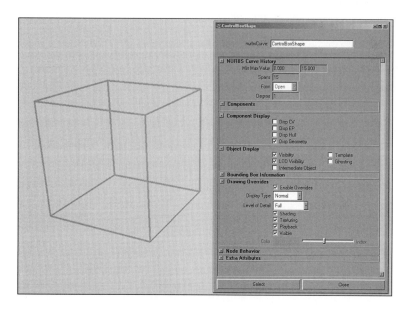

Figure 17.15   A control box.

You can hook up a control box to a rigged character in several ways. Basically, the main goal is to in some way connect the transformation controls of the control box into the transformation controls of the character rig. You can achieve this through expressions, complex node networks, or just simple constraints or parenting relationships.

The most common and straightforward methods for hooking up control boxes to your character are the following:

- **Transform (object) parenting**—Simply parent your control as a child of your control box. This works easily and efficiently for things such as IK handles and constrained locators, as well as groups that are meant to control translation or rotation.

- **Shape parenting**—You do this by parenting the NURBS curves' shape nodes (not the transform, but the shape, which you have to load into the Hypergraph and graph input and output connections to see and select). Making the NURBS curve shape a child of the actual transform that you are trying to hook up the control box for enables you to use the curve as a selection handle for the actual joint or hierarchical animation control.

   You can do this by first point-snapping the NURBS curve to the joint that you want to hook it onto. Next, parent the NURBS curve transform to the joint and click Modify, Freeze Transformations on the NURBS curve. Select the NURBS curve shape. (Make sure the node says Shape at the end, in Hypergraph, Graph, Input and Output Connections. Also be sure you have the shape selected, not the transform.) Then Shift+select to add to the current selection the joint (or any other transform node) that you want to hook up the NURBS curve as a selection handle for. Then perform this MEL command:

   ```
   parent -r -shape;
   ```

   This parents the NURBS curve shape node under the transform for the joint. Now you should be able to select the curve in the view port window, but in actuality you are selecting the transform of the object that you just parented the NURBS curve shape onto.

- **Grouped control boxes with constraints**—Create a group node that has the same orientation and translation space as the joint or node that you are hooking up the control box. Then make this node the parent of your control box. You then freeze transforms on the control box and point-constrain it to the joint that you are hooking up to. Orient-const˅˅˅˅ the joint to the control box so that it controls the rotations.

You can create a group node that has the same orientation and translation space as the joint or node that you are hooking up the control box to in two different ways. First, you can create a null transform by selecting nothing and then hitting Ctrl+g. Next, you can give the null the same transform pivots as the joint or node you are trying to hook up to. You do that in two ways:

- Point-, orient-, and scale-constrain the null transform node to the joint. Then immediately delete the constraint nodes to give the null transform node the same transform space as the joint.

- Point-snap the null transform node directly on top of the joint. Then temporarily parent the null to the joint, freeze transforms on the null, and unparent it back into its original hierarchy to give the null transform node the same transform space as the joint.

- **Grouped control boxes with direct connections**—Create a null group node, and point- and orient-constrain it to the parent node of the actual joint or transform that you are trying to hook the control box onto. Next, create a group node that has the same orientation and translation space as the joint or node that you are hooking the control box up to; make this node the parent of your control box. Parent your control box group node under the constrained null. Then freeze transforms on the control box and open the Connection Editor. Load the NURBS curve's rotates on the left side and the joint's rotates on the right, and directly connect them to one another so that the control box is driving the rotations of the joint. Even though they are directly connected, they will always move together properly because the parents are linked with constraints and the nodes are both in the same transform space.

Connecting your control boxes is really a crucial element of rigging your character because it is one of the last steps before your character is ready for animation testing. treat the process of hooking them up to your character accordingly. One thing to remember, though, is that it really doesn't matter how you get your control boxes hooked up to control your character, as long they work correctly and move the correct nodes around. Sometimes on simple characters you can get away with purely parenting techniques or direct connections alone (which is perfectly acceptable). Another good idea when it comes to hooking up your control boxes is to keep the translates and rotates of the con-trol boxes transforms capable of going back to zero as the default attribute state. Therefore, if you need to move, scale, or position your control box, simply enter Component mode and shape it using the control vertices. This also usually means freezing the transforms before actually going through the process of connecting the box to control a joint or other transform node.

Also remember that control boxes are simply used to select animation controls for your character and to move the character around. The goal of these controls is that they be immediately accessible and selectable from any view. Sometimes it is difficult, but do whatever you can to make the controls easy to see and select from most angles. This includes making controls somewhat uneven in shape or asymmetrical, as well as color-coding so that if one is right on top of the other, it is still quite intuitive to differ-entiate between the two control boxes.

Here are a few easy ways to color-code your control boxes in Maya:

- By clicking Display, Wireframe Color with the object selected, you can easily change the color of just about any object without modifying attributes that other parts of Maya directly use to change the color of the node as well (such as the Layer Editor).

- Open the Attribute Editor of the node and expand the Object Display frame layout. Then expand the Display Overrides subsection of the Object Display lay-out. Next, turn on the check box that reads Enable Overrides. Now the lower section that reads Color becomes enabled, and you can drag the slider and choose any color that you want.

- Simply make a layer and assign your objects to that layer. Then just change the layer color. This is the least preferred method because you really don't want to have to make a layer for every single object whose wireframe color you want to change.

Note

Changing the wireframe display color affects only the OpenGL display of the node, not any look or color attributes of the shader or the software-rendered elements. However, it affects the "hardware"-rendered wireframe color.

Figures 17.16 and 17.17 show the control boxes for The Jerk and Spot models, respectively.

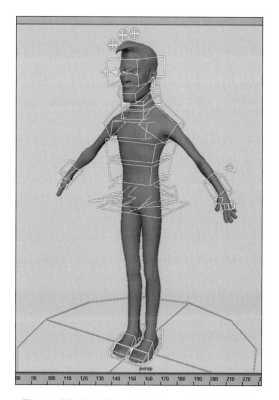

Figure 17.16   The control boxes for The Jerk.

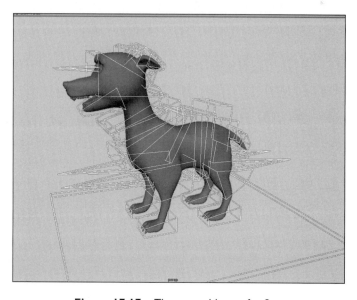

Figure 17.17   The control boxes for Spot.

Creating Advanced Bipedal Character Controls

This section covers several more advanced approaches, some that lend themselves very nicely to the stretching characters into any pose needed by the animators. We know that our human character will need to stand on two feet, sit down and drive a car, get sprayed by a fire hydrant, get knocked down, and interact with several objects and props in his environment. The fact that the character might need to be animated with a touch of cartooned style, per his character design, is also a consideration for the design of the controls. A special type of rig involving a stretchy spline IK setup that reacts with the intuitive controls of an FK hierarchy will be used for the back (spine) of The Jerk. It will give him the ability to stretch his back evenly, similar to the real stretching ability of a spine. It will also allow normal, traditional FK-style rotations of the controls for certain poses that should not be controlled by an IK rotational element. The ability to stretch more than would be anatomically correct will exist, and it will be the animator's job to decide how much the back will stretch, bend, and so on.

The legs of the character will be rigged using IK because The Jerk will need to stick mostly to the ground for walking. The arms will also be rigged using IK, but a simple IK parenting technique will be used to allow for FK-style rotation of the shoulders, as well as IK-style translation placement for The Jerk's clavicle and hand. This will give the character animator full control to pose the characters. Both the arms and the legs of The Jerk will have automatic stretching built into their IK rigs as well. This adds another level of control for the animators, especially when sticking the feet or hands onto objects, because the legs and arms will actually stretch to any length to meet the placement of the hands or feet.

The Advanced Biped Spine

Let's start the first advanced character setup exercise with creating what I have coined "the Divine Spine." There has been much talk about spine controls over the years, and several techniques in Maya lend themselves to achieving promising results, but these techniques are missing key elements from other styles of rigging that many animators and riggers prefer. Thus arises the basic dilemma of character rigging: How do you really manipulate the transformation space to achieve the ultimate combination of motion capabilities, while still successfully maintaining straightforward ease of use and production-level stability?

This advanced spine setup solves many, if not all, of the problems that certain pre-existing techniques for spine setups contain. It also combines the best of both FK controls and IK controls, which enabling the animator to operate in both FK and IK seamlessly at the same time while animating the character. No uncomfortable or unintuitive switching on and off of weighted attributes is required. I designed the Divine Spine setup with these requirements:

1. Be able to move the hips of the character without changing the location or moving the shoulders, and be able to move the shoulders without changing the position of the hips.

2. Still be able to grab a control and rotate it in any direction. It should intuitively rotate the character's back hierarchically as if it were a simple FK joint hierarchy.

3. Be able to grab the same character control and translate it, and intuitively translate the character's spine like a spline IK setup.

4. Be able to compress and stretch uniformly between vertebrae when the controls are animated.

5. Be controlled by a minimal number of control joints, yet still allow for a large number of actual spine joints.

6. Be stable, predictable, and production-worthy. It should not use some forced mathematical function to compute secondary motion that will make the animator "fight" with the motion.

This spine setup is a versatile approach and can be used effectively to rig extremely realistic spine controls as well as cartooney ones.

Without further ado, let's begin.

Exercise 17.4   The Divine Spine Setup

1. First, create your joint hierarchy and orient the joints. I usually use a total of 12 to 18 joints for the base hierarchy of the spinal column, but you can use more or less, depending on your character's requirements. For this setup to work properly, you must be sure of the following things:

   • Scale Compensate is turned on in the Joint tool options before you draw your joints.

   • All your joints have been properly oriented before proceeding, with the Scale option checked on in the Orient Joint options window before you perform the Orient Joint operation (see Figure 17.18).

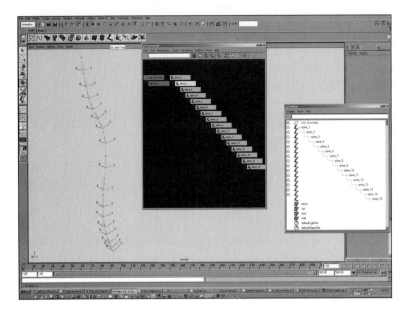

Figure 17.18 Make sure Scale Compensate is turned on and that you properly orient all your joints before proceeding.

Note

If you prefer to start with a precreated joint hierarchy, you can open the file Jerk_DivineSpine_Begin.mb on the CD that comes with this book.

2. Create a spline IK handle from the first to the last joints in the hierarchy using the Skeleton IK Spline Handle Tool options. Make sure that Auto Simplify Curve is turned off in the spline IK options (see Figure 17.19).

3. Select the spline IK curve that the IK Spline Handle Tool created for you automatically. Then create a curve info node by executing the following MEL command in the command line (by all probability, your curve might actually be named curve1):

```
arclen -ch on;
```

4. Select the Spline IK curve, open the Hypergraph, and select the menu item Graph, Input and Output Connections to view upstream in the Hypergraph.

You should see a node attached to your curve called curveInfo. This node contains the length of your curve (see Figure 17.20).

Figure 17.19   Make sure that Auto Simplify Curve is turned off in the spline IK options.

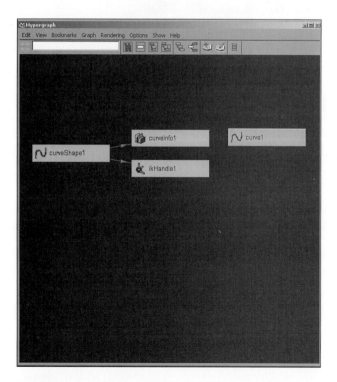

Figure 17.20   The curveInfo node contains the length of your curve.

5. From the Utilities tab of the createRenderNode window (accessible from the menu path Create, Create New Node in the Hypershade), create a multiplyDivide node.

6. Double-click the multiplyDivide node to display the Attribute Editor and set Operation to Divide. Open the Hypergraph and display the input and output connections along with the spline IK's NURBS curve (see Figure 17.21).

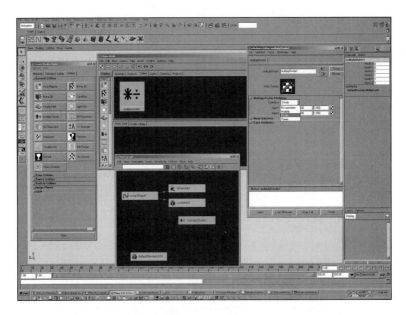

Figure 17.21 Switching the multiplyDivide node's Operation attribute to Divide mode in the Attribute Editor.

Note

If at any time you lose sight of your utility node (such as multiplyDivide) and you can't seem to find it for selection, you can usually find it in the Hypershade window's Utilities tab. If this fails (because the node isn't connected to the defaultRenderUtilityList), you can always select all the nodes of that type or with that name, and then find the one you want by using MEL and either node type or wildcard name using the select command.

To select by node type, execute this MEL command:

```
select -add `ls -type multiplyDivide`;
```

To select by wildcard name, execute this MEL command:

```
select -add "*multiplyDivide*";
```

You can then click Graph, Input and Output Connections and see all the nodes you are looking for. This easy technique works for any node type or node name in your Maya scene, by the way.

7. Next, open the Connection Editor, load the curveInfo node in the left side, and load the multiplyDivide node on the right.

8. Figure out which axis is pointing down your joint hierarchy so that when you scale your joints, they scale along the axis that is pointing toward the next child joint. This determines which attributes you connect in the next step. For this example, if you used the default xyz for the Orient Joint command, the axis you need to use to connect will be the X axis (see Figure 17.22).

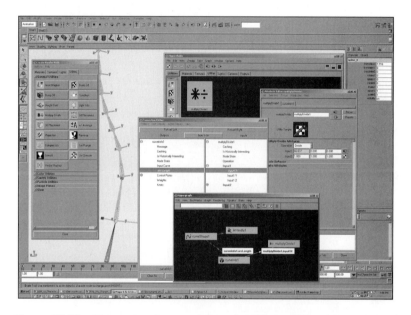

Figure 17.22 Connecting the curveInfo node with the Orient Joint command.

9. Connect the arcLength attribute of the curveInfo node to the multiplyDivide node's input1 attribute. Be sure to use the axis (X, Y, or Z) that your joint should scale along—you took note of this in the last step. For this example, use input1X.

10. Now look at the number that is in the multiplyDivide node's input1 attribute (by looking at the yellowed number in the Attribute Editor). In this case, it is 66.637. This is the output value of the arcLength, which returns the current length of your spline IK curve's length. If the spline's curve length changes (by pulling CVs or deforming it in some way), this arclen node will continue to update the curve length and feed the current new distance into the multiplyDivide node.

Now you want to create a normalized ratio that represents the amount that the curve length is scaling (if a CV of the curve gets moved) to drive the scale attribute of each joint in the hierarchy. This is easily achieved by dividing the current distance (the yellow one) by the initial distance before the deforming took place. So, as common sense would dictate, the output at the default state always equals a scale of 1. The curve has not yet been deformed, so the current distance just happens to also be exactly what you need for the initial distance.

11. Copy/paste the attributes from the yellow input attribute of your multiplyDivide node (the curve's current length) into the corresponding input2 channel directly below in the Attribute Editor for the correct division action to take place.

This results in a value that will represent the amount by which the joint's length should be changed to approximate the curve's current length. You can then simply use this to drive the scaleX attribute of each joint (see Figure 17.23).

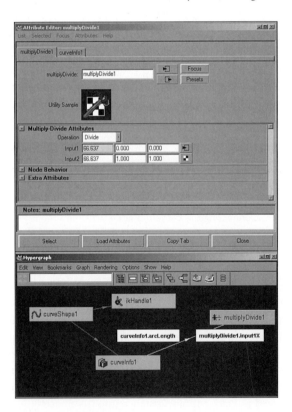

Figure 17.23 Resulting value that represents the length that the joints will be changed to.

12. Open the Connection Editor again, load the multiplyDivide node on the left and the joints on the right, and then connect the multiplyDivide node's division outputX attribute into each joint's scaleX. Skip the very last joint in the hierarchy (the bottommost child at the tip). Because it is the very last end joint, it doesn't need to have any scale attached (see Figure 17.24).

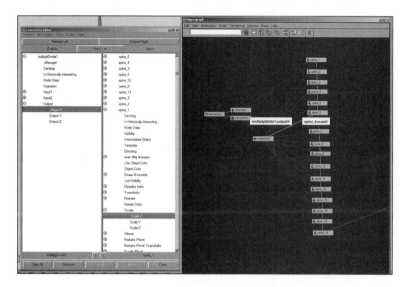

Figure 17.24   In the Connection Editor, connect the multiplyDivide node's division outputX attribute into each joint's scaleX.

Now you will create a second skeleton hierarchy. This will be the low-res, control joint hierarchy that controls all the high-res spine's motion through a series of binding and weighted pole vector constraints. Usually about four to six joints will do just fine for this low-res hierarchy.

13. Create the joints, and make sure they are spaced evenly and are placed in the locations that you want the back to pivot and bend from. Also make sure that they are placed directly on top of the spline IK curve by using the Joint tool with holding down the c key; this activates Curve Snapping mode while drawing your joints directly on top of the spline IK curve. Make sure that the new low joint count hierarchy that you just built has the same start position as the spline IK's root and has a similar end position as the very last child joint in the spline IK hierarchy.

14. Make sure you are happy with the orientation and placement of your new low-res joint hierarchy; reorient these new low-res spine joints, if necessary. Click Modify, Prefix Hierarchy Names to rename this new joint hierarchy with the prefix lowRes_Control_ (see Figure 17.25).

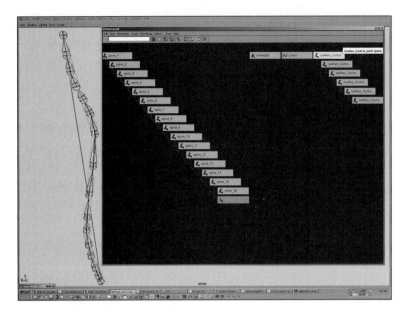

Figure 17.25   Rename the low-res joint hierarchy.

15. Now select the spline curve and Shift+select the lowRes joint hierarchy's root. Smooth-bind the curve to the lowRes joint hierarchy.

16. Test how the low-res joint hierarchy bends your spline IK setup so far. If you are unhappy with the arc or curve of the bend, hit Undo (the z key) a few times until you are back to the point where you can start rebuilding your low-res joint hierarchy. Do this test a few times until you get the right placement and number of joints for your low-res joint hierarchy (see Figure 17.26).

17. Next, even out the weighting of your smooth bound curve by distributing the curve's CV weights more evenly across the joints. Do this by selecting the CVs of the curve and using the Smooth Skins tab under General Editors, Component Editor. Modify the weights by changing some of the values at 1 to .5, or .75, depending on how close they are to the neighboring joint (see Figure 17.27).

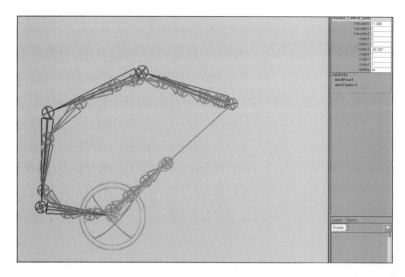

Figure 17.26   Testing the low-res joint hierarchy on the spline IK setup.

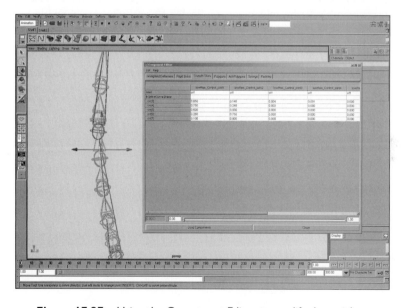

Figure 17.27   Using the Component Editor to modify the weights.

Now the problem you have is that the spline IK hierarchy bends and compresses really nicely, but it doesn't twist (due to the nature of the spline IK solver's pole vector). Although the spline IK solver has a rotation plane implemented and is controllable by using the twist attribute, you don't want to use this attribute to drive the twisting of the spine—it will violate the intuitive control that an animator expects to have when he rotates one of the single joint controls of the low-res skeleton. At this point you really need a rotate plane at every single joint, which has a weighted average to control the twisting of the spine based on the twisting of the low-res control joints. Unfortunately, the spline IK allows only a single rotate plane that is distributed evenly over the entire hierarchy.

So, in the following steps you will create yet one more hierarchy of joints. This time it will be an exact duplicate of the spline IK hierarchy—but *without* the spline IK and *with* a weighted pole vector–constrained ikRPsolver IK handle at every single joint.

18. Select the root joint of the original spine's spline IK joint hierarchy and duplicate it using the default duplicate options. Delete the unused effector node in the new duplicated hierarchy, which got duplicated from the other spline hierarchy. (Make sure you delete only the effectors of the duplicated hierarchy, not the effector that the IK spline solver is connected to.)

19. Click Modify, Prefix Hierarchy Names to rename this duplicated hierarchy to have a new prefix of Ik_Bind_Spine_. This is the spine that the character mesh eventually will be bound onto (see Figure 17.28).

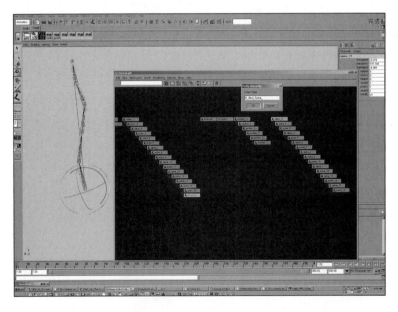

Figure 17.28 This is the spine that the character mesh eventually will be bound onto.

Note

This situation will result in the creation of three hierarchies in the end. One of them (the one you just duplicated) will have the character's skin bound to it and will be partially controlled by the original stretchy spine splinelk hierarchy. These two hierarchies will need to stay unparented from any group that will transform with the character because these two hierarchies will be entirely controlled by the lowRes spine that is currently smooth-skinned to the spine's spline curve. If you transform the bound IK spline hierarchy as well as the low-res control spine, you get double transforms. I discuss this later, but hopefully this helps enlighten things a little bit more for now.

20. Translate this duplicated Ik_Bind_Spine_ hierarchy's root node away from the spline IK hierarchy so that this whole situation isn't completely confusing when you try to select and rig up your joints in the 3D view window.

You now want to create rotate plane IK handles at each joint of the new Ik_Bind_Spine_ hierarchy by starting with the root and then making an IK handle that is *a single joint long* using the IK Handle tool.

21. Select the first joint and then the very next joint in the hierarchy going up the spine. Then start the next IK handle's base at the end location of the previous IK handle that was just created; continue this process until the end of the spine hierarchy is reached (see Figure 17.29). This procedure should exactly result in the same number of IK handles as there are joints in your hierarchy, minus one—the only joint that does not have an IK handle stuck directly on top of it should be the root (which will later be point-constrained).

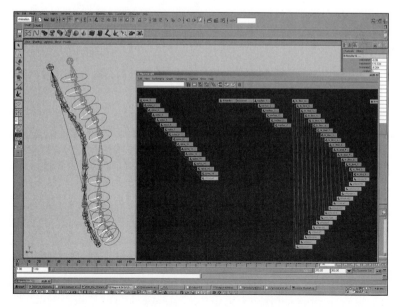

Figure 17.29 Creating rotate plane IK handles at each joint of the new Ik_Bind_Spine_ hierarchy.

Now you will perform a few steps to perfectly line up the rpIk spine with the spline IK spine.

22. First, point-constrain each one of the rpIk handles to the corresponding joint that is part of the spline IK hierarchy. Then point-constrain the root of the Ik_Bind_Spine_ rpIk hierarchy directly to the root of the spline IK hierarchy (see Figures 17.30 and 17.31).

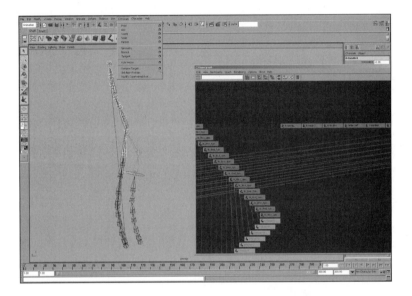

Figure 17.30   This image shows half of the IK handles as they are being point-constrained to the corresponding splineIk spine joints.

23. Next, connect the scale attributes from each original joint in the spline IK hierarchy to the scale attributes of the corresponding duplicate joint in the Ik_Bind_Spine_ rpIk joint hierarchy.

Because these two hierarchies are right on top of each other in the 3D view, the easiest way to select them is by looking at the two hierarchies side by side in the Hypergraph's Graph, Scene Graph mode. Then hit the Toggle Free Form Layout button and move the hierarchies side by side. By doing this, you can see exactly which nodes you need to connect to each other because each node in the hierarchy is right next to the corresponding one. Because the hierarchies are exactly the same, you simply need to open the Connection Editor, select a single spine joint first, and load it into the left side. Select the corresponding duplicate Ik_Bind_Spine_ joint second, and load it into the right side. Then quickly connect the scale attribute of the spine to the scale attribute of the corresponding IK_Bind_Spine.

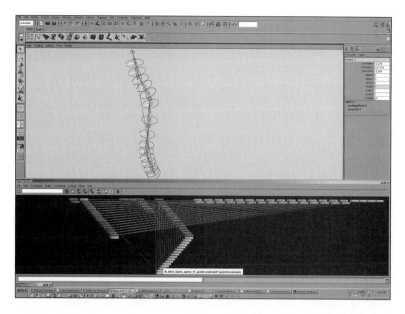

Figure 17.31 This image shows all of the IK handles after they have been point-constrained to the corresponding splineIk spine joints. The root of the Ik_Bind_Spine_ has been point-constrained to the root of the splineIk's spine joint root.

24. Next, group all the rpIk handles under one node by selecting them all and hitting Ctrl+g (see Figure 17.32).

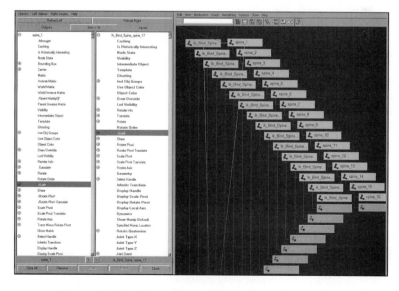

Figure 17.32 Group all the rpIk handles under one node.

You should now have three joint hierarchies that, for the most part, all move together and are controlled by the low-res control hierarchy. They have the capability of stretching and compressing, as well as rotating using an FK approach and translating using an IK approach. The only part missing is the FK capability to actually twist the low-res joint hierarchy and have the joints in the high-res joint hierarchy get the separate portions driven by the twist.

To achieve the desired twisting capability, you will create locators to serve as weighed poleVector constraints for each rotate plane IK handle in the rpIk Ik_Bind_Spine_ hierarchy.

25. Before beginning, hide the lowRes control hierarchy temporarily so that it doesn't confuse things in the 3D view. Do this by selecting the root of the lowRes hierarchy and hitting Ctrl+h.

26. Start by creating a single locator, and name it poleVector1. Next, activate the Move tool, and with the middle mouse button on your mouse, and the v key on your keyboard depressed, drag your mouse to snap the locator directly on top of the root joint of the high-res hierarchies. When the locator is directly on top of the root joint, translate it along the Z-axis direction that moves it backward so that it is directly behind the character's back. Be sure that it is moving only on a single axis and that you are moving it behind the character.

27. Next, hit Ctrl+d to duplicate the locator and snap this new duplicated locator to the next joint, which should also have an IK handle right on top of it. Perform the exact same step, moving the locator backward about the same distance on the same axis as the first locator that you just moved behind the character. Repeat this step for each joint in the hierarchy except for the very last one.

28. When you are finished duplicating, snapping, and moving all the locators behind the character, check that you have the correct number of locators. You should have a single locator for each rpIk handle, and each locator should be located directly behind each one of the character's spine joints, with a single IK handle for each joint except the root. Your locators should be situated something like the ones shown in Figure 17.33.

29. Next, unhide the low-res control joints by setting the root node's visibility attribute to on. Parent each one of the poleVector# locators to the nearest low-res control joint (see Figure 17.34).

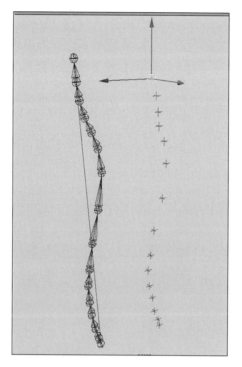

Figure 17.33 Your locators should be situated something like this.

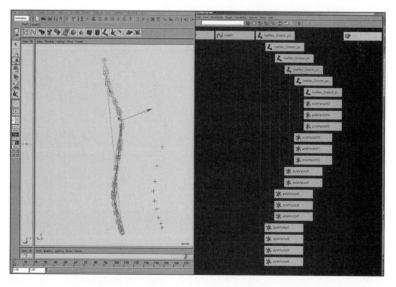

Figure 17.34 Parenting each poleVector locator to the nearest low-res control joint.

30. Now pole vector–constrain each rpIk handle so that it is constrained to all of the locators. Do this by first selecting all the locators that you have situated and parented behind your character's back; then add to the last selection the rpik handle and perform the command Constrain, Pole Vector.

This creates a single weighted pole vector constraint with weight attributes for each locator, which constrains the IK handle onto all the locators situated behind your character.

31. Perform Step 31 for each IK handle on your character's back: Select all the locators and then select a single IK handle, and perform Constrain, Pole Vector. When you are finished, you should have each one of your IK handles pole vector–constrained to all of the locators behind your character, as in Figure 17.35.

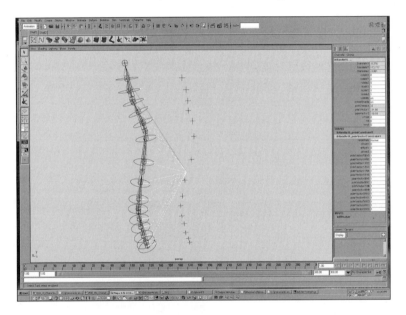

Figure 17.35 Each rotate plane IK handle pole vector is constrained to all the locators that have been placed behind the back.

Now it's time to manually change each of the pole vector constraint weights to weight them with a nice fall-off toward the corresponding low-res joints that the locators are parented onto.

32. To do this, select each IK handle and click the pole vector constraint in the Channel box to modify the pole vector constraint weight attributes (or, just select the pole vector constraint that is a child of your IK handle).

Now look at the weight values that show up in the Channel box. Each weight represents how much the current IK handle's twisting is controlled by each locator that it is constrained to (the locators are children of the low-res back).

33. Set each weight value to a number that will distribute the rotation of the pole vector to be controlled evenly by two to four of the locators.

Rotating a low-res joint causes the pole vector constraint locator that is a child to orbit around the pivot of the low-res joint you are rotating. This, in turn, causes any of the IK handles that are constrained to the locator to twist or rotate along the IK handle's rotate plane. The idea is to determine which low-res joint's rotations you want to have affect the twisting of the high-res joints.

Determining which joints should receive weighting is quite simple: If the joint is at the top of the hierarchy, weight it toward the locators that are children of the top low-res joint. The best part about all this is that the poleVector constraint has weights, so it can have weights that are falling off from one locator to the next, across multiple joints. If one of your rpIk handles is in between the top low-res joint and one of the middle low-res joints, give it weights that are averaged between locators that are children of these two hierarchies. For example, if you are distributing the weights across four locators, choose weights that are falling off from low values to higher values, such as .1, .35, .75, and 1; the rest of the weights should be set to 0. The only rule for which constraint weights you should give higher weights to is this: Set the weights of the pole vector constraints so that when you twist the low-res hierarchy, the high-res joints rotate with an appealing and desirable fall-off between them.

Figure 17.36 shows what your pole vector constraints should look like when you are finished changing their weights.

34. Next, group all of your IK handles and curves together. Then group both of your high-res IK hierarchies under the same group and name it spineRigIkNodes. Keep your low-res hierarchy outside of this spineRigIkNodes group because this group will never be moved or translated. The lowRes hierarchy will be the joints that are hooked up to control boxes and that are used to animate the character.

35. Point-constrain the root of the lowRes hierarchy to the root of the character, and group and constrain the rest of the lowRes hierarchy to control boxes so that it is kept free from the translations of the root.

This keeps the hips free from moving with the shoulders, and vice versa. An additional parent of both hierarchies should eventually also be used when the rest of the character controls are built, to move both the root and the upper spine together.

You can find a completed file, titled Jerk_DivineSpine_Finished.mb, on the accompanying CD for this chapter.

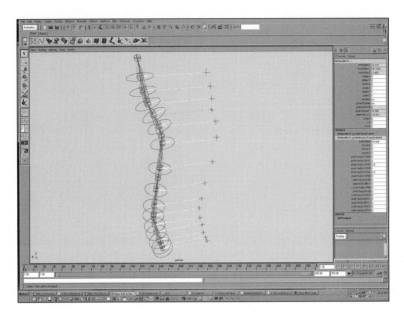

Figure 17.36   When you are finished changing their weights, your pole vector constraints should look like this.

Advanced Stretchy IK Legs and Classic Reverse Foot

The Jerk's legs will be rigged up in a similar way to the spine: They will be capable of stretching when the distance between the foot and the hips becomes larger. This is an interesting setup because it causes the foot to stay stuck to the ground, even if the character's root is causing the leg to stretch just a small amount. This capability allows for the animator to hit nice key poses in a walk, or any other pose that involves planting one foot and moving another, without having to worry too much about the terrible "IK snapping" of joints as the IK handle moves too far away from the joint and it can no longer bend to achieve the pose.

In the next exercise, you set up the leg joints so that they will stretch and the animator will never have to worry about this problem.

Exercise 17.5   Classic Reverse Foot Setup

The foot will be set up using a classic reverse foot setup. This simple technique allows the foot to be rotated from all three pivots that a real foot's weight lands upon while walking: the heel, the ball, and the toe. This makes for a very straightforward time when animating the feet for a walk cycle of a character.

1. Start by opening the file Jerk_IkLegs_Begin.mb on the CD for this chapter.

2. Next, activate the rotate plane IK Handle tool by going to Skeleton, IK Handle Options and hitting the Reset Tool button. Using the IK Handle tool, create an IK handle from the leg joint to the ankle joint, then from the ankle joint to the ball joint, and finally from the ball joint to the toe joint. Your result should look like Figure 17.37.

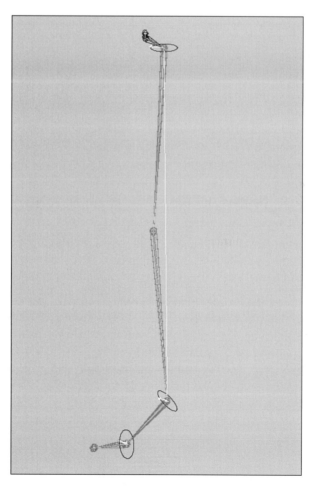

Figure 17.37   The leg after creating the necessary IK handles.

3. Next, rename all your IK handles to match the portions of the leg and foot that they correspond to—ankle_ikHandle, ball_ikHandle, and toe_ikHandle.

4. Now create the reverse foot. Start by drawing a backward foot joint hierarchy. The root of this new joint hierarchy should start at the base of the heel and then move to the toe, the ball, and the ankle. Name your hierarchy reverseHeel, reverseToe, reverseBall, and reverseAnkle, accordingly. Your result should look like Figure 17.38.

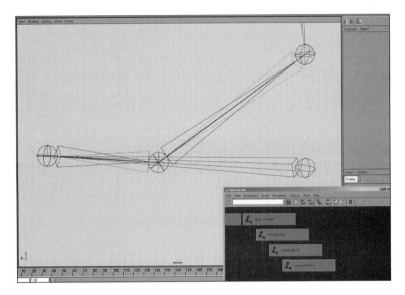

Figure 17.38 The reverse foot joint hierarchy.

5. Next, parent the ankle IK handle to the reverseAnkle joint. Parent the ball IK handle to the reverseBall joint, and parent the toe IK handle to the reverseToe joint, as in Figure 17.39.

6. Create three locators that will be pole vector constraints for the leg and feet IK handles. Name the first locator ballPoleVector. Keeping the v key pressed down and using the middle mouse button with the Move tool, point-snap this locator to the reverseAnkle node and make it a child of reverseAnkle. Next, select the ballPoleVector locator that you just parented, Shift+select the ball_ikHandle, and perform Constrain, Pole Vector. Move the locator so that it is off to the side of the foot, not right on top of the ankle joint.

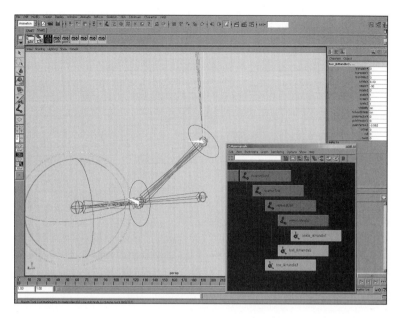

Figure 17.39   IK handle relationship in the reverse foot joint hierarchy.

7. Name the second locator toePoleVector, and point-snap and parent it to the reverseBall joint. Next, select it along with the toe_ikHandle and perform Constrain, Pole Vector. Also move this locator so that it is off to the side of the foot, not right on top of the ball joint.

8. Finally, name the third locator legPoleVector, and point-snap it to the legJoint; then move it out in front of the knee joint. Parent this locator to the Hips joint. Select this locator, and Shift+select the ankleIk handle and again perform Constrain, Pole Vector. Your result should look like Figure 17.40

The reverse foot setup is completed, and is ready to be animated.

9. You can animate the reverseHeel, reverseToe, and reverseBall joints to make the character's foot roll as it is walking. Also hide the locators and IK handles that are children of the reverse foot hierarchy so that they aren't accidentally animated or selected.

Now you can create your stretchy legs setup.

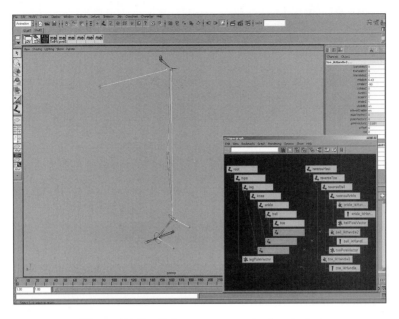

Figure 17.40 Pole vector constraint for the leg.

10. Create a distance dimension node from the leg to the ankle with the measuring tool by using the menu command Create, Measuring Tools, Distance Tool. Click first on the leg joint and then on the ankle joint. Now point-constrain the first locator of the distance tool to the leg joint; point-constrain the second locator of the distance tool to the ankle_ikHandle, which spans from the leg joint to the ankle joint, using Constrain, Point (see Figure 17.41).

11. Next, open the Create Render Node window from the Hypershade window under Create, Create New Node, and create the following utility nodes:

- Three multiplyDivide nodes
- Two plusMinusAverage nodes
- One condition node

Figure 17.42 shows the result.

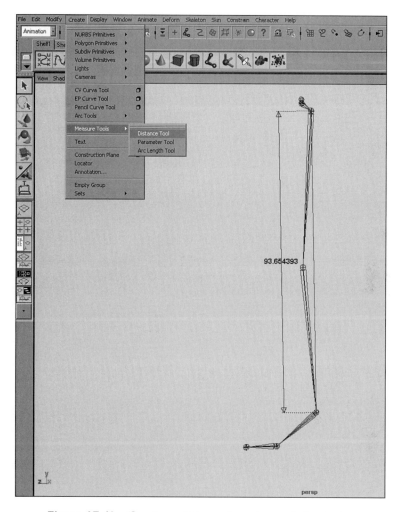

Figure 17.41   Creating a distance dimension node for the leg.

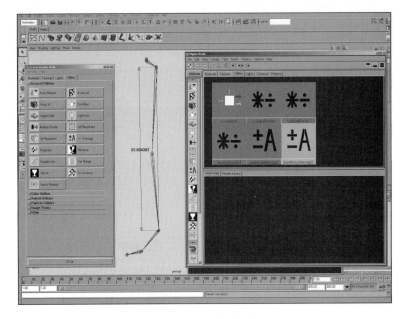

Figure 17.42 Creating utility nodes for the leg.

Next, you'll hook up a node network that will allow the legs to stretch as the distance between the ankle's IK handle and the leg joint becomes greater.

To start, you'll create some attributes that can be used to easily control the stretching capabilities of the leg.

12. Select the reverseHeel joint. This will be the node that you add the additional attributes onto because this is also the joint that you can use to animate the position of the foot. Go to the menu item Modify, Add Attributes and add the following attributes:

> autoStretch min: 0, max: 1—This is so that the automatic stretching can be blended on and off.

> shortenTolerance min: 0, max: 1—This attribute will control how short the leg gets before it starts to bend.

> legScale min: 0, max: 10—This is an extra control that allows the leg to scale on top of the automatic scale.

Figure 17.43 shows the result.

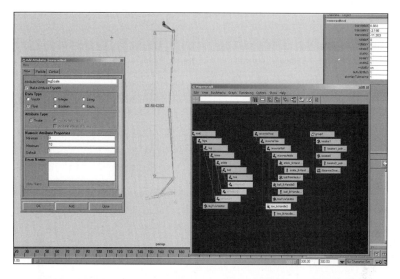

Figure 17.43 The new leg attributes are ready to be connected.

Now you'll connect all the nodes and attributes that you just created to get the controllable automatic stretchy reaction that you want from the leg.

13. Connect the distanceDimensionShape.distance attribute to the multiplyDivide1.input1Y attribute. Set the operation mode of multiplyDivide1 node to Divide. Next, copy and paste the number from input1Y (using Ctrl+c and Ctrl+v) into the input2Y attribute of the multiplyDivide1 node.

14. Next, connect the multiplyDivide1 outputY to the plusMinusAverage1 input1D[0] attribute. Make sure that the plusMinusAverage1 node's operation is set to Subtract. Also make sure that the multipyDivide1 node's input2Z attribute is set to 1. Then connect it to the plusMinusAverate input1D[1] attribute (to subtract 1 from the output).

15. Connect the plusMinusAverage1 node's output1D to the multiplyDivide2 node's input2Y. Connect the reverseHeel's autoStretch attribute into the input1Y attribute of the multiplyDivide2 node.

16. Connect the multiplyDivide node's outputY attribute to the plusMinusAverage node's input1D[0]. Then set the multiplyDivide2 node's input2z attribute to 1 and connect it to the input1D[1] attribute of the plusMinusAverage2 node.

17. Set the operation mode of the condition1 node to Less Than, and connect the plusMinusAverage2 node's output1D attribute to the condition node's colorIfFalseG attribute. Then connect the plusMinusAverage2 node's output1D attribute to the condition node's firstTerm attribute. Next, connect reverseHeel's shortenTolerance attribute to the condition node's secondTerm attribute, and also connect reverseHeel's shortenTolerance attribute to the condition node's colorIfTrueG attribute.

18. Next, connect the condition1 node's outColorG to the last multiplyDivide3 node's input1Y attribute. Connect reverseHeel's attribute legScale to multiplyDivide3's input2Y attribute.

19. Finally, connect the outputY attribute of the multiplyDivide3 node into the scaleX attributes of the leg and the knee joint nodes.

Your final node network should look similar to Figure 17.44.

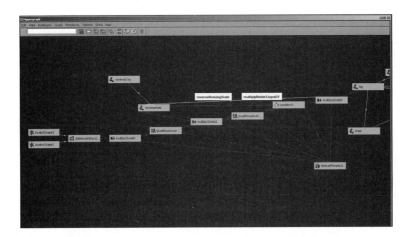

Figure 17.44 The final node network for the stretchy leg.

You can now animate the reverse feet, and the leg will actually stretch to compensate for the overextension of the foot. The attributes to control this reaction are right on the reverseHeel, so you can keyframe this behavior on and off and scale the legs on top of it. The completed scene file appears on the accompanying CD as Jerk_IkLegs_Finished.mb.

Advanced IK Arms and Clavicular Triangle

In the next exercise, you will see how I chose to rig The Jerk's shoulders and arms. The technique used enables the arms to stretch and the shoulder to rotate as if it were an FK arm. Separate controls exist for posing the arm using IK from the scapula, the clavicle, and the shoulder, as well as the traditional IK handle at the wrist. Two locators both have the wrist's IK handle constrained to them, adding the capability to plant the character's hand any place we choose. Two extra joints were inserted as children of the shoulder and elbow but were not connected (not made parents) with the rest of the hierarchy of the arm. These unparented children joints were used for better deformations on the twisting of the shoulder and the wrist, to avoid the painful washboard effect.

Exercise 17.6   Advanced Stretchy IK Arms and the Clavicular Triangle

Begin by opening the file Jerk_ArmSetup_Begin.mb, which you'll find on the accompanying CD. Take a look at how the arm joints are laid out to create the hierarchy.

Examine this file closely: It contains the joint placement for the entire skeletal hierarchy that will create the final arm for The Jerk. The only thing missing is the controls, which you will add to the rig now. You begin with the shoulder area of the character, which I refer to as "the clavicular triangle." Then you tackle the advanced stretchy IK arm controls that will allow the character's arms to stretch to any length. You'll also transition the hand to be stuck on any object and stay there while the rest of the body is animated. So, let's get started with the clavicular triangle.

1. Beginning with the file Jerk_ArmSetup_Begin.mb from the CD, create an IK handle from the clavicularTriangle joint node to the scapulaJoint node. Do this by clicking Skeleton, IK Handle Tool Options; first hit the Reset Tool button and then select the nodes in order from the 3D view port window. Rename the newly created IK handle scapulaClavicle_IkControl.

2. Next, select the scapulaJoint and use the Ctrl+h key combination to temporarily hide it so that you can select the correct node in the view port window. Now, using the same settings in the IK Handle tool from above, create another IK handle from the clavicleJoint node to the clavToShoulder joint node. Rename the newly created IK handle clavicleStretch_IkHandle.

3. Next, use the Ctrl+Shift+h keyboard combination to unhide the last hidden node (the scapulaJoint node). Then select the clavicleJoint node and use Ctrl+h to temporarily hide it.

4. Using the same settings, create an IK handle from the scapulaJoint node to the shoulderJoint node. Rename this newly created IK handle clavicleShoulder_IkControl.

5. Create one last IK handle from the shoulderJoint node all the way down to the bottom of the arm to the wristJoint node. Rename the newly created IK handle armWrist_IkControl. Now Ctrl+Shift+h to unhide the previously hidden clavicleJoint.

6. Next, parent the clavicleShoulder_IkControl under the scapulaClavicle_IkControl node. Then parent the clavicleStretch_IkHandle and the armWrist_IkControl nodes to the clavicleShoulder_IkControl. Finally, parent the entire group of the scapulaClavicle_IkControl node to the connectToSpine joint node. Your hierarchy so far should look like Figure 17.45.

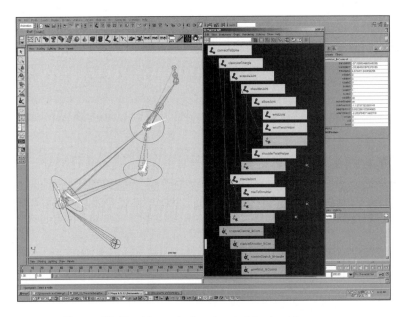

Figure 17.45   Hierarchy for the clavicle shoulder setup.

7. Now that you've parented all your IK appropriately, select all four IK handles and perform the Modify, Freeze Transformations menu command. Next, with all the IK still selected, highlight the poleVectorX, poleVectorY, and poleVectorZ attributes in the Channel box and set them all to 0 (zero).

8. Next, click Create, Measure Tools, Distance Tool. While holding down the v key on your keyboard (Snap mode), snap a distance locator from the clavicleJoint to the clavToShoulder joint. Rename each locator appropriately: clavicleJointPoint and clavToShoulderPoint. Also rename the distanceDimension node that was created to clavToShoulder_distanceDimension.

9. Select the shoulderJoint and the clavToShoulderPoint and perform the Constrain, Point menu command. Next, select clavicleJoint and then clavicleJointPoint, and again perform the Constrain, Point menu command. Now select the two locators and the distance dimension, and hit the Ctrl+g keyboard combination to group them. Rename the group clavicleDistanceGroup and make it a child of the connectToSpine joint node. Your hierarchy so far should look like Figure 17.46.

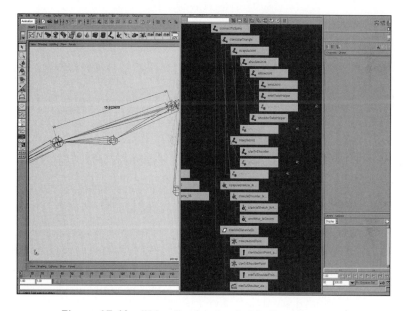

Figure 17.46   IK handles for the clavicle shoulder setup.

10. Next, execute this command:

```
createNode multiplyDivide;
```

11. Be sure to hold down the Shift key, and Shift+click, selecting the clavToShoulder_distanceDimension node. Open the Hypergraph window and click Graph, Input and Output Connections.

Your screen should look like Figure 17.47.

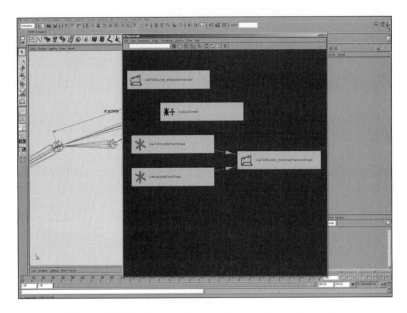

Figure 17.47   Connecting the distanceDimension node.

12. Next, using Shift plus the middle mouse button, drag and drop the clavToShoulder_distanceDimensionShape onto the multiplyDivide1 node. This should bring up the Connection Editor window. Inside the Connection Editor, connect the distance attribute from the clavToShoulder_distanceDimensionShape into the Input1X attribute of the multiplyDivide node.

13. Next, select the multiplyDivide node and open the Attribute Editor. Change Operation to Divide, and copy the yellow input1X attribute (using the Ctrl+c keyboard combination) and paste it into the input2X field so that you are dividing the current distance by the initial distance. This creates a ratio that you can use to scale the clavicle joint down its axis. Your hierarchy so far should look like Figure 17.48.

14. Select the multiplyDivide node and Shift+select the clavicleJoint. Open the Hypergraph window and click Graph, Input and Output Connections. Using Shift and the middle mouse button, drag and drop the multiplyDivide node onto the clavicleJoint node. Again, this opens the Connection Editor for you to connect the appropriate attributes.

15. In the Connection Editor, highlight the OutputX attribute from the multiplyDivide node, and connect it with the scaleX attribute of the clavicleJoint node. This should appear to do nothing because the outputX attribute should be currently equal to 1.

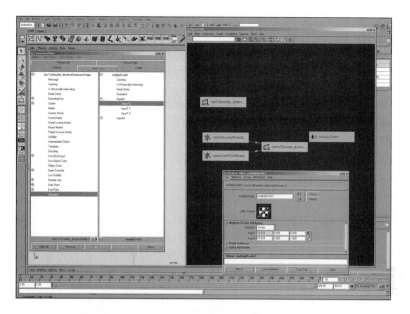

Figure 17.48   Connecting the multiplyDivide node.

16. Finally, select the shoulderJoint, Shift+select the clavicleStretch_IkHandle, and perform Constrain, Point.

That is about it for the clavicle setup. If you move or rotate the clavicleShoulder_IkControl IK handle, you will see that the clavicleJoint actually scales to keep its length between the shoulder and its point of origin at the clavicle. Although this is not anatomically correct, it can prove very helpful for achieving appealing deformations in this area when the character points his arm forward in front of his body, reaches his hand across his chest, or lifts his arm above his head. The key is to spread the weighting of this joint smoothly and sparingly across certain portions of the frontal geometry.

In the next exercise, you will set up some of the controls for the entire arm itself.

Exercise 17.7 Arm Twist Setup

Begin by connecting the joints that will help the arm's twisting deformations look more believable.

1. Using the Connection Editor, connect the wristJoint.rotateX attribute to control the wristTwistHelper.rotateX attribute (highlighting in the Connection Editor, just like in the last example). Then connect the shoulderJoint.rotateX attribute to control the shoulderTwistHelper.rotateX attribute using the same method (see Figure 17.49).

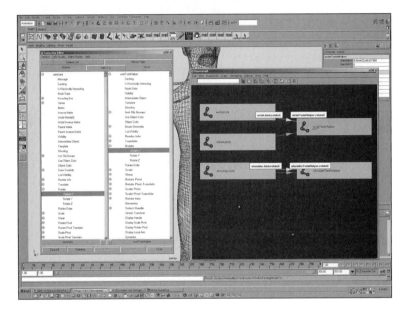

Figure 17.49 Connecting the joints that will help the arm's twisting deformations.

Next, you will create a standard IK control for the arm, which will enable the animator to control the twisting of the shoulder and the orientation that the elbow is pointing. You will pole vector–constrain the wrist's IK handle onto a locator that is situated behind the character, which can be grabbed and translated around to control the arm's orientation.

2. Create a locator (click Create, Locator) and rename it armPoleVectorConstraint. Now, with the Move tool activated, hold down the v key (Point Snap mode) on the keyboard and, holding down the middle mouse button, click and drag the locator toward the shoulderJoint until it snaps into place on top of the shoulderJoint. Then, no longer holding the v key, translate it backward a few units behind the character.

3. Make the armPoleVectorConstraint locator a child of the connectToSpine node by selecting the armPoleVectorConstraint and then the connectToSpine; then hit the p key on your keyboard.

4. Select the armPoleVectorConstraint locator and Shift-click the armWrist_IkControl node to add it to the selection. Create a pole vector constraint by using the menu command Constrain, Pole Vector.

5. Select the armPoleVectorConstraint locator and perform Modify, Freeze Transformations to zero the locator's transforms.

   Next, you will create the extra controls that will allow the hand to be "planted" or stuck on any object. For example, if the character needs to lean his hand against the wall, grab onto a pole and swing around on it, or even just hold on to a steering wheel, this setup will easily allow for it.

   The way you'll accomplish this is very simple indeed. First, you'll create two locators and parent them under the same group as the armWrist_IkControl. Then you will create weighted point and orient constraints from these two locators onto the armWrist_IkControl node. Finally, you will add an attribute that will control the weight of the constraints that were added, to determine which locator the IK handle gets constrained onto. Let's get started.

6. First, create two locators. Rename one locator plantIkHand. Rename the other locator freeIkHand.

7. With the Move tool activated, hold down the v key (Point Snap mode) on the keyboard and, holding down the middle mouse button, click and drag both locators toward the wrist's armWrist_IkControl in the 3D view port until they snap into place directly on top of the armWrist_IkControl.

8. Next, parent both the plantIkHand and freeIkHand locators under the same parent as the armWrist_IkControl node (the scapulaClavicle_IkControl) by selecting the two locators and Shift+selecting the scapulaClavicle_IkControl to add it to the selection last; then hit the p key on your keyboard.

   Next, you will create an empty "null" transform node that you'll use to parent the IK handle and both locators under so that they are in the same orientation and position as the wristJoint node. You can then orient-constrain the wrist to the IK handle without changing the current orientation of the wrist.

9. Create the null transform by first being sure that nothing is selected and then hitting the Ctrl+g keyboard combination.

10. With the new null node created, point-snap it to the wristJoint node using the Snap mode of the Move tool by holding down the v key while clicking and dragging with the middle mouse button held down. Zero the null node's transforms by selecting it and performing Modify, Freeze Transformations.

To put this null node into the same orientation as the wristJoint, you will point- and orient-constrain it and immediately delete these constraints by executing a single line of MEL code supplied in the next step.

11. A quick and easy way to do this is to execute the following MEL command in the command line (first select the wristJoint node and Shift+select the null node to add to the selection). Now execute the following bit of tricky code (which actually creates constraints for you and then automatically deletes them immediately afterward so that they will line up your nodes but not keep them controlled via a constraint relationship—all at the same time):

```
delete 'orientConstraint';  delete 'pointConstraint';
```

12. Rename the null node to be called wristTransformCompensation. Parent it under the same node as the armWrist_IkControl IK handle and plantIkHand and freeIkHand locators by first selecting the wristTransformCompensation, Shift+selecting the clavicleShoulder_IkControl node, and hitting the p key on the keyboard.

The null transform is now in the same orientation space as the wristJoint, but it will travel correctly under the clavicleShoulder_IkControl IK handle node. You will now make this new wristTransformCompensation null node the parent of the armWrist_IkControl IK handle and plantIkHand and freeIkHand locators.

13. Select all three of these nodes (armWrist_IkControl, plantIkHand, and freeIkHand), and Shift+select the wristTransformCompensation null node to add it to the selection last. Hit the p key to parent the IK and locators to this null node.

Note

If the wrist and elbow seem to pop into a different spot when you parent the armWrist_IkControl IK handle, you can correct this. Simply select the armPoleVectorConstraint, highlight all its translate channels in the Channel box, and then hit 0 and the Enter key. This update problem occurs because of the nature of Maya's lazy dependency graph evaluations.

14. Now select the armWrist_IkControl, plantIkHand, and freeIkHand nodes; perform Modify, Freeze Transformations to zero out the IK handle and locator's transforms; and put them in the same transformation space as the wristTransformCompensation null node. You should remember that this is also in the same orientation space as the wristJoint node. This whole step is important because you will next orient-constrain the wrist to the armWrist_IkControl IK handle node.

15. Select the armWrist_IkControl, Shift+select the wristJoint node, and perform the menu command Constrain, Orient. So far, your nodes should look like Figure 17.50 in the Hypergraph window.

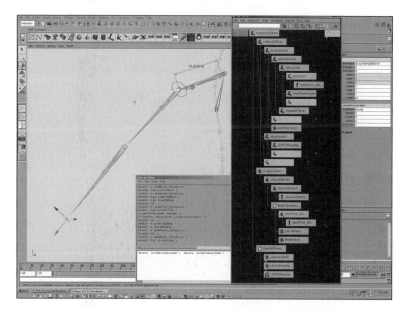

Figure 17.50   Arm and wrist IK control hierarchy.

Now that you have all your controls in the proper transformation space, you will finally create the constraints that enable you to animate the hand freely and then plant it so that it sticks somewhere. Again, you'll do this by using the weights of orient and point constraints.

16. Select the plantIkHand and freeIkHand nodes, and Shift+select the armWrist_IkControl to add it to the selection last. Now perform the two menu commands Constrain, Point and Constrain, Orient.

So far, if everything was done properly, you should have your wristJoint orient constrained to your arm's IK handle. The IK handle, in turn, is point- and orient-constrained to both plantIkHand and freeIkHand locators, which both currently constrain it with a weighted average of 1.

17. Next, select the armWrist_IkControl and use Modify, Add Attribute to create a float attribute. Name that float attribute handPlant, and give it a min of 0, max of 1, and default of 0. The settings should look like those in Figure 17.51.

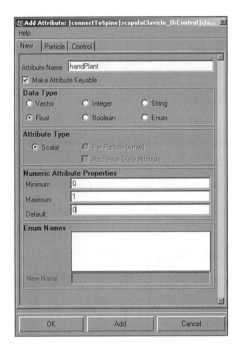

Figure 17.51 Adding attributes to the armWrist_IkControl.

Now that you have created the handPlant attribute on the armWrist_IkControl IK handle, you want to make it control the weights of the constraints between the plantIkHand and freeIkHand locators. This is achieved using set-driven keys.

18. Go to the menu item Animate, Set-Driven Key, Set option box to bring up the UI for creating set-driven keys.

19. Next, select the armWrist_IkControl IK handle and click the Load Driver button. Be sure to highlight the handPlant attribute in the upper-left section of the window.

20. Open the Hypergraph and select the two bottom constraints that are children of the armWrist_IkControl node (the point and orient constraints that you just finished creating in Step 16). These should be named armWrist_IkControl_pointConstraint1 and armWrist_IkControl_orientConstraint1. Hold the Shift key and add to the selection the plantIkHand and freeIkHand nodes. Next, in the Set-Driven Key window, click Load Driven. Your window should look like Figure 17.52.

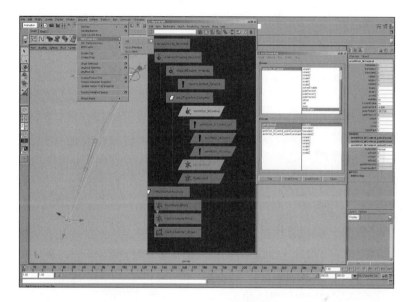

Figure 17.52   Preparing to use the Set-Driven Key window.

The next few steps are very important for applying the set-driven keys correctly.

21. First, be sure that the armWrist_IkControl IK handle's handPlant attribute is set to 0 and is loaded as the driver node/attribute. Also be sure that the node name armWrist_IkControl is highlighted on the upper left and that the attribute name handPlant is highlighted on the upper right of the Set-Driven Key window.

22. Now set the attributes on your nodes to the following values:

> *Driver attribute:*
>
> armWrist_IkControl.handPlant: 0
>
> *Driven attributes:*
>
> freeIkHand.visibility: on
>
> plantIkHand.visibility: off
>
> armWrist_IkControl_pointConstraint1.plantIkHandW0: 0
>
> armWrist_IkControl_pointConstraint1.freeIkHandW1: 1

armWrist_IkControl_orientConstraint1.plantIkHandW0: 0

armWrist_IkControl_orientConstraint1.freeIkHandW1: 1

23. Now that your attributes are set exactly from the previous list, with your driver node actively highlighted, go through the driven nodes in the Set-Driven Key window and, one by one, click each node/attribute in the Driven section. Highlight each name on the lower left, highlight the attribute that you just set on the lower right, and hit the Key button. For example, the first node to highlight on the bottom left is the freeIkHand; on the bottom right, it is the attribute visibility. With both highlighted, hit the Key button. Do this for each node's attribute that you previously loaded and set, including each constraint separately (see Figure 17.53).

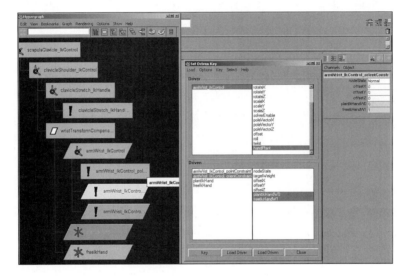

Figure 17.53 Using the Set-Driven Key window.

Now that you have hit the Key button for each driven attribute value when the driver is set to 0, you will set the values for the driven attributes when the driver is set to 1.

24. Set the following node attribute's values:

Driver attribute:

armWrist_IkControl.handPlant: 1

Driven attributes:

freeIkHand.visibility: off

plantIkHand.visibility: on

armWrist_IkControl_pointConstraint1.plantIkHandW0: 1

armWrist_IkControl_pointConstraint1.freeIkHandW1: 0

armWrist_IkControl_orientConstraint1.plantIkHandW0: 1

armWrist_IkControl_orientConstraint1.freeIkHandW1: 0

25. Finally, repeat the previous step, but using the current values, and set a driven key on each one of your driven node/attributes. One by one, highlight them in the Driven section of the Set-Driven Key window; one by one, highlight their attributes. Then hit the Key button to set the driven node's attribute key at the current driver node's attribute value.

Two locators control the location of the arm's IK handle as well as the orientation of the wrist. For the most part, the freeIkHand locator can be used to animate the hand when it does not need to be planted on something. But now there's an extra node to use to plant and orient the hand on a shot-by-shot basis, without ever needing to add extra controls to the character. When you need the hand to transition from being free moving to being planted somewhere, simply parent or point-constrain the plantIkHand onto the object that the hand needs to be stuck to and then animate the .handPlant attribute over a couple of frames, from 0 to 1. This hides the freeIkHand locator, which you no longer need to animate, and makes visible the plantIkHand locator, which you have stuck onto something.

In the next exercise, you will tackle the stretchy arm setup, which includes creating all the controls, attributes, and node networks involved to make an automatically stretchy IK arm that will stretch to maintain the distance between the IK handle and the shoulder. Regardless of whether the location of the shoulder or the location of the IK handle causes this distance to become greater, the arm will still stretch automatically. You will also add all the controls needed by an animator to animate this behavior blended on and off, while still exposing manual controls to scale the length on top of these controls.

Exercise 17.8   Stretchy Arm Setup

Begin by creating a distance dimension node for the arm. You will do this the same way you created the distance dimension for the clav to shoulder. This begins the controls that cause the arm to stretch.

1. Go to Create, Measure Tools, Distance Tool to activate the Distance tool.

2. Now click with the mouse once in the general area of the shoulder and again in the general area of the wrist. You will get two locators, most likely named locator1 and locator2. Rename these locators shoulderPoint for the locator near the shoulder, and wristPoint for the locator near the wrist. Also rename the distanceDimension node armDistance_distanceDimension.

3. Select the shoulderJoint node, Shift+select the shoulderPoint locator, and point-constrain the locator to the shoulder by using Constrain, Point. Next, point-constrain the wristPoint locator to the armWrist_IkControl by selecting the armWrist_IkControl, Shift+selecting the wristPoint locator, and again performing the menu command Constrain, Point. Finally, select the two locators and the distanceDimension node, and group them using the Ctrl+g keyboard combination. Name this new group armDistanceGroup (see Figure 17.54).

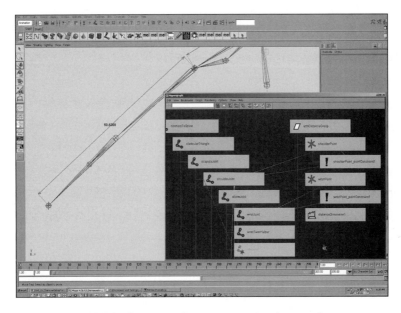

Figure 17.54 Setting up the constraints for the stretchy arm.

4. Parent the armDistanceGroup node under the connectToSpine joint node so that it is part of the hierarchy that will comprise the arm.

Next, you will create a bunch of math utility nodes to create a node-based expression network. These nodes were built in Maya traditionally for rendering, but they are more commonly being used for character rigging as well.

5. Open the Hypershade window by clicking Window, Rendering Editors, Hypershade, and go to the Create, Create New Node menu. This launches the Create Render Node window. Next, click the tab labeled Utilities and create the following series of nodes (you will create four total utility nodes—see Figure 17.55):

Create three multiplyDivide nodes and rename them armScaleRatio, autoStretchMultiplier, and armScaleMultiplier.

Create one Condition node and rename it shortenToleranceCondition.

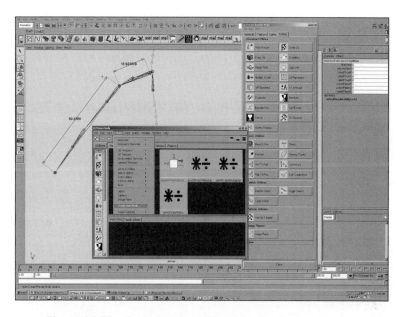

Figure 17.55   Setting up the utility nodes for the stretchy arm.

Next, you will create a few attributes that an animator can use to control the stretchiness of the character's arms.

6. Select the armWrist_IkControl and load up the Add Attribute window by going to Modify, Add Attribute.

7. In the Add Attribute window, create three float data type attributes with the following names and settings:

autoStretch (min 0, max 1, default 1)

shortenTolerance (min 0, max 1, default 1)

armScale (min 0, max 10, default 1)

Now it is time to get started connecting some attributes to create our stretchy IK arm.

Because you already have the Hypershade window open, you will use it (instead of the Hypergraph) to make all of your node connections.

8. Choose the Utilities tab from the Hypershade, and select all four of the new utility nodes that you just created. Shift+add to the selection the armDistance_distanceDimension node and the armWrist_IkControl node from either the Hypergraph or the 3D view port. Now, with the current active selection in the Hypershade, click the menu item Graph, Input and Output Connections. You get a somewhat disorganized display of nodes. Organize the nodes in your window so that they are visually lined up similar to the order pictured, to make it easier to connect the appropriate attributes (see Figure 17.56).

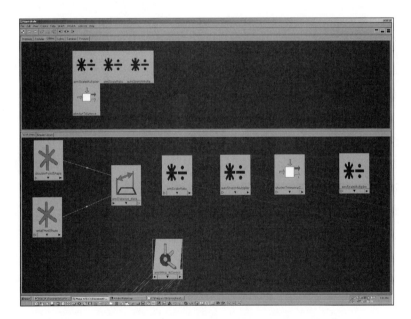

Figure 17.56 Preparing the utility nodes for the stretchy arm.

9. Holding down the Shift key and the middle mouse button, drag and drop the distanceDimensionShape node onto the armScaleRatio multiplyDivide node. Using the Connection Editor, connect the distance attribute to the input1X attribute of the multiplyDivide node.

10. Now select the armScaleRatio multiplyDivide node that you just connected to, and hit Ctrl+a to launch the Attribute Editor. Change the multiplyDivide node's operation mode from Multiply to Divide. Now copy the number from the input1X channel and paste it into the input2X channel so that you are dividing the current distance by the original distance.

The node's output should currently equal 1; as the distance grows, the output will be a normalized ratio equal to how much the initial distance has scaled (starting from 1). This output will eventually be the number that you use to drive the scale of the arm joints, but you will set up a few extra nodes to add a small amount of logic and control over the stretchiness.

11. Using the Connection Editor window, connect the following attributes to create an expression-based node network:

The armWrist_IkControl.autoStretch attribute into the autoStretchMultiplier.input1X attribute

The armScaleRatio.outputX attribute into the autoStretchMultiplier.input2X attribute (The output of this autoStretchMultiplier node enables you to blend the stretchy behavior from on to off, and vice versa.)

The autoStretchMultiplier.outputX attribute into the shortenToleranceCondition.firstTerm attribute

The autoStretchMultiplier.outputX attribute also into the shortenToleranceCondition.colorIfFalseR attribute

The armWrist_IkControl.shortenTolerance attribute into the shortenToleranceCondition.secondTerm attribute

The armWrist_IkControl.shortenTolerance also into the shortenToleranceCondition.colorIfTrueR attribute (The output of the shortenToleranceCondition node's outColorR attribute now keeps the arm from shrinking shorter than the shortenTolerance attribute specifies.)

The shortenToleranceCondition.outColorR attribute into the armScaleMultiplier.input1X attribute

The armWrist_IkControl.armScale attribute into the armScaleMultiplier.input2X attribute

12. Next, select the shortenToleranceCondition node and open the Attribute Editor by hitting Ctrl+a. Change the operation mode of this condition node to Less Than.

This condition node keeps the arm from scaling any shorter than what the armWrist_IkControl.shortenTolerance attribute is set to by making a decision for you. The logic behind how the condition node works is as follows: If the First Term is Less Than the Second Term, use Color If True; otherwise, use Color If False. This output, which goes into the armScaleMultiplier, enables you to manually stretch the arm longer or shorter by changing this attribute.

All that is left is to connect the output of this scale multiplier to each of the arm joints (the shoulder and the elbow).

13. Again, using the Connection Editor, connect the armScaleMultiplier.outputX attribute into both the shoulderJoint.scaleX and elbowJoint.scaleX attributes. Figure 17.57 shows a Hypershade and Hypergraph Input and Output Connections view of what your final node network should look like.

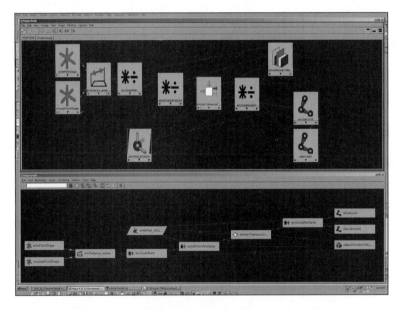

Figure 17.57 A Hypershade and Hypergraph Input and Output Connections view of what your final node network should look like.

Figure 17.58 shows a Hypergraph Scene Hierarchy view of what your node's groupings should look like.

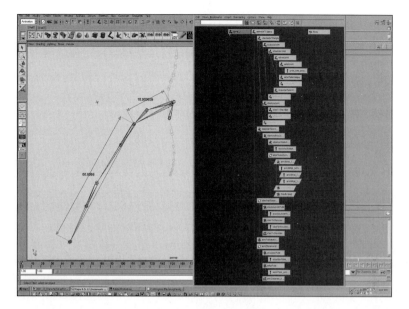

Figure 17.58   A Hypergraph Scene Hierarchy view of what your node's groupings should look like.

Now spend a few minutes testing the controls and attributes that you just created. Try moving around the freeIkHand locator while the handPlant attribute on the IK handle is set to 0. Experiment with your controls to make sure you didn't miss a step and that everything is functioning properly. If something seems to be working incorrectly, go back and retrace your steps to troubleshoot what might have gone wrong. This completed exercise with all the rigging finished is found in the file Jerk_ArmSetup_Finished.mb in the CD folder for this chapter.

In the next exercise, you will add the hand to the arm setup and, finally, put in all the control boxes that the character animator will ultimately use to animate the entire arm and hand.

Exercise 17.9   Rigging an Advanced Additive Hand and Fingers

Before you start this exercise, take a moment to examine the hierarchy of the hands for this setup, as in the file Jerk_HandJoints.mb in this chapter's folder on the CD. Note that at each knuckle there is an additional joint that is directly on top of the child knuckle joint. This technique allows for two things. It zeroes out the transforms of the children knuckles (which will be directly animated), and it also allows for layered animation on the parent knuckles if this becomes necessary for later shot requirements.

Also note that the knuckles have control boxes around them. The technique of using control boxes for the animators to set keys on is a great idea when setting up a character. Control boxes can be added to a character in many ways; this is covered later in this chapter. For now, you should know that these control boxes are actually NURBS curves shape nodes that were made children of the joint's transform by selecting the curve shape and then the joint, and using the –shape flag with the parent MEL command. (See the section in this chapter, " Hooking Up Control Boxes to Your Character Rig," for more information.)

For the hand setup, you want it to be super-easy for an animator to use, as well as have all the extra controls needed for the animator to hit any hand pose necessary. You will set up a hand control that will allow the animator to rotate the fingers individually or together, add a full-finger curl, and add individual controls for each knuckle. You will use added attributes that are connected to plusMinusAverage nodes, which add together the attributes that control the rotations of the knuckles.

1. Start by opening the completed previous exercise, which is found in the file Jerk_ArmSetup_Finished.mb (or, you can start from your own completed file). With the arm setup file open, import the file Jerk_HandJoints.mb that is on the CD for this chapter.

2. Select each parent joint node that makes up the fingers and thumb hierarchies. They are the thumb_1, index_DoubleKnuckle, middle_DoubleKnuckle, ring_DoubleKnuckle, and pinkyFinger_1 nodes. Parent them directly to the wristJoint node, and delete the empty handGroup group node that is left.

3. Now select each knuckle control box from the 3D view port, and go to Modify, Add Attribute. Add the following float data type attributes (just leave the min, max, and default options blank):

> fingerFullCurl
>
> fingerMidBend
>
> fingerTipBend

Figure 17.59 shows the result.

You will use the double-jointed knuckle, along with the addition operation of the plusMinusAverage nodes, to allow the fingerCurl attribute to make the whole finger bend each joint. This also will cause the finger to flex closed, while still providing individual control over each joint in each finger so that the animator can pose the hand very explicitly. For each of the four fingers, you will create two plusMinusAverage nodes and then connect the same attributes on each finger. The following steps go through one finger; you should repeat the steps for the rest of the fingers in the exact same fashion (except for the thumb, which is slightly different and is covered separately).

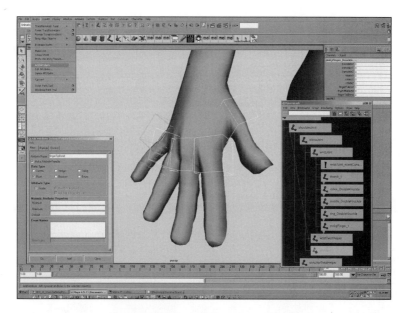

Figure 17.59   Knuckle control boxes.

4. Create two plusMinusAverage nodes by opening the Hypershade window and going to Create, General Utilities, Plus Minus Average.

5. Select the two new plusMinusAverage nodes that you just created, as well as the pinkyFinger_Knuckle node. Open the Hypergraph window and select Graph, Input and Output Connections.

6. Use the Hypergraph and Connection Editor to connect the fingerFullCurl attribute of the pinkyFinger_Knuckle node into the input1D[0] attributes of both plusMinusAverage nodes. Also connect the fingerFullCurl attribute to the pinky_DoubleKnuckle rotateX attribute.

7. Next, connect the fingerMidBend attribute of the pinkyFinger_Knuckle node to the input1D[1] attribute of one of the plusMinusAverage nodes. Now connect the output1D of this node into the rotateX attribute of the pinkyFinger_2 joint.

Tip

Sometimes array attributes can be tricky to connect to because the Connection Editor doesn't always show you the next available element. To connect an output attribute to the input1D[1] attribute, try selecting and loading both nodes into the Inputs and Outputs view of the Hypergraph. Next, right-click and hold down the mouse on the very rightmost side of the output node. A pop-up menu should appear that displays at the very top Connect Output Of and that gives you a list of attributes. Continuing to hold down the mouse button, highlight the appropriate attribute from the list and then let go of the mouse button. The mouse turns into an active dragging line with a little square icon at the end.

Now right-click on top of the node that contains the input array attribute, and hold down the mouse button. You should see a menu labeled Connect Input Of. While still holding down the right mouse button on top of your input node, select the appropriate input array attribute. That's it—you just made a connection. This technique takes a little practice, but it is really fast once you get the hang of it. And it takes less effort because you don't need to load the Connection Editor just to connect a few attributes.

8. Connect the fingerTipBend attribute of the pinkyFinger_Knuckle node to the input1D[1] attribute of the other plusMinusAverage node. Now connect the output1D of this node into the rotateX attribute of the pinkyFinger_3 joint.

   Figure 17.60 is an example of what the node network looks like for the finger.

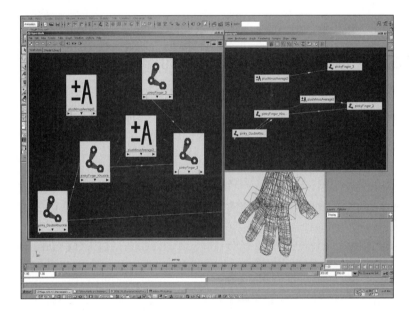

Figure 17.60 This is what the node network looks like for the finger.

Perform steps 2 through 8 for each of the other four fingers.

9. For the thumb, create three plusMinusAverage nodes. Select them along with the thumb_Knuckle joint, and load them in the Input Output Connections view of the Hypergraph.

10. Connect (using the Hypergraph and the Connection Editor) the thumb_Knuckle rotateY and rotateZ attributes directly to control the thumb_1 rotateY and rotateZ attributes.

11. Connect the fingerFullCurl attribute of the thumb_Knuckle to the input1D[0] attribute of one of the unused plusMinusAverage nodes. Then connect the fingerMidBend attribute to the input1D[1] attribute of the same plusMinusAverage node. Now connect the output1D of this plusMinusAverage into thumb_DoubleKnuckle rotateX.

12. Connect the fingerFullCurl attribute of the thumb_Knuckle to the input1D[0] attribute of one of the other unused plusMinusAverage nodes. Then connect the thumb_Knuckle rotateX attribute to the input1D[1] attribute of the same plusMinusAverage node; connect its output1D into the rotateX of the thumb_1 node.

13. Connect the fingerFullCurl attribute of the thumb_Knuckle to the input1D[0] attribute of the last unused plusMinusAverage node. Then connect the fingerTipBend attribute to the input1D[1] attribute of the same plusMinusAverage node. Now connect the output1D of this plusMinusAverage into the thumb_2 rotateX attribute. Your result should look like Figure 17.61.

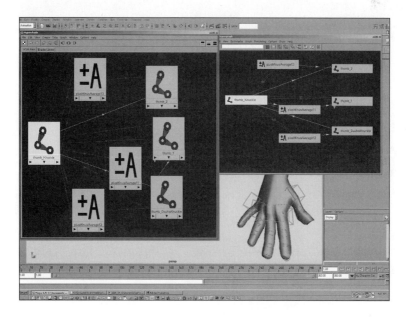

Figure 17.61 Utility nodes set up for the hand.

This completes the hand setup. For a finished example file of this rig, open the scene file Jerk_HandSetup_Finished.mb, which is included in this chapter's folder of the CD.

Hooking Up the Head Skeletal Hierarchy

For the head of a character, you can create a separate hierarchy that is point-constrained to a locator that is a child of the spine or neck. This leaves the rotational controls free from the hierarchy and enables the animator to animate them by hand (see Figure 17.62). You will do this in the next exercise.

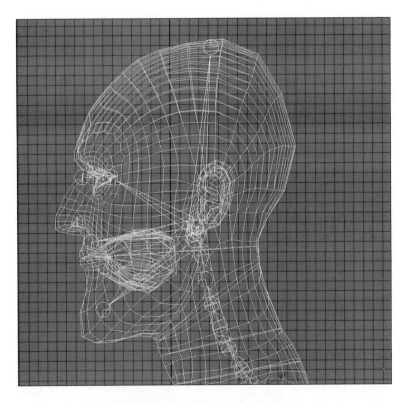

Figure 17.62   IK layout for the head.

Exercise 17.10 Attaching the Head Setup

This is a short exercise that goes through a few simple steps to create a joint hierarchy for the head. The head is created first. Then it is connected to the neck using a combination of constraints that allow for additional freedom when animation occurs, giving the character's head extra flexibility later.

1. Create the head joints for your character using a similar joint layout as shown in Figure 17.62.

   It is a good idea to place the jaw's point of rotation slightly in front of and below the side view of the ear lobe. Usually you should include a few extra joints that stem from the jaw, as well as a joint that goes up to the top of the head of your character, for extra weighting of the facial geometry.

2. Next, create a locator and point-snap it to the root of the head skeleton that you just created. Make this locator a child of the nearest neck joint.

3. Point-constrain the head's root to this new child locator by selecting the locator and then the head's root joint, and performing Constrain, Point (see Figure 17.63).

   This setup allows the character's head to rotate freely from the spine and neck, but it still translates around with the neck and spine appropriately. If you need to translate the neck by any small amount, the ability is there by moving the locator that the head is constrained onto.

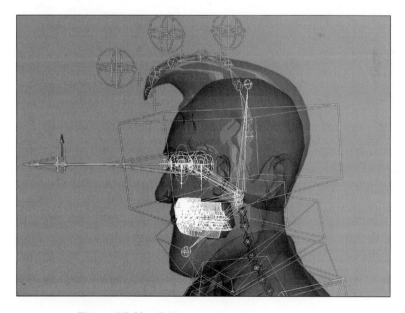

Figure 17.63 Full head setup with control boxes.

Facial Controls and Blend Shape Deformers

Although facial rigging was a smaller portion of the setup for this project, the way that the rigging was accomplished can also be used for complex scenarios of lip-synching and high-range emotional facial animation. All facial expression controls can be successfully implemented in a very traditional way. You first model them as separate models and apply them as blend shapes targets. Then you rig each attribute of your blend shape into a single faceController node simply and quickly by adding attributes. Then you use the Connection Editor to quickly hook them all into the single faceController node so that they are easily accessible to the animator.

Eye blinks can also be modeled as blend shapes and hooked up using set-driven key onto attributes of a driver. Each eye should have a separate blink control so that the eyes can blink at an offset of each other (see Figure 17.64).

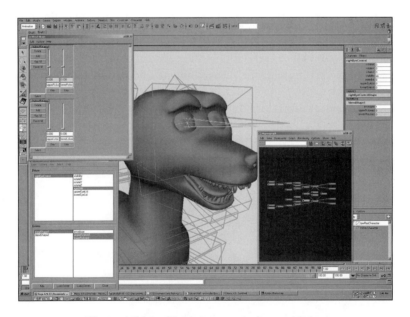

Figure 17.64 Blend shape setup for eye blinks.

The opening and closing of the jaw can be achieved using joints and painting the smooth bind weights to achieve an appropriate and appealing opening and closing of the mouth corners.

It is important to note that all the blend shapes for the lips must be modeled with the geometry in the default pose, with the mouth closed, to avoid double transformations of the jaw being double deformed while opening.

Tip

To create blend shapes for a character that has already been bound to a skeleton, you will want to be sure of two things:

- Be sure that you are using an exact duplicate of the character's geometry before it was bound to the skeleton to begin modeling your blend shapes.

- When you create the blend shape, go into the Advanced tab in the Create Blend Shape options box and choose the Front of Chain options in the deformation order pull-down menu. Or, after you create the blend shape, choose Inputs, All Inputs and use the middle mouse button to drag your blend shape to the bottom of the deformation order list (just above any tweak nodes there—see Figure 17.65).

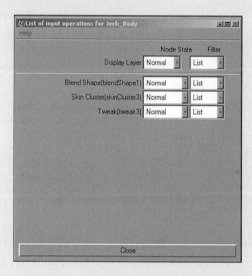

Figure 17.65   List of history operations window.

Creating Eye Controls

The eye's "look at" controls were set up simply with two joints for each eye. RPK IK handles were point- and pole vector–constrained to a locator that is a child of the "look at" control.

The next exercise takes you through this process. Start with a new scene and create two spheres, evenly placed as your eyeball objects.

Exercise 17.11   Eye Setup

Begin by creating the joints for the eyes.

1. Create two joints for each eye.

   The crucial aspect of where these joints get placed is that the parent joint (the one that will control the rotations of the eye) has its location in the exact same location of the eye geometry's pivot. Therefore, it is also extremely important that the eye be capable of rotating around its own pivot without visibly intersecting any of the face's external geometry. In other words, make sure the eyes can look around correctly by simply rotating around. If the eyes are perfect spheres and are carefully placed inside the head, and if the head is modeled correctly around the eyes, centering the pivot of the eyes should work just fine.

   An easy way to make sure your parent joint is in the exact same place as your eyeball joint is to turn on handles for the node that should rotate the eyes. You can do this by selecting the joint and going to Display, Component Display, Selection Handles. Then use the v key to point-snap the joint directly on top of the location during creation and layout of the joint.

2. Create two locators, and place each locator directly in front of each eye.

3. Name the joints and the two children locators appropriately according to which eye they are in front of: leftEyeJoints and leftEyeAim.

4. Next, create an IK handle from the parent joint to the end joint at the end of the eye.

5. Now select the "look at" locator first and the IK handle second; click Constrain, Point to point-constrain the IK handle onto the locator.

6. With the same selection active, click Constrain, Pole Vector to pole vector–constrain the IK handle to the same target.

7. Select the eyeball geometry group. Shift+select the parent eyeball joint, and hit p to parent the eyeball geometry to the joint (see Figure 17.66).

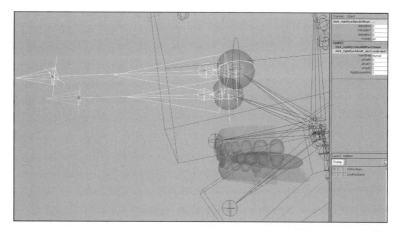

Figure 17.66   Parenting the eyeball to the eyeball joint hierarchy.

You can now hook up some parented control boxes to make the eyes look around. You can add an additional parent to the aim locator that is point-constrained to the location of the eyes. An animator can use this to have FK-style rotations and then actually translate the locator to have the IK style look at control as well.

This technique involves several really cool things. First, you will not get flipping because you will have control over the IK handle's rotate plane much better than a mere aim constrain could provide. Second, you can actually bind those joints that are rotating the eyes to the face geometry. When you weight the character, you will want to carefully distribute the weighting of the eye joints just around the lids of the character, somewhere between .2 and .4, so that the fleshy area around the eyes actually deforms subtlety enough when his eyes look around.

The Hair of the Jerk

For the hair of The Jerk, the overlapping action rig setup was used (loaded straight from the finished example file from Chapter 13, "Making Advanced Connections"). This was simply imported from the completed file from Chapter 13, chapter13_OverlappingAction_finished.mb, and then was translated, rotated, and scaled into place using the TRANS_ROTATE_SCALE_MATRIX node. Then the mainAttachNode was constrained to the end of the head hierarchy to attach it to the main skeleton. See Chapter 13 for a detailed step-by-step tutorial on how to create this dynamically driven floppy IK setup.

Note

If you do not want the dynamics mode of this rig during actual animation testing, you can turn the dynamicFlopOnOff and addMoreFlopiness attributes found on the FloppyChainContoller locator node to 0 until the actual playblasted animation occurs. Then you can begin testing how high you want to set these attributes. Note that because this portion of the rig is using soft body particle dynamics, it is necessary to start the animation at least 10 to 15 frames earlier so that the dynamics get a chance to calculate their initial position correctly.

Smooth Binding Proxy Geometry

The characters were modeled using subdivision surfaces in Maya, but when it came to production, we chose to convert our properly modeled sub-d meshes into medium-resolution polygon meshes for the purposes of our rendering pipeline going out to Mental Ray. We were also fortunate enough to not need to deal with the hassle of binding Maya's sub-d surfaces or doing any deformations on sub-d geometry at all because we had a pure polygon conversion before skinning occurred. I strongly recommend doing things this way, unless there is a strong reason to not to. The level of simplification on a geometric level becomes a real time saver and improves the quality of your final result.

This might not be the case for some productions using Maya, though. Because subdivision surfaces are going for a full-blown implementation in Maya, I have included the workflow that is involved with rigging a character that is actually built from Maya's native subdiv mesh node. The following exercise was not necessarily used for our production, but it is an important step to take if you are planning to skin a subdivision mesh in Maya.

The basic premise for the workflow is this: We do not want to bind the Maya subdivision surface itself to the joint's skinCluster because it will be much too slow to deform or to paint weights onto. The difficulty of working with the model is truly overwhelming when compared with simply binding the polygon control mesh shape node. You will bind only the joints that need to deform the character by implicitly selecting them and then selecting the polygon control mesh shape node, instead of binding directly the subdivision surface.

Exercise 17.12   How to Bind a Subdiv Mesh's Polygon Proxy Control Mesh

This exercise was written to work with any character as a general workflow tutorial. Therefore, it is not file-specific. You will simply need to start with a scene that contains any Maya subdivision surface geometry and some joints to bound the geometry onto.

1. Go to your current 3D view panel. Under the Show menu, turn off everything except joints. This makes it easier to see and select only joints.

2. Carefully select only the joints that are important for the character to deform.

   This means that anywhere there are overlapping or point-constrained joints, select only the single joint that should be causing the deformations. Never select two joints that are overlapping (double joints). You also usually don't need to select the tips of the joint hierarchies. Keep the Hypergraph open to make sure you are selecting only the joints you need. The fewer joints you select, the fewer you will have to paint weights for later.

3. When you have made sure your selection is correct, save a quick-select set by going to Create, Sets, Quick Select Set. Call your new set bindJoints. This is just a way of saving a selection so that you can go back and select it again later.

4. Now select the subdivision character and open the Hypergraph window. To select the polygon control mesh, you must be in Scene Hierarchy mode of the Hypergraph. Turn on Options, Display, Shape Nodes by making sure there is a check box next to it in the menu window.

5. Next, you should see two shape nodes. One is a subdiv shape that is being fed its data by a polyToSubdiv node (which you can see if you select it and click Graph, Input and Output Connections). Below it is another shape node, which is a polygon mesh shape. The polygon mesh shape node is your poly control cage (as seen in Figure 17.67).

   You can select the polygon proxy control mesh of your native Maya subdivision geometry by viewing the shape nodes, as previously stated. Or, you can find it in the tangled node network that shows up in the Input/Output Connections view of the Hypergraph. Or, you can use a quick MEL command by selecting it in the View window and executing the following line in the Script Editor window:

   ```
   select -r 'listRelatives -c -type mesh';
   ```

Note

If your subdiv surface is not in polyProxy mode, you will need to switch it to this mode before any of this will appear. Select your surface and go to Subdiv Surfaces, Polygon Proxy Mode.

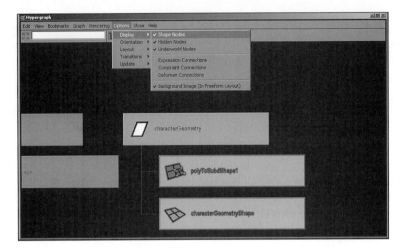

Figure 17.67 Viewing geometry shapes with the Hypergraph.

6. With the polygon shape node visible in the Hypergraph, select your bind joint selection set by going to Edit, Quick Select Sets, bindJoints.

7. Hold down the Shift key and select the polygon shape node in the Hypergraph.

8. Go to the options for Skin, Bind Skin, Smooth Bind Options Box, change the Bind To options to Selected Joints, and hit the Bind Skin button.

9. Before you can paint weights, you must assign a shader to the poly proxy mesh. Select the poly proxy control mesh again. Open the multilister, right-click the initialShadingGroup, and choose Edit, Assign.

10. Under your current 3D view, go to the Show menu and turn off Subdiv Surfaces. This makes it easier to deform your character and visibly see what is going on.

Painting Smooth Skin Weights

Painting weights is one of the single most important stages for your character's deformations to look believable and appealing. The process of painting weights basically involves using the Artisan paint brush architecture in Maya to paint on a value somewhere between 0 and 1. This will tell your skin cluster which joints will have an influence on the movement of which vertices.

The following text describes the process I use to paint weights on a smooth bound character. Then following exercise elaborates on the specifics involved to achieve good character weighting.

First, just as if you were doing a painting, rough in your general values by blocking out your weights, going through groups of vertices as well as each joint, and flooding them with either 0 or 1 values. Next, paint with a medium-size brush around the edges of your weights so that all the influences are at a value of 0 or 1. When you are finished and you have painted every single joint at either 1 or 0, you set the Artisan value to 1 but turn the opacity down to about .33.

Then go through and lightly soften the edges of all your weights by painting with this partially opaque brush. Every once in a while, use the smooth brush at this stage to also soften the edges. The last stage is to go through and use the smooth brush exclusively to really soften the weights on the joints that you want to have a lot of fall-off to their weighting. During this entire process, you should be testing your character's deformations by bending the joints and testing the controls. When you get things looking pretty good, you should do major motion and extreme poses for your character; test the weighting on an animated character that is hitting really exaggerated poses (with hands way up in the air, bending over and touching the head to the toes, and so on). At this point, you can go back and paint in the weights to fix any problems you see.

As a general workflow process, painting weights can seem somewhat repetitive, tedious, and often frustrating. It can feel like as soon as you change one joint's weights to look good in one pose, the other pose no longer works. It is important to note that sometimes it is simply a process of finding an acceptable state in between. Usually, though, if you follow the workflow outlined in the steps ahead, the painting of your character's weights should end up being a very smooth process (no pun intended!).

Exercise 17.13   Common Workflow for Effectively Painting Smooth Skin Weights

1. Select the smooth-bound polygon mesh and begin to paint weights using the Artisan options found under the Skin, Edit Smooth Skin, Paint Skin Weights Tool options box (see Figure 17.68).

2. Select the bound character. Under Skin, Edit Smooth Skin, Prune Small Weights (with a setting of about .4), get rid of all traces of pointlessly weighted vertices before you begin your weight painting. This enables you to see exactly which joints are the major influences deforming the geometry of your character. You will have a better idea of which joints you need to paint weights for the most (see Figure 17.69).

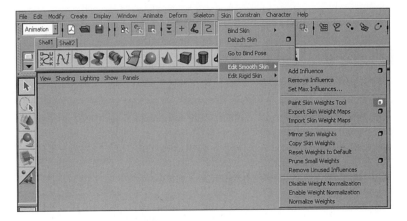

Figure 17.68 The Paint Skin Weights menu.

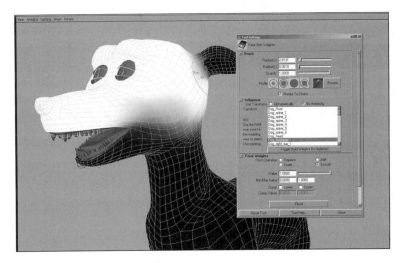

Figure 17.69 Painting weights with Artisan.

3. Deform the character by placing it into several extreme poses and setting keys across the timeline.

A common sequence of poses during this phase would be a "jumping-jack" sequence, with the character's legs and arms reaching their full upward and downward extensions. This is known as range-of-motion testing. You want to paint the weights for your character so that they look decent even at the most extreme poses. This way, you will be sure that they will look good when the animators pose the character in a more normal, expected pose (see Figure 17.70).

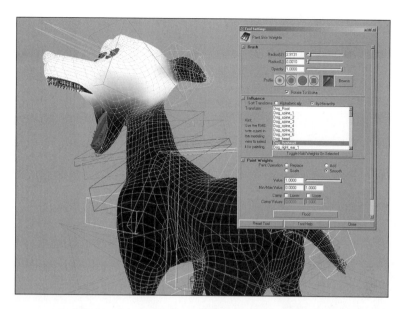

Figure 17.70   Testing deformations while painting weights.

4. Paint the weights for only half of the mesh, until deformations are acceptable on that half. I almost exclusively use Replace mode and Smooth mode in Artisan to paint skin weights. These modes are set in the Paint Weights section of the Paint Skin Weights tool options.

5. When you have the weights painted for half of the character, select the skin and use the Mirror Weights feature under the Skin, Edit Smooth Skin, Mirror Skin Weights options box (see Figure 17.71). Be sure to use the correct axis settings that you want to mirror across.

6. Now you can clean up your mirrored weights (they never come out perfect) by checking all the deformations and going through the same steps that you did previously to make sure all your weights are perfect on both sides. Painting precise and sparing brush strokes with the Smooth mode of the Paint Weights tool only where it's needed is crucial at this stage for really well-painted smooth skin weight deformations.

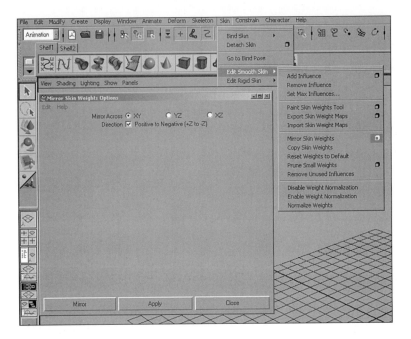

Figure 17.71 Use the Mirror Weights feature to create your mirrored weights.

Tip

Use the Toggle Hold Weights on Selected button in the Paint Weights window to keep a joint's weights from changing after you have painted them (see Figure 17.72).

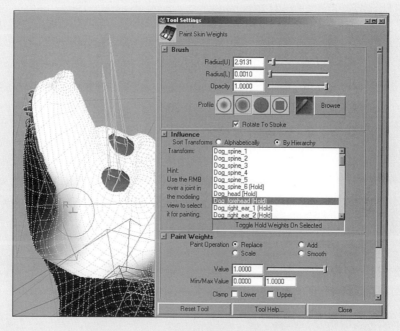

Figure 17.72   Using Toggle Hold Weights.

Paint Weights Using per-Vertex Selections

You can use the Skin, Edit Smooth Skin, Paint Skin Weights tool on a per-vertex level as well as an entire object level. Many people are not aware that you actually can use the Paint Weights tool on a per-vertex level by selecting the vertices and loading the paint weights tool. This is extremely useful when you first start painting the weights on your character and you are trying to lay out your initial weights, or when you are trying to "point-tweak" certain vertices and leave others alone. Select the vertices whose weights you want to change, and use the Flood button to flood those vertices in Replace mode with a value of 1; this is a great first step at very quickly roughing in your character's weights. You can then go in and use low opacity in Replace mode with a value of 1, as well as Smooth mode with flooding, to really disperse the gradual fall-offs of your joints' weighting.

Sometimes it is difficult to paint or select the correct vertices on a character that you are trying to change the weights on because those areas are in little crevices, such as under the armpits, in folds of skin, between the legs, or between crevices in fingers. These most difficult areas to paint the weights on also end up becoming the most crucial areas for making the best-looking deformations on your character. So, having a quick and easy way of selecting and editing these areas ends up being crucial as well. A great tip for selecting these difficult vertices of your polygon character is to use the UV Texture Editor, but still select it using Vertex Component Selection mode. The geometry is literally unwrapped in UV space. If your modeling and texturing departments have done a good job laying out your UVs, the process of selecting vertices using this unwrapped representation of your character becomes an extremely quick and easy trick to use.

Figure 17.73 shows difficult vertices to select in 3D space and the exact same vertices selected in UV space. This is an example of how much easier and quicker it can be if you have the right UV layout at hand.

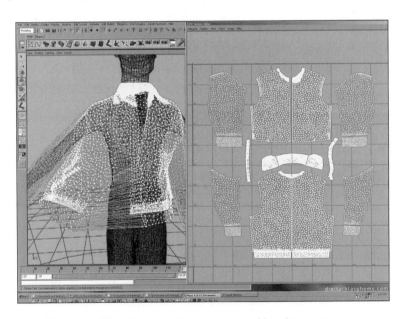

Figure 17.73 Using the UV layout to quickly select vertices.

Using Additional Influence Objects

The smooth binding in Maya works quite nicely because it enables you to use multiple influence objects. It even allows geometry to become an influence object that you can paint weights for.

Although it wasn't necessary to use influence objects for our character rig, I highly recommend using them to achieve complex deformations. Check them out in the Maya documentation. You create an influence object from any transform node in Maya by selecting the smooth bound mesh and then the object that you want to become an influence. Then you choose Skin, Edit Smooth Skin, Add Influence (see Figure 17.74).

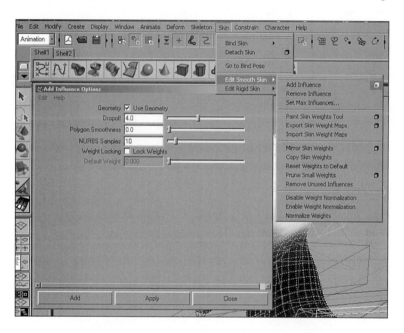

Figure 17.74   The Add Influence menu command.

When you have finished painting weights and you have done all the other steps necessary to finish setting up your character, such as parenting low-res geometry and creating control boxes (as explained in earlier sections of this chapter), you are ready to hand off your file to the animator.

Summary

Character rigging can be a very fun and interesting process. The one thing to remember about this entire process, though, is that it will always be a collaboration between you and other teams. The way that the file is set up, as well as the controls there, will ultimately be used by the animator; thus, they need to be easily understood and controllable. The deformations of the character will ultimately change the shape and nature of the character's model and must therefore stay true to the design and style in which the character was originally modeled. The character that you set up must eventually be textured, lit, and rendered, so it absolutely must not have geometric problems such as bad normals or bad UVs when you bind it to the skeleton. The difficult part in setting up a character is being able to systematically take all of this into consideration, with the final goal being a stable character whose transformation space has been manipulated to offer full control to the animator.

Character animation is a long and difficult process, and the capability to have the character react in a desirable and predictable way is the most valuable thing that can be achieved. To make the character's controls and deformations predictable, and to give the character the capability to be textured, lit, and rendered are all vital in their own ways. The process of character animation will continue to become more simplified—and, therefore, capable of more sophistication—as time goes by. The same can be said of the techniques to rig a good character that is capable of achieving more types of motion. Always remember that, much like a puppet, there is a human behind the controls of your character breathing the appeal of artificial life into its computer-generated soul.

Chapter 18

Shading

By Max Sims

All the animation is complete, and now it is time to give life to the surfaces with shaders. Shader creation inside Maya is extremely fun—and equally confusing at times. You will want to take a ground-up approach, both literally and figuratively, to avoid confusion. You will start shading and texturing the scene with a multitude of techniques. You will work your way up figuratively by first understanding the visual qualities of the materials needed for the shaders.

On the literal side, you will build shaders for the road, sidewalk, cars, characters, props, and buildings. To show the elements of Maya that are needed to achieve a desired look, we discuss the Hypershade in a logical progression along with material and texture editing. In this chapter, procedural and hand-painted maps are shown and placed in 2D and 3D on your surfaces.

A matrix of possibilities exists to create rich surface textures. This chapter guides you through the shader creation process and helps you understand these salient ideas in Maya:

- Visual concepts to approach a shading problem
- The differences in painted and procedural shaders
- The process of creating shaders from the ground up
- Texture mapping via projection and UVs
- Production-proven techniques for achieving good-looking, efficient shaders

Seeing the World in Shaders

When you start to learn about color, a sunset never quite looks the same. You start to analyze how the spectacular vista is created from the chromatic progression of analogous colors of orange to red to blue and the high-contrast value levels. The same observation and analytical skills are needed to create shaders that will look like the material you are trying to describe.

Your goal is to have accurate shaders for the entire street scene in the *Parking Spot* short film. Taking a ground-up approach, think of the surfaces that you need to create. The roadbed is the first item. Work your way up to the sidewalk, the storefront, and then the building. You must consider what materials these items are made of. Asphalt on the roadbed will have painted stripes, oil spots, and skid marks. The concrete on the sidewalk will have generous cracks. Likewise, close observation shows the complex mixture of rocks that concrete is made of. Are weeds growing in the cracks? Buildings will contain stone and wood. Will they be perfectly clean, or will they need a lot of irregularity factored in? The shop window's glass will have signs inside, and the glass might not be as green as glass in the car.

Use the same bottom-up approach to think about how a shader would be created. The asphalt of the road will be dark, but will it be completely black? A mottled dark gray is more likely the candidate. Think of the procedural texture or the scanned-in image that you need to get that color. Layer on top of that the painted stripe. There will be a thickness to it, and its sheen will be different from that of the asphalt. A bump map might be needed to raise it off the surface, and a specular map might be needed to differentiate the shininess. The edge of the painted stripe will have a deckled edge and will not be laser-perfect; this will have to be done on the original texture maps. The oil spots and skid marks also need this kind of attention. A reflectivity map will control the level of the oil's reflections. An iridescent highlight can be seen if the light glints it at just the right angle. The skid marks will have a worn rubber shader that the Blinn material type might best accommodate.

Use this systematic approach to all the varied surfaces in your scene. Work your way up the different objects in the scene, and write some notes about what each type of material is and what special properties you want it to convey. You are trying to capture a feel for what the surface will look like. This can be done in an impressionistic rather than literal manner. We start down this path with the end goal in mind: the look.

Achieving a Look

A "look" is the way surfaces are shaded to have a particular visual quality. It is the melding of production design and shader creation. Computer graphics opens up endless possibilities in looks that were impossible to achieve with live action and cel animation. The process of creating the shaders that will imbue a film with a specific visual quality is called *look development*. The shaders repeatedly are created and evaluated, to give a film a balance of the director's vision and art department's criteria. This is done even for photorealistic effects in movies such as the *Star Wars* and *Matrix* films.

Think of the visual quality differences in two similar CG films: PDI's *Antz* and Pixar's *A Bug's Life*. The lighting obviously was much darker and yet softer in *Antz*. *A Bug's Life* reflected the micro world and the wonder at that scale. Lighting contributed a great deal, but the shaders were always in the art department's eye. The two disciplines work in conjunction with each other.

The way Pixar treated a leaf in terms of shaders is an excellent example. The leaf has a translucent quality, and it was a critical test in the beginning of the production to see if that effect could be accomplished. The test piece was based on a piece of artwork that had ants crossing a twig. Translucency tests were done to see if the ants' shadows could come through the leaf. A simple cycle animation loop was done to test render. The shader meisters at Pixar then went to work to see if the effect was attainable. It was, and production could commence. The team felt confident that it could get the desired "look."

To get this leaf look, the team programmed a shading model for translucency that accepted the shadow maps to the surfaces. You can see the test and artwork on the "Making Of" DVD for *A Bug's Life*. During production, the shader department also decided that, for modeling efficiency, the leaves needed to have the thickness put into the shader so that everything could be done on a single piece of geometry. The shader was programmed to find the surface edge and render a thickness by making it lighter. The art department provided detailed artwork of what the veins of the leaf would look like, as well as the coloring during different seasons. The texture painters followed that guidance to paint the vein maps and the color maps. The highlights on the surface and bumps were also added to the mix. In addition, the leaf might need bite marks from some munching caterpillar. Would that be modeled in, or was it easier to put that in a transparency map? All these items were designed and resolved before it got to a final render.

To achieve a look, think of your overall artistic goal. Create artwork that embodies the look, and then critically and logically break down the problem to its simplest elements.

The first consideration of any shader creation is keen observation. Start by looking at your tabletop, and you will see fingerprints, smudges, and dirt, and so on. What would you need to do to affect the way light is disturbed over these irregularities? What shader type comes close to the specular controls you need? Will a custom map need to be painted and added to the specular?

Note

Try to find a real example of the material you are trying to reproduce. This will permit you to closely observe how light affects your surface. If the material is too large, try to get a photograph online or go out in the field and take images for your project. Photograph a material in different light and at different times of the day to see how it looks. If you will use the photo as the basis for maps on the shader, take the picture in overcast light or in the shadow. Take pictures in detail and then from far away, to scrutinize macro and micro patterns.

The next thing to do is observe the textures of the surfaces around you. Is it a fine-grain, molded plastic texture or a wet, glossy highlight? See if it is necessary to bump-map the surface. Which of the myriad choices in Maya's Create Texture Node is the right type and height of graininess for a bump map? I like to use the granite texture for simulating grained plastic; it can be sized up or down depending on the fineness needed. Another great texture is to use leather for a cobblestone effect. Think of the material types in terms of what overall effect they have rather than by their names. The almost limitless combination of textures against the channels in the shader menu can be overwhelming.

The hardest part to wrap your mind around is the notion of infinite recursion. That means that, for a color map, a ramp can use a ramp within a ramp within a ramp, ad infinitum. The other possibility is that this ramp within ramp can be used for any other shader channel, such as transparency, bump, or specular channels. This is where the fun comes in. A matrix of possibilities exists for creating rich surface textures.

Note

Experience and playful experimentation are the best ways to learn the different textures in Maya. Try every one, and look at all the attributes for them. You might end up transposing the snow for a dust coating.

Let's play with the shaders to get an idea of what is possible in terms of looks by observing material differences in Maya. This will get you accustomed to the different material types.

Exercise 18.1   Observing Material Differences

How does the light hit the surface? That is a trick question. Light strikes a surface in very complex ways. A novice sees light as a smooth-to-rough highlight on a shader ball. An expert sees complex mottling and interaction. The main differences in shader types in Maya lie in the specular shading. This is the main way to affect how light strikes the surface. This exercise gets you thinking about how the shaders vary in these terms. In this exercise, you learn about the visual differences in shader types by creating new materials. This also acclimates you to the material editors. You don't need to open a file; look at Figure 18.1 to see all the shader possibilities.

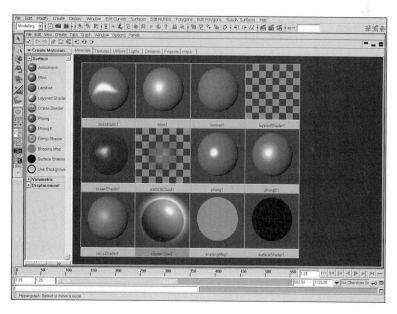

Figure 18.1   The different shader types are shown here. Look at the highlights especially.

1. In the Hypergraph window, select Create, Materials, Anisotropic.

2. Open the Attribute Editor and display the Specular Shading attributes. Adjust the sliders for Angle, X&Y, Roughness, and Fresnel Index, and observe the changes.

You'll see that the highlight on the material sample is curved (see Figure 18.2). Go down the list of attributes to look at the material samples and see the specular shading differences. Anisotropic materials distribute the light in differing directions. This is good for brushed-metal finishes or hair.

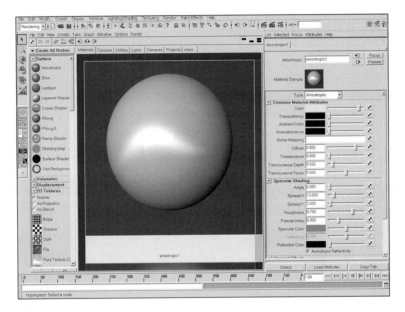

Figure 18.2 The highlight on the Anisotropic Material Sample is curved.

3. Pick Blinn on the Type pull-down menu in your Shader Attribute window. Dial the Eccentricity and Specular Roll Off back and forth to see the highlight on the shader ball increase and decrease. (See Figure 18.3.)

Note

A Blinn shader is based on planetary surface reflectance albedo. This is the amount of light that hits the surface and bounces back. Earth's value is 0.39, and a perfect reflector is 1.00. The shader was created for the Voyager flyby simulations at Jet Propulsion Laboratory (JPL). It was named after my first computer graphics teacher, Jim Blinn, back at Art Center College of Design in the mid-1980s. Blinn shaders are nice for materials such as the metallic paint and rubber on The Jerk's car.

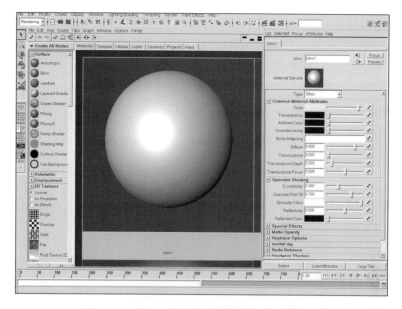

Figure 18.3   A Blinn shader is nice for materials such as metallic paint and rubber.

4. Switch to a Lambert type (see Figure 18.4). You will not see a Specular Shading tab.

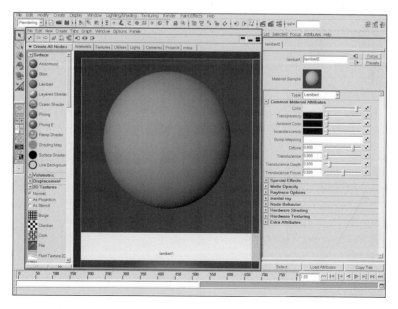

Figure 18.4   A Lambert shader is great for matte surfaces.

Lambert shaders are great for very matte surfaces. There is no highlight on the material, just as a matte surface should behave. You still do use other material types, such as Blinn, for matte appearing surfaces, such as cloth, to "sell" the look.

5. The next type is a Layered shader. It will have a default green color.

   With this material, you can composite two or more shader types on a surface. If you need velvet and chrome on one surface, a layered shader is your answer (see Figure 18.5). Think of a transparency channel as the mask to show through the underlying material.

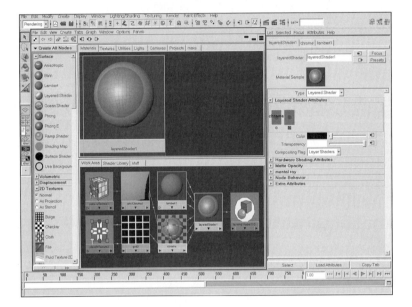

Figure 18.5   This Layered shader demonstrates how the chrome shader needs to let the velvet shader show through the transparent areas.

6. When you create new materials in Hypershade, you will see a new Shader type since Maya 4.5: the Ocean shader. You will see some new tabs for Ocean, Common Material, and Environment Attributes. It is fairly daunting to see so many choices, but try to move the slider bars to see what they can do to change the material (see Figure 18.6).

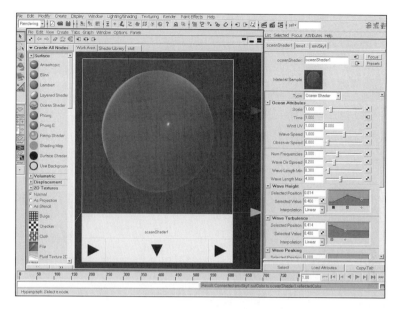

Figure 18.6   A recently new shader type since Maya 4.5 is the Ocean shader.

Playing is a great way to learn anything in Maya. With experience and good memory, you will gain ideas of preset values to plug in to achieve a specific look. The Ocean shader was made for fluid dynamics, but it can be used on regular surfaces as well. Its name should be self-explanatory for its use.

7. Switch the type to Phong. The only new attribute is Cosine Power. Slide that attribute all the way to the right; it will be at 100. Type in **10,000** and then start sliding. Notice that at c. 6000, you will see the highlights again. The Cosine value goes right up to infinity. Talk about shiny! (See Figure 18.7.)

Tip

This example shows that presets on Maya slider bars are factory-set by their software engineers. Always try to increase the value in any attribute by typing a higher value. You also get fine control by holding down Ctrl+LMB and dragging the number window.

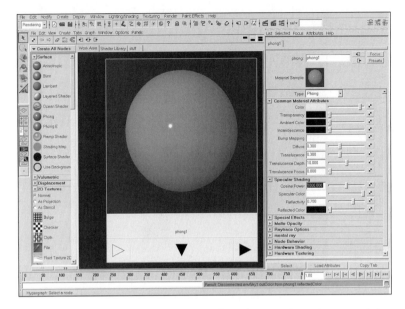

Figure 18.7   The Phong shader excels at shiny things such as chrome and glass. A surface that is very polished, with hard specular highlights and reflections, is ideal.

8. Turn Material Type now to Phong E. This has the most control for the specularity. Play with the Roughness and Highlight Size. You have further control with Whiteness; start to change color there. Notice the neat effect of the highlight gradation (see Figure 18.8).

Note

A Phong E shader renders faster than a Phong shader, and traditionally provides the most possibilities for specular control.

9. Switch to the Ramp shader. You will see a great deal of attributes and a very new Ramp interface (see Figure 18.9).

10. Expand the Color tab and click your cursor in the Ramp Editor three times. Choose a set of continuing lighter colors, with the lightest to the right.

11. Change Color Input to Brightness, and change Interpolation to None on all three colors.

You have infinite control on the color of each shader to create very special effects here on the Ramp Shader type. It can be used as a cel shader or a way of modulating chroma in any color theory that you espouse. This will be a primary means of getting a specific look for the *Parking Spot* short. A ramp can be used to gradate Specular Roll Off, Color, and Reflectivity. It can also map an environment.

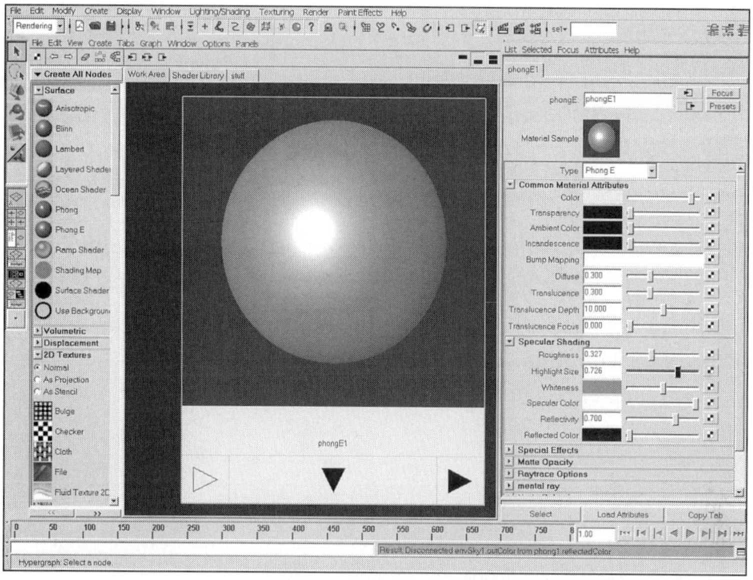

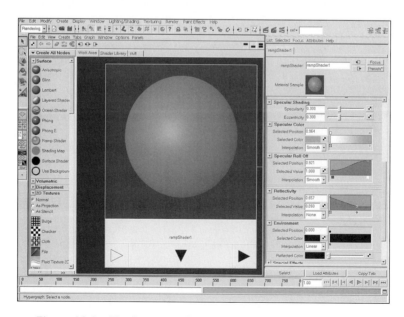

Figure 18.8   Notice the neat effect of the highlight gradation with the Phong E material type.

Figure 18.9   The Ramp interface in Maya 5. You have tremendous control over the color and highlights using the ramp graphs.

Now you will add and experiment with more of these effects.

12. Switch Color Input to Light Angle. In the Transparency tab, add a white color to the left of the Ramp Editor. Move the default black tab close to it.

13. Repeat Step 12 with Incandescence, Specular Color, Specular Roll Off, and Reflectivity.

14. In the Environment tab, make it black on the left to blue to white. Add another black tab and set the tabright next to the white 75% of the way there.

You should have a rich opalescent material that defies description (see Figure 18.10). The Ramp shader is a staple for creating special effects in your future projects. Explore this relatively new shader type in Maya 5, and see what cool looks you can achieve.

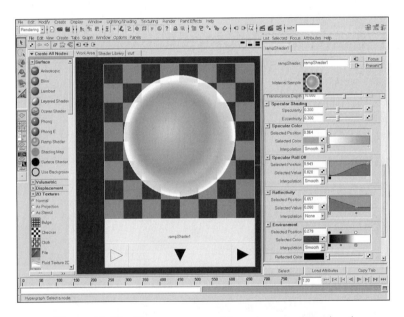

Figure 18.10   You can create a rich opalescent material such as this using the tools in the new Ramp interface.

15. Go to the Attribute Editor for shaders and keep the Type pull-down menu on. The next two types of shaders have specialized uses. Until the Ramp shader was available, a Shading Map shader was used to do cel effects. Skip over to the Surface Shader; it is a wrapper node that permits you to pass attributes from a shader to objects. This is useful in animation effects when an animated attribute shader can drive an effect.

16. Repeat all the steps in this exercise, this time using a fractal texture mapped to the specular channel across the various types of shaders. The specularity will be speckled and affected based on the white-to-black values (see Figure 18.11).

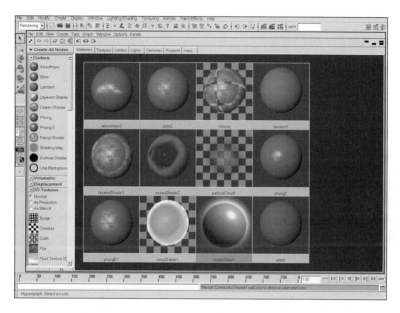

Figure 18.11   The fractal map adds a subtle richness in the specular mapping.

The subtle application of mapping the specular channels really makes any shader material look compelling. No surface is perfect, even in the computer world. Digital feature films need to pay particular attention to this level of shader creation because the images will be closely scrutinized.

I find that playing with all these shader types is extremely fun and leads in labyrinthine directions. The salient part of the previous exercise is to keep looking at the way the light hits the surfaces. See how Maya shaders can help in your quest for interesting visual qualities.

Note

The most neglected part of shader creation is seeing the effect of light when it strikes a surface. This is by no means a treatise on texturing or shading, of course. An excellent set of books to get much further in depth are *[Digital] Lighting and Rendering* (New Riders, 2000), by Jeremy Birn, and *[Digital] Texturing and Painting* (New Riders, 2001), by Owen Demers. Another great resource is www.dvgarage.com, which has excellent tutorials and sells DVDs and toolkits designed to help you understand the complexity of surfaces. The founder of the site, Alex Lindsay, is a former ILM rebel unit crewmember who excels at modeling, compositing, and rendering. We have included a sample image map from the Surface toolkit on the CD accompanying this book; named dvGSTK_063_512.tif, this image map is in the Shading/Source Images folder.

Considerations Before Shading

Before any shading commences, you must consider a few criteria. First is the quality of your surfaces. Second is file organization. For our project, Mark Adams, who has decades of experience in digital model making, did most of the models. His results are at the highest level of professionalism. In many cases, though, you are creating the model yourself or have a less experienced team member than Mark. Before applying shaders, check your model's surface quality for good parameterization, tessellation, and UVs. Then get your files organized for smoother shader production.

Surface Quality

Parameterization should have an even spacing and regular flow. Check to see that the isoparameter curves are evenly gridded or that the detail is only where it is needed. Look for waves and oscillations on the surface (see Figure 18.12). Also avoid what is called a "skinny" patch, with two or more isoparameters closely spaced for no reason. Open the Attribute Editor to count how many spans the surface is composed of if it is a NURBS surface. The span count should seem reasonable. The number of spans should be as high as will be needed to get the detail. This could be as high as hundreds of spans for a large creature's belly for a feature film, or just one span in each direction in U and V. It all depends on your criteria.

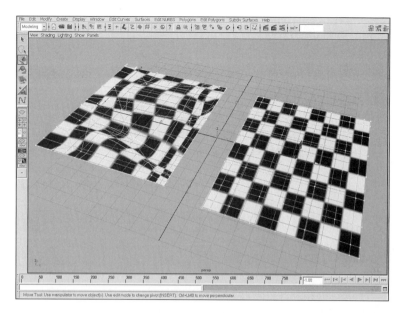

Figure 18.12   The surface on the left is poorly parameterized,
so the texture gets distorted. The right image is a much better result.

Tip

A NURBS surface is infinitely smooth. A large flat plane might be a 1-by-1 span NURBS surface that is sufficient to describe a ground plane. The maximum tessellation for a single patch is 128 by 128 polygons, and that can cause artifacts when rendering. It might need to be rebuilt to a 10-by-10 span surface just so that enough detail is seen close to the camera. This permits finer tessellation between the patches and holds up better when the camera is moving. This is one of the rare times when you need to increase the resolution of the surface.

Polygonal and subdivision surfaces also merit inspection before applying materials. You need to see what the poly count is in the Attribute Editor. Are the polygons well distributed and evenly spaced? Are there too many polygons for something that will be seen only very far away? Are UVs correct? Use the Polygon Cleanup tool to identify anything can be streamlined. Refer to Chapter 7, "Methods," for more detail.

To plan your shaders, think of what artwork you will need and where will it reside on your network. Working from your conceptual artwork and reference images, plan the various textures required. If painted artwork is needed, can it also help generate additional channels with image processing? Also think of the possibilities in creating shaders strictly through procedural means; you might not want to paint a perfect leather map every time.

Shading Process and Tools

The models are in good working order. The next step is to give the surfaces an authentic quality. The fundamental process involves creating the various textures and applying them to the various channels in the shader. The next step is to map the textures on the UVs based on the size of the surfaces. This might mean applying graphics or making a 3D bump map the right size. Throughout this process, you are evaluating the shader quality by lighting and render testing. In this section, first you will look at the common shading elements in Maya; then you will focus on the specific shaders for the production.

The shading process in Maya can take a circuitous route. Every user of the software has a favorite path while meandering to the final images. Legacy users of the software might embrace traditional routines and avoid anything that smacks of new. There is merit in exposing yourself to your colleagues' workflow and liberally adapting it to your own. Let's discuss how you can go about the shader-creation process and manage your pipeline efficiently.

Multilister, Hypershade, and Visor

Shaders can be created in two main ways. One is with the Hypershade/Visor; the other is with Multilister. If you used the old Alias PowerAnimator, Multilister should look very familiar. The materials are on top and the textures are at the bottom. You can expand the materials to see the underlying textures. The only advantage is seeing all your textures and materials easily. Don't get married to using Multilister, however, it will disappear in the next release. If you use only Multilister now, be sure to learn about Hypershade.

Hypershade is the best way to map relationships and edit shading networks. In a way, you are a programmer because you are connecting coded elements to produce an algorithm to describe a material to render. The result is a shader that has certain visual properties that are then applied to a surface. That point of view might make you think that creating shaders is highly technical, but it doesn't have to be. Hypershade simply graphs the elements that comprise your shader.

When you open Hypershade, you are presented with three areas. The first is Create Nodes, on the left. The second is the top tabs, where materials, textures, and other related materials are located. The bottom tab contains a work area as well as tabs such as the Shader Library; this is where most of the mapping of relationships occurs.

My personal procedure is to create a number of materials and map only the textures that I need per shader. I try to reuse as many textures as possible. A general course of action is to open the Attribute Editor for the shader and then go to the channel, such as the color channel. Pick the Create Render Node icon to the right of the channel. You can create the exact 2D or 3D texture that you want for that shader, and it will create the proper texture placement node as well. If you want to use the same texture to map to another channel in your shader—such as a bump map—you simply do it in the work area below. You can pick the material in the work area and graph the upstream and downstream connections. This shows the entire chain of procedures. You can reuse the color texture by Middle Mouse Button (MMB) dragging the texture on the material ball and then selecting Bump on the scrolldown menu. This is described in greater detail in the following exercises. The key is to see how the chain of texture placement feeds into the texture itself and then is wired into the material. Placing your cursor over the connecting arrow tell you a lot about how things can be connected. Double-click the arrow, and you can see the Connection Editor. This shows even more nonstandard connections that you can make.

Tip

To see a shader in extreme detail, you can use your Alt+LMB+MMB drag zoom control on a full-screen pane, just as you would zoom in a 3D window.

The power of Hypershade is that you can wire up the shaders in a myriad of ways. The beauty of Hypershade is that you can visually program your shaders in the work area. Try the shader programming exercise 18.2 later in this chapter to learn this. To avoid confusion in Hypershade, you must have a clean, concise project setup and plan your shaders.

Efficient Shader Setups

Render times will always be an issue. The shaders should be set up to use and reuse the computer's resources as efficiently as possible. One excellent way to get that done is to use the same texture map for different parts of the final shader. As a simple example, you might use the same Checker pattern for the bump and specular channel on one shader and again as a color map on another. Normally, you could create each one separately, creating three Checker and three 2D Texture Placement nodes. If the pattern doesn't vary for all three, why not just use it once? If you need to tweak one of the

Checker patterns to make it slightly different from the other, you can insert a utility such as a Switch node to reverse the pattern. You would still retain only one Checker pattern that could be changed universally once, and all the dependent shaders would comply. Another measure of efficiency is to convert a complex texture into its final 2D result. This is like "flattening" layers in Photoshop. The complex program that makes the map takes its toll at render time. (See Figure 18.13.)

Note

A simple example of flattening a texture, use a procedural cloth color texture that has ramps mapped to the gap and threads color. Pick the cloth texture and the surface that it is assigned to. Then go to the Edit, Convert to File Texture. This means fewer calculations at render time. If you want to edit the shader's textures again, you have to edit the original.

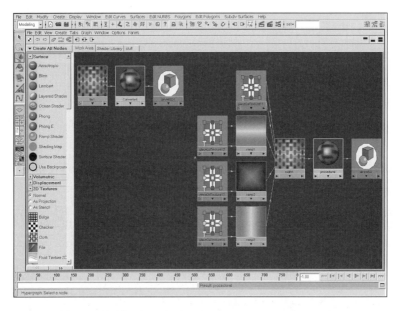

Figure 18.13 The shaders have the same result, but the left one has fewer nodes and connections.

Having the final texture map rather than the procedural network that created it results in faster render times. This economy of scale is multiplied by 300 frames for a 10-second animated piece.

Creating Libraries

Another way of ensuring efficiency is to create and manage your assets. I prefer to do this in two different ways. The first is to set the current project that I am working on at the time. The other is to store away elements that I want to reuse for other projects. You can create a project in Maya with a name such as Library to keep shaders and texture maps as well as other frequently used models.

This is easily done by following these steps:

1. Create a Library project by going to File, Project New. Set the Use Defaults button on.

2. Make a tab in your Hypershade window by selecting Tabs, Create New.

3. Type **Library** in the New Tab Name text box.

4. Set Initial Placement to Bottom, and set Tab Type to Disk.

5. Click the Root Directory folder icon to browse to the Library project.

6. Click Create to see the new tab in the lower Hypershade panel.

Now you have the central area to store any model and shader and fill your hard disk. The visor can see the entire drive, and you can cull anything that Maya can accept (see Figure 18.14).

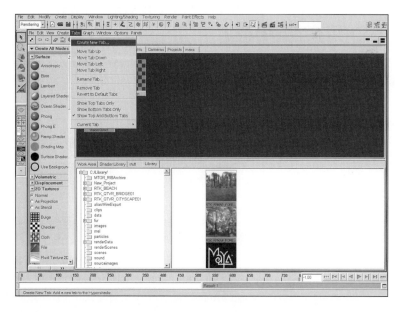

Figure 18.14   A Library tab in Hypershade and a visor make a central repository.

This is useful for images because you will see a small preview picture. MMB over the image, and it can be imported as a texture straight into Hypershade.

Tip

Select all your shaders and use the Export Selected network. This stores all these shaders in one easy file.

For a specific project's texture maps, a central repository should be your project's Source Images folder, which is created in a project by default. This is where texture maps should be stored. If you are so inclined, create subfolders for Bump, Color, and so on. Use a standard naming convention that describes the texture and its use. For our project, this was as simple as brick_bump120502.jpg. The first name is descriptive, the second tells what texture channel it is used for, and the third gives the date it was created.

Material Assignment

Now that all your files are organized, let's talk quickly about material assignment. This can be done before texturing so that surfaces can have already distinguished colors and less boring Lambert grayness everywhere. In Maya, there are always several ways of getting the same thing done. You might end up falling into a routine and not using alternate methodologies. After you create a shader, you can Shift+select the material along with the model's surfaces. Right Mouse Button (RMB) over the shader material to pull down the Assign Material to Selection menu. This is excellent for getting many surfaces to one shader. An alternate method is to MMB drag the material to a specific surface in a modeling window. This can be tricky because you might have a lot of overlying surfaces, and the wrong one might receive the shader. To guarantee that the right shader is assigned, RMB over the desired surface. The bottom menu includes Materials, Assign Existing or Assign New. Confirm the type of material that you want to make; the Attribute Editor comes up. This is a great time to differentiate surfaces by a unique color.

Tip

After a texture is assigned to a shader, the Color Balance, Default Color option can be set to any color to help distinguish the shader in the shaded view.

You should have varied colors now for your models, and you can use this setup for your layout rendering and general motion testing. Next you will want to see how the shaders look before heavy texturing and long renders ensue.

Evaluating Shaders

Throughout the shader-making process, you will constantly be adjusting your shaders to the lighting and rendering. Shaders are usually done before lighting, but a preliminary lighting set up that represents the scene should be taken into consideration. The next chapter deals with lighting, although the shading, lighting, and rendering process happen in tandem. Consider them started together and then polished sequentially, with minor tweaks to accommodate a past phase. The shading will be completely done before lighting, although there might be adjustments back and forth.

Seeing the shader ball in your Hypershade window is strictly a preview of things to come. The next step is to see it on the actual surfaces that you designed it for. Scale is usually the discrepancy between the Hypershade and the rendered model. A 3D or 2D texture might look just right on the shader ball, yet is too fine grained on the model. The quickest way to get texture preview is to use the hardware shading. This displays your shader map according to the channel that you set in the Attribute Editor under Hardware Texturing. You have the option there to see any channel, such as color, and then the resolution. This is a great way to position maps or see the 3D placement of textures.

When the hardware lighting is switched on with the 7 key, it enhances the shader's look. You might consider a simple lighting setup before your real lighting is in place. A directional light and ambient light will suffice. This gives you two-point lighting, with a key light with the directional and then a fill with the ambient. If someone else is doing the lighting, that person might already have a preliminary setup that could be used. The shader must look a certain way, and lighting will only enhance it. You will find that the shader will not need to be modified that much from the basic light set to the finished lighting.

To test and retest the shader, use the IPR render for constant changes. IPR caches the scene into memory and then rerenders the changes much quicker than in a real render. You can also crop an area in the picture where the current shader is, so that modifications update rapidly in your scene. Remember that you are trying to get your shader to look right for that instance. When you are satisfied with the way the shader looks, first render with the software render at low-resolution settings, and then move on to your final settings to make sure. Try to scrub your animation to different frames to make sure that all is right with your world.

Creating Texture Maps

Color is the most obvious thing you will see on a shader. The choices here are numerous. A painted texture map can be created in Maya Paint Effects—for example, a scanned source or some form of procedural, such as wood. You will get very different looks by creating your color maps using these three main techniques. An additional consideration is how the maps will be applied to the surface. This applies to all types of map types, including bump and specular maps. Let's look at these in detail and then see where Maya can help.

Note

You can combine all the texture types in the following sections to build a credible shader. Keep the layers on a map somewhat related, or reuse the texture in a different channel. Alternatively, you can use the same or a slight variation of a map for bump, specular, and reflectivity maps. Your choices are endless.

Painted Texture Maps

A painted texture map is hand-done with digital or real paint. On the digital side, popular applications such as Right Hemisphere's Deep Paint, Procreate Painter, and Adobe Photoshop excel at giving artists control. These can be used to image process, and Deep Paint can be used as a 3D paint application with nice Maya integration. I notice that my students tend to be more comfortable with full-value ranges and outlandish color schemes using these packages rather than real paint. A higher level of detail can be inferred into the model in just the color channel. You can extrapolate a bump or a specular map by image-processing the base image further. For instance, you can strip out the color and then sharpen the image. This has many advantages for production efficiency and for getting an integrated look. Because the color of skin can be related to the graining, a simple black-and-white map can be used for a reflectivity map. The registration will be perfect.

A hand-painted map is equally useful. There is a difference still when I see someone's real painting compared to something done with a Wacom tablet and a paint program. This is evident in backgrounds for modern 2D animated films. Artists use hand-painted art and then apply it digitally as a 2D or 3D layer. Paint mixes up in the brush and on the board, combining to make a rich, varied color. The confidence that comes with applying paint with a brush versus a Wacom stylus is very subtle, but I can tell the difference. Have someone sign his name on paper and then with a stylus: You will see a big difference. The pen signature always looks more confident than the Stylus version. That being said, I created many of my texture maps with gouache and then scanned them in for the *Parking Spot*. I retouched them in Painter and then applied them as a projection map.

Scanned Textures

A scanned source is a photograph or just about anything put on your scanner or digital camera. The beauty of photographic material is that it reinforces the notion of realism. The more photographic information is in the texturing, the more photorealistic it can appear to be. Having a photo reference nearby is great for truly matching that look. However, I often feel that, with 3D CG, photorealism is just one of the millions of looks you can get. The nice aspect of a photographic source is the true-life randomness that is in the picture; the nicks and scratches are hard to guesstimate in a painting. Even if the goal is something stylized, photos make a great source for maps. Remember that your hand-drawn work can also be scanned and that all of this can be processed with your digital toolset.

Maya Paint Effects Textures

Maya Paint Effects is also a great way of generating texture maps in 2D and 3D. The brushes are quite unique: Check out the visor and see all of the presets. Open the brush templates and start to experiment. Another possibility is to use the Preset Blending tool to blend the brushes with a user-tunable percentage of the previous brush. This can be done with shape and color. One thing that I love to do with Paint Effects is create a re-peating tile image in the Canvas mode. Just activate the arrowlike icons above the panel; a brush that goes past the right border appears on the left. The Paint Effects brushes can be invoked with the 3D Texture tool in the Render level as well; that lets you 3D paint on the surfaces in any channel. Be careful with adjacent NURBS borders, though: It is still not as accurate as Studio Paint, another Alias|Wavefront product. The seams might not match up perfectly, and you might need to retouch it.

Procedural Textures

Another way to generate textures is to get the computer to do the work and use the built-in procedures. Procedural textures are simply mini computer programs that generate images. Instead of scanning in a sample of wood, you can use the Wood Texture program, which generates the rings and colors and then algorithmically projects them on multiple surfaces. This can very quickly create a texture that would take a long time to paint or find a sample. Another advantage is that it is easy to change and animate the settings. There is a rendering time impact, but using Convert to File Texture can obviate that. This is the equivalent of flattening the procedural map to a file texture.

Tip

Using procedural versus hand-painted textures can be a point of argument. Some studios hand-paint every map; others use procedurals any chance they can. I test this by assigning an exercise. Do the same image once hand-painted only and the other procedurals only. Hopefully you will find that you like a bit of both.

Now that you've learned the basics of textures, you're ready to create your own procedural material. For the car model in our short film, we needed to create a shader for the grill. Instead of modeling a complete grill that would be a heavy-trimmed model, we decided to use a shader. The challenge here was to create something that is done with one surface and yet has a thickness.

Exercise 18.2 Creating a Grill with a Procedural Material

This exercise teaches you how to use some of Maya's features to generate an all-procedural material. You use the same maps or variations of them to get the right texture. You also start to wire up connections to program the shader.

1. In the Hypershade window, select Create, Materials, Blinn and then Create, 2D Textures, Ramp. Show the top and bottom tabs using the icons in the upper-right area, and MMB drag the Blinn shader to the work area.

2. In the Attribute Editor for the Ramp, delete the green color between the red and the blue on the default colors. Turn the top color to white and the bottom color to black. Drag the white ramp color up to a Selected position of .5. Ramp Type should be set to Circular Ramp, and Interpolation should be set to None.

3. MMB the on the new black and white texture in the Hypershade and then click it and drag it onto the Blinn shader. Set it to the Transparency Map pull-down.

   Your shader should look like an almost clear object (see Figure 18.15). Name the shader perfshader.

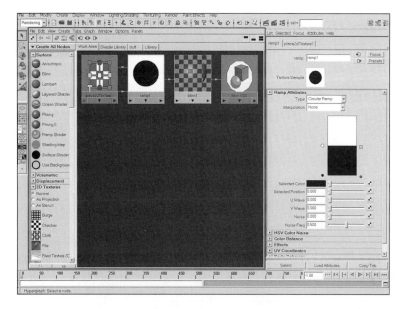

Figure 18.15 After completing Steps 1–3, your shader should look like this.

Now repeat the pattern. Instead of just plugging in a formula, try this:

4. Assign the shader to a primitive plane. Select the Ramp again and go to the Place 2D Texture node. Double-click the Place 2D Texture node to display the Attribute Editor. Click the Interactive Placement button.

You should see a red border on your primitive (see Figure 18.16). This is like a 2D decal placement icon. You can also use the 6 key to display the texture in shaded mode.

5. Set the texture shading in Maya by clicking the 5 key and then the 6 key. Use your MMB on the center dot of the red outline, and drag it around. Look at the numbers change around the Translate Frame in the Attribute Editor. Pick the red outline in the corner, and see the Rotate Frame spin about. Pick the vertical edge; either the U or the V coverage will start updating.

This is almost all you need to know about 2D texture placement. You can plug any numbers into the appropriate box to round off the value to a whole value, such as 45° instead of 43.77906°.

Now we need to get the right kind of repetition of the white circles. There are now small circle patterns in a grid instead of just one large circle. This looks more like the perf patterns we want.

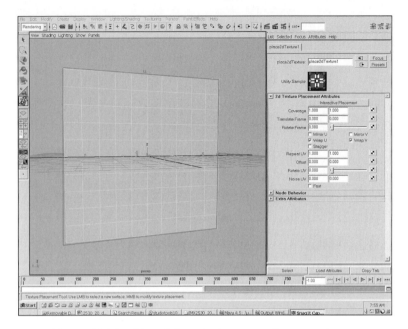

Figure 18.16 After clicking the Interactive Placement button,
you should see a red border on your primitive.

6. Set the Repeat UV value to 10 and 10. The texture on the Blinn should now have some small holes on it (see Figure 18.17). Check the Stagger box so that the circles are centered at 45°. Stagger is a setting to offset the placement of tiled maps so that they repeat at half the placement every other line, kind of like the way bricks are laid.

   Two things to notice are that the highlights are still on the transparent areas and that a surface thickness is lacking. We will use and modify the ramp texture to make the bump and specular maps.

7. Open the bottom Hypershade window to full-screen. Pick the Blinn material and click the Input/Output Connections icon. MMB drag the ramp onto the Blinn material and map it to the bump map.

8. Repeat the MMB drag process and map it to the specular map.

   Notice now that the one ramp controls the bump around the hole's edge, but we might need more finesse. Also, the specular is backward; we want the holes to be dulled and the material to be shiny.

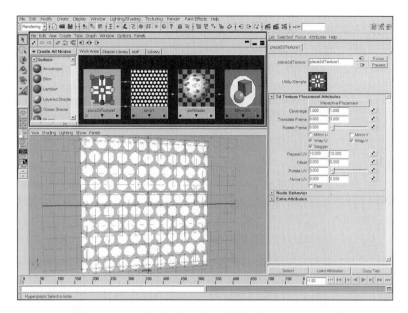

Figure 18.17   At this point, the highlights remain on the transparent areas and the object lacks a surface thickness.

9. Pick the line that connects the ramp out the alpha node to the bump2D color node, and click the Delete key.

You have disconnected the two nodes; now you need to rewire things slightly with a mild variation of the ramp.

10. Select the ramp and click Edit, Duplicate, Shading Network.

11. MMB drag the new ramp copy to the bump 2d node. You are prompted to click Other or Default. Select Default. This establishes a standard connection. Ctrl+drop will do this faster the next time.

Now you can modify the bump ramp separately from the transparency ramp. You have still retained the 2d placement information.

12. Add a medium gray to the middle of the ramp and change it to a smooth interpolation. Add white at the bottom and then move it up to near the gray (see Figure 18.18).

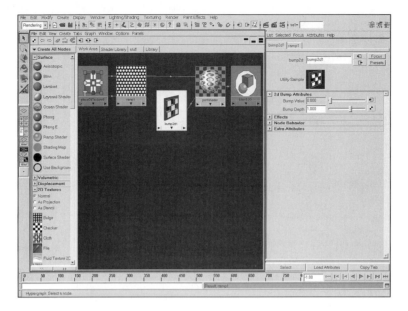

Figure 18.18   The shader thus far is starting to look like a perf pattern.

You now have a material that looks like the highlights appear only on the transparent areas. You need to use the same mapping, but you must invert the specular map by using a utility.

13. The highlights need to be suppressed by inverting the specular map. To invert the specular map, select Create, General Utilities, Reverse. Place it in the work area.

14. Mouse over the ramp1 out color to the Blinn Specular color to see the connection as it is now. Highlight the connecting wire and delete it.

15. MMB drag ramp1 to the Reverse node, and select Input.

16. MMB drag the Reverse node to the Blinn shader, and choose specularColor.

Notice now that the two channels for the mapping are controlled by one channel. The problem concerns changing the placement on the multiple ramps. Here is where Maya shines: It's all in reusing its nodes and being as efficient as possible.

17. Disconnect the bump ramp from the Place 2Dtexture. It reverts to one circle rather than the 10 by 10 previously set at Step 6.

18. Ctrl+drop Place 2dTexture to the Ramp for the bump map. The coordinates can now be reused. (See Figure 18.19.)

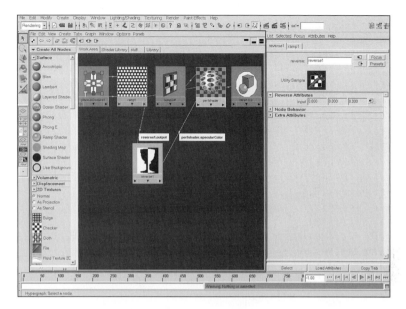

Figure 18.19   The final perf shader is much easier to create than to model.

As you can see, Maya can be wired and rewired to suit your needs. You can call this type of shader creation "modeling by shaders." This means that sometimes it is easier and more efficient to create the detail with textures rather than to model it.

The next sections take a brief look at the application of color maps by discussing some other shaders created for the *Parking Spot* piece.

Shader Example

Open the file candy_apple.mb to see one of the shaders created for the *Parking Spot* project. Each one has a unique problem and solution.

I created a candyApple shader for The Jerk's car (see Figure 18.20). The unique aspect of it was that I wanted a real warm/cool bias. Because The Jerk drives quite a flamboyant car, he needs a killer paint job. The shader has a cubic environment for the color, utilizing a cool red for the top. It then gradates down the side with a ramp that matches the top and bottom colors, with a neutral red at the center. That ramp is used along the sides, ensuring perfect color registration.

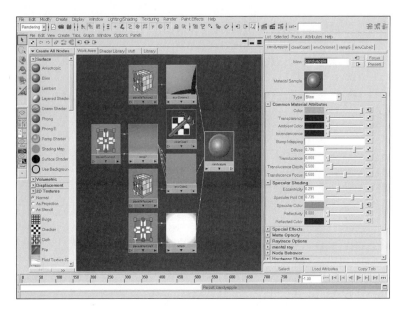

Figure 18.20 This is the shader that I created for The Jerk's car in the *Parking Spot* piece.

The specular has a circular ramp using something I learned from Winslow Homer, who painted a fisherman at sea with a hat. I looked closely at the highlight on the fisherman's hat and saw that Homer had put a tiny dab of green and red paint next to the white. He was using simultaneous contrast. This is where the complementary colors clash and excite your eye, giving a shimmering effect. The red-green ramp around the white achieves the same effect.

The shader also has a slight glow intensity. This would normally give an overall glow, but in the shader glow area, I set the threshold to .419 so that only the brightest areas glow. A Clearcoat utility is mapped to the reflectivity, which is ideal for painted metal. The material is more reflective as it is seen at a shallower angle. In real life, if you look down the road at a very shallow angle, you will start to see reflections; this is the same effect that Clearcoat achieves.

The environment around the painted metal is seen in the Reflected Color map. I used a Chrome environment with Sky Zenith black and Sky Color a summer's afternoon blue. With these settings, the reflected environment would give nice dark cores on the normals facing the top of the sky and high-contrast horizon-line reflections. In other words, if you can't make it good, make it shiny.

Projection Mapping

As a production exercise, we wanted to show how we would get a real project done; we did not want to just show a smorgasbord of toolsets. The online docs provide a good description and starting point, but Alias|Wavefront makes you pay extra if you want to learn a workflow. I am consciously avoiding the UV mapping in polygons and subdivs because I rarely use this for my production. I use projection maps much more frequently as my workflow. These are like slide projectors on the surfaces that I can precisely position in 3D. They offer the following advantages:

- They can be tiled seamlessly across multiple surfaces.
- They can be limited to a 3D volume.
- They can be projected from a perspective view.
- They can be converted back to 2D in NURBS.
- One piece of artwork can be used for multiple surfaces.

In the next exercise, you will see that I can use the projection technique for realistic or nonphotorealistic images. The only difference is the underlying artwork. The basic idea is to grab a screen image and use that as the basis for artwork. The image can then be reprojected with precise registration.

Exercise 18.3   Creating a Nonphotorealistic Painted Shader

For this tutorial, you will use a file created for you, called dawg_shade.mb, on the CD that accompanies this book.

1. Open the dawg_shade.mb file and go to the Front1 view.

2. In the Create Textures area of the Hypershade panel, select a 2D texture with the As projection checked on, and then click File. We want a 3D projection with a 2D file.

    This makes a registration for your projected file (see Figure 18.21). There is no 2D image file yet, until you paint one in. It is represented by a gridded cube called the Transformation Matrix.

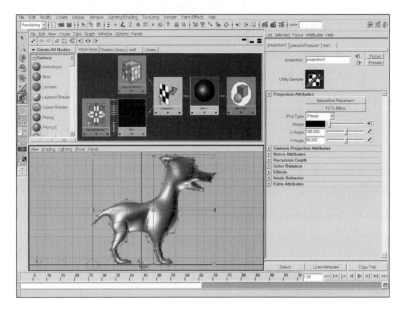

Figure 18.21   Here is the side view of the dog with the
Projection matrix, to help in aligning the picture.

3. Scale and move the Transformation matrix (the gridded cube) that just appeared to overlap the dog's boundaries.

4. Make the Front panel as large as possible on your screen. Zoom in to get as close as possible to the matrix (see Figure 18.22).

5. Get a screen grab with your favorite screen grabber. Mine happens to be Snagit, by Techsmith (www.techsmith.com).

6. Otherwise, go to Window, Rendering Editors, Hardware Render Buffer.

   In Render, Attributes, set the following:

   File Name: side paint

   End Frame: 1

   Resolution: Full_1280

   Draw Style: Smooth

   Full Image Resolution: On

   Display Options, Background Color: White

   Display Options, Transform icons—on

   Set Cameras, Front1 in the Render Buffer window

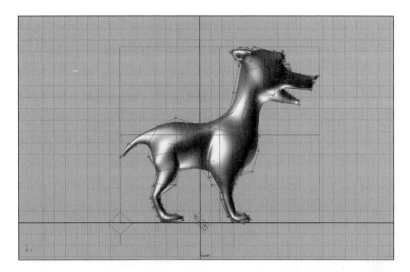

Figure 18.22   The side view shows where the projection map will be.

7. Click Render, Render Sequence to get a picture. To see it, move over to Flipbooks, sidepaint.1 (see Figure 18.23).

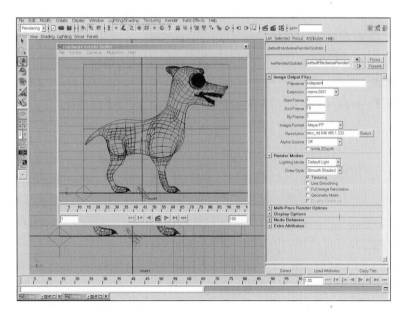

Figure 18.23   The hardware render window can be used for screen grabbing.

8. Save the image to disk.

9. Crop the picture to the exact borders of your Transformation matrix grid in your favorite image-editing application.

10. In that package or in Paint Effects canvas mode, paint in the colors you would like to see for your dog. We went with a black Spot, of course (what other color could you associate with fire hydrant–loving Dalmatians? (See Figure 18.24.)

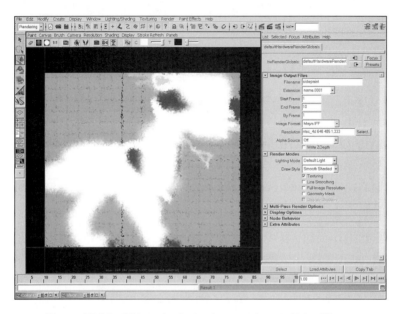

Figure 18.24 This is the final color map done in Paint Effects.

11. Save the image and load it as the file for the projection. Create a new material and then assign the projection to the color map. Assign the material to the dog model.

   The image and the matrix are now in the same space (see Figure 18.25). The only problem is what to do when the character moves and flexes. In the final step, you make a copy of the model and save it as a template. This maintains the proper mapping even when the dog moves or the skin is stretched.

12. Pick the dog and the assigned shader. Go to From the Render menu set, and select Texturing, Create Texture Reference Object. It will first be an active pink template; unpick it.

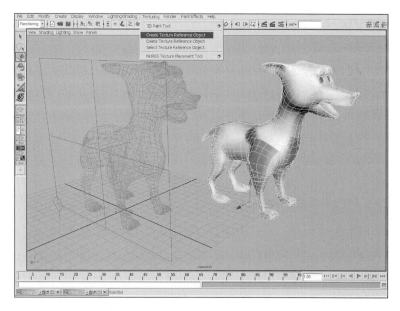

Figure 18.25   The dog can move without the projection swimming across the surface.

13. Test the mapping by displaying the hardware texturing (6 key) and then moving isolated points and the entire model. Your final figure should look like Figure 18.26.

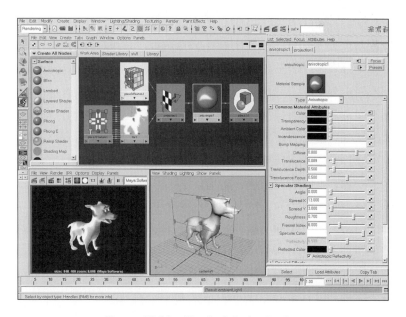

Figure 18.26   The final shader for Spot.

Summary

Shader creation can be a very rewarding endeavor. Remember to carefully and critically observe all surfaces, and apply that observation to each shader you create. Experiment heavily to see what type of look you can attain in Maya. Try to use the best of both the procedural and painted world to get the best effect in your maps, and reuse the images in the other types of maps. Try to be as efficient as possible to program your shaders by reusing redundant nodes. If you do need a complex painted map, consider a projection technique due to its multiple advantages.

Chapter 19
Lighting

By Adrian Dimond

In this chapter, you learn about technical issues associated with achieving photorealistic lighting. I walk you through some advanced lighting techniques and show you a few very new ways to light inside Maya using the recently adopted Mental Ray for Maya plug-in. If you need more in-depth information on lighting issues, you might read *Digital Lighting and Rendering* (New Riders Publishing, 2000) by Jeremy Birn; or, check out Birn's web site, www.3drender.com/.

Lighting is the single most important aspect of creating any type of image. Without lights, you obviously cannot see the image. Standard lights will at least illuminate your subject matter, but not much more. That's why the plethora of lighting types in Maya is so beneficial. All of Maya's lighting tools provide more control than most users take advantage of, however. This chapter discusses how to use Maya's lights so that you can gain the kind of control you need to make seminal images. Specifically, this chapter teaches you the following:

- How to create a lighting style using Maya
- How to use specific controls of Maya's lighting parameters
- How to interpret a color script to do master lighting
- How to control shadows
- How to define global illumination
- How to fake global illumination with Maya's standard renderer
- How to use Final Gathering and high dynamic range (HDR) images in Mental Ray

The World in Lights

Everything we see is illuminated. A large directional light, the sun, illuminates everything naturally outdoors. Even though it's illuminated by the same light source, however, an outdoor environment can look different, and the mood it evokes can change. The season of the year and the time of day vary greatly based on atmospherics and other light properties. The latitude and longitude also affect the light outdoors. Imagine being in the Arctic Circle during the winter months, when the sun comes up for a very short while. Think of the colors you would describe to someone. Now think of a bright summer day on a late afternoon in the Tropics. How would you go about describing that? This is the problem we presented ourselves with when doing the lighting for our *Parking Spot* animation. The story would take place on such a summer day. The Jerk's car would block out Spot's space basking in the sun. Confrontation would ensue and the hilarity would begin. How does one go about turning this description into Attribute Editor settings for the lights?

You can find the answer to that question by knowing what you can do with Maya's lights, as well as through keen observation.

The most commonly used default lights in Maya are the directional and ambient lights. A directional light has an infinite decay. In other words, it never falls off in intensity. Therefore, all surfaces are illuminated. The ambient light takes in the bounce light that fills in every shadow. Yes, everything will be lit, but the results will be the typical mundane CG scene.

It is better to get an idea of what your scene will look like by first observing nature. Notice that I didn't say to get photographic reference yet. First you should go out to see the scene in which you think the action will take place. Look at how the sunlight falls on the ground. Do the trees' shadows move about? Documentation should happen after observation. Photos tend to overexpose the light areas and underexpose the darks. If you take photos, bracket the exposures for the shadow and the light side. When a movie is being filmed even outdoors, the filmmaker needs to compensate for the dynamic range. Our eyes can see a 1:100 contrast ratio; this means that the human eye can distinguish 100 levels of black to white. Film—and, to a lesser extent, video—can't yet capture and reproduce the full dynamic range of our eyes. However, the proper usage of high dynamic range images can compensate for this and bring an element of realism to CG that is otherwise difficult to obtain.

The director of photography will tell the key grip that he needs to use lights that will retain a natural sunlit feel. This might mean using a bounce card or light banks on the shadow side so that the exposure to film will look like the way we perceive the world. The same thing needs to be done with computer lighting: The shadows can't be lifeless black.

In the following tutorials, I discuss how to set up basic lighting and how to create and utilize HDR images in Maya using Mental Ray and, to a limited degree, the standard Maya renderer.

Shadow Control

Shadows are actually where the real action is. Don't be afraid to be in the shadow and do interesting things there. The first matter is that the shadow color. In Maya, you want to make sure that the shadow is something other than black. In general, you use the complementary color of the light you are shining for the shadow color.

Shadow and light can be broken up to make more interesting patterns. As a good example, look at the sidewalk and see the tree shadows. Observe how the leaves flicker and diffuse the light to the ground. There is even a focus effect where shadow is dappled. Think of the cloud patterns as they dance across the landscape and then what this looks like at the local level. The intensity nearby rises and falls.

The best way to achieve these effects in Maya is to map the shadows and color in the lights. This is exactly what you'll do in this first exercise.

Exercise 19.1   Gobos and Shadows

This exercise shows you how to get more interesting shadow effects and how to animate them. Begin this exercise by opening the file Gobo.mb in the Scenes directory of the Lighting project on the accompanying CD. The scene comprises some simple geometry to give a clearer picture when doing tests to show to the director before proceeding to the final lighting setup.

1. After you open the Gobo.mb file, select the spotlight and then go to Windows, Attribute Editor. Have the Window, Hypershade; Window, Rendering Editors, Render View; and Perspective windows open (see Figure 19.1).

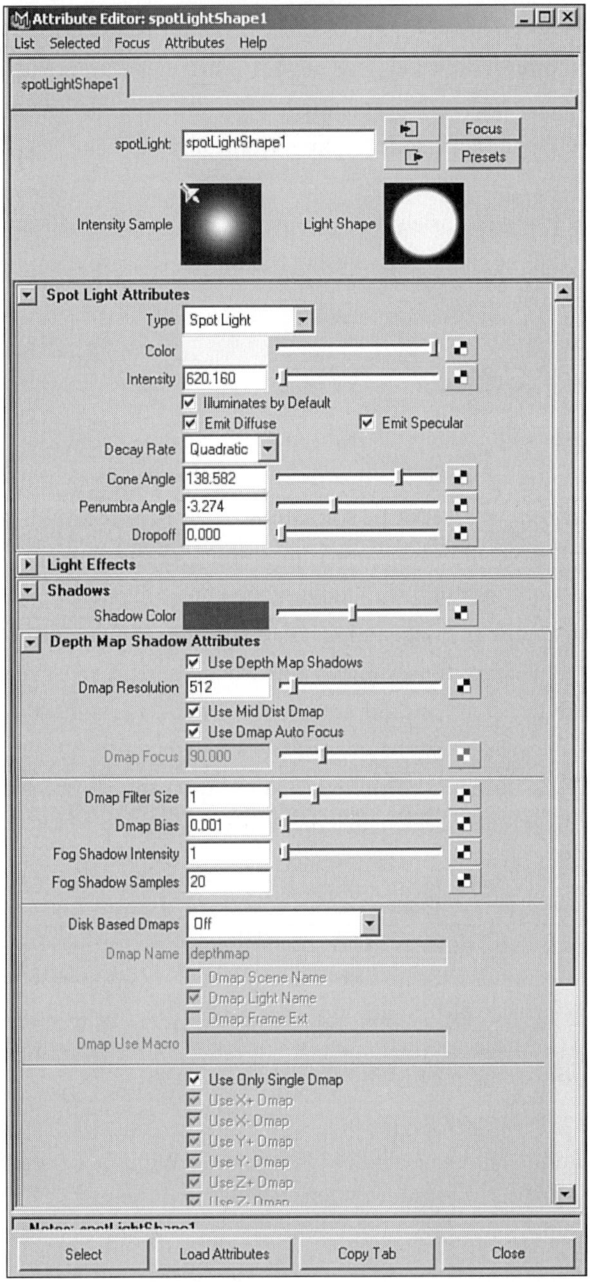

Figure 19.1   This is a simple scene with a standard three-point light set up.
Notice the settings for the spotlight.

Figure 19.2 shows a simple light setup comprising orange with purple shadows. The settings are not for a full-on, saturated color, but a light tint of orange and a deep, rich purple. Look to the art world, and you will observe that there is a large spectrum of colored shadows.

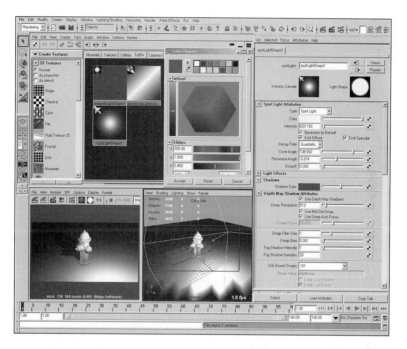

Figure 19.2   In this simple light setup, the shadow color is set to purple and the light color is set to a light orange.

2. Pick the spotlight and hit t on the keyboard. This enables the manipulators for the spotlight. Now click the target manipulator, and you can move the target and aim of the light. Position the light target so that you can see a shadow in the render (see Figure 19.3).

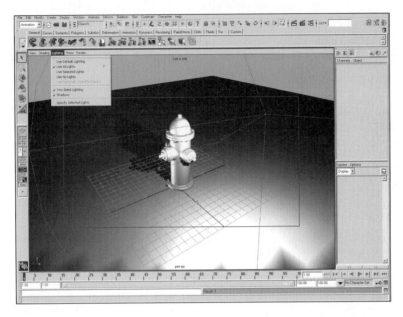

Figure 19.3   Positioning the light and the target makes it easier to control shadow placement.

3. In the Render window, hit the IPR Render icon. Then drag a marquee around a smaller area in the IPR window for fine-tuning. Adjust the drop-off in the spotlight Attribute Editor, and you will see it fading away from the center of the light. Set the intensity value to any negative number. The higher the negative value is, the more light is sucked out.

Notice how the drop-off can control the fade and how the negative intensity makes a nice soft shadow (see Figure 19.4). The beauty of this is that you can't do this in nature, yet it's so easy in Maya.

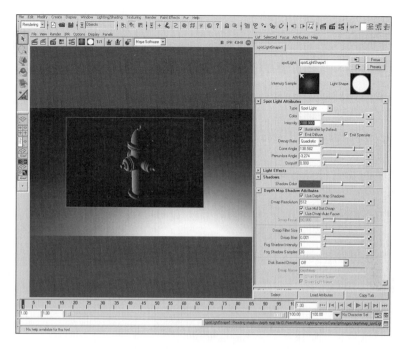

Figure 19.4 A negative value on the spotlight sucks away light and helps add contrast to a scene.

Tip

Even though the implementation of OpenGL and the quality of video cards have increased significantly since the days of insanely expensive SGI reality engines, do not rely on what you see in the GUI interface because it is not truly WYSIWYG. Using hardware shading and lighting will help you position lights with shadows and generally adjust values, but this will not show you accurately what your render will look like. IPR gets you a step closer, but because it is incapable of dealing with ray tracing, it, too, cannot be relied upon solely for adjusting settings. However, it is a great way to interactively set your lights and textures, and it is invaluable despite its shortcomings.

Next, you will start to do something that most people forget is possible in Maya: add motion to the lights. Shadows and colors can be animated over time in subtle ways.

4. Set the Intensity back to the positive value it was before (or something close), and then map a fractal texture to the color (see Figure 19.5).

Tip

One typical place to put a negative light is inside a character's mouth: The inside of the mouth is usually not illuminated, but it might pick up illumination from other light sources if you are not careful.

You might also consider doing this for nostrils if you can see them in a close-up.

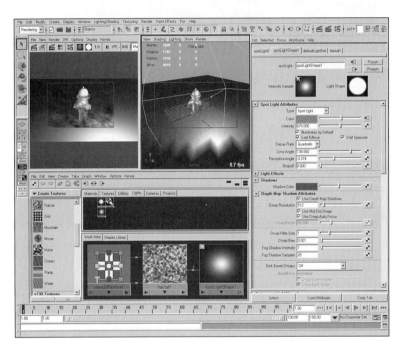

Figure 19.5 The fractal texture breaks up the light unevenly and makes the image a bit more interesting.

5. In the Fractal tab, set the Amplitude to 6 and check Animated.

6. Click with the RMB on the Time option and set a key. Scrub the timeline to 60, and then move the Time value slider to 5. and set another key (see Figure 19.6).

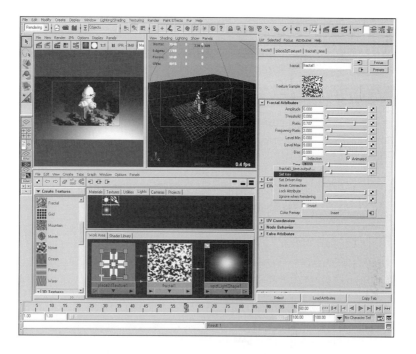

Figure 19.6   Set the key for time here in the Attribute Editor. You can animate all of these slider bars by clicking them with the RMB and selecting Set Key from the pop-up menu.

7. Click the timeline. You will notice that the animated light effect updates when you go to the new point in time. However, some changes will not update in IPR until you hit the IPR button again. You need to rerender the depth map shadows any time a change is made to the shadow parameters so that you can see those changes reflected in the IPR window.

8. To make this effect subtler, reverse the color offset and color gain, but don't make the color gain completely black (see Figure 19.7).

9. Set Render Globals to render frames 1–60. Go to Render, Batch Render and view the scene in fcheck (see Figure 19.8). Uncompress the file Gobo.zip in your Images folder. It produces a rendered sequence called Gobo.#.tif, which you can then load into fcheck.

   On most systems that can run Maya, you can type **fcheck** at the command line or command console to launch the program. On Windows, Maya now takes advantage of the Start menu and places a link for fcheck there.

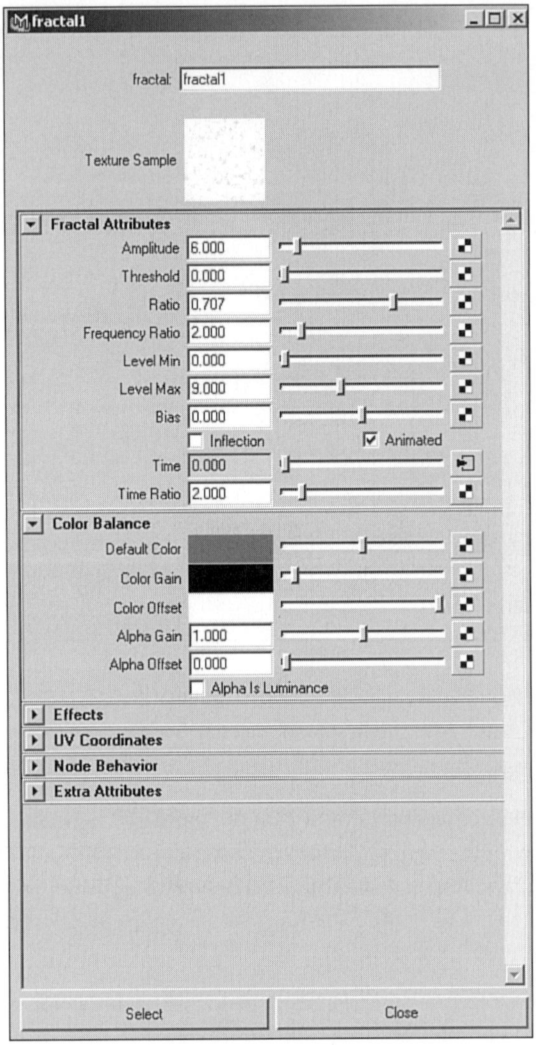

Figure 19.7 Change the color offset and the gain to make the effect subtler.

Tip

fcheck views a wide range of image formats and image sequences, and it can also be used for image conversions. In addition, you can use imgcvt, which is a command line–only program for converting images and image sequences that comes standard with all distributions of Maya. However, neither supports AVI or QuickTime formats, so you will need a third-party program such as QuickTime Pro or a compositing program to do more sophisticated manipulations.

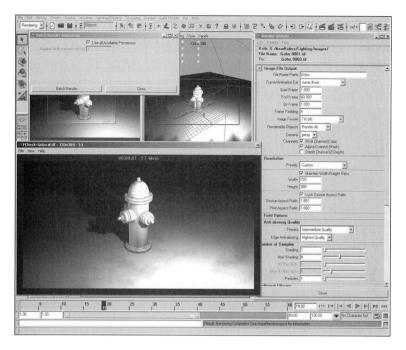

Figure 19.8   Open the finished sequence here in fcheck by going to Open, Animation.

The variation in the lighting moves quickly with the animated fractal. The idea, though, is that a subtle variation will bring life to an animated piece. When doing this for production, keep the changes very subtle and make them occur over a greater length of time. In general, the ambient movement in real life is very subtle. You can speed up movement in post, but it is more difficult to slow something down.

Maya Lights in Production

It is a good idea to follow a set methodology for lighting scenes. Here are some guidelines to follow:

- **Use quadratic decay for added control**—This gives the most control for attaining precise light-intensity values. It falls off like real lights using the inverse square law. This law states that if light is transmitting in all directions from the source, such as a bulb, the farther the light is from the source, the more spread out it will be. Light that is twice as far from the surface at any given point will be four times as strong. Light naturally drops off this way, and the quadratic falloff treats lighting in Maya realistically. Using quadratic falloff helps when calculating lights for other rendering plug-ins such as Mental Ray and Pixar RenderMan.

Note

Even though inverse square attenuation provides the most natural fallout for a light source, it is not always the most efficient or easiest to work with. Because it spreads the light values over a wide range, surfaces close to the light source might get blown out or have extreme hotspots on them. Because the attenuation allows light to travel very far even though it might have little effect on surfaces far away, the computer still has to calculate it and thus can be wasting CPU cycles that could be used elsewhere.

- **Vary the RGB setting**—Never let any of the lights be exactly R 255 G 255 B 255—sometimes that will cause banding errors and looks too perfect. Even if one of the RGBs is set to 254, it will mix up the color just enough.

- **Use as few lights as possible**—Most users don't have 2 teraFLOPS of computing power for their projects. Renders go faster with fewer lights. Anything you can do to shave a few minutes off one render will be multiplied by 30 frames per second.

In terms of the individual lights themselves, these are some general rules of thumb:

- **Use of directional lights**—To make sure something is definitely lit, use directional lights. These are fairly versatile because they never decay. Duplicate the directional and face it toward the other light at 180°; then set it to be a cool color at 25% to 50% of the intensity of its doppelganger. Group them so that they will rotate simultaneously.

- **Use of area lights**—Use area lights for highly reflective objects to simulate the studio product photography look. Area lights also simulate a nice bounce light if you uncheck specular reflections and aim them upward.

- **Use of volume lights**—The new volume lights in Maya 4.5 are great for achieving little pools of emphasis. Volume lights contain their effect within the geometric boundaries of a sphere, box, cylinder, or cone. They can be used to highlight just a small area, such as a character's eye. The light can be used to simulate what spills over in a room on a sunny day.

Tip

To start setting your lights, you need a blank slate. Simply put the same white Blinn shader on all your objects and then light them. To test the value range, I look at the render in the render window with only the luminance turned on. Try to get a three-value contrast from white to midtones to black in every image. Think of it as having a 1-2-3 or light-medium-dark value scheme. This gives your images a vitality that most observers will subconsciously register as a compelling image.

With Maya lighting, you get nothing for free, except practically an unlimited number of rendering licenses. Because Maya does not support radiosity out of the box, the key light does not automatically fill out your shadows by bouncing light from surface to surface. Many alternative renderers can do global illumination and radiosity and compute the lights differently. You learn how to do this with Mental Ray shortly. Luckily, Mental Ray and Pixar's RenderMan can be used to get good global illumination. However, using true radiosity in production can still be prohibitive due to the intensity of computation. Most studios still use bounce lighting with conventional light placement and an observant eye of the artist to achieve these effects. As faster processors and more efficient software come around, using radiosity on a regular basis will become a reality. Upcoming feature films will use global illumination, but they currently rely on tricks and fakes and an artistic eye to simulate the look of global illumination.

A basic way of thinking about lighting is to first show the model and its environs. After that, think about visual interest and the basic storytelling that the lighting will help motivate. Here are six good lighting rules to keep in mind:

- **Key lights**—Use these for your main source for shadows. This models the surfaces to show off the forms. A Maya directional and spot are the best for this.

- **Fill lights**—These add detail to the shadow area. Bounce light also should be separately taken into account. The Maya ambient light is good for this because it has an omnidirectional source. Also try using spots and area lights with Specular unchecked.

- **Rim lights**—These create a backlit edge on the subject to help pull it from the background. A directional light set to values slightly above 1 and to a fairly cool color will do nicely. You can set a shader glow with the threshold up a bit to get a nice bloom effect.

- **Kickers**—These emphasize another plane in your subject matter, such as the side of a head. Maya's point lights and area lights are good candidates for this type of duty. Area lights are especially good for this because they can easily simulate the scale of an unnatural light source, as opposed to the sun.

- **Background lights**—These set the foreground-to-background lighting ratios. The background needs to be lit so that the foreground elements are set apart. The background should complement the main elements in a shot. Try dark against light, or vice versa, and then use a warm-to-cool color scheme to set things off. Directional and spots are the primary workhorses in Maya for this. Sometimes point and volume lights are used.

- **Eye lights**—These add warmth to a character's eyes, which is the part of the character that you relate to the most. This brings up the moist specular highlights in the eye and keeps the shadows in the eye socket minimized. Point and volume lights are the primary Maya lights to use for this.

You can work with just two- or three-point lighting as you go down the list. The rest can be considered secondary. Start with the key first and work down the list. Start from darkness and slowly add the lights. Turn off the other lights occasionally to see the effect of each light. Use the Window, General Editors, Attribute Spreadsheet to manipulate the lights in concert.

Defining GI, Radiosity, FG, IBL, and HDRI

These terms are often thrown around, and the meanings of each get confused. Global illumination, otherwise known as diffuse indirect illumination, refers to a range of techniques such as Final Gather and radiosity. Light bounces all around off every surface indirectly. This bouncing of light energy is referred to as *radiosity*. Various algorithms exist for calculating radiosity, such as matrix, progressive, and wavelet. Specific techniques, such as Monte Carlo, have become well known. Photon maps can be calculated and optimized in a wide range of ways as well.

In Mental Ray, Final Gathering is an accelerated technique of using photon mappings for approximating radiosity. It simulates the emission of radiant light energy using a ray-tracing renderer. This allows any surface to be a light source. These light values are stored in a photon map and are referred to by the renderer when it creates the color for any given surface, rather than calculating it each time an area of surface is shaded.

Another aspect of global illumination in computer graphics is the use of image-based lighting (IBL) to achieve realistic lighting by referring to a specific environment. This process literally enables you to take a "snapshot" of an environment and reproduce the same qualities of light using radiosity, Final Gathering, or a dome light rig in the CG environment. Any image can be used for image-based lighting, but to truly reproduce the full range of values, you will need to use high dynamic range images for your IBL. HDR images can represent a wider range of values than video or even film. Essentially, an HDR image is a single file with multiple exposures built into it to accommodate the huge range that natural light can have. With a little help from Paul Debevec, you can create HDR images in many ways. Take a look at his web site, www.debevec.org.

To learn more technical explanations of these terms, check my links page at www.gmask.com/newriders/links/.

Faking GI with Maya's Standard Renderer

Most often when people refer to a global illumination fake, they are using a dome light and light probe images to create realistic lighting for a CG environment. This is very easy to do in most programs, including Maya. It is even possible to use a similar setup in Mental Ray, but you don't need to because Final Gathering is essentially an automated form of IBL using a dome light. In Maya, you literally create a dome of lights with shadows and then use the pixel color values of an image to control the color of the lights in your dome light rig.

Radiosity dictates that objects will pick up color from one another, given certain parameters. In many cases, this effect is not always that noticeable, and it might be unnecessary to reproduce it for all surfaces. When you need to have "bounced" light, it is easy enough to reproduce by placing a light source that emits the color of the surface.

Maya does not understand HDR-formatted images, but there is a trick for that, thanks to Emmanuel Campin (www.pixho.com). Because the HDR-formatted image starts out as a series of images, you can utilize multiple images in Maya to create certain effects, such as the particular qualities of specular highlights that you get using a true HDR image. But it can be quite easy to reproduce this misunderstood quality of light.

Finally, you can simulate the effect of Final Gathering and create your own photon map of a sort by using the baked lighting feature of Maya. This might not always be practical when there are many moving objects or lights in the scene, but it is common to use this feature when creating lighting for games when the need for real-time performance prohibits using a large number of lights or shadows, let alone radiosity.

Faking Global Illumination with Dome Lights

It is possible to achieve practically any look with the Maya renderer. In some cases, this can be faster than using physically correct calculations such as radiosity to achieve the same look using Mental Ray. Mental Ray can create photorealistic images with less effort from the user, but at a cost. For individual users and small shops, you can get a lot of bang for your buck using the standard Maya renderer, but it will require more effort and, in many, cases a lot of compositing. These skills are valuable no matter what renderer you choose because there are more than these two to choose from.

In the next exercise, you will experiment with a dome lighting rig using some of the props from the *Parking Spot* project. No final decision has been made about the type of lighting to go with yet; the director has asked to see some samples.

Exercise 19.2 Creating a Dome Light

The basic process is to create a dome made up of lights pointing inward. These lights all have shadows turned on, but with very small depth maps. Then one directional light source is added to simulate the sun.

1. Open the DomeLight_Start.mb file from the accompanying CD and select the spotlight. I have already placed the pivot point for this light to be in the center of the worldspace. Go to Edit, Duplicate Options. This opens the options window for the Duplicate tool. Reset the settings under the window's File, Reset Settings menu. Enter 4 for the number of copies, and enter −22 in the X rotation box. Then hit Apply (see Figure 19.9).

Note

I derived the aforementioned numbers by dividing 90° in the arc to be created by 4, and I then subtracted .5 because the first light was already rotated −2° so that is not parallel to the ground plane.

2. Now select the first four lights, but not the last one at the very top, and group them. Choose Edit, Reset Settings in the Duplicate panel. Then enter **45** into the rotate Y and **7** into the number of copies to be made (45 is 360 ÷ 8). Then hit Apply. You now have a dome light (see Figure 19.10).

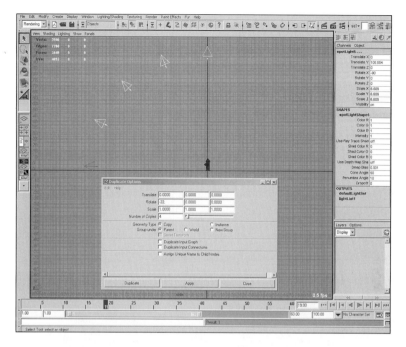

Figure 19.9 Creating an arc of lights using Duplicate.

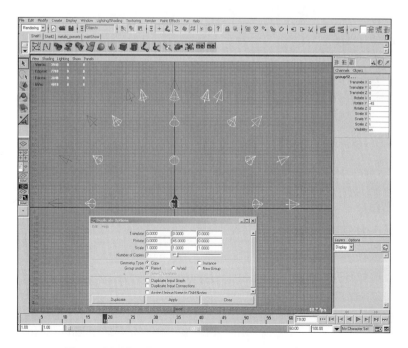

Figure 19.10 The completed dome light with 33 lights.

If you were to render this scene now, it would be completely blown-out white. Because these lights are supposed to be only ambient light, their combined intensities should equal no more than 1 in this case, not 33.

3. To correct this, go to Edit, Select All by Type, Lights, and make sure you have the Channel box open (Display, UI Elements, Channel box). Enter **.08** for intensity and **.9** into the R and G color channels to give the ambient light a blue tint. This enters the same value into all the lights selected (.03 is 1 ÷ 33).

4. Now do an IPR render and play around with the settings of the lights (see Figure 19.11). It is also a good idea to make a set for the lights so that you can easily reselect them later. Go to Window, Relationship Editors, Sets. Under Edit, Create Set Options, name the set as dome light and hit Apply.

Now you can just type **select dome light** into the command line or create a shelf button for it when you want to select this set of lights.

Figure 19.11   IPR rendering with the dome light.

The next step is to enable depth map shadows for the lights. You can do this by typing **on** into the Use Depth Map Shadow portion of the Channel box with the dome light set selected, but you cannot set the Dmap resolution. To simplify things, you need to use a MEL script.

5. Enter the following MEL script into the Script Editor while the light is selected:

```
string $selection[]=`ls -l -sl`;

for ($node in $selection){

setAttr ($node+".useDepthMapShadows") 1;
setAttr ($node+".dmapResolution") 128;
setAttr ($node+".dmapFilterSize") 2;

}
```

6. Hit Ctrl+a to select all the text in the Script Editor, and then hit Enter on the key-pad. Now rerender the IPR render. Notice the subtle shadowing starting to develop (see Figure 19.12).

Figure 19.12   IPR rendering with the dome light after enabling shadows.

7. Create a directional light from the Create, Lights, Directional menu. In the viewport, choose Panels, Look Through Selected, and then position the light to look down at the hydrant. Open the lights' Window, Attribute Editor and choose a light yellowish/orange color for the light color and a dark purple for the shadow color. Then check Use Depth Map Shadows, set Dmap Resolution to 1024, and set Dmap Filter Size to 4. Rerender the IPR view of the scene and tweak it to your satisfaction (see Figure 19.13).

You must find a fine balance between the dome light and the directional light. Otherwise, the directional light will cancel out the shadowing created by the dome light. You could also render a separate pass of the dome light shadows to boost them in compositing.

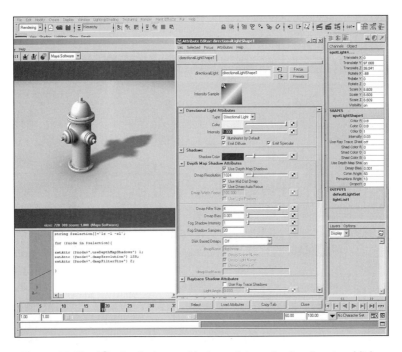

Figure 19.13 The fire hydrant with dome light and solar directional light.

This is a very simplified version of dome lighting, but it is effective for most projects. For a more complex dome light rig that has far more features than are discussed here, check out Emmanuel Campin's GI Joe script at `www.pixho.com`. Emmanuel is a brilliant lighting artist who has made a great contribution to the Maya community by sharing his skills and insights into the complexities of working with the Maya standard renderer.

Another benefit of the GI Joe script is that you can load any image, and it will sample colors from that image to simulate global illumination using an image-based lighting system without requiring HDR images. You do this by creating a dome and then using the position and number of the CVs in the dome to create an array of lights that point inward. The position of the lights is then linked to the UV coordinates of the texture, and the pixel color at the location is linked to each corresponding light. This enables you to easily swap out images and try different lighting scenarios via image-based lighting.

The next step in faking radiosity in the Maya standard render is to simulate bounced color that will occur between surfaces. This is what you'll do in the next short exercise.

Exercise 19.3   Bounce Lighting

In this exercise, you will essentially place lights that are tinted the color of the surface that the light is bouncing from and point them toward the receiving surface. All surfaces do this to some degree, but most are not very noticeable. However, when used in key places, this can be very effective.

1. Open the BounceLight_Start.mb file from the accompanying CD. Create an IPR render and keep the current render using the Save Image button in the Render window (you will use this saved image for comparison so that you can see the subtle effect that using the bounce light adds). Create a spotlight and place it so that it is centered in the hydrant, pointing at the ground (see Figure 19.14).

2. Check off Illuminates by Default. Then select the light and the ground plane, and use Lighting/Shading, Make Light Links so that the light illuminates only the ground.

3. Choose a red color such as the hydrant, set the intensity to .2, check off Emit Specular (because you do not need to contribute specular highlights), and set the cone angle to 20 and the Penumbra Angle to 20, to make a very soft diffusion of light. Because the color bouncing will affect only very close objects, set the dropoff to .1 and draw a box around the hydrant so that the IPR refreshes. Now you can use the scrollbar at the bottom of the IPR window to compare the bounce light version against the version you saved earlier (see Figure 19.15).

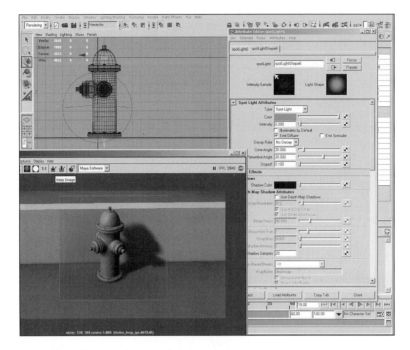

Figure 19.14   The fire hydrant before the bounce light is added.

Figure 19.15   A side–by–side comparison: before and after adding the bounce light.

4. The final step for this scene is to duplicate the first bounce light and point it down at the wall so that you do not get a distinct red spot on the wall. Then, as before, link it to illuminate only the wall (see Figure 19.16).

These effects might seem subtle, but they can go a long way toward grounding an object into its environment, along with the soft shadows created by the dome light. You will start to notice interesting interactions of light and shadow, such as the red bleeding from the wall and into the shadow being cast by the hydrant.

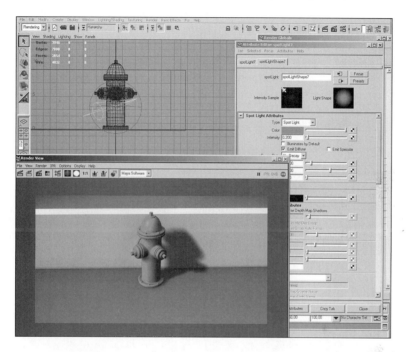

Figure 19.16   The final hydrant with two bounce lights.

Another fine detail that is hard to reproduce is correct highlights for extremely bright light sources. This is one area in which being able to work with HDR images is really great, but out of the box Maya does not recognize any of the common formats. However, there is a rather simple way around this using a rarely known feature called Reflection Specularity. You'll use this feature in the next exercise.

Exercise 19.4 HDR Specular Highlights

In a nutshell, in this exercise you'll create two spheres—one that is your reflection map and a second smaller one that is the high-intensity specular map.

To start off, I took a picture in my backyard (see Figure 19.17) using my Nikon CoolPix 990 with its Fisheye Converter FC-E8 0.21x lens. This lens has practically a 180° range of view and is great for creating ball maps. I did some preprocessing on the images before using them in Maya. You can use your own image and use Photoshop to desaturate it, and then use levels to remove all but the brightest values in the image. For simplicity, however, I have provided my image on the accompanying CD (see the files wideangle_highlight_map.tif and wideangle_reflection_map.tif).

Figure 19.17 The reflection and specular map images preprocessed in Photoshop.

I. After you've preprocessed your image (or opened the CD file), open the HDR_Specular_Start.mb scene file from the CD. Then select a primitive from Create, NURBS, Sphere and scale it up so that it is larger than the dome light you created in the previous tutorial (included in the scene file you opened).

Actually, it is important only for it to be larger than any of the objects that might be reflecting it, so that they do not intersect. But go ahead and scale it up to 150 units on the X, Y, and Z.

2. Open Window, General Editors, Attribute Spread Sheet Editor, and click the Render tab. Set Cast Shadows, Receive Shadows, and Primary Visibility to Off.

3. Open Window, Rendering Editors, Hypershade window, and create a surface shader. Name the surface shader HDR_amb. Select the sphere you created previously, and then click with the RMB on the surface shader and let go on Assign Material to Selection from the pop-up menu.

4. Double-click the surface shader and click the texture box next to Out Color. Choose a file texture with the As projection option.

5. Locate the wideangle_reflection_map.tif file on the accompanying CD. In the Projection node, change the projection type to Ball. Then click the place3dTexture1 tab for the projection in Windows, Attribute Editor and type **–90** into the X rotation field. By default, the ball projection's pinch point is on its side, and you want it to point down. Go ahead and render a frame in the Window, Rendering Editors, Render View without IPR because it will not render with ray tracing enabled (see Figure 19.18). Make sure that ray tracing is enabled in the Window, Rendering Editors, Render Globals, Raytracing section. It looks pretty good, but the highlights on it are not bright enough. Use the Keep Image button to save this image for comparison later.

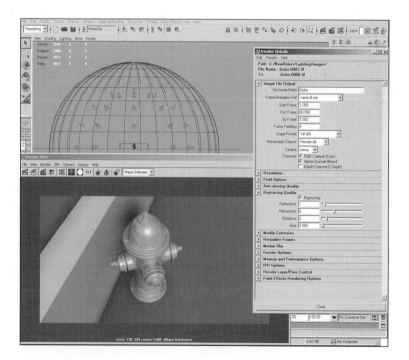

Figure 19.18   The fire hydrant with ray-traced reflections.

Note

The ball projection node works by pulling the four corners of the map into a point. It is like laying a handkerchief over a ball and pulling the corners tight underneath. That is why the image you are using is spherical rather than panoramic. If you were using a spherical mapping or the inherent UV mappings of the NURBS sphere, however, this would be a perfectly valid way to go if the image was prepared that way.

6. Use Edit, Duplicate to create a copy of the first reflection sphere and make it slightly smaller in scale. Then, in the Window, Rendering Editors, Hypershade window, use Create, Materials, Blinn Shader and name it HDR_spec. Use the RMB to assign it to the selection. Duplicate the previous ball projection by RMB-clicking the surface shader, and choose Graph Network. Then click the projection1 and, from the Hypershade panel, choose Edit, Duplicate, Shading Network.

7. Double-click the new projection node and then click the tab for the file node. In the file node, replace the previous reflection map with the wideangle_highlight_map.tif file from the CD.

8. Double-click the blinn4 shader you created earlier, and then drag and drop the new projection3 node onto the Specular Color. Set the transparency of blinn4 to full white.

9. For the last bit of magic, go to the ray-tracing settings of HDR_spec shader, RMB-click in the Reflection Specularity field, and choose Create New Expression.

   This opens the Expression Editor, where you should type **reflectionSpecularity=30**.

   The final step is to align the reflection map and specular map with the light source in the scene.

10. Select both spheres and both 3dplacement nodes for both ball projections, and group them. Then, from the top view with Hardware Texturing turned on in the perspective viewport, rotate the group of spheres and 3dtexture nodes; see where the sun is in the reflection map, and align it to the directional light. It is hard to see, but a lighter area is visible in the reflection map—that is the sun. Do another render, and compare it to the previously saved image (see Figure 19.19).

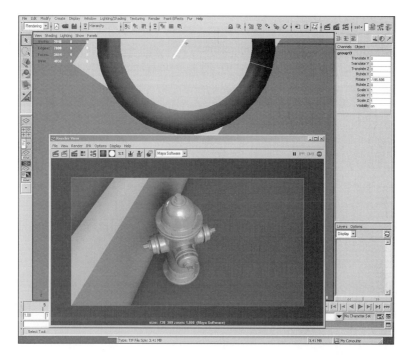

Figure 19.19   The fire hydrant with ray-traced reflections and HDR specular highlights.

The rigs and shaders created in the previous tutorials can be reused for pretty much any situation, although the dome lighting rig is mainly for outdoors because it simulates Earth's atmosphere, which is spherical. A simplified version can be created for indoors. The main issue is to use light linking so that your light rig does not interfere with walls enclosing a room. In other words, you could use six directional lights to simulate global illumination in a room, but you need to turn off Illuminate by Default for each light and link them so that they illuminate only the opposite wall and objects in the room. If your light from the north is illuminating the north and south walls, you will get the proper results. You need to exclude the north wall from the north lights list of linked surfaces.

Creating and Preparing HDR Images

You can use global illumination, Final Gathering, and radiosity in Mental Ray without using HDR images, but it is definitely something to take advantage of. It is especially useful when trying to match location-based lighting such as live-action shoots when you need to combine CG with a live-action backplate.

Of course, you can manually sample color from a live-action backplate and, from observation, determine what direction light is coming from and assign those lights color. In the final tutorial in this chapter, you will do this with a color script. However, when compositing for live action, you will have to deal with matching natural light or incandescent light, or both. In these cases, having references beyond the filmed or videographed backplates is essential. However, on a shoot, you might not always have the time to take detailed photos of the environment, or you might not even be present at the shoot. If the goal of your project is to wedge CG into a live-action backplate as seamlessly as possible, it is a really good idea to integrate as much data collection into the schedule as possible. Often live-action shoots have a prelight day, and this could be an opportune time for you as a CG artist to go to the set (preferably with an assistant) and collect your data.

Data to collect is as follows:

- Even if you are not doing 3D tracking, it is a good idea to take measurements of the set and props. Bring a long tape measure and a notepad. Things will go easier and quicker if you have three people—two to operate the tape measure and one to take notes. Measure the dimensions of the set, props, and lights. You can use these measurements when creating your light setup so that your physically correct lighting adjustments will be accurate.

- Take images of the set using a digital still camera. I mentioned the Nikon Coolpix 990 earlier. It has been superceded by a higher-res version, but the great thing about this camera is that it has interchangeable lenses and exposure control. It is also a good idea to get a battery pack because they tend to eat up batteries. Actually, buy two battery packs so that one can be charging while you use the other. You can use a power line, but then it becomes cumbersome if you need to move around a lot, which you will, and it becomes a hazard for foot traffic. You do not need to use a flash unless there is extremely poor light. This camera is incredible for capturing the existing lighting conditions. Buy at least two 128MB or 256MB compact flash cards or equivalent, and a laptop or other device so that you can download your stills to a large hard drive and still be able to shoot at the same time. When you are taking pictures of surfaces for texture maps, try to use a telephoto lens because this will flatten them. Take pictures of everything from the walls of the set to the props, to the placement of lights on the set, and even to the talent.

- Collect light probe information. For this you'll need to bring several different light probes. Three basic types of light probes exist—reflective, ambient, and skin. The reflective light probe can be any ball that has a mirrorlike surface. I have found that most garden and variety stores have "gazing globes" that are cheap and reasonably large, and these work well. You can also use holiday ornaments, but they tend to be the size of tennis ball, which is a bit small. For a highly reflective surface, you can get large steel ball bearings, but they will be heavy and expensive and require a tripod or some other sturdy mount. It is a good idea to use a sturdier mount for the lighter light probes because if you are shooting outdoors, a slight wind can make it hard to get alignment between exposures. Ambient light probes can be a white Styrofoam ball or even the reflective probe covered with a nice bright white piece of cloth such as a new T-shirt. These are mainly used for indoor color sampling, not so much for HDRI lighting. However, they are good for measuring the radiant light coming off various surfaces when placed near them. The last light probe type is for skin. You can make a skin light probe using moleskin, which is popular for hikers to prevent blisters and happens to react to light like human skin. You can apply this material to a ball or any surface and sample color from it. Again, this is not so much for HDRI, but it is useful for determining bounced light and gauging translucence when actual human skin is not in the shot. If the shoot is primarily being done against a blue or green screen, light probe information might not be especially helpful because the light probes tend to pick up mostly those two intense colors. The pictures you take of these light probes will contain color values that you can sample with an eyedropper in the Maya Color Chooser or use directly as image-based lighting bases.

To create an HDR image for image-based lighting, you need to take multiple exposures of your probe or use a fish-eye lens as a light probe substitute to get the proper range of values. Values that fall into shadows need a high exposure, and an extremely bright light source needs a low exposure. Then you need a range of exposures in between. Another feature on the Nikon Coolpix is that you can manually choose between +2 and −2 levels of exposure (see Figure 19.20).

Figure 19.20 An exposure sheet and layered alignment file.

Various formats exist for the projections. We have already discussed ball maps. Panoramic maps can be created in several ways. For instance, you could place your camera in the middle of the environment and take a series of images, taking a range of exposures at some division of 360° and then stitching them together in Photoshop.

To convert the range of exposures into an HDRI format, you will need either Paul Debevec's HDRShop (`www.debevec.org/HDRShop/`) or mkhdr from `http://athens. ict.usc.edu/FiatLux/mkhdr/`.

If you do not have a digital camera, you can also create HDR images in programs such as Bryce using multiple camera views. Or, if you only have one image to work with, you can create the different exposures in Photoshop using various Levels settings. You can also download various HDR images from the Internet (`www.debevec.org/ Probes/` or `http://radiosity.tripod.co.jp/`). After you have gotten some HDR images, you can use HDRview to preview them (`www.debevec.org/FiatLux/ hdrview/`).

After you have created or acquired an HDR image, you must convert it to a format that Mental Ray understands. Mental Ray comes with a commandline utility that will convert .hdr files to .map files.

On the commandline type `imf_copy campus_probe.hdr campus.map map rgb_fp`. The `imf_copy` command is stored in your Maya 5.0/bin directory.

Maya does not understand either of these formats and gives you a warning when you load, but you can simply ignore the warning. You do not need to use an HDR image to take advantage of image-based lighting with global illumination, Final Gathering, or radiosity, but, as described earlier, the look will not be entirely the same. In the next exercise you'll learn the difference in look between the two.

Exercise 19.5   Using Final Gathering in Mental Ray for Maya 5

To get started, install the Mental Ray for Maya plug-in. If it is not already installed or did not come with your Maya installation, you can download it for free from www.aliaswavefront.com/. Next you need an HDR image. We have provided one of Debevec's light probe images on the CD in a file called campus_probe.hdr. Making HDR images from scratch is difficult, and the software you need to create them is not entirely user-friendly today. However, you can download a growing number of HDR images—for free or for a fee. To get a list of various HDR, Final Gathering, global illumination, image-based lighting, and radiosity resources on the Net, go to www.gmask.com/newriders/links/, or you can retrieve the HDR_links.htm file from the accompanying CD.

1. Open the MR_HDR_Start.mb file from the CD.

   This is a short tutorial. (We have already set many rendering settings to facilitate this exercise; we discuss these in more detail in Chapter 20, "Rendering.") Basically, you are using the same dome approach we used before, except that you need only one light source that will emit your photons. The Final Gathering feature of Mental Ray and an HDRI map will do the rest of the work of lighting the scene (see Figure 19.21).

2. The next step is to create a single point light, via Create, Lights, PointLight. It does not matter where you place it. Give the light an intensity of 0.

3. Now double-click the Domeshader in the Hypershade window. The Domeshader is just a surface shader, like the one you used in the previous tutorials. Click the Texture button next to Out Color, and choose a file texture with the As projection option turned on.

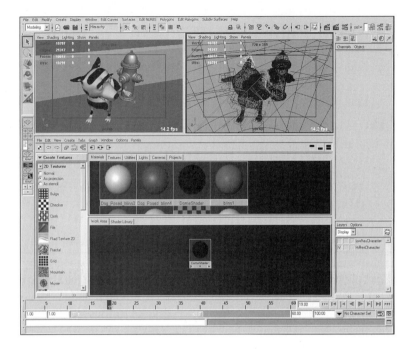

Figure 19.21 The dog gets familiar with the fire hydrant before you apply an HDRI map to the dome.

4. In the Attribute Editor, click the Projection tab and select Ball Proj Type.

   Depending on whether the orientation of your light probe image is horizontal or vertical, your map needs a certain projection type (see Figure 19.22). The map on the left was taken with a fish-eye lens pointing up at the sky and is vertical. If you were using a map with this orientation, you would need to rotate the ball projection –90 on the X. However, in this case you will use a map similar to the image on the right, which was shot off a light probe and has a horizontal orientation; you need to make a change to the projection.

5. Go to the File tab and click the folder icon next to the Image Name field. Browse to the CD-ROM and load the campus.map file.

   This can vary from one platform to the next, but on Windows, after you have opened the file browser, you must choose Best Guess (*.*) from the Files of Type pull-down menu (see Figure 19.23). Double-click the campus.map file.

   You will see this warning printed in the command feedback:

   ```
   "// Warning: Failed to open texture file sourceimages/campus.map //".
   ```

Just ignore it; Mental Ray does know how to read this file. I already converted this file from .hdr to .map for you using the imf_copy program. If you need to have a regular 8-bit image file so that you can see where you are placing the map first, you can use the HDRview.exe program to save the .hdr file as a .bmp file. I have included a converted version of the file called campus.bmp if you want to view the map file directly.

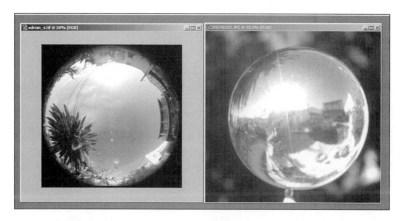

Figure 19.22 Two light probe images. The one on the right is vertical, and the one on the left is horizontal.

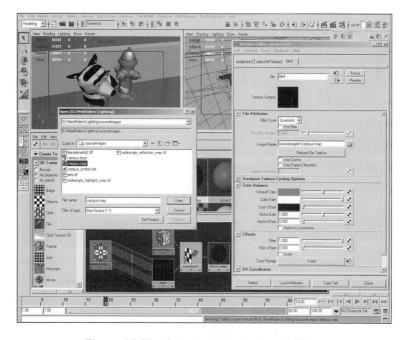

Figure 19.23 Selecting the HDRI map in Maya.

6. Render the perspective view. It will take Mental Ray a few moments to create the Final Gathering map. You will see a thermometer in the lower-left side of the Maya interface. When it is done rendering, use the Keep Image button to save the current render.

If the image appears blown out or too bright you can adjust the overall brightness of the HDR image by adjusting the Color Gain slider under Color Balance for the selected file node.

For comparison, replace campus.map with campus.bmp, rerender, and then compare the difference between the two images (see Figure 19.24).

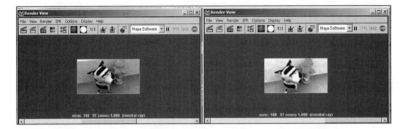

Figure 19.24   Comparing a Final Gathering render with and without HDRI.

You can see that the color in the HDRI version on the left is much richer. Notice that you have the prominent highlights in the fire hydrant that are the evidence of HDRI usage. We talk more about the rendering settings for Mental Ray in Chapter 20. This was just an introduction to this fascinating new option in Maya. In general, your lighting approaches with discrete lights will be the same; however, some adjustments will have to be made to take advantage of Mental Ray's speedier ray tracing and special features.

Color Scripts

A *color script* is an image or set of images that will describe an entire movie in terms of color. A fully saturated beginning might turn to a despondent monochromatic blue and end with a triadic celebration. A good example of this is the painting in Figure 19.25, which expresses the color and mood of light throughout the piece. You can find the color piece in the source images folder of the Lighting project on the CD.

Figure 19.25   The color script image for our *Parking Spot* animation was based on an Edward Hopper painting. Max painted in water-based gouache, scanned it, and then made the script through image processing. In black and white, there is still a full range of values.

The image is attempting to sum up the quality of light on a summer day. The shadows have a bluish purple color, and all of the light is a warm orange tone. This will help us set up our lighting style. Now the lights will have an orange bias with blue-violet shadows. The next thing to think about is color bounce. This is the phenomenon in which a white object on a red rug will have a pink color subtly bouncing up to it. In the color script, I want the ground colors to bounce up into the props and set pieces. This helps shape the forms and gives an interesting richness. In Maya, the lights need to be placed in the scene to bounce up into the shadows. Your best bet is to have the scanned color script image as an image plane in Maya so that you can grab the exact colors from it.

In a digital studio environment, the art department provides a color script and color key paintings that the lighting department can use to match. The goal is to get the look and feel of the color, mood, and other intangible qualities. The first step is to create a master lighting in which all of the scenes in a sequence are continuous. Each shot is then individually adjusted to the camera based on that master lighting. You will find some excellent resources on this subject in the "making of" section that accompanies Pixar, Dreamworks, and Disney DVDs. The best one I have ever seen on color scripts is on the Dreamworks animated film *Eldorado*. Also check out the books that come out with these movies—the artwork is fantastic.

In the next exercise, you will light a scene from *Parking Spot*. The season is summer, and the sun is in its last bright phase before sunset starts moving in.

Exercise 19.6 Lighting a Bright Summer's Day

First you will set up the master lighting to get the entire scene properly lit. Then you will focus on the specific shot.

1. Load the StreetScene_Start.mb file from the CD. This image shows The Jerk character with his car in front of the Last Minute Gift Shop.

2. Create a directional light and scale it up so that you can see the icon for it in the large scene. Then set the hardware shading to use your lights by pressing 5 and then 7 on your keyboard. In the Channel box, rotate the light so that the dog is in the shadow of the car. Rename the light Key. This is your key light.

3. Set the directional color to a creamy orange and set the shadows to a dark purple. Make sure the depth map shadows are checked on. Set the shadow Dmap resolution to 1024 and the Dmap filter size to 10. At this point, your scene should look like Figure 19.26.

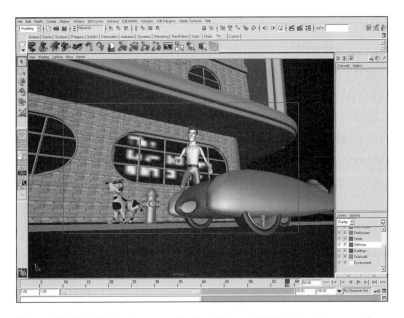

Figure 19.26 The Jerk gets to the Last Minute Gift Shop a minute too late.

4. Now you will create a fill light. Begin by creating another directional light, but turn it facing 180° from your key light. Set the color to a medium blue and the intensity value to .25. Check off Specular. Call the light you just created Fill.

5. Open the Hypershade, Perspective, Render window. Then go to Window, General Editors, Attribute Spreadsheet and select all the lights in Hypershade. Try an IPR render to see how all of this balances out. You can adjust the intensities of all the lights in the attribute Spread Sheet Editor and look at the IPR render. The bounce light from the directional fill should have a lightening effect on the shadow areas (see Figure 19.27). More special kickers will be achieved later.

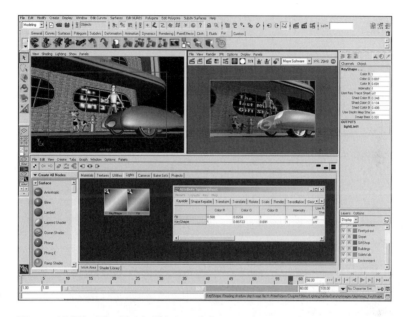

Figure 19.27   The bluish fill light is lightening the areas that were in shadow.

This is the bare minimum for lighting the background. Next you will emphasize the shot for the dog. A strong color bounce from the red car will help add to Spot's anger.

6. Create an area light and place it between the actors and the car. Face it toward them and name it RedCarBounce.

7. Set the light to match the red of the car. Set Decay Rate to Quadratic and Intensity to 33. Check off Emit Specular and Illuminates by Default.

8. Open the Outliner and select the characters, pavement, sidewalk, and area light. Then, in the Render menu, click Lighting/Shading, Make Light Links.

   One major advantage of CG lighting is that shadows can be eliminated entirely and lights can be linked to specific surfaces. Visually, you can cheat a shadow or light effect this way. A seamless backdrop can be burned with a bright light and the subject can be in nice, soft, subtle light. If you want to edit these relationships in Maya, just use the object- or light-centric Light Linker in the Lighting/Shading menu.

   Next you will start to suck in some light where you don't want it, for soft value transitions.

9. Create a spot light and place it above the dog. Then set the drop-off to 4 and make it a bright orange color; name it DogShadow. Set the intensity to −.4. This creates a dark blue area under the car, to remove light.

10. Turn off Illuminates by Default and link the light to the pavement only. Repeat step 9 for the car, The Jerk, and the fire hydrant, but link the light to the sidewalk (see Figure 19.28).

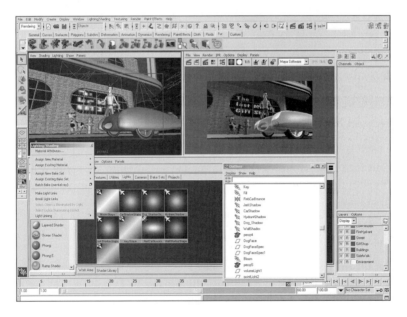

Figure 19.28 The characters are now well grounded with the economical use of negative lights, to replace the use of rendered shadows.

Now the secondary lighting will enhance the subjects' illumination. You can establish a pattern of light linking and see the results via iterations in IPR with the Attribute spreadsheet for the lights. This is the best way to get immediate feedback and see the "big picture."

11. Create a volume light and place it close to The Jerk's eyes.

12. Link the volume light to the face and eyes. Check Emit Specular to Off. See Figure 19.29.

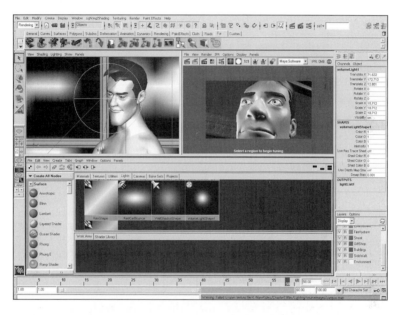

Figure 19.29   Adding a light source to illuminate the eye of a character draws in the viewers' focus and creates drama.

13. Create a point light and place it near the eye with Emit Specular checked to On. Link it to the eye, and repeat by creating another light for the second eye.

14. Adjust the attribute spreadsheet for the new eye lights to get the right balance of light on the eyes without drawing too much emphasis (see Figure 19.30).

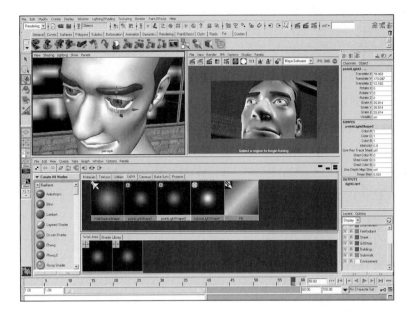

Figure 19.30 Tweak the positions of the point lights to create an attractive highlight for The Jerk's eyes.

Subtlety is the key here. This takes a lot of experimentation and rendering. If you want to get a sneak peek, open the StreetScene_Finished.mb file to see the final results.

Next you will add a rim light to get the characters to pop to the foreground.

15. Create a directional light facing toward the camera, and link it only to the characters. Set the light's intensity to a 1.3 value and a light blue color.

16. Double-click shaderGlow in the HyperShade window. In the Attribute Editor, set Threshold to .6.

17. Select the Dog Fur shader and set Glow Intensity to .5.

18. Start a new IPR render and play with the shaderGlow Threshold and the Dog Fur shader's Glow Intensity, as shown in Figure 19.31. You should get a nice bloom effect. You can take it further by adjusting the glow and halo attributes to your heart's content.

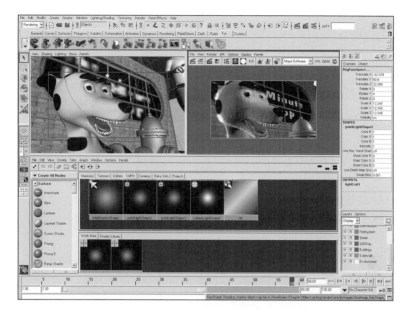

Figure 19.31   Using the Threshold feature of the shaderGlow prevents the glow from covering too much of the surface and creates a controlled "bloom" effect.

Summary

Hopefully, you have gained some insight into using and controlling Maya's lights and have learned some new techniques that you can add to your lighting arsenal. For very precise lighting, think in terms of two-, three-, and possibly six-point lighting, and be as restrained as possible without sacrificing fidelity. Be bold with shadows, and always use good reference to get excellent results. Remember that light linking can easily reduce your burden. Lighting is an art form that will always be a journey in both CG and real-world production.

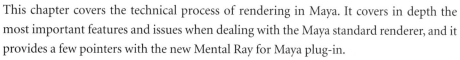

Chapter 20

Rendering

By Adrian Dimond

This chapter covers the technical process of rendering in Maya. It covers in depth the most important features and issues when dealing with the Maya standard renderer, and it provides a few pointers with the new Mental Ray for Maya plug-in.

Specifically, this chapter discusses the following topics:

- How to render efficiently with Maya's standard renderer
- How to render with mental ray for Maya
- Multipass rendering
- Render farms
- How to prepare for final output

Note

Besides the Maya standard renderer and Mental Ray for Maya, you can choose from several RenderMan-compliant renderers and interfaces:

- Pixar RenderMan and Mtor (www.pixar.com)
- BMRT (http://groups.yahoo.com/group/bmrt)
- Mayaman (www.animallogic.com/research/mayaman)
- 3delight (www.3delight.com)
- Air (www.sitexgraphics.com)
- Aqsis (www.aqsis.com)
- RenderDotC and Maitai (www.dotcsw.com)

Rendering Efficiently with Maya's Standard Renderer

A lot of work goes into preparing a scene to be rendered, but this careful attention to detail is worth it because it will prevent you from getting unexpected errors after waiting several hours for a scene to be rendered. By getting into the habit of applying custom settings in the Maya standard renderer, you will achieve better results than you would if you used Maya's default settings. Despite its flaws, the Maya standard renderer enables you to render on a practically unlimited number of CPUs for every seat of it that you have. For smaller shops and individuals, this is a cost-effective way to deal with the expense of rendering.

A large part of working efficiently with the Maya standard renderer is to understand what it can and can't do. Knowing this will help you prepare and plan for creating those effects before you get halfway into your project and realize that you can't just turn on an effect and expect it to be rendered in a one-pass render. There are solutions for most of the Maya standard renderer's known limitations. In the following section, we list and discuss these issues.

Known Limitations

Although you can render efficiently with the Maya standard renderer, it is limited in some ways. But you can get around these limitations with some clever techniques.

For instance, many functions in Maya are called post effects. Some effects also can be rendered only with Window, Rendering Editors, Hardware Render Buffer.

PaintFX, Fur, Glows, and OptiFX such as lens flares, depth of field, and 2D motion blur are examples of such post processes. That means that the effects are added to the image after the main rendering process is done. As a result, these effects cannot be a part of ray-tracing effects such as reflection or refraction, and they cannot even be behind transparent surfaces.

Most of these effects use Z-depth files so that they can be composited behind and in front of the correct objects, but Z-depth does not understand transparency. This on or off information stored in a Z-depth file can also create some jagged edges when the effect is behind another object.

To work around this limitation in Maya, you can render double size and then half size; scale down the image afterward, and this smoothes it out. To deal with effects that cannot be behind transparencies or that cannot be seen in reflections or refractions, you can render in passes or use reflection maps to fake the effects.

To fake a reflection, you render from a second camera's point of view and then use that as a reflection map on the surface that you would have ray-traced. Normally you would just ray-trace these effects if you could, but if you want fur to appear in a reflection, for example, this is what you have to do.

Another limitation is that PaintFX and Fur do not render properly if you use the Field Render feature of the Maya standard renderer. To work around this, you can render those effects at a step value of .5 and then use a compositing program to create fields.

You can use glows to create some stunning effects. However, sometimes you might want to use a glow function in composite rather than in camera, so to speak. When you are rendering elements for composite, it is usually a good idea to not use the glow in Maya because the bloom from it usually does not composite well. You can get around this by doing a glow pass for the object, by saving a separate scene in which the object's shader has Hide Source checked on under Special Effects. This renders the glow without the object. You then can use this pass in composite on top of the original non-glowed version using an additive composite mode.

If your glows flicker, it is because of the Automatic Exposure feature of the shaderGlow node, in the Hypershade window. You can fix this flickering by first doing a render at your target resolution and then making note of two values that are produced by the Automatic exposure in the Output window. In the report that is generated for the frame you just rendered, you will see two values: the glow intensity normalization factor and the halo intensity normalization factor. These are the global values for glows and halos. To use them, you need to enter the result into their respective Intensity fields in the shaderGlow node in the Hypershade window.

2D and 3D motion blurs also are limited in Maya because they do not affect a moving object's shadow. There's a good tutorial for faking this online at www.3dluvr.com/ pixho/tutorials/mb_shdws/MBShdw_main.html. Maya's motion blur is also not seen in refractions or reflections. However, you can use Pixho's fake for motion-blurred shadows to get them in reflections and refraction.

Another great trick for dealing with effects that do not respond to motion blur is to render them as a background plate. Then use that background plate as a camera plane in Maya, and place an object with a transparent shader and no specular in front of the area that you want to be blurred. Animate the "blur object" so that it moves with the area of your background image sequence. When you use 2D motion blur, Maya blurs all pixels that are in the path of movement. So, even though your object is transparent, the background image is blurred.

You also fake motion blur by rendering the separate objects that need to be blurred with a Render Globals, Image File Output, By Frame setting of .1. This renders out 10 times as many frames as you would normally have. Then in your compositing program, you time-stretch the long sequence to be one tenth of the speed it was at so that it is the correct speed when playing back. When you render this sequence with interlacing or with frame blending in Adobe After Effects, you get a really smooth motion.

When you are working with 3D titles, render more frames than you think you need so that you can retime a sequence without having to rerender. It is usually easy to speed something up, but if you need to slow something down, you will need those in-between frames; you can get them using the Render Globals, Image File Output, By Frame setting. The problem with this setting, though, is that it renumbers your frames in a way that some render farm software does not understand. To compensate for this, you can either stretch out your keyframes manually or use a script such as ajrTimeWarp, by Andy Rawling, available from `www.highend3D.com`.

Another issue that confuses many Maya users is that there are two types of particles: software and hardware. If you pick a hardware particle type and you do a software render, you get an error similar to "Hardware rendering selected for particleShape1. Skipped." To render the hardware particle render type, select Window, Rendering Editors, Hardware Render Buffer. The hardware renderer has its own render attributes. You must render these separately and composite them. One of the options of the hardware renderer is a geometry mask that makes it possible to composite particles that go around and in front of other objects.

Antialiasing

In your Render Globals, you have many settings to adjust to get optimal performance. First, we cover the antialiasing settings, which you can access by going to Antialiasing, Number of Samples. You'll see the following:

- **Presets**—This is a basic set of preferences for antialiasing. The Preview set is good for tests, but the higher-quality settings might not be the most efficient for large or complicated scenes because many per-object or per-shader adjustments should be made for performance. If you choose the Highest Quality preset it assigns the same high settings to everything, whether they need it or not. Use the following as guidelines on how to adjust on a per-object or shader basis.

- **Edge Antialiasing**—This setting controls how well the edge of an object is smoothed. Highest Quality is the highest value possible.

- **Shading and Max Shading**—The Shading value controls the minimum number of samples used to antialias texture maps and shaders. The Max Shading value is the maximum number of samples that are used to antialias texture maps and shaders. You need to keep both of these shading values as low as possible for optimal performance. Because more shader samples might be needed for only a few textures or shaders in your scene, there is no need to force the renderer to apply the same level to all of them using high values set here.

  You can set Max Shading to a higher value, and the adaptive algorithm will catch color differences only when they need to be fixed. Setting the Shading value, on the other hand, would force it to treat all pixels the same way and, thus, would slow things down.

  If you have some specific textures that are noisy or that have fine detail, select the objects that they are assigned to and open Window, General Editors, Attributes Spread Sheet Editor. Then turn on the Shading Samples Override in the Render tab, and set the Shading Samples and Max Shading Samples to appropriate values for that texture to render smoothly.

- **Multipixel Filtering**—This applies a blur to the entire rendered image and is available only when you choose the High or Highest Edge Antialiasing. In most cases, this is not really the best way to deal with an image that is flickering, but it will reduce the roping effect. You have a choice of filter types when performing multipixel filtering. The Box filter is the softest, and Guassian is only slightly soft. If you cannot solve problems with flickering or roping by applying a filter and adjusting shading samples per object, your next best solution might be to render the image at twice the resolution and scale it down.

  Maya does not use multipixel filtering when rendering with fields. If you are getting artifacts, you can use a By Frame setting of .5 in Render Globals, Image File Output to render twice as many frames, and then use your compositing package to retime those frames into a field-rendered sequence.

- **Contrast Threshold**—The Red, Green, and Blue settings are relevant only when Edge Antialiasing is set to Highest Quality. Contrast Threshold represents the number of samples taken during the second pass of the render. These settings can be adjusted to bring out small highlights and shadows, but they can increase render times. Coverage is relevant only when 3D Motion Blur is turned on. Lowering the value improves the quality of 3D motion blur but increases the render time (see Figure 20.1).

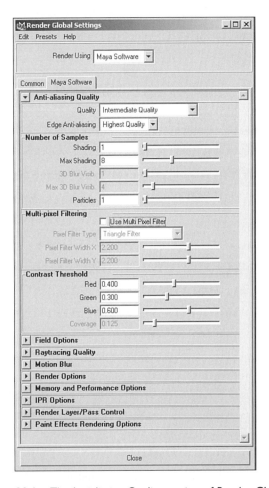

Figure 20.1   The Antialiasing Quality section of Render Globals.

Ray Tracing

Maya's ray-tracing capabilities are decent, and you will get the most from them if you use them wisely.

For instance, try to use ray tracing for those effects that only it can do. For casting light through transparent surfaces or semiopaque but colored surfaces, ray tracing is necessary to get the right effect. Do not use soft ray-traced shadows because they are far more time consuming than the same effect achieved with depth map shadows.

Because ray-traced shadows are created during the render, the whole scene will have to be ray-traced, which is more time consuming than selecting just surfaces that have reflective or refractive properties for ray tracing. Transparent shaders that have a refractive value of 1 do not have to be ray traced, so check off Refractions in the shader's Ray Trace options. Objects that do not ray-trace, that do not reflect, or that can be seen in either of those processes are not included in the ray-traced voxel and, thus, speed up the process. It is also a good idea to avoid using a large amount of world space unnecessarily. Large objects that extend the horizon of your world but then focus only on geometry in one small area slow down ray tracing; either delete those objects or make them smaller.

You can change many of these settings by using each surface's Attribute Editor, by using the Attribute Spread Sheet Editor, or by creating MEL scripts and a ray-tracing scripts shelf for easy access in the future.

Ray-Tracing Quality

To ensure optimal results when ray tracing in Maya, keep the following values as low as you can:

- **Reflections** can be achieved with a setting as low as 1. Raising this value can greatly increase the amount of time for a render. If you have only one reflective surface, it might not be necessary to set it any higher, unless you need the surface to reflect itself.

- **Refractions** can require higher values to achieve certain effects. Glass generally requires a setting of 9 or 10. If you set black areas in your rendering where there are supposed to be refractions, set this value higher.

- **Shadows** level is the maximum number of times a light ray can reflect or refract and still force an object to cast a shadow. Normally 1 should be sufficient if you have one reflective surface. If you are using reflections and you want to have your ray-traced shadows appear in reflections or refractions, this value and the value of Ray Trace Shadow Attributes, Ray Depth Limit of the light casting the shadow need to be set to 2 or higher. When you are working with cloud or tube particles and you are getting either incorrect or missing shadows, you might need to increase this value as well.

- **Bias** is relevant only if you have 3D motion-blurred objects and ray-traced shadows. If you see artifacts or incorrect shadows, try setting Bias to .05 or .1. Otherwise, leave it set to the default of 0.

Memory and Performance Options for Ray Tracing

The following settings control how the ray tracer works internally. In most cases, you must change these from the defaults unless you are using a lot of memory or have a very complicated scene. These settings are found under Memory and Performance Options, Ray Tracing.

- **Recursion Depth**—This setting determines how many times or levels the voxel will be recursed. For simple scenes, a setting of 1 is fine. The default is 2; for more complex scenes with more geometry, a setting of 2 or 3 might be in order. Each new level is the result of multiplying the previous level by itself, and that resulting number is how many voxels it creates. This exponential increase in voxels can add up to more than a gigabyte of RAM at Level 6.

- **Leaf Primitives**—Whereas Recursion Depth determines the number of recursions required for each voxel, this setting controls how many triangles are allowed in each voxel before recursion to the next level. The higher the number of triangles, the longer the ray will take to intersect with them. The default setting is 200 triangles.

- **Subdivision Power**—This sets the cubic resolution of the voxels. The value is the power at which the voxels will be created. The default is .2500, and it can be raised slightly for very complicated scenes (see Figure 20.2).

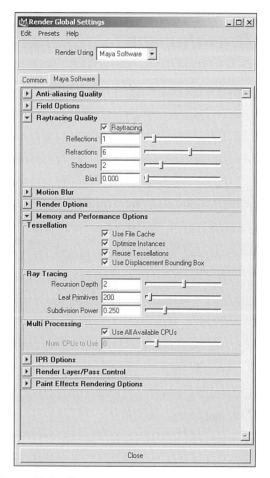

Figure 20.2   The ray-tracing sections of Render Globals.

Motion Blur

A big difference exists between 2D and 3D motion blur. One difference is time: 3D blur is very slow. Another difference is that 3D blur can take into account the rotation of objects, whereas 2D blur can blur only on the linear vector that an object travels between frames. One benefit of 2D motion blur is speed: It is a post process, so you can adjust its setting quite easily after rendering if you use the correct options. This prevents having to rerender the entire scene because the motion blur is too strong or too weak. It is capable of doing this by storing motion vectors in the rendered file itself.

When you turn on 2D motion blur in Window, Rendering Editors, Render Globals, you are given the option to keep motion vectors. For video resolution files, this can double and even triple the size of the rendered file, depending on how many objects have motion blur enabled. After you have rendered the sequence, use the blur2d command that comes with every install of Maya to adjust your 2D blur settings without having to rerender the sequence from scratch.

Whether you use 2D or 3D motion blur, it is a good idea to limit blur to only the objects that are moving, rather than leave it on for all objects by default.

Number of Samples for 3D Motion Blur

Two more settings are relevant to 3D motion blur and are available only when you have 3D motion blur enabled. Samples are the numbers of passes that the renderer takes for any given pixel. If you look at a television screen up close, you will notice that it is made up of lots of red, green, and blue dots. From a distance, you don't notice that they are individual dots. But when looking at it close-up, you would need more dots—or, in this case, more samples—to have a clear picture.

If your blurs look blocky, most likely it's because you have too few samples. To solve this problem, try increasing the Max 3D Blur Visib rather than the Min samples (see Figure 20.3). The method for sampling is adaptive, so if you increase the Max, it gives more where only it is needed; if you raise the minimum, it gives more to everything, whether it needs it or not.

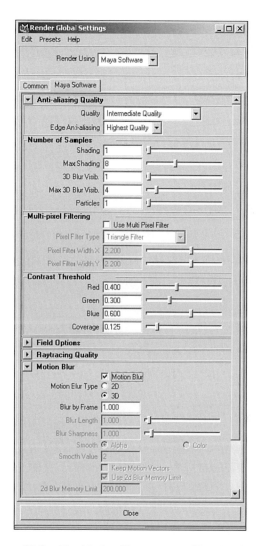

Figure 20.3   The Motion Blur sections of Render Globals.

Depth of Field

Depth of field uses Z-depth information generated by Maya to create a blur like what you would see with a real camera lens. Many compositing programs enable you to use Z-depth files to add DOF, so you gain more control without having to rerender your 3D scene. You can enable the saving of Z-depth files in Render Globals, Image File Output; check the Depth Channel (Z Depth) box on (see Figure 20.4).

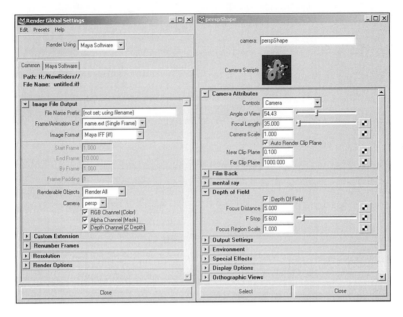

Figure 20.4 The DOF section of the Render Globals and Camera Attributes.

To enable DOF during the render, you have to go to your camera attributes and, under Depth of Field, check it on. If you render the effect in camera, note that the greater the blur is, the longer the post blur render will take.

Tip

To get a better handle on your DOF settings, download the "DOF Control" MEL script, by Dirk Bialluch, from `www.highend3d.com/maya/mel/`. This script creates a DOF control object (polyCube) for selected cameras, so you can easily adjust/animate depth of field settings.

Tessellation

When you model objects in a scene, make sure they are as light as possible. That means giving the models the least amount of data needed to describe the surface. Heavy models will generate heavy render times, so don't overtessellate. Also remember to delete anything that will not be seen in the shot.

On the models themselves, adjust the tessellation in the Attribute Editor. You can get good results by setting the Advanced Tessellation attribute of a surface to Best Guess Based on Screen Size, which adjusts the tessellation based on the distance from the camera. For geometry that will always be a certain distance from camera, you might want to just set it to a standard amount. For precise tessellation, such as when you are working with complex patch models for a character, you need to set specific tessellation values to prevent "cracking."

For some models, you might need to open Window, Attribute Editor and, under Tessellation, Options, check Smooth Edge. However, you need to do this for all the surrounding surfaces as well, and doing this for each might be tedious. Using Window, General Editors, Attribute Spread Sheet Editor, Tessellation is a much faster way to change this for many objects. You could also make a MEL script and keep it in a shelf for future use. Smooth Edge does create more geometry, so it should be used wisely. A Smooth Edge ratio of .999 produces precise results but also uses a lot of memory and time to build during the render. These are all settings that can be implemented through a MEL script so that whenever you need to apply a specific setting to a large number of objects, you can do it with one click.

Here are the Tessellation settings found in Render Globals, Memory and Performance Options (see Figure 20.5):

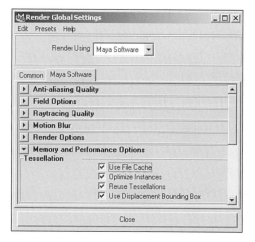

Figure 20.5   The Tessellation section of Render Globals.

- **Use File Cache**—This function allows the renderer to do its own form of memory swapping outside of your system's virtual memory or swap space. This is especially helpful with ray tracing because it can store less frequently visited voxels to disk and reserve memory for the more frequented ones. In this case, you can increase the Maximum Memory parameter for the renderer (use the -mm flag for the command-line renderer), and the renderer will need to do less disk caching. However, if you have multiple processes on the same system with disk I/O, using the File Cache can be counterproductive.

- **Optimize Instances**—This tells the renderer to reuse the same tessellation for similar objects, such as primitives and objects that have duplicate or instanced geometry. This saves on time tessellating the geometry and on drive space as well.

- **Reuse Tessellations**—This setting saves tessellations that are created for lights when they are casting shadows. If you have more than one light, this can speed up things by using the same tessellation for all the shadows being cast. This function does use more memory, so if memory is really low, you might want to turn this off.

- **Use Displacement Bounding Box**—This forces the renderer to use the Bounding Box settings you have set for a surface that is being displaced. Normally the renderer must tessellate the surface to calculate the size of the Bounding Box Scale, which wastes time. To set this for an object, you can use the Attribute Spread Sheet Editor, but the Window, Attribute Editor has a Calculate Bounding Box Scale button under the displacement map. You can use a MEL script to automatically calculate and set this value for all selected objects using the command:

  ```
  `displacementToPoly -findBboxOnly`
  ```

Memory

When you are ready to render, it is usually a good idea to quit out of the GUI portion of Maya because it is using available memory that you might need for your render.

If you have a lot of RAM, you might want to increase the maximum memory limit. This can be done when you are issuing a render from the command line using the -mm ### parameter of the Render command (### is the number of megabytes you want to increase it to). Depending on which platform you are on, the Render command might have slightly different syntax.

To increase performance, you can increase this number. If you find that you are going into swap excessively, you might want to lower this number and force the renderer to use less RAM. By default, the renderer uses a base of 64MB of RAM. You can also use the -tw -th flags at the commandline and give them each a value of 64 up to 256 in situations where you are running out of RAM. Here's an example: `Render -th 64 -w 64 myseenfile.ma`. These flags are listed in the help for the render command if you type **render-h** in the operating system's commandline. The full list of flags is also in the Rendering Utilities section of the electronic help.

Animation Efficiencies

When you animate, delete the static animation channels, as described in Chapter 19, "Lighting," to keep your data clean. If you have animation that can be baked down in the Graph Editor, consider doing it for an approved shot, and then store the baked and unbaked file just in case. This is especially important when you are working with dynamic simulations because if you are rendering on a network by sending out packets, each computer will have to run up to the frame it starts rendering from. This is a huge waste of CPU time.

However, one issue with baking channels for dynamics is that sometimes rotational values fail due to limitations in Eular math. Anytime you bake channels generated from dynamics, you will need to examine them with Windows, Animation Editors, Graph Editor to see if the rotation channels have failed and then run Curves, Eular Filter to fix them. If you do not do this, effects such as motion blur will have strange moments where the object is totally blurred because the channel is interpreted going from 180° to −180°. Even though the motion seems correct in playback, something can be horribly wrong in the GUI and must be intercepted before time is wasted rendering.

Shaders and Texture Maps

Shaders can be excellent tools for exploring what a render will look like. However, they can be deeply procedural and highly recursive. This means that a layered shader could be made up of a lot of programmed render nodes, such as fractals, that nest inside each other. The final effect might be wonderful but costly because, at render time, the CPU has to run the calculations on a procedural texture. Although basic procedurals are very effective and fun to work with, as they become more complex, they can become devastatingly slow. At this point, optimization will become a disuse.

Luckily, Maya has a great solution: Convert to File Texture. This gets all the procedural textures and utilities and renders down to a 2D map of the final effect (see Figure 20.6). This is a great time saver. You simply pick the surfaces that are affected, along with the shader, and then select Convert to File Texture from the Hypershade Edit menu. You are given options for the size of the texture map and can determine whether you want to bake in the lighting. If you have a bump map that is illuminated by a colored light, the Bake Lighting option the bumps facing the colored light in the 2D map. The result is like an automated trompe l'oeil. This utility is worth the price of admission.

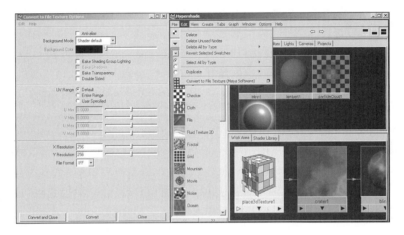

Figure 20.6   The Convert to File Texture options.

Of course, many times the nature of the procedural texture might more than make up for any extra computational time. If your camera moves from far away to very close to several procedural surfaces, it might be prohibitive to create image maps large enough to provide the same detail. There is a balance between memory usage and CPU time. Depending on the length of the scene or how many times the object is reused throughout a production, the benefits of baking textures can be negligible. In games, baking is essential, and rarely can you use any procedural textures or large numbers of lights, so they all must be baked.

If you reuse the same file texture in multiple shaders, try to link that same file texture node to all of them. It will also help to use IFF textures because they are the native format for Maya.

It is also a good idea to try to use perfectly square texture maps because nonsquare ones will not look as good as they should in some situations. It is also better usage of RAM to use Base 2 squared images. Image resolutions of 256×256, 512×512, and 1024×1024 are examples of Base 2 dimensions.

In Maya 4.5, Alias|Wavefront has changed the default filtering for file textures. In previous versions, the default was Mipmap, but now it is Quadratic. Quadratic provides a much higher quality and is an efficient way to antialias your bitmap texture files, but it is slightly slower than Mipmap.

Block Order Texture (BOT) Files

BOT files reduce the need for RAM when using large texture maps because the structure of the format breaks the texture into chunks that the renderer can easily cache to disk. BOT files allow the render to only load what it needs during the render—rather than loading an entire 40MB file, it loads only several hundred kilobytes. Unfortunately, you cannot read BOT files in external programs, so you will probably want to do this only to files that will not be edited after they are assigned.

For larger texture maps, you can save on memory by converting just those images to a BOT file. You can use the MEL command `makebot -i "in_image" -o "out_bot_file"` to convert single textures at a time, or you can use `maya -optimizeRender [options] mayaFile optimizedMayaFile` to automatically convert all the textures to BOT files and automatically assign them to the texture nodes that they will replace. To get more information about this command, type **'maya -optimizeRender –help'** in the command prompt or console of your operating system.

Tip

The MEL script "Make BOT," by Yuya Sugiyama and downloadable from www.highend3d.com/maya/mel/, gives you a GUI for converting all file textures or selected file textures to BOT files.

Shadows

Try not to turn on shadows for every light, and use depth map shadows instead of ray-traced shadows whenever possible. Although we are using quite a few shadow maps for the dome light rig discussed in Chapter 19, those maps were very economical because they use very small resolutions for the depth maps. If the light rig had consisted of ray traced shadows or area lights, it would have taken much longer to render.

Turning off shadow casting for surfaces can also decrease render times. Creating lights that use a smaller worldSpace will have denser shadow maps and use less memory. Spotlights are very efficient because you can precisely control their worldSpace by decreasing the cone angle.

Reusing shadow maps also decreases render time and can free up some RAM. You can reuse only shadows that are not animated or that do not have other objects passing through them.

Any shadow or surface that is not animated can decrease render times if you baked it. This converts the combined effect of the shadow and the surface's color into a single texture file. This is the Bake Shading Group Lighting option in the Convert to File Texture function found under the Edit menu in the Hypershade window. You can also enable the Bake Shadows option; this function uses only depth map rendered shadows.

If you are using a point light for casting shadows, you can economize by turning off all but one of the six directions in which it can cast a shadow. To turn off the extra shadows, select the point light and open Window, Attribute Editor. Under Depth Map Shadow Attributes is a list of check boxes for each possible direction (see Figure 20.7).

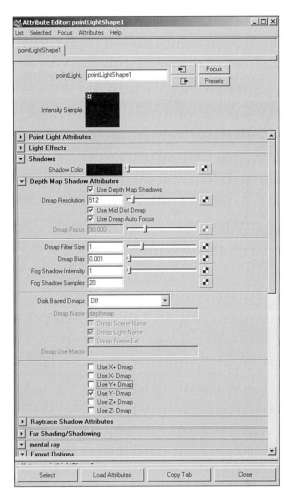

Figure 20.7   Disabling unnecessary Dmaps for a point light.

Render Diagnostics

Another very useful utility in the standard Maya renderer is Render Diagnostics (see Figure 20.8). This looks at your entire scene, checks for a long list of criteria, and then generates a message. Many of the typical warnings are related to ray tracing, shadows, and overall settings that are set too high. Render Diagnostics also checks to see that shading groups are connected properly, and it analyzes cameras and Render Global settings. This utility can be helpful, but it cannot solve all rendering problems, so do not rely on it. Many issues are better solved in the workflow in the pipeline before rendering.

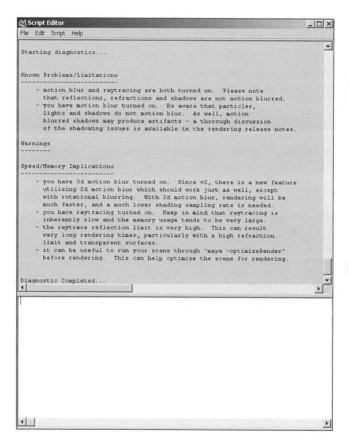

Figure 20.8   The results of Render Diagnostics are printed in the Script Editor window.

When creating models, the issue of using double-shaded faces and making sure that all the normals are facing in the correct directions could come back to haunt you at this point if you did not set them properly in the first place. If so, you can fix these problems using Window, General Editors, Attribute Spread Sheet Editor and clicking the Render tab. Here you can control whether a surface is rendered double-sided and can flip which side is out, as well as many other features. However, if it has to do with a complex model such as a character, in most cases the modeler should have set this in an intuitive manner to prevent headaches down the road.

Command-Line Rendering

You can launch renders in various ways besides the Batch Render command inside Maya. You can use the command line of your operating system to run `render.exe` (as it would be on Windows—this varies from system to system). Running the `render` command from the command line (see Figure 20.9) gives you access to some parameters not accessible through Render Globals. It also gives you the capability to quickly change parameters instead of having to open scene in the program. Type `render.exe -h` at the Windows command prompt. You will see all the options of the `render` command; Figure 20.9 shows some.

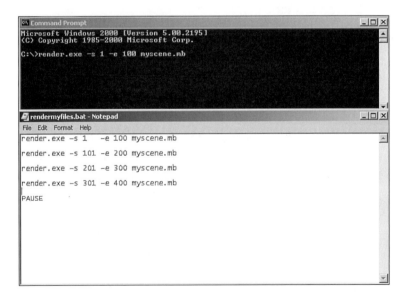

Figure 20.9 Executing a render from the command prompt in Windows 2000 and the Windows BAT file.

On Windows, you can create a batch file and queue several renders to launch one after another. Sometimes it is a good idea to break long sequences into packets. Sometimes the renderer might not free up memory properly, and restarting the renderer every once in a while cleans up the RAM. The batch file (or BAT file, as it is called, because of its .bat suffix) is basically a text file with a series of commands on each line. On UNIX systems, you typically use a shell script, which requires you to declare which shell type you are using and where it is located in the first line—for example, `#! /usr/bin/ksh`. When you add .bat to the end of a file in Windows, the file is made executable and can be double-clicked to launch. On UNIX, however, you will need to use the command `chmod` to make the file executable. A neat trick in Windows is that you can RMB a scene file and launch a render, but it will use only the options set in the Render Globals saved with the file.

Tip

Creating batch script files for renders can be a little intimidating, but it is really quite easy when you get used to it. The "Batch Maker" MEL script, by Yuya Sugiyama, creates BAT files for Windows with a nice GUI interface inside Maya and saves an executable .bat file in your project directory. This script can be found at `www.highend3d.com/maya/mel/`.

Previewing Renders

Here are some tips for getting the speediest of renders when previewing your scene.

When previewing, you should always preview at a lower resolution than your final output, or render only a small portion of the area you are working on. Some effects might not look correct when you render them at half resolution, but this is fine when you are simply trying to rough out your settings.

The defaults of Maya's IPR render are pretty much the way they should stay. You can do speed it, though, by rendering only select objects. You can do this several ways. For instance, you can use the option Render Globals, Image File Output, Renderable Objects, Render Active. This renders only the objects that you currently have selected. The renderer automatically uses any lights in the scene, so they do not have to be selected. A better way is to use your display layers to focus on the area you are currently tuning. Because the IPR renderer does work with ray tracing, you might need to just do a standard render.

Tip

There's a neat MEL script at www.highend3d.com/maya/mel/ called "Hide Til Render Partition Tools," by Matt Gidney. With it, you can assign objects that you will not need to see until the final render to be hidden while working in Maya.

Turn off any lights that do not affect the area you are focusing on. Again, you can simplify this by putting your lights in their own layers or sets.

Turn off all depth map shadows with the Render Globals, Render Options, Enable Depth Maps option by checking it off. To disable all ray-traced shadows, simply set Render Globals, Ray Tracing Quality, Shadows slider to 0 (see Figure 20.10).

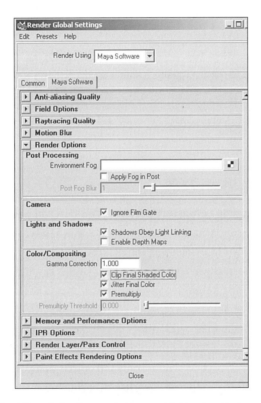

Figure 20.10 Disabling all depth map shadows with Render Options in Render Globals.

If you need to use depth map shadows, you can choose Reuse Existing Dmaps(s) from the pull-down menu in the Shadow Casting Lights attributes under Depth Map Shadow Attributes, Disk Based Dmaps. After the lights have rendered the shadow map once, the renderer will reuse the map until you tell the renderer otherwise.

Another obvious speed enhancement for preview is to use low or no antialiasing. The Preview Quality setting in Render Globals, Antialiasing Quality, Presets is fine for this. Turn off ray tracing, or set the values in Render Globals, Ray Tracing Quality to lower numbers.

Tip

Another handy MEL script, located at `www.highend3d.com/maya/mel/`, is "enableMaterials," by Bryan Ewert. enableMaterials temporarily disconnects the materials from their surfaces, forcing them to render a neutral gray.

As you create many versions of a render for review, it gets difficult to keep track of them. Therefore, it's helpful to "brand" or do a "burn in" in the lower area of the render that gives information about the name of the scene file and counts time code. This can be accomplished in several ways. For notes, you can create a simple text object in Maya, give it a white surface shader, and then group it to the camera. For time code, you can render a counting sequence in a program such as Adobe After Effects and use a camera plane.

Preflight Checklist

The following is a list of things you should check before you render your file. Some of them might be obvious, but it pays to be careful and get into the habit of checking these issues before saving the file.

- Check your Render Globals settings. These include Fine Name Prefix, Frame/Animation Ext; Start Frame, End Frame, By Frame; Frame Padding; Image Format; Renderable Objects; Camera; Channels; Resolution; Field Options; Antialiasing Quality; Ray Tracing Quality; Render Options; and Render Layer/Pass Control.

- Select all objects and check them with Window, Attribute Spread Sheet Editor, Render tab and Tessellation tab.

- Make sure your file paths are local if you are placing the scenes on a server for rendering, and ensure that any other linked file paths will not be broken before rendering.

You might want to reboot your computer before starting a long render and check to make sure that you will not run out of disk space.

Tip

Download the MEL script "Conform Textures," by Robin Escher, from `www.highend3d.com/maya/mel/`. It helps convert file paths for textures from being absolute to relative. This aids in renders that are cross-platform or when your drive mappings on different Windows systems vary.

Conducting Rendering Tests

In preparation for rendering, you need to test the scene files, for several reasons. First, doing so helps you make sure that any external files, such as textures or references, are still correctly linked. Even if it is 3 A.M. and you desperately want to go home and sleep, it is important to do this to ensure that your renders look right and that the process doesn't stop after the first frame. If this is going to be your full-time job, it should be possible for you to do this test by logging in remotely. It is even possible to have your render farm software send you emails or pages so that no matter where you are, you are informed about the status of your renders. However, some problems can be more difficult to solve remotely—believe me, it can be frustrating to try to talk to somebody who has never used UNIX through a command-line session over the phone.

Another reason to conduct rendering tests is so that you can time some frames and approximate the rendering time required. Because the time that a given frame takes to render can vary in a sequence, you need to render several frames and average their time in your estimate. Three frames are the minimum, unless it is a really short sequence. Your formula for estimating the render time is as follows:

(Frame1 time + Frame2 time + Frame3 time) / Total number of test frames (in this case, 3) × Number of frames in the sequence

The number of systems or CPUs that you have to render with then divides your total. So if X, Y, and Z are your test frames; T is the number of test frames; R is the number of computers in the render farm; and S is the total number of frames, the equation would be as follows:

$totalrendertime=((($X + $Y + $Z) / $T) * $S) / $R;

This formula is not perfect, but it will get you reasonably close to the actual required time. It is a good idea to make note of average times versus the complexity of any given scene to budget for future projects or to try to get a quote from a render farm service.

Rendering with Mental Ray

Many of the issues discussed previously about working efficiently with the Maya standard renderer also apply to Mental Ray for Maya—or any other renderer, for that matter. However, Mental Ray for Maya is capable of some effects that Maya's renderer is not, such as Radiosity and Final Gather. Although these effects are very impressive, both can be extremely time consuming. The docs included with the install are fairly extensive but do not include tutorials. I will be keeping a list of Mental Ray for Maya links with tutorials and a list of books about Mental Ray at `www.gmask.com/newriders/mr`.

This section covers the basics of rendering with Mental Ray for Maya.

Known Limitations

There have been many improvements since the release of Mental Ray for Maya plug-in, but there are still so many issues to deal with; we discuss them here. Since Version 1, support for the following has been added.

- Volumetric effects: light fog, environment fog, volume fog
- Maya's noise/volumeNoise shaders
- Image planes
- Ocean Shader
- Ramp Shader
- Volume Light
- Particle instancing
- New support for mental ray custom shaders

For future versions of the software, check the FAQ for Mental Ray in the `www.aliaswavefront.com` Maya support section, as well as the documentation for the actual Mental Ray for Maya plug-in that is included with its install, for further improvements and possible workarounds.

As of this writing, the following features are not supported in the Mental Ray for Maya plug-in:

- Maya's area lights
- Paint effects, shader/light glow, optical effects, 2D motion blur, and fur rendering
- Hardware rendering of particle systems
- Interactive photorealistic rendering (IPR)
- Field rendering
- Block Ordered Textures (BOT) files

The sections that follow give you workarounds to some of these limitations.

Area Lights

The Mental Ray for Maya plug-in also does not understand Maya's area lights. However, you can still create a Mental Ray area light by using a regular point light or spotlight and then going to Window, Attribute Editor, Mental Ray, Area Light and checking on Area Light. This creates an area light icon at the origin of the spotlight.

BOT Files

The Mental Ray for Maya plug-in does not support BOT files, but it does have memory-mapped textures. The imf_copy utility included with the installation turns your image file into a filtered .map file. Keep in mind that you will not be able to see these images in the Maya GUI, and it will report an error, but Mental Ray will still be capable of using the image. You can use a standard file format for placement and, when you are ready to render, create the memory-mapped textures. The syntax for this command is `imf_copy -p inimage outimage`.

Common Settings

The Mental Ray plug-in shares your basic settings for Maya. This makes it easy to switch between the two. Most of Maya's shader nodes are converted for use with Mental Ray. To take advantage of Mental Ray's special features, though, you will need to dig a little deeper. Lights, shaders, and Render Globals all have their own Mental Ray counterpart to ones that you are familiar with using for the Maya standard renderer.

To explore the many extra nodes mentalray provides you with, launch Maya and go to Hypershade, Create, Create Render Node and get a rather huge list of custom shader attributes (see Figure 20.11).

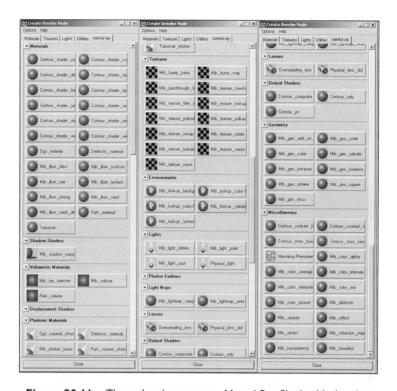

Figure 20.11   The rather long custom Mental Ray Shader Node tab.

Under Window, Rendering Editors, Mental Ray, you will find two other menus: Approximation Editor and Custom Text Editor.

The Approximation Editor is where you assign a surface its approximation. This is Mental Ray's equivalent of Maya's tessellation settings that it uses by default. The Mental Ray Text Editor is used for creating special Maya nodes to store information such as custom shaders that only Mental Ray can understand (see Figure 20.12).

You can select the Mental Ray renderer in two places: either in Window, Rendering Editors, Render View, or through the Render Global Setting (see Figure 20.13).

Figure 20.12 The Mental Ray Approximation Editor and Custom Text Editor.

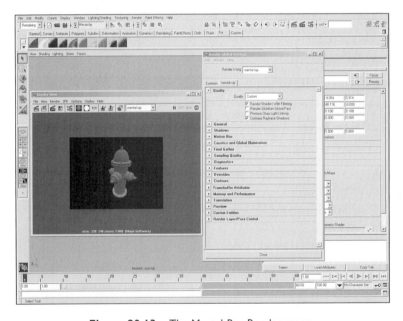

Figure 20.13 The Mental Ray Render menu.

Each light has its own Mental Ray section. Spotlights and point lights have several options, but area lights do not because they are not directly supported. However, you can turn either of the aforementioned lights into an area light (see Figure 20.14).

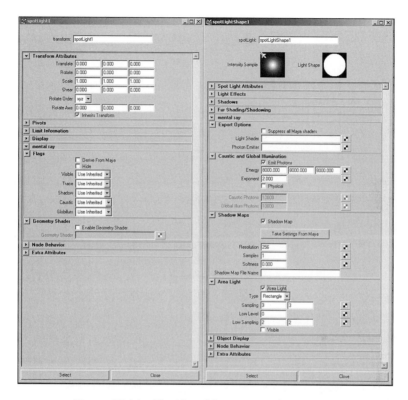

Figure 20.14   The Mental Ray section of a spotlight.

Each shader has its own Mental Ray section. To really make use of Mental Ray's capabilities, you will need to use these settings rather than derive them from Maya. However, you will need to use the Take Settings from Maya button so that you can tweak Ray Tracing settings (see Figure 20.15).

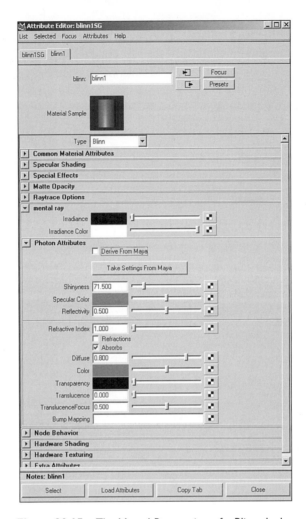

Figure 20.15   The Mental Ray section of a Blinn shader.

To use Mental Ray for rendering you must choose it in Window, Rendering editors, Render Globals choose, Render Using or in the IPR window. You can derive typical settings from Maya's Render Globals (see Figure 20.16). The defaults here are a good start. The main place you will need to focus on is in the area of quality; generally, you will want to use the Production preset.

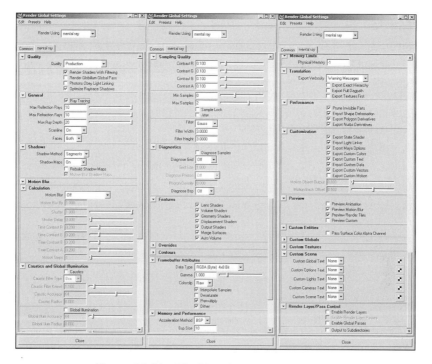

Figure 20.16   The Mental Ray Render Globals.

The Production preset is where you fine-tune all aspects of your render and enable the major effects, such as ray tracing, shadows, motion blur, caustics, global illumination, and Final Gather.

Ray Tracing

Mental Ray can selectively ray-trace an object in the scene because it is a hybrid renderer and is very fast. The settings here are very similar to Maya's.

Shadows

These settings give you some general choices for your shadows rendered with Mental Ray. If you turn on Motion Blur in the following section, notice that you can check on Motion Blur Shadows.

Motion Blur

Again, some of these settings look familiar. You have two choices for motion blur: Linear and Exact. Linear blurs in the direction that the object is moving, whereas Exact blurs the position of every moving vertex, taking into account surface deformations.

Caustics/Global Illumination

To use Caustics, Global Illumination, and Final Gather, you must have Ray Tracing enabled; to do so, check it on under Rendering in the Production settings. To enable Caustics in Mental Ray, simply check it on under Caustics. However, to take advantage of it, you need to access the settings of at least one light, shader, and object (see Figure 20.17).

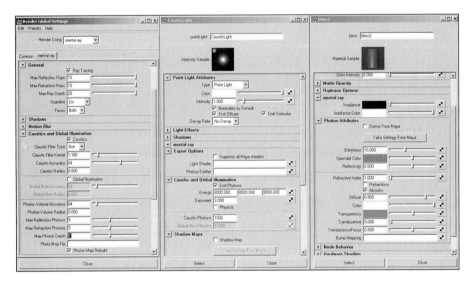

Figure 20.17   The Mental Ray Caustics settings.

Basically, you need a transparent surface and a light that is emitting caustic photons. Notice that when you use the Mental Ray settings for a shader, its preview icon does not represent those settings. You need to enable the surfaces that you want to cast or to receive caustic photons. You can do this in several ways. You can do it on a per-object basis by opening each object's Mental Ray attributes and selecting an option under the Caustic flag. You an enable it for all objects by going to the Overrides, Caustics/Global Illumination, Caustics Generating and Receiving pop-up menus in the Mental Ray Render Globals and making the appropriate choice. You can also go to the Window, Attribute Spread Sheet, All tab and select the options there under MI Caustic (see Figure 20.18).

Figure 20.18   Enabling objects to cast or receive caustics.

For fine-tuning your caustics, use the Mental Ray, Caustic and Global Illumination settings for your lights that emit photons, and the Production, Caustics/Global Illumination section of the Mental Ray Render Globals.

If your caustics are spotty, you need to emit more photons. Go to the Mental Ray, Caustics and Global Illumination settings of your lights, and increase the number of caustic photons. The more photons there are, the longer the render will take. A setting of 10,000 is a good on to start with; 100,000 seems medium, and 500,000 is very fine but will be noticeably slower. To increase or decrease the brightness of the photons, use the Energy levels. Increasing or decreasing these values does not impact render time.

To increase the quality—and, thus, the rendering time—you can lower the Production, Caustics/Global Illumination, Caustic Accuracy setting from its default of 64. If your caustics details are too soft, you can lower this value. If you want to soften them, you can either increase this value or increase the Caustic Radius setting. When you have finished tweaking your settings, check off Photon Map Rebuild. This allows the renderer to reuse previous photon maps and speeds up rendering on animation sequences. This is great for a fly-through in which there is no movement except for the camera.

I have included a little test caustics scene for you to experiment with. Just imagine what a glass fire hydrant would look like. Open the file MR_Caustics.mb from the accompanying CD, and play around with the settings previously mentioned. Figure 20.19 shows three test images with settings of 1000, 100,000, and 500,000 photons emitted from a single point light. There is a very big difference between the first image and the other two, but the middle and last picture are very similar except that the render with 500,000 photons took much longer. The lower number makes for an interesting disco ball effect and is fast for previewing caustic placement.

Figure 20.19   Caustic photon emissions of 1,000, 100,000, and 500,000.

To enable Global Illumination in Mental Ray, simply check it on under Caustics/Global Illumination. The setup is similar to enabling caustics in Maya: You must set the Mental Ray flags for the objects to Cast or Receive. Notice that the PhotonLight in the scene has an intensity of 0. You can use the light source, but with Global Illumination, you need to use it only to emit photons. The main difference is that if your image is spotty, you need to decrease Production, Caustics/Global Illumination, Global Illum Accuracy. Adding more photons increases render time. To have a nice, even illumination, you must raise the Global Illum Accuracy value. If your illumination becomes too mottled, it can have artifacts if you are rendering moving objects. To reduce the mottled illumination, you can reduce the number of photons; increase the Global Illum Accuracy value; increase Production, Caustics/Global Illumination, Max Photon Depth; and increase the Global Illum Radius, which softens the illumination from each photon.

The Global Illumination scene with the fire hydrant is on the CD for your experimentation. Open the file MR_GI.mb from the CD, and play around with the settings previously mentioned. Figure 20.20 shows the three test images of our GI test scene with settings of 1000, 100,000, and 500,000 photons emitted from a single point light. You will see a big difference between the first image and the other two, but the middle and last picture are very similar except that the image that used 500,000 photons took much longer to render. I made other adjustments as well for each number of photons. For the first image, the Global Illum Accuracy is 64, the Global Illum Radius is 0, and the Max Photon Depth is 10. For the second image, those settings are 512, 40, and 40. The last image has settings of 1024, 20, and 20.

Final Gather

Final Gather uses the ray tracer to send random rays whenever the original ray hits a surface. These random rays collect color from the surrounding surfaces and use them to compute the resulting color. This effectively turns surfaces into light sources.

Final Gather is enabled in the Production, Final Gather section of the Mental Ray Render Globals. Besides turning it on, you need to have at least one light—with a setting of 0 intensity—and you need to create some surfaces that emit ambient or diffuse color. You can apply a surfaceShader to any object, and it will become a bright light source. Other shaders such as Blinn will need Mental Ray, Irradiance set for it to emit color or bounce light.

Figure 20.20 Global Illumination with photon light emissions of 1000, 100,000, and 500,000.

The three main settings that you will need to tweak are Production, Final Gather, Final Gather Rays; Min Radius; and Max Radius. Final Gather Rays is the number of rays used in the calculation. You do not need too many rays, unless it is a really large scene. Depending on the scale of the scene, you might need to adjust the Min and Max Radius settings. These units are worldSpace, so if your scene is very small, you need only a small range. If you can narrow the range to only what you need. you can use fewer rays. The larger the scene is, the higher the Max will be; the finer the detail is, the smaller the Min and the longer the render will be.

As with Global Illumination, you can keep the Final Gather map by checking off the Final Gather Rebuild check box. This is great for architectural fly-throughs as long as no objects are animated.

Open the Final Gather test scene, called MR_FG.mb, from the accompanying CD. I tried three Production, Final Gather, Final Gather Rays settings of 1, 100, and 1000 (see Figure 20.21).

Figure 20.21   Final Gather Ray values *of* 1, 100, and 1000.

The director of our *Parking Spot* project has decided to use the Maya standard renderer and wants to be able to control as much of it as possible in the composite stage. The next section covers multipass rendering.

Multipass Rendering

Several reasons exist for using multipass rendering, the first of which is to give the compositor more control of each element. This is especially important when you are trying to wedge CG elements into a live-action background. You would also use multipass rendering if you needed to revise certain elements. Creating everything in layers gives you the option of rerendering only what is needed, rather than the whole scene. Another reason is that certain effects can be completed only in compositing, so it is absolutely a requirement to render that element as a separate pass.

Render Layers

Render layers are like display layers, except that they tell the renderer to render only what is in that layer. If multiple render layers are enabled, the renderer still saves a separate file for each of those render layers. A convenient feature of this is that the render can create directories for each sequence. Even if you are not rendering separate passes, you might want to use this feature just for the automatic output directory. In Render Globals, Render Layer/Pass Control, if you check on Enable Render Layers, you will get a list of render layers (see Figure 20.22).

There is always a defaultRenderLayer that contains all objects in the scene that were not assigned to their own render layer. If you then check on Output to Subdirectories, all passes will be put in their own folder. So, with two clicks in the Render Globals, you can have directories automatically made for your rendered files. Using this function can be really handy for projects because you can rerender the changes and they will replace the files in the hierarchy that you have already established. Then you can simply reload your composite project, and those files will be automatically replaced in composite. You might want to back up the old version, which you can do by duplicating the folder structure or by dragging the folders on your desktop to a backup hard drive and adding "_BAK" to the end of the name of the copied folder.

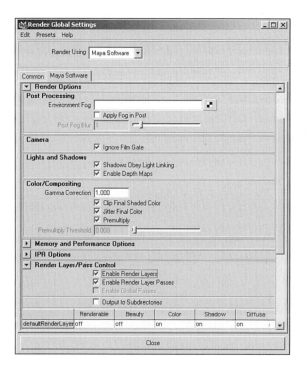

Figure 20.22   Render Layer/Pass Control options.

Tip

A setting that you will need to use when working with render layers is the Composite option, under Render Globals, Render Options. Two types of alpha or matte channels exist: premultiplied and straight. By default, Maya creates premultiplied alpha channels. If your background color in Maya is black and you composite the image over a white background, you will get a slight black halo because premultiplied mixes the background color with the color of your smooth edge. Checking on Composite with a Composite Threshold value of 0 creates a straight alpha channel by not antialiasing the edges of your image's color channel that border the alpha channel. This way, when you composite the image, the colors are mixed correctly with the new background color. However, if you view your image in fcheck, it might appear as if you forgot to turn on antialiasing because the edges will look jagged, but this is not the case.

One caveat to mention about render layers is that when you have shadows being cast from objects that are in two separate render layers, ray-traced shadows from the object that is not in the current render layer are ignored. Depth map shadows work perfectly, as do ray-traced reflections of objects that are not in the current render layer. If you need a ray-traced shadow in a render layer that does not contain the object casting the shadow, create a duplicate of that object and include it in the current render layer. Then turn off that object's primary visibility in the Render Stats section of the object's Attribute Editor.

Another reason to use render layers and to composite your elements is that the size of your scene might make rendering in one pass prohibitive. Some renderers are more efficient than others with memory, but even those that are more efficient are often subject to render passes. Anytime you have an element that does not move—especially entire backgrounds—they should not be rerendered for an entire scene. Scenes with thousands of characters are often rendered in passes with small groups of the characters, to conserve memory and to make the project more manageable.

Global Passes

Besides creating render layers, you can choose Enable Global Passes. Globals passes create separate renders for a beauty pass, a color pass, a specular pass, a diffuse pass, and a shadow pass.

A beauty pass is one that renders all the attributes listed, and it is the same as rendering without the global passes. Often you can render this pass and maybe only the specular or shadow pass if those areas are of particular concern, such as when you want to darken the shadows or brighten the highlights in post. The color pass involves only the color information, such as texture maps.

The specular pass renders just the specular parts of those shaders that have specular properties, such as Phong, Blinn, and Anisotropic shaders. This pass is rendered without a mask or alpha channel, so you must use your compositing software's compositing mode, often called screen. Screen takes only the light areas of your image and applies the image in a nonadditive manner. The effect is somewhat like that of an optical printing technique, in which two pieces of film are stacked and then the combination is printed.

The diffuse pass contains the diffuse and ambient shading of a surface, or the Diffuse Coif, if you are rendering a software particle type.

The shadow pass creates a mostly dark image (or whatever color your shadows are) with an alpha channel for compositing them. In previous versions of Mental Ray and in certain situations, you had to use a "background" shader to create a shadow pass, but now it is much easier.

Lighting Passes

Lighting passes are yet another type of pass that you can create, but lighting passes require a little more work from you because Maya does not handle this with a feature. The idea is that you can obtain further control over your lighting adjustments much faster in composite by rendering your scene or objects with only one light at a time and creating a separate pass for each light. When you create display layers and render layers, Maya does not ignore lights that are not in the current layer. All layers will be rendered with any lights that are enabled. You must manually turn off all but the lights that you want to render with and then save that as a separate scene file to be rendered.

Which Technique?

Obviously, using all of the aforementioned techniques could produce a horrendous number of layers to manage and composite, so you need to be selective. You can plan your approach using some of the following criteria.

Backgrounds and crowd scenes usually require a lot of memory to render, so they would benefit from render layers. Most scenes have a "hero" object or character that is in focus. Heroes demand good lighting and more attention to detail, so in this case using global passes (as well as lighting passes) would be a good idea. This gives you the maximum control over the quality of light and combination of shading. Finally, a scene that is matching a CG element to a live-action backplate often requires global passes and lighting passes. Given a particular effect, you might need to treat one object in a scene separately from the others; this is another case for render layers.

Tip

An issue that you might encounter when using render layers is how to handle objects that need to be rendered separately but intersect with one another. This can be handled with a "blackhole" shader. This is basically a surface shader with the Out Matte Opacity set to black. To cut out the section where the two objects intersect, you must duplicate one of the objects, assign the "blackhole" shader, and place it in the render layer of the other object. Typically, you move this object with the shader into the render layer of the object that will be placed in front of the other object in composite (see Figure 20.23).

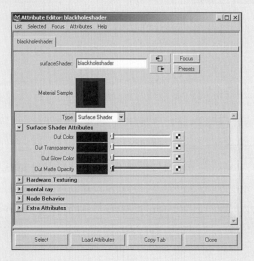

Figure 20.23   A surface shader set up to be a "blackhole" shader.

Exercise 20.1   Multipass Rendering

Begin by opening the RenderPasses.mb file from the accompanying CD. You will be rendering from several POVs, and the compositors want specific layers to help them tweak the scenes to the director's satisfaction.

One of the shots is a wide shot; the other is a close-up. In the wide shot, you want to be able to control the characters separately from the background, which might get replaced when a more complete background is done. For the close-ups, you want global passes and lighting passes; you need a mask only for the foreground to separate the background.

The first thing you have to do is separate the various elements into render layers. Fortunately, all the objects and characters in the scene are in their own groups already.

1. Simply select the objects and characters in the scene in Window, Outliner. Hold down Ctrl (or the equivalent, if you are not on Windows) and click the Fire_Hydrant, Jerk_Character, Dog_Character, Car, Pavement, Sidewalk, and Buildings1 (see Figure 20.24).

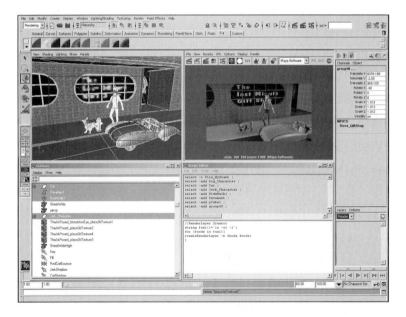

Figure 20.24   Selecting the major components for render layers in the scene.

2. You could have gone through one at a time, clicking each group and making a render layer for it, and then manually naming each. But you are in a big hurry. So, use the following short MEL script to place all these groups in a render layer named after the group:

```
//RenderLayer Creator

string $sel[]='ls -sl -l';

for ($node in $sel){
createRenderLayer -n $node $node;
 }
```

This script stores the selection in an array. You then step through the array and assign each entry—or, in this case, each group name—to a single variable. You use that variable with the createRenderlayer command and its On flag to name the layer after the group. Execute the script. The render layers automatically are created (see Figure 20.25).

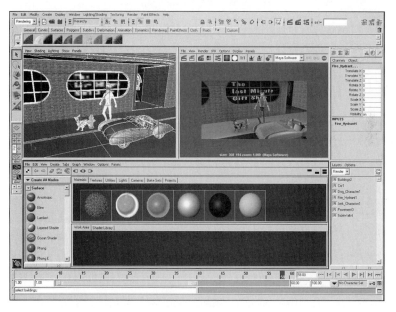

Figure 20.25   The new set of render layers after using a little MEL script.

Next, you need to enable ray tracing so that the Last Minute Gift Shop will reflect the action going on in front of it.

3. Enable ray tracing in Window, Rendering Editors, Render Globals (Maya Software) and check it on. You need a Reflections level of only 2; because you aren't using any ray-traced shadows, set Shadows to 0. Only a few of the surfaces in this scene need to be reflective. So, open Window, Rendering Editors, Hypershade and check that only the shaders for the door, window, car, and fire hydrant have any reflectivity (see Figure 20.26).

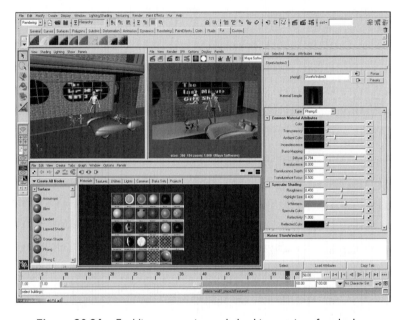

Figure 20.26   Enabling ray tracing and checking settings for shaders.

4. Go back to Render Globals, Render Layer/Pass Control. If they are not enabled, check on Enable Render Layers, Enable Render Passes, and Output to Subdirectories. Under the Renderable tab, type **off** into the field next to the defaultRenderLayer. For all the other layers, click the tab above all the columns and type **on**. Turn on Renderable, Beauty, Color, Shadow, Diffuse, and, to the far right, Specular. Also make sure that Composite is turned on in the render options (see Figure 20.27).

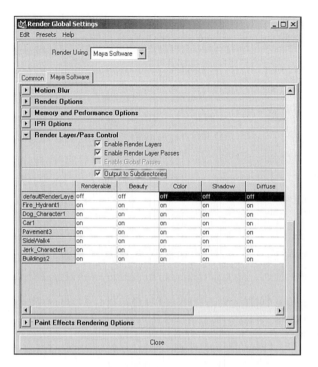

Figure 20.27   Render Layer/Pass Render globals.

You are almost ready to save the first scene file to be rendered, but first you must check the Image File Output preferences. There are several cameras in the scene, but you want to render only the StreetWideHigh camera.

5. Click the pop-up menu next to Camera and pick StreetWideHigh. If any other cameras say (renderable) next to them, you must go to the Output settings of each camera's attributes and check off Renderable so that they do not render more than one camera (see Figure 20.28).

6. Go to File, Save As, and save this scene as RenderPasses_WH.mb.

   You can now render this file. If you are planning to render several files using a render farm or a batch script, you should test the scene that you prepared by rendering some test frames. An easy way to render the scene with different parameters than what you saved in is to use the command-line options of the renderer. The result is a neat set of subdirectories ready to be dragged and dropped into your favorite compositing program (see Figure 20.29).

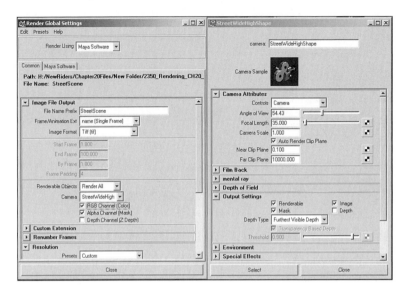

Figure 20.28 Setting Image File Output and Camera Output.

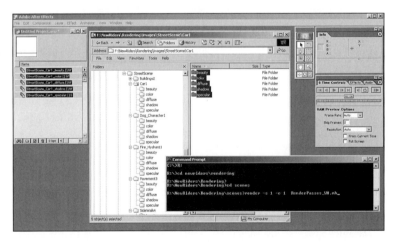

Figure 20.29 Dragging and dropping subdirectories of render passes into Adobe After Effects.

You will now prepare the close-up of The Jerk's face.

7. Open the RenderPasses_JCU.mb file from the accompanying CD. As you can see, most of the other characters and props are not visible in the scene, so you want to turn them off. Then you want to render several lighting passes—one for each major lighting source. Start by turning off the render layers for everything but Buildings2 and Jerk_Characters1 (see Figure 20.30).

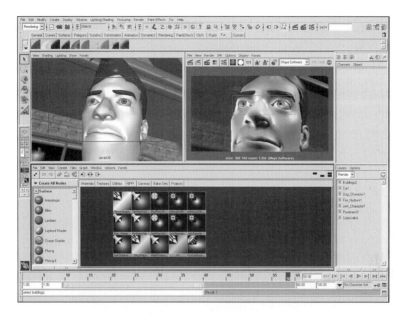

Figure 20.30   The close-up of The Jerk scene file.

Next you need to turn off the lights that we are not concerned with—in this case, BloomShape, CarShadowShape, DogFaceShape, DogFaceSpec, DogFaceSpec1, Dog_ShadowShape, and HydrantShadowShape.

8. Select the lights in the Hypershade window and then choose Display, Hide, Hide Selection to disable them.

9. Check your Render Globals and make sure that Enable Render Layers and Enable Render Layer Passes are turned on.

The first scene file that you are going to save is for the Building render layer. Because you do not need multilight passes of the building, you will save it as a separate render. Save the scene as RenderPasses_JCU_B.mb.

10. Turn off the Buildings2 render layer and then turn the Jerk_Character1 render layer back on. You can hide the WallShadowShape light as well at this point.

11. Now save a scene file for each of the following lights and name then as follows:

JerkFaceShape only enabled, save as RenderPasses_JCU_JF.mb

JerkFaceSpec and JerkFaceSpec1 only enabled, save as RenderPasses_JCU_JFS.mb

KeyShape and JerkShadowShape only enabled, save as RenderPasses_JCU_K.mb

Fill and JerkShadowShape only enabled, save as RenderPasses_JCU_F.mb

RedCarbounce only enabled, save as RenderPasses_JCU_RCB.mb

You are now ready to start your render engines and create a bunch of material for your compositor to work with. In this case, it might be more than necessary, but it is better to have more material than not enough. You might want to spend some time with these renders in a compositing package and see what you really need to gain more control.

Render Farms

A render farm has nothing to do with animals, nor should managing one be anything like trying to herd sheep. The following section should give you some heads-up details on how to plan to build or wrangle a render farm.

Essentially, a render farm is a collection of computers that have been networked and set up with appropriate software to automatically divide the tasks of an animation sequence among the participating computers. These computers are often referred to as render nodes or render clients, and they often take orders from the server or master computer.

Render Farm Services

There are not many render farm services to choose from, but it always pays to do a search online for new vendors. Shop around and contact each vender for a quote based on your project specs. You usually have a good chance of a volume discount.

Here are some to get you started:

- **EFX**—`http://ren3d.com/Pages/Services1.html`. For Windows, the cost is $0.75 per CPU hour for Maya; it's a flat rate of $91.50 per hour for Maya for the whole farm.

- **The Render Factory**—`www.therenderfactory.net`. Students get a 50% discount.

- **ResPower**—`www.respower.com/`. Cost is $0.75 per CPU hour for Maya.

Render Farm Software

You have many packages to choose from when it comes to render-farm software. If you use Windows, you can choose from the following; the Maya Dispatcher software does not run on Windows:

- **Maya Net Render v4.0, by Nitisara**—`www.highend3d.com/maya/tools/`. Free. *Best feature:* Supports Mental Ray. Supports Windows only.

- **Smedge 2, by Überware**—`www.uberware.net/smedge2`. $40 per client to allow renders on that machine (for 2–25 clients); $1000 for an unlimited number of render clients (26 or more). *Best feature:* Supports other commandline applications. Supports Windows only. Downloadable demo.

- **Muster, by Virtual Vertex**—`www.vvertex.com/`. $899 for Muster V 3.0, full-site unlimited client license for Maya; $45 for Muster V 3.0, multiplatform, single-client CPU for Maya. *Best feature:* Supports multiple platforms, including Mac OS X, Windows, Irix, and Linux. Downloadable demo.

- **Rush, by Greg Ercolano**—`www.3dsite.com/people/erco/rush/`. $150 per host, with volume discounts. *Best feature:* Can be scripted to support any renderer that has a command line. Supports Windows, Linux, Irix, and OS X.

- **Lemonpro, by Martin P. Heigan**—`www.ice.org/~martin/lemon_pro.html`. $180 per computer. Supports Windows only. Downloadable demo.

- **Rendermax, by Rendercorp**—`www.rendercorp.com`. $65 for each CPU; $995 unlimited special introductory price. *Best feature:* Uses Image Scatter, which allows the network to render chunks of a single image. Supports Windows, Irix, and Linux. Downloadable demo.

- **Spider, by Spider Networks, Inc.**—`www.stationx.com/`. $99 for each CPU (Freelance), or $6000 Unlimited (Freelance); Pro version. *Best features:* Supports image slicing and command-line scripting. Supports Windows only. Downloadable demo.

- **ButterflyNetRender v2.0, by Liquid Dream Solution**—`metanerd.bizland.com/`. Various licensing options. *Best Feature:* Split frames. Supports Windows, Linux, and OS X.

Picking the Platform

You might not have the option to pick your operating system when designing a render farm if your only hardware is what you currently have. In that case, it probably makes more sense to buy new systems that use the same OS that you already have. This will not only be convenient, but it will prevent incompatibilities that some aspects of your renders might have in a mixed-platform scenario.

A known issue with mixing platforms is big-endian versus little-endian floating-point math. You will encounter this issue when trying to set up your render farm when not all computers are the same platform. The same operation on one platform might not be rendered equally on another. In the case of particles, the differences can be very dramatic. If you are trying to mix big-endian and little-endian machines, you will have problems. Typically, servers such as those made by SGI are big-endian, meaning that they place the highest-level byte in the lowest or first position in a byte string. As you might expect, little endian follows the opposite scheme. There are actually middle-endian systems as well. This plays havoc with floating-point math over which particle systems are reliant. In this case, it is best to use render pools to separate those systems from one another and prevent renderings that have jumps between packets due to this incompatibility between platforms.

Windows is by far the dominant platform for 3D animation these days. However, its limitations with RAM are beginning to reveal it as a weak platform as projects grow larger and more memory hungry. Generally, you should not notice variances between rendering on AMD and rendering on Intel processors, as you would when rendering between an Intel and a MIPS processor.

Mac OS X is still a favorite of a wide range of graphic artists, and it can be a convenient platform in an environment that already has a large number of Macs set up. It is probably not the least expensive compared to hardware such as Intel and AMD systems.

Linux can run on a wide range of processors but is qualified to run on only certain versions of Red Hat Linux. Be sure to visit www.aliaswavefront.com and check the Qualification Charts for the correct version to use. In general, Linux is the least expensive and most powerful operating system you can choose. It has much better memory management than Windows, enables you to use much more than 2GB per process for rendering. For large networks, it is much easier to manage because it is UNIX.

Irix is still out there and kicking, but these systems are still far too expensive for render farms. Some of SGI's multiprocessor systems rival, if not beat, anything else on the market, but at a high cost.

Hardware

Several factors can influence how you build your machines for a render farm. You must find a balance with ease of use, space, cost, and scalability.

Many animators have developed a random collection of computers over the years as they bought new systems. The great thing is that most of the computers are perfectly happy to chug along and spit out a few frames or act as a file server. However, if you are building a farm, your budget and floor space probably are the main factors in your decision. If you're budget-minded and have a lot of space, you can get the old beige box with last year's CPU in it. These are cheap and plentiful. Those wire baker's shelves that are pretty common and cheap make excellent shelving for tower-style computers. Otherwise, if space is a concern and price is not as much of an issue, you can go rack-mount and try to cram as many units into a vertical tower as possible.

When it comes to buying your components, you have many options. Some companies specifically build systems for rendering, or you can get generic desktop systems. The more technically minded might want to build their own computers. Often you can get the same power as in a preconfigured system, but for much less money than a name brand. It always pays to shop around, but when checking out a new online vendor, be sure to find out what it charges for shipping, and make sure that you understand all policies before you place an order. Most places welcome your phone calls if you have questions. I also recommend that you buy most of your computer components from the same vendor. This not only saves you on time and shipping costs, but some vendors do more testing than others to make sure that the parts you are buying work together. A good online vendor generally makes it easy for you to assemble the correct parts using a configurator or online customization form.

For a machine that mainly will be used for rendering, you should have at least 512MB of RAM and a 10–20GB hard drive installed in it. Get whatever processor makes the most sense for your budget, and consider multiprocessor machines. When you have two or more CPUs, your frames will not only render faster, but you also will have fewer systems to maintain. You need only minimal 8MB 24-bit color video cards. These days, some motherboards come with a video card of this level built in.

10/100BaseT, Gigabit, Firewire

Most computers these days come with 10/100BaseT Ethernet ports. Many motherboards designed today even have them built in as a standard feature. For the small render farm of fewer than eight computers, 100BaseT probably will be fast enough for your projects.

Gigabit Ethernet has come down in price significantly in the past few years, and Apples are starting to come with it as a standard. If your farm is larger and uses many shared resources, such as animated texture files and cached particle systems, it might make sense for you to upgrade to Gigabit Ethernet. Unfortunately, multiport Gigabit switches are still fairly expensive.

Firewire networking is another possibility because it provides as much speed as Gigabit and does not require a hub or switch. It is fairly inexpensive and also works with the PC and the Mac. The main issue is that it is a daisy-chain system might limit the number of computers that can be in the chain. This is an inexpensive way to get a fast network, but it's still an experimental one.

Switches and Hubs

If you have more than one computer, you will undoubtedly have a hub to connect your computers. When you decide to build a render farm, you will need to get a switch. A switch is like a hub, except that it generally has a higher internal bandwidth and is designed to manage the bandwidth more efficiently than a hub. Network rendering can require a great amount of bandwidth and activity. If you will start out with 8 computers, you should go ahead and buy a 16-port switch and give yourself room to grow. Stacking multiple switches creates a bottleneck unless they are especially designed to allow higher-bandwidth communications between switches such as fiber links.

Uninterrupted Power Supply

Every computer animator should have a UPS for the computer and most peripherals. A good number of the buildings and cities I have worked in have experienced serious power problems or voltage underage and brownouts. You need proper protection to prevent hardware from being fried or from work being lost. You most likely have a surge-protected power strip, but these wear out with no warning and do not prevent hardware failure.

Your typical UPS has a volt amps (VA) rating. The UPS provides the VA for a variable number of minutes, depending on the model. You need enough time to either manually shut down your computers or have the proper software and hardware installed for the computers to shut down automatically if there is a power outage.

To figure out how many VAs you need, list the equipment to be protected by writing down their names and, next to them, their VA rating. Some products list the power requirements as watts; multiply watts by 1.4 to get VA. If the power requirements are listed in amps, multiply by 120. Total these figures, and you will have the minimum VA that your UPS must cover.

If you have added internal hard drives to your computers or built them yourself, you must find the VA rating for each component and add them. Your typical IDE HD uses less than 28 VA when in use; large CRT computer monitors might use as much as 360 VA, and LCD monitors use only approximately 56 VA. More than 1600 AMD CPUs use around 90 VA, and Intel 733mHz Itanium 64-bit CPUs use 164 VA. Here is an example worksheet for calculating your minimum VA requirements for a UPS (see Figure 20.31).

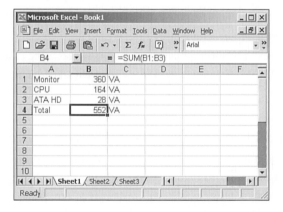

Figure 20.31   Example worksheet for calculating minimum VA requirements for a UPS.

When you are creating a render farm, your requirements can become large overall, but the computers built for a render farm should not need as many peripherals or a monitor, and they require fewer VAs per computer than a single desktop system.

KVM stands for keyboard, video, and mouse. These boxes come in a wide range of flavors and are essential for managing your render farm from a central location. You do not need to buy a monitor for every computer in your farm. Even if you can log into these machines remotely to issue commands, you will need to be able to get to their desktops if there are problems. Some KVMs enable you to monitor hundreds of computers by chaining the individual units together. Most KVMs enable you to switch between systems using special keyboard commands, or you can press a button on the box.

Farm Layouts

The layout for a render farm varies depending on the size of the network.

Small Network

For a small network, most likely you have one switch and one system designated as the server where project files and frames are stored.

Medium or High-Traffic Network

On a slightly larger network or one that is using a large number of resources, you might need to alter your configuration so that each computer is reading those files off their local hard drive. Most render farm software does not manage distributing the project files to all the render clients. This is when use of MEL or customized rendering software becomes necessary. By placing the source files for the render on each render client's local drive, little, if any, bandwidth will be used on the network, but then you must manage files on a certain number of computers—and doing that manually is not fun. Distributing those files to each computer also could take hours.

Massive Network

A massive network might have hundreds of computers to manage on any given render. At this level, you need customizable software. In this environment, you might need to send packets of frames to be divided by a cluster of computers that have their own server and switch. All the switches are connected to a master where the distribution of frames is controlled. Project files are copied to each cluster's file server. Another option is to have each cluster up-linked to the master server via high-speed connections so that the combined data transfer from each cluster does not max out.

Internet Network

It is also possible to have any number of computers on the Internet rendering. But unless all of your rendering nodes have fast connections to the Internet, projects with large source files will bring the process to a halt. It is certainly convenient to take advantage of the Internet to manage and monitor your render farm when you are not on the premises.

Preparing for Final Output

Rendering can take a lot of space, especially when you are creating a lot of render passes. Fortunately, hard drives are cheap these days. IDE drives are great for large capacity, and even though you can still get a lot of mileage these days with CD-ROMs, just buying more hard drives makes the most sense. Most cases these days still have a 5-inch drive bay that is perfect for removable drive sleds. When you fill up one drive, you can just put another one in. Always make backup copies of your project files and deliverables: Disaster usually strikes in the final hours of a project when you need problems the least.

Video

Various standards exist for video. The ones most familiar are NTSC, PAL, and SECAM. These formats use fields to refresh the television screen. Different formats also use different frame rates. NTSC uses 29.97fps, while PAL and SECAM uses 25fps. These standards have their own resolutions as well. NTSC is a maximum of 720×486; while PAL and SECAM have a maximum of 720×576.

The main issue here when discussing fields is reproduction of motion. Certain types of motion suffer when not rendered using fields. Horizontal movement is typically the most noticeable when not rendered with fields; it exhibits itself as a hurky, jerky kind of movement. Titles are prone to this problem. Film, however, smoothes this type of movement with motion blur. In some cases in film, it is desirable to have very crisp frames with no motion blur. This creates a very jarring type of movement that is great for horror and music videos.

You have the option to render with fields in Maya, but first you must find out what the Field Dominance is for the hardware that you are using to output the video. Then you set it accordingly in Render Globals, Field Options. However, if you got them mixed, a quick fix is to open the sequence in a compositing program and nudge the file up or down 1 pixel; this reverses the field dominance.

High Definition and Digital Video

Other formats, such as those for HD and DV, can use what is called progressive scanning. This means that they can display a full frame without using fields. This is more like what you see when you see a film projected on a screen.

These days, practically any computer is capable of outputting real-time full-frame video. If your computer is not equipped for this out of the box, it is very inexpensive to buy a composite video card for output to low-end devices such as VHS decks.

For professional output, the cost to get uncompressed digital output is still rather expensive, so it might not be practical for freelancers, festival contestants, and small shops to own a digital beta deck or even a beta-sp deck. Your option at this point is to find your local post-production house. Most editorial houses these days have Avid systems or some other desktop-based nonlinear editing system, making it easy to import your animation as a QuickTime, AVI, or image sequence. CD-ROM is a great format for delivery of small projects. For larger projects, many facilities are willing to connect your drive to their system. Remember to keep backups of your work and to never send your original or your only copy.

Film

Outputting to film is not as easy to do as outputting to video because you do not really know exactly what it will look like until it has been printed to film. For one thing, film can be color-timed to control color and density. You will want to do a test by preparing a few frames from each scene and having them printed. If you are intercutting footage with nonprocessed live-action footage, it will help to have the director of photography available to examine the test, to aid in matching them back to the original film.

If you are integrating CG with filmed live action and you are getting scans from the negative, you do not want to process the live-action plate if it will be matched back to another piece of footage. In any case, the scan should use a dynamic range in which the darkest blacks and brightest whites are not clipped when scanned to a bitmap format. Most likely this will be a 16-bit–per-channel Cineon file if you are using a Kodak film scanner.

Summary

Rendering is almost always rushed because it is the last process in the creation of animation. Some of the suggestions given here might seem like more work than is necessary to render an animation. However, if you work in a large production or one that is subject to client review, you will find that maximizing your flexibility by using rendering passes will save you huge amounts of time when it comes to revisions. Plus, many effects and photorealistic lighting cannot always be achieved by rendering in one pass.

Part V

Appendix

A Intermediate and Advanced MEL   833

Appendix A

Intermediate and Advanced MEL

By Erick Miller

This appendix is meant for the technical users of Maya, who might already have discovered the power of using MEL and would like to expand upon that power even further. Writing scripts and using Maya with MEL in a production environment can require versatility on the part of the artist, and the more advanced tricks that you have up your sleeve, the better. This appendix is meant to further sharpen your already rich knowledge of Maya and MEL. Following the MEL topics is a special section on using Maya's application programming interface (API) to write a custom deformer node in C++.

The following is covered in this appendix:

- Script nodes
- `scriptJobs`
- Ways to launch executables and get data
- Error handling
- Distributed jobs: Scripting and error logging
- Intro to the API: Writing a deformer

What Is a Script Node?

Have you ever wondered how Maya remembers your UI settings on a per-file basis? When you open one file, the Multilister might load, and when you open another file, the Graph Editor might be open. Maya accomplishes this by storing this information in MEL, inside a completely editable node called a script node. A script node is actually a type of expression, although it is not an expression because it is not evaluated at every frame. Instead, a script node can be evaluated as soon as you open the file that contains it. This gives you an easy and safe way to embed whatever MEL code your heart desires directly into the file that the code is appropriate to execute with. This works especially well for character UI scripts.

A character UI is the type of script that you simply don't want to have to explain to the user: how to source it, where to source it from, how to execute the procedure, how to keep the script versions updated, and so on. It's all a really messy hassle and can be completely solved by embedding your supercool character UI directly into a script node.

Creating and Using a Script Node

You can create a script node interactively from within the Script Editor. You can also create a script node from within a MEL procedure using the `scriptNode` MEL command, which can be found in the MEL command documentation. Figure A.1 shows how to access, view, and edit script nodes from within Maya's UI.

Say that you want to have a UI that has slider bars as well as a Set Key button for a character's special attributes. You also want this code to load automatically when the scene loads, and you want to be able to save a shelf button of your character's poses to go back to while animating.

The following simple tutorial shows you how to do just that: create a script node and embed some simple customized UI code into your scene.

Figure A.1   The Expression Editor, where you can view
and edit all the script nodes currently in your file.

Exercise A.1   Creating a Script Node

1. First, load the scene myLocatorWithAttrs_begin.mb from the Appendix A folder on the CD that accompanies this book.

2. Then go to Window, Animation Editors, Expression Editor. Inside the Expression Editor, go to the menu command Select Filter, By Script Node Name.

You should see a couple script nodes, sceneConfigurationScriptNode and uiConfigurationScriptNode. These two nodes are automatically created and updated by Maya when you save your scene, and they are in charge of saving and setting your UI preferences so that the next time you open your file, you can pick right back up where you left off. Feel free to explore through the uiConfiguration script node: It is very large and tells you a lot about how Maya's UI preferences are built and saved.

continues

Now that you have quickly looked over these nodes, it's time to create your own. You should never add to the already existing default script nodes because Maya will automatically overwrite these nodes and your additions will be lost the next time the scene is saved.

3. Click the New Script Node button and type a name for your new node in the Script Node Name text field. I called the script node CustomEmbeddedUI, but the name is pretty much irrelevant, as long as it is a name that you feel is suitable.

4. Next, open the file customControlWindow.mel from the accompanying CD into your favorite text editor. Copy/paste (by right-clicking or using Ctrl+c and Ctrl+v) the following code into the script node window in the Expression Editor:

```
global proc customControlWindow()
{
    string $selected[] = `ls -sl`;
    if ( !`size($selected)` ){
        return;
    }
    if(`window -ex custCntrlWin`){ deleteUI custCntrlWin; }
//    else if(`windowPref -ex custCntrlWin`){ windowPref -r custCntrlWin; }
    window
        -wh 550 650
        -title ("Custom Attribute Control Window")
        -s 1 custCntrlWin;
    scrollLayout;
    columnLayout;
    int $count = 0;
    for ($node in $selected)
    {
        string $keyableAttrs[] = `listAttr -r -w -k -u -v -m -s $node`;
        if ( !`size($keyableAttrs)` ){
            continue;
        }
        string $fl = `frameLayout
                    -label ("Custom Controls::"+$node )
                    -collapsable true
                    -cl true
                    -labelAlign "top"
                    -borderStyle "in"`;
        if ( !$count ){ frameLayout -e -cl false $fl; $count++; }
        rowColumnLayout
            -nc 2
            -columnWidth 1 450
            -columnWidth 2 60;
```

```
                        button -label ("Select Node: "+$node) -c
                        ➥("select -r "+$node+";");
                        button -label "Key All " -c ("select -r "+$node+";
                        ➥SetKey;");
                for ($attr in $keyableAttrs)
                {
                        string $buffer[];
                        $numTokens = `tokenize ($node +"."+$attr) "." $buffer`;
                        if ( $numTokens <= 2 )
                        {
                                attrFieldSliderGrp
                                        -at ($node +"."+$attr);
                                button
                                        -label ("Set Key")
                                        -c ("setKeyframe \""+$node +"."+$attr+"\"");
                        }
                }
                setParent ..;
                        setParent ..;
        }
        rowColumnLayout
                -nc 2
                -columnWidth 1 450
                -columnWidth 2 60;
        button
        -h 50
        -label "Save Selected Node's \"setAttr\" Commands to a Shelf Button."
        -c ("saveSelectedNodeAttrsToShelf
        ➥( `textField -q -tx "+$node +"_custCntrlWin` );");
        textField ($node +"_custCntrlWin");
        setParent ..;
                setParent ..;
        showWindow;
}


global proc string saveSelectedNodeAttrsToShelf(string $label)
{
        string $selected[] = `ls -sl`;
        if ( !`size($selected)` ){
warning "Nothing is currently selected. No shelf button created, or action
➥taken.";
                return "Nothing is currently selected. No shelf button created,
                ➥or action taken.";
        }
        string $safeShelfCommand;
        for ($node in $selected)
        {
                string $keyableAttrs[] = `listAttr -r -w -k -u -v -m -s $node`;
                if ( !`size($keyableAttrs)` ){
                        continue;
```

```
        }
        for ($attr in $keyableAttrs)
        {
                string $value = string ( `getAttr ($node+"."+$attr)` );
                $safeShelfCommand = ("catch (`setAttr \""+$node
            ➥ +"."+$attr+"\" "+$value+"`);\n")+$safeShelfCommand;
        }
    }
    print "\n\n\n";
    print "// Command to put in shelf: \n\n";
    print $safeShelfCommand;
    print "\n";
    global string $gShelfTopLevel;
    if (`tabLayout -exists $gShelfTopLevel`)
    {
        if ($label == ""){ $label = "ATTR";  }
        shelfButton
                -parent ($gShelfTopLevel + "|" + `tabLayout -q -st
                ➥$gShelfTopLevel`)
                -enableCommandRepeat 1
                -enable 1
                -width 34
                -height 34
                -manage 1
                -visible 1
                -annotation ("Will set attributes into a stored pose for the
                ➥previously selected nodes (for all keyable attributes)." )
                -label $label
                -iol $label
                -image1 "menuIconCharacters.xpm"
                -style "iconOnly"
                -command $safeShelfCommand;
    }
    else
    {
        error "You need a visible shelf for this work, dude!  Show your
        ➥shelf, man!";
    }
    return $safeShelfCommand;
}
```

This code builds a nice little custom UI for any keyable attributes on all nodes selected at the time the script is called. I wrote it to be generic enough to use on basically any selected node with keyable numeric attributes so that it could be reused.

The function `customControlWindow()` basically just loops over the currently selected nodes. For each selected node with keyable attributes, it loops again over the attributes and builds a slider and button for each attribute. The function `saveSelectedNodeAttrsToShelf` simply loops over all the keyable attributes in the currently selected nodes and builds a MEL command string to `setAttr` for those attribute values. Then it puts the string that it built into a shelf button on your currently visible Maya shelf.

5. After you have copied the code into the Expression Editor's Script text field, hit the Create button.

6. Next, go to the Execute On drop-down enumeration menu. Currently it is set to Demand. Click it and change it to GUI Open/Close (see Figure A.2).

This causes the code that you just put into the Script field to execute as soon as the file loads. In this case, so far you have only sourced the script when the file loads.

Figure A.2   The Expression Editor script node's Execute On options, which enable you to define exactly when the code will get executed.

7. Next, at the very end of the script node, after all the UI code, type the following into the Script text field in the Expression Editor and click the Edit button:

```
select -r"myLocatorWithAttributes";
evalDeferred "customControlWindow()";
```

If you are guessing that this will select the locator as soon as the file is loaded and then launch the UI code, you are correct! So, you can source, load, and execute completely file-specific code when the file loads.

Tip

What if you don't want to write, or have time to write, your own supercustom character UI?

If you don't do character UIs simply because you think it is a waste of time to write all this code that will never be used again, you are actually pretty wise! At the same time, I recommend using character UIs for any characters that have multiple controls because it makes the animator's job much easier. So how do you get around this dilemma and embed a character UI without having to write one? Simple! Feel completely free to use mine! That's what I wrote it for.

If you don't want to use mine, there are also several other great character UIs out there, free, totally customizable, and available for download. They mostly have different functionality—some have much more functionality than the simple (but very reusable) one included here. No matter what, though, you can always embed one into your file in a script node. There is a general rule out there when it comes to writing code: Don't reinvent the wheel! If someone else already wrote it, you have a much better starting place by using what is already out there than trying to start all over yourself (of course, unless what is already out there is really poorly implemented—but the only way you'll find that out is by checking it out first). If I don't use my own UI, I often use a script called attributeCollection.mel, which can be downloaded for free directly from Alias|Wavefront's free MEL script downloads at its web site. This is a powerful UI script that can be embedded as an integrated scriptedPanel, is fully customizable, and works quite nicely. There is nothing wrong with writing your own character GUI. But often your time is much better spent doing real work (such as writing real algorithms and solving real problems with your code) than it is writing flashy UIs—although I love flashy UIs and cool custom icons as much as the next guy!

The animators will really appreciate a nice, consistent, embedded UI, especially if they don't have to do any extra work and it just loads automatically. In fact, they probably won't even realize that it is custom and will often just think it is automatically built into Maya (until they get into a different file and whine about where their favorite UI went!).

Now we'll move on to the last step necessary to make the UI load automatically whenever the appropriate nodes are selected. For this we will use something called a `scriptJob`.

Combining *scriptJobs* with Script Nodes

A `scriptJob` is a job you can run from MEL that watches predetermined events or conditions and then reacts to those events or conditions by triggering the code that you tell it to trigger. It is a job that attaches to your instance of Maya while you have it open, and it has a unique job ID so that you can kill it without having to restart Maya. I strongly suggest reading the MEL command reference documentation for `scriptJob` because the list of predefined conditions and events is much too long to list. Here are a few really useful examples of `scriptJob`:

```
scriptJob -event "SelectionChanged" "doIt";

scriptJob -conditionTrue "SomethingSelected" "doIt"`;

scriptJob -attributeChange "object.attribute" "doIt";
```

Whenever the event or condition occurs, the fictional function `doIt` is executed. Maya has a large list of events and conditions that can easily be found in the online documentation for the MEL command `scriptJob`:

Note

I am using `doIt` as a fictional function that I can launch to exemplify things. `doIt` is the triggered procedure.

In the next exercise, you will create a simple `scriptJob` to launch your UI code based on the `SelectionChanged` event.

Exercise A.2   Launching the UI Code

You want to launch the UI based on a certain group of predefined objects in a scene. Usually the animators are animating a certain group of objects/locators or character icons. Because these are the only objects that you want the UI to get displayed for, you need to filter through your selection list and determine whether the currently selected object matches one of the preselected objects. When you have a way of differentiating the objects that you want to draw the UI for, you can simply start a scriptJob that is based on the SelectionChanged event. Whenever the selection changes, this code gets executed. The final result is that you get a UI that pops up into display only when the selection changes, and it contains the currently selected object only if the currently selected object is one of the objects on the list.

Here is how you will do it:

1. First, make sure you are still using the file from the previous exercise, myLocatorWithAttrs_begin.mb. Open the Expression Editor. Make sure you have all the code from the last exercise in your script node expression and that the Expression Editor's script node window Execute On drop-down enumeration menu is currently set to GUI Open/Close.

2. Next, delete the following old line of code from your script node; you no longer need it after this next step to get the UI to automatically load:

```
evalDeferred "customControlWindow()";
```

3. Add the following code (copy and paste it from the customControl Window.mel file found on the accompanying CD) in front of the code that is already in your existing `CustomEmbeddedUI` code from the last exercise:

```
int $jobNum = 'scriptJob -ct "SomethingSelected"
"objFilterCustomUiCode()"';
```

Note

You must type this first line (`int $jobNum = ...;`) manually because it is not a part of the customControl Window.mel file. This is because this line actually starts your script job for you the next time the file is opened.

```
global proc objFilterCustomUiCode()
{
    if(`window -ex custCntrlWin`){ return; }
    string $predefinedObjects[] = { "myLocatorWithAttributes" };
    string $selected[] = `ls -sl -dag`;
    if ( !`size($selected)` ){
        return;
    }
    int $foundMatch = 0;
    for ($obj in $selected)
    {
        for ($predefinedObj in $predefinedObjects)
        {
            if ($predefinedObj == $obj){
                $foundMatch = 1;
                break;
            }
        }
        if ( $foundMatch ){
            customControlWindow();
```

```
        return;
    }
  }
}
```

The previous code simply loops through the currently selected objects and compares them against a list of predefined objects—in this case, the only predefined object is `myLocatorWithAttributes`. If a match is found, the function `customControlWindow()` is called, which creates the custom UI window. The last line is the actual declaration of the script job. The `scriptJob` command returns an integer number that will be used to kill the job later, so it is important to save this data into a variable.

4. Next, click the Script radio button labeled After. This switches the Script text box to make it blank. Don't worry—you have not just lost all of your code; it is still there. You have merely switched modes. Any code that you paste into this section will be clean-up code that basically should do anything that needs to happen immediately after the scene is closed. You could add a reminder message at the end here, reminding the user to check his file into a version-control system. Basically, any code that you want to execute after the file is closed should go here. You could even add code that checks the file into a database for the user automatically. In this case, you will simply do clean-up and kill the `scriptJob` that you launched in the previous code so that you do not have random or duplicate `scriptJobs` running, in case the user reopens the file during the same session of Maya.

5. Write the following in the Expression Editor, with its mode set to After:

```
scriptJob -kill $jobNum -force;
```

That's it. You should now have a `scriptJob` that will launch an event-based trigger that loads a UI element only for the objects that you specify, and that will clean up after itself when the file closes. A finished version of this file is included on the CD, called myLocatorWithAttrs_finished.mb.

Note

For `scriptJobs` to work, you must have Execute Script Nodes in your File, Open Scene options box checked (see Figure A.3). This is the default in Maya, but in case it has been changed, your embedded script will not execute when a scene with script nodes is loaded.

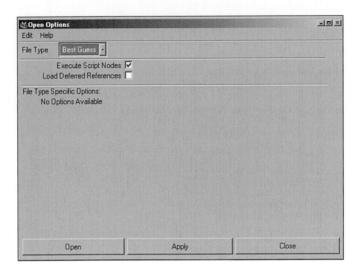

Figure A.3 Execute Script Nodes checked in the File, Open options box, for script nodes to execute when the file is opened.

Launching an Executable and Returning Its Output

Now that we are finished with script nodes, let's talk about other ways of using Maya to interact with your computing environment. Often you will find that you need to launch an external tool or executable from within Maya (such as Perl or another renderer). Maya has a system command that will do this, but, unfortunately, the system command returns immediately back into the script and does not always wait for the output to be returned from the system process that it launched (depending, of course, on the executable you are launching). Occasionally, this might be desired behavior. If it is, just use the system optionally with the start command. In most cases, though, you need to send information to the executable and then have information returned. This process of guaranteeing input/output can be achieved in MEL by simply using a pipe to open the executable. The only behavior that the pipe can have is to wait for the output before proceeding. Because this is exactly the behavior we want, our problem is solved with the following code:

```
//
// Launches an executable and pipes any output returned into
// an array of strings. Any arguments to the exe should be
// contained (and escaped) in the $exe argument variable
// from a procedure that would call this procedure:
//
global proc string[] processOutStream( string $exe )
{
     // create a pipe to the passed-in file
int $standardOutput = popen( $exe, "r" );
     string $catchOutput[];
     // loop over and add each line to the next element
     // of an array, until "end of file" is true.
     while ( !feof( $standardOutput ) )
     {
          $catchOutput[size( $catchOutput )] =
fgetline( $standardOutput );
     }
     // close the pipe:
     pclose( $standardOutput );
     // return the array of data:
     return ( $catchOutput );
}
```

Here is an example of calling the previous function, along with what the output of the program returns:

```
// This is a standard program that ships with Maya
// to do the post-process blurring after rendering:

string $output[] = processOutStream( "blur2d"  );

//Result (stored in the array variable $output):

Usage: blur2d [-l blur_length] [-s blur_sharpness]
[-m smooth_value] [-r smoothColor] [-n start end step]
[-f input_file_name] ... use blur2d -h for more help
```

Error Handling

Error handling is the task of constantly checking your code for failure, unwanted behaviors, or input/output errors. If a failure occurs, being able to recognize it and react to it in some kind of controlled or predetermined manner is the best way to handle a "runtime" error (other than simply exiting with no trace that an error occurred).

A runtime error is an error that is outside the initial logic of the programmer and that occurs because of some unanticipated change or combination of unknown circumstances. Often runtime errors are completely avoidable in MEL because all memory allocation and garbage collection is done by Maya's command interpreter. Nonetheless, errors often occur, and when they do, it's good to be prepared.

Sometimes errors in MEL are actually okay; other times they are not. Sometimes you know that there will be an error in the code that you execute because the nature of the code does something that results in an error in the interpreter but not a logic error in your actual code. The catch MEL command is perfect for this very instance, as well as for catching any real error. It gives you, the programmer, the opportunity to react to the error, as well as the option of immediately exiting from the code or continuing if the error will not affect the outcome of the code in an incorrect fashion.

Error-handling code is added on top of your script's algorithm, usually after the main code is running smoothly and any logic bugs have been tracked and removed. You can write error-handling code at the same time you are writing the main functions of your code. But you should do so only if you are very comfortable with the code you are writing and can defiantly plow right through it with no questions about how it will work at the end. Otherwise, error-handling code should be added after the first version of the script is already working and you have someone else on your team give it a real test for the very first time (ideally outside a production, of course). Any code that is truly "production-worthy" is bound to contain a fair deal of error-handling code.

Error handling is usually done line by line, and it can become quite tedious and make your code much more difficult to read than most people would prefer. Usually error handling is done with a simple if( ) condition, which checks whether an error, or unwanted circumstance, occurred. The more complex the logic is, most likely the more complex your error handling is. Therefore, in any real code, you could potentially have one third of it as only error-handling code. But this would guarantee that when some clueless user sat down to use your script and did something that the script was never designed to do, you will never have to apologize because the script will tell him what he did wrong and will exit (or react accordingly to avoid the error) before the real error ever occurs. Some people like to call this "bulletproofing" your code.

Here is an example of a script that I wrote, called complimentaryLightShadow.mel, that incorporates an acceptable amount of error handling. To make it production-safe code, it does a moderate amount of common error checking, including checking for selections, checking for correct nodeTypes, checking attribute connections, keeping track of errors, and then returning a simple code as well as a message based on the status. All is common to error handling.

Here is a description of what the script actually does:

A basic principal of painting/illustration is to use subtle complementary color within a light's shadow to emphasize deep contrast and give a richer color value to the entire painting so that the shadows don't look dull. This script creates a complementary shadow color node network, derived from your light's color value. The node network uses an editable curve to remap color into complementary hues based on the light's color. It updates as you change your light's color and creates extra attributes for you to modify the shadow's saturation (amount of color) and value (lightness/darkness) according to the mood of the final lighting. This script was an idea/request from two colleagues, Aaron and Bec.

This script can be found and tested on the included CD (complimentary LightShadow.mel) as well:

```
global proc int complimentaryLightShadow()
{
     int $returnStat = 0;
//
// Save initial selection...
//
     string $selected[] = `ls -sl`;
     string $lights[];
//
// Get all possible selected light shape nodes:
//
     $lights = `ls -sl -lt`;
     string $shapeBuffer[] =
`listRelatives(eval("ls -tr -o -sl"))`;
     select -cl;
     for ( $lightShape in $lights ){ select -add $lightShape; }
     for ($shape in $shapeBuffer){ select -add $shape; }
     $lights = `ls -sl -lt`;
//
// If no lights are selected, use all lights in scene:
//
     if ( !`size ($lights)` ){
          $lights = `ls -lt`;
     }
//
// Node connections inside the following loop
// simply convert RGB to HSV, and uses the
// complementary Hue, derived from shifting
// the color space (with a simple curve
// editable in Graph Editor). It then converts
```

```
// color back with HSV to RGB, and drives the light
// shape's shadow Rgb... Two attributes "shadowSaturation"
// and "shadowValue" are added as new editable
// shadow color attributes:
//
    if (!`size($lights)` ){
//
// Using catch allows me to still return an error code to
// the calling function, while still generating an "error"
// in the output of the Script Editor. If I did not use
// catch, then Maya would exit before the return statement
// could execute, and therefore that would be the end of my
// script if this function was used inside of another
// function:
    //
    catch (`error "There are no lights in your scene. This"+
"script will operate on the shadow color of any light type."`);
        $returnStat=2;
    }
    else
    {
        for ( $light in $lights )
        {
            select -r $light;
            if (`connectionInfo -id ($light+".sc")`){
                warning ($light+": Skipped "+$light+", because it's
                ➥shadow color is already connected to another
                ➥attribute.");
                continue;
            }
            //
            // Safely add attributes for later connections:
            //
            int $attrExistWarning = 0;
            if (!`attributeExists "lHue" $light`){
                addAttr -sn "lHue" -ln "lightHue"
-min 0 -max 360 -at "double";
            }
            else { $attrExistWarning++; }
            if (!`attributeExists "sHue" $light`){
                addAttr -sn "sHue" -ln "shadowHue"
-min 0 -max 360 -at "double";
            }
            else { $attrExistWarning++; }
            if (!`attributeExists "sSat" $light`){
                addAttr -sn "sSat" -ln "shadowSaturation"
-min 0 -max 1 -at "double";
                setAttr -e -keyable true ".sSat";
            }
            else { $attrExistWarning++; }
            if (!`attributeExists "sVal" $light`){
```

```
                    addAttr -sn "sVal" -ln "shadowValue"
-min 0 -max 1 -dv 0.333 -at "double";
                    setAttr -e -keyable true ".sVal";
            }
            else { $attrExistWarning++; }
            //
            // Print warning if any above attributes
// already existed:
            //
            if ($attrExistWarning){
                    warning ($light+": "+$attrExistWarning+
" attributes were not created because they already existed.\n");
                    $returnStat=1;
            }
            //
            // Create color utilities:
            //
            string $rgbToHsv = `createNode rgbToHsv -n
➥($light+"_rgbToHsvInfo")`;
            string $hsvToRgb = `createNode hsvToRgb -n
➥($light+"_hsvToRgbInfo")`;
            //
            // Draw the curve that will be used to drive the
// complementary hue.
// You can find and edit this curve in the Graph
// Editor, if you want to add keys, or change the
// key tangents,  or just do general tweaks...
// all the real fun is here:
            // (think of it as a set-driven key)
string $shadowHueShift = `createNode animCurveUU
-n ($light+"_ShadowHueShift")`;
            float $indexedKeyValues[] = {
                    0.0, 120, 30, 210, 60, 275, 120, 360,
                    159.9999, 300, 160, 25, 180, 45, 250, 40,
                    275, 60, 300, 70, 330, 90, 360, 120
            };
            int $i;
            for ($i = 0; $i < size($indexedKeyValues); $i++ ){
                    setKeyframe -itt flat -ott flat
-f $indexedKeyValues[$i] -v $indexedKeyValues[++$i];
            }
            //
            // Safely make necessary attribute connections:
            //
            int $attrConnectedWarning = 0;
            if (! `connectionInfo -id ($light+".sc")`){
                connectAttr ($hsvToRgb+".o") ($light+".sc");
            }
            else { $attrConnectedWarning++; }
            if (! `connectionInfo -id ($light+".lHue")`){
                connectAttr ($rgbToHsv+".oh") ($light+".lHue");
            }
            else { $attrConnectedWarning++; }
```

```
                    if (! `connectionInfo -id ($light+".sHue")`){
                        connectAttr ($shadowHueShift+".o") ($light+".sHue");
                    }
                    else { $attrConnectedWarning++; }
                    if (! `connectionInfo -id ($rgbToHsv+".i")`){
                        connectAttr ($light+".cl") ($rgbToHsv+".i");
                    }
                    else { $attrConnectedWarning++; }
                    if (! `connectionInfo -id ($shadowHueShift+".i")`){
                        connectAttr ($light+".lHue") ($shadowHueShift+".i");
                    }
                    else { $attrConnectedWarning++; }
                    if (! `connectionInfo -id ($hsvToRgb+".ir")`){
                        connectAttr ($light+".sHue") ($hsvToRgb+".ir");
                    }
                    else { $attrConnectedWarning++; }
                    if (! `connectionInfo -id ($hsvToRgb+".ig")`){
                        connectAttr ($light+".sSat") ($hsvToRgb+".ig");
                    }
                    else { $attrConnectedWarning++; }
                    if (! `connectionInfo -id ($hsvToRgb+".ib")`){
                        connectAttr ($light+".sVal") ($hsvToRgb+".ib");
                    }
                    else { $attrConnectedWarning++; }
                    //
                    // Print warning if any above attributes were
// not connected:
                    //
                    if ($attrConnectedWarning){
                        warning ($light+": Connection failure on current light.
                        ➦"+$attrConnectedWarning+" attributes were not
                        ➦connected because they were already destinations of
                        ➦another attribute connection.\n");
                        $returnStat=1;
                    }
                    //
                    // Get default shadow saturation from light
// saturation.
                    //
                    setAttr ($light+".sSat")
(`getAttr ($rgbToHsv+".outHsvS")`);
                }
        }
        //
        // Restore original selection if there was one:
        //
        select -cl;
        if (`size ($selected)`){
            for ($each in $selected){ select -add $each; }
        }
        return ( $returnStat );
}
```

Distributed Jobs: Scripting and Error Logging

Often you will want to run scripts in a distributed system, such as in a render farm, as a distributed batch script, or in some sort of distributed network-queuing setup that your company might be using. In this case, your distributed queuing software would need to build the command to call Maya and pass to it the command to source your script. It also would have to pass the arguments to execute your script using the -script flag, like this (using a fictional script, myScript.mel, which takes a fictional argument, arg):

```
mayabatch.exe -script "myscript.mel" -command "myscript(\"arg\")"
```

This entire process of submitting distributed jobs often can be done from within another script. In such a case, you'd have one MEL script that is called to gather data to send submission commands to your distributed job system. Alternatively, you could have an image-compositing script, a Perl script, or a shell script sending off commands to your distributed queuing system and telling it to run the next script on a batch of files that have just been finished by the last process. This is known as job chaining. This is a great way to automate repetitive and scriptable duties, such as autocompositing a bunch of files after they have been rendered, or sending a large series of geometry files through a custom exporter. Unfortunately, as cool as this is, the process remains almost wholly unsupervised across a large network in most respects. Therefore, it is prone to file errors and data loss if a substantial amount of error handling is not built into each part of your system with a generalized mechanism in place to catch and handle the errors that might occur while inside Maya.

MEL exposes its general mechanism in the catch command, mentioned previously. When you have "caught" an error, you must decide what to do with it. In different sections of your code, you should be responsible as the author of your script for making sure that you catch any errors that could occur. This is especially true if your code will run over a long period of time and performs a very specifically reusable and generalized function. Error handling is less important, of course, if you just hacked some code together to fix some bug in a bunch of files and you will never use the script again. But even in this case, you want your code to work; if it fails, you want to know why.

Here is an example of catching a simple error and then writing an error log that tells the user who is troubleshooting any problems the basic information that he will need to trace the error back to its point of origin. A group of little helper functions us included, but the main error handling occurs in the procedure importFileAndDoIt.

This procedure checks whether the file passed into it exists and is readable. If this is true, it then proceeds to the import code. If this is `false`, it detects and generates an error, which includes writing an error log to the directory where the file is located, which includes the date and time as well as the name of the file and what error occurred. This is a general case of error handling and also should give you some good insight on using `fopen` to write a text file to disk. `fopen` is the MEL command that enables you to create and write files to disk (such as ASCII text files for error logging).

```
//
// import a file:
//
global proc string importFileAndDoIt( string $filePathToImport )
{
     int $ERROR = 1;
     string $pathToSucess;
     if ( `filetest -r $filePathToImport` )
     {
          $ERROR   = catch ($pathToSucess =
`file -import $filePathToImport`);
          if ( ! $ERROR ) // no error, successful import:
{
               //
               // Your main algorithm, or chunk of code,
// that performs the logic of your script;
               // your fictional procedure "DoIt" would go
               // here, doIt can do anything you want:
               doIt();
          }
     }
     if ( $ERROR )
     {
          string $dt = `getDateAndTime`;
          string $err =
               `outputStringToAsciiTxtInFilesDir
               ($dt+"Bad file, unable to import:   "
+$filePathToImport+"  \n")
               "Import_Error_Log" "txt"`;
          error ("Import file failed. "+$filePathToImport
+" .  Wrote to error log file "+$err+" ");
     }
     return $pathToSucess;
}


// Here is a helper function to write a text file into the
// directory  where the scene file lives. Used for error logs
// or any other file-related ASCII text that needs to be
// written to disk:
```

```
global proc string outputStringToAsciiTxtInFilesDir(
                        string $outputString,
                        string $fileName,
                        string $fileType )
{
string $pathToCurrentFile =
getFullUnixPathToOpenMayaScene();

     // If Maya file is not saved, then it has no name:
// this is error-handling code inside of my error-
// handling function!
     if ($pathToCurrentFile == ""){
          $pathToCurrentFile = `pwd`;
          $pathToCurrentFile = $pathToCurrentFile+"/";
     }
     string $outputFile = ( $pathToCurrentFile + $fileName
+ "." + $fileType );
     pause -sec 3;
     if (`filetest -r $outputFile` && !`filetest -w $outputFile`)
     {
          int $ver = 1;
          while ( `filetest -r $outputFile`
&&
 !`filetest -w $outputFile`)
          {
                string $newName = $outputFile + $ver;
                $outputFile = $newName;
                $ver++;
          }
     }
     int $fileId;
     if ( `filetest -w $outputFile` ){
          $fileId = `fopen $outputFile "a"`;
     }
     else{
          $fileId = `fopen $outputFile "w"`;
     }
     fprint $fileId ("\n"+$outputString+"\n");
     fclose $fileId;
     return $outputFile;
}


// extra helper function for error logs:
// works only on Windows, but getting the formatted
// date and time is just as trivial on a UNIX-based machine:
global proc string getDateAndTime()
{
     string $returnDateAndTime;
     if (`about -os` == "nt"){
          string $dateIn[] = `processOutStream "date /T"`;
```

```
            string $timeIn[] = `processOutStream "time /T"`;
            string $date = `removeAllStringsFromString $dateIn[0] "\n"`;
            string $time = `removeAllStringsFromString $timeIn[0] "\n"`;
            $returnDateAndTime = ( $date+$time + " : ");
        }
        else{
            $returnDateAndTime = "Unknown system date / time : ";
        }
        return $returnDateAndTime;
}


// Here is a quick helper function that will return the
// path only with the scene name removed, to the current
// open scene file inside of Maya:
global proc string getFullUnixPathToOpenMayaScene()
{
        string $pathToFile = `file -q -sn`;
        string $temp = $pathToFile;
        string $fileName = `substitute ".*/" $temp ""`;
        string $unixPath = `substitute $fileName $pathToFile ""`;
        return $unixPath;
}
// quickly get rid of newlines, tabs, spaces, etc...
// converts string to lowercase for personal consistency
// remove the tolower for case-sensitive character removal
global proc string removeAllStringsFromString( string $string,
string $badWord )
{
        string $newstring = tolower($string);
        $badWord = tolower($badWord);
        for ($i = 0; $i < size($string); $i++){
            $newstring = `substitute $badWord $newstring ""`;
        }
        return  $newstring;
}
```

A good way to test this code is to try out the function and send it both a file path that does exist and one that does not exist or is incorrectly written, such as in the following two examples:

```
//A bad file path will output an error log file:
importFileAndDoIt("C:\Temp\mayaFile.mb");
//A good file path will import correctly (if the Maya file actually exists):
importFileAndDoIt("C:/Temp/mayaFile.mb ")
```

Note

Maya 5 also has a brand new MEL Keyword, called catchQuiet. This new keyword yields the exact same features as the regularly used catch, except that catchQuiet will automatically suppress the error or warning messages so that they do not appear in the output of the script editor at all. This can be very useful for those errors or warnings that you want to completely hide from the user, or a program that may be watching output for the "error" keyword.

The reason that the first file path in the previous example failed is because of the difference in slashes in the passed-in strings. This is a common problem in coding; the \ character is recognized by the compiler as an escape character, discussed earlier in Chapter 5, "MEL." Because the \ is not interpreted as a literal character, the import fails. The second example does not fail because Maya uses the standard forward slashes as its directory path delimiters. If you want the first example to work and still use forward slashes, you must escape each slash. The escape sequence for an escape character is \ \, is interpreted as the literal string \.

Here is an example of a properly escaped string with backward slashes:

```
importFileAndDoIt("C:\\Temp\\mayaFile.mb");
```

Advanced MEL

This section provides a somewhat more advanced breakdown of a script's functions, which are really the script's three functional algorithms. Many of you might recognize this script, called fitMorph.mel, as one of my many scripts that can be found on highend3d.com (the well-known high-end 3D software resource and community web site). Here I explain how I used many of Maya's already existing functions to solve the specific problems that I was being challenged with, using creative solutions and knowledge of Maya's behavior to write a script more efficiently, quickly, and easily.

We'll start with a perfect example of using one of Maya's built-in functions and getting the required behavior from it every time, with no chance that something might go wrong. Your script will be guaranteed to work properly. In most cases, the software architects of Maya have put much more effort into ensuring that things will work together appropriately—more effort than a single MEL scripter can afford to invest. So, the moral is: Use the built-in functionality of Maya to solve your problems. Make sure you investigate the "best" way to solve a problem that will require the least amount of code. Never reinvent the wheel.

The following function is quite simple: It point-constraints the selected objects (in reverse order because of the selection order consistency that I needed to match with for the rest of my script). Then it deletes the point-constraint node and reselects the objects in the order they were originally selected.

```
global proc snapObjToObj()
{
    //
    // if selected is equal to two:
    //
    string $sel[] = `ls -sl`;
    if (size ($sel)!= 2)
    {
        error "Select 2 geometry objects, the object to move, and the
target object last.";
    }
    // select them in opposite order:
    select -r $sel[1] $sel[0];
    // perform a point constraint to snap the objects together and then
delete it:
    string $pConstraints[] = `pointConstraint -weight 1`;
    delete $pConstraints[0];
    select -r $sel[0] $sel[1];
    //select -cl;
}
```

Here is an example of not finding an "automatic" built-in solution to my problem. What I really needed was a "bounding box" constraint because a scale constraint actually uses the numeric attributes of the object's scale instead of the bounding boxes of the objects. I wanted to have a quick and "scale-independent" way to match two objects close enough to each other's bounding box size. I didn't care if this was super accurate, but it did need to be close, so I used an approximation of within .1 in unit size. This seemed acceptable to me. Then I simply looped through and scaled the object by this increment in each axis until the bounding boxes hit greater than, equal to, or less than the range of the declared increment value. That's a pretty simple algorithm, but it's a good example of not finding an "automatic" solution directly built into Maya and needing to write my own.

```
global proc boundingBoxFitter( string $object, string $target )
{
    // bbox buffer array
```

```
float $bbox[6];

// object's original bbox
eval ("select -r "+$object);
$bbox = `xform -q -ws -bb`;
float $sizeX = $bbox[3] - $bbox[0];
float $sizeY = $bbox[4] - $bbox[1];
float $sizeZ = $bbox[5] - $bbox[2];

// the target bbox
select -r $target;
$bbox = `xform -q -ws -bb`;
float $targetX = $bbox[3] - $bbox[0];
float $targetY = $bbox[4] - $bbox[1];
float $targetZ = $bbox[5] - $bbox[2];

// conform bboxes within an
// incremented tolerance range
// not a perfect fit, but fast.
//
float $incrmnt = .1;

// each while loop below scales on a certain axis until
// the difference is less than or equal to .15:
// conform bounding box x
while ( (abs($sizeX - $targetX) >= .15 ) &&
        (abs($targetX - $sizeX) >= .15 )){
    eval ("select -r "+$object);
    if ($targetX < $sizeX)
    scale -r (1-$incrmnt) 1 1 ;
    if ($targetX > $sizeX)
    scale -r (1+$incrmnt) 1 1 ;
    eval ("select -r "+$object);
    $bbox = `xform -q -ws -bb`;
    $sizeX = $bbox[3] - $bbox[0];
    select -r $target;
    $bbox = `xform -q -ws -bb`;
    $targetX = $bbox[3] - $bbox[0];
}
// conform bounding box y
while ( (abs($sizeY - $targetY) >= .15 ) &&
        (abs($targetY - $sizeY) >= .15 )){
    eval ("select -r "+$object);
    if ($targetY < $sizeY)
    scale -r 1 (1-$incrmnt) 1 ;
    if ($targetY > $sizeY)
    scale -r 1 (1+$incrmnt) 1 ;
    eval ("select -r "+$object);
    $bbox = `xform -q -ws -bb`;
    $sizeY = $bbox[4] - $bbox[1];
    select -r $target;
```

```
            $bbox = `xform -q -ws -bb`;
            $targetY = $bbox[4] - $bbox[1];
    }
    // conform bounding box z
    while ( (abs($sizeZ - $targetZ) >= .15 ) &&
              (abs($targetZ - $sizeZ) >= .15 )){
        eval ("select -r "+$object);
        if ($targetZ < $sizeZ)
        scale -r 1 1 (1-$incrmnt) ;
        if ($targetZ > $sizeZ)
        scale -r 1 1 (1+$incrmnt) ;
        eval ("select -r "+$object);
        $bbox = `xform -q -ws -bb`;
        $sizeZ = $bbox[5] - $bbox[2];
        select -r $target;
        $bbox = `xform -q -ws -bb`;
        $targetZ = $bbox[5] - $bbox[2];
    }
}
```

What follows are the real meat and potatoes of the script. So many people have emailed me about how I wrote this script! Well, here is the secret: This function is absolutely a perfect example of using both built-in functionality of Maya and some special tricks to solve a problem.

This function gives a single vertex as well as a surface in the scene (poly, NURBS, or subdivs). It snaps the vertex to the closest point on the surface. Let's talk a little about how this is achieved.

First, I am able to use NURBS, polygons, or subdivs. I also can use any other type of surface that Maya implements later, and I won't have to update this function. How is this possible? I know that the behavior of Maya's geometry constraint and the implementation of Maya's geometry constraint is all I need to do the job. Therefore, I get all the geometry constraint's core implementation compatibility features for free. If the geometry constraint is compatible with some type of geometry, so is my function. It's that simple.

So, the only limitation of the geometry constraint is that it doesn't work on vertex types. Therefore, all my function does to get around this is snap a null group node to the location of the vertex exactly; then it geometry-constrains the null and moves the vertex to the new location where the null is after it has been constrained. Again, it's actually quite simple. When this function is combined with a loop over the selected vertices, it snaps all the vertices to the object—and that was the basic challenge of what I was faced with. I didn't want to make the user have to load a plug-in, and I wanted a simple quick solution, so this was the best I could find. This is also a good example of learning to break your problems into smaller, more generic problems that can then be easily represented by generic, reusable functions.

Note

If you ever need to actually calculate the distance from one location to another in 3D, you simply calculate the magnitude of the difference between the two positional vectors. If you need a way to linearly calculate the nearest point from a list of objects, you can simply do a double loop on each group of objects and just store the names of the two that return the shortest distance calculation. Doing stuff like this gets extremely slow and uses a lot of system resources, and it is much better handled in the API, with memory references, pointers, and some data structures that are more versed for these kinds of calculations. It is totally fine to perform this calculation in MEL, though, as long as you don't need to calculate it on a repetitive per-frame basis, or as an input to the geometry's creation history. The node called closestPointOnSurface is a pretty helpful node to look into (by typing **createNode closestPointOnSurface**) for this kind of thing as well.

```
global proc float[] snapToClosestPointOnSurface( string $vertex, string
➥$surface)
{
    // Tricky hack to calculate closest point on surface
    // by using Maya's fast native integrated constraint system;
    // this saves us from having to loop through all vertices
    // and compare the magnitude of the difference between
    // two vector positions for n squared vertex/geometry
    // locations, geometry constraint algorithm already does
    // this for us:
    //
    float $location[3] = `xform -ws -q -t $vertex`;
// create a null, and move it to the location of the vertex:
    string $null = `group -em`;
    xform -os -piv 0 0 0;
    xform -ws -t $location[0] $location[1] $location[2];
    select -r $surface $null;
// create a geometry constraint from the null onto the surface
    string $geoConst[] = `geometryConstraint -weight 1`;
    clear ( $location );
// get the new location:
    $location = `xform -ws -q -t $geoConst[0]`;
    select -r $vertex;
// move the vertex to that location:
    xform -ws -t $location[0] $location[1] $location[2];
// delete the null node:
    delete $null;
// return the location:
    return ( $location );
}
```

Example usage:

```
snapToClosestPointOnSurface("pCube1.vtx[5]", "pSphere1");
```

The full source code for fitMorph.mel is included on the CD. These example functions are the basis of the only real algorithms in the script. The rest of the functions are really just either UI code, wrapper functions for the previous functions for UI buttons to call, or error-handling code. Take a look at all the other functions for a good idea of how much extra code is necessary to get a script going with a simple UI and a couple simple options that call the same basic functions. The final first version of the script was around 500 lines of code, which really isn't so bad for a pretty cool script.

Intro to the API: Writing a Deformer

Maya's API is an object-oriented API, written in C++, and built on the design principle of class factories. When using an API (in any language, not just C++), it is quite important to be familiar with the paradigms that the language is based on.

If you are not familiar with object-oriented programming or the concept of inheritance, overloading, or virtual functions, I will give a brief explanation. In fact, the following explanation should be generalized and brief enough to give you a very basic idea of C++ and what object-oriented programming is. It also should give you enough information to write a deformer node, but that will be all. I strongly suggest that you read a couple really good C++ books—and maybe even take a class or two at a community college—if you really want to write a powerful plug-in that incorporates true principles of object-oriented design. Keep in mind that there are genius programmers out there who can also help you learn C++ if you ask the right questions. If you are familiar with C++ and object-oriented programming, feel free to skip this next section. A couple good books on C++ are *C++: How to Program*, by Harvey M. Deitel and Paul J. Deitel (good for beginners), or *The C++ Programming Language (Special 3rd Edition)* *(Addison-Wesley, 200)* , by Bjarne Stroustrup (good for experienced programmers).

What Is *Object Oriented*?

Object-oriented programming is a paradigm of programming that bases its design on the concept that everything in the real world exists as a separate object. When things in the real world are built, they are built from several different objects or pieces that are glued together to create a new object. A brick is an object, and when you stack a bunch of them together with some cement and water in the right way, you have a brick wall, which is another object. All objects consist simply of data and behaviors. It's like cement: When you combine it with water, it automatically forms a thick liquid that can be used as glue.

Objects are represented by the keyword `class` in C++. Classes are made up of both private and public data of any type, as well as inherited and programmer-defined functions that can manipulate the class's data. Objects in a C++ API can have what is known as a "base" class. The base class is a class that you can "inherit" from, to gain all the default behavior of that class's implementation for free. To write your own functionality into Maya, you do something called virtual function overloading. Most of this happens automatically by the compiler; you just go about your business, writing your plug-in by rewriting the appropriate class functions according to the specs in the API documentation. The compiler does the rest for you, as long as you have included the correct paths to all the appropriate "header" files in your code. Whenever you use the `#include` statement, you are telling the complier exactly what external code it is supposed to "link" with to compile the binary .mll correctly. Because you are inheriting from the deformer in this example, one file that you need to include is the header file for the deformer base class. A .mll file is simply a binary library file. It is really just a dynamic load library for Maya, known as an mll, for Maya load library, or a Maya plug-in.

Maya represents its API in several robust base classes. Maya has a pretty mature API, used by many programmers in both the games and film industries. Some people have given it quite a bit of work, and it is relatively simple to write your own node or deformer by simply inheriting from the base MPx classes. So, instead of talking more about how to program in C++ and object-oriented design principles, which is far beyond the scope of this book, let's learn by example. You'll take a close look at the code that it takes to write a simple yet pretty cool deformer node in Maya's API using C++.

Note

Compiling is the process of converting your high-level programming code into actual bits and bytes that your computer can recognize as the instructions to begin execution of a process. You will need a compiler installed that is completely specific to the language you are writing in (in this case, C++), as well as your operating system's platform. You should also have the developer's kit installed with your installed version of Maya, and you should know how to link and compile in your compiler before attempting to write a plug-in. Because there are many different compilers, and each compiler is different, I will not begin talking about how to do this. Consult the manuals for your specific compiler for your specific platform for more details. I use Microsoft Visual Studio C++ 6.0 on Microsoft Windows 2000 professional as my compiler, and It append to the include and link paths by clicking Alt+F7 and adding custom paths to the C/C++ tab's PreProcessor option and the Link tab's Input option.

Here is the anatomy of the rippleDeformer plug-in. This source code can be found in the C++ source code file rippleDeformer.cpp on the accompanying CD-ROM. The entire Visual Studio project and workspace has been included (the .dsp and .dsw files), in case you are using Windows; you can open this project in Visual Studio 6.0+ and directly compile from there.

```cpp
///////////////////////////////
//
// These are the include statements that tell the
// compiler what code to automatically include in
// its evaluations as the compile takes place.
//
//
#include <string.h>
#include <iostream.h>
#include <math.h>

#include <maya/MPxDeformerNode.h>
#include <maya/MItGeometry.h>

#include <maya/MTypeId.h>
#include <maya/MPlug.h>
#include <maya/MDataBlock.h>
#include <maya/MDataHandle.h>

#include <maya/MFnNumericAttribute.h>
#include <maya/MFnEnumAttribute.h>
#include <maya/MFnPlugin.h>
#include <maya/MFnDependencyNode.h>

#include <maya/MPoint.h>
//#include <maya/MMatrix.h>

////////
// error handling macro:
//


#define McheckErr(stat,msg)\
      if ( MS::kSuccess != stat ) {       \
            cerr << msg;                  \
            return MS::kFailure;          \
      }



/////////////////////////////////////////////
//
// Inherit from Maya's MPxDeformerNode
```

```
// to create a derived deformer class
// object:
//
class ripple : public MPxDeformerNode
{

    public:
                                        ripple();
            virtual                     ~ripple();

            static  void*       creator();
            static  MStatus       initialize();

            /////
            // Deformation function
            //
            virtual MStatus     deform      (       MDataBlock&             block,
                                                    MItGeometry&        iter,
                                                    const MMatrix&      mat,
                                                    size_t
multiIndex  );

            /////
            //
            // Ripple Deformer Attributes (these MObjects actually
            //represent the attributes that will get created on the
            // deformer node itself:
            //

            static  MObject     rippleXtype;

            static  MObject     rippleXx;
            static  MObject     rippleXy;
            static  MObject     rippleXz;

            static  MObject     rippleYtype;

            static  MObject     rippleYx;
            static  MObject     rippleYy;
            static  MObject     rippleYz;

            static  MObject     rippleZtype;

            static  MObject     rippleZx;
            static  MObject     rippleZy;
            static  MObject     rippleZz;

            static  MObject     amplitude;

            static  MObject     frequency;
```

```
          static   MObject       multiplier;

          static   MObject       waveScale;

          static   MObject       offsetX;
          static   MObject       offsetY;
          static   MObject       offsetZ;

          static   MTypeId          id;

     private:
     //
     // no private data members
     //
};


MTypeId   ripple::id( 0x8000e );

////////////
// global attribute definitions:
//
MObject   ripple::rippleXtype;

MObject   ripple::rippleXx;
MObject   ripple::rippleXy;
MObject   ripple::rippleXz;

MObject   ripple::rippleYtype;

MObject   ripple::rippleYx;
MObject   ripple::rippleYy;
MObject   ripple::rippleYz;

MObject   ripple::rippleZtype;

MObject   ripple::rippleZx;
MObject   ripple::rippleZy;
MObject   ripple::rippleZz;

MObject   ripple::amplitude;
MObject   ripple::frequency;
MObject   ripple::multiplier;
MObject   ripple::waveScale;

MObject   ripple::offsetX;
MObject   ripple::offsetY;
MObject   ripple::offsetZ;



////////////////
```

```
//      Constructor:
ripple::ripple(){}

///////////////
// Destructor:
ripple::~ripple(){}

///////////////
// Creator... this uses the operator new
// which helps with dynamic memory allocation:
void* ripple::creator(){ return new ripple(); }


///////////////
//
// Initialize and create deformer
// node's internal attributes
// - this function gets called when the deformer is
// first created, before the deform function gets called:
//
MStatus ripple::initialize()
{

    //
    // Create attribute function set objects:
    //
    MFnNumericAttribute nAttr;
    MFnEnumAttribute eAttr;

    //
    // Create and set properties using
    // MFnNumericAttribute member functions:
    //

    rippleXtype     = eAttr.create( "rippleXType", "rxt" );
    eAttr.addField(    "sine", 0);
    eAttr.addField(    "cosine", 1);
    eAttr.setKeyable(true);
    eAttr.setStorable(true);
    eAttr.setReadable(true);
    eAttr.setWritable(true);

    rippleXx = nAttr.create( "rippleXx", "rxx", MFnNumericData::kDouble );
    nAttr.setDefault(.33);
    nAttr.setSoftMin(-1.0);
    nAttr.setSoftMax(1.0);
    nAttr.setKeyable(true);
    nAttr.setStorable(true);
    nAttr.setReadable(true);
    nAttr.setWritable(true);
```

```
  rippleXy = nAttr.create( "rippleXy", "rxy", MFnNumericData::kDouble );
nAttr.setDefault(.33);
nAttr.setSoftMin(-1.0);
nAttr.setSoftMax(1.0);
nAttr.setKeyable(true);
nAttr.setStorable(true);
nAttr.setReadable(true);
nAttr.setWritable(true);

  rippleXz = nAttr.create( "rippleXz", "rxz", MFnNumericData::kDouble );
nAttr.setDefault(.33);
nAttr.setSoftMin(-1.0);
nAttr.setSoftMax(1.0);
nAttr.setKeyable(true);
nAttr.setStorable(true);
nAttr.setReadable(true);
nAttr.setWritable(true);

  rippleYtype     = eAttr.create( "rippleYType", "ryt", 1 );
  eAttr.addField(    "sine", 0);
  eAttr.addField(    "cosine", 1);
eAttr.setKeyable(true);
eAttr.setStorable(true);
eAttr.setReadable(true);
eAttr.setWritable(true);

  rippleYx = nAttr.create( "rippleYx", "ryx", MFnNumericData::kDouble );
nAttr.setDefault(.33);
nAttr.setSoftMin(-1.0);
nAttr.setSoftMax(1.0);
nAttr.setKeyable(true);
nAttr.setStorable(true);
nAttr.setReadable(true);
nAttr.setWritable(true);

  rippleYy = nAttr.create( "rippleYy", "ryy", MFnNumericData::kDouble );
nAttr.setDefault(.33);
nAttr.setSoftMin(-1.0);
nAttr.setSoftMax(1.0);
nAttr.setKeyable(true);
nAttr.setStorable(true);
nAttr.setReadable(true);
nAttr.setWritable(true);

  rippleYz = nAttr.create( "rippleYz", "ryz", MFnNumericData::kDouble );
nAttr.setDefault(.33);
nAttr.setSoftMin(-1.0);
nAttr.setSoftMax(1.0);
nAttr.setKeyable(true);
nAttr.setStorable(true);
```

```
nAttr.setReadable(true);
nAttr.setWritable(true);

 rippleZtype     = eAttr.create( "rippleZType", "rzt" );
 eAttr.addField(      "sine", 0);
 eAttr.addField(      "cosine", 1);
eAttr.setKeyable(true);
eAttr.setStorable(true);
eAttr.setReadable(true);
eAttr.setWritable(true);

 rippleZx = nAttr.create( "rippleZx", "rzx", MFnNumericData::kDouble );
nAttr.setDefault(.33);
nAttr.setSoftMin(-1.0);
nAttr.setSoftMax(1.0);
nAttr.setKeyable(true);
nAttr.setStorable(true);
nAttr.setReadable(true);
nAttr.setWritable(true);

 rippleZy = nAttr.create( "rippleZy", "rzy", MFnNumericData::kDouble );
nAttr.setDefault(.33);
nAttr.setSoftMin(-1.0);
nAttr.setSoftMax(1.0);
nAttr.setKeyable(true);
nAttr.setStorable(true);
nAttr.setReadable(true);
nAttr.setWritable(true);

 rippleZz = nAttr.create( "rippleZz", "rzz", MFnNumericData::kDouble );
nAttr.setDefault(.33);
nAttr.setSoftMin(-1.0);
nAttr.setSoftMax(1.0);
nAttr.setKeyable(true);
nAttr.setStorable(true);
nAttr.setReadable(true);
nAttr.setWritable(true);

 amplitude = nAttr.create( "ripplePower", "amp", MFnNumericData::kDouble );
nAttr.setDefault(0.0);
nAttr.setSoftMin(-1.5);
nAttr.setSoftMax(1.5);
nAttr.setKeyable(true);
nAttr.setStorable(true);
nAttr.setReadable(true);
nAttr.setWritable(true);

 frequency = nAttr.create( "frequency", "frq", MFnNumericData::kDouble );
nAttr.setDefault(99.0);
 nAttr.setSoftMin(-10000.0);
nAttr.setSoftMax(10000.0);
nAttr.setKeyable(true);
```

```
    nAttr.setStorable(true);
    nAttr.setReadable(true);
    nAttr.setWritable(true);

    multiplier = nAttr.create( "multiplier", "mlt", MFnNumericData::kDouble );
    nAttr.setDefault(1.0);
    nAttr.setSoftMin(-100.0);
    nAttr.setSoftMax(100.0);
    nAttr.setKeyable(true);
    nAttr.setStorable(true);
    nAttr.setReadable(true);
    nAttr.setWritable(true);

    waveScale = nAttr.create( "waveScale", "wvs", MFnNumericData::kDouble );
    nAttr.setDefault(1.0);
    nAttr.setSoftMin(-100.0);
    nAttr.setSoftMax(100.0);
    nAttr.setKeyable(true);
    nAttr.setStorable(true);
    nAttr.setReadable(true);
    nAttr.setWritable(true);

    offsetX = nAttr.create( "offsetX", "osx", MFnNumericData::kDouble );
    nAttr.setDefault(0.0);
    nAttr.setKeyable(true);
    nAttr.setStorable(true);
    nAttr.setReadable(true);
    nAttr.setWritable(true);

    offsetY = nAttr.create( "offsetY", "osy", MFnNumericData::kDouble );
    nAttr.setDefault(0.0);
    nAttr.setKeyable(true);
    nAttr.setStorable(true);
    nAttr.setReadable(true);
    nAttr.setWritable(true);

    offsetZ = nAttr.create( "offsetZ", "osz", MFnNumericData::kDouble );
    nAttr.setDefault(0.0);
    nAttr.setKeyable(true);
    nAttr.setStorable(true);
    nAttr.setReadable(true);
    nAttr.setWritable(true);

    //
    // Add the attributes, and define what other attributes the
    // MObjects will affect:
    //
    addAttribute( amplitude );
    attributeAffects( ripple::amplitude, ripple::outputGeom );

    addAttribute( frequency );
```

```
attributeAffects( ripple::frequency, ripple::outputGeom );

addAttribute( multiplier );
attributeAffects( ripple::multiplier, ripple::outputGeom );

addAttribute( waveScale );
attributeAffects( ripple::waveScale, ripple::outputGeom );

addAttribute( rippleXtype );
attributeAffects( ripple::rippleXtype, ripple::outputGeom );

addAttribute( rippleXx );
attributeAffects( ripple::rippleXx, ripple::outputGeom );

addAttribute( rippleXy );
attributeAffects( ripple::rippleXy, ripple::outputGeom );

addAttribute( rippleXz );
attributeAffects( ripple::rippleXz, ripple::outputGeom );

addAttribute( rippleYtype );
attributeAffects( ripple::rippleYtype, ripple::outputGeom );

addAttribute( rippleYx );
attributeAffects( ripple::rippleYx, ripple::outputGeom );

addAttribute( rippleYy );
attributeAffects( ripple::rippleYy, ripple::outputGeom );

addAttribute( rippleYz );
attributeAffects( ripple::rippleYz, ripple::outputGeom );

addAttribute( rippleZtype );
attributeAffects( ripple::rippleZtype, ripple::outputGeom );

addAttribute( rippleZx );
attributeAffects( ripple::rippleZx, ripple::outputGeom );

addAttribute( rippleZy );
attributeAffects( ripple::rippleZy, ripple::outputGeom );

addAttribute( rippleZz );
attributeAffects( ripple::rippleZz, ripple::outputGeom );

addAttribute( offsetX );
attributeAffects( ripple::offsetX, ripple::outputGeom );

addAttribute( offsetY );
attributeAffects( ripple::offsetY, ripple::outputGeom );

addAttribute( offsetZ );
attributeAffects( ripple::offsetZ, ripple::outputGeom );
```

```
        return MS::kSuccess;
}




//////////////////////////////////////////////////
//
// "deform" Overloaded Member Function:
//
// This function gets called whenever the deformer
// node receives a "dirty" message, telling it that
// incoming dg data has changed and, therefore, it needs
// to re-compute to refresh its output data.
//
// This function is the "compute" or the brains of the
// node and tells the vertices how to deform:
//
//Arguments:
//block: the datablock of the node (this hold all the node's accessible data
//       including its attributes and all of its connected plugs)
//iter: an iterator for the geometry to be deformed (this is all of
//     the geometry's vertices)
//m   : matrix to transform the point into world space ( only by
//       post multiplying the point by the matrix, you will translate
//       it into world space coordinates)
//multiIndex: the index of the geometry that we are deforming
//
MStatus ripple::deform( MDataBlock& block,
                                MItGeometry& iter,
                                const MMatrix& m,
                                size_t multiIndex )


{
     MStatus status = MS::kSuccess;

     // Get deformer's attribute values:
     //
     MDataHandle ripXtypeData = block.inputValue(rippleXtype, &status);
     McheckErr(status, "Error getting rippleXtype data handle.\n");
     short ripXtype = ripXtypeData.asShort();

     MDataHandle rxxData = block.inputValue(rippleXx, &status);
     McheckErr(status, "Error getting rippleXx data handle.\n");
     double rxx = rxxData.asDouble();

     MDataHandle rxyData = block.inputValue(rippleXy, &status);
     McheckErr(status, "Error getting rippleXy data handle.\n");
     double rxy = rxyData.asDouble();

     MDataHandle rxzData = block.inputValue(rippleXz, &status);
```

```
McheckErr(status, "Error getting rippleXz data handle.\n");
double rxz = rxzData.asDouble();

MDataHandle ripYtypeData = block.inputValue(rippleYtype, &status);
McheckErr(status, "Error getting rippleYtype data handle.\n");
short ripYtype = ripYtypeData.asShort();

MDataHandle ryxData = block.inputValue(rippleYx, &status);
McheckErr(status, "Error getting rippleYx data handle.\n");
double ryx = ryxData.asDouble();

MDataHandle ryyData = block.inputValue(rippleYy, &status);
McheckErr(status, "Error getting rippleYy data handle.\n");
double ryy = ryyData.asDouble();

MDataHandle ryzData = block.inputValue(rippleYz, &status);
McheckErr(status, "Error getting rippleYz data handle.\n");
double ryz = ryzData.asDouble();

MDataHandle ripZtypeData = block.inputValue(rippleZtype, &status);
McheckErr(status, "Error getting rippleZtype data handle.\n");
short ripZtype = ripZtypeData.asShort();

MDataHandle rzxData = block.inputValue(rippleZx, &status);
McheckErr(status, "Error getting rippleZx data handle.\n");
double rzx = rzxData.asDouble();

MDataHandle rzyData = block.inputValue(rippleZy, &status);
McheckErr(status, "Error getting rippleZy data handle.\n");
double rzy = rzyData.asDouble();

MDataHandle rzzData = block.inputValue(rippleZz, &status);
McheckErr(status, "Error getting rippleZz data handle.\n");
double rzz = rzzData.asDouble();

MDataHandle ampData = block.inputValue(amplitude, &status);
McheckErr(status, "Error getting amplitude data handle.\n");
double amp = ampData.asDouble();

MDataHandle freqData = block.inputValue(frequency, &status);
McheckErr(status, "Error getting frequency data handle.\n");
double magnitude = freqData.asDouble();

MDataHandle multData = block.inputValue(multiplier, &status);
McheckErr(status, "Error getting multiplier data handle.\n");
double mult = multData.asDouble();

MDataHandle wScaleData = block.inputValue(waveScale, &status);
McheckErr(status, "Error getting waveScale data handle.\n");
double wScale = wScaleData.asDouble();

MDataHandle osxData = block.inputValue(offsetX, &status);
```

```
        McheckErr(status, "Error getting offsetX data handle.\n");
        double osX = osxData.asDouble();

        MDataHandle osyData = block.inputValue(offsetY, &status);
        McheckErr(status, "Error getting offsetY data handle.\n");
        double osY = osyData.asDouble();

        MDataHandle oszData = block.inputValue(offsetZ, &status);
        McheckErr(status, "Error getting offsetZ data handle.\n");
        double osZ = oszData.asDouble();

        MDataHandle envData = block.inputValue(envelope,&status);
        McheckErr(status, "Error getting envelope data handle.\n");
        float env = envData.asFloat();


/////
//
// Ripple deformer algorithm:
// Here is a loop that uses the MItGeometry iterator's functions
// to retrieve the point position of the current vertex and
// to advance to the next vertex in the loop.  This is the basic way that
// all deformer nodes in Maya work.  Get the point position and then
// modify the point position using some sort of algorithm.  In this case,
// I am using a completely non-linear (yet simple) equation to re-compute
// a new position for the point, based on the current settings of the node's
// attributes - if the settings are set to 0, then a sine function is used,
// and if the settings are set to 1, then a cosine function is used (for
each axis).

        //
        for ( ; !iter.isDone(); iter.next())
        {

            MPoint pt = iter.position(  MSpace::kObject );

            if (! ripXtype )
            {
                pt.x = (pt.x + env * (( sin( (pt.x * rxx) + (pt.y * rxy) +
                ➡(pt.z * rxz) + magnitude * mult) * (amp/2) ) +
                ➡((sin(pt.y+osX)* (amp/2) )+osX) )) * wScale;
            }
            else if ( ripXtype == 1 )
            {
                pt.x = (pt.x + env * (( cos( (pt.x * rxx) + (pt.y * rxy) +
                ➡(pt.z * rxz) + magnitude * mult) * (amp/2) ) +
                ➡((cos(pt.y+osX)* (amp/2) )+osX) )) * wScale;
            }

            if (! ripYtype )
            {
```

```
                pt.y = (pt.y + env * (( sin( (pt.x * ryx) + (pt.y * ryy) +
                ➥(pt.z * ryz) + magnitude * mult) * (amp/2) ) +
                ➥((sin(pt.z+osY)* (amp/2) )+osY) )) * wScale;
            }
            else if ( ripYtype == 1 )
            {
                pt.y = (pt.y + env * (( cos( (pt.x * ryx) + (pt.y * ryy) +
                ➥(pt.z * ryz) + magnitude * mult) * (amp/2) ) +
                ➥((sin(pt.z+osY)* (amp/2) )+osY) )) * wScale;
            }

            if (! ripZtype )
            {
                pt.z = ( pt.z + env * (( sin( (pt.x * rzx) + (pt.y * rzy) +
                ➥(pt.z * rzz) + magnitude * mult) * (amp/2) ) +
                ➥((sin(pt.x+osZ)* (amp/2) )+osZ) )) * wScale;
            }
            else if ( ripZtype == 1 )
            {
                pt.z = ( pt.z + env * (( cos( (pt.x * rzx) + (pt.y * rzy) +
                ➥(pt.z * rzz) + magnitude * mult) * (amp/2) ) +
                ➥((sin(pt.x+osZ)* (amp/2) )+osZ) ))   * wScale;
            }

    // set the new position of the vertex; this is actually
    // performing the deformation on the vertex and moving it
    // through space into the new position:
            iter.setPosition( pt, MSpace::kObject );
        }

    return status;
}




///////////////////////////////////////
//
// Standard plug-in initialization:
//
MStatus initializePlugin( MObject obj ){
    MStatus result;
    MFnPlugin plugin( obj, "www.erickmiller.com", "4.5", "Any");
    result = plugin.registerNode( "ripple", ripple::id, ripple::creator,
                                        ripple::initialize,
MPxNode::kDeformerNode );
    // set the MEL procs to be run when the plug-in is loaded / unloaded
result = plugin.registerUI("source rippleDeformerCreateUI.mel;
rippleDeformerCreateUI;", "rippleDeformerDeleteUI");
    if (!result) {
        result.perror("registerUIScripts");
        return result;
```

```
    }
    return result;
}
MStatus uninitializePlugin( MObject obj){
    MStatus result;
    MFnPlugin plugin( obj );
    result = plugin.deregisterNode( ripple::id );
    return result;
}
```

Note

To create your deformer node in Maya (after you have compiled the previous C++ code and loaded it as a plug-in from the Plug-In Manager), you can simply use the `deformer` MEL command. Here is an example:

```
deformer -type ripple;
```

(Alternately you can use `createNode ripple`, but the `deformer` command automatically hooks up your deformer to your geometry, so it is recommended that you use the `deformer` command instead.)

For the ripple deformer example, I have gone a step further and have written some small MEL scripts that get sourced and create a `rippleDeformer()` MEL function as well as a menu item under Maya's Main Deform Menu (for more information on how to create a custom menu item, see Chapter 5). Examples of the full implementation (that is, the additional MEL code), which is really just some UI code and some error handling to make sure the plug-in is loaded, can be found in the CD-ROM files rippleDeformer.mel and rippleDeformerCreateUI.mel. Notice that these scripts are fully required only because they are sourced by name in the `initializePlugin()` API code.

Summary

The code and ideas presented in this chapter focused upon common issues that can occur or that have the capacity to become slightly challenging in a production environment. The idea was to present possible solutions to some of these intermediate and advanced Maya and MEL issues in generic forms that can then be applied to your specific instances of these problems. For almost every issue found in Maya, there is a solution that can be either scripted in MEL or written as a command or a node in the API. The world of Maya's customizable architecture is an ever-growing and complex maze, and it can be fully appreciated only through the compounded hours of exploration and experimentation that finding the solutions to specific production problems will bring. With that in mind, let the true exploration begin.

Index

Symbols
\ (backslash), 54, 855
\\ (double backslashes), 855
/ (forward slash), 54
~ (tilde), 54
10/100BaseT, render farms, 825
180 rule, 337
2D motion blur, 783
    Maya standard renderer, 777
3D, calculating distance, 859
3D animation, 481
3D layout, 334
3D motion blur, 783-784
    Maya standard renderer, 777
    software rendering, 444-447
3D reference geometry, 149
3D titles, 778

A
A.S.A.F.E, 510
    anticipation, 510
    arc, 511-512
    exaggeration, 512-513
    follow-through, 512
    secondary action, 510-511
accessing
    commands, 53
    Script Editor, 85-88
acting, 500-501
    capturing your vision for animation, 492
acting researching, 497
actions, 501
    definition of, 65
    overlapping action. *See* overlapping action
    primary action, 511
    secondary action, 510-511
Add Attribute window, 375, 428
adding
    attributes, 428
    goal objects to particles, 460
    items to default menus, 102-104
    new menus to global UI, 104-106
    soft body curves, 400-406
    time to poses, 561-565
adjusting
    attributes in Render Stats, 423
    clipping planes, 211
    directional emitters, 420
    intensity of light, 769
aesthetic criteria for characters, 290

aim constraints, 387
aiming cameras where you want them, 76-77
Align tool, 279
aligning
    images planes, 263
    sketches, 263
    splines, 642
alpha channels
    green-screen technique, 443
    hardware rendering, 440-444
    luminance, 440
anatomy of characters, 576-577
animals, dogs. *See* quadrupeds
animate to the camera, 547-548
animatics
    layout, 334
    from storyboards, 339-341
animating
    characters. *See* character animation
    reverse foot, 651-656
    shot sequences, 345-348
animation, 46
    3D animation, 481
    characters, 696
    computer animation, 481-482
    facial animation, 682-683
    joints, 610-614
    Maya standard renderer, 789
    MEL, 482
    motion. *See* motion
    planning, 486-487
        acting, 492
        capturing your vision, 487-489, 493-497
        drawings, 490-491
        imagination, 493
        mannequins, 490
        researching motion, 497-498
        text, 491-493
    pose-to-pose, 514-516
    principles. *See* principles of animation
    puppet animation, 481
    setting up characters for, 610
    straight-ahead versus pose-to-pose, 514-516
    traditional animation, 485
    weight, communicating, 513
    Western animation, 521
animation curves, set-driven keys, 402
Anime and Manga, 516, 521
anisotropic materials, 702
antialiasing Maya standard renderer, 778-780
anticipation, principles of animation, 510

appeal, principles of animation, 509-510
appendages, testing, 538
    Jerk_left_armIK, 542-544
    Jerk_left_armPoleVector, 545-546
    Jerk_left_clavicleControlNode, 546
    Jerk_left_legPoleVector, 541-542
    Jerk_left_pinkyFinger_4, 544-545
    Jerk_left_reverseHeel, 538-539
    Jerk_left_reverse_ball, 539-540
    Jerk_left_reverse_toe, 540
applying set-driven keys, 667
approach to learning Maya, 15
Approximation Editor, Mental Ray, 801
arc, principles of animation, 511-512
area lights, 744
    Mental Ray, 800
arguments, MEL, 93-100
arms
    IK arms, 657-660
        stretchy arms, 669-674
        twisting, 662-669
    testing, 542-546
array attributes, connecting, 677
arrays, MEL, 93-100
Art Deco designs, 201
articulation, 40-42
artists, roles of layout artists, 335-336
artwork
    image plances, setting up, 147-148
    modeling, 143-144
    orthographic line drawings, 143
        preparing scans, 145-146
aspect ratios, 344
assigning materials, shading, 716
Attach Surfaces, 154-155, 278
attaching
    heads, 681
    surfaces, 153-155
attenuation, inverse square attenuation, 744
Attribute Editor, 634
attributes
    adding, 428
    adjusting in Render Stats, 423
    array attributes, connecting, 677
    Conserve, 426
    controlling behavior of attributes with
      set-driven keys, 378
    customizing, 399
    goalPP, 460
    hiding, 375
    highlighting, 395-396
    locking, 375
    of nodes, viewing, 363
    Pressure, 428
    removing from Channel Box, 398
    Speed, 431

    traceDepthPP, 460
    values, changing, 397
Auto Simplify Curve, 632
Autokey, 552
automagically, 509
automatic in-betweening, 570
avoiding
    degenerate surfaces, 192
    inadvertent transforms, 223
    sharp edges, 151
axis, 177
    local rotation axis, 375
    of orientation and scale, joints, 585-587
axis rotations, joints, 612

B

B-splines, 121-122
    nonuniformed B-splines. *See* NURBS
    uniform B-splines, 121
background lights, 746
backplates, 760
backslash (\), 54, 855
backstories, 499
batch script files, creating for renders, 795
beaches, creating, 198-200
beauty passes, 814
behaviors of scripts, changing, 54
Bettencourt, James, 493
bevel, 152
Bezier basis, 120
bias, ray tracing, 782
big timing, 518
binding
    character meshes, 640
    characters, node history, 596
    polygon proxy control meshes, 687-688
    smooth binding, influence objects, 695
bipedal characters, 630
    joints, 637
    modeling, 311-329
    modifying weights, 638
    spines, 630-632, 635-644, 647
        twisting, 640, 644-646
Birail 3+ tool, 270
blend shapes
    creating, 683
    eyes, 682
blinking eyes, 682
Blinn shader, 703
blobby particles, 137
    motion blur, 447
blobby surfaces, 112
Block Order Texture files. *See* BOT files
body panels of cars. *See* cars, body panels

body parts
  arms, 657-660
    stretchy arms, 669-674
    testing, 542-546
    twisting, 662-669
  clavicle, 657
  clavicular triangle, 657-660
  ears, 323
    quadruped characters, 620-622
  eyes, 324, 683-685
  feet. *See* feet
  fingers, 326, 675-679
    testing, 544-545
  hair, 328, 685
  hands. *See* hands
  heads. *See* heads
  hips
    controlling, 529-530
    quadruped characters, 615-616
  jaws, 536-537
  joints. *See* joints
  legs
    IK, 648-656
    quadruped characters, 616-620
    testing, 541-542
  mouths, 323
  necks, controlling, 534
  noses, 321
  shoulders, testing, 546
  skin, 294
  spines
    bipedal characters, 630-632, 635-647
    controlling, 532-533
    quadruped characters, 615-616
  tails, quadruped characters, 620-622
  toes, 540
  waists, controlling, 527-528
  wrists. *See* arms
bolts, 257-260
booleans, Polygon Booleans, 172
borrowing code, 840
BOT (Block Order Texture) files
  Maya standard renderer, 791
  Mental Ray, 800
bounce lighting, 753-755
boundaries
  detach boundaries, 285
  for viewing, 75
bounding box constraints, 856
Box filter, 779
breaking models, 523-526
  viewing results of, 525
breaking the character, 525
budgets, Parking Spot project, 31-32
A Bug's Life, **699**
buildings, 201
  details, 206
  doors, 206-207

  downspouts, 211
  footings, 211
  foundations, 202-206
  planning, 201-202
  windows, 208-210
bulletproofing
  character setup, 582-583
  definition of, 582
business, 548

C

C++
  object-oriented programming, 860
  writing deformer nodes, 861-874
caching
  particle disk caching, 455
  software rendering, 454
calculating distance in 3D, 859
Camera Attribute Editor, 341-343
cameras, 341-345
  aiming where you want them, 76-77
  digital still cameras, 760
  lenses, 342
  Nikon Coolpix, 760-761
  resolution, 344
Campin, Emmanuel, 752
capped surfaces from open ends, 160-161
CAPS, 509
  A.S.A.F.E., 510
    anticipation, 510
    arc, 511-512
    exaggeration, 512-513
    follow-through, 512
    secondary action, 510-511
  character, 509-510
  physics, 513
    slow in, slow out, 513
    squash and stretch, 513-514
  STS, 514
    staging, 516-518
    straight-ahead versus pose-to-pose, 514-516
    timing, 518
caps, NURBS, 160-161
cars, 261-262
  body panels
    building, 263-272, 278-287
    building fenders, 272-276
    building wheel wells, 268-269
  fenders, 272-276
  modeling in Parking Spot production,
    134-136
  wheel wells, 268-269
case sensitivity, 93
catch MEL command, 846, 851
Caustics, Mental Ray, 806-808
changing
  attribute values, 397
  behavior of scripts, 54
  channels, 147

commands with caution, 57-58
defaults for commands, 55
geometry after smooth binding, 590-591
hotkeys, 58
menus, 73
pole vector constraint weights, 646-647
Channel Box, removing attributes, 398
channels, changing, 147
character, CAPS, 509-510
character animation, 479-481
breaking the model, 523-526
viewing results of, 525
controls, 526-527. *See also* Jerk, controls
defining character's nature, 498-500
definition of, 482
floor plans, 522
planning. *See* planning, character animation
poses. *See* poses
production processes, 523
starting from a dead stop, 523
testing appendages, 538
Jerk_left_armIK, 542-544
Jerk_left_armPoleVector, 545-546
Jerk_left_clavicleControlNode, 546
Jerk_left_legPoleVector, 541-542
Jerk_left_pinkyFinger_4, 544-545
Jerk_left_reverseHeel, 538-539
Jerk_left_reverse_ball, 539-540
Jerk_left_reverse_toe, 540
waist controls, 527-528
character lines, 267, 280
character mesh, binding, 640
character roots, 526
character setup, 575
common pitfalls, 585
changing geometry after smooth
binding, 590-591
character compatibility for data
transfers, 601
deformers, 597-598
designing skeletal controls, 592
gimbal locking, 594-595
joints, axis of orientation and scale, 585-587
joints, moving after creation or smooth
binding, 587-589
node history, 595-596
normals, 599-600
parameterization, 599-600
pose compensation, 593
rotation order, 594-595
transforms, 599
UV texture coordinates, 599-600
when to use IK and FK, 591-592
IK legs and reverse foot, 648-651
animating, 651-656
rules of, 576
anatomy of characters, 576-577
bulletproofing, 582-583

controls of characters, 578-579
keeping files clean, 579-582
motion requirements of characters, 577
character setup pipelines, 583-584
character UIs, 834
writing, 840
characteristics of Maya, 7-8
characters. *See also* **body parts; models**
aesthetic criteria for, 290
animation, 696
bipedal characters. *See* bipedal characters
bound, smooth-skinned characters,
transferring UVs to, 412-417
details, 292
extraordinary points, 292-293
functional criteria, 289
heads. *See* heads
modeling in Parking Spot production, 134
in Parking Spot project, 25-27
quadruped characters. *See* quarupeds
rigging, 696
sculpting, 326
setting up for animation, 610
subdivision surfaces, 290-291
time to create, 326
checking
merges, 255
normals, NURBS surfaces, 250
checklists, preflight checklist for renders,
797-798
child locators, creating, 383
chmod command, 795
choosing
modeling formats, 113-115
multipass rendering techniques, 815
platforms, render farms, 824
chunkiness in particle systems, 431-432
Circular Fillet tool, 236
circular fillets, 236
city blocks
curbs, 182-184
creating, 184-189
sidewalks, 190-196
street lamps, 211
street signs, 211
streets, 197
Clark, Scott, 290, 483-486
clavicle, 657
clavicular triangle, 657-660
cleaning
files, character setup, 579-582
node history, 596
clipping planes, 75
adjusting, 211
close-out poses, 566
closing UI elements, 70-71

code
borrowing, 840
for error handling, example of, 847-850
executing as files load, 839
fitMorph.mel, 855-860
for rippleDeformer plug-in, 862-874
UI code, launching, 841-843
collecting data for HDR images, 760-761
collisions, 423-425
goal objects, 474-475
goals, 458
hit points, 457
particles, 461, 463
resilience, 425
tessellation, 465
water. *See* water
collisionU, 460
collisionV, 460
color, color scripts. *See* color scripts
color passes, 814
color scripts, 766-767
creating a summer day, 768-772
color-coding control boxes, 628
Combine command, 254
Combine operation, creating smooth edges, 158-159
combining scriptJob with script nodes, 841-843
Command Feedback line, 246
command options, shelves, 65-67
command scripts, comments, 57
command-line rendering, Maya standard renderer, 794-795
commands
accessing, 53
changing using caution, 57-58
chmod, 795
Combine, 254
Conform, 255
Convert NURBS to Polygons, 248
Create, Annotation, 579
createNode, 360
defaults, 53-54
changing, 55
solving command mysteries, 55-57
Duplicate menu, 58
MEL commands
catch, 846, 851
duplicate, 58
joint, 586-587
whatIs, 55, 65
named commands, hotkeys, 62
Normals, 250
Orient Joint, 611
print, 92
Scale, 246
for sourcing scripts shelf buttons, 90
Union, 171, 249-251
xform, 856

comments
in command scripts, 57
MEL, 94-100
communicating
with team, 292
weight, 513
compatibility for data transfers, character setup, 601
compiling, 861
components, 352
grouping, 222
naming, 222
Composite option, render layers, 813
compositing
hardware-rendered particles, 438-439
water, 476
computer animation, 481-482
conditions, if(), 846
conducting rendering tests, 798-799
Conform command, 255
Conform Textures, 798
connecting
array attributes, 677
control boxes to character rigs, 625-629
distanceDimension node, 659
multiplyDivide node, 660
nodes, 364
DAG, 364-367
per-particle values to the transparency of shaders, 453
soft bodies, 401
spline IK rigs, 407-410
Connection Editor, 635
connections
nodes, 355
viewing, 362
Conserve attribute, simulating loss of motion, 426
constraints, 386
aim constraints, 387
bounding box constraints, 856
geometry constraints, 387, 858
grouped control boxes, 626
normal constraints, 387
orient constraints, 387-389
point constraints, 355, 371, 386
pole vector constraints, 388
scale constraints, 387, 856
tangent constraints, 388
weighted constraints
driving, 394-395
overlapping action, 390
continuity
choosing modeling formats, 114
G1 continuity, subdivision surfaces, 131-133
G2, 133
geometric continuity, NURBS, 126-128

Contrast Threshold, 780
control boxes, 625
    color-coding, 628
    hooking up to character rigs, 625-629
    knuckles, 676
control nodes, particle systems, 427-428
control structures, MEL, 93-100
controlling
    eyes, 683-685
    faces, 682
    heads, 535-538
    jaws, 536-537
    necks, 534
    spines, 532-533
    UI with MEL, 100-102
controls
    character animation (examples from Parking
        Spot project), 526-527
        Jerk_CharacterMainRoot, 527-528
        Jerk_ElvisControlBox, 530-532
        Jerk_frontHairControl, 537-538
        Jerk_HeadControlBox, 535-537
        Jerk_HipsAndPartialRootControl, 529-530
        Jerk_jawControlBox, 536-537
        Jerk_mainNeckControlBox, 534
        Jerk_midBackHairControl, 537-538
        Jerk_midFrontHairontrol, 537-538
        Jerk_NeckMiddleControlBox, 534
        Jerk_SpineBottomControlBox, 532-533
        Jerk_SpineMiddleControlBox, 532-533
        Jerk_SpineTopControlBox, 532-533
    of characters, 578-579
conventions for hotkeys. *See* hotkeys
Convert NURBS to Polygons command, 248
Convert to File Texture, 790
converting NURBS surfaces
    to polygon meshes, 247-248
    to subdivision surfaces, 241, 283
coordinate space, 350
coordinates, UV texture coordinates, 599-600
corners, 152
    curbs, 188
    miters, 162-164
    radiused corners, 202
    sidewalks, 191, 194
Cosine Power, 705
Create Render Node window, 102
createNode command, 360
creating
    DG nodes, 357-358
    Multiply/Divide utility nodes, 358
    nodes, createNode command, 360
    script nodes, 834-840
criteria for characters, 289-290
curbs, 182-184
    corners, 188
    creating, 184-189
    expansion joints, 184

curves. *See also* edges
    character lines, 267
    isoparameter curves, 267
    single-span edit point curves, 280
    soft body curves, adding, 400-406
customControlWindows(), 839
customizations, removing, 56
customizing attributes, 399
CV Curve tool, 225
CVs
    grids, 149
    placement of, 265
    scaling, 160
cycles in dependency graphs, 359

D

DAG (directed acyclic graph), 355
DAG nodes, connecting, 364-367
dailies, 509
    scene evaluations, 520
data
    collecting for HDR images, 760-761
    referencing, 602
data transfers, character compatibility, 601
datatypes, numeric integers, 94
Debevec, Paul (HDRShop), 762
deco windows, 209
Deep Paint, 718
defaults for commands, 53-54
    changing, 55
    solving command mysteries, 55-57
deformability, NURBS, 126-128
deformation history, 597
deformation order, character setup, 597-598
deformations
    reordering, 597
    rotation, 530
deformer nodes, writing, 861-874
deformers, character setup, 597-598
degenerate surfaces, 192
deleting history from nodes, 362
dependency graphs
    cycles in, 359
    input output, 356-357
    viewing, 363
depth of field (DOF), Maya standard renderer,
    785-786
design references, 140-142
designing skeletal controls, 592
detach boundaries, 285
details
    in characters, 292
    of modeling, avoiding sharp edges, 151
developing your Maya skills, 10
    approach to learning, 15
    backgrounds, 11

education, 13-15
experimentation, 12-13
DG (dependency graph) nodes, 355
creating, 357-358
input output, 356-357
diffuse indirect illumination. *See* global
illumination
diffuse passes, 814
digital cameras, 760
digital video (DV), 829
direct connections, grouped control boxes, 627
directed acyclic graph (DAG), 355
directional emitters, adjusting, 420
directional lights, 734, 744, 768
creating, 752
disk space, props, 220
Disney Animation: The Illusion of Life, 508
displaying Attribute Editor, 634
distance, calculating in 3D, 859
Distance tool, 427
distanceDimension node, connecting, 659
distributed jobs
error logging, 851-855
scripting, 851-855
submitting, 851
Divine Spine setup, 631
DOF (depth of field), Maya standard renderer,
785-786
dog bones, building, 225-238
dogs. *See* quadrupeds
dome lights
creating, 748, 750-752
faking global illumination, 748
doors, 206-207
Dope Sheet, 563
timing of poses, 566-568
downloading Mental Ray, 763
downspouts, 211
drawing joints, 610
drawing skills, 11
drawings
capturing your vision, 489-490
planning animation, 491
drift pose, 567
driving weighted constraints, 394-395
duplicate MEL command, 58
Duplicate menu command, 58
duplicating locators, 644
DV (digital video), rendering final output, 829

E

ears, 323
quadrupeds, rigging, 620-622
EchoAll Commands, 55
Edge Antialiasing, 779

edgePath script, 159-160
edges
attaching, 153-155
corners, 152
fillets, doing it yourself, 156-158
point spreads, 152-153
removing, 253
rounded edges, 151-152. *See also* rounded
edges
filets, 156
row creation, 159
sharp edges, avoiding, 151
smooth edges, polysets, 158-159
editing
geometry after smooth binding, 590-591
subdivision surfaces, 308-311
editors
Camera Attribute Editor, 341-343
Graph Editor, 569-570
effects
post effects, 776
ray-tracing effects, 776
special effects, 48-49
efficiency, choosing modeling formats, 113
EFX, 822
emissions, 420
adjusting directional emitters, 420
multistreaks, 422
emit function, 447-448
emitter particles, trail particles, 450
emitters, speed of, 471
emitting
particles, 447-448
water trails, 469-474
energy sources, 488
Ercolano, Greg (Rush), 823
error handling
if( ) conditions, 846
MEL, 845-850
error logging distributed jobs, 851-855
error logs, 851
errors
runtime errors, 846
troubleshooting, 93
escape sequences for escape characters, 855
evaluating
scenes, dailies, 520
shaders, 717
exaggeration, principles of animation, 512-513
examining
objects to be modeled, 141
photos of objects to be modeled, 141-142
executables, launching and returning output,
844-845
executing code as files load, 839

exercises
5.1 Executing Your First MEL Command: Launching the Script Editor Using a MEL Command, 86
8.1 Curbs and Gutters, 183-189
8.2 Creating Sidewalks, 190-194
9.1 Building the BigBone, 225-238
9.2 Building a Fire Hydrant, 239-260
9.3 Creating the Car Body Panels, 264-287
10.1 Creating a Custom Modeling Menu Shelf, 295-297
10.2 Subdivision Surface Sketching, 300-303
10.3 Modeling Spot, the Dog, 303-307
10.4 Subdiv Surface Editing, 308-310
10.5 Building the Jerk, 317-329
11.1 Camera Tutorial, 341-345
11.2 Animating a Quick Shot Sequence, 345-348
12.1 Connecting Two DAG Nodes, 364-367
13.1 Creating the Standard Set-Driven Key Hand Control, 370-381
13.2 Using Weighted Constraints to Grab a Randomly Moving Object, 381-386
13.3 Using Particle Dynamics, Weighted Constraints, and Inverse Kinematics to Create an Overlapping Action Skeleton Rig, 389-412
13.4 Transferring UVs onto a Bound, Smooth-Skinned Character, 412-417
14.1 Water Flow Control Setup, 428-432
14.2 Sliding Water Down a Surface, 457-461
14.3 Emitting a Water Trail, 469-474
15.1 Setting the Poses to Match the Planning Poses, 547-548
15.2 Keying the Poses, 548-551
15.3 Posing the Jerk, 552-561
15.4 Adding Time to Poses, 561-565
16.1 Cleaning Up Node History, 596
17.1 Creating Spot's Hind Right Leg, 617-620
17.10 Attaching the Head Setup, 681
17.11 Eye Setup, 684-685
17.12 How to Bind a Subdiv Mesh's Polygon Proxy Control Mesh, 687-688
17.13 Common Workflow for Effectively Painting Smooth Skin Weights, 689-692
17.2 Character Setup for Spot's Tail and Ears, 621-622
17.3 Creating Low-Res Stand-In Geometry, 623-624
17.4 The Divine Spine Setup, 631-648
17.5 Classic Reverse Foot Setup, 649-656
17.6 Advanced Stretchy IK Arms and the Clavicular Triangle, 657-661
17.7 Arm Twist Setup, 662-669
17.8 Stretchy Arm Setup, 669-675
17.9 Rigging an Advanced Additive Hand and Fingers, 675-679
18.1 Observing Material Differences, 701-709
18.2 Creating a Grill with a Procedural Material, 720-725
18.3 Creating a Nonphotorealistic Painted Shader, 727-731
19.1 Gobos and Shadows, 735-743
19.2 Creating a Dome Light, 748-752
19.3 Bounce Lighting, 753-755
19.4 HDR Specular Highlights, 756-759
19.5 Using Final Gathering in Mental Ray for Maya 5, 763-766
19.6 Lighting a Bright Summer's Day, 768-773
20.1 Multipass Rendering, 816-822
A.1 Creating a Script Node, 835-840
A.2 Launching UI code, 841-844
expansion joints, curbs, 184
expectations, 188. *See also* **visions, for animation**
experimenting
with Maya, 12-13
with shaders, 700
exporting objects as references, 213
extraordinary points, 292-293
eye lights, 746
eyes, 324
blinking, 682
controlling, 683-685

F

facePathSplit script, 158
faces
controlling, 682
eyes, 324, 683-685
mouths, 323
noses, 321
facial controls, 682-683
failure of rotational values, 789
faithfulness to materials, 514
faking
global illumination, 747-748
motion blurs, Maya standard renderer, 778
radiosity in standard renderer, 753-755
reflections, Maya standard renderer, 777
familiarizing yourself with Maya, 52-53
fcheck, 742
feet
quadruped characters, rigging, 616-620
reverse foot, 648-656
testing, 538-540
toes, 540
fenders, creating, 272-276
fidelity, choosing modeling formats, 113
Field Render feature, Maya standard renderer, 777
file reference system, 338
file referencing, 213-214
files
batch script files, creating for renders, 795
BOT files
Maya standard renderer, 791
Mental Ray, 800

keeping clean for character setup, 579-582
managing, 77
    naming files, 77-79
overwriting files, hotkeys, 60
Z-depth files, 776
fill lights, 745
fillet, 152
filleted holes, 170-171
fillets, 238
circular fillets, 236-238
disadvantages of, 156
doing it yourself, 156-158
tangents, 157
film, rendering final output, 830
Final Gather, Mental Ray, 809-812
Final Gathering, 746-747
Mental Ray, 763-766
finding
utility nodes, 634
what is being executed, 55-57
fingers, 326. *See also* **hands**
knuckles, 676
moving, 379-381
rigging, 675-679
spreading open, 377
testing, 544-545
fire hydrants
bolts, building, 257-260
building, 238-260
modeling in Parking Spot production, 136
Firewire, render farms, 826
fitMorph.mel, 855-860
fixed orientation, 177
FK (forward kinematics), 371
when to use, 591-592
flattening textures, 714
flexibility
choosing modeling formats, 114
polygon meshes, 115-117
flexible topology, subdivision surfaces, 129-131
floor plans, character animation, 522
flow of water, 428-432
follow-through, principles of animation, 512
footings on buildings, 211
forces of motion, 570
formula for render times, 798
forward kinematics. *See* **FK**
forward slash (/), 54
foundations of buildings, 202-206
fractal maps, 709
freezing
transforms, 224
transforms of nodes, 350
full shots, 547
functional criteria for characters, 289

functions
customControlWindow(), 839
emit, 447-448
linstep, 450-452
mag, 449
noise, zigzagging motion, 465-468
solving problems with Maya's already existing
    functions, 855-860
unit, 448
Fur tool, 138

G

G1 continuity, subdivision surfaces, 131-133
G2 continuity, 133
**generating alpha channels, green-screen
    technique, 443**
geoConnector node, 465
geometric continuity, NURBS, 126-128
geometry
3D reference geometry, 149
changing after smooth binding, 590-591
low-res stand-in geometry, 622-624
minimizing in props, 221
modifying after it is smooth-skinned, 412-417
smooth binding proxy geometry, 686
updating character setup, 579
geometry constraints, 387, 858
Geometry mask, 438
GI Joe script, 752
Gigabit Ethernet, render farms, 826
**gimbal locking, pitfalls of character setup,
    594-595**
global illumination, 746-747
faking, 747-748
Mental Ray, 806, 809
simulating, 759
global passes, 814
glows, Maya standard renderer, 777
goal objects, collisions, 474-475
goal weight, 457
goalPP attribute, 460
goals
collisions, 458
objects, adding to particles, 460
of research, 498
water, 457-458
goalU, 460
goalUV, 463
goalV, 460
grabbing moving objects, 381-386
Graham, Don, 570
Graph Editor, poses (motion), 569-570
gravity, 426-427
green-screen technique, 443
grids, 149-150
grooves, 239

grouped control boxes
  with constraints, 626
  with direct connections, 627
grouping, 407
  components, 222
  overlapping action, 407-410
guidelines
  for lighting, 743-746
  for props, 217
    location, 219-220
    scaling, 218
    simplicity, 220-221
    spatial orientation, 218-219
    structure, 222-224
gutters, 184-189

H

hair, 328, 685
hands
  creating set-driven key hand controls, 370-381
  fingers. *See* fingers
  grabbing moving objects, 381-386
  rigging, 675-679
  rotating, 372-374
hardware, render farms, 825
  10/100BaseT, 825
  Firewire, 826
  Gigabit Ethernet, 826
  hubs, 826
  switches, 826
  UPS, 826-827
Hardware Alpha, 440, 442
hardware lighting, 717
hardware particles, 778
Hardware Render Buffer, 433
hardware rendering, 433, 436
  alpha channels, 440-444
  compositing hardware-rendered particles,
    438-439
  sprites, 435
  types of, 436
hardware-rendered multipoints, 436
hardware-rendered particles, tessellation, 439
**HD (high definition), rendering final
  output, 829**
HDR, highlights, 756-758
HDR images, 759
  collecting data, 760-761
  creating for image-based lighting, 761-762
HDRShop, 762
HDRview, 762
heads, 680
  attaching, 681
  controlling, 535-538
  ears, 323
  eye controls, 683-685
  facial controls, 682-683

  hair, 328
  rotation, 535
Heigan, Martin P. (Lemonpro), 823
hiding. *See also* **bulletproofing**
  attributes, 375
  UI elements, 70-71
hierarchies
  heads, attaching, 681
  joints, 610-614
  low-res joints, 637
  renaming, 390
  subdivision surfaces, 131
high definition (HD), 829
high-resolution models, 338
highlighting attributes, 395-396
highlights, 756-758
hips
  controlling, 529-530
  quadruped characters, rigging, 615-616
history
  deformation history, 597
  deleting from nodes, 362
  of Maya, 8-9
  nodes, 362, 595-596
  viewing, 362
hit points, 457
holding poses, 496
holes, 164. *See also* **potholes**
  nonplanar holes, 169-170
  planar holes, 168-169
  polymesh holes, 167-168
  scooping out of surfaces, 171
  tunneling, 165
    NURBS, 165-166
Hotbox, 68
  marking menus, 68-69
Hotkey Editor, 58
hotkeys, 58
  changing, 58
  creating, 58-61
  defining by referring to procedures in
    scripts, 63-64
  examples of, 60
  MEL scripts, 63
  named commands, 62
  overwriting files, 60
  planning for future, 61, 64
  setting only for duration of Maya session, 61
hubs, render farms, 826
hulls
  repairing, 185
  viewing on NURBS surfaces, 186
hybrids, 516
hydrants. *See* **fire hydrants**
Hypergraph, 363, 470
Hypergraph Scene Hierarchy view, 674

Hypergraph window, 394
Hypershade, 363, 712-713
    libraries, 715
Hypershade window, opening, 671

I

IBL. *See* image-based lighting
icons, tool boxes, 65
IDE drives, 829
if() conditions, 846
IK (inverse kinematics), 371
    arms, 542-544, 657-660
        stretchy arms, 669-674
        twisting, 662-669
    rotate plane IK handles, 641
    spline rigs, connecting, 407-410
    splines, 400
    when to use, 591-592
IK handles, 641
IK splines, tails, 620-622
image plane display toggles, 148
image planes
    aligning, 263
    setting, 243
    setting up, 147-148
image-based lighting (IBL), 747
    creating HDR images, 761-762
images
    HDR images. *See* HDR images
    resolutions, 790
imagination, capturing your vision for
    animation, 493
Implied Tangent, 275
improvisation, 500, 504
in-betweening, 515
    automatic in-betweening, 570
infinite recursion, 700
influence objects, smooth binding, 695
intensity of light, adjusting, 769
internal motivation, 501
Intersect Surfaces tool, 234
interviews
    Clark, Scott, 483-486
    Schnitzer, Adam, 335-336
    Thuriot, Paul, 602-607
inverse kinematics. *See* IK
inverse square attenuation, 744
.inverseScale connections, 586
IPR render, 717, 795
Irix, rendering, 824
isoparameter curves, generating, 267
isoparameters, 710

J

jaws, controlling, 536-537
Jerk
    breaking models, 523-526
    controls, 526-527
        Jerk_CharacterMainRoot, 527-528
        Jerk_ElvisControlBox, 530-532
        Jerk_frontHairControl, 537-538
        Jerk_HeadControlBox, 535-537
        Jerk_HipsAndPartialRootControl, 529-530
        Jerk_jawControlBox, 536-537
        Jerk_mainNeckControlBox, 534
        Jerk_midBackHairControl, 537-538
        Jerk_midFrontHairControl, 537-538
        Jerk_NeckMiddleControlBox, 534
        Jerk_SpineBottomControlBox, 532-533
        Jerk_SpineMiddleControlBox, 532-533
        Jerk_SpineTopControlBox, 532-533
    posing, 552-561
    testing arms
        Jerk_left_armIK, 542-544
        Jerk_left_armPoleVector, 545-546
    testing feet
        Jerk_left_reverseHeel, 538-539
        Jerk_left_reverse_ball, 539-540
        Jerk_left_reverse_toe, 540
    testing fingers, Jerk_left_pinkyFinger_4,
        544-545
    testing legs, Jerk_left_legPoleVector, 541-542
    testing shoulders,
        Jerk_left_clavicleControlNode, 546
Jerk Null, 526
Jerk_CharacterMainRoot, 527-528
Jerk_ElvisControlBox, 530-532
Jerk_frontHairControl, 537-538
Jerk_HeadControlBox, 535-537
Jerk_HipsAndPartialRootControl, 529-530
Jerk_jawControlBox, 536-537
Jerk_left_armIK, 542-544
Jerk_left_armPoleVector, 545-546
Jerk_left_clavicleControlNode, 546
Jerk_left_legPoleVector, 541-542
Jerk_left_pinkyFinger_4, 544-545
Jerk_left_reverseHeel, 538-539
Jerk_left_reverse_ball, 539-540
Jerk_left_reverse_toe, 540
Jerk_mainNeckControlBox, 534
Jerk_MAIN_TRANSFORM, 526-527
Jerk_midBackHairControl, 537-538
Jerk_midFrontHairControl, 537-538
Jerk_NeckMiddleControlBox, 534
Jerk_SpineBottomControlBox, 532-533
Jerk_SpineMiddleControlBox, 532-533
Jerk_SpineTopControlBox, 532-533
Jet Propulsion Laboratory (JPL), 702
job chaining, 851

Johnston, Ollie, 486, 508
joining polymeshes, 285
joint MEL command, 586-587
Joint tools, 610
joints
    axis of orientation and scale, 585-587
    axis rotations, 612
    bipedal characters, 637
    clavicle joints, scaling, 660
    creating hierarchies for animation, 610-614
    drawing, 610
    low-res joint hierarchies, 638
    moving, 589
        after creation or smooth binding, 587-589
    orienting, 611
    overlapping action, 391
    rotate plane IK handles, 641
    rotating, 586
    weighting, 647
    weights, 693
JPL (Jet Propulsion Laboratory), 702
jump-start poses, 566

K

Kabuki, 519
Kahler, Taibi, 501
key lights, 745
keyframes. See also keys
    setting, 551
keying poses, 548-551
keys, setting for poses, 566
kickers, 746
kinematics, 516
knot intervals, 121-122
knuckles, 676. See also hands
KVM (keyboard, video and, mouse), 827

L

Lambert shader, 703
launching. See also accessing
    executables and returning its output, 844-845
    UI code, 841-843
Layered shader, 704
layering, 515
    motion, 572
layers, 180
    planning modeling, 149
    render layers, 812-815
layout, 333-335
    3D, 334
    animatics, 334
    of animation, 43-44
    artists, roles of, 335-336
    of render farms, 828
    storyboards, 334
    visual clarity, 337-338
Leaf Primitives, 782

learning Maya, approach to, 15
Left Mouse Button (LMB), 545
legs
    IK legs, 648-651
    quadruped characters, rigging, 616-620
    testing, 541-542
Lemonpro, 823
lenses, cameras, 342
libraries
    creating, 715-716
    pose libraries, 519
light linking, 759
light probe information, 761
lighting, 735
    areas lights, 744
    background lights, 746
    bounce lighting, faking radiosity, 753-755
    color scripts. See color scripts
    directional lights, 734 744, 768
        creating, 752
    dome lights
        creating, 748-752
        faking global illumination, 748
    eye lights, 746
    fill lights, 745
    Final Gathering, Mental Ray, 763-766
    global illumination, 746-748
    guidelines for, 743-746
    hardware lighting, 717
    HDR images. See HDR images
    highlights, 756-758
    image-based lighting, creating HDR images,
        761-762
    key lights, 745
    kickers, 746
    Mental Ray, 803
    negative light, 740
    outdoor lighting, 734
    in photographs, 734
    point lights, shadows, 792
    projects, 47-48
    quadratic decay, 743
    radiosity, 746
    rim lights, 745
    setting lights, 745
    shaders, 710
    shadows. See shadows
    three-point lighting, 746
    two-point lighting, 746
    volume lights, 744
lighting passes, 814
lights, street lamps, 211
limit surfaces, subdivision surfaces, 129
limitations
    of Maya standard renderer, 776-778
    of Mental Ray, 799-800
line of action, 494-496
linear interpolation, 570

linking, light linking, 759
linstep function, 450-452
Linux, rendering, 824
liquids. *See* water
live-action backplates, 760
living forces, 571
LMB (Left Mouse Button), 545
local rotation axis, 375
location of props, 219-220
location scout, 339
locations, 178. *See also* sets
locators
    creating, 393
    duplicating, 644
locking attributes, 375
lofting troubleshooting, 168
logical holes, 171-172
look development, 699-700
loss of motions, simulating with Conserve
    attribute, 426
low-res joint hierarchies, 637
    testing, 638
low-res stand-in geometry, 622-624
low-resolution models, 338
luminance, alpha channels, 440
Luxo, Jr., 514

M

Mac OS X, rendering, 824
mag function, 449
magnitude of gravity, 427
Make BOT, 791
Make Hole tool, 167
managing files, 77
    naming files, 77-79
Manga, 516, 521
mannequins, capturing your vision, 490
mapping shadows, 735-743
maps
    fractal maps, 709
    panoramic maps, 762
    projection maps, 727-730
    texture maps. *See* texture maps
marking menus, 68-69. *See also* shelves
    Mixed mode, 69
Marsh, Tom, 566
material assignment, shading, 716
materials, anisotropic materials, 702
.matrix[], 588
Max Shading, 779
maximizing camera's window, 75
Maya
    common applications of, 4-5
    history of, 8-9
Maya Embedded Language (MEL), 81. *See also*
    MEL

Maya Net Render v4.0, 823
Maya Paint Effects, texture maps, 719
Maya Personal Learning Edition, 15
Maya standard renderer, 776
    animation, 789
    antialiasing, 778-780
    BOT files, 791
    command-line rendering, 794-795
    depth of field, 785-786
    faking reflections, 777
    Field Render feature, 777
    glows, 777
    limitations of, 776-778
    memory, 788
    motion blurs, 777, 783-784
        3D, 784
        faking, 778
    preflight checklist, 797-798
    ray tracing, 781-782
    Render Diagnostics, 793-794
    rendering tests, conducting, 798-799
    shaders, 789-791
    shadows, 791-792
    tessellation, 786-788
    texture maps, 790
Mckee, Robert, 512
measurements for sets, 179-180
measuring gravity, 426
MEL (Maya Embedded Language), 81-84
    adding
        items to default menus, 102-104
        menus to global UI, 104-106
    animation, 482
    arguments, 93-100
    arrays, 93-100
    catching return values into variables, 92-93
    commands, 351
        catch, 846, 851
        emit, 447
        joint, 586-587
        setting rotate pivots, 224
        whatIS, 65
    comments, 94-100
    control structures, 93-100
    controlling user interfaces, 100-102
    error handling, 845-850
    hotkeys, 63
    programming, 91-92
    runtime errors, 846
    Script Editor, accessing, 85-88
    script nodes. *See* script nodes
    scriptJob, 841-843
    scripts
        Make BOT, 791
        Conform Textures, 798
    solving problems with Maya's already existing
        functions, 855-860
    troubleshooting errors, 93
    writing scripts, 85
        with external editors, 88

MEL Command Reference, 7, 56

memory
  Maya standard renderer, 788
  options for ray tracing, 782

Mental Ray, 748, 799
  Approximation Editor, 801
  area lights, 800
  BOT files, 800
  Caustics, 806-808
  downloading, 763
  Final Gather, 809-812
  final gathering, 763-766
  Global Illumination, 806, 809
  limitations of, 799-800
  motion blurs, 806
  ray tracing, 805
  settings, 800-801, 804-805
    lights, 803
    shaders, 803
  shadows, 805
  Text Editor, 801

menus
  adding
    new menus to global UI, 104-106
    items to default menus, 102-104
  changing, 73
  marking menus, 68-69
  UI, 73-74

merges, checking, 255
merging vertices, 255
metaball modeling tools, 112
microexpressions, 501
Middle Mouse Button (MMB), 545
Miles, Ace, 501
Miller, Erick, 290
Miller, George A., 509
mini-script theory, 501-503
minimizing geometry in props, 221
mirror command icons, 243
mirror threshold, 310
mirrors in performance environments, 504
miters, 162-164
Mixed mode, marking menus, 69
MMB (Middle Mouse Button), 45
mnemonics, hotkeys. *See* hotkeys, creating
modeling, 39-40
  artwork, 143-144
    image planes, 147-148
    preparing scans, 145-146
  bipedal characters, 311-329
  cars. *See* cars
  characters in Parking Spot production, 134
  fire hydrants in Parking Spot production, 136
  from polygonal shapes, 298
  image planes, setting up, 147-148
  planning, 148-151
    planning projects, 140-144

  quadrupeds, 298-299, 303-307
    subdivision surface editing, 308-311
    subdivision surface sketching, 300-303
  storefronts in Parking Spot production, 136-137

modeling formats
  blobby surfaces, 112
  choosing, 113-115
  NURBS. *See* NURBS
  octrees, 112
  point clouds, 112-113
  polygon meshes. *See* polygon meshes
  subdivision surfaces. *See* subdivision surfaces

modeling menu shelves, creating, 294-297
models. *See also* **characters**
  breaking, 523-526
    viewing results of, 525
  cars. *See* cars
  modeling menu shelves, creating, 294-297
  sets, 177, 181
    organizing, 212-214
  texturing, 294

modifying
  geometry after it is smooth-skinned, 412-417
  weights, bipedal characters, 638

motion
  controlling motion of water trails, 472
  follow-through, 512
  forces of, 570
  Jerk_ElvisControlBox, 532
  layering, 572
  living forces, 571
  loss of, simulating with Conserve attribute, 426
  photography, 505
  poses, 569-570
  requirements of characters, 577
  researching, 497-498
  tips for, 572
  transitioning from poses, 570-572
  zigzagging, 465-468

motion blurs
  2D, 783
  3D, 783
    software rendering, 444-447
  blobby particles, 447
  faking Maya standard renderer, 778
  hardware-rendered particles, 439
  Maya standard renderer, 777, 783-784
    3D, 784
  Mental Ray, 806

motion capture, 506-507
motion paths, 571
motion research, planning character animation, 504
mouths, 323
movies, 507. *See also* **video**

moving
  fingers, 379-381
  holds, 567
  joints, 589
  objects in surface space, 463-464
moving objects, grabbing, 381-386
Multilister, 712
multipass rendering, 812
  choosing a technique, 815
  exercises, 816-822
  global passes, 814
  lighting passes, 814
  render layers, 812-814
Multipixel Filtering, 779
multiple passes, software rendering, 455
Multiply/Divide utility nodes, 358
multiplyDivide node, connecting, 660
multipoints, hardware rendered, 436
multistreaks, 422, 436, 461
Muster, 823
Muybridge, Edwierd, 505

N

named commands, hotkeys, 62
naming
  components, 222. *See also* structures
  files, 77-79
  hierarchies, 390
  subobjects, 212
natural terrain, beaches, 198-200
nature of characters, defining, 498-500
necks, 534
negative light, 740
networks, render farms, 828
new features
  Create, Annotation command, 579
  joint MEL command, 586
  Notes, 579
Nikon Coolpix, 760-761
Nitisara, Maya Net Render v4.0, 823
node connections, set-driven keys. *See*
  set-driven keys
nodes, 355
  attributes, viewing, 363
  components, 352
  connecting, 364
    DAG nodes, 364-367
  connections, 355
  DG nodes, 355
    creating, 357-358
    input output, 356-357
  distanceDimension node, connecting, 659
  freezing transforms of, 350
  geoConnector, 465
  history, 362, 595-596
  Multiply/Divide utility nodes, 358

multiplyDivide node, connecting, 660
non-DAG nodes, viewing, 361
null nodes
    creating, 406
    orientating, 664
object-level nodes, creating parent/child relationships, 350
parent nodes, 351-352
particleSamplerInfo, 453
read-only, default non-DAG scene nodes, 361
script nodes. *See* script nodes
shape nodes, 353
    creating parent/child relationships, 351
transform nodes, 351-352
tweak nodes, 598
types of, viewing, 360
viewing relationships of, 353-354
noise function, zigzagging motion, 465-468
non-colliding particles, 461-463
non-DAG nodes, viewing, 361
nonplanar holes, 169-170
nonuniform rational B-splines. *See* NURBS
normal constraints, 387
normals
  character setup, 599-600
  viewing, 250
Normals command, 250
noses, 321
Notes, 579
null nodes
  creating, 406
  orientating, 664
null transforms, creating, 663
numeric integer datatypes, 94
NURBS (nonuniform rational B-splines),
  111, 120
  caps, 160-161
  geometric continuity, 126-128
  holes
    creating between planar NURBS
      surfaces, 168
    tunneling, 165-166
  nonplanar holes, 169-170
  parameterization, 120-123
  planar holes, 168-169
  rectilinear topology, 124
  shape parenting, 626
  single-surface NURBS, disadvantages of, 166
  smooth surfaces, 125-126
  Surface Fillet commands, 156
  surfaces
    checking normals, 250
    converting to polygon meshes, 247-248
    converting to subdivision surfaces, 241, 283
    hulls, viewing, 186
    shading, 711
    tessellation, 465
  trimming, 125, 233-234, 237

O

object-oriented programming, 860
objectives of Parking Spot project, 20-23
objects
  exporting as references, 213
  moving in surface space, 463-464
  moving objects, grabbing, 381-386
  naming, 212
  parenting, 223
  pivots, setting, 189
  removing, 196
observation, 700
  looking for material differences, 701-709
Ocean shader, 704
octrees, 112
Open/Close Curve tool, 244
opening
  Hypershade window, 671
  UI elements, 70-71
ordering UI elements, 71-73
organizing
  files, 77
  models of sets, 212-214
orient constraints, 387-389
Orient Joint command, 611
orientating null nodes, 664
orienting joints, 611
orthographic line drawings, 143
  preparing scans, 145-146
outdoor lighting, 734
output, launching executables and returning
  output, 844-845
overhead, reducing, 38
overlapping action, 388-390
  driving weights of constraints, 394-395
  grouping, 407-410
  highlighting attributes, 395-396
  joints, 391
  locators, creating, 393
  particle goals, 400, 403
  soft body particles, 400
  weighted constraints, 390
overwriting files, hotkeys, 60

P

Paint Effects, 137
Paint Skin Weights tool, 693-694
painted shaders, creating nonphotorealistic
  shaders, 727-730
painted texture maps, 718-719
painting
  smooth skin weights, 688-691
  weights using per-vertex selections, 693-694

panoramic maps, 762
parameterization
  character setup, 599-600
  NURBS, 120-123
parent nodes, 351-352
parent/child relationships, 350-351
parenting, 626
  objects, 223
Parking Spot production, 134
  cars, 134-136
  characters, 134
  fire hydrants, 136
  storefronts, 136-137
Parking Spot project, 18
  details of, 24
    characters, 25-27
    scenes, 27-28
  dog bones, 225-238
  history of, 18-23
  Jerk. *See* Jerk
  objectives of, 20-23
  plans, 29
    budget, 31-32
    storyboards, 29-30
    the book, 30-31
  presentation of, 24
  shader example, 725-726
  Spot the dog. *See* quadrupeds
  water trails. *See* water, water trails
particle disk caching, 455
particle goals, 400, 403
particle rendering
  hardware rendering, 433, 436
    alpha channels, 440-444
    compositing hardware-rendered particles,
      438-439
    sprites, 435
    types of, 436
  software rendering. *See* software rendering
particle systems
  chunkiness, 431-432
  collisions, 423-425
  control nodes, 427-428
  emissions. *See* emissions
  gravity, 426-427
  noise function, 465-468
  trail particles, 450
  water. *See* water
particles, 778
  adding goal objects to, 460
  blobby particles, motion blur, 447
  collisions, 461-463
  emitting, 447-448
  multistreaks, 422
  non-colliding, 461-463
particleSamplerInfo, 453-454

passes, 814
Pencil Generated Imagery (PGI), 481
people. *See* bipedal characters
per-particle values, connecting to shaders, 453
per-vertex selections, painting weights, 693-694
performance, options for ray tracing, 782
PGI (Pencil Generated Imagery), 481
Phong E shader, 706
Phong shader, 705
photographs
    lighting, 734
    of objects to be modeled, examining, 141-142
photography, motion, 505
photon mappings, 746
physics, CAPS, 513-514
pipelines, character setup, 583-584
pivots
    of objects, setting, 189
    setting, 223-224
Pixar, shaders, 699
placement of CVs, 265
placing tools or actions on shelves, 65
planar holes, 168-169
planar NURBS holes, 168
planar surfaces, 156-158
planes, setting image planes, 243
planning, 148
    animation, 486-487
        acting, 492
        capturing your vision, 487-489, 493-497
        drawings, 490-491
        imagination, 493
        mannequins, 490
        researching motion, 497-498
        text, 491-493
    buildings, 201-202
    character animation
        capturing your vision, 488
        final plan, 522-523
        mini-script theory, 501-503
        motion capture, 506-507
        motion research, 504
        reference footage, 505
        researching motiion, 497-498
        story research, 503
        video research, 507
    hotkeys, 61, 64
    modeling, 148-151
    modeling projects. *See* modeling
projects
        preproduction. See preproduction
        production, 39, 523
    sets, 176
platforms, choosing for render farms, 824

plug-ins
    Mental Ray. *See* Mental Ray
    rippleDeformer, 862-874
point clouds, 112-113
point constraints, 371, 386, 855
    creating, 382
    roots, 390
point lights, shadows, 792
point spreads, edges, 152-153
pole vector constraint weights, changing,
    646-647
pole vector constraints, 388
Polygon Booleans, 172
polygon meshes, 111, 115, 134
    converting from NURBS surfaces, 247-248
    flexible topology, 115-117
    positional continuity, 117-118
    shading, 119
polygon proxy control meshes, binding, 687-688
polygonal proxies, 302
polygonal shapes, modeling from, 298
polymesh holes, 167-168
polymeshes. *See* polygon meshes
polyProxy mode, 687
polysets, 158-159
pose compensation, 593
pose-to-pose animation, 514-516
Poser, 491
poses, 496, 519-521, 547
    adding time to, 561-563, 565
    adjusting timing of, 566-568
    character animation, 523
    closc-out poses, 566
    Dope Sheet, timing of poses, 566-568
    drift pose, 567
    Graph Editor, 569-570
    holding, 496
    jump-start poses, 566
    keying, 548-551
    motion, 569-570
    pose libraries, 519
    posing the Jerk, 552-561
    setting keys, 551-561, 566
    setting to match planning poses, 547-548
    transitioning to motion, 570-572
positional continuity, polygon meshes, 117-118
post effects, 776
potholes, 170-172
precision, choosing modeling formats, 114
preflight checklist, renders, 797-798
preparing scans, 145-146
preproduction, 34
    stories, 34-35
    technical considerations, 37-38
    visual considerations, 36-37

Pressure attribute, 428
previewing
    renders, 795-797
    subdivision surfaces, 254
previsualization, 149
primary action, 511
principles of animation, 508-509
    anticipation, 510
    appeal, 509-510
    arc, 511-512
    CAPS, 509
    exaggeration, 512-513
    follow-through, 512
    secondary action, 510-511
    slow in, slow out, 513
    solid drawing, 509-510
    squash and stretch, 513-514
    staging, 516-518
    straight-ahead versus pose-to-pose, 514-516
    timing, 518
print command, 92
printing lists of node's attributes, 364
problem solving, 11
problems with character setup. *See* **character setup, common pitfalls**
procedural textures, 720
    creating a grill, 720-724
production of animated products, 39, 46
    animation, 46
    articulation, 40-42
    effects, 48-49
    layout, 43-44
    lighting, 47-48
    modeling, 39-40
    rendering, 49
    set dressing, 44-45
    shading, 42-43
production processes of characater animation, 523
productions, Parking Spot production, 134
    cars, 134-136
    characters, 134
    fire hydrants, 136
    storefronts, 136-137
programming
    in MEL, 91-92
    object-oriented programming, 860
progressive scanning, 829
projection maps, 727-730
projects, production of, 39, 46
    animation, 46
    articulation, 40-42
    effects, 48-49
    layout, 43-44
    lighting, 47-48
    modeling, 39-40

rendering, 49
set dressing, 44-45
shading, 42-43
props
    bolts, 257-260
    cars. *See* cars
    disk space, 220
    dog bones, building, 225-238
    fire hydrants, building, 238-260
    guidelines for, 217
        location of, 219-220
        scaling, 218
        simplicity, 220-221
        spatial orientation, 218-219
        structure, 222-224
    minimizing geometry, 221
    scaling, 225, 245-246
    shading, 221-223
    simplicity, 220-221
    space, 218-220
    structure, 222-224
psychological research, mini-script theory, 501-503
puppet animation, 481

Q

quadrapeds, 614
    hooking up control boxes, 625-629
    IK legs and feet, 616, 618-620
    IK spline tails and ears, 620-622
    modeling, 298-307
        subdivision surface editing, 308-311
        subdivision surface sketching, 300-303
    setting up spine and hips, 615-616
quadratic decay, lighting, 743
quality
    of ray tracing, Maya standard renderer, 781-782
    surface quality, shading, 710-711
    visual quality of surfaces, 699-700

R

radiosity, 746
    faking in standard renderer, 753-755
radius of a curvature, 170
radiused corners, 202
Ramp shader, 706
range-of-motion testing, 690
ratios, aspect ratios, 344
ray tracing
    Maya standard renderer, 781-782
    memory and performance options, 782
    Mental Ray, 805
ray-traced shadows, 781
ray-tracing effects, 776
read-only, default non-DAG scene nodes, 361

rearranging UI elements, 71
Rebuild Surfaces, 155
rectilinear topology, NURBS, 124
Recursion Depth, 782
reducing overhead, 38
reference footage, 505
referencing, 602
Reflection Specularity, 755-758
reflections, 18
    faking with Maya standard renderer, 777
    ray tracing, 781
refractions, ray tracing, 781
relationships, parent/child, 350-351
removing. *See also* bulletproofing
    attributes from Channel Box, 398
    customizations, 56
    edges, 253
    objects, 196
    ridges, 229
    surfaces, 277
    transform nodes, 352
renaming hierarchies, 390
render buffers, Hardware Render Buffer, 433
Render Diagnostics, Maya standard renderer, 793-794
The Render Factory, 822
render farms, 822
    choosing platforms, 824
    hardware, 825-827
    layout of, 828
    services, 822
    software, 823
Render Globals, antialiasing Maya standard renderer, 778-780
render layers, 812-815
    Composite option, 813
render times
    formula for, 798
    shading, 713-714
Rendercorp, Rendermax, 823
renderers, standard renderer. *See* Maya standard renderer
rendering, 49
    command-line rendering, 794-795
    final output, 829-830
    with Mental Ray. *See* Mental Ray
    multipass rendering. *See* multipass rendering
    particle rendering. *See* particle rendering
    water drops, 475
rendering tests, conducting, 798-799
RenderMan-compliant renderers, 775
Rendermax, 823
renders
    Mental Ray. *See* Mental Ray
    preflight checklist, 797-798

previewing, 795-797
RenderMan-compliant renderers, 775
reordering
    deformations, 597
    UI elements, 71-73
repairing hulls, 185
repeating last used menu command, 392
researching
    motion, 497-498, 504
    stories, 503
    video, 507
Reset Options menu command, 55
resilience, collisions, 425
resolution, 790
    cameras, 344
resources for learning Maya, 13-14
ResPower, 822
results of breaking-the-character activities, viewing, 525
return values, catching into variables, 92-93
reverse foot, 648-651
    animating, 651-656
Reverse Surface Direction tool, 237
Revolve tool, 227
RGB, varying settings, 744
ridges, removing, 229
rigging. *See also* articulation
    bipedal characters. *See* bipedal characters
    characters, 696
    faces, 682-683
    hands and fingers, 675-679
    quadruped characters, 614
        hooking up control boxes, 625-629
        IK legs and feet, 616-620
        IK spline tails and ears, 620-622
        setting up spine and hips, 615-616
Right Hemisphere, Deep Paint, 718
rigs. *See* skeleton rigs
rim lights, 745
rippleDeformer plug-in, 862-874
RMB-scrub, 348
roles of layout artist, 335-336
roots, point constraints, 390
Rotate Plane (RP), 388
rotate plane IK handles, 641
rotating
    hands, 372-374
    joints, 586
rotation
    deformations, 530
    heads, 535
    local rotation axis, 375
    of necks, 534
    order, pitfalls of character setup, 594-595
    of spines, 533

rotational values, failure of, 789
rotoscoping, 506
rounded edges, 151-153
    Attach Surfaces, 155
    edgePath, 159-160
    fillets, 156
row creation, edges, 159
rows, tangent rows, 284
RP (Rotate Plane), 388
rubber hose movement, 509
rules of character setup, 576
    anatomy of characters, 576-577
    bulletproofing, 582-583
    controls of characters, 578-579
    keeping files clean, 579-582
    motion requirements of characters, 577
runtime errors, 846
Rush, 823

S

Scale command, 246
Scale Compensate, 631
scale constraints, 387, 856
scaling
    clavicle joints, 660
    CVs, 160
    props, 218, 225, 245-246
scanned texture, 719
scans, preparing, 145-146
scenes, 178
    in Parking Spot project, 27-28
Schnitzer, Adam, 335-336
scooping holes out of surfaces, 171
Script Editor (MEL)
    accessing, 85-88
    sourcing scripts, 88-91
script nodes, 834
    combining with scriptJob, 841-843
    creating, 834-838, 840
scripting distributed jobs, 851-855
scriptJob, combining with script nodes, 841-843
scripts
    changing behavior of, 54
    edgePath, 159-160
    facePathSplit, 158
    sourcing into Script Editor, 88-91
    writing MEL scripts with external editors, 88
sculpting characters, 326
seasons, lighting a summer day, 768-772
secondary action, principles of animation, 510-511
selecting vertices, 694
sequences, animating shot sequences, 345-348
services, render farms, 822
set dressing, 44-45

set models, 218
set-driven keys, 370
    animation curves, 402
    applying, 667
    controlling attributes, 378
    creating hand controls, 370-381
sets, 175, 178
    buildings. *See* buildings
    city blocks. *See* city blocks
    measurements, 179-180
    mockups of, 180-182
    models, 177, 181
        organizing, 212-214
    planning, 176
    standards for, 177-179
shaders
    Blinn, 703
    connecting per-particle values to transparency of shaders, 453
    creating, 698
    evaluating, 717
    example of, 725-726
    experimentation, 700
    Lambert, 703
    Layered, 704
    lighting, 710
    Maya standard renderer, 789-791
    Mental Ray, 803
    nonphotorealistic painted shaders, creating, 727-730
    observation of live objects, 700
        looking for material differences, 701-709
    Ocean, 704
    Phong, 705
    Phong E, 706
    Ramp, 706
    visual quality of surfaces, 699-700
shading, 42-43
    choosing modeling formats, 115
    considerations before beginning, surface quality, 710-711
    Hypershade, 712-713
    Multilister, 712
    polygon meshes, 119
    process of, 712
        creating libraries, 715-716
        evaluating shaders, 717
        material assignment, 716
        setups, 713-714
    props, 221-223
    render times, 713-714
    setups, 713-714
    subdivision surfaces, 133-134
    texture maps. *See* texture maps
Shading value, 779
shadow passes, 814

shadows, 735
mapping, 735-743
Maya standard renderer, 791-792
Mental Ray, 805
point lights, 792
ray tracing, 782
ray-traced shadows, 781
shape nodes, 353
parent/child relationships, 351
shape parenting, 626
shapes, modeling from polygonal shapes, 298
sharp edges, avoiding, 151
shelf buttons for sourcing script commands, 90
shelves, 64-65
command options, 65-67
marking menus. *See* marking menus, 64
placing tools or actions of, 65
text-mode shelves, 67
Shift key, setting keys, 552
shortcut keys, repeating last used menu
command, 392
shot sequences, animating, 345-348
shots, 178
shoulders, testing, 546
sidewalks
corners, 191, 194
creating, 190-196
simplicity, props, 220-221
simulating
global illumination, 759
loss of motion, Conserve attribute, 426
single-span edit point curves, 280
single-surface NURBS, disadvantages of, 166
skeletal controls, designing, 592
skeleton rigs
creating, 389
grouping, 407
with spline IK and soft body curves, 399-406
skeletons. *See* body parts
sketches, aligning, 263
sketching subdivision surfaces, 300-303
skills
developing your Maya skills, 10-15
drawing skills, 11
skin, 294
skin cluster, 588
skinny patches, 710
slow in, slow out (principles of animation), 513
small timing, 518
Smedge 2, 823
smoke, alpha channels, 440
smooth binding
changing geometry, 590-591
influence objects, 695
moving joints, 587-589

smooth binding proxy geometry, 686
smooth skin weights, painting, 688-691
smooth surfaces, NURBS, 125-126
smooth-skinned characters, transferring UVs
onto, 412-417
snapping CVs to grids, 149
soft bodies, connecting, 401
soft body curves, adding, 400-406
soft body particles, 400
software
Poser, 491
render farms, 823
software particles, 778
software rendering, 444
3D motion blur, 444-447
caching, 454
emitting particles, 447-448
linstep function, 450-452
mag function, 449
multiple passes, 455
particleSamplerInfo, 453-454
unit function, 448
water drops, 475
solid drawing, principles of animation, 509-510
solving problems with Maya's already existing
functions, 855-860
sourcing scripts into Script Editor, 88-91
space, props, 218-220
spatial orientation, props, 218-219
special effects, 48-49
specular passes, 814
speed of emitters, 471
Speed attribute, 431
Spider, 823
Spider Networks, Inc., 823
spines
bipedal characters, 630-632, 635-644, 647
twisting, 640, 644-646
controlling, 532-533
quadruped characters, rigging, 615-616
rotation, 533
spline IK rigs, connecting, 407-410
splines
aligning, 642
IK, 400
Split Polygon tool, 158, 253
spreading fingers, 377
Spreaed Sheet Editor, adjusting light
intensities, 769
Sprites, hardware rendering, 435, 438
Square tool, 274, 277
squash and stretch, principles of animation,
513-514
stage lines, 338
staging, principles of animation, 516-518

standard render, faking radiosity, 753-755

Standard Renderer, faking global illumination, 747

standard renderer. *See* Maya standard renderer

standards for sets, 177-179

Stanford, Leyland, 505

Starewich, Ladislas, 481

staying on model, 485

storefronts, modeling in Parking Spot production, 136-137

stories
  backstories, 499
  preproduction, 34-35

story arcs, 503

story research, planning character animation, 503

storyboards, 35
  to animatics, 339-341
  layout, 334
  of Parking Spot project, 29-30

straight-ahead versus pose-to-pose, 514-516

street lamps, 211

street signs, 211

streets, creating, 197. *See also* city blocks

stretchy arms, 669-674

structures, props, 222-224

STS, 514
  staging, 516-518
  straight-ahead versus pose-to-pose, 514-516
  timing, 518

Studio Tools, point clouds, 113

sub-d geometry, 686

Subdivision Power, 782

subdivision surfaces, 111, 129, 283, 290-291
  converting from NURBS surfaces, 241, 283
  disadvatanges of, 291
  editing, 308-311
  extraordinary points, 292-293
  G1 continuity, 131-133
  hierarchies, 131
  hydrants, building, 240
  limit surfaces, 129
  previewing, 254
  shading, 133-134
  sketching, 300-303

subdivisional meshes, binding polygon proxy control meshes, 687-688

submitting distributed jobs, 851

subobjects, naming, 212

Subtract tool, 171

Surface Fillet commands, NURBS, 156

surface quality, shading, 710-711

surface space, moving objects, 463-464

surfaces
  attaching, 153-155
  creating capped surfaces from open ends, 160-161
  removing, 277
  scooping holes out of, 171
  subdivision surfaces. *See* subdivision surfaces
  visual quality of, 699-700

surfacing flow, NURBS, 165-166

switches, render farms, 826

T

tableau gag, 496

tail particles, 450

tails, rigging quadruped characters, 620-622

tangent constraints, 388

tangent rows, grabbing, 284

tangents, fillets, 157

team work, communication, 292

technical considerations, preproduction, 37-38

templates, 149

tessellation
  collisions, 465
  hardware-rendered particles, 439
  Maya standard renderer, 786-788

tessellationFactor, 465

testing
  appendages, 538
    Jerk_left_armIK, 542-544
    Jerk_left_armPoleVector, 545-546
    Jerk_left_clavicleControlNode, 546
    Jerk_left_legPoleVector, 541-542
    Jerk_left_pinkyFinger_4, 544-545
    Jerk_left_reverseHeel, 538-539
    Jerk_left_reverse_ball, 539-540
    Jerk_left_reverse_toe, 540
  low-res joint hierachies, 638
  range-of-motion, 690
  rendering tests, conducting, 798-799

text, capturing your vision for animation, 491-493

Text Editor, Mental Ray, 801

text-mode shelves, 67

texture coordinates, 119, 600

texture maps, 718
  Maya Paint Effects, 719
  Maya standard renderer, 790
  painted texture maps, 718-719
  procedural textures, 720
    creating a grill, 720-724
  scanned textures, 720
  shaders, example of, 725-726

texture shading, setting, 721

textures, 700
  assigning to shaders, 716
  characters, 294
  flattening, 714

texturing models, 294
Thomas, Frank, 508
three-layer walls, 204
three-point lighting, 746
thresholds, mirror threshold, 310
thumbs. *See* fingers
Thuriot, Paul (interview with), 602-607
tilde (~), 54
time
    adding to poses, 561-565
    of poses, adjusting, 566-568
timelines, 569
times, formula for render times, 798
timing, principles of animation, 518
Tippet Studios, 602
titles, 3D titles, 778
tool boxes, icons, 65
Tool Settings window, 65
tools, 5-7
    Align, 279
    Attach Surfaces, 278
    Birail 3+, 270
    Circular Fillet, 236
    CV Curve, 225
    defined, 65
    Distance, 427
    Fur, 138
    Intersect Surfaces, 234
    Joint tools, 610
    Make Hole, 167
    metaball modeling tools, 112
    Open/Close Curve, 244
    Paint Skin Weights, 693-694
    Reverse Surface Direction, 237
    Revolve, 227
    Split Polygon, 158, 253
    Square, 274, 277
    Subtact, 171
    Tumble, 199
topology
    flexible topology, subdivision surfaces,
      129-131
    rectilinear topology, 124
traceDepthPP, 460
trail particles, 450
trails, water. *See* water, water trails
transform nodes, 351-352
transform parenting, 626
Transformation matrix grid, 728-730
transformations, parent/child relationships,
  350-351
transforms
    character setup, 599
    freezing, 224
    inadvertent transforms, avoiding, 223

transitioning from pose orientation to motion
  orientation, 570-572
trimming, 233-234, 237
    NURBS, 125
troubleshooting
    errors, 93
    lofting, 168
    typos, 93
Tumble tool, 199
tunneling, 165
    nonplanar holes, 169-170
    NURBS, surfacing flow, 165-166
    planar holes, 168-169
    polymesh holes, 167-168
tweak nodes, 598
twisting
    arms, 662-669
    spines, bipedal characters, 640, 644-646
two-point lighting, 746
types of nodes, 360
typos, 93

U

Uberware, Smedge 2, 823
UI (user interfaces), 69
    adding new menus to global UI, 104-106
    character UIs, 834
      writing, 840
    MEL controlling, 100-102
    menus, 73-74
    viewing relationships of nodes, 353-354
UI code, launching, 841-843
UI elements, 70
    hiding, 70-71
    ordering, 71-73
undos, 12
uniform B-splines, 121
uninterrupted power supply (UPS), 826-827
Union command, 171, 249-251
unit function, 448
up-axis, 177
updating geometry, character setup, 579
UPS (uninterrupted power supply), 826
    render farms, 826-827
user interfaces. *See* UI
utility nodes, finding, 634
UV layout, 694
UV parameterization, 459, 463
UV texture coordinates, character setup,
  599-600
UVs, transferring onto bound, smooth-skinned
  characters, 412-417

V

vanishing normals, 132
variables, catching return values, 92-93
vertical parameters scale, 569
vertices
  merging, 255
  selecting, 694
video, rendering final output, 829
video research, 507
videotaping performances, 504
viewing, 74
  aiming where you want it, 76-77
  boundaries, 75
  connections, 362
  dependency graphs, 363
  hulls on NURBS surfaces, 186
  maximizing camera's window, 75
  node types, 360
  nodes, 362-363
  non-DAG nodes, 361
  normals, 250
  relationships of nodes through the UI, 353-354
  results of breaking-the-character activities, 525
virtual function overloading, 861
Virtual Vertex, Muster, 823
visions for animation, 487-489, 493-497. *See also* expectations
  acting, 492
  drawings, 490-491
  imagination, 493
  mannequins, 490
  text, 491-493
visual clarity, 337-338
  storyboards to animatics, 339-341
visual considerations, preproduction, 36-37
volume lights, 744

W

waist controls, 527-528
walls, three-layer walls, 204
water
  blobby particles, 137
  collisions, 423-425, 456, 474-475
    goals, 458
    hit points, 457
  compositing, 476
  emissions, 420-422
  flow control, 428-432
  goals, 457-458
  moving in surface space, 463-464
  noise function, 465-468
  rendering water drops, 475

water trails, 469
  controlling motion of, 472
  creating, 455-456
  emitting, 469-474
  speed of, 471
weighted constraints
  blending between moving objects, 381-386
  driving, 394-395
  overlapping action, 390
weights
  communicating, 513
  joints, 647, 693
  modifying in bipedal characters, 638
  painting using per-vertex selections, 693-694
  pole vector constraints, changing, 646-647
  smooth skin weights, painting, 688-691
Western animation, 521
whatIs Mel command, 55, 65
Williams, Richard, 508
window frames as single surfaces, 162
windows, 208-210
  Add Attribute window, 375, 428
  Create Render Node window, 102
  Hypergraph, 363, 394
  Hypershade, 363
    opening, 671
  maximizing for viewing, 75
Windows, rendering, 824
world transform identity matrix, 350
wrists. *See* arms
writing
  character UIs, 840
  deformer nodes in Maya's API using C++, 861-874
  MEL scripts, 85
    with external editors, 88

X-Y-Z

X and Y positioning, 178
xform, 856
Z height, 178
Z-depth files, 776
zigzagging motions, 465-468

informIT

www.informit.com

YOUR GUIDE TO IT REFERENCE

New Riders has partnered with **InformIT.com** to bring technical information to your desktop. Drawing from New Riders authors and reviewers to provide additional information on topics of interest to you, **InformIT.com** provides free, in-depth information you won't find anywhere else.

Articles

Keep your edge with thousands of free articles, in-depth features, interviews, and IT reference recommendations—all written by experts you know and trust.

Online Books

Answers in an instant from **InformIT Online Books'** 600+ fully searchable online books.

POWERED BY

Safari

Catalog

Review online sample chapters, author biographies, and customer rankings and choose exactly the right book from a selection of over 5,000 titles.

New Riders

www.newriders.com

VOICES THAT MATTER

HOW TO CONTACT US

VISIT OUR WEB SITE

WWW.NEWRIDERS.COM

On our web site, you'll find information about our other books, authors, tables of contents, and book errata. You will also find information about book registration and how to purchase our books, both domestically and internationally.

EMAIL US

Contact us at: **nrfeedback@newriders.com**

- If you have comments or questions about this book
- To report errors that you have found in this book
- If you have a book proposal to submit or are interested in writing for New Riders
- If you are an expert in a computer topic or technology and are interested in being a technical editor who reviews manuscripts for technical accuracy

Contact us at: **nreducation@newriders.com**

- If you are an instructor from an educational institution who wants to preview New Riders books for classroom use. Email should include your name, title, school, department, address, phone number, office days/hours, text in use, and enrollment, along with your request for desk/examination copies and/or additional information.

Contact us at: **nrmedia@newriders.com**

- If you are a member of the media who is interested in reviewing copies of New Riders books. Send your name, mailing address, and email address, along with the name of the publication or web site you work for.

BULK PURCHASES/CORPORATE SALES

The publisher offers discounts on this book when ordered in quantity for bulk purchases and special sales. For sales within the U.S., please contact: Corporate and Government Sales (800) 382-3419 or **corpsales@pearsontechgroup.com**. Outside of the U.S., please contact: International Sales (317) 581-3793 or **international@pearsontechgroup.com**.

WRITE TO US

New Riders Publishing
201 W. 103rd St.
Indianapolis, IN 46290-1097

CALL/FAX US

Toll-free (800) 571-5840
If outside U.S. (317) 581-3500
Ask for New Riders
FAX: (317) 581-4663

New Riders

WWW.NEWRIDERS.COM

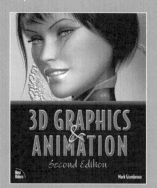

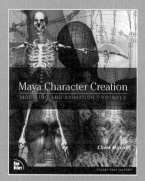

Maximize Your Impact

1592730094
George "Fat Man" Sanger
US$35.00

As THE game resource, NRG books explore programming, design, art, and celebrity savvy. NRG takes you behind the scenes... revealing insider secrets like never before.

1592730078
David Freeman,
Foreword by Wil Wright
US$39.99

0131460994
Chris Crawford
US$39.99

1592730019
Jessica Mulligan,
Bridgette Patrovsky
US$49.99

0131018167
Richard A. Bartle
US$49.99